DATE DUE

MY 27 00			
DE 18 '09			

DEMCO 38-296

International Organization
A Reader

Friedrich Kratochwil
University of Pennsylvania

Edward D. Mansfield
Columbia University

⬛ HarperCollins*CollegePublishers*

Acquisitions Editor: Maria Hartwell
Project Editor: Shuli Traub
Design Supervisor: Jill Yutkowitz
Cover Design: Kay Petronio
Cover Illustration/Photo: Ken Condon
Production Manager: Willie Lane
Compositor: University Graphics, Inc.
Printer and Binder: R. R. Donnelley & Sons Company
Cover Printer: The Lehigh Press, Inc.

International Organization: A Reader

Library of Congress Cataloging-in-Publication Data

International organization : a reader / [edited by] Friedrich
    Kratochwil, Edward D. Mansfield.
        p.   cm.
    Includes bibliographical references.
    ISBN 0–06–501214–3
    1. International organization.   2. International agencies.
3. International relations. I. Kratochwil, Friedrich V.
II. Mansfield, Edward D., 1962–   .
JX1954.I483   1994
341.2—dc20   93-6032
                                              CIP

95 96   9 8 7 6 5 4 3

Contents

Preface

Friedrich Kratochwil

1. International Organization: Subfield or Approach to the Study of International Politics?

The study of international organization has often been identified with the examination of particular international organizations, whose number has dramatically
increased over the last few decades. But while the growth of both intergovernmental and nongovernmental international organizations (ranging from Amnesty
International to Green Peace) is central to the study of international organization,
an understanding of how international politics is organized entails more than the
examination of transnational interest groups, international bureaucracies, or more
or less formalized intergovernmental exchanges. The periodically recurring "summits," the establishment and dissolution of international alliances, and the convening of ad hoc conferences to address specific problems such as ecology (Rio 1992)
or to negotiate a comprehensive regime for the oceans (UNCLOS III) all suggest
that the web of interactions among government and subnational groups is much
richer than the imagery of an international anarchy, in which states face each
other in a "state of nature." Consequently, the purpose of this reader is to present
a variety of studies that analyze how global politics is organized and what effects
various organizational forms have on international relations. The *study* of international organization, therefore, can be conceived of as the investigation of the various organizational forms that populate the international arena, rather than as representing merely a subfield of traditional international relations theory.

  This remark has two implications for this book. First, if we examine international politics from this perspective, we notice that the international system is not
created by one organizing principle alone (territorial sovereignty). Several other
principles, such as nationalism and self-determination, contest the legitimacy and
exclusivity of territoriality as the fundamental organizing principle. Indeed much
of the dynamics of the international system is created by the interaction effects of
these principles. If the nation does not coincide with the territory it occupies, imperial formations come under pressure and are likely to disintegrate, as the case of
Austria-Hungary demonstrates. Similarly, if self-determination of subnational
groups becomes the principle upon which the differentiation of the "units" of the
international system is based, then even the classical nation-state might no longer
be able to contain the dynamics of ethnic conflicts. The emerging minority prob-

lems in the aftermath of the Soviet Republics' declaration of "independence" suggest that this may be the case.

Second, not only are a variety of patterns of organization present in the international arena, but many scholars of international organization also argue that the notion of "anarchy" and its corollaries of contrasting hierarchical and vertical modes of organizing might not be particularly useful for understanding international politics. Part of the problem results from the lack of conceptual clarity which the characterization of the international arena as an anarchy implies.

In fact, the term anarchy contains two distinct meanings. The technical meaning concerns the absence of central institutions. In this sense, the analogy of the international system to the market is appropriate, since no central governmental structures are charged with making binding choices on behalf of the actors in the international arena. (The competence of the United Nations [UN] Security Council under Chapter 7 of the UN Charter can be treated as a sufficiently marginal exception.) But we also use the concept of anarchy to characterize a situation in which order itself is lacking, and in which even the most fundamental preconditions for social coexistence are violated by continuous and widespread normless (anomic) behavior. This is the meaning of anarchy which comes close to the Hobbesian "war of all against all." However, the first meaning of anarchy is incompatible with the second one. Markets could not come into existence without the assignment of property rights, without the emergence of a convention which allows for the exchange of all goods and services via one universal medium of exchange (money), or without the economic actors being socialized enough to let prices fluctuate according to demand and supply instead of increasing their profits by holding guns to the heads of their customers.

Consequently, the simple dichotomy between horizontal and vertical forms of organization (anarchy versus hierarchy) may need refinement if we want to explain both order and the variety of organizational forms that we encounter in the international and the domestic arena. Often scholars attempt to solve the problem of order by little more than a definitional exercise, that is, by making order dependent upon hierarchy. But the existence of strong hierarchical organizations is not tantamount to instituting order, even if states as hierarchical organizations have organized the means of violence rather effectively. The old adage that "one can do a lot with bayonets, but one cannot sit on them" reminds us that there is a much more contingent relationship between order and the hierarchical organization of force than is usually assumed.

Since many scholars of international organization view the dichotomy between horizontal and vertical forms of organization as being overly crude, the variety of organizational forms also needs to be explicitly addressed. For example, the institution of multilateralism, which in the postwar era has given rise to the General Agreement on Tariffs and Trade (GATT), the European Community (EC), or even the North Atlantic Treaty Organization (NATO), represented a demanding organizational form that is quite at odds with the simple bilateralism which we would expect if (structural) realism were indeed the sole organizational model for international politics.

Consequently, international organization as an approach has both a critical and a constructive function for the development of theories of international politics. Its critical function consists in the examination of fundamental assumptions on which theories of international politics rest. Its more constructive function lies in the development of a conceptual framework that includes the questions raised above in a systematic analysis of world politics.

2. The Contributions of an Organizational Approach

Taking the problem of "organizing" as the central problem to study in international politics has several advantages. Instead of taking the "units" as given and then analyzing a system comprised of them, the study of international organization is concerned with the very constitution of these units, as well as the practices by which they interact. One implication of this approach is that we must pay attention to the way in which the system and the units are co-constituitive of each other. For example, the emergence of the territorial state and the creation of the European state system occurred simultaneously. Sovereignty thus became the most important notion for both domestic and international politics. Domestically, sovereignty signified the establishment of hierarchical patterns of authority; internationally, it denoted the equality of autonomous actors, analogous to the status of property holders in Roman private law.[1]

The close connection between international organization as a field of study and international law thereby becomes visible. However, it would be fallacious to assume that since the international system was constituted by legal norms, the analysis of international politics or relations can be reduced to legal issues and methodologies. After all, the rule structure which constitutes a game does not tell us what the various moves of the actors will be, or which strategies they will choose, or even who will win. In the same vein, the recognition of the role of norms in international politics by itself tells us little about the process and the outcomes of international interactions.

Nevertheless, the conceptualization of politics in terms of a game constituted by rules and norms also allows us to analyze issues regarding power more adequately. As power theorists have pointed out, the conceptualization of power as capabilities or, even further, as a universal "currency" of international politics, is highly problematic because several of the preconditions for making money a universal medium of exchange do not exist in either domestic or international politics. For example, the massive firepower of tanks and bombers is of no use against guerrillas or for laying the foundations for a policy of economic growth. Similarly, as the Vietnam War showed, such power will do little in helping to win the hearts and minds of people in a civil war. Indeed, in the absence of the convention analogous to money as a universal medium of exchange, certain capabilities are non-fungible across issue-areas. In addition, what represents a true capability rather than an impediment is often indeterminate unless we know the nature of the game we are playing. Thus, being heavier than the average person is likely to be a useful resource for a football player but it is also most likely to be a handicap for a runner.

Another basic conceptual distinction of the approach underlying this reader is the distinction between "organizing" and "organizations," or between the problem of international organization (used in the collective singular) and the problem of international organizations (in the plural). Assessing organizational efforts in international politics is obviously a broader task than assessing the role of formal organizations in that process. The study of international organization has therefore distinguished between the role of *institutions*, defined here as settled practices, and *formal organizations* that possess formal hierarchies of decision making and that are palpable entities, such as bureaucracies with headquarters that issue directives and might administer certain programs or activities.

3. Regimes and the Study of International Organization

The conceptual distinctions discussed above explain how and why the study of international organization exhibits continuity and identity despite the fact that its foci of interest as well as its methods show some rather remarkable discontinuities. One of the most significant changes in this respect was the decline of interest in intergovernmental organizations (IGOs) and the increased interest in international regimes. Since many of the contributions in this reader are concerned with regimes, it is useful to briefly discuss why interest in regimes arose, what regimes are, and how they function.

Interest in international regimes arose, in part, because some scholars found that classical institutional analysis provided an incomplete framework with which to understand the functioning of even formal intergovernmental organizations. Earlier studies had argued that, because hierarchical organizations are more efficient than other types of organizations, this form of organizing will in the long run supplant other, alternative modes of organizing. In this sense, formal hierarchical organizations are seen as responses to informational deficiencies and other "market failures" that obtain when a multiplicity of actors interact with incomplete information. Since they possess some degree of formal authority vis-à-vis their constituent members, formal organizations (like national governments) can facilitate transparency and help to overcome market failures.

Regime theorists often argue, however, that the efficiency fostered by increased transparency is not necessarily due to the establishment of formal hierarchies. They maintain that certain informal information-sharing agreements can insure greater transparency, and that the assignment of exclusive property rights might also be a solution to market failures. For example, if exclusive property rights to a certain fish stock are assigned to a state, that state will neither have an incentive to cheat in its annual catch of fish nor will it want to exhaust its stock of fish by exceeding the sustainable yield. The reassignment of property rights (as occurred in UNCLOS III through the creation of the exclusive economic zone) is more likely to prevent overfishing than is the creation of a supranational bureaucracy.

Furthermore, regime theorists also significantly modified the identification of hierarchy with order in international relations. This identification is based on the argument that social order exists because recalcitrant actors can be forced to comply. Analyses of the problem of compliance by regime theorists suggest, however, that this issue is far more complicated than is implied by the usual "enforcement" argument. In order to have effective compliance, norms must be clearly established and sufficient monitoring capabilities must exist to establish conformity with the regime. Finally, agencies (courts, domestically, and tribunals, internationally) are crucial for compliance because they can render authoritative decisions of whether or not an infraction of the regime norms has occurred.

Viewed from this perspective, the weakness of international regulations does not seem to lie solely in the lack of central enforcement but rather in the lack of adequate measures for monitoring and arriving at authoritative decisions. For example, even if it is agreed that a certain authority should be charged with the responsibility of punishing aggressors, international organizations must establish who initiated the aggressive act, determine the intentions of the aggressor (Was the transgression really an indication of the intention to commence hostilities, or a simple error by soldiers in the field?), and commence appropriate enforcement proceedings.

Two further issues are central to the role of international regimes. They concern the delineation of a domain or activity which is regulated by a regime, and the assessment of proper actions within a given domain. The first concerns defining the boundaries of the issue-area of the regime; the second concerns problems of legitimacy of the regime itself and the (im)permissibility of actions taken within that domain. As some of the contributions in Chapters 1, 4, and 8 argue, the formation of regimes is influenced not only by the demands for transparency but also by patterns of consensus and by the availability of knowledge about causal connections between actions and outcomes.

4. Organization of the Book

This reader addresses the issues raised above. Chapters 1 and 8 examine how scholars have studied international relations within an organizational context. Taking up the problem of theory building at the outset and conclusion of this reader provides the opportunity to examine more closely the traditional assumptions underlying the analysis of international relations. In this respect, realist attempts to explain "cooperation under anarchy" and some alternative views on this topic (in Chapter 2) serve as our point of departure after a brief review of the development of the field of international organization (in Chapter 1).

In Chapter 3, the roles of regimes in structuring international interactions are investigated. Chapter 4 then elaborates on the linkages between formal organizations and regimes. In Chapter 5, our focus shifts from the investigation of the role of norms and rules for structuring international interactions to the role of specific international organizations in changing the international environment. While the conventional wisdom has been that the appropriate case study for such a task would be the examination of international organizations as actors (agencies empowered to take action or make and administer policy), the contributions in this chapter point to the importance of the legitimization and delegitimization functions of universal international organizations in the issue-areas of decolonization, human rights, and communications.

Chapter 6 investigates the role international organizations play in settling disputes, peacekeeping, and promoting global welfare. In particular, efforts at mediation on the part of the Secretary-General of the United Nations, preventive diplomacy, peacekeeping operations, and global policies are examined. While the record of both the UN and regional organizations is not impressive, the renewed interest in the UN by the former Soviet Union and the recent collective response in the Persian Gulf might indicate a halt to the regime decay.

Chapter 7 investigates the process of integration that has occurred in Europe. While integration followed neither the path of functionalist logic nor that of neofunctionalist spillovers, the emergence of the Europe of 1992 remains a challenge to theory building in international relations even if no new super-state is likely to develop. Fundamental to this process is the creation of several overlapping sets of organizational and institutional decision-making centers. While certain powers have devolved from the state upward to the community organs, other powers were delegated downward to regional decision centers. Chapter 8 focuses on the structures of international politics and their transformation rather than on the more specific regimes in a specific issue-area.

One final note is in order regarding the division of labor between the editors of this volume. This preface and the introductions to Chapters 4, 6, 7, and 8 were written by Friedrich Kratochwil; the introductions to Chapters 1, 2, 3, and 5 were written by Edward Mansfield. All editing of the articles in this book was done jointly.

ACKNOWLEDGMENTS

We would like to thank Donald Puchala, John Ruggie, Mark Zacher, Goodwin Cooke, Pernilla M. Neal, Curtis G. Reittel, and several anonymous reviewers who provided many useful comments and suggestions on this book. We also owe a debt of gratitude to the project heads and editors at HarperCollins who encouraged us to edit this reader, and who guided this project from its inception. In this respect, we are particularly grateful to Lauren Silverman, Maria Hartwell, and Catherine Woods. We deeply appreciate the editorial and research assistance of Reynolds Koslowski, and the support provided by the Lawrence B. Simon chair, without which this project could not have been completed. Finally, we would like to thank Lydia, Liv, and Katherine for their contributions to this book.

Friedrich Kratochwil
Edward D. Mansfield

NOTE

1. See, e.g., John G. Ruggie, "Continuity and Transformation: Toward a Neo-realist Synthesis," *World Politics*, vol. 35 (January 1983), pp. 261–285.

Chapter
1

The Organization of International Relations

Edward D. Mansfield

*T*his chapter provides an introduction to the study of international organization. The articles contained in this chapter display a number of different perspectives on the rationale for analyzing the "organization" of international relations, rather than focusing solely on the role of formal organizations in the international arena. Each paper reflects the view that the defining characteristic of the field of international organization is its concern with governance, which is distinct from both the anarchy problematique stressed by realism and the world order or government approach to international politics that forms the basis of classical studies of international organization. The central theme that runs through these papers is that focusing on the way that the units in the international system are constituted and how their interactions are institutionalized yields a richer account of this system and systemic change than is provided by various alternative approaches to the study of international relations.

Traditional approaches to the study of international relations often draw analogies between domestic and international politics. Since the global system lacks a formal government, such as that which exists in the domestic arena, we are led to expect that international relations will be characterized by the absence of hierarchy, norms, and common values. Indeed, this is why many scholars argue that the international system is "anarchic." Given that most of us live in domestic societies in which law and order seem to prevail, we are led to believe that order itself is the outcome of a certain way of organizing, particularly the organization of force.

It is clear that fundamental differences exist between domestic and international settings. However, scholars of international organization often argue that the stark distinctions that are drawn between hierarchy and anarchy overstate matters. They point out that there is a considerable amount of cooperation in international politics. The fact that we can, for example, board a French plane in New York in order to fly to Europe (using a Brazilian passport which guarantees us certain rights abroad), with fuel extracted in the Middle East by a Dutch company, suggests that legal norms governing interactions regulate certain interactions across domestic systems. Similarly, these scholars point out that states conclude alliances, treaties of friendship and commerce; exploit common resources; and assign exclusive property rights, even in the absence of a central global government. States also occasionally cede certain rights to "federations" or supranational institutions and even shoulder expense and hardship in order to vindicate particular fundamental principles of international conduct. Conversely, the existence of a central government is not a guarantor of order. It also fails to ensure that upheavals will not both change the type of government that exists and the very nature of the members of a political system. This is illustrated by the difficulties that the former Soviet Union is encountering in establishing a new form of association between the state and society and among various republics.

Many studies of international relations argue that the underlying features of the international system have been much the same over time. They maintain that, at least in modern times, the global arena has been characterized by anarchy; and that the states which comprise the international system can be treated as functionally similar since each state must ensure its own security and is a sovereign entity. The issues that scholars of international organization have raised suggest that the situation may be more complex than is implied by this approach. As noted above, they often argue that the distinction between hierarchy and anarchy is too stark to capture adequately the dynamics underlying international politics. Further, scholars of international organization often maintain that the concept of sovereignty is more complex than is implied by alternative analyses. As an organizational principle, sovereignty established both the domestic hierarchy of authority—the sovereign was "absolved" from all laws apart from those governing his conscience—and the legal equality of states. But it also left unanswered questions such as which actors were to be designated sovereign, by which methods could sovereign leaders legitimately assume power, and vis-à-vis whom could leaders establish sovereign authority. Finally, traditional analyses of international relations generally argue that states are the actors on which we should focus attention. These analyses therefore place little emphasis on the importance of non-state actors such as international organizations and subnational groups and societies. As a result, scholars of international organization generally view as inadequate those approaches to international relations that focus solely on states.

Central to the study of international organization is the role of norms. The important contribution of norms for constituting international relations is not well captured when we think of norms in regulative terms. Injunctions such as "do not steal" or "do not use force" are proper examples of regulative rules which often require formal organizations for their implementation. These organizations serve to prohibit actions and punish transgressors. For this reason we are justified in thinking that rules and norms that are not enforced quickly lose their effectiveness in governing international interactions. What is often less appreciated, but equally important, is that many rules and norms function quite differently. Rather than enjoining actors from acting in a certain way, they are "constitutive" of a certain activity. It is therefore useful to distinguish between regulative and constitutive rules and norms. The rules setting up an activity or game and determining, for example, what constitutes a legal move for a knight in a game of chess, a goal in soccer, a promise, or a contract in law are constitutive. Similarly, the basic organizing principles of international politics (that is, those rules and norms that establish the international "game") are constitutive. Although their character might be hotly contested, they function quite differently from regulative rules.

With these considerations in mind, scholars of international organization often maintain that the organization of international relations is anarchical in the technical sense (that is, lacking central decision-making institutions), while, at the same time, not lacking rules and norms. These considerations also contribute to their view that various intermediate forms of governing arrangements exist that fall outside the familiar dichotomy between hierarchy and anarchy. For example, regimes that govern a specific issue area do not establish a hierarchy within this issue area, but it is often argued that they can mitigate the effects of global anarchy.

The selections in this chapter develop these points. Friedrich Kratochwil and John Gerard Ruggie's contribution discusses the evolution of the study of international organization. They show that the various shifts of emphasis in this field were driven by the interest in issues of international governance. This not only established the core concern for scholars of international organization but also provided for the development of an alternative approach to realism for the study of international relations. Finally, the authors attempt to clarify several theoretical issues that arose out of the latest shift in interest to regimes.

Yosef Lapid's article elaborates on these arguments. He argues that the dynamics of the international system cannot adequately be understood with reference to the conceptual dichotomy between hierarchy and anarchy. Further, he maintains that a wide variety of organizational principles characterize the units in the international system.

Finally, John Gerard Ruggie's article provides an additional critique of realist thinking and an exploration of a demanding form of international organization. Despite its importance and the explicit pursuit of multilateral goals by policymakers for the purpose of reconstructing the postwar order, traditional analyses of international relations have not come to grips with these issues. Defining multilateralism in terms of three normative principles (indivisibility, generalized principles of conduct, and diffuse reciprocity) rather than formally (number of parties or voting procedures), Ruggie distinguishes between the institution of multilateralism and specific multilateral organizations. This conceptual elaboration (following the distinction between institution and organization made above) is then used to explore the historical developments within Europe and the international system.

International Organization: A State of the Art on an Art of the State

Friedrich Kratochwil and John Gerard Ruggie

International organization as a field of study has had its ups and downs. . . . In the interwar period, the fate of the field reflected the fate of the world it studied: a creative burst of work on "international government" after 1919, followed by a period of more cautious reassessment approaching the 1930s, and a gradual decline into irrelevance if not obscurity thereafter. . . . The fate of theory and the fate of practice were never all that closely linked after World War II. Indeed, it is possible to argue, with only slight exaggeration, that in recent years they have become inversely related: the academic study of international organization is more interesting, vibrant, and even compelling than ever before, whereas the world of actual international organizations has deteriorated in efficacy and performance. Today, international organization as a field of study is an area where the action is; few would so characterize international organizations as a field of practice.

Our purpose in this article is to try to figure out how and why the doctors can be thriving when the patient is moribund. To anticipate the answer without, we hope, unduly straining the metaphor, the reason is that the leading doctors have become biochemists and have stopped treating and in most cases even seeing patients. . . .

What we are suggesting, to pose the issue more directly, is that students of international organization have shifted their focus systematically away from international institutions, toward broader forms of international institutionalized behavior. We further contend that this shift does not represent a haphazard sequence of theoretical or topical "fads" but is rooted in a "core concern" or a set of puzzles which gives coherence and identity to this field of study.[1] The substantive core around which the various theoretical approaches have clustered is the problem of international governance. And the observable shifts in analytical foci can be understood as "progressive problem shifts," in the sense of Imre Lakatos's criterion for the heuristic fruitfulness of a research program.[2] This evolution has brought the field to its current focus on the concept of international regimes. To fully realize its potential, the research program must now seek to resolve some serious anomalies in the regime approach and to link up the informal ordering devices of international regimes with the formal institutional mechanisms of international organizations.

In the first section of this article, we present a review of the literature in order to trace its evolution. This review draws heavily on articles published in *International Organization,* the leading journal in the field since its first appearance in 1947, and a source that not only reflects but in considerable measure is also responsible for the evolution of the field. The second section critiques the currently prevalent epistemological practices in regime analysis and points toward lines of inquiry which might enhance the productive potential of the concept as an analytical tool. Finally, we briefly suggest a means of systematically linking up regimes and formal organizations in a manner that is already implicit in the literature.

PROGRESSIVE ANALYTICAL SHIFTS

As a field of study, international organization has always concerned itself with the same phenomenon: in the words of a 1931 text, it is an attempt to describe and explain "how the modern Society of Nations governs itself."[3] In that text, the essence of government was assumed to comprise the coordination of group activities so as to conduct the public business, and the particular feature distinguishing international government was taken to lie in the necessity that it be consistent with national sovereignty. . . .

However, there have been identifiable shifts in how the phenomenon of international governance has been conceived, especially since World War II—so much so that the field is often described as being in permanent search of its own "dependent variable." Our reading of the literature reveals four major analytical foci, which we would place in roughly the following logical—and more or less chronological—order.

Formal Institutions

The first is a formal institutional focus. Within it, the assumption was made or the premise was implicit that (1) international governance is whatever international organizations do; and (2) the formal attributes of international organizations, such as their charters, voting procedures, committee structures, and the like, account for what they do. To the extent that the actual operation of institutions was explored, the frame of reference was their constitutional mandate, and the purpose of the exercise was to discover how closely it was approximated.[4]

Institutional Processes

The second analytical focus concerns the actual decision-making processes within international organizations. The assumption was gradually abandoned that the formal arrangements of international organizations explain what they do. This perspective originally emerged in the attempt to come to grips with the increasingly obvious discrepancies between constitutional designs and organizational practices. . . .

Over time, this perspective became more generalized, to explore overall patterns of influence shaping organizational outcomes.[5] The sources of influence which have been investigated include the power and prestige of individual states, the formation and functioning of the group system, organizational leadership positions, and bureaucratic politics. The outcomes that analysts have sought to explain have ranged from specific resolutions, programs, and budgets, to broader voting alignment and the general orientation of one or more international institutions.

Organizational Role

In this third perspective, another assumption of the formal institutionalist approach was abandoned, namely, that international governance *is* whatever international organizations *do*. Instead, the focus shifted to the actual and potential roles of international organizations in a more broadly conceived process of international governance.[6] This perspective in turn subsumes three distinct clusters.

In the first cluster, the emphasis was on the roles of international organizations in the resolution of substantive international problems. Preventive diplomacy and peace-keeping were two such roles in the area of peace and security,[7] nuclear safeguarding by the International Atomic Energy Agency (IAEA) was another.[8] Facilitating decolonization received a good deal of attention in the political realm,[9] providing multilateral development assistance in the economic realm.[10] The potential role of international organizations in restructuring North-South relations preoccupied a substantial number of scholars throughout the 1970s,[11] as did the possible contributions of international organizations to managing the so-called global commons. . . .[12]

The second cluster of the organizational-role perspective shifted the focus away from the solution of substantive problems per se, toward certain long-term institutional consequences of the failure to solve substantive problems through the available institutional means. This, of course, was the integrationist focus, particularly the neofunctionalist variety.[13] It was fueled by the fact that the jurisdictional scope of both the state and existing international organizations was increasingly outstripped by the functional scope of international problems. And it sought to explore the extent to which institutional adaptations to this fact might be conducive to the emergence of political forms "beyond the nation state." . . . [14]

The third cluster within the organizational-role perspective began with a critique of the transformational expectations of integration theory and then shifted the focus onto a more general concern with how international institutions "reflect and to some extent magnify or modify" the characteristic features of the international system.[15] Here, international organizations have been viewed as potential dispensers of collective legitimacy,[16] vehicles in the international politics of agenda formation,[17] forums for the creation of transgovernmental coalitions as well as instruments of transgovernmental policy coordination,[18] and as means through which the global dominance structure is enhanced or can possibly come to be undermined.[19]

The theme that unifies all works of this genre is that the process of global governance is not coterminous with the activities of international organizations but that these organizations do play some role in that broader process. The objective was to identify their role.

International Regimes

The current preoccupation in the field is with the phenomenon of international regimes. Regimes are broadly defined as governing arrangements constructed by states to coordinate their expectations and organize aspects of international behavior in various issue-areas. They thus comprise a normative element, state practice, and organizational roles. . . . The focus on regimes was a direct response both to the intellectual odyssey that we have just traced as well as to certain developments in the world of international relations from the 1970s on.

When the presumed identity between international organizations and international governance was explicitly rejected, the precise roles of organizations *in* international governance became a central concern. But, apart from the focus on integration, no overarching conception was developed *of* international governance itself. And the integrationists themselves soon abandoned their early notions, ending up with a formulation of integration that did little more than recapitulate the condition of interdependence which was assumed to trigger integration in the first place.[20] Thus, for a time the field of international organization lacked any systematic conception of its traditional analytical core: international governance. The introduction of the concept of regimes reflected an attempt to fill this void. International regimes were thought to express both the parameters and the perimeters of international governance.[21]

The impact of international affairs during the 1970s and beyond came in the form of an anomaly for which no ready-made explanation was at hand. Important changes occurred in the international system, associated with the relative decline of U.S. hegemony: the achievement of nuclear parity by the Soviet Union; the economic resurgence of Europe and Japan; the success of OPEC together with the severe international economic dislocations that followed it. Specific agreements that had been negotiated after World War II were violated, and institutional arrangements, in money and trade above all, came under enormous strain. Yet—and here is the anomaly—governments on the whole did not respond to the difficulties confronting them in beggar-thy-neighbor terms. Neither systemic factors nor formal institutions alone apparently could account for this outcome. One way to resolve the anomaly was to question the extent to which U.S. hegemony in point of fact had eroded.[22] Another, and by no means entirely incompatible, route was via the concept of international regimes. The argument was advanced that regimes continued in some measure to constrain and condition the behavior of states toward one another, despite systemic change and institutional erosion. In this light, international regimes were seen to enjoy a degree of relative autonomy, though of an unknown duration.[23]

In sum, in order to resolve both disciplinary and real-world puzzles, the process of international governance has come to be associated with the concept of international regimes, occupying an ontological space somewhere between the level of formal institutions on the one hand and systemic factors on the other. Hence, the notion that the concern with international regimes is but another academic fad from which the field has suffered throughout the postwar period itself betrays a misunderstanding of the considerable intellectual continuity that has brought the field to the present point. . . .[24]

Conflict and Cooperation

These shifts in analytical foci have been accompanied by an analytical shift of a very different sort, perhaps most clearly expressed in the premises of recent methodological approaches. Take the rational-choice approach as one instance.[25] It raises the promise and offers the possibility that two strands of thinking about international relations which have been distinct if not oppositional in the past may become unified. Typically, the opposition has been expressed in the conflict/cooperation dichotomy. . . . Moreover, it has been inferred from this premise that these two realms of international life require (from the vantage point of conflict studies) or make possible (from the vantage point of cooperation studies) two very different modes of analysis. Realism and to a lesser extent Marxism have tended to dominate the former strand, and liberalism in its many guises—Ricardian trade theory, Wilsonian idealism, functionalism, and interdependence imperatives—the latter.

What we find in the recent literature inspired by the rational-choice perspective, on the contrary, is the claim that *both* conflict *and* cooperation can be explained by a *single* logical apparatus.[26] Moreover, the differences between the two branches now are understood to reflect situational determinants not structural determinants. . . . Interestingly, developments in some neo-Marxist approaches have proceeded on precisely analogous lines, insofar as the traditional opposites, unity and rivalry, have been collapsed within a single "world system" framework. . . . Approaches informed by hermeneutics and language philosophy are reaching much the same conclusions as well.[27] And in each case, the concept of regimes is found to be a useful focal point for analysis.

In summary, that branch of the study of international relations which calls itself international organization is lively and productive. It is once again focusing squarely on the phenomenon of international governance, and it is pursuing its object of study in innovative ways that are bringing it closer to the theoretical core of more general international relations work. These are no mean accomplishments. And they are not diminished by the fact that serious problems remain to be resolved.

PROBLEMS IN THE PRACTICE OF REGIME ANALYSIS

One of the major criticisms made of the regimes concept is its "wooliness" and "imprecision."[28] The point is well taken. There is no agreement in the literature even on such basic issues as boundary conditions: Where does one regime end and another begin? What is the threshold between nonregime and regime? Embedding regimes in "meta-regimes," or "nesting" one within another, typifies the problem; it does not resolve it. . . .[29]

The only cure for wooliness and imprecision is, of course, to make the concept of regimes less so. Definitions can still be refined, but only up to a point. Two fundamental impediments stand in the way. One is absolute: ultimately, there exists no external Archimedian point from which regimes can be viewed as they "truly" are. This is so because regimes are conceptual creations not concrete entities. As with any analytical construction in the human sciences, the concept of regimes will reflect commonsense understandings, actor preferences, and the particular purposes for which analyses are undertaken. Ultimately, therefore, the concept of regimes, like the concept of "power," or "state," or "revolution," will remain a "contestable concept."[30]

Well short of this absolute impediment stands another. It is not insuperable, but a great deal of work will have to be done in order to overcome it. The problem is this: the practice of regime analysis is wracked by epistemological anomalies— anomalies that more often than not go unnoticed in the literature. These anomalies debilitate any endeavor to achieve clarity and precision in the concept of regimes and to enhance its productive capacity as an analytical tool. In the paragraphs that follow, we flag three related epistemological problem areas. . . .

Ontology Versus Epistemology

International regimes are commonly defined as social institutions around which expectations converge in international issue-areas. The emphasis on convergent expectations as the constitutive basis of regimes gives regimes an inescapable intersubjective quality. It follows that we *know* regimes by their principled and shared understandings of desirable and acceptable forms of social behavior. Hence, the ontology of regimes rests upon a strong element of intersubjectivity.

Now, consider the fact that the prevailing epistemological position in regime analysis is almost entirely positivistic in orientation. Before it does anything else, positivism posits a radical separation of subject and object. It then focuses on the "objective" forces that move actors in their social interactions. Finally, intersubjective meaning, where it is considered at all, is inferred from behavior.

Here, then, we have the most debilitating problem of all: epistemology fundamentally contradicts ontology! Small wonder that so much disagreement exists on what should be fairly straightforward empirical questions: Did Bretton Woods "collapse" in 1971–73, or was the change "norm governed"? Are recent trade restraints indicative of dangerous protectionism or not? . . .

In many such puzzling instances, actor *behavior* has failed adequately to convey intersubjective *meaning*. And intersubjective meaning, in turn, seems to have had considerable influence on actor behavior. It is precisely this factor that limits the practical utility of the otherwise fascinating insights into the collaborative potential of rational egoists which are derived from laboratory or game-theoretic situations.[31] To put the problem in its simplest terms: in the simulated world, actors cannot communicate *and* engage in behavior; they are condemned to communicate *through* behavior. In the real world, the situation of course differs fundamentally. Here, the very essence of international regimes is expressed in cases such as that of France in 1968, asking for "sympathy and understanding" from its trading partners, as France invoked emergency measures against imports after the May disturbances of that year—and getting both from GATT (General Agreement on Tariffs and Trade) even though *no* objective basis existed in fact or in GATT law for doing so. But a positivist epistemology simply cannot accommodate itself to so intersubjective an ontology. Hence, the case is treated in the literature as illustrating cynicism, complicity, and the erosion of respect for the GATT regime.[32]

The contradiction between ontology and epistemology has elicited surprisingly little concern in the regimes literature. Once it is realized just how problematical the contradiction is, however, what options exist to deal with it? One possibility would be to try to deny it somehow. Theodore Abel's classic neopositivist response to the challenge posed by Weber's concept of *Verstehen* might serve as a model: the concept aids in "the context discovery," Abel contended, but ultimately it is not a method relevant to "the context of validation." Hence it poses no challenge.[33] This response may have been viable a generation ago, but it no longer is. Interpretive epistemologies . . . are simply too well developed today to be easily dismissed by charges of subjectivism[34]—or . . . of idealism.

A second possibility would be to try to formulate a rendition of the intersubjective ontology which is compatible with positivist epistemology. In view of the influence currently enjoyed in international relations theory by analogies and metaphors drawn from microeconomics, one plausible means of executing this maneuver would be to follow the economists down the road of "revealed preferences"—that consumption behavior, for example, reveals true consumer preferences. If our epistemology does not enable us to uncover meaning, the analogous reasoning would hold, then let us look for "revealed meaning," that is, for "objective" surrogates. It should suffice to point out that this is a solution by displacement: it displaces the problem into the realm of assumption—namely that "objective" surrogates can capture "intersubjective" reality—which of course is not uncharacteristic of the manner in which economists handle difficult problems.

That leaves us with the third and only viable option, of opening up the positivist epistemology to more interpretive strains, more closely attuned to the reality of regimes. . . .

Norms in Explanation

There is a closely related problem having to do with models of explanation. The standard positivist model works with an initial condition plus a covering law, on the basis of which it hypothesizes or predicts an occurrence. Even a single counterfactual occurrence may be taken to refute the covering law.[35] (A probabilistic formulation would, of course, appropriately modify the criteria for refutation, but it would not alter the basic structure of the explanation.)

Now consider the fact that what distinguishes international regimes from other international phenomena—from strategic interaction, let us say—is a specifically normative element.[36] Indeed, one of the four analytical components of the concept of regimes is specified to be norms—"standards of behavior defined in terms of rights and obligations." And it has become customary to maintain that change in the normative structure of regimes produces change *of*, as opposed merely to *within*, regimes.[37]

The positivist model of explanation is not easily applied to cases in which norms, so defined, are a significant element in the phenomena to be explained. . . . Two problems in particular need to be raised.[38]

First, unlike the initial conditions in positivist explanations, norms can be thought of only with great difficulty as "causing" occurrences. Norms may "guide" behavior, they may "inspire" behavior, they may "rationalize" or "justify" behavior, they may express "mutual expectations" about behavior, or they may be ignored. But they do not effect cause in the sense that a bullet through the heart causes death or an uncontrolled surge in the money supply causes price inflation. Hence, where norms are involved, the first component of the positivist model of explanation is problematical.

The second is even more so. For norms are counterfactually valid. No single counterfactual occurrence refutes a norm. Not even many such occurrences necessarily do. Does driving while under the influence of alcohol refute the law (norm) against drunk driving? Does it when half the population is implicated? To be sure, the law (norm) is *violated* thereby. But whether or not violations also invalidate or refute a law (norm) will depend upon a host of other factors, not the least of which is how the community assesses the violation and responds to it. What is true of drunk driving is equally true of the norms of nondiscrimination in international trade, free and stable currency exchanges, and adequate compensation for expropriated foreign property. . . .

Let it be understood that we are not advocating a coup whereby the reign of positivist explanation is replaced by explanatory anarchy. But we would insist that, just as epistemology has to match ontology, so too does the explanatory model have to be compatible with the basic nature of the particular scientific enterprise at hand. The impact of norms within international regimes is not a passive process, which can be ascertained analogously to that of Newtonian laws governing the collision of two bodies. Hence, the common practice of treating norms as "variables"—be they independent, dependent, intervening, or otherwise—should be severely curtailed. So too should be the preoccupation with the "violation" of norms as the beginning, middle, and end of the compliance story. Precisely because state behavior within regimes *is* interpreted by other states, the rationales and justifications for behavior which are proffered, together with pleas for understanding or admissions of guilt, as well as the responsiveness to such reasoning on the part of other states, all are absolutely critical component parts of any explanation involving the efficacy of norms. Indeed, such communicative dynamics may tell us far more about how robust a regime is than overt behavior alone. And only where noncompliance is widespread, persistent, and unexcused—that is, presumably, in limiting cases—will an explanatory model that rests on overt behavior alone suffice.[39]

To be sure, communicative dynamics may be influenced by such extracontextual factors as state power, but that is no warrant for ignoring them. On the contrary, it suggests a potentially important relationship to be explored.[40] Similarly, the fact that verbal behavior may lend itself to manipulation suggests only that it be treated as judiciously as any other piece of scientific evidence.

The Hierarchy of Analytical Components

The concept of international regimes is said to be a composite of four analytical component parts: principles ("beliefs of fact, causation, and rectitude"), norms ("standards of behavior defined in terms of rights and obligations"), rules ("specific prescriptions and proscriptions for action"), and decision-making procedures ("prevailing practices for making and implementing collective choice").[41] At first blush, the four fit together neatly in the specific case that was uppermost in everyone's mind when this conception was initially hammered out: the GATT-based trade regime.[42] The principle that liberalized trade is good for global welfare and international peace was readily translated by states into such norms as nondiscrimination, which in turn suggested the most-favored-nation rule, all of which led to negotiated tariff reductions based on reciprocal concessions. But matters were complicated right from the start by the fact that GATT contained not one but at least *two* such "scripts," and that the second stood in stark contrast to the first. The second ran from the responsibility of governments to stabilize their domestic economies on through the norm of safeguarding the balance of payments and, under certain circumstances, domestic producers, to rules defining specific GATT safeguarding provisions, and finally to establishing mechanisms of multilateral surveillance over their operations.[43] Different governments of course weighted these two scripts differently, but over time they seem not to have been unduly perturbed by the need to live with the ambiguity of their juxtaposition. Ambiguity, however, *is* more troublesome for analysts, *even when* it is a deliberate creation of policy makers.[44] And therein lies another epistemological tale.

The notion still prevails in the regimes literature that the four analytical components are related instrumentally and that the greater the coherence among them is, the stronger the regime will be.[45] There is an a priori attractiveness to this notion, in the sense that our collective research program would be eased considerably were it to obtain. But reality is not so obliging. Let us take up first the instrumentalist idea.

A basic epistemological problem with instrumentalism is its presumption that it is always possible to separate goals (presumably expressed in principles and norms) from means (presumably expressed in rules and procedures), and to order them in a superordinate-subordinate relationship. But this relationship need not hold. As R. S. Summers has aptly remarked: "However true this might be of constructing houses or other artifacts, it is not always so in law. In law when available means limit and in part define the goal, the means and the goal thus defined are to that extent inseparable.". . . [46] Thus, notions such as reciprocity in the trade regime are *neither* its ends *nor* its means: in a quintessential way, they *are* the regime—they *are* the principled and shared understandings that the regime comprises.

The idea that the four regime components should also be coherent, and that coherence indicates regime strength, is even more profoundly problematical. The basic epistemological problem with this notion is its presumption that, once the machinery is in place, actors merely remain programmed by it. But this is clearly not so. Actors not only reproduce normative structures, they also change them by their very practice, as underlying conditions change, as new constraints or possibilities emerge, or as new claimants make their presence felt. Lawyers call this "interstitial lawmaking,"[47] and sociologists, the process of "structuration."[48] Only under extremely unusual circumstances could we imagine parallel and simultaneous changes having taken place in each of the four component parts of regimes such that they remained coherent—assuming that they were so at the outset. In any case the robustness of international regimes has little to do with how coherent they remain—how coherent is the very robust U.S. Constitution?—but depends on the extent to which evolving and even diverging practices of actors express principled reasoning and shared understandings.

We have now reached the same conclusion through three different routes: the conventional epistemological approaches in regime studies do not and cannot suffice. . . .

REGIMES AND ORGANIZATIONS

The progressive shift in the literature toward the study of international regimes has been guided by an abiding concern with the structures and processes of international governance. Despite remaining problems with this framework of analysis, the most serious of which were flagged in the previous section, a great deal has been accomplished in a relatively short span of time. Along the way, however, . . . international institutions of a formal kind have been left behind. This fact is of academic interest because of the ever-present danger of theory getting out of touch with practice. But it is also of more than academic interest. The Secretary General of the United Nations, to cite but one serious practical instance, has lamented that the malfunctioning of that institution seriously inhibits interstate collaboration in the peace and security field. . . .[49] In order for the research program of international regimes *both* to contribute to ongoing policy concerns *and* better reflect the complex and sometimes ambiguous policy realm, it is necessary to link up regimes in some fashion with the formal mechanisms through which real-world actors operate. In point of fact, the outlines of such linkages are already implicit in the regime approach. Our purpose in this final section is no more than to underscore the specific dimensions that are highlighted by an interpretive epistemology.

There has been a great deal of interest in the regimes literature recently in what can be described as the "organizational-design" approach. The key issue underlying this approach is to discern what range of international policy problems can best be handled by different kinds of institutional arrangements, such as simple norms of coordination, the reallocation of international property rights, or authoritative control through formal organizations. For example, an international fishing authority would probably be less appropriate and less able to avoid the early exhaustion of fisheries' stock than would the ascription of exclusive property rights to states. Where problems of liability enter the picture, however, as in ship-based pollution, authoritative procedures for settling disputes would become necessary. The work of Oliver Williamson and William Ouchi is very suggestive here, demonstrating the relative efficacy of the institutionalization of behavior through "hierarchies" versus through transaction-based informal means. . . .[50]

For its part, an interpretive epistemology would emphasize three additional dimensions of the organizational-design issue. The intersubjective basis of international regimes suggests that *transparency* of actor behavior and expectations within regimes is one of their core requirements. And, as has been shown in such diverse issue-areas as international trade, investment, nuclear nonproliferation, and human rights, international organizations can be particularly effective instruments by which to create such transparency. . . .[51]

The second is *legitimation*. A regime can be perfectly rationally designed but erode because its legitimacy is undermined.[52] Or a regime that is a logical non-starter can be the object of endless negotiations because a significant constituency views its aims to be legitimate.[53] If a regime enjoys both it is described as being "stable" or "hegemonic." The important point to note is that international organizations, because of their trappings of universality, are the major venue within which the global legitimation struggle over international regimes is carried out today. . . .

The third dimension we would describe as *epistemic*. Stephen Toulmin has posed the issue well: "The problem of human understanding is a twofold one. Man knows, and he is also conscious that he knows. We acquire, possess, and make use of our knowledge; but at the same time, we are aware of our own activities as knowers."[54] In the international arena, neither the processes whereby knowledge becomes more extensive nor the means whereby reflection on knowledge deepens are passive or automatic. They are intensely political. And for better or for worse, international organizations have maneuvered themselves into the position of being the vehicle through which both types of knowledge enter onto the international agenda. . . .[55]

In short, the institutional-design approach, complemented by a concern with transparency creation, the legitimation struggle, and epistemic politics, can push the heuristic fruitfulness of the regime research program "forward" yet another step, linking it "back" to the study of international organizations.

CONCLUSION

In this article, we set out to present a "state of the art" of the field of international organization circa 1985. Our conclusions can be restated very quickly. In the first section, we tried to dispel the notion that the field has been floundering from one "dependent variable" to another, as academic fashions have dictated. On the contrary, the analytical shifts have been progressive and cumulative and have been guided by an overriding concern with what has always preoccupied students of international organization: how the modern society of nations governs itself.

In the second section we pointed out, however, that the currently ascendant regimes approach is internally inconsistent in a manner that has deleterious effects. The reason for its inconsistency is the tension between its ontological posture and its prevailing epistemological practices. In contrast to the epistemological ideal of positivism, which insists on a separation of "object" and "subject," we proposed a more interpretive approach that would open up regime analysis to the communicative rather than merely the referential functions of norms in social interactions. Thus, what constitutes a breach of an obligation undertaken within a regime is not simply an "objective description" of a fact but an intersubjective appraisal. . . .

Finally, in our third section, we identified some linkages between the analytical construct of international regimes and the concrete entities of international organizations. Students of international organization have already assimilated from the organizational design school the lesson that the provision of routine and predictable policy frameworks is not synonymous with the construction of formal hierarchies. An interpretive epistemology would suggest further that international organizations can contribute to the effectiveness of informal ordering mechanisms, such as regimes, by their ability to enhance (or diminish) intersubjective expectations and normatively stabilized meanings, which are the very bases of regimes. International organizations do so, we pointed out, through the modalities of transparency creation, focusing the legitimation struggle, and devising future regime agendas via epistemic politics. Thus reinvigorated, the study of formal organizations may yet come to reinvigorate the practice of formal organizations.

NOTES

1. Thomas Kuhn uses the notion "sets of puzzles" in his discussion of preludes to paradigms; see Kuhn, *The Structure of Scientific Revolutions* (Chicago: University of Chicago Press, 1962), and *The Essential Tension* (Chicago: University of Chicago Press, 1977).
2. The criterion of the fruitfulness of a research program, and issues connected with progressive versus degenerative problem shifts, were introduced by Imre Lakatos, "Falsification and the Methodology of Scientific Research Programmes," in Lakatos and Alan Musgrave, eds., *Criticisms and the Growth of Knowledge* (Cambridge: Cambridge University Press, 1970).
3. Edmund C. Mower, *International Government* (Boston: Heath, 1931).
4. A distinguished contribution to this literature is Leland M. Goodrich and Anne P. Simons, *The United Nations and the Maintenance of International Peace and Security* (Washington, DC: Brookings, 1955). See also Klaus Knorr, "The Bretton Woods Institutions in Transition," *International Organization* [hereafter cited as *IO*] 2 (February 1948); Walter R. Sharp, "The Institutional Framework for Technical Assistance," *IO* 7 (August 1953); and Henri Rolin, "The International Court of Justice and Domestic Jurisdiction," *IO* 8 (February 1954).
5. The most comprehensive work in this genre remains Robert W. Cox and Harold K. Jacobson, eds., *The Anatomy of Influence: Decision Making in International Organization* (New Haven: Yale University Press, 1973).
6. Inis L. Claude's landmark text, *Swords into Plowshares* (New York: Random House, 1959), both signaled and contributed to this shift.

7. Lincoln P. Bloomfield, ed., *International Force—A Symposium, IO* 17 (Spring 1973); James M. Boyd, "Cyprus: Episode in Peacekeeping," *IO* 20 (Winter 1966); Robert O. Matthews, "The Suez Canal Dispute: A Case Study in Peaceful Settlement," *IO* 21 (Winter 1967); Yashpal Tandon, "Consensus and Authority behind UN Peacekeeping Operations," *IO* 21 (Spring 1967); David P. Forsythe, "United Nations Intervention in Conflict Situations Revisited: A Framework for Analysis," *IO* 23 (Winter 1969); John Gerard Ruggie, "Contingencies, Constraints, and Collective Security: Perspectives on UN Involvement in International Disputes," *IO* 28 (Summer 1974); and Ernst B. Haas, "Regime Decay: Conflict Management and International Organization, 1945–1981," *IO* 37 (Spring 1983).

8. Robert E. Pendley and Lawrence Scheinman, "International Safeguarding as Institutionalized Collective Behavior," in John Gerard Ruggie and Ernst B. Haas, eds., special issue on international responses to technology, *IO* 29 (Summer 1975); and Joseph S. Nye, "Maintaining a Non-Proliferation Regime," in George H. Quester, ed., special issue on nuclear nonproliferation, *IO* 35 (Winter 1981).

9. Ernst B. Haas, "The Attempt to Terminate Colonization: Acceptance of the UN Trusteeship System," *IO* 7 (February 1953); John Fletcher-Cooke, "Some Reflections on the International Trusteeship System," *IO* 13 (Summer 1959); Harold K. Jacobson, "The United Nations and Colonialism: A Tentative Appraisal," *IO* 16 (Winter 1962); and David A. Kay, "The Politics of Decolonization: The New Nations and the United Nations Political Process," *IO* 21 (Autumn 1967).

10. Richard N. Gardner and Max F. Millikan, eds., special issue on international agencies and economic development, *IO* 22 (Winter 1968).

11. Among many other sources, see Branislav Gosovic and John Gerard Ruggie, "On the Creation of a New International Economic Order: Issue Linkage and the Seventh Special Session of the UN General Assembly," *IO* 30 (Spring 1976).

12. David A. Kay and Eugene B. Skolnikoff, eds., special issue on international institutions and the environmental crisis, *IO* 26 (Spring 1972); Ruggie and Haas, eds., special issue, *IO* 29 (Summer 1975); and Per Magnus Wijkman, "Managing the Global Commons," *IO* 36 (Summer 1982).

13. Various approaches to the study of integration were summarized and assessed in Leon N. Lindberg and Stuart A. Scheingold, eds., special issue on regional integration, *IO* 24 (Autumn 1970).

14. Ernst B. Haas, *Beyond the Nation State: Functionalism and International Organization* (Stanford: Stanford University Press, 1964).

15. The phrase is Stanley Hoffmann's in "International Organization and the International System," *IO* 24 (Summer 1970). A similar position was advanced earlier by Oran R. Young, "The United Nations and the International System," *IO* 22 (Autumn 1968).

16. Inis L. Claude, Jr., "Collective Legitimization as a Political Function of the United Nations," *IO* 20 (Summer 1966); cf. Jerome Slater, "The Limits of Legitimization in International Organizations: The Organization of American States and the Dominican Crisis," *IO* 23 (Winter 1969).

17. A representative sampling would include Kay and Skolnikoff, eds., special issue, *IO* 26 (Spring 1972); Robert Russell, "Transgovernmental Interaction in the International Monetary System, 1960–1972," *IO* 27 (Autumn 1973); Thomas Weiss and Robert Jordan, "Bureaucratic Politics and the World Food Conference," *World Politics* 28 (April 1976); Raymond F. Hopkins, "The International Role of 'Domestic' Bureaucracy," *IO* 30 (Summer 1976); and John Gerard Ruggie, "On the Problem of 'The Global Problematique': What Roles for International Organizations?" *Alternatives* 5 (January 1980).

18. The major analytical piece initiating this genre was Robert O. Keohane and Joseph S.

Nye, "Transgovernmental Relations and International Organizations," *World Politics* 27 (October 1974); cf. their earlier edited work on transnational relations and world politics, *IO* 25 (Summer 1971).

19. Robert Cox's recent work has been at the forefront of exploring this aspect of international organization: "Labor and Hegemony," *IO* 31 (Summer 1977); "The Crisis of World Order and the Problem of International Organization in the 1980's," *International Journal* 35 (Spring 1980); and "Gramsci, Hegemony and International Relations: An Essay in Method," *Millennium: Journal of International Studies* 12 (Summer 1983).

20. Robert O. Keohane and Joseph S. Nye, "International Interdependence and Integration," in Fred I. Greenstein and Nelson W. Polsby, eds., *Handbook of Political Science*, vol. 8 (Reading, MA: Addison-Wesley, 1975). The point is also implicit in Ernst Haas's self-criticism, "Turbulent Fields and the Theory of Regional Integration," *IO* 30 (Spring 1976).

21. John Gerard Ruggie, "International Responses to Technology: Concepts and Trends," *IO* 29 (Summer 1975).

22. This is the tack taken by Susan Strange, "Still an Extraordinary Power: America's Role in a Global Monetary System," in Raymond E. Lombra and William E. Witte, eds., *Political Economy of International and Domestic Monetary Relations* (Ames: Iowa State University Press, 1982); and Bruce Russett, "The Mysterious Case of Vanishing Hegemony: Or, Is Mark Twain Really Dead?" *IO* 39 (Spring 1985).

23. See Stephen D. Krasner, "Introduction," in Stephen D. Krasner, ed., *International Regimes* (Ithaca, NY: Cornell University Press, 1983); and Robert O. Keohane, *After Hegemony* (Princeton: Princeton University Press, 1984), for discussions of this thesis.

24. The fad-fettish is argued by Susan Strange, "Cave! Hic Dragones: A Critique of Regime Analysis," in Krasner, ed., *International Regimes.*

25. The public-choice approach to the study of international organization began with the use of public goods theory in the early 1970s, went on to explore the theory of property rights later in the decade, and has come to focus on game theory and microeconomic theories of market failure to explain patterns of international governance. See, respectively, Bruce M. Russett and John D. Sullivan, "Collective Goods and International Organizations," *IO* 25 (Autumn 1971), and John Gerard Ruggie, "Collective Goods and Future International Collaboration," *American Political Science Review* 66 (September 1972); John A. C. Conybeare, "International Organization and the Theory of Property Rights," *IO* 34 (Summer 1980); and Keohane, *After Hegemony.* A useful review of the relevant literature may be found in Bruno S. Frey, "The Public Choice View of International Political Economy," *IO* 38 (Winter 1984).

26. In the context of rational-choice theory generally, the argument was first articulated by John Harsanyi, "Rational Choice Models of Political Behavior vs. Functionalist and Conformist Theories," *World Politics* 21 (July 1969). In the international relations literature, it is implicit in Robert Jervis, "Cooperation under the Security Dilemma," *World Politics* 30 (January 1978), and explicit in Robert Axelrod, "The Emergence of Cooperation among Egoists," *American Political Science Review* 75 (June 1981), as well as in Keohane, *After Hegemony.*

27. Richard K. Ashley, "The Poverty of Neorealism," *IO* 38 (Spring 1984), and Friedrich Kratochwil, "Errors Have Their Advantage," *IO* 38 (Spring 1984).

28. See Susan Strange, in Krasner, ed., *International Regimes.*

29. This route is taken by Vinod K. Aggarwal, *Liberal Protectionism: The International Politics of Organized Textile Trade* (Berkeley: University of California Press, 1985).

30. On "contestable concepts," see William Connally, *The Terms of Political Discourse,* 2d ed. (Princeton: Princeton University Press, 1983).

31. Most notable among such works is Robert Axelrod's *Evolution of Cooperation* (New

York: Basic, 1984), and Axelrod, "Modeling the Evolution of Norms" (Paper delivered at the annual meeting of the American Political Science Association, New Orleans, 29 August–1 September 1985). For an attempt to incorporate progressively more "reflective" logical procedures into sequential Prisoner's Dilemma situations and to expose them to more realistic data sets, see Hayward R. Alker, James Bennett, and Dwain Mefford, "Generalized Precedent Logics for Resolving Insecurity Dilemmas," *International Interactions* 7, no. 2 (1980), and Hayward Alker and Akihiro Tanaka, "Resolution Possibilities in 'Historical' Prisoners' Dilemmas" (Paper delivered at the annual meeting of the International Studies Association, Philadelphia, 18 March 1981).

32. This case, and the more general problem of interpretation which it reflects, are discussed by John Gerard Ruggie, "International Regimes, Transactions, and Change: Embedded Liberalism in the Postwar Economic Order," in Krasner, ed., *International Regimes*.

33. Theodore F. Abel, "The Operation Called *Verstehen*," *American Journal of Sociology* 54 (November 1948).

34. For a good selection of readings that begins with Weber, includes the neopositivist response, the Wittgensteinian school, phenomenology, and ethnomethodology, and ends with hermeneutics and critical theory, see Fred R. Dallmayr and Thomas A. McCarthy, *Understanding and Social Inquiry* (Notre Dame: University of Notre Dame Press, 1977).

35. On the importance of the logical form of *modus tollens* in the hypothetical deductive explanation scheme, see Karl Popper, *The Logic of Scientific Discovery* (New York: Harper & Row, 1968), chaps. 3 and 4.

36. One of the distinctive characteristics of strategic interaction is that ultimately it rests upon a *unilateral* calculation of verbal and nonverbal cues: "A's expectation of B will include an estimation of B's expectations of A. This process of replication, it must be noted, is not an interaction between two states, but rather a process in which decision-makers in one state work out the consequences of their beliefs about the world; a world they believe to include decision-makers in other states, also working out the consequences of their beliefs. The expectations which are so formed are the expectations of one state, but they refer to other states." Paul Keal, *Unspoken Rules and Superpower Dominance* (London: Macmillan, 1984), p. 31.

37. See Krasner, "Introduction," *International Regimes*.

38. Some of these and related issues are discussed more extensively in Kratochwil, "The Force of Prescriptions," *IO* 38 (Autumn 1984).

39. Account should also be taken of that fact that different types of norms—implicit versus explicit, constraining versus enabling, and so on—function differently in social relations. Consult Edna Ullman-Margalit, *The Emergence of Norms* (Oxford: Clarendon, 1977), and H. L. A. Hart, *The Concept of Law* (Oxford: Oxford University Press, 1961). Moreover, compliance too is a variegated and complex phenomenon, as discussed by Oran R. Young, *Compliance and Public Authority* (Baltimore: Johns Hopkins University Press, 1979).

40. It is well established that the so-called hegemonic stability thesis, for example, leaves a good deal about regimes still to be accounted for. See the original formulation and test by Robert O. Keohane, "Theory of Hegemonic Stability and Changes in International Economic Regimes," in Ole Holsti et al., eds., *Change in the International System* (Boulder: Westview, 1980); and, most recently, Duncan Snidal, "The Limits of Hegemonic Stability Theory," *IO* 39 (Autumn 1985).

41. Krasner, "Introduction," *International Regimes*, p. 2.

42. These issues were discussed at length at the October 1980 UCLA conference in preparation for the regimes book edited by Krasner.

43. The interplay between these two scripts forms the basis of Ruggie's interpretation of the postwar trade and monetary regimes presented in "Embedded Liberalism."

44. The proclivity of international relations theorists to resolve ambiguity and contradiction in images of international order, and the schema on the basis of which they do so, are explored by John Gerard Ruggie, "Changing Frameworks of International Collective Behavior: On the Complementarity of Contradictory Tendencies," in Nazli Choucri and Thomas Robinson, eds., *Forecasting in International Relations* (San Francisco: Freeman, 1978).

45. Cf. Haas, "Regime Decay."

46. R. S. Summers, "Naive Instrumentalism and the Law," in P.S. Hacker and J. Raz, eds., *Law, Morality, and Society* (Oxford: Clarendon, 1977).

47. This is simply another name for the role of precedent in legal interpretation and development.

48. Anthony Giddens, *A Contemporary Critique of Historical Materialism* (Berkeley: University of California Press, 1981), p. 19: "According to the theory of structuration, all social action consists of social practices, situated in time-space, and organized in a skilled and knowledgeable fashion by human agents. But such knowledgeability is always 'bounded' by unacknowledged conditions of action on the one side, and unintended consequences of action on the other. . . . By the duality of structure I mean that the structured properties of social systems are simultaneously the *medium and outcome of social acts.*"

49. United Nations, *Report of the Secretary-General on the Work of the Organization, 1982* (A/37/1).

50. Oliver Williamson, *Markets and Hierarchies* (New York: Free, 1975), and William Ouchi and Oliver Williamson, "The Markets and Hierarchies Program of Research: Origins, Implications, Prospects," in William Joyce and Andrew van de Ven, eds., *Organization Design* (New York: Wiley, 1981). From the legal literature, see Guido Calabresi and Douglas Melamed, "Property Rules, Liability Rules, and Inalienability: One View of the Cathedral," *Harvard Law Review* 85 (April 1972); Philip Heyemann, "The Problem of Coordination: Bargaining with Rules," *Harvard Law Review* 86 (March 1973); and Susan Rose-Ackerman, "Inalienability and the Theory of Property Rights," *Columbia Law Review* 85 (June 1985).

51. The GATT multilateral surveillance mechanisms are, of course, its chief institutional means of establishing intersubjectively acceptable interpretations of what actors are up to. For a treatment of investment which highlights this dimension, see Charles Lipson, *Standing Guard: Protecting Foreign Capital in the Nineteenth and Twentieth Centuries* (Berkeley: University of California Press, 1985); for nonproliferation, see Nye, "Maintaining a Nonproliferation Regime," and for human rights, John Gerard Ruggie, "Human Rights and the Future International Community," *Daedalus* 112 (Fall 1983). The impact of intergovernmental information systems is analyzed by Ernst B. Haas and John Gerard Ruggie, "What Message in the Medium of Information Systems?" *International Studies Quarterly* 26 (June 1982).

52. Puchala and Hopkins, "International Regimes," in Krasner, ed., *International Regimes*, discuss the decline of colonialism in terms that include this dimension.

53. The New International Economic Order is a prime example.

54. Stephen Toulmin, *Human Understanding* (Princeton: Princeton University Press, 1972), p. 1.

55. Ruggie analyzes this process in "On the Problem of 'The Global Problematique.'"

Theorizing the "National" in International Relations Theory:
Reflections on Nationalism and Neorealism

Yosef Lapid

INTRODUCTION

In international relations theory—neorealism in particular—nations and nationalisms register as a key area of empirical neglect and theoretical infertility (Howard, 1989; Ryan, 1990). The "neglect-of-nationalism" problem has not passed totally unnoticed by the IR discipline (Holsti, 1980; Haas, 1986; Jervis, 1989). The remarkable aspect of our story is, however, that even when noted, this glaring lacuna has nonetheless failed to generate a sustained disciplinary effort to eliminate it. Indeed—despite the salience of the national factor in the extraordinary transformations of our global political landscape since 1989—we have yet to see a serious theoretical effort to reconsider nationalism in light of contemporary transformations.[1]

In view of the above, we have reasons to suspect that in the case of nationalism we are not facing a typical manifestation of random scholarly neglect. The dynamics of misinterpretation by which the neorealist omission of nationalism has been produced and reproduced may not be observational or theoretical in any narrow sense. They may be embedded instead in sets of underlying premises which continue to shape IR theoretical thinking on nationalism. Arguably, such "second-order" obstacles are not easily corrigible by improved "first-order" definitions of what we mean by nationalism (Riggs, 1990:578), nor by enhanced rationales of why we should study it more carefully in the future (Haas, 1986).

This study sets out to explore the possibility that major metatheoretical blockages may account for the otherwise puzzling absence of nations and nationalisms from the current neorealist agenda (Lapid, 1989). Submitting that the national phenomenon is not one that any major IR theory can currently afford to ignore, the analysis locates and unpacks the misguided paradigmatic logic which can be held largely responsible for our postulated neglect-of-nationalism problem. We proceed in three consecutive stages. The first section deals with broad definitional issues in an attempt to delimit the complex and changing profile of contemporary nationalism. The second part locates the specific sense in which nations and nationalism can be shown to be missing from neorealism in some theoretically interesting way. The third section shows that the neorealist omission of nationalism is a product of guiding theoretical premises, as opposed to random scholarly neglect. We conclude with preliminary thoughts on how theorizing the "national" in international relations theory, along the lines suggested in this paper, may help render the neorealist game of "catching up with the new realities" a less desperate one.

I. NATIONALISM: THE PROFILE OF AN ELUSIVE PHENOMENON

Ironically enough, countless attempts to deal with the "semantic" problem of nationalism have only succeeded to render it ever less manageable. As put by a justly exasperated observer, the terminological problem is by now "not only gigantic but also insoluble" (Riggs, 1987:109). So, rather than committing our discussion to some narrowly gauged ("operational") definitions, we shall try to restore the lost clarity of some fundamental distinctions concerning the national phenomenon.

With respect to nationalism it seems essential to differentiate between two interrelated, but analytically distinct, meanings (Seton-Watson, 1977:3). In its first and more interesting meaning, nationalism is a "theory" (Cobban, 1969:35), a "core doctrine" (Smith, 1983:150), a "global political programme" (Hobsbawm, 1990:181), and/or a "generative order for geopolitical organization" (Portugali, 1988:154) that designates the "nation-state" as the archetypical modern polity. In its second meaning, nationalism refers to behavioral "facts" produced by political movements seeking to defend or to advance the interests of their respective "nations." Both of these meanings stand in need of further clarifications.

The "Theory" of Nationalism

As a "theory" or as a "generative order," nationalism affirms at least three cardinal tenets. First, it holds that the world is divided into "nations," each with its own character. Second, it prescribes that each "nation" ought to constitute an independent polity and become coextensive with it. And in the third place, it holds that the coincidence of nations and states on a one-to-one basis is highly desirable from both the perspective of individual nations and from the point of view of a successful global political order. The following observations about nationalism as a "generative order" seem relevant for our purposes.

1. The "generative order" interpretation postulates a qualitative discontinuity between nationalism as a *modern normative doctrine* and earlier forms of ethnonational collective identifications (Worsley, 1984:187–203). The French Revolution is the earliest point of reference for its historical appearance as a coherent and fully articulated blueprint for global political order (Cobban, 1969:35). Expressions of what may look like nationalism in the pre–eighteenth century era are hence to be recognized as *qualitatively* different phenomena. For in the absence of a nation-state "blueprint," sociological expressions of collective identity cannot possibly result in the potent behavioral pattern characteristic of modern nationalism.[2]

2. Nationalism thus understood emerges as a potentially revolutionary doctrine (Bibo, 1976:73). Depending on the degree to which extant political realities do in fact approximate the "nation-state" desideratum, nationalism may have formidable disruptive, or powerful reproductive, implications. When state boundaries do not actually coincide with national boundaries, the ascendance of nationalism as a "generative order" will set into motion a disruptive dual-track process that predisposes "stateless-nations" and "nationless-states" to embark in energetic efforts to "normalize" their existence. To the extent, however, that this disruptive upheaval does take its grim course—and results in a world of actual nation-states—nationalism can then be expected to lose much of its revolutionary potential. It could then be expected to mutate into a stabilizing force, institutionalizing the smooth reproduction of a global order consisting of "nonproblematic" nation-states. In this context, the nationalist doctrine also upholds the "dogma of homogeneity" and presents itself as a great would-be simplifier at the global level (Cobban, 1969:125). For the success of the "programme" would signify a degree of stability, uniformity, and symmetry in the basic makeup of the "legitimate" constituents of our global political order ("nations-states") which is both unprecedented and unimaginable in view of extant realities.

3. As a model of global political organization, nationalism is marred, however, by a strong element of indeterminacy which continues to bedevil the course of contemporary world politics. The "nation-state" blueprint is inherently problematic for it combines territorial and ethnic principles of sociopolitical organization. These two principles are potentially contradictory in a world, like ours, which is intricately multiethnic and which permits, stimulates, and frequently necessitates movements of large numbers of people across territorial boundaries. "A purely territorial state," explain H. M. Hughes and E. C. Hughes, "claims sovereignty over all within its boundaries including the ethnic strangers within its gates. A purely national state would claim sovereignty over its members no matter where they go. It would disregard territory. The nation-state suffers from continual strain because it combines these two contradictory principles" (Hughes and Hughes, 1952:116).

4. Theoretical contradictions notwithstanding, the "generative-order" interpretation of nationalism has considerable merit in that it renders intelligible the remarkable modern propensity of states to form nations and of nations to establish themselves as states (McNeill, 1986). The current political order would look much different without this doomed desire to seek "national congruence" by fusing together cultural identities with corresponding territorial polities. The active involvement of over 800 million persons (or about 25% of the world's population) in ethnicity-based identity group conflicts (Gurr, 1990)—as well as the actual or near breakup of "multinational states" (the former Soviet Union, Yugoslavia, Canada, etc.) and the reunification of "multistate nations" (Germany, Korea?)—dramatically attest to the enduring "generative" power of nationalism in the expanding structural fluidity of the post–cold war era.[3] For there is arguably nothing inherent in either "nations" or "states" to feed these deadly dynamics, were it not for the bitterly contested sets of contradictory "entitlements" derived from the ambiguities of the (nationalist) "generative order."

5. Available evidence strongly supports the conclusion that "[t]he attempt to make the culturally united nation-state the one and only basis of legitimate political organization has proven untenable in practice. It was never tenable in theory" (Cobban, 1969:129). The historical verdict on this matter seems crystal clear. Most of the attempts to implement the nationalist programme have met with near-total failure. Properly utilized, the term "nation-state" applies even today to a mere handful of sovereign polities. The gap between the "nation-state" ideal and political reality seems, moreover, to be actually growing rather than narrowing (Nielsson, 1984). And it is precisely this paradoxical inability to either implement or repudiate the national "blueprint" which renders necessary a closer look to the "observational"—as opposed to "institutional"—facts of nationalism (Kratochwil, 1989). We turn now to the second important sense in which nations and nationalisms should figure in any theory of international relations hoping to catch up with long existing and newly emerging realities.

The "Facts" of Nationalism

Even if a pessimistic reading of the current status and future prospects of nationalism as a blueprint for global political organization turns out to be valid, it does not necessarily follow that we can safely ignore a rather different set of "facts" concerning contemporary nationalism. The historical evidence suggests that "national" activism need not, and does not always, occur in a coherent "nation-state" matrix. Rather than automatically dismissing such "neo-nationalisms" as theoretically uninteresting, the recognition that the *actual* relationship between "nation" and "state" is not as static as suggested by the generative model should simply force us to take seriously some fundamental sociological differences between "nations" and "states" as would-be referents of modern "national" activism (Wiberg, 1991). The following observations on the "sociological facts" of contemporary nationalism seem relevant for our purposes.

1. As a partial result of the internal contradictions of the nation-state "programme," contemporary world politics is animated by the predicaments of two interrelated, but nonetheless distinct, forms of nationalism: (a) *State-nationalism* attached to extant sovereign states and (b) *Ethnonationalism* expressing the rising aspirations of nonsovereign forms of ethnic nationhood.

These two forms of nationalism are not conditioned by the same set of explanatory factors. More importantly, they impact world politics in distinctly different ways. Hence they cannot be lumped in the same analytical containers without risking serious theoretical omissions. Since "nation" and "state" are neither in potentiality nor in actuality one and the same kind of thing, it follows that the haphazard interchanging of "nation" and "state" is unacceptable for theoretical, as opposed to merely semantic, reasons. Nations, in short, do not exist only in reference to the "nation-state" model, and the desire for statehood is not the sole defining characteristic of nationhood (Smith, 1988; Armstrong, 1990).

2. State-nationalism and ethnonationalism seem to differ in some of their generic characteristics. Their territorial, psychological, and political prerequisites, in particular, are very different. Of these two, even when it operates *outside* the nation-state matrix, state-nationalism must insist on territorial ownership, exclusive loyalty, and undiluted sovereignty. It will therefore invariably strengthen the reproductive, as opposed to transformative, logic of the existing world order. It will also invariably increase the stability, the symmetry, and the homogeneity of its constituent units. In notable contrast, especially when it distances itself from the orbit of the nation-state programme, ethnonationalism seems able to absorb considerable levels of territorial division, dispersion, and/or overlap, without a corresponding loss of collective identity.[4] As opposed to sovereign states which can deviate only marginally from Western notions of exclusive territorial ownership, once formed, "nations" have qualitatively greater latitude in this respect (Berry, 1981; Galtung, 1980:255). For unlike "states," "nations" do not necessarily derive their viability and their vitality from exclusive ownership of well-demarcated pieces of territory. In the case of nations, the normative basis of identity rests "not in *space,* but in *time*" (Berry, 1981:80). Other, theoretically relevant, differences derive from the fact that in contrast to state-nationalism, ethnonationalism must normally adjust to a condition of multiple loyalties and sub-sovereign levels of political control. All this renders ethnonationalism interesting as a possible agent of systemic transformation, as opposed to merely systemic disruption and/or reproduction (Isaacs, 1979:52).[5]

3. Recent technological, economic, and social developments have posed enormous challenges to the capacity of territorial states to fulfill their traditional functions of security, welfare, and identity (Poggi, 1990). It is at the identity level, in particular, that both highly-developed polities with solid economies of abundance (Canada, Belgium, Spain) and less-developed states trapped in economies of scarcity (the former Soviet Union, Yugoslavia, Jordan, India) have been experiencing difficulties in recent years (Isaacs, 1979; Armstrong, 1990). On the other hand, the relative magnetism of ethnonationalism may have been considerably enhanced by an obsessive search for community (Rothschild, 1981). "The identity dimension of ethnicity," says Manning Nash, "rests on the fact that fellow members of ethnic groups are thought to be 'human' and trustworthy in ways that outsiders are not. The ethnic group provides refuge against a hostile, uncaring world" (1989:128–29).

4. Two final clarifications seem necessary at this point. First, ethnicity is not, in principle, the only force animating the current lust for community. Other bases for "imagining community" are clearly possible and have been historically exercised (Anderson, 1983). For the time being, however, ethnicity has eclipsed all would-be competitors. This, I submit, is not to be explained by some "deep" psychological roots separating ethnicity from all other group solidarities. Rather, it is related to the fact that the still ruling "nation-state" generative order "entitles" and "empowers" (ethno)nations in ways which are clearly not applicable to any other nonstate "actors." Second, although it is true that ethnicity has not emerged yet as "an alternative principle for the political restructuring of the world in the twenty-first century" (Hobsbawm, 1990:173), it is in no way precluded that ethnicity will figure rather saliently—albeit in a transformed sense—when such a "principle" finally crystallizes.

II. NATIONALISM AND NEOREALISM: A PROBLEMATIC ENCOUNTER

We are now in a better position to specify the nature and scope of the neorealist problematic encounter with contemporary nationalism. Two points seem noteworthy in this context. First, in assessing the ability of neorealism—or any other IR theory—to make room for the national phenomenon, we must keep in mind the fundamental distinctions drawn between nationalism as a "generative order" and "political movement" on the one hand, and between "state-nationalism" and "ethnonationalism" on the other. Any IR theory that collapses these distinctions will not pass the test as set by this paper. This seems particularly important with respect to "state-nationalism" which, in one way or another, is bound to figure rather prominently in any "state-centric" theory. Although, when properly defined, state-nationalism does differ in significant ways from reified "statism," the two are—in some ways—largely compatible and mutually reinforcing. Far from resulting in embarrassing anomalies, state-nationalism may, in fact, be summoned in last-minute efforts to rescue embattled premises in the realist "hard-core" (Gilpin, 1986). The "state-centric" assumption and the "anarchy/hierarchy" distinction are perfect cases in point.

The situation is, however, radically different with respect to *ethnonationalism*. Whereas *state-nationalism* can facilitate realist and neorealist hard-core articulation, with respect to cardinal realist premises, *ethnonationalism* consistently throws up embarrassing "anomalies."[6] The reason becomes readily apparent once we recall that the theoretical apparati of both realism and neorealism were devised with sovereign states—as opposed to ethno-nations—in mind. It follows that if our intention is to determine the degree to which realist discourses have successfully accommodated the current complexities of the national phenomenon, we are better off focusing on the problematic *realism/ethnonationalism* nexus than on the *realism/state-nationalism* nexus where the national phenomenon melts quietly into indiscriminate state-centrism.

Second, we recall, however, that our target in this paper is not traditional realism, but structural neorealism in particular. This clarification shifts our attention back to nationalism as a *"generative order."* A careful reader will have realized by now that state-nationalism and ethnonationalism are unmistakably *unit-level* terms. Nationalism as a *"generative-order"* is, however, a *systemic-structural* construct par excellence. As a "generative order," nationalism has, as indicated, a generative role in the production and reproduction of the problematic "social totality" in which it operates. It has in addition recurrent behavioral implications for its relevant constituent units, in this case: (ethno)nations, nations, states, nation-states, multi-nation states, empires, and so on.

Whereas in the case of traditional realism (which is primarily an attempt at *unit-level* theorizing) we have no apparent reason to expect concern with nationalism as a generative structure, this is precisely the sense in which nationalism would have to figure, if at all, in neorealism. For as succinctly put by Waltz, "The idea that international politics can be thought of as a system with a precisely defined structure is neorealism's fundamental departure from traditional realism" (1990:30).

We have now determined both the shape of the missing parts (nationalism as a "generative order" and "ethnonationalism") and the place where we could possibly fit them in the neorealist puzzle (i.e., the neorealist concept of "structure" as defined by Professor Waltz). What remains to be shown is why the task, as defined, is mission impossible.

III. GENERATIVE ORDER VERSUS GENERATIVE STRUCTURE: INCOMPATIBLE?

The critical component of nationalism as a "generative order" is the *contestable prescription* that states should be nations and nations should be states. This "national congruence" prescription is historically specific and conventional. It has little to do with objective positivist laws. It operates as a "generative" producer of certain recurrent patterns, not through (mechanical) causation, but through its role in the contested set of constitutive norms which currently determine the "international game" (Kratochwil, 1991; Dessler, 1989; Jackson, 1990). Inconsistencies and ambiguities notwithstanding, the "nation-state" prescriptive formula institutionalizes national congruence as a positive and feasible political project. Both would-be nations *and* extant states feel *empowered* by this prescriptive formula to function as survival-oriented, macro-level conflict groups.

Some parallels with the institution of sovereignty are instructive in this context. As noted by John Ruggie (1983), the breakup or disintegration of any individual state cannot affect the institution of the state, or the interstate system itself, as long as the prescriptive force of *"sovereignty"* (as *the* master "generative order"?) is not significantly weakened. Likewise, as long as *nationalism* persists as a relevant "generative order," the elimination of any single unit of (ethnic) nationhood—through either assimilation or sovereign statehood—cannot affect the institutional permanence of an *international* (as opposed to interstate) tier in world politics.

It should be evident that thinking about nationalism as a "generative order" rests on a basic ontological position which "insists that *all* social action depends on the preexistence of rules, implying that even under anarchy, rules are an essential prerequisite for action" (Dessler, 1989:458). This ontological position seems clearly incompatible with the "positional ontology" which grounds the Waltzian construct of "generative structure." Nationalism as a "generative order" operates through norms, rules, and conventions which "institutionalize" social behavior. By contrast, Waltz's "generative structure" operates through (mechanical) acts of "arrangement," and/or "positioning," which highlight mainly the *unintended* results of systemic organization (Dessler, 1989:444). In generative terms, it is hence the "deepest" structural level (Ruggie, 1983)—"anarchy" as the *principle* by which the constituent units of the international system are organized—which banishes "conventionalist" variables (such as nationalism as a "generative order") from Waltz's "generative structure."

In conclusion, the neorealist omission of nationalism as a "generative order" is not accidental. In this sense, the neglect of nationalism does not seem to be corrigible without major modifications of the neorealist ontology (Wendt, 1987). Nor is the core trouble, at this level, limited to nationalism. It is all part of a large-scale neorealist "problem-shift" determined to bring the realist tradition "within the theoretical pale" (Waltz, 1990:29), even at the cost of rendering it virtually irrelevant to some of the most important epochal changes witnessed in world politics.

Theorizing Ethnonationalism: Restoring Actor Differentiation?

Is structural neorealism equally incapacitated with respect to *ethnonationalism?* The answer seems to be a qualified "no." Starting with the distribution of capabilities across actors, it is evident that ethnonationalism can be easily accommodated by neorealist analysis when it is perceived to affect gravely the capabilities of major powers in particular. Neorealism posits that for theory-building purposes sovereign states differ only in power capabilities and international systems only in their configurations of capability distributions. At the level of capabilities, ethnonationalism can significantly affect systemic processes and outcomes either through changing the number—or through augmenting or diluting the power base—of extant sovereign states. The "implosion" of Soviet power, as well as German reunification, has demonstrated the potential impact of such dynamics on even the central balance of power. The rising importance of regional and local balances in the foreseeable future further elevates the theoretical significance of ethnonationalism in the context of capabilities and power balancing (Horowitz, 1991:232). However, in the vast majority of cases, situating ethnonationalism in a narrow "control-of-capability" matrix will simply reduce (ethno)nations to minor epiphenomena of state power.

In contrast with its minor theoretical role at the level of capabilities, there is apparently *no theoretical* room for ethnonationalism at the deepest structural level of anarchy as the organizational principle of international systems. Anarchy, as aptly pointed out by Richard Ashley (1988), denotes an absence (of world government) and a presence (of sovereign states). Given that the "presence" consists of "like-units," ethno-nations cannot be considered constituent units of the anarchic realm because of their sovereignty lag. They are hence relegated, by default, to the "hierarchic" realm, where they typically seem equally out of place.[7]

To be truly compatible with the neorealist anarchy/hierarchy distinction, stateless nations must be expected either to succeed in their bid for independent statehood, or to disappear through voluntary or coerced assimilation. As (mis)conceived by Waltz, ethnonationalism must indeed be seen in a perpetual process of gravitation toward one of the two "stable" poles (i.e., anarchy or hierarchy) of a sharply dichotomized political universe. However, the historical experience does not validate this expectation. Nationless states are poor assimilators of ethnic pluralism. And national movements are no better at producing "genuine" nation-states. The ethnonational phenomenon simply refuses to dissolve itself into a bifurcated political universe of mutually exclusive "anarchies" and "hierarchies." In sum, far from benefiting from the "generative power" of the "anarchy/hierarchy" dichotomy, ethnonationalism is rendered less comprehensible by it.

This brings us to our main concern with the second component of the tripartite structural construct which dominates neorealist theorizing. This second-level component, which covers the extent of functional differentiation of units in a given political order, was declared stillborn at delivery by Professor Waltz himself. In a masterful act of theoretical resuscitation, John Ruggie has restored this level to life, designating it "as a dimension of possible future transformation, from the modern to a postmodern international system" (1983:146). Kenneth Waltz has yet to accept as viable the impressive signs of vitality produced by Ruggie's effort (Waltz, 1990:30). But in the absence of a second structural level, there is nothing to resist the conclusion that neorealism "contains only a reproductive logic but no transformational logic" (Ruggie, 1983:285).

The debate over reproductive versus transformational logics in neorealism (Haggard, 1991) is relevant in this context in view of the fact that we have differentiated between state-nationalism and ethnonationalism along this very dimension. That state-nationalism can be a major reproductive force needs no further elaboration. That ethnonationalism may evolve into disruptive directions is also self-evident. It is, however, the above-mentioned transformative vector implicit in the global rise of ethnonationalism which is particularly intriguing from both a practical and a theoretical point of view. By opting to block its second-level structural component as a possible source of systemic transformation, neorealism voluntarily abdicates the theoretical tool needed to capture the transformative dimensions of contemporary ethnonationalism.[8]

CONCLUSIONS

What are the wider implications of this analysis? Are the revealed flaws inherent and immutable, or contingent and transcendable? Is one to proceed mainly in the direction of revising neorealism in order to augment its analytical sensitivity to contemporary nationalism (Buzan, 1991)? Or is one better advised to move to a radically different research tradition (Mayall, 1990)? Only tentative reflections seem justified at this stage. It was certainly not our intention to proclaim the irrelevance of realist theoretical discourses to the politics of contemporary nationalism. Nor was it to issue an open-ended invitation for atheoretical additions of nations and nationalisms to an ever-expanding shopping list of would-be actors, processes, and structures in world politics (Waltz, 1990:29–31). The question is, How to theorize the "national" in international relations theory? How are basic realist and neorealist variables (such as anarchy, sovereignty, security, rationality, power, etc.) modified, if at all, by the current mutations of the national phenomenon? We have not tried to answer these questions. We have simply indicated where and why neorealism must engage in some serious rethinking if it wants to contribute, as it should, to better theorizations of the "national" in international relations theory.

NOTES

1. See, however, Mearsheimer's skeletal attempt to offer a neorealist account of nationalism in his provocative "Back to the Future" (1990) thesis. Despite considerable weaknesses, Mearsheimer's effort is salutary in focusing theoretical attention on nationalism.
2. Some Western European states such as England, France, the Netherlands, Denmark, and Sweden, for example, have been evolving over a longer period of time as prototypes of modern nationalism. However, as their emergence was not closely guided by a conscious aim of implementing the nation-state blueprint, they were missing a decisive element.
3. For a different view see Eric Hobsbawm's conclusion that the nationalist programme "is no longer a major vector of historical development" (1990:163). Michael Walzer and many others disagree in very strong terms (Walzer, 1990).
4. Indeed, despite dramatically increased levels of mobility at both intra- and inter-state levels, the overall level of global ethnic activism has been rising, rather than diminishing, in recent years.
5. With respect to territoriality, consider, for instance, John A. Armstrong's observation: "For much of the world, the dominant concept is adherence to ethnic communities coexisting in the same space. Superficial transference of Western notions of territorial exclusivity can grossly impair relationships among such groups, while the evolving Western postindustrial society may profitably learn a good deal about modes of group affiliation which do not presuppose territorial monopolies" (Armstrong, 1990:167).
6. This is readily apparent, for instance, with respect to state-centrism. Because of its role as a demystifier of would-be state coherence and "national unity" (Connor, 1972), ethnic nationalism raises serious questions as to the possibility of treating states as united and sovereign actors. The same holds true, however, with most other realist and neorealist hardcore assumptions. See Lapid, "The Richness of Nationalism and the Poverty of Neorealism" (unpublished manuscript).
7. As illustrated by Quebec nationalism, ethnonational movements show a recurrent propensity to activate both anarchic and hierarchic impulses in the political arenas in which they operate.
8. The problem seems, however, less irreversible than in the case of nationalism as a "generative structure." As anticipated by Ruggie's critique (1983), and as demonstrated by Barry Buzan's insightful work on "mature" versus "immature" anarchies (1991), it is possible to use the second structural level to give greater determinate content to the general constraints of anarchy deduced by Waltz.

BIBLIOGRAPHY

Anderson, B. (1983) *Imagined Communities.* London: Verso Editions.

Armstrong, J. A. (1990) Contemporary Ethnicity: The Moral Dimension in Comparative Perspective. *The Review of Politics* 52(2): 183–188.

Ashley, R. K. (1988) Untying the Sovereign State: A Double Reading of the Anarchy Problematique. *Millennium* 17:227–262.

Berry, C. J. (1981) Nations and Norms. *The Review of Politics* 43(1):75–87.

Bibo, I. (1976) *The Paralysis of International Institutions and the Remedies.* New York: John Wiley & Sons.

Buzan, B. (1991) *People, States, and Fear.* Boulder, CO: Lynne Rienner Publishers.

Cobban, A. (1969) *The Nation State and National Self-Determination.* New York: Thomas Y. Crowell Company.

Dessler, D. (1989) What's at Stake in the Agent-Structure Debate?" *International Organization* 43(3):441–473.

Galtung, J. (1980) *The True Worlds.* New York: Free Press.

Gellner, E. (1983) *Nations and Nationalism.* Oxford: Billing and Sons.

Gilpin, R. (1986) The Richness of the Tradition of Political Realism. In Keohane, ed. (1986), pp. 301–321.

Haas, E. B. (1986) What Is Nationalism and Why Should We Study It? *International Organization* 40(3):707–744.

Haggard, S. (1991) Structuralism and Its Critics: Recent Progress in International Relations Theory. In E. Adler and B. Crawford, eds., *Progress in Postwar International Relations,* pp. 403–437. New York: Columbia University Press.

Hobsbawm, E. J. (1990) *Nations and Nationalism Since 1780.* New York: Cambridge University Press.

Holsti, K. J. (1980) Change in the International System: Interdependence, Integration, and Fragmentation. In O. R. Holsti et al., eds. (1980), pp. 23–53.

Holsti, O. R. et al., eds. (1980) *Change in the International System.* Boulder, CO: Westview Press.

Horowitz, D. L. (1991) Ethnic and Nationalist Conflicts. In M. T. Klare and D. C. Thomas, eds., *World Security,* pp. 225–236. New York: St. Martin's Press.

Howard, M. (1989) Ideology and International Relations. *Review of International Studies* 15:1–10.

Hughes, E. C. and H. M. Hughes. (1952) *Where People Meet.* Glencoe, IL: The Free Press.

Isaacs, H. R. (1979) Power and Identity. *Headline Series* No. 246, pp. 3–64. New York: Foreign Policy Association.

Jackson, R. H. (1990) *Quasi-States: Sovereignty, International Relations and the Third World.* Cambridge: Cambridge University Press.

Jervis, R. (1989) Political Psychology—Some Challenges and Opportunities. *Political Psychology* (September):481–494.

Keohane, R. O., ed. (1986) *Neorealism and Its Critics.* New York: Columbia University Press.

Kratochwil, F. V. (1991) Man, the State, and International Order. Mimeograph. Philadelphia: University of Pennsylvania.

Kratochwil, F. V. (1989) *Rules, Norms, and Decisions.* Cambridge University Press.

Lapid, Y. (1989) The Third Debate: On the Prospects of International Theory in a Post-Positivist Era. *International Studies Quarterly* (September):235–254.

McNeill, W. H. (1986) *Polyethnicity and National Unity in World History.* Toronto: University of Toronto Press.

Mayall, J. (1990) *Nationalism and International Society.* New York: Cambridge University Press.

Mearsheimer, J. (1990) Back to the Future. *International Security,* 15(1):5–56.

Nash, M. (1989) *The Cauldron of Ethnicity in the Modern World.* Chicago: University of Chicago Press.

Nielsson, G. P. (1984) The Role of "Nation-Groups" in Political Integration and Disintegration: Toward Global Systemic Comparative Analysis. In E. Tiryakian and R. Rogowski, eds., *New Nationalisms of the Developed West.* Winchester, MA: Allen and Unwin.

Poggi, G. (1990) *The State.* Stanford, CA: Stanford University Press.

Portugali, Y. (1988) Nationalism, Social Theory and the Israeli/Palestinian Case. In *Nationalism, Self-determination and Political Geography,* pp. 151–165. London: Croom Helm.

Riggs, F. (1990) Interdisciplinary Tower of Babel. *International Social Science Journal* 126:577–592.

Riggs, F. (1987) A Conceptual Encyclopedia for the Social Sciences. *International Social Science Journal* 123:109–126.

Rothschild, J. (1981) *Ethnopolitics.* New York: Columbia University Press.

Ruggie, J. G. (1983) Continuity and Transformation in the World Polity: Toward a Neorealist Synthesis. In Keohane, ed. (1986), pp. 131–157.

Ryan, S. (1990) *Ethnic Conflict and International Relations.* Brookfield, USA: Dartmouth.

Seton-Watson, H. (1977) *Nations and States.* Boulder, CO: Westview Press.

Smith, A. D. (1988) The Myth of the "Modern Nation" and the Myths of Nations. *Ethnic and Racial Studies* 11(1):3–26.

Smith, A. D. (1983) Ethnic identity and World Order. *Millennium* 12:149–161.

U.S. Institute of Peace. (1990) Identity Group Conflicts with Sovereign States: Incidence, Dynamics, and Resolution. International Studies Association Conference, Omni Shoreham Hotel, Washington, DC.

Waltz, K. N. (1990) Realist Thought and Neorealist Theory. *Journal of International Affairs* 44(1):21–38.

Waltz, K. N. (1979) *Theory of International Politics.* Reading, MA: Addison-Wesley.

Walzer, M. (1990) Only Connect. *The New Republic* (August 13):32–34.

Wendt, A. E. (1987) The Agent-Structure Problem in International Relations Theory. *International Organization* 41(3):335–370.

Wiberg, H. (1991) States and Nations as Challenges to Peace Research. *Journal of Peace Research* 28(4): 337–343.

Worsley, P. (1984) *The Three Worlds: Culture and World Development.* Chicago: University of Chicago Press.

Multilateralism: The Anatomy of an Institution

John Gerard Ruggie

In 1989, peaceful change, which a leading realist theorist had declared a very low-probability event in international politics less than a decade before,[1] accommodated the most fundamental geopolitical shift of the postwar era and perhaps of the entire twentieth century: the collapse of the Soviet East European empire and the attendant end of the cold war. Many factors were responsible for that shift. But there seems little doubt that multilateral norms and institutions have helped stabilize their international consequences. Indeed, such norms and institutions appear to be playing a significant role in the management of a broad array of regional and global changes in the world system today.

In Europe, by one count at least fifteen multilateral groupings are involved in shaping the continent's collective destiny. . . .[2]

At the level of the global economy, despite sometimes near-hysterical predictions for twenty years now of imminent monetary breakup and trade wars that could become real wars, "just like in the 1930s,"[3] the rate of growth in world trade continues to exceed the rate of growth in world output; international capital flows dwarf both; and the eighth periodic round of trade negotiations, which had been prematurely pronounced dead, is moving toward completion. . . .

Moreover, after years of being riveted by the cold war, the United Nations (UN) has been rediscovered to have utility in international conflict management. . . .

Thus, there exists a compound anomaly in the world of international relations theory today. An institutional phenomenon of which conventional theories barely take note is both widespread and significant; but at the same time, the particular features that make it so are glossed over by most students of international institutions themselves. This article is intended to help resolve both parts of the anomaly.

. . . The argument, in brief, goes something like this: Multilateralism is a generic institutional form of modern international life, and as such it has been present from the start. The generic institutional form of multilateralism must not be confused with formal multilateral organizations, a relatively recent arrival and still of only relatively modest importance. Historically, the generic form of multilateralism can be found in institutional arrangements to define and stabilize the international property rights of states, to manage coordination problems, and to resolve collaboration problems. The last of these uses of the multilateral form is historically the least frequent. In the literature, this fact traditionally has been explained by the rise and fall of hegemonies and, more recently, by various functional considerations. Our analysis suggests that a permissive domestic environment in the leading powers of the day is at least as important and, in some cases, more important. When we look more closely at the post–World War II situation, for example, we find that it was less the fact of American *hegemony* that accounts for the explosion of multilateral arrangements than it was the fact of *American* hegemony. Finally, we suggest that institutional arrangements of the multilateral form have adaptive and even reproductive capacities which other institutional forms may lack and which, therefore, may help explain the roles that multilateral arrangements play in stabilizing the current international transformation.

THE MEANINGS OF MULTILATERALISM

At its core, multilateralism refers to coordinating relations among three or more states in accordance with certain principles. But what, precisely, are those principles? And to what, precisely, do those principles pertain? To facilitate the construction of a more formal definition, let us begin by examining an historical instance of something that everyone agrees multilateralism is not: bilateralism.

Earlier in this century, Nazi Germany succeeded in finely honing a pure form of bilateralism into a systemic organizing principle. . . . In 1934, Hjalmar Schacht devised a scheme of bilateralist trade agreements and clearing arrangements.[4] The essence of the German international trade regime was that the state negotiated "reciprocal" agreements with its foreign trading partners. These negotiations determined which goods and services were to be exchanged, their quantities, and their price. Often, Germany deliberately imported more from its partners than it exported to them. But it required that its trading partners liquidate their claims on Germany by reinvesting there or by purchasing deliberately overpriced German goods. Thus, its trading partners were doubly dependent on Germany. . . .

Let us examine next an institutional arrangement that is generally acknowledged to embody multilateralist principles: a collective security system. None has ever existed in pure form, but in principle the scheme is quite simple. It rests on the premise that peace is indivisible, so that a war against one state is, ipso facto, considered a war against all. The community of states therefore is obliged to respond to threatened or actual aggression, first by diplomatic means, then through economic sanctions, and finally by the collective use of force if necessary. Facing the prospect of such a community-wide response, any rational potential aggressor would be deterred and would desist. Thus, the incidence of war gradually would decline.

A collective security scheme certainly coordinates security relations among three or more states. But so, too . . . did the League of the Three Emperors, which was nothing more than a set of traditional alliances.[5] What is distinct about a collective security scheme is that it comprises, as Sir Arthur Salter put it a half-century ago, a permanent potential alliance "against the *unknown* enemy"[6]—and, he should have added, on behalf of the *unknown* victim. . . .

We are now in a position to be more precise about the core meaning of multi-lateralism. Keohane has defined institutions, generically, as "persistent and con-nected sets of rules, formal and informal, that prescribe behavioural roles, con-strain activity, and shape expectations."[7] Very simply, the term "multilateral" is an adjective that modifies the noun "institution." Thus, multilateralism depicts a *generic institutional form* in international relations. How does multilateral modify institution? Our illustrations suggest that multilateralism is an institutional form which coordinates relations among three or more states on the basis of "general-ized" principles of conduct—that is, principles which specify appropriate conduct for a class of actions, without regard to the particularistic interests of the parties or the strategic exigencies that may exist in any specific occurrence. MFN treatment is a classic example in the economic realm: it forbids discrimination among coun-tries producing the same product. Its counterpart in security relations is the re-quirement that states respond to aggression whenever and wherever it occurs. . . .

Bilateralism and multilateralism do not exhaust the institutional repertoire of states. Imperialism can be considered a third generic institutional form. Imperial-ism also is an institution that coordinates relations among three or more states though, unlike bilateralism and multilateralism, it does so by denying the sover-eignty of the subject states.[8]

Two corollaries follow from our definition of multilateralism. First, general-ized organizing principles logically entail an indivisibility among the members of a collectivity with respect to the range of behavior in question. . . . But note that in-divisibility here is a *social construction,* not a technical condition: in a collective security scheme, states behave as if peace were indivisible and thereby make it so. . . . Bilateralism, in contrast, segments relations into multiples of dyads and compartmentalizes them. Second, as discussed in further detail below, successful cases of multilateralism in practice appear to generate among their members what Keohane has called expectations of "diffuse reciprocity.". . . [9] Bilateralism, in con-trast, is premised on specific reciprocity, the simultaneous balancing of specific quid-pro-quos by each party with every other at all times.[10]

It follows from this definition and its corollaries that multilateralism is a highly demanding institutional form. Its historical incidence, therefore, is likely to be less frequent than that of its alternatives; and if its relative incidence at any time were to be high, that fact would pose an interesting puzzle to be explained.

The obvious next issue to address is the fact that . . . the generic concept of in-ternational institution applies in practice to many different types of institutional-ized relations among states.[11] So too, therefore, does the adjective multilateral. . . . Common usage in the literature distinguishes among three institutional domains of interstate relations: international orders, international regimes, and interna-tional organizations. Each type can be, but need not be, multilateral in form.

The literature frequently refers to international economic orders, interna-tional security orders, international maritime orders, and so on. An "open" or "lib-eral" international economic order is multilateral in form, as is a maritime order based on the principle of *mare liberum*. The New Economic Order of the Nazis was not multilateral in form, for reasons that have already been suggested, and neither was the European security order crafted by Bismarck. The concept of multilateralism here refers to the constitutive rules that order relations in given domains of international life—their architectural dimension, so to speak. Thus, the quality of "openness" in an international economic order refers to such characteristics as the prohibition of exclusive blocs, spheres, or similar barriers to the conduct of international economic relations. . . .

A regime is more concrete than an order. Typically, the term "regime" refers to a functional or sectoral component of an order. Moreover, the concept of regime encompasses more of the "how" question than does the concept of order in that, broadly speaking, the term "regime" is used to refer to common, deliberative, though often highly asymmetrical means of conducting interstate relations. That much is clear from common usage. But while there is a widespread assumption in the literature that all regimes are, ipso facto, multilateral in character, this assumption is egregiously erroneous. For example, there is no reason not to call the Schachtian schemes for organizing monetary and trade relations international regimes; they fully meet the standard criteria specified by Stephen Krasner and his colleagues. . . .[12]

Finally, formal international organizations are palpable entities with headquarters and letterheads, voting procedures, and generous pension plans. They require no conceptual elaboration. But, again, their relationship to the concept of multilateralism is less self-evident than is sometimes assumed. Two issues deserve brief mention. The first issue . . . is that there have been international organizations that were not multilateral in form. The Comintern and the Cominform come to mind. . . . The second issue is more problematic even today. There is a common tendency in the world of actual international organizations, and sometimes in the academic community, to equate the very phenomenon of multilateralism with the universe of multilateral organizations or diplomacy. The preceding discussion makes it clear why that view is in error. It may be the case empirically that decisions concerning aspects of international orders or, more likely, international regimes in fact are made in multilateral forums. The EC exhibits this empirical pattern most extensively. . . .

MULTILATERALISM IN HISTORY

The institutional form of multilateralism has now been defined. What can we say about its specific expressions over time, their frequency distribution, and some possible correlates? . . . To organize the discussion, I adapt a standard typology of institutional roles from the literature: defining and stabilizing international property rights, solving coordination problems, and resolving collaboration problems.[13]

Property Rights

Not surprisingly, the earliest multilateral arrangements instituted in the modern era were designed to cope with the international consequences of the novel principle of state sovereignty. The newly emerged territorial states conceived their essence, their very being, by the possession of territory and the exclusion of others from it. But how does one possess something one does not own? And, still more problematic, how does one exclude others from it?

The world's oceans posed this problem. Contiguous waterways could be shared, administered jointly, or, more than likely, split down the middle; the international property rights of states thereby were established bilaterally. The oceans were another matter. States attempted to project exclusive unilateral jurisdiction, but they failed. Spain and Portugal tried a bilateral solution, whereby Spain claimed a monopoly of the western trade routes to the Far East and Portugal claimed the eastern routes. But they, too, failed. All such efforts failed for the simple reason that it is exceedingly difficult if not impossible in the long run to vindicate a property right that is not recognized as being valid by the relevant others in a given community, especially when exclusion is as difficult as it was in the oceans. Attempts to do so lead to permanent challenge and recurrent conflict. A multilateral solution to the governance of the oceans, therefore, was inescapable. The principle which was first enunciated by Hugo Grotius at the beginning of the seventeenth century and which states slowly came to adopt was . . . that . . . all states were free to utilize the high seas, provided only that they did not thereby damage the legitimate interests of others.[14] And each state had the same rules for all states, not one rule for some and other rules for others.

An even more profound instance of delimiting the property rights of states—more profound because it concerned internal, as opposed to external, space—was the invention of the principle of extraterritoriality as the basis for organizing permanent diplomatic representation. . . . As a result, grave breaches of the principle of extraterritoriality are, ipso facto, deemed to be a violation against the entire community of states. . . .[15]

Coordination Problems

. . . A paradigmatic case of a coordination problem in the mid-nineteenth century was posed by electronic telegraphy and concerned what would happen to a message as it came, for instance, to the border between France and the Grand Duchy of Baden. The following procedure was instituted: "A common station was established at Strasbourg with two employees, one from the French Telegraph Administration, the other from Baden. The French employee received, for example, a telegram from Paris, which the electric wires had transmitted to him with the speed of light. This message he wrote out by hand onto a special form and handed it across the table to his German colleague. He translated it into German, and then sent it again on its way."[16] However, with the intensification of trade, the desire for the latest stock market information from London, Paris, and Berlin, and important diplomatic messages that governments wished to send to one another, this arrangement became untenable. . . . The initial response was to negotiate a series of bilateral treaties. But in the dense communications complex of the European continent, bilateral solutions soon also proved inadequate. Several multilateral arrangements were therefore constructed and were subsequently combined in 1865, when the International Telegraph Union was established.

The multilateral arrangement for telegraphy consisted of three parts. First, the parties devised rules concerning the network of telegraph lines that were to connect countries within Europe (and, later, in other parts of the world), the codes to be used, the agreed priorities of transmission, the languages that were permissible, the schedule of tariffs to be levied, the manner in which proceeds would be divided, and so on. Second, they established a permanent secretariat to administer the day-to-day implementation of these rules and to coordinate the technical operations of the system. And, third, they convened periodic conferences to make any such revisions in the basic system as became necessary over time. . . .

Collaboration Problems

Where the definition and stabilization of at least some international property rights is concerned, there appears to exist an ultimate inevitability to multilateral solutions, although "ultimate" may mean after all possible alternatives, including war, have been exhausted. In cases of coordination problems, there appears to exist an ultimate indifference as to which one of several outcomes is selected, although "ultimate" here may mask such concrete problems as sunk investments that individual states may have in the "equally acceptable" outcome that did not get adopted.

Between the two extremes of inevitability and indifference lies the domain of mixed-motive, conflict of interest situations. Even in this domain, however, cooperation occurs. And sometimes it occurs on a multilateral basis. Before 1945, however, it did not do so very often.

In the security realm, the most celebrated case is the Concert of Europe, a case in which students of international relations have paid far more attention to the issue of whether or not it constituted a security regime than to the fact that it exhibited elements of the multilateral form. . . .

Between the Napoleonic and the Crimean wars, from 1815 to 1854, peace in Europe was maintained, in Henry Kissinger's words, by an institutional "framework" that was regarded by participants as being "legitimate," so that "they sought adjustment within [it] *rather than in its overthrow.*"[17] In doing so, according to Robert Jervis, they "behaved in ways that sharply diverged from normal 'power politics.'". . . [18]

How were these feats achieved? The five powers constituted themselves as "an executive body" of the European international system,[19] convening extensive multilateral consultations through which they acted on matters that could have undermined the peace. . . .

What could account for this unusual institutional development? It seems that the threat posed by Napoleon's imperial ambitions to the very principle of the balance of power proved weightier than the usual risks and uncertainties that plague cooperation in the security realm. Moreover, the threat posed by the French revolutionary wars to the very principle of dynastic rule seems to have proved weightier than the differences in domestic social formations, such as those existing between liberal and protestant England on the one hand and the more conservative and catholic Austria and orthodox Russia on the other. . . .

The Concert of Europe gradually eroded not only because the memory of the initial threats faded but also because over time the parameters of the situation were transformed. Above all else, the revolutions of 1848 seriously shook the prevailing concept of legitimate political order from within, and the sense of international cohesion diverged sharply thereafter. . . .

In the economic realm, the nineteenth century witnessed what economists consider to be paradigms, if not paragons, of multilateralism: free trade and the gold standard. By free trade is meant two things: a minimum of barriers to trade, including tariff and nontariff barriers; and nondiscriminatory treatment in trade. An international gold standard exists when two sets of conditions are approximated. First, the major countries must maintain a link between their domestic money supply and gold at substantially fixed ratios. Second, in principle they must allow the outflow of gold to liquidate an adverse balance of current obligations and must accept a corresponding inflow in case of a favorable balance. These conditions also establish the convertibility of currencies at relatively fixed rates, and they facilitate international adjustment insofar as the initial imbalance in the current account in principle will be rectified automatically in both surplus and deficit countries by the appropriate domestic measures that follow from the inflow and outflow of gold. . . .

The multilateralism of free trade and the international gold standard appears to have been created and sustained by two sets of factors. Although it may appear paradoxical, these paragon cases of multilateralism were not achieved by multilateral means. The decisive factor seems to have been Britain's unilateral move toward free trade and the gold standard and its bilateral dealings to achieve both goals. Britain thereby signaled its willingness to bear the costs of an open trading order and a stable monetary order and thus reduced the distributive and strategic uncertainties of these arrangements for others. . . .

This brief overview of multilateralism prior to the twentieth century suggests several broad generalizations that shed further light on the character of the multilateral institutional form. First, the strategic task environment has an impact on the form that agreements take. Defining and delimiting the property rights of states is as fundamental a collective task as any in the international system. The performance of this task on a multilateral basis seems inevitable in the long run, although in fact states appear to try every conceivable alternative first. . . . At the other extreme, limiting transaction costs by solving coordination problems is institutionally neither complex nor particularly demanding, and it was the domain in which multilateralism in all three institutional expressions—orders, regimes, and organizations—flourished in the nineteenth century. Between these two lies the problematic terrain of significant conflict of interest situations, in which states *sometimes*, but prior to the twentieth century not often, construct multilateral arrangements *even though* alternatives are available and viable. The major powers could have selected bilateral alliances in the early nineteenth century and selected discriminatory economic arrangements in the mid-nineteenth century, as they had done before and as they would do again subsequently. But at those particular points in time, they did not. Why not? Presumably, multilateralism was in their interest. But what, concretely, does that mean? . . . As noted above, it seems that the

Concert of Europe was due in part to exogenous shocks to both the international system and the system of domestic rule. Free trade and the gold standard in part seem to have been due to the willingness and the capability of Great Britain to take the lead. Both cases also were made possible by the existence of compatible or at least permissive domestic settings.

Second, as was alluded to earlier, it seems that successful instances of multilateralism come to exhibit "diffuse reciprocity."[20] For example, what was crucial to the success of the Concert of Europe, according to Jervis, "is that 'self-interest' was broader than usual [and] also longer-run than usual. . . . For this system to work, each state had to believe that its current sacrifices would in fact yield a long-run return, that others would not renege on their implicit commitments when they found themselves in tempting positions."[21]

Third, the record shows that prior to the twentieth century, very few instances of multilateralism generated formal organizations. The Concert of Europe never went beyond great power consultations, while free trade and the international gold standard were instituted and sustained by even more ad hoc bilateral and unilateral means. . . .

The Twentieth-Century Discontinuity

An important break in this third pattern occurred with the twentieth-century "move to institutions," as the critical legal theorist David Kennedy has described it—by which he means a move to formal organizations.[22]

Above all, a completely novel form was added to the institutional repertoire of states in 1919: the multipurpose, universal membership organization, instantiated first by the League of Nations and then by the UN. Prior international organizations had but limited membership, determined by power, function, or both, and they were assigned specific and highly circumscribed tasks. In contrast, here were organizations based on little more than shared aspirations, with broad agendas in which large and small had a constitutionally mandated voice. Moreover, decision making within international organizations increasingly became subject to the mechanism of voting, as opposed to treaty drafting or customary accretion; and voting itself subsequently shifted away in most instances from the early unanimity requirement that was consistent with the traditional mode of conducting international proceedings. Finally, the move amplified a trend that had begun in the nineteenth century, a trend toward multilateral as opposed to merely bilateral diplomacy, especially in the form of "conference diplomacy.". . . [23]

In short, as a result of the twentieth-century move to institutions, a multilateral political order that is "capable of handling at least some collective tasks in an *ex ante* co-ordinated manner" has emerged.[24] I might add in conclusion that while numerous descriptions of this "move to institutions" exist, I know of no good explanation in the literature of why states should have wanted to complicate their lives in this manner. And I would think it particularly difficult to formulate any straightforward explanation within the currently ascendant logic of instrumental rationality.

NOTES

1. See Robert Gilpin, *War and Change in World Politics* (New York: Cambridge University Press, 1981), p. 15: "Although . . . peaceful adjustment of the systemic disequilibrium is possible, the principle mechanism of change throughout history has been war, or what we shall call hegemonic war (i.e., a war that determines which state or states will be dominant and will govern the system)."

2. See William M. Clarke, "The Midwives of the New Europe," *Central Banker* 1 (Summer 1990), pp. 49–51; and Bruce Stokes, "Continental Shift," *National Journal*, nos. 33 and 34, August 1990, pp. 1996–2001.

3. This refrain was begun by C. Fred Bergsten in "The New Economics and U.S. Foreign Policy," *Foreign Affairs* 50 (January 1972), pp. 199–222. For a recent rendition, see "Echoes of the 1930s," *The Economist*, 5 January 1991, pp. 15, 16, and 18.

4. The classic and appropriately titled study of the Nazi system is Albert O. Hirschman's *National Power and the Structure of Foreign Trade* (1945; reprint, Berkeley: University of California Press, 1980). See also Leland B. Yeager, *International Monetary Relations: Theory, History, and Policy* (New York: Harper & Row, 1976), pp. 357–76.

5. A. J. P. Taylor, *The Struggle for Mastery in Europe* 1848–1918 (Oxford University Press, 1971), chap. 12.

6. Arthur Salter, *Security* (London: Macmillan, 1939), p. 155; emphasis in original.

7. Robert O. Keohane, "Multilateralism: An Agenda for Research," *International Journal* 45 (Autumn 1990), p. 732.

8. See Michael Doyle, *Empires* (Ithaca, NY: Cornell University Press, 1986), pp. 19–47. Some of the more predatory expressions of the Nazi arrangements came very close to if they did not actually constitute the imperial form.

9. Robert O. Keohane, "Reciprocity in International Relations," *International Organization* 40 (Winter 1986), pp. 1–27.

10. Bilateral balancing need not imply equality; it simply means establishing a mutually acceptable balance between the parties, however that is determined in practice. For an extended discussion of this difference, see Karl Polanyi, "The Economy as Instituted Process," in Karl Polanyi, Conrad M. Arensberg, and Harry W. Pearson, eds., *Trade and Market in the Early Empires* (Glencoe, IL: Free Press, 1957), pp. 243–70.

11. Robert O. Keohane, "International Institutions: Two Approaches," *International Studies Quarterly* 32 (December 1988), pp. 379–96.

12. Stephen D. Krasner, ed., *International Regimes* (Ithaca, NY: Cornell University Press, 1983).

13. The distinction between coordination and collaboration was proposed by Arthur Stein in "Coordination and Collaboration: Regimes in an Anarchic World," in Krasner, *International Regimes*, pp. 115–40. . . .

14. It took until the early eighteenth century before piracy, frequently state-sponsored, came to be generally defined as being inherently damaging to the legitimate interests of states. See Robert C. Ritchie, *Captain Kidd and the War Against the Pirates* (Cambridge, MA: Harvard University Press, 1986).

15. Note in this connection that UN Security Council Resolution 667 "*strongly* condemns" Iraq for "*aggressive acts perpetrated* . . . against diplomatic premises and personnel in Kuwait," whereas Resolution 660, passed in response to Iraq's invasion of Kuwait, merely "condemns" the invasion, without embellishment. The full texts are contained in UN Security Council, S/RES/667, 16 September 1990, and S/RES/660, 2 August 1990; emphasis added.

16. International Telecommunications Union (ITU), *From Semaphore to Satellite* (Geneva: ITU, 1965), p. 45.

17. See Henry A. Kissinger, *A World Restored* (New York: Universal Library, 1964), p. 5. Kissinger concentrates on the *Congress* system, a subset of the Concert of Europe, which ended by about 1823, but my commentary holds for the entire concert system.

18. See Robert Jervis, "Security Regimes," in Krasner, *International Regimes*, p. 178. See also Jervis, "From Balance to Concert: A Study of International Security Cooperation," *World Politics* 38 (October 1985), pp. 58–79; and Richard B. Elrod, "The Concert of Europe: A Fresh Look at an International System," *World Politics* 28 (January 1976), pp. 159–74.

19. The term is used by Gordon A. Craig and Alexander L. George in *Force and Statecraft* (New York: Oxford University Press, 1983), p. 31.

20. Keohane, "Reciprocity in International Relations."

21. Jervis, "Security Regimes," p. 180.

22. David Kennedy, "The Move to Institutions," *Cardozo Law Review* 8 (April 1987), pp. 841–988.

23. For a brief though excellent review, see Volker Rittberger, "Global Conference Diplomacy and International Policy-Making," *European Journal of Political Research*, vol. 11, no. 2, 1983, pp. 167–82.

24. Ibid., pp. 167–68.

Chapter
2

Anarchy and Cooperation

Edward D. Mansfield

*I*ssues regarding cooperation among states are fundamental to the study of international relations. Scholars disagree over the extent to which cooperation is a common feature of international relations. They also differ regarding how to foster cooperation among states. Many explanations of international relations draw heavily on political theory and the fundamental distinctions which theorists such as Aristotle and Thomas Hobbes introduced. A variety of contemporary controversies regarding international cooperation have roots in these different traditions and their underlying assumptions.

Classical political theorists have long suggested that the reason for cooperation lies in humanity's social nature. Cooperation among actors who share a common goal that cannot be achieved single-handedly by each leads them to pool their efforts. However, classical theorists recognized that instances often existed in which actors with common goals failed to cooperate. This led them to distinguish between the ability of groups inside a political community and across communities to cooperate. Cooperation inside the community was possible among families, households, tribes, citizens, and compatriots. Cooperation across communities was limited by the existence of enemies and other factors.

Modern political theory, beginning with Hobbes, dispensed with the notions of "sociality" and the "good life," which gave coherence to a political community. Instead of the habits and practices which served as the foundation of a political community, the interests of actors, who pursue strategies designed to realize these interests, form the cornerstone of modern political theory. Instead of deliberating and reflecting on the goals as well as the means of action, modern political theory views the interests and goals of actors as given by assumption, and it explains the choices of actors in terms of instrumental and strategic rationality.

These two traditions therefore treat the issue of cooperation quite differently. While cooperation in classical theory is largely the result of habits and practices among persons who share common traditions and meanings, cooperation among rational egoists is largely the result of the organization of force. Self-interested actors, having become through the social contract "subjects" of a sovereign, are dis-

42

suaded by penalties and their enforcement from pursuing strategies to advance their myopic interests. In the absence of such a sovereign authority, anarchy obtains. Under these conditions, cooperation is particularly difficult to generate and sustain.

These insights have done much to shape modern theories of international relations. It is interesting, however, that realists and liberals—both of whom share the modern interest paradigm described above—have, nevertheless, arrived at very different conclusions regarding the implications of this paradigm for the study of international relations. For example, realists often rely on Hobbes's classic analysis of the "state of nature" in their attempts to explain how and why anarchy guides the behavior of states. Anarchy, in their opinion, is the reason why cooperation among states is relatively rare. In the absence of a superordinate authority to guide international relations, states which engage in cooperative behavior must worry about whether cooperation will undermine their security.

On the other hand, it is often argued that scholars in the liberal tradition emphasize the relative ease of cooperation among sovereign states and neglect the security concerns that realists highlight. But, while liberals do view cooperation as being less rare and less problematic than realists, many of them appreciate the need to attend to matters of security in a global system in which no supraordinate authority exists. For example, Adam Smith, who was one of the fathers of liberalism, recognized that "defense is more important than opulence." Their appreciation of the need for security also explains why liberals such as Immanuel Kant did not believe that the creation of a world government provided a solution to the dilemmas of international politics. Instead, they argued that the establishment of republics would create the conditions conducive to a perpetual peace. The existence of republics would not only avoid costly dynastic wars but would also foster commerce, which would, in turn, cultivate "manners" and sentiments of general sympathy toward other states.

The selections in this chapter address a number of the issues raised above. First, Robert Keohane provides a rich analysis of the issue of cooperation in international politics and of the roles that international institutions play in this regard. He draws a distinction between two competing schools of thought, each of which seeks to explain the emergence and role of international institutions. One school is indebted to the "modern" Hobbesian paradigm of self-interest and power. Institutions ensure cooperation because, as in the case of the threat of the Hobbesian sovereign, they affect calculations of costs and benefits on the parts of states. The other school explains cooperation in more sociological terms. It focuses on the "reflective" character of choices, on the emergence and transformation of interests, and on the institutional underpinnings that constitute the international system. Keohane analyzes the strengths and limitations of each of these approaches to the study of cooperation.

Second, Duncan Snidal emphasizes the importance of strategic interactions among states in fostering or impeding international cooperation. He argues that much research on international cooperation has been guided by analyses that rely on insights drawn from the Prisoners' Dilemma. After explaining the central features of this approach, Snidal suggests that many aspects of international cooperation can be better understood as a coordination game, rather than a Prisoners' Dilemma. He compares and contrasts these approaches and demonstrates that they can be used in conjunction with each other to explain many aspects of cooperation and international institutions. This, in turn, allows us to address issues concerning what type of political institutions will be created under various circumstances, as well as to assess their expected stability and performance.

Third, Alexander Wendt addresses international cooperation using what Keohane refers to as a reflective approach. Wendt argues that there are many similarities between neoliberal and neorealist approaches, which are usually viewed as being largely incompatible. By tracing these similarities to a common set of underlying assumptions, Wendt identifies the factors which hinder the expansion of traditional analyses of international relations. He argues, for example, that because realists assume that anarchy, competitive power politics, and self-help are endemic to the international system, they neglect the roles of both political practice and history in the construction and evolution of international systems. In contrast to this view, Wendt maintains that the structure of the international system emerges and evolves through the interaction among states; and that this structure depends on historical experiences and the lessons that actors learn from their interactions.

International Institutions: Two Approaches

Robert O. Keohane

. . . To understand the conditions under which international cooperation can take place, it is necessary to understand how international institutions operate and the conditions under which they come into being. This is not to say that international institutions always facilitate cooperation on a global basis: on the contrary, a variety of international institutions, including most obviously military alliances, are designed as means for prevailing in military and political conflict. Conversely, instances of cooperation can take place with only minimal institutional structures to support them. But all efforts at international cooperation take place within an institutional context of some kind, which may or may not facilitate cooperative endeavors. To understand cooperation and discord better, we need to investigate the sources and nature of international institutions, and how institutional change takes place.

"Cooperation" is a contested term. As I use it, it is sharply distinguished from both harmony and discord. When harmony prevails, actors' policies *automatically* facilitate the attainment of others' goals. When there is discord, actors' policies hinder the realization of others' goals, and are not adjusted to make them more compatible. In both harmony and discord, neither actor has an incentive to change his or her behavior. Cooperation, however, "requires that the actions of separate individuals or organizations—which are not in pre-existent harmony—be brought into conformity with one another through a process of policy coordination" (Keohane, 1984:51). This means that when cooperation takes place, each party changes his or her behavior *contingent* on changes in the other's behavior. We can evaluate the impact of cooperation by measuring the difference between the actual outcome and the situation that would have obtained in the absence of coordination: that is, the myopic self-enforcing equilibrium of the game. Genuine cooperation improves the rewards of both players.

International cooperation does not necessarily depend on altruism, idealism, personal honor, common purposes, internalized norms, or a shared belief in a set of values embedded in a culture. At various times and places any of these features of human motivation may indeed play an important role in processes of international cooperation; but cooperation can be understood without reference to any of them. This is not surprising, since international cooperation is not necessarily benign from an ethical standpoint. Rich countries can devise joint actions to extract resources from poor ones, predatory governments can form aggressive alliances, and privileged industries can induce their governments to protect them against competition from more efficient producers abroad. The analysis of international cooperation should not be confused with its celebration. As Hedley Bull said about order, "while order in world politics is something valuable, . . . it should not be taken to be a commanding value, and to show that a particular institution or course of action is conductive of order is not to have established a presumption that that institution is desirable or that that course of action should be carried out" (Bull, 1977:98).

Cooperation is in a dialectical relationship with discord, and they must be understood together. Thus to understand cooperation, one must also understand the frequent absence of, or failure of, cooperation, so incessantly stressed by realist writers. But our awareness of cooperation's fragility does not require us to accept dogmatic forms of realism, which see international relations as inherently doomed to persistent zero-sum conflict and warfare. . . .

Realist and neorealist theories are avowedly rationalistic, accepting what Herbert Simon has referred to as a "substantive" conception of rationality, characterizing "behavior that can be adjudged objectively to be optimally adapted to the situation" (Simon, 1985:294). But adopting the assumption of substantive rationality does not commit the analyst to gloomy deterministic conclusions about the inevitability of warfare. On the contrary, rationalistic theory can be used to explore the conditions under which cooperation takes place, and it seeks to explain why international institutions are constructed by states (Axelrod, 1984; Keohane, 1984; Oye, 1986).

That rationalistic theory can lead to many different conclusions in international relations reflects a wider indeterminacy of the rationality principle as such. As Simon has argued, the principle of substantive rationality generates hypotheses about actual human behavior only when it is combined with auxiliary assumptions about the structure of utility functions and the formation of expectations. Furthermore, rationality is always contextual, so a great deal depends on the situation posited at the beginning of the analysis. Considerable variation in outcomes is therefore consistent with the assumption of substantive rationality. When limitations on the cognitive capacities of decision-makers are also taken into account—as in the concept of bounded rationality—the range of possible variation expands even further.

... Traditionally counterposed to rationalistic theory is the sociological approach to the study of institutions, which stresses the role of impersonal social forces as well as the impact of cultural practices, norms, and values that are not derived from calculations of interests (Barry, 1970; Gilpin, 1981). Yet the sociological approach has recently been in some disarray, at least in international relations: its adherents have neither the coherence nor the self-confidence of the rationalists. Rather than try in this essay to discuss this diffuse set of views about international relations, I will focus on the work of several scholars with a distinctive and similar point of view who have recently directly challenged the predominant rationalistic analysis of international politics. These authors, of whom the best-known include Hayward Alker, Richard Ashley, Friedrich Kratochwil, and John Ruggie, emphasize the importance of the "intersubjective meanings" of international institutional activity (Kratochwil and Ruggie, 1986:765). In their view, understanding how people think about institutional norms and rules, and the discourse they engage in, is as important in evaluating the significance of these norms as measuring the behavior that changes in response to their invocation.

These writers emphasize that individuals, local organizations, and even states develop within the context of more encompassing institutions. Institutions do not merely reflect the preferences and power of the units constituting them; the institutions themselves shape those preferences and that power. Institutions are therefore *constitutive* of actors as well as vice versa. It is therefore not sufficient in this view to treat the preferences of individuals as given exogenously: they are affected by institutional arrangements, by prevailing norms, and by historically contingent discourse among people seeking to pursue their purposes and solve their self-defined problems.

In order to emphasize the importance of this perspective, and to focus a dialogue with rationalistic theory, I will treat the writers on world politics who have stressed these themes as members of a school of thought. ... I have ... coined a phrase for these writers, calling them "reflective," since all of them emphasize the importance of human reflection for the nature of institutions and ultimately for the character of world politics.

My chief argument in this essay is that students of international institutions should direct their attention to the relative merits of two approaches, the rationalistic and the reflective. Until we understand the strengths and weaknesses of each, we will be unable to design research strategies that are sufficiently multifaceted to encompass our subject-matter, and our empirical work will suffer accordingly.

The next section of this essay will define what I mean by "institutions," and introduce some distinctions that I hope will help us to understand international institutions better. Defining institutions entails drawing a distinction between specific institutions and the underlying practices within which they are embedded, of which the most fundamental in world politics are those associated with the concept of sovereignty. I will then attempt to evaluate the strengths and weaknesses of the rationalistic approach, taking into account the criticism put forward by scholars who emphasize how actors are constituted by institutions and how subjective self-awareness of actors, and the ideas at their disposal, shape their activities. . . .

INTERNATIONAL INSTITUTIONS: DEFINITIONS AND DISTINCTIONS

"Institution" is an even fuzzier concept than cooperation. Institutions are often discussed without being defined at all, or after having been defined only casually. Yet it sometimes seems, as a sociologist lamented half a century ago, that "the only idea common to all usages of the term 'institution' is that of some sort of establishment of relative permanence of a distinctly social sort" (Hughes, 1936:180, quoted in Zucker, 1977:726). In the international relations literature, this vagueness persists. We speak of the United Nations and the World Bank (part of the "United Nations System"), IBM and Exxon, as institutions; but we also consider "the international monetary regime" and "the international trade regime" to be institutions. Hedley Bull refers to "the balance of power, international law, the diplomatic mechanism, the managerial system of the great powers, and war" as "the institutions of international society" (Bull, 1977:74).[1] John Ruggie discusses "the institutional framework of sovereignty" (Ruggie, 1986:147), and Stephen Krasner writes about "the particular institutional structures of sovereignty" (Krasner, 1987:11).

It may help in sorting out some of these troubling confusions to point out that "institution" may refer to a *general pattern or categorization* of activity or to a *particular* human-constructed arrangement, formally or informally organized. Examples of institutions as general patterns include Bull's "institutions of international society," as well as such varied patterns of behavior as marriage and religion, sovereign statehood, diplomacy, and neutrality. Sometimes norms such as that of reciprocity, which can apply to a variety of situations, are referred to as institutions. When we speak of patterns or categorizations of activity as institutions, the particular instances are often not regarded themselves as institutions: we do not speak of the marriage of the Duke and Duchess of Windsor, international negotiations over the status of the Panama Canal, or the neutrality of Sweden in World War II as institutions. What these general patterns of activity have in common with specific institutions is that they both meet the criteria for a broad definition of institutions: both involve persistent and connected sets of rules (formal or informal) that prescribe behavioral roles, constrain activity, and shape expectations.

Specific institutions, such as the French state, the Roman Catholic church, the international nonproliferation regime, or the General Agreement on Tariffs and Trade, are discrete entities, identifiable in space and time. Specific institutions may be exemplars of general patterns of activity—the United Nations exemplifies multilateral diplomacy; the French state, sovereign statehood; the Roman Catholic church, organized religion. But unlike general patterns of activity, specific institutions have unique life-histories, which depend on the decisions of particular individuals.

General patterns of "institutionalized" activity are more heterogeneous. Some of these institutions are only sets of entities, with each member of the set being an institution. Bull's institution of international law, for instance, can be seen as including a variety of institutions codified in legal form. In this sense, all formal international regimes are parts of international law, as are formal bilateral treaties and conventions. Likewise, the institution of religion includes a variety of quite different specific institutions, including the Roman Catholic church, Islam, and Congregationalism. Other general patterns of activity can be seen as norms that are applicable to a wide variety of situations, such as the norm of reciprocity (Keohane, 1986b).

It is difficult to work analytically with the broad ordinary-language definition of institutions with which I have started, since it includes such a variety of different entities and activities. In the rest of this essay, therefore, I will focus on institutions that can be identified as related complexes of rules and norms, identifiable in space and time. This conception of the scope of my analytical enterprise deliberately omits institutions that are merely categories of activity, as well as general norms that can be attached to any of a number of rule-complexes. It allows me to focus on *specific institutions* and on *practices*. As explained below, it is the mark of a practice that the behavior of those engaged in it can be corrected by an appeal to its own rules. This means that practices are deeply embedded—highly institutionalized in the sociological sense of being taken for granted by participants as social facts that are not to be challenged although their implications for behavior can be explicated.

Specific institutions can be defined in terms of their rules. Douglass North (1987:6) defines institutions as "rules, enforcement characteristics of rules, and norms of behavior that structure repeated human interaction." Institutions can be seen as "frozen decisions," or "history encoded into rules" (March and Olson, 1984:741). These rules may be informal or implicit rather than codified: in fact, some very strong institutions, such as the British constitution, rely principally on unwritten rules. To be institutionalized in the sense in which I will use the term, the rules must be durable, and must prescribe behavioral roles for actors, besides constraining activity and shaping expectations. That is, institutions differentiate among actors according to the roles that they are expected to perform, and institutions can be identified by asking whether patterns of behavior are indeed differentiated by role. When we ask whether X is an institution, we ask whether we can identify persistent sets of rules that constrain activity, shape expectations, and prescribe roles. In international relations, some of these institutions are formal orga-nizations, with prescribed hierarchies and the capacity for purposive action. Oth-ers, such as the international regimes for money and trade, are complexes of rules and organizations, the core elements of which have been negotiated and explicitly agreed upon by states.[2]

This definition of specific institutions incorporates what John Rawls has called the "summary view" of rules, in which "rules are pictured as summaries of past decisions," which allow the observer to predict future behavior (Rawls, 1955:19). Rules such as these can be changed by participants on utilitarian grounds without engaging in self-contradictory behavior. This definition is useful as far as it goes, but it does not capture what Rawls calls "the practice conception" of rules. A practice in the sense used by Rawls is analogous to a game such as baseball or chess: "It is the mark of a practice that being taught how to engage in it involves being instructed in the rules that define it, and that appeal is made to those rules to correct the behavior of those engaged in it. Those engaged in a practice recognize the rules as defining it" (Rawls, 1955:24). Were the rules of a practice to change, so would the fundamental nature of the activity in question.

Someone engaged in a practice has to explain her action by showing that it is in accord with the practice. Otherwise, the behavior itself is self-contradictory. As Oran Young points out, "It just does not make sense for a chess player to refuse to accept the concept of checkmate, for a speaker of English to assert that it makes no difference whether subjects and predicates agree, or for an actor in the existing international society to disregard the rules regarding the nationality of citizens." In international relations, the "menu of available practices" is limited: "a 'new' state, for example, has little choice but to join the basic institutional arrangements of the states system" (1986:120).

The concept of a practice is particularly applicable to certain general patterns of activity such as sovereignty and multilateral diplomacy. Their rules, many of which are not codified, define what it means to be sovereign or to engage in mul-tilateral diplomacy.[3] Like the rules of chess and the grammar of the English lan-guage, respect for state sovereignty and multilateral diplomacy are taken for granted by most of those who participate in them. When fundamental practices are violated, as in the seizure of the American Embassy in Teheran in 1979, disap-proval is virtually universal. . . .

Rawls' distinction helps us to see the specific institutions of world politics, with their challengeable rules, as embedded in more fundamental practices. Just as the actors in world politics are constrained by existing institutions, so are insti-tutions, and prospects for institutional change, constrained by the practices taken for granted by their members. For each set of entities that we investigate, we can identify institutionalized constraints at a more fundamental and enduring level.

Consider, for instance, the practice of sovereign statehood, which has been fundamental to world politics for over three hundred years. At its core is the prin-ciple of sovereignty: that the state "is subject to no other state and has full and ex-clusive powers within its jurisdiction without prejudice to the limits set by applica-ble law" (*Wimbledon* case, Permanent Court of International Justice, series A, no. 1, 1923; cited in Hoffmann, 1987:172–73). Sovereignty is thus a relatively precise legal concept: a question of law, not of fact, of authority, not sheer power. As a legal concept, the principle of sovereignty should not be confused with the empirical claim that a given state in fact makes its decisions autonomously. . . .

Sovereign statehood is a practice in Rawls' sense because it contains a set of rules that define it and that can be used to correct states' behavior. These rules are fundamental to the conduct of modern international relations. Extraterritorial jurisdiction for embassies is such a central rule, implied by the modern conception of sovereignty; immunity from ordinary criminal prosecution for a state's accredited diplomats is a corollary of this principle. More generally, as Martin Wight has argued, the norm of reciprocity is implied by that of sovereignty, and respect for reciprocity is therefore part of the practice of sovereign statehood: "It would be impossible to have a society of sovereign states unless each state, while claiming sovereignty for itself, recognized that every other state had the right to claim and enjoy its own sovereignty as well. This reciprocity was inherent in the Western conception of sovereignty" (Wight, 1977:135).

Treating sovereign statehood as a practice does not imply that the process of recognizing entities as sovereign is automatic: on the contrary, states follow political convenience as well as law in deciding which entities to regard as sovereign. But once an entity has been generally accepted by states as sovereign, certain rights and responsibilities are entailed. Furthermore, acceptance of the principle of sovereignty creates well-defined roles. Only sovereign states or entities such as international organizations created by states can make treaties and enforce them on subjects within their jurisdictions, declare and wage wars recognized by international law, and join international organizations that are part of the United Nations System.

. . . I have begun with a broad definition of institutions as persistent and connected sets of rules that prescribe behavioral roles, constrain activity, and shape expectations. I have focused my attention, however, on specific institutions and practices. Specific institutions can be defined in the first instance in terms of rules; but we must recognize that specific institutions are embedded in practices. In modern world politics, the most important practice is that of sovereignty. To understand institutions and institutional change in world politics, it is necessary to understand not only how specific institutions are formulated, change, and die, but how their evolution is affected by the practice of sovereignty.

THE RATIONALISTIC STUDY OF INTERNATIONAL INSTITUTIONS

Rationalistic research on international institutions focuses almost entirely on specific institutions. It emphasizes international regimes and formal international organizations. Since this research program is rooted in exchange theory, it assumes scarcity and competition as well as rationality on the part of the actors. It therefore begins with the premise that if there were no potential gains from agreements to be captured in world politics—that is, if no agreements among actors could be mutually beneficial—there would be no need for specific international institutions. But there are evidently considerable benefits to be secured from mutual agreement—as evidenced for millennia by trade agreements, rules of war, and peace treaties, and for the last century by international organizations. Conversely, if cooperation were easy—that is, if all mutually beneficial bargains could be made without cost—there would be no need for institutions to facilitate cooperation. Yet such an assumption would be equally as false as the assumption that no potential gains from agreements exist. It is the combination of the potential *value* of agreements and the *difficulty* of making them that renders international regimes significant. In order to cooperate in world politics on more than a sporadic basis, human beings have to use institutions.

Rationalistic theories of institutions view institutions as affecting patterns of costs. Specifically, institutions reduce certain forms of uncertainty and alter transaction costs: that is, the "costs of specifying and enforcing the contracts that underlie exchange" (North, 1984:256). Even in the absence of hierarchical authority, institutions provide information (through monitoring) and stabilize expectations. They may also make decentralized enforcement feasible, for example by creating conditions under which reciprocity can operate (North, 1981; Williamson, 1981, 1985; Keohane, 1984; Moe, 1987). At any point in time, transaction costs are to a substantial degree the result of the institutional context. Dynamically, the relationship between these institutionally affected transaction costs and the formation of new institutions will, according to the theory, be curvilinear. If transaction costs are negligible, it will not be necessary to create new institutions to facilitate mutually beneficial exchange; if transaction costs are extremely high, it will not be feasible to build institutions—which may even be unimaginable.

In world politics, sovereignty and state autonomy mean that transaction costs are never negligible, since it is always difficult to communicate, to monitor performance, and especially to enforce compliance with rules. Therefore, according to this theory, one should expect international institutions to appear whenever the costs of communication, monitoring, and enforcement are relatively low compared to the benefits to be derived from political exchange. Institutions should persist as long as, but only so long as, their members have incentives to maintain them. But the effects of these institutions will not be politically neutral: they can be expected to confer advantages on those to whom their rules grant access and a share in political authority; and insofar as the transaction costs of making agreements outside of an established institution are high, governments disadvantaged within an institution will find themselves at a disadvantage in the issue area as a whole. More generally, the rules of any institution will reflect the relative power positions of its actual and potential members, which constrain the feasible bargaining space and affect transaction costs.[4]

These transaction-cost arguments have been applied in qualitative terms to international relations. As anticipated by the theory, effective international regimes include arrangements to share information and to monitor compliance, according to standards established by the regime; and they adapt to shifts in capabilities among their members (Finlayson and Zacher, 1983; Keohane, 1984: chapter 10; Aggarwal, 1985; Lipson, 1986; Haggard and Simmons, 1987). Furthermore, the access rules of different international regimes affect the success of governments in the related issue areas (Krasner, 1985:123). As a general descriptive model, therefore, this approach seems to do quite well: international regimes work as we expect them to.

However, the rationalistic theory has not been used to explain why international institutions exist in some issue areas rather than in others. Nor has this theory been employed systematically to account for the creation or demise of such institutions. Yet the theory implies hypotheses about these questions: hypotheses that could be submitted to systematic, even quantitative, examination. For instance, this theory predicts that the incidence of specific international institutions should be related to the ratio of benefits anticipated from exchange to the transaction costs of establishing the institutions necessary to facilitate the negotiation, monitoring, and enforcement costs of agreements specifying the terms of exchange. It also predicts that in the absence of anticipated gains from agreements, specific institutions will not be created, and that most specific institutions in world politics will in fact perform the function of reducing transaction costs. Since the theory acknowledges the significance of sunk costs in perpetuating extant institutions, and since its advocates recognize that organizational processes modify the pure dictates of rationality (Keohane, 1984: chapter 7), its predictions about the demise of specific institutions are less clear.

The rationalistic theory could also help us develop a theory of compliance or noncompliance with commitments.[5] For international regimes to be effective, their injunctions must be obeyed; yet sovereignty precludes hierarchical enforcement. The game-theoretic literature suggests that reputation may provide a strong incentive for compliance (Kreps and Wilson, 1982). But we do not know how strong the reputational basis for enforcement of agreements is in world politics, since we have not done the necessary empirical work. What Oliver Williamson calls "opportunism" is still possible: reputations can be differentiated among partners and violations of agreements can often be concealed. Historically, it is not entirely clear to what extent governments that renege on their commitments are in fact punished for such actions. Indeed, governments that have defaulted on their debts have, it appears, not been punished via higher interest rates in subsequent periods for their defections (Eichengreen, 1987; Lindert and Morton, 1987).

Rationalistic theory can often help us understand the direction of change in world politics, if not always its precise extent or the form that it takes. For instance, there are good reasons to believe that a diffusion of power away from a hegemonic state, which sponsored extant international regimes, will create pressures on these regimes and weaken their rules—even though it is dubious that hegemony is either a necessary or a sufficient condition for the maintenance of a pattern of order in international relations (Keohane, 1984). . . .

Yet even on its own terms, rationalistic theory encounters some inherent limitations. The so-called Folk Theorem of game theory states that for a class of games that includes 2×2 repeated Prisoners' Dilemma, there are many feasible equilibria above the maximum points of both players (Kreps, 1984:16). We cannot predict which one will emerge without knowing more about the structure of a situation—that is, about the prior institutional context in which the situation is embedded. This means that the conclusions of formal models of cooperation are often highly dependent on the assumptions with which the investigations begin—that they are context-dependent. To be sure, once we understand the context, it may be possible to model strategies used by players to devise equilibrium-inducing institutions (Shepsle, 1986). The literatures on bureaucratic politics and agency theory complicate matters further by suggesting that the organizational "actor" will not necessarily act as "its" interests specify, if people within it have different interests (Moe, 1984; Arrow, 1985). Thus even on its own terms rationalistic theory seems to leave open the issue of what kinds of institutions will develop, to whose benefit, and how effective they will be.

Even within the confines of the rationalistic research program, therefore, formal theory alone is unlikely to yield answers to our explanatory puzzles. Rationalistic theory is good at posing questions and suggesting lines of inquiry, but it does not furnish us with answers. . . .[6]

Rationalistic theory also needs to extend its vision back into history. To do so in a sophisticated way entails a departure from the equilibrium models emphasized by neoclassical economic theory. It requires intellectual contortions to view the evolution of institutions over time as the product of a deterministic equilibrium logic in which rational adaptation to the environment plays the key role. Institutional development is affected by particular leaders and by exogenous shocks—chance events from the perspective of a systemic theory. Theories of "path-dependence" in economics demonstrate that under specified conditions, accumulated random variations can lead an institution into a state that could not have been predicted in advance (David, 1985; Arthur, Ermoliev and Kaniovski, 1987; see also March and Olson, 1984:745). From a technological standpoint, path-dependence occurs under conditions of increasing rather than decreasing returns—resulting for instance from positive externalities that give established networks advantages over their competitors, from learning effects, and from the convergence of expectations around an established standard. Examples include the development of the typewriter keyboard, competition between different railroad gauges or between Betamax and VHS types of video recorders, and between gasoline and steam-powered cars. Viewed from a more strictly institutional perspective, path-dependence can be a result of sunk costs. Arthur Stinchcombe (1968:120–21) points out that if "sunk costs make a traditional pattern of action cheaper, and if new patterns are not enough more profitable to justify throwing away the resource, the sunk costs tend to preserve a pattern of action from one year to the next."

Surely the General Agreement on Tariffs and Trade (GATT), the International Monetary Fund (IMF) and the United Nations are not optimally efficient, and they would not be invented in their present forms today; but they persist. In some cases, this may be a matter of sunk costs making it rational to continue involvement with an old institution. Sometimes the increasing returns pointed to by path-dependence theorists may account for this persistence. Or considerations of power and status may be more important than the functions performed by the institutions. . . .

REFLECTIVE APPROACHES

Scholars imbued with a sociological perspective on institutions emphasize that institutions are often not created consciously by human beings but rather emerge slowly through a less deliberative process, and that they are frequently taken for granted by the people who are affected by them. In this view the assumption of utility maximization often does not tell us much about the origins of institutions; and it also does not take us very far in understanding the variations in institutional arrangements in different cultures and political systems. Ronald Dore, for instance, suggests that Oliver Williamson's attempt to construct "timeless generalizations" perhaps "merely reflects the tendency of American economists to write as if all the world were America. Or perhaps [Williamson] does not have much evidence about America either, and just assumes that 'Man' is a hard-nosed short-run profit maximizer suspicious of everyone he deals with" (Dore, 1983:469).

Values, norms and practices vary across cultures, and such variations will affect the efficacy of institutional arrangements. This point can be put into the language of rationalistic theory: institutions that are consistent with culturally accepted practices are likely to entail lower transaction costs than those that conflict with those practices. But such a statement merely begs the question of where the practices, or the preferences that they reflect, came from in the first place. The most ambitious form of rationalistic theory, which takes fundamental preferences as uniform and constant, is contradicted by cultural variation if preferences are meaningfully operationalized. The more modest form of this theory, which treats variations in preferences as exogenous, thereby avoids seeking to explain them.

Similar problems arise with explanations of changes in institutions over time. Rationalistic theories of specific institutions can be applied historically, as we have seen. Each set of institutions to be explained is viewed within an institutional as well as material context: prior institutions create incentives and constraints that affect the emergence or evolution of later ones. Change is then explained by changes in opportunity costs at the margin, as a result of environmental changes.

Such an approach has been highly revealing, as the literature on institutional change in economics demonstrates (North, 1981). However, these rationalistic theories of specific institutions have to be contextualized before they are empirically useful: that is, they must be put into a prior framework of institutions and practices. Only with this prior knowledge of the situation at one point in time to guide us, can we use this theory effectively to improve our knowledge of what is likely to happen next. We can then work our way back through the various levels of analysis—explaining actor behavior by reference to institutional constraints and opportunities, explaining specific institutions by reference to prior institutions, explaining those institutions by reference to fundamental practices. Up to a point, rationalistic theory can pursue its analysis backwards in time; and it can only gain by becoming more historically sensitive. But as Field (1981) pointed out and as North (1981) has recognized in the field of economic history, at some point one must embed the analysis in institutions that are not plausibly viewed as the product of human calculation and bargaining. And ultimately, the analysis has to come to grips with the structures of social interaction that "constitute or empower those agents in the first place" (Wendt, 1987:369).

International institutions are not created *de novo* any more than are economic institutions. On the contrary, they emerge from prior institutionalized contexts, the most fundamental of which cannot be explained as if they were contracts among rational individuals maximizing some utility function. These fundamental practices seem to reflect historically distinctive combinations of material circumstances, social patterns of thought, and individual initiative—combinations which reflect "conjunctures" rather than deterministic outcomes (Hirschman, 1970), and which are themselves shaped over time by path-dependent processes. Rationalistic theory can help to illuminate these practices, but it cannot stand alone. Despite the ambitions of some of its enthusiasts, it has little prospect of becoming a comprehensive deductive explanation of international institutions.

Quite apart from this limitation, the writers whom I have labeled "reflective" have emphasized that rationalistic theories of institutions contain no *endogenous* dynamic. Individual and social reflection leading to changes in preferences or in views of causality—what Hayward Alker refers to as *historicity* (Alker, 1986) and what Ernst Haas discusses under the rubric of *learning* (Haas, 1987)—is ignored. That is, preferences are assumed to be fixed. But this assumption of fixed preferences seems to preclude understanding of some major changes in human institutions. For example, as Douglass North points out, "the demise of slavery, one of the landmarks in the history of freedom, is simply not explicable in an interest group model" (North, 1987:12). Nor, in the view of Robert Cox, is American hegemony explicable simply in power terms: on the contrary, it implies a "coherent conjunction or fit between a configuration of material power, a prevalent collective image of world order (including certain norms) and a set of institutions which administer the order with a certain semblance of universality" (Cox, 1986:223).

From this perspective, rationalistic theories seem only to deal with one dimension of a multidimensional reality: they are incomplete, since they ignore changes taking place in consciousness. They do not enable us to understand how interests change as a result of changes in belief systems. They obscure rather than illuminate the sources of states' policy preferences. The result, according to Richard Ashley, has been a fundamentally unhistorical approach to world politics, which has reified contemporary political arrangements by denying "history as process" and "the historical significance of practice" (Ashley, 1986:290; see also Alker, 1986; Kratochwil, 1986).

Some analysts in the reflective camp have sought to correct this lack of attention to historicity and learning. In analyzing Prisoner's Dilemma, Alker (1985) emphasizes not merely the structure of payoff matrices but the sequential patterns of learning taking place between actors over the course of a sequence of games. And Ruggie (1986) has argued that only by understanding how individuals think about their world can we understand changes in how the world is organized—for instance, the shift from medieval to modern international politics. Socially influenced patterns of learning are crucial, as Karl

Deutsch and Ernst Haas—the teachers, respectively, of Alker and Ruggie—have always emphasized.

Reflective critics of the rationalistic research program have emphasized the inadequacies of rationalism in analyzing the fundamental practice of sovereign statehood, which has been instituted not by agreement but as a result of the elaboration over time of the principle of sovereignty. Sovereignty seems to be *prior* to the kinds of calculations on which rationalistic theory focuses: governments' strategies assume the principle of sovereignty, and the practice of sovereign statehood, as givens. Indeed, according to some critics of rationalistic thinking, sovereignty is of even more far-reaching significance, since it defines the very nature of the actors in world politics. Ruggie conceptualizes sovereignty as a "form of legitimation" that "differentiates units in terms of juridically mutually exclusive and morally self-entailed domains." Like private property rights, it divides space in terms of exclusive rights, and establishes patterns of social relationships among the resulting "possessive individualists," whose character as agents is fundamentally shaped by sovereignty itself (Ruggie, 1986: 144–47).. . .

The criticisms of rationalistic theory, both from within the framework of its assumptions and outside of them, are extensive and telling. The assumption of equilibrium is often misleading, and can lead to mechanical or contorted analysis. Rationalistic theory accounts better for shifts in the strength of institutions than in the values that they serve to promote. Cultural variations create anomalies for the theory. It does not take into account the impact of social processes of reflection or learning on the preferences of individuals or on the organizations that they direct. Finally, rationalistic theory has had little to say about the origins and evolution of practices, and it has often overlooked the impact of such practices as sovereignty on the specific institutions that it studies.[7]

Yet the critics have by no means demolished the rationalistic research program on institutions, although taking their argument seriously requires us to doubt the legitimacy of rationalism's intellectual hegemony. To show that rationalistic theory cannot account for changes in preferences because it has omitted important potential explanatory factors is important, but it is not devastating, since no social science theory is complete. Limiting the number of variables that a theory considers can increase both its explanatory content and its capacity to concentrate the scholarly mind. Indeed, the rationalistic program is heuristically so powerful precisely because it does not easily accept accounts based on post hoc observation of values or ideology: regarding states as rational actors with specified utility functions forces the analyst to look below the surface for interests that provide incentives to behave in apparently anomalous ways. In quite a short time, research stimulated by rationalistic theory has posed new questions and proposed new hypotheses about why governments create and join international regimes, and the conditions under which these institutions wax or wane. A research program with such a record of accomplishment, and a considerable number of interesting but still untested hypotheses about reasons for persistence, change, and compliance, cannot be readily dismissed.

Indeed, the greatest weakness of the reflective school lies not in deficiencies in their critical arguments but in the lack of a clear reflective research program that could be employed by students of world politics. Waltzian neorealism has such a research program; so does neoliberal institutionalism, which has focused on the evolution and impact of international regimes. Until the reflective scholars or others sympathetic to their arguments have delineated such a research program and shown in particular studies that it can illuminate important issues in world politics, they will remain on the margins of the field, largely invisible to the preponderance of empirical researchers, most of whom explicitly or implicitly accept one or another version of rationalistic premises. Such invisibility would be a shame, since the reflective perspective has much to contribute.

As formulated to date, both rationalistic and what I have called reflective approaches share a common blind spot: neither pays sufficient attention to domestic politics. It is all too obvious that domestic politics is neglected by much game-theoretic strategic analysis and by structural explanations of international regime change. However, this deficiency is not inherent in the nature of rationalistic analysis: it is quite possible to use game theory heuristically to analyze the "two-level games" linking domestic and international politics, as Robert Putnam (1988) has done. At one level reflective theory questions, in its discussion of sovereignty, the existence of a clear boundary between domestic and international politics. But at another level it critiques the reification of the state in neorealist theory and contemporary practice, and should therefore be driven to an analysis of how such reification has taken place historically and how it is reproduced within the confines of the domestic-international dichotomy. Such an analysis could lead to a fruitful reexamination of shifts in preferences that emerge from complex interactions between the operation of international institutions and the processes of domestic politics. Both Kenneth Waltz's "second image"—the impact of domestic politics on international relations—and Peter Gourevitch's "second image reversed" need to be taken account of, in their different ways, by the rationalist and reflective approaches (Waltz, 1959; Gourevitch, 1978). . . .[8]

NOTES

1. Bull also declares that "states themselves are the principal institutions of the society of states" (1977:71), which implies that he subscribed to the view, discussed below, that the international institution of sovereignty is prior to the state.
2. *International regimes* are specific institutions involving states and/or transnational actors, which apply to particular issues in international relations. This is similar to the definition given by Krasner (1983), but makes it clearer that regimes are institutions, taking advantage of the definition of institutions given above. *Formal international organizations* are purposive institutions with explicit rules, specific assignments of roles to individuals and groups, and the capacity for action. Unlike international regimes, international organizations can engage in goal-directed activities such as raising and spending money, promulgating policies, and making discretionary choices.
3. These practices have evolved over the course of decades or centuries and can therefore be considered in Young's terminology to be *spontaneous* orders: "the product of the action of many men but . . . not the result of human design" (Young, 1983:98, quoting Hayek, 1973:37).

4. The assertion that hegemony is necessary for institutionalized cooperation, and the less extreme view that hegemony facilitates cooperation, can both be interpreted within this framework as declaring transaction costs to be lower when a hegemon exists than when power resources are more fragmented.
5. For a pioneering exploration of these issues, see Young (1979).
6. The theoretical indeterminacy of rationalistic theory suggests that in international relations, as in the economics of institutions, "theory is now outstripping empirical research to an excessive extent" (Matthews, 1986:917).
7. This does not mean, however, that rationalistic theory is incapable of contributing to our understanding of the evolution of practices. As Wendt argues, "there is no a priori reason why we cannot extend the logic of [rationalistic] analysis to the analysis of generative structures" (Wendt, 1987:368). In notes to the author, Barry Weingast has illustrated this point by sketching a functional, transaction-cost argument for the existence of sovereignty, as a set of relatively unambiguous conventions, known to all players and not revisable ex post, which facilitate coordination and signaling.
8. Recently major work has been done on links between domestic and international politics, by scholars trained in comparative politics. Unlike the critics of rationalistic theory discussed above, however, these writers emphasize international structure, material interests, and state organization as well as the role of ideas and social patterns of learning. Also unlike the critics of rationalist international relations theory, these writers have engaged in extensive and detailed empirical research. See Zysman (1983), Katzenstein (1985), Gourevitch (1986), and Alt (1987).

BIBLIOGRAPHY

Aggarwal, V. K. (1985) *Liberal Protectionism: The International Politics of Organized Textile Trade.* Berkeley: University of California Press.

Alker, H. R. Jr. (1985) From Quantity to Quality: A New Research Program on Resolving Sequential Prisoner's Dilemmas. Paper delivered at the August meeting of the American Political Science Association.

Alker, H. R. Jr. (1986) The Presumption of Anarchy in World Politics. Draft manuscript, Department of Political Science, M.I.T., August.

Alt, J. A. (1987) Crude Politics: Oil and the Political Economy of Unemployment in Britain and Norway, 1970–85. *British Journal of Political Science* 17:149–99.

Arrow, K. J. (1985) The Economics of Agency. In *Principals and Agents: The Structure of Business,* edited by J. W. Pratt and R. J. Zeckhauser, pp. 37–51. Boston: Harvard Business School Press.

Arthur, W. B., Y. M. Ermoliev and Y. M. Kaniovski. (1987) Path-Dependent Processes and the Emergence of Macro-Structure. *European Journal of Operational Research* 30:294–303.

Ashley, R. K. (1986) The Poverty of Neorealism. In *Neorealism and Its Critics,* edited by R. O. Keohane, New York: Columbia University Press.

Axelrod, R. (1984) *The Evolution of Cooperation.* New York: Basic Books.

Barry, B. (1970) *Sociologists, Economists and Democracy.* London: Macmillan.

Bull, H. (1977) *The Anarchical Society.* New York: Columbia University Press.

Cox, R. W. (1986) Social Forces, States and World Orders: Beyond International Relations Theory. In *Neorealism and Its Critics,* edited by R. O. Keohane, pp. 204–55. New York: Columbia University Press.

David, P. A. (1985) Clio and the Economics of QWERTY. *American Economic Review Proceedings* 75:332–37.

Dore, R. (1983) Goodwill and the Spirit of Market Capitalism. *British Journal of Sociology* 34:459–82.

Eichengreen, B. (1987) Till Debt Do Us Part: The U.S. Capital Market and Foreign Lending, 1920–1955. Cambridge: NBER Working Paper no. 2394 (October).

Field, A. J. (1981) The Problem with Neoclassical Institutional Economics: A Critique with Special Reference to the North/Thomas model of pre-1500 Europe. *Explorations in Economic History* 18:174–98.

Finlayson, J. A. and M. W. Zacher (1983) The GATT and the Regulation of Trade Barriers: Regime Dynamics and Functions. In *International Regimes,* edited by S. D. Krasner, pp. 273–315. Ithaca: Cornell University Press.

Gilpin, R. (1981) *War and Change in World Politics.* New York: Cambridge University Press.

Gourevitch, P. A. (1978) The Second Image Reversed: International Sources of Domestic Politics. *International Organization* 32:881–912.

Gourevitch, P. A. (1986) *Politics in Hard Times.* Ithaca: Cornell University Press.

Haas, E. B. (1987) Adaptation and Learning in International Organizations. Manuscript. Berkeley: Institute of International Studies.

Haggard, S. and B. A. Simmons. (1987) Theories of International Regimes. *International Organization* 41:491–517.

Hayek, F. A. (1973) *Rules and Order.* Vol. 1 of *Law, Legislation and Liberty.* Chicago: University of Chicago Press.

Hirschman, A. D. (1970) The Search for Paradigms as a Hindrance to Understanding. *World Politics* 22(3):329–43.

Hughes, E. C. (1936) The Ecological Aspect of Institutions. *American Sociological Review* 1:180–89.

Katzenstein, P. J. (1985) *Small States in World Markets.* Ithaca: Cornell University Press.

Keohane, R. O. (1984) *After Hegemony: Cooperation and Discord in the World Political Economy.* Princeton: Princeton University Press.

Keohane, R. O., ed. (1986a) *Neorealism and Its Critics.* New York: Columbia University Press.

Keohane, R. O. (1986b) Reciprocity in International Relations. *International Organization* 40:1–27.

Krasner, S. D., ed. (1983) *International Regimes.* Ithaca: Cornell University Press.

Krasner, S. D. (1985) *Structural Conflict: The Third World against Global Liberalism.* Berkeley: University of California Press.

Krasner, S. D. (1987) Sovereignty: An Institutional Perspective. Manuscript. Stanford, CA: Center for Advanced Study in the Behavioral Sciences, October.

Kratochwil, F. (1986) Of Systems, Boundaries and Territoriality: An Inquiry into the Formation of the State System. *World Politics* 39:27–52.

Kratochwil, F. and J. G. Ruggie. (1986) International Organization: A State of the Art on an Art of the State. *International Organization* 40:753–76.

Kreps, D. M. (1984) Corporate Culture and Economic Theory. Manuscript. Stanford, CA: Graduate School of Business, Stanford University.

Kreps, D. and R. Wilson (1982) Reputation and Imperfect Information. *Journal of Economic Theory* 27:253–79.

Lindert, P. H. and P. J. Morton (1987) How Sovereign Debt Has Worked. University of California, Davis, Institute of Governmental Affairs, Research Program in Applied Macroeconomics and Macro Policy, Working Paper series no. 45, August.

Lipson, C. (1986) Bankers' Dilemmas: Private Cooperation in Rescheduling Sovereign Debts. In *Cooperation under Anarchy*, edited by K. Oye, pp. 200–25. Princeton: Princeton University Press.

March, J. and J. Olson (1984) The New Institutionalism: Organizational Factors in Political Life. *American Political Science Review* 79:734–49.

Matthews, R. C. O. (1986) The Economics of Institutions and the Sources of Growth. *Economic Journal* 96:903–18.

Moe, T. M. (1984) The New Economics of Organization. *American Journal of Political Science* 28:739–77.

Moe, T. M. (1987) Interests, Institutions and Positive Theory: The Politics of the NLRB. *Studies in American Political Development* 2:236–99.

North, D. C. (1981) *Structure and Change in Economic History.* New York: W. W. Norton.

North, D. C. (1984) Government and the Cost of Exchange in History. *Journal of Economic History* 44:255–64.

North, D. C. (1987) Institutions and Economic Growth: An Historical Introduction. Paper prepared for the Conference on Knowledge and Institutional Change sponsored by the University of Minnesota, Minneapolis, November.

Oye, K. A., ed. (1986) *Cooperation under Anarchy.* Princeton: Princeton University Press.

Putnam, R. D. (1988) Diplomacy and Domestic Politics: The Logic of Two-Level Games. *International Organization* 42:427–60.

Rawls, J. (1955) Two Concepts of Rules. *Philosophical Review* 64:3–32.

Ruggie, J. G. (1986) Continuity and Transformation in the World Polity: Toward a Neorealist Synthesis. In *Neorealism and Its Critics*, edited by R. O. Keohane, pp. 131–57. New York: Columbia University Press.

Schepsle, K. (1986) Institutional Equilibrium and Equilibrium Institutions. In *Political Science: The Science of Politics*, edited by H. F. Weisberg, pp. 51–81. New York: Agathon Press.

Simon, H. A. (1985) Human Nature in Politics: The Dialogue of Psychology with Political Science. *American Political Science Review* 79:293–304.

Stinchcombe, A. L. (1968) *Constructing Social Theories.* New York: Harcourt, Brace and World.

Waltz, K. N. (1959) *Man, the State and War.* New York: Columbia University Press.

Wendt, A. E. (1987) The Agent-Structure Problem in International Relations Theory. *International Organization* 41:335–70.

Wight, M. (1977) *Systems of States*, edited with an introduction by H. Bull. Leicester: Leicester University Press.

Williamson, O. E. (1981) The Modern Corporation: Origins, Evolution, Attributes. *Journal of Economic Literature* 19:1537–68.

Williamson, O. E. (1985) *The Economic Institutions of Capitalism.* New York: Free Press.

Young, O. R. (1979) *Compliance and Public Authority.* Washington: Resources for the Future.

Young, O. R. (1983) Regime Dynamics: The Rise and Fall of International Regimes. In *International Regimes,* edited by S. D. Krasner, pp. 93–114. Ithaca: Cornell University Press.

Young, O. R. (1986) International Regimes: Toward a New Theory of Institutions. *World Politics* 39:104–22.

Zucker, L. G. (1977) The Role of Institutionalization in Cultural Persistence. *American Sociological Review* 42:726–43.

Zysman, J. (1983) *Governments, Markets and Growth.* Ithaca: Cornell University Press.

Coordination Versus Prisoners' Dilemma: Implications for International Cooperation and Regimes

Duncan Snidal

The problem of international cooperation is essentially one of collective action applied to the particular circumstances of the international system. The formation of international regimes raises the same general issues that surround the development of political institutions for resolving collective action problems in various spheres of human activity. . . .

One explanation of institutional variation lies in the possibility that different regime forms may provide different solutions to the same problem; that is, given any particular problem of collective action, a solution might be achieved in any number of different ways and be reflected in correspondingly different institutional development. For example, the problem of maintaining free trade among states might be resolved by formal contract and enforcement through international treaties and organizations. Alternatively, the same trade problem might be resolved through the emergence of norms and conventions that provide informal guides for state conduct. In fact, the current international trade regime seems to fall somewhere between these extremes (Lipson, 1982). . . .

A second explanation for regime variation is that regimes in different issue areas represent different solutions to fundamentally different problems. Different histories and contexts of particular international issues may facilitate certain types of solutions in some issues and other solutions in other issues. For example, the historical development of the norm of open access to ocean transportation routes provides a solid foundation for an informal norm-based regime, whereas in international trade, discrimination against foreign goods is a well-recognized right of states, and so the norm of nondiscrimination is inadequate as the sole basis of a regime. But an even more important source of this type of regime variation lies in the possibility that the underlying strategic structure of issues is fundamentally different; this will occur when the nature of interdependence between states, as reflected in the ways in which they affect and are affected by one another, differs across issue areas. If this is the case, then there is no longer any single problem of collective action. Instead, multiple different problems of collective action need to be recognized. These multiple problems may be soluble by similar types of regimes, or they may each require different institutional forms for their resolution.

Both explanations of variation in regime type are important, but the impact of strategic structure is generally less well understood than are other sources of regime variation. In large part this is because a particular model of collective action, the Prisoners' Dilemma (PD), has incorrectly come to be treated as the problem of collective action. Indeed, sometimes even a very special case of PD—the public good problem—is treated as if it were the sole problem. A wide range of issues have been analyzed this way without careful scrutiny to check that their underlying strategic structure corresponds to this particular formalization. Although PD (and public goods) provide an important category of collective action problems, inappropriate analysis and erroneous conclusions result when other issues are treated as if they are PD when in fact they are not. Other collective action problems hold very different implications for the likely nature and performance of regime institutions. . . .

The diverse structures of collective action problems will be analyzed in terms of two simple situations represented in game theoretic format—the PD and coordination games—which pose fundamentally different problems for cooperation. Starting from the basic 2×2 representation of these games, the restrictive assumptions of the two-actor, two-choice, one-play game are each relaxed. The implications for (international) political institutions that emerge from these expanded games demonstrate that differences in the underlying strategic structures of international issues provide an important source of regime variation. . . .

USING GAMES TO STUDY THE DIVERSITY OF COLLECTIVE ACTION PROBLEMS

Ordinal 2×2 games provide a useful way to investigate the variety and diversity of collective action problems. . . .

Considering all possible combinations of ordinal preferences, there are 78 different 2×2 games which provide an exhaustive listing of the possible relations of interdependence in a two-state, two-choice, one-play world (Rapoport & Guyer, 1966). To investigate the implications of different types of strategic interdependence for regimes, I consider two of these: the PD and coordination games. Although the choice of these particular games may seem arbitrary (which in itself would not matter for showing that *some* different situations of interdependence lead to different implications for regimes), there are compelling reasons why a comparison of these two games is germane. First, these two games have been widely discussed as important problems both in the game theory literature and in substantive discussions of problems of international cooperation. Second (although it will not be developed here), in a typology of cooperation problems in 2×2 games, these two games emerge as the two polar cases of assistance and coordination problems as discussed below (Snidal, 1981, chap. 2). Third, they are analytically more tractable and fruitful than many other simple games. . . .[1]

THE ASSISTANCE PROBLEM: PRISONERS' DILEMMA

PD is well known as a problem of collective action and so is dealt with only briefly here. The normal (or strategic) game form is presented in Figure 1, where policy alternatives are indicated in boldface (**0,1**) for each of the two states, and the entries in each cell represent ordinal payoffs for States A and B, respectively. (The ordinal payoffs are represented as ranging from 4 = "Most Preferred Outcome" to 1 = "Least Preferred Outcome".)

PD is an archetypical example of the disjuncture between individual and group rationality which characterizes many problems of collective action: Pursuit of individual self-interest by states (represented by their each choosing their dominant strategy **1**) results in their being worse off than if both abstain from pursuit of their narrow self-interest and cooperate (represented by their each choosing strategy **0**). The dilemma persists even if cooperation is achieved, because both states will continue to have strong incentives to defect and the system is likely to return to the stable noncooperative and deficient equilibrium (i.e., outcome (2,2) in Figure 1).

The PD is the standard representation of externalities (including public goods) where in the pursuit of their own private gains actors impose costs on each other *independently of each other's action;* that is, in the pursuit of its national interest State A makes State B worse off regardless of what the latter does, and vice versa. Because each is affected more by the other's move than by its own move (e.g., State A's choice alters B's outcome by two ordinal rankings, whereas B's choice can affect B's outcome by only one ordinal ranking), they both need assistance from the other in the form of forbearance from its individually rational

Figure 1 Prisoners' Dilemma.

		STATE B	
		0	**1**
0		3, 3	1, 4
STATE A			
1		4, 1	2, 2

choice. Because each gains more by participating in a program of mutual assistance than by acting independently, there is room for cooperation in PD.[2]

The outcome of the single-shot PD depends heavily on the social-political context. If enforceable agreements are not possible, then neither state will cooperate, because each will be better off not cooperating regardless of what the other does. If binding agreements can be made, then both states will find it in their interests to enter into an agreement to cooperate. This notion of *contracting* out of PD depends on some equivalent to a Hobbesian sovereign able to enforce agreements. The sovereign might accomplish this by forcing states to perform on their promises or by imposing sanctions on failures to perform, so that the strategic structure is changed, and states find it in their self-interest to comply "voluntarily." Obviously such a sovereign is rarely present in international politics. However, as one extends the underlying analytic model beyond the single-shot PD, other factors appear that may allow for less centralized cooperation (e.g., iterated play) or otherwise affect the ease of solution by contract (e.g., bargaining problems in graduated games). Investigating these possibilities requires relaxing the underlying assumptions. . . .

Multiple States and Asymmetries in Prisoners' Dilemma

The extension of the two-actor PD to the *n*-actor situation is straightforward and well known; it corresponds to the standard case of (separable) externalities where each state imposes costs or benefits on others independent of their own behavior. . . . Standard examples include the "tragedy of the commons" where every state has an individual incentive to overexploit the commons even though this is contrary to the collective interests of all states.

The two standard results from *n*-actor PD are: (1) that larger numbers of states inhibit cooperation; and (2) that asymmetries (usually implicitly defined in terms of the impact of one state on another but, in fact, also a result of differences in preferences and intensities) facilitate cooperative and efficient outcomes. This latter result is often elaborated with the specific claim that smaller countries will benefit disproportionately in such asymmetric situations (i.e., the small exploit the large). However, these results are based specifically on public goods assumptions and are not valid as universal generalizations for all PD. Again, confusion of public goods as the problem of collective action is misleading for understanding the diversity of cooperation problems. But a precise specification of the conditions under which these generalizations apply does provide further insight into international cooperation. Not surprisingly, these conditions are closely related to the defining characteristics of public goods of "jointness" (i.e., that consumption by one state does not diminish the quantity or quality of the benefit available to the other) and, especially, of nonexclusion (i.e., that there is no way to prevent any state from receiving benefits).[3] When these conditions do not apply—and PD problems need involve neither jointness nor nonexclusion—then the generalizations need to be qualified or changed.

First, consider the claim that larger group size impedes cooperation. Insofar as this refers to the problems of organization that arise as a result of the different social-political features of large as opposed to small groups, the assertion is valid. As the number of members in any social grouping increases, there is likely to be a commensurate increase in problems of communication, in the tendency for states to perceive that their individual actions are less visible so that they can renege or cheat on cooperative arrangements without being noticed, and in the problems of resolving bargaining disputes over the distribution of benefits from cooperation. Even with an extensive and institutionalized apparatus for negotiation and diplomacy, states are not able to overcome such problems easily. Therefore, in general, multilateral negotiations involving greater numbers of states can be expected to increase the difficulty of cooperation.

However, an increased number of states also may have an opposite effect by opening up new areas (or levels) of potential cooperation which are not accessible to smaller numbers of states. There will be some projects on which no small group of states has incentive to cooperate but on which a larger group will find room for cooperation (e.g., projects such as the European airbus might not have been undertaken if, for example, there had been only two interested states). Even in public goods problems, an increased number of participants will not only increase the problems of organizing collective action, it will also increase the benefits from cooperation as reflected in the corresponding increase in the optimal level of provision. This beneficial impact of increased numbers of states may hold independently of any assumptions of jointness (e.g., where there are economies of scale in cooperation), but jointness will further enhance incentives for cooperation.

The possibility of exclusion will be especially important in mitigating the adverse effects of increased numbers of states on the prospects for international cooperation. If the benefits of cooperation can be restricted to states that behave cooperatively, then such exclusion will make provision in large groups hardly more difficult than in small groups. Indeed, in some sense exclusion makes the problem a small group one of agreement between any single country and the group of already-cooperating states. Admission to the group of benefiting states (or continued membership in the group) will be made contingent upon contribution to the collective effort. Many international organizations involving such diverse issues as trade, money, military alliances, or health regulation are in fact able to practice such exclusion to different degrees. Although difficult bargaining problems over what constitutes a "fair" contribution by various members persist, such exclusionary principles do facilitate substantial levels of cooperation.

Second, consider the impact of asymmetry within a group of states.[4] Hardin

(1982, pp. 40–41, 73) demonstrates that the likelihood of cooperation depends not only on the size of the group but on the net benefits received by each cooperating member and hence on the minimum-sized subgroup that can benefit from cooperation. For a given average payoff, a more asymmetric distribution of benefits means that a smaller subgroup is able to benefit from cooperation and therefore that cooperation within the group is more likely. If the issue involves public goods, then other states can get a free ride off this provision (and the distributive implications of the theory of hegemonic stability pertain); if the good is not joint, then there will not be benefits to noncontributors and only the larger states will benefit from their ability to cooperate; and if the good exhibits jointness but exclusion is possible, then noncontributors may be induced to contribute to the cooperative venture (perhaps at a cost they may see as exploitative).[5]

Therefore, the general conclusions that cooperation in PD is less likely as group size increases or as asymmetry decreases depend heavily on the exact context of the issue. These conclusions are not universally applicable whenever the issues do not meet the public good conditions of jointness or nonexclusion or both. Moreover, sometimes the cooperation that large numbers serve to impede is only a possibility because there are a large number of states involved in the issue. Only with these important caveats, can one conclude that *in PD large numbers tend to inhibit cooperation.* In addition, *asymmetries increase the likelihood of some cooperation but the distribution of benefits from cooperation will also be affected by the asymmetry.* Sometimes the distribution will favor smaller states, but in other cases they will favor larger states. Thus generalizations such as the "theory of hegemonic stability" need to be tightly circumscribed by careful specification of the properties of particular issue areas. This is true even within the realm of PD situations, and I demonstrate below that it applies even more forcefully in the coordination problem.

The Role of Time in Prisoners' Dilemma

One limitation of 2×2 games is that their inherently static, one-shot nature is inadequate for analyzing problems where considerations of play through time are important. Although it falls short of a truly dynamic analysis, some understanding of cooperation in a more dynamic world is provided by considering the situation where the same 2×2 game is played (or "iterated") through time.[6] Normally this involves looking only at the impact of future time, but it is also relevant to look at the impact of past and present time as discussed below.

It is now widely understood that the prospect of repeated play into the future increases the likelihood of cooperation in PD even in the absence of centralized enforcement (Axelrod, 1984; Hardin, 1982; Shubik, 1970; Taylor, 1976). Although noncooperation is a rational strategy in single-play PD, repeated play of the game into the future makes it worthwhile to take a chance on cooperating today in the hope that other states will do likewise and mutual cooperation will prevail over the deficient noncooperative equilibrium in the longer term. This possibility is more likely: (1) the longer the time horizon (or expected number of iterations of the game), since, as the final game approaches, the incentive to cooperate because of future considerations diminishes; (2) the lower the temporal discount rate or, equivalently, the more future benefits from cooperation are valued relative to the prevailing incentive not to cooperate; and (3) the greater the benefits from cooperation relative to the gains to be had from not cooperating (or the losses to be incurred from cooperating while other states do not).[7] To the extent that these conditions are fulfilled, *the fact that a PD issue is recurring through time will facilitate cooperative behavior.*

If we treat "present" time as the duration of a particular simple PD game embedded within an ongoing issue area, it becomes apparent that the speed with which states can adjust their policies (i.e., the duration of any single PD) has an impact similar to that of a longer future time horizon. The faster that states adapt to each others' actions, the more iterations of the game there are in any fixed length of time. Thus *when states in PD can adapt quickly to cooperative or noncooperative actions by the other side, there are greater prospects for cooperation* for precisely the same reasons that future play improves prospects for cooperation in PD. Improved information and communication—including preparations for policy changes—may be an important aspect of regimes for this reason.

Finally, past experience in PD may either encourage or hinder cooperation because of the mixed effects of learning and building trust between states. This is directly related to the incentives to cooperate because of "reputational" effects that encourage cooperation when games are repeated into the future. Generally, past success at cooperation will positively reinforce cooperation because of the increased reputational costs of reneging on longstanding arrangements. However, past success at cooperation also enhances the stability of a regime so that states may begin to feel they can cheat on cooperation without disrupting the tendency of other states to cooperate. . . .

The Coordination Problem and the Coordination Game

The coordination problem is generally less well understood as a problem of collective action and so will be dealt with in some detail here. Sometimes coordination is presented simply as the problem of two or more actors matching policies where they are indifferent about where they match (or have perfectly correlated preferences over alternative matches). A good example is a meeting problem where two friends are indifferent about where they meet for lunch as long as they both go to the same restaurant. Here there is no disjuncture between individual and collective rationality and no problem of collective action. It requires no more than communication and common sense to achieve an outcome that is both individually and collectively optimal.[8]

A more deep-seated problem of coordination arises when actors have a strong desire to coordinate but some differences over exactly where to coordinate. This problem is introduced into the meeting problem when friends wish to meet for lunch but each prefers meeting at a different restaurant or at a different time. The normal form of this game is presented in Figure 2.[9]

This game poses a different problem of collective action than does PD. The problem in PD is that in pursuing its own self-interest, each state imposes costs on

Figure 2 Coordination Game.

	STATE B	
	0	**1**
0	4, 3	2, 2
STATE A		
1	1, 1	3, 4

the other independent of the other state's policy choice, whereas *in the coordination game each imposes costs or benefits on the other contingent upon the other's policy.* The collective action problem is that neither state can choose its best policy without knowing what the other intends to do, but there is no obvious point at which to coordinate. Easy resolution of the problem (as in the simple meeting problem) is hindered by the inherently opposed interests about where coordination should occur. (State A prefers the northwest cell and State B the southeast cell.) However, once a cooperative solution is achieved, it does not need to be enforced (as did the cooperative outcome in simple PD), but is self-enforcing, because neither state has any incentive to depart from the coordination point in the single-play coordination game. Thus one can appreciate that the problem of coordination is fundamentally different from that of assistance in PD. (Stated more formally, the problem in the coordination game is one of choice between multiple stable and efficient equilibria over which states have opposed interests, whereas in PD the problem is getting away from a single stable but inefficient equilibrium.)

Cooperation in the coordination game depends on the surrounding social-political context. Established traditions or shared principles are likely to provide the basis for the emergence of norms or *conventions* which will guide individual national behavior in an issue area. No centralized enforcement is necessary, because neither state has incentive to depart from an established convention: The prevailing expectations of how the other state will behave which are conveyed by the convention provide a compelling reason for each state to adhere to it in order to gain the benefits of coordination. Any role for centralized authority in coordination problems is likely to be less concerned with enforcement than with codification and elaboration of an existing or latent convention and with providing information and communication to facilitate the smooth operation of the convention. Moreover, because the need for enforcement that exists in PD is absent, in coordination states will be more resistant to surrendering autonomy to a central agency because an alternative decentralized resolution is available. Finally, unlike PD where an obvious "cooperation point" exists, a sovereign would have no clear criterion (independent of conventions) upon which to base a choice between alternative coordination points. Therefore the simple coordination problem is almost certain to result in a decentralized solution.

Although this simple model of coordination applies to an important class of international cooperation problems (e.g., standardization of measurement systems, standardization of equipment within NATO, or recent European attempts to adopt common standards in telecommunications equipment), it is far too restrictive and unrealistic for many other important problems of international coordination. Consider the nature of attempts at international economic cooperation reflected in the recent string of economic summit meetings between leaders of the largest capitalist economies. In essence, the shared objective has been to agree on broad macroeconomic objectives and to coordinate policies in order to achieve them.[10] Two important differences distinguish this situation from the simple coordination game presented in Figure 2: (1) available policies are neither dichotomous nor discrete but involve states choosing over a broad policy continuum (e.g., from "contractionary" to "expansionary"); and (2) coordination is not an all-or-nothing problem and there is no need to meet exactly, provided that policies fall within a range of compatibility. Instead, states might be better characterized as preferring to coordinate policies as closely as possible where, in general, closer is better, *ceteris paribus*. However, at the same time different states will prefer to coordinate at different points (e.g., the West Germans may have a relatively greater concern with price stability than the French) and so some opposition of interests remains within the overall desire to coordinate. . . .

TWO DIFFERENT REGIMES: COORDINATION AND ASSISTANCE

Table 1 summarizes the main differences between the problems of collective action posed by coordination and PD. The entries are necessarily simplified and do not capture all of the nuances that may occur within each basic game situation according to particular contextual differences. As a result, the differences between the two situations are drawn somewhat more starkly than they may actually appear in real world situations. Nevertheless, the table usefully summarizes the fundamentally different natures of the two problems of collective action.

In comparing these two problems of collective action, we have also (directly and indirectly) been comparing the problems each poses for international cooperation and the implications for resolution of these problems through international regimes. . . .

The most basic distinction between the two categories of regimes is that between contract and convention as forms of solutions to cooperation problems. This distinction is often treated as one between the need for centralized enforcement versus the possibility of decentralized outcomes. Although this is the case in many circumstances, it is not a hard and fast rule. As I have discussed, cooperative outcomes to PD sometimes can be achieved without centralized enforcement when a problem recurs through time; similarly, centralized institutions could provide the basis for conventional outcomes. Instead of being viewed as a defining characteristic of the two situations, the occurrence of centralized versus decentralized resolutions is better treated as a consequence of the underlying nature of solutions by contract and by convention. Contract is a solution to a particular type of cooperation problem of assistance (i.e., separable externalities) and is based on the mutual performance (or forbearance) of particular acts so as to benefit others. States surrender some of their authority or autonomy in return for other states doing the same. For example, states might agree to surrender the right to produce

TABLE 1 SUMMARY OF KEY DIFFERENCES AND SIMILARITIES BETWEEN PD AND COORDINATION

	Prisoners' Dilemma	Coordination
Basic problem	Assistance: states interdependent because each imposes costs on the other independent of the other's actions	Coordination: states interdependent because impact of each state's choice contingent on other's choice
Basic solution	Contract	Convention
Effect of graduation	Strategic structure unaltered: game is same in small as in large	Strategic structure altered: game is fundamentally different in small than in large
Effect of multiple players	Generally inhibits cooperation: alleviated by asymmetries and possibility of exclusion	May inhibit formation of regimes; enhances stability of regimes
Effect of asymmetries	i. Facilitates cooperation ii. Without exclusion favors smaller states; with exclusion favors larger states	i. Slightly facilitates cooperation ii. Favors larger states
Impact of time	Future time and rapid adjustment increase prospects for cooperation	Past time increases whereas future time and rapid adjustment decrease prospects for cooperation

certain sorts of weapons or to impose certain restrictions on imports. Convention is a solution to a different problem of cooperation (i.e., nonseparable externalities) and is based on the coordination or harmonization of policies among states. It does not require that states give up any autonomy per se although negotiation of coordination points will affect the choices they will want to make independently. For example, states might agree on target macroeconomic policies and for that reason find it in their self-interest to pursue those targets even though they are still free to pursue other targets. Thus contract and convention provide different categories of basic solutions to fundamentally different problems of interdependence. As Stein (1982, p. 316) points out, cooperation in such issues depends on "rational self-interested calculation [which] leads actors to abandon independent decision-making in favor of joint decision-making." But the underlying differences in the two situations result in important differences in the nature of joint decision-making and hence in the nature of regimes.

Institutionalization

A first distinction concerns the nature of the basic rules and the extent of institutionalization (i.e., the nature of formal political arrangements) which characterize an issue area. In convention, rules will be largely self-enforcing and states will obey them (which is in the collective interest) because it is in their own self-interest. In contract, rules are not self-enforcing and there will be a tendency for them to be weakened by states cheating. . . .

Regimes pertaining to coordination problems, and based on convention, will generally have low levels of institutionalization concerned primarily with facilitating the choice, interpretation, and observance of a particular convention. This will involve information gathering and informal consultation about the preferences and policies of states as well as providing a forum for the resolution of bargaining problems pertaining to the choice of a particular convention. Enforcement in the large will not be necessary, and exclusion does not make sense given the nature of the problem. (However, a subset of states may try to exclude others from the process of selecting a convention in order to impose one that corresponds more closely to their own preferences.) Some local enforcement may be desirable to prevent minor deviations from the convention in the small. States may be willing to accept this enforcement although adherence may be achieved through (negotiated) voluntary restraint since it entails only a small sacrifice to reinforce a convention producing much larger benefits.

Contract solutions to PD will likely require much higher levels of institutionalization in order to overcome the continuing incentives for states to defect from cooperative arrangements. This will be reflected in formal agreements restricting national behavior (i.e., akin to Hart's primary rules of law) as well as procedures to support these rules through centralized processes of adjudication (i.e., akin to Hart's secondary rules). Needless to say, the centralized powers of sanction are typically very limited and contract is sustained more by needs of maintaining ongoing cooperation and reputational considerations than through fear of any international sovereign. One notable exception to this is the sanction of exclusion from a regime. Threat of exclusion, if credible, may be an important device for ensuring that states behave cooperatively. The credibility of the threat will depend in part on the properties of the particular issue area (e.g., impossible for many international commons problems but not for trade issues) and in part on the nature of the political arrangements (e.g., a military alliance able to determine precisely the scope of its membership). . . .

The second source of cooperation in assistance problems is the noncentralized enforcement that arises from reputational considerations and the prospects of playing through time. Indeed, one consequence of playing through time (or, alternatively, of the reaction time to each other's policies becoming exceedingly rapid) is that the strategic structure of the situation is transformed into one similar to that of the coordination game (Snidal, 1981; Taylor, 1976).[11] To the extent that these other incentives are adequate for maintaining cooperation, then solution by contract and centralized enforcement is not necessary. However, uncertainty about the possibility of maintaining cooperation over the long run, and the lack of trust among states coupled with continuing incentives to defect in any single play of the game (especially in issues involving large numbers of states), may make some form of centralized monitoring efficacious for maintaining cooperation. Therefore, even in this situation of repeated play through time, a greater level of enforcement is required (in PD) than in the pure coordination situation.

However, reputations and considerations of ongoing cooperation are not restricted to single-issue areas but are important across issue areas (cf. Hardin, 1982, pp. 186–187). A horizontal proliferation of PD games may provide a more important incentive for cooperation than the vertical continuation of any single

PD issue area through time. Fear that noncooperation will spread into other issue areas provides incentives for states not to succumb to immediate temptations to defect for short-run, issue-specific benefits. Indeed, this is a much more important aspect of issue-linkage than the more often discussed exchange form of linkage based on the linking of issues in a bargaining context. It is directly related to broader questions about the emergence of an international society with multiple overlapping interests and concerns. To the extent that such a society is emerging, the individual PD situation becomes embedded in a broader social context, and cooperation is increasingly possible with less formal centralized enforcement. In the extreme, variation between issues according to their strategic structure would tend to be dominated by the similarity imposed by these broader social considerations. But in less fully articulated international societies such as the present one, important regime variations will persist. Social considerations may be sufficient to enforce cooperation in PD issue areas of relatively minor importance where costs and risks of cooperation are low relative to benefits (e.g., international copyright law) but not in vital issue areas where they are high (e.g., military cooperation). Thus, in the current situation, successful resolution of major PD problems will require a higher level of institutionalization than in coordination problems.

Regime Stability and Transformation

Because a comprehensive international society is not fully developed, questions pertaining to the stability of regimes within particular issue areas are important. Sources of instability could include any of a wide range of changes in the circumstances or context of an issue area, but two potential sources of instability stand out as being of particular interest. The first is the stability of the regime in the face of underlying changes in the issue area itself.[12] The second is the stability of the regimes and their rules also to change. . . . But in analyzing each of these potential sources of instability one must be somewhat wary of the presumption that stability—even stability of cooperative outcomes—is always a virtue. First, changes in an issue area may affect the nature of desired cooperative outcomes so that it is desirable for regimes and their rules to also change. Second, different states may have different evaluations of the outcomes produced under various regimes, and those relatively least advantaged under particular regimes may welcome change. . . .

The striking feature of the coordination game is its stability in the single-play version, which is only slightly decreased when the situation recurs through time. If issue change is so substantial that the prevailing convention becomes dysfunctional (i.e., worse than no coordination) for regime members, then the regime will dissolve or transform. But for less dramatic issue change (which leaves the prevailing convention suboptimal but still better than no coordinating agreement whatsoever), the stability of the regime combined with likely disputes over which new convention to adopt will make it difficult to initiate a change to a better convention. This stability means that the regime will not always be sufficiently flexible in responding to new conditions which affect an issue area. This problem will be difficult to resolve because by their nature conventions cannot change quickly if they are to be effective. It can be mitigated through greater reliance on centralized institutions to adapt conventions to particular prevailing issue circumstances, but this negates many of the other advantages of conventional solutions which resulted from decentralized regimes. Alternatively, the existence of a single or small number of dominant actors may enable them to act as leaders in adapting new coordination points to changes in underlying conditions. However, except for this role of leadership, a decrease in the dominance of a single state is unlikely to be destabilizing to coordination outcomes. Therefore, coordination regimes are likely to be stable but, in the absence of leadership, may suffer from a lack of adaptability as issue circumstances change.

The situation in PD is very different. The inherent instability of PD outcomes will be aggravated by changes in issue areas which affect the distribution of costs and benefits of cooperation—and perhaps even the precise definition of cooperative behavior by the individual state. Because it can be profitably abandoned by the individual state, success and stability of a regime depend on its ability to deliver benefits from cooperation relative to those available from alternative regime arrangements. This adjustment will be facilitated by the higher degree of institutionalization associated with contract regimes which enhances their capacity for adaptation and transformation. Centralized institutions will provide a framework for modifying the contract while a past history of cooperation will facilitate the emergence of new arrangements. But, especially with regard to larger adjustments, these transformations will be controversial since states have substantial conflict of interest in PD problems. Bargaining over the exact nature of new regimes will be intense and only well-established contract regimes will be able to orchestrate a successful transition without disruption of cooperation. The exception to this rule will be the special case of regimes concerned with public goods provision where leadership is provided by a single dominant actor.

Changes in the Distribution of Power Among States

The impact of changes in the distribution of power among states can be usefully discussed in terms of the theory of hegemonic stability. The first (static) claim of the theory that the prospects for emergence of cooperative regimes are likely to be enhanced by asymmetries among states is essentially supported in both PD and coordination situations although it is subject to some refinement. In PD, the applicability of the generalization will depend heavily on the possibility for exclusion. If there is no exclusion, then we are in the public good case (which is the analytical underpinning of the theory) and the importance of dominant members to regime stability is explained by Olson's [1965] "privileged group" analysis. Nevertheless, a problem of cooperation will remain because the dominant member will not provide the collectively optimal level of the good except in concert with other states. If exclusion is possible, then cooperation may be possible without a dominant state although such asymmetry will likely facilitate cooperation. In the coordination problem, conventions are likely to emerge without dominant states which are therefore not as important to cooperation as in PD. However, cooperation may be facilitated through the prominence of dominant states in establishing conventions—especially if changing circumstances require modification in the convention. Therefore, the claim of hegemonic stability theory about the role of dominant states in facilitating cooperation is largely valid, although it should not be over-stated to suggest that hegemony is necessary for, or always leads to, cooperative outcomes. . . .

The second (static) claim that regimes based on the leadership of a dominant state will favor small states is not generally valid. The case where it does apply is again that of international public good provision where exclusion is impossible. But if exclusion is possible in a PD situation, then small countries will not have a free ride, and there is no reason to suppose that they will bear less than their fair share of the costs of cooperation through the regime. Finally, the claim is simply wrong in the coordination problem where regime outcomes will favor larger states which have a greater influence in determining coordination outcomes. . . .

Strictly speaking, a static model is inadequate to assess the dynamic claim that international regimes will emerge and decline in response to shifts in the concentration of power in an issue area. (The same applies to the derivation of hegemonic stability arguments themselves.) However, comparative statics analysis allows some observations about the reasonableness of the claim in terms of the preceding discussion of regime stability and transformation. . . .

NOTES

1. The other compelling game which arises for these very same reasons is "Chicken." In terms of the typology of 2×2 games it is the case involving simultaneous assistance and coordination problems. It is discussed in Snidal (1981), but is excluded here because it is analytically more complicated than the other two models.
2. This is not true for all cases where one or both states need "assistance" from the other. For example, in the game of "Deadlock" (formed by interchanging the payoff pairs in the northwest and southeast cells of Figure 1), each is better off by foregoing the other's assistance rather than by accepting it at the cost of foregoing its own dominant strategy.
3. I use the term "closely related" here because there are some subtle distinctions between the technical and institutional aspects of the relevant restrictions. Within the analysis of market economies, nonexclusion is treated as a technical property of goods (within an otherwise perfect set of property rights), whereas at the international level, problems of nonexclusion may also arise as a consequence of political-institutional factors (e.g., lack of control over exclusion reflected in imperfect property rights). Furthermore, the concepts of jointness and nonexclusion are not analytically distinct since jointness is a necessary but not sufficient condition for nonexclusion (Snidal, 1979). Such distinctions are essential for a more fine-tuned analysis of particular issue areas, although for the more general analysis below we will concentrate on the property of nonexclusion.
4. In doing this I implicitly move from ordinal to interval-level payoffs.
5. Smaller states will be willing to join at any cost less than their benefit from participating in the cooperating group. As a result, imposing sufficiently high admission costs on

smaller states will have the effect of ensuring that all of the profits of cooperation (i.e., excess of benefits over costs) accrue to the larger states.

6. Iterated games have important limitations as approximations of dynamic situations since, for example, they do not allow for the possibility that the structure of the system itself may change over time. This is an important consideration when we are trying to analyze issues where institutional and political changes may be involved. Ultimately the supergame formed by looking at simple games iterated through time is only slightly more dynamic than the simple game itself (where strategies can be thought of as dynamic insofar as they represent a listing of how the state will act through time). Nevertheless, the supergame does provide an important first step in looking at the impact of playing through time.

7. The formal conditions for cooperation induced through repeated play are quite stringent and would not appear to offer much help for international cooperation (Taylor, 1976). In large part this is because the purely logical analysis misses some of the important features of the social context which facilitate cooperation, and perhaps even distorts the nature of the problem (cf., Hardin, 1982, chap. 9). Other extensions of the basic supergame model may also enhance possibilities for cooperation (Axelrod, 1984).

8. Two important discussions of the coordination game are Lewis (1969) and Schelling (1960). Their examples of such coordination problems all revolve around problems of information and communication. Although these are certainly important in some international problems (e.g., see Schelling's military examples), they are not widely applicable to issues of longer-term cooperation failures in regimes where communication is possible.

9. Figure 2 shows one symmetric version of the coordination problem. Minor variations (and different coordination games) can be created by interchanging the two lowest payoffs in various combinations, although not all of the resulting games are symmetric. However, the basic analytical results are the same as reported here.

10. Of course, many other international economic issues—for example, beggar-thy-neighbor trade policies—will fall into the PD category of collective action problem. But problems such as demand management are closer to the coordination problem. For a discussion of this see Whitman (1977) and Gordon and Pelkmans (1979, part II). Pelkmans's argument is particularly relevant in distinguishing the different nature of international economic problems of what he calls "foreign economic policy" such as trade policy and (international) "demand management policies." He argues that the former require mutual assistance (or "negative cooperation") in the form of mutual restraint from policies that hurt others; the latter require coordination (or "positive cooperation") and meshing of policies between states. However, he fails to draw the corresponding analytical distinctions and often seems to be treating both problems as equivalent to PD.

11. This observation opens up important considerations for understanding how different solutions are possible for the same problem of collective action. Except for brief comments in the present and next paragraphs, I will not investigate that here. For a discussion of this, see Hardin's (1982) discussion of "contract by convention" as well as Snidal (1981).

12. This sort of change must be limited to changes that occur within the basic strategic structure of the game. For example, an increase in the external military threat might increase the optimal level of security provision in an alliance or a change in economic conditions might require some common shift in economic policies. But changes so dramatic as to alter the underlying strategic structure cannot be analyzed in the same way.

BIBLIOGRAPHY

Axelrod, R. *The evolution of cooperation.* New York: Basic Books, 1984.

Gordon, R., & Pelkmans, J. *Challenges to interdependent economies.* New York: McGraw-Hill, 1979.

Hardin, R. *Collective action.* Baltimore: Johns Hopkins University Press, 1982.

Lewis, D. *Convention: A philosophical study.* Cambridge, Mass.: Harvard University Press, 1969.

Lipson, C. The transformation of trade: The sources and effects of regime change. *International Organization,* 1982, *36,* 417–456.

Olson, M. *The logic of collective action: Public goods and the theory of groups.* Cambridge, MA: Harvard University Press, 1965.

Rapoport, A., & Guyer, M. A taxonomy of 2×2 games. *General Systems Yearbook,* 1966, *11,* 203–214.

Schelling, T. *The strategy of conflict.* Cambridge, MA: Harvard University Press, 1960.

Shubik, M. Game theory, behavior and the paradox of prisoners' dilemma: Three solutions. *Journal of Conflict Resolution,* 1970, *14,* 181–193.

Snidal, D. Public goods, property rights and political organizations. *International Studies Quarterly,* 1979, *December,* 532–566.

Snidal, D. Interdependence, regimes and international cooperation. New Haven, CT: Yale University, Ph.D. dissertation, 1981.

Stein, A. Coordination and collaboration: Regimes in an anarchic world. *International Organization,* 1982, *36,* 299–324.

Taylor, M. *Anarchy and cooperation.* New York: Wiley, 1976.

Whitman, M. v. N. Sustaining the international economic system: Issues for U.S. policy. *Essays in International Finance, No. 121.* Princeton, NJ: Princeton University Press, 1977.

Anarchy Is What States Make of It: The Social Construction of Power Politics

Alexander Wendt

. . . Does the absence of centralized political authority force states to play competitive power politics? Can international regimes overcome this logic, and under what conditions? What in anarchy is given and immutable, and what is amenable to change?

The debate between "neorealists" and "neoliberals" has been based on a shared commitment to "rationalism."[1] Like all social theories, rational choice directs us to ask some questions and not others, treating the identities and interests of agents as exogenously given and focusing on how the behavior of agents generates outcomes. As such, rationalism offers a fundamentally behavioral conception of both process and institutions: they change behavior but not identities and interests. In addition to this way of framing research problems, neorealists and neoliberals share generally similar assumptions about agents: states are the dominant actors in the system, and they define security in "self-interested" terms. Neorealists and neoliberals may disagree about the extent to which states are motivated by relative versus absolute gains, but both groups take the self-interested state as the starting point for theory.

This starting point makes substantive sense for neorealists, since they believe anarchies are necessarily "self-help" systems, systems in which both central authority and collective security are absent. The self-help corollary to anarchy does enormous work in neorealism, generating the inherently competitive dynamics of the security dilemma and collective action problem. Self-help is not seen as an "institution" and as such occupies a privileged explanatory role vis-à-vis process, setting the terms for, and unaffected by, interaction. Since states failing to conform to the logic of self-help will be driven from the system, only simple learning or behavioral adaptation is possible; the complex learning involved in redefinitions of identity and interest is not.[2] Questions about identity- and interest-formation are therefore not important to students of international relations. A rationalist problématique, which reduces process to dynamics of behavioral interaction among exogenously constituted actors, defines the scope of systemic theory.

By adopting such reasoning, liberals concede to neorealists the causal powers of anarchic structure, but they gain the rhetorically powerful argument that process can generate cooperative behavior, even in an exogenously given, self-help system. Some liberals may believe that anarchy does, in fact, constitute states with self-interested identities exogenous to practice. . . .

Yet some liberals want more. When Joseph Nye speaks of "complex learning," or Robert Jervis of "changing conceptions of self and interest," or Robert Keohane of "sociological" conceptions of interest, each is asserting an important role for transformations of identity and interest in the liberal research program and, by extension, a potentially much stronger conception of process and institutions in world politics.[3] "Strong" liberals should be troubled by the dichotomous privileging of structure over process, since transformations of identity and interest through process are transformations of structure. Rationalism has little to offer such an argument, which is in part why, in an important article, Friedrich Kratochwil and John Ruggie argued that its individualist ontology contradicted the intersubjectivist epistemology necessary for regime theory to realize its full promise. . . .[4]

The irony is that social theories which seek to explain identities and interests do exist. Keohane has called them "reflectivist";[5] because I want to emphasize their focus on the social construction of subjectivity and minimize their image problem, following Nicholas Onuf I will call them "constructivist.". . . [6] Constructivism's potential contribution to a strong liberalism has been obscured, however, by recent epistemological debates between modernists and postmodernists, in which Science disciplines Dissent for not defining a conventional research program, and Dissent celebrates its liberation from Science.[7] Real issues animate this debate, which also divides constructivists. With respect to the substance of international relations, however, both modern and postmodern constructivists are interested in how knowledgeable practices constitute subjects, which is not far from the strong liberal interest in how institutions transform interests. They share a cognitive, intersubjective conception of process in which identities and interests are endogenous to interaction, rather than a rationalist-behavioral one in which they are exogenous.

My objective in this article is to build a bridge between these two traditions (and, by extension, between the realist-liberal and rationalist-reflectivist debates) by developing a constructivist argument, drawn from structurationist and symbolic interactionist sociology, on behalf of the liberal claim that international institutions can transform state identities and interests. . . .

My strategy for building this bridge will be to argue against the neorealist claim that self-help is given by anarchic structure exogenously to process. . . . I argue that self-help and power politics do not follow either logically or causally from anarchy and that if today we find ourselves in a self-help world, this is due to process, not structure. There is no "logic" of anarchy apart from the practices that create and instantiate one structure of identities and interests rather than another;

structure has no existence or causal powers apart from process. Self-help and power politics are institutions, not essential features of anarchy. *Anarchy is what states make of it.* . . .

ANARCHY AND POWER POLITICS

Classical realists such as Thomas Hobbes, Reinhold Niebuhr, and Hans Morgen-thau attributed egoism and power politics primarily to human nature, whereas structural realists or neorealists emphasize anarchy. The difference stems in part from different interpretations of anarchy's causal powers. Kenneth Waltz's work is important for both. In *Man, the State, and War,* he defines anarchy as a condition of possibility for or "permissive" cause of war, arguing that "wars occur because there is nothing to prevent them."[8] It is the human nature or domestic politics of predator states, however, that provide the initial impetus or "efficient" cause of conflict which forces other states to respond in kind.[9] Waltz is not entirely consistent about this, since he slips without justification from the permissive causal claim that in anarchy war is always possible to the active causal claim that "war may at any moment occur."[10] But despite Waltz's concluding call for third-image theory, the efficient causes that initialize anarchic systems are from the first and second images. This is reversed in Waltz's *Theory of International Politics,* in which first- and second-image theories are spurned as "reductionist," and the logic of anarchy seems by itself to constitute self-help and power politics as necessary features of world politics.[11]

This is unfortunate, since whatever one may think of first- and second-image theories, they have the virtue of implying that practices determine the character of anarchy. In the permissive view, only if human or domestic factors cause A to attack B will B have to defend itself. Anarchies may contain dynamics that lead to competitive power politics, but they also may not, and we can argue about when particular structures of identity and interest will emerge. In neorealism, however, the role of practice in shaping the character of anarchy is substantially reduced, and so there is less about which to argue: self-help and competitive power politics are simply given exogenously by the structure of the state system. . . .

Anarchy, Self-help, and Intersubjective Knowledge

Waltz defines political structure on three dimensions: ordering principles (in this case, anarchy), principles of differentiation (which here drop out), and the distribution of capabilities.[12] By itself, this definition predicts little about state behavior. It does not predict whether two states will be friends or foes, will recognize each other's sovereignty, will have dynastic ties, will be revisionist or status quo powers, and so on. . . . Put more generally, without assumptions about the structure of identities and interests in the system, Waltz's definition of structure cannot predict the content or dynamics of anarchy. Self-help is one such intersubjective structure and, as such, does the decisive explanatory work in the theory. The question is whether self-help is a logical or contingent feature of anarchy. In this section, I develop the concept of a "structure of identity and interest" and show that no particular one follows logically from anarchy.

A fundamental principle of constructivist social theory is that people act toward objects, including other actors, on the basis of the meanings that the objects have for them. States act differently toward enemies than they do toward friends because enemies are threatening and friends are not. Anarchy and the distribution of power are insufficient to tell us which is which. U.S. military power has a different significance for Canada than for Cuba, despite their similar "structural" positions, just as British missiles have a different significance for the United States than do Soviet missiles. The distribution of power may always affect states' calculations, but how it does so depends on the intersubjective understandings and expectations, on the "distribution of knowledge," that constitute their conceptions of self and other. . . . It is collective meanings that constitute the structures which organize our actions.

Actors acquire identities—relatively stable, role-specific understandings and expectations about self—by participating in such collective meanings.[13] Identities are inherently relational: "Identity, with its appropriate attachments of psychological reality, is always identity within a specific, socially constructed world," Peter Berger argues. . . .[14]

Identities are the basis of interests. Actors do not have a "portfolio" of interests that they carry around independent of social context; instead, they define their interests in the process of defining situations. . . .[15] Sometimes situations are unprecedented in our experience, and in these cases we have to construct their meaning, and thus our interests, by analogy or invent them de novo. . . . This seems to be happening today in the United States and the former Soviet Union: without the cold war's mutual attributions of threat and hostility to define their identities, these states seem unsure of what their "interests" should be.

An institution is a relatively stable set or "structure" of identities and interests. Such structures are often codified in formal rules and norms, but these have motivational force only in virtue of actors' socialization to and participation in collective knowledge. Institutions are fundamentally cognitive entities that do not exist apart from actors' ideas about how the world works.[16] This does not mean that institutions are not real or objective, that they are "nothing but" beliefs. As collective knowledge, they are experienced as having an existence "over and above the individuals who happen to embody them at the moment."[17] In this way, institutions come to confront individuals as more or less coercive social facts, but they are still a function of what actors collectively "know." Identities and such collective cognitions do not exist apart from each other; they are "mutually constitutive." . . .[18]

Self-help is an institution, one of various structures of identity and interest that may exist under anarchy. Processes of identity-formation under anarchy are concerned first and foremost with preservation or "security" of the self. Concepts of security therefore differ in the extent to which and the manner in which the self is identified cognitively with the other, and, I want to suggest, it is upon this cognitive variation that the meaning of anarchy and the distribution of power depends. Let me illustrate with a standard continuum of security systems.

At one end is the "competitive" security system, in which states identify negatively with each other's security so that ego's gain is seen as alter's loss. Negative identification under anarchy constitutes systems of "realist" power politics: risk-averse actors that infer intentions from capabilities and worry about relative gains and losses. At the limit—in the Hobbesian war of all against all—collective action is nearly impossible in such a system because each actor must constantly fear being stabbed in the back.

In the middle is the "individualistic" security system, in which states are indifferent to the relationship between their own and others' security. This constitutes "neoliberal" systems: states are still self-regarding about their security but are concerned primarily with absolute gains rather than relative gains. One's position in the distribution of power is less important, and collective action is more possible (though still subject to free riding because states continue to be "egoists").

Competitive and individualistic systems are both "self-help" forms of anarchy in the sense that states do not positively identify the security of self with that of others but instead treat security as the individual responsibility of each. Given the lack of a positive cognitive identification on the basis of which to build security regimes, power politics within such systems will necessarily consist of efforts to manipulate others to satisfy self-regarding interests.

This contrasts with the "cooperative" security system, in which states identify positively with one another so that the security of each is perceived as the responsibility of all. This is not self-help in any interesting sense, since the "self" in terms of which interests are defined is the community; national interests are international interests. In practice, of course, the extent to which states identif[y] with the community varies, from the limited form found in "concerts" to the full-blown form seen in "collective security" arrangements. Depending on how well developed the collective self is, it will produce security practices that are in varying degrees altruistic or prosocial. This makes collective action less dependent on the presence of active threats and less prone to free riding.[19] Moreover, it restructures efforts to advance one's objectives, or "power politics," in terms of shared norms rather than relative power.[20]

On this view, the tendency in international relations scholarship to view power and institutions as two opposing explanations of foreign policy is therefore misleading, since anarchy and the distribution of power only have meaning for state action in virtue of the understandings and expectations that constitute institutional identities and interests. . . .

Because states do not have conceptions of self and other, and thus security interests, apart from or prior to interaction, we assume too much about the state of nature if we concur with Waltz that, in virtue of anarchy, "international political systems, like economic markets, are formed by the coaction of self-regarding units."[21] We also assume too much if we argue that, in virtue of anarchy, states in the state of nature necessarily face a "stag hunt" or "security dilemma."[22] These claims presuppose a history of interaction in which actors have acquired "selfish" identities and interests; before interaction (and still in abstraction from first- and second-image factors) they would have no experience upon which to base such definitions of self and other. To assume otherwise is to attribute to states in the state of nature qualities that they can only possess in society.[23] Self-help is an institution, not a constitutive feature of anarchy. . . .

Anarchy and the Social Construction of Power Politics

If self-help is not a constitutive feature of anarchy, it must emerge causally from processes in which anarchy plays only a permissive role. This reflects a second principle of constructivism: that the meanings in terms of which action is organized arise out of interaction. This being said, however, the situation facing states as they encounter one another for the first time may be such that only self-regarding conceptions of identity can survive; if so, even if these conceptions are socially constructed, neorealists may be right in holding identities and interests constant and thus in privileging one particular meaning of anarchic structure over process. In this case, rationalists would be right to argue for a weak, behavioral conception of the difference that institutions make, and realists would be right to argue that any international institutions which are created will be inherently unstable, since without the power to transform identities and interests they will be "continuing objects of choice" by exogenously constituted actors constrained only by the transaction costs of behavioral change.[24] Even in a permissive causal role, in other words, anarchy may decisively restrict interaction and therefore restrict viable forms of systemic theory. I address these causal issues first by showing how self-regarding ideas about security might develop and then by examining the conditions under which a key efficient cause—predation—may dispose states in this direction rather than others. . . .

Consider two actors—ego and alter—encountering each other for the first time. Each wants to survive and has certain material capabilities, but neither actor has biological or domestic imperatives for power, glory, or conquest (still bracketed), and there is no history of security or insecurity between the two. What should they do? Realists would probably argue that each should act on the basis of worst-case assumptions about the other's intentions, justifying such an attitude as prudent in view of the possibility of death from making a mistake. Such a possibility always exists, even in civil society; however, society would be impossible if people made decisions purely on the basis of worst-case possibilities. Instead, most decisions are and should be made on the basis of probabilities, and these are produced by interaction, by what actors *do*.

In the beginning is ego's gesture, which may consist, for example, of an advance, a retreat, a brandishing of arms, a laying down of arms, or an attack.[25] For ego, this gesture represents the basis on which it is prepared to respond to alter. This basis is unknown to alter, however, and so it must make an inference or "attribution" about ego's intentions and, in particular, given that this is anarchy, about whether ego is a threat.[26] The content of this inference will largely depend on two considerations. The first is the gesture's and ego's physical qualities, which are in part contrived by ego and which include the direction of movement, noise, numbers, and immediate consequences of the gesture. The second consideration concerns what alter would intend by such qualities were it to make such a gesture itself. Alter may make an attributional "error" in its inference about ego's intent, but there is also no reason for it to assume a priori—before the gesture—that ego is threatening, since it is only through a process of signaling and interpreting that the costs and probabilities of being wrong can be determined. Social threats are constructed, not natural. . . .

It is through reciprocal interaction, in other words, that we create and instantiate the relatively enduring social structures in terms of which we define our identities and interests. . . .

The simple overall model of identity- and interest-formation . . . applies to competitive institutions no less than to cooperative ones. Self-help security systems evolve from cycles of interaction in which each party acts in ways that the other feels are threatening to the self, creating expectations that the other is not to be trusted. Competitive or egoistic identities are caused by such insecurity; if the other is threatening, the self is forced to "mirror" such behavior in its conception of the self's relationship to that other.[27] Being treated as an object for the gratification of others precludes the positive identification with others necessary for collective security; conversely, being treated by others in ways that are empathic with respect to the security of the self permits such identification.[28]

Competitive systems of interaction are prone to security "dilemmas," in which the efforts of actors to enhance their security unilaterally threatens the security of the others, perpetuating distrust and alienation. The forms of identity and interest that constitute such dilemmas, however, are themselves ongoing effects of, not exogenous to, the interaction; identities are produced in and through "situated activity.". . . [29] We do not *begin* our relationship with the aliens in a security dilemma; security dilemmas are not given by anarchy or nature. Of course, once institutionalized such a dilemma may be hard to change (I return to this below), but the point remains: identities and interests are constituted by collective meanings that are always in process. . . .

Predator States and Anarchy as Permissive Cause

The mirror theory of identity-formation is a crude account of how the process of creating identities and interests might work, but it does not tell us why a system of states—such as, arguably, our own—would have ended up with self-regarding and not collective identities. In this section, I examine an efficient cause, predation, which, in conjunction with anarchy as a permissive cause, may generate a self-help system. In so doing, however, I show the key role that the structure of identities and interests plays in mediating anarchy's explanatory role.

The predator argument is straightforward and compelling. For whatever reasons—biology, domestic politics, or systemic victimization—some states may become predisposed toward aggression. The aggressive behavior of these predators or "bad apples" forces other states to engage in competitive power politics, to meet fire with fire, since failure to do so may degrade or destroy them. One predator will best a hundred pacifists because anarchy provides no guarantees. . . .

In an anarchy of two, if ego is predatory, alter must either define its security in self-help terms or pay the price. This follows directly from the above argument, in which conceptions of self mirror treatment by the other. In an anarchy of many, however, the effect of predation also depends on the level of collective identity already attained in the system. If predation occurs right after the first encounter in the state of nature, it will force others with whom it comes in contact to defend themselves, first individually and then collectively *if* they come to perceive a common threat. The emergence of such a defensive alliance will be seriously inhibited if the structure of identities and interests has already evolved into a Hobbesian world of maximum insecurity, since potential allies will strongly distrust each other and face intense collective action problems; such insecure allies are also more likely to fall out amongst themselves once the predator is removed. If collective security identity is high, however, the emergence of a predator may do much less damage. If the predator attacks any member of the collective, the latter will come to the victim's defense on the principle of "all for one, one for all," even if the predator is not presently a threat to other members of the collective. If the predator is not strong enough to withstand the collective, it will be defeated and collective security will obtain. But if it is strong enough, the logic of the two-actor case (now predator and collective) will activate, and balance-of-power politics will reestablish itself.

The timing of the emergence of predation relative to the history of identity-formation in the community is therefore crucial to anarchy's explanatory role as a permissive cause. Predation will always lead victims to defend themselves, but whether defense will be collective or not depends on the history of interaction within the potential collective as much as on the ambitions of the predator. . . . "Mature" anarchies are less likely than "immature" ones to be reduced by predation to a Hobbesian condition, and maturity, which is a proxy for structures of identity and interest, is a function of process. . . .

The role of predation in generating a self-help system, then, is consistent with a systematic focus on process. Even if the source of predation is entirely exogenous to the system, it is what states *do* that determines the quality of their interactions under anarchy. In this respect, it is not surprising that it is classical realists rather than structural realists who emphasize this sort of argument. The former's emphasis on unit-level causes of power politics leads more easily to a permissive view of anarchy's explanatory role (and therefore to a processual view of international relations) than does the latter's emphasis on anarchy as a "structural cause"; neorealists do not need predation because the system is given as self-help.

This raises anew the question of exactly how much and what kind of role human nature and domestic politics play in world politics. The greater and more destructive this role, the more significant predation will be, and the less amenable anarchy will be to formation of collective identities. Classical realists, of course, assumed that human nature was possessed by an inherent lust for power or glory. My argument suggests that assumptions such as this were made for a reason: an unchanging Hobbesian man provides the powerful efficient cause necessary for a relentless pessimism about world politics that anarchic structure alone, or even structure plus intermittent predation, cannot supply. One can be skeptical of such an essentialist assumption, as I am, but it does produce determinate results at the expense of systemic theory. A concern with systemic process over structure suggests that perhaps it is time to revisit the debate over the relative importance of first-, second-, and third-image theories of state identity-formation. . . .

INSTITUTIONAL TRANSFORMATIONS OF POWER POLITICS

Let us assume that processes of identity- and interest-formation have created a world in which states do not recognize rights to territory or existence—a war of all against all. In this world, anarchy has a "realist" meaning for state action: be insecure and concerned with relative power. Anarchy has this meaning only in virtue of collective, insecurity-producing practices, but if those practices are relatively stable, they do constitute a system that may resist change. . . .

In the remainder of this article, I examine three institutional transformations of identity and security interest through which states might escape a Hobbesian world of their own making. In so doing, I seek to clarify what it means to say that "institutions transform identities and interests," emphasizing that the key to such transformations is relatively stable practice.

Sovereignty, Recognition, and Security

In a Hobbesian state of nature, states are individuated by the domestic processes that constitute them as states and by their material capacity to deter threats from other states. In this world, even if free momentarily from the predations of others, state security does not have any basis in social recognition—in intersubjective understandings or norms that a state has a right to its existence, territory, and subjects. Security is a matter of national power, nothing more.

The principle of sovereignty transforms this situation by providing a social basis for the individuality and security of states. Sovereignty is an institution, and so it exists only in virtue of certain intersubjective understandings and expectations; there is no sovereignty without an other. These understandings and expectations not only constitute a particular kind of state—the "sovereign" state—but also constitute a particular form of community, since identities are relational. The essence of this community is a mutual recognition of one another's right to exercise exclusive political authority within territorial limits. These reciprocal "permissions" constitute a spatially rather than functionally differentiated world—a world in which fields of practice constitute and are organized around "domestic" and "international" spaces rather than around the performance of particular activities. . . .

Sovereignty norms are now so taken for granted, so natural, that it is easy to overlook the extent to which they are both presupposed by an ongoing artifact of practice. When states tax "their" "citizens" and not others, when they "protect" their markets against foreign "imports," when they kill thousands of Iraqis in one kind of war and then refuse to "intervene" to kill even one person in another kind, a "civil" war, and when they fight a global war against a regime that sought to destroy the institution of sovereignty and then give Germany back to the Germans, they are acting against the background of, and thereby reproducing, shared norms about what it means to be a sovereign state.

If states stopped acting on those norms, their identity as "sovereigns" (if not necessarily as "states") would disappear. The sovereign state is an ongoing accomplishment of practice, not a once-and-for-all creation of norms that somehow exist apart from practice. . . .[30] Thus, saying that "the institution of sovereignty transforms identities" is shorthand for saying that "regular practices produce mutually constituting sovereign identities (agents) and their associated institutional norms (structures)." Practice is the core of constructivist resolutions of the agent-structure problem. . . .

This may tell us something about how institutions of sovereign states are reproduced through social interaction, but it does not tell us why such a structure of identity and interest would arise in the first place. Two conditions would seem necessary for this to happen: (1) the density and regularity of interactions must be sufficiently high and (2) actors must be dissatisfied with preexisting forms of identity and interaction. Given these conditions, a norm of mutual recognition is relatively undemanding in terms of social trust, having the form of an assurance game in which a player will acknowledge the sovereignty of the others as long as they will in turn acknowledge that player's own sovereignty. Articulating international legal principles such as those embodied in the Peace of Augsburg (1555) and the Peace of Westphalia (1648) may also help by establishing explicit criteria for determining violations of the nascent social consensus. . . .[31] But whether such a consensus holds depends on what states do. If they treat each other as if they were sovereign, then over time they will institutionalize that mode of subjectivity; if they do not, then that mode will not become the norm.

Practices of sovereignty will transform understandings of security and power politics in at least three ways. First, states will come to define their (and our) security in terms of preserving their "property rights" over particular territories. We now see this as natural, but the preservation of territorial frontiers is not, in fact, equivalent to the survival of the state or its people. Indeed, some states would probably be more secure if they would relinquish certain territories—the "Soviet Union" of some minority republics, "Yugoslavia" of Croatia and Slovenia, Israel of the West Bank, and so on. The fact that sovereignty practices have historically been oriented toward producing distinct territorial spaces, in other words, affects states' conceptualization of what they must "secure" to function in that identity, a process that may help account for the "hardening" of territorial boundaries over the centuries.

Second, to the extent that states successfully internalize sovereignty norms, they will be more respectful toward the territorial rights of others. This restraint is *not* primarily because of the costs of violating sovereignty norms, although when violators do get punished (as in the Gulf War) it reminds everyone of what these costs can be, but because part of what it means to be a "sovereign" state is that one does not violate the territorial rights of others without "just cause." A clear example of such an institutional effect, convincingly argued by David Strang, is the markedly different treatment that weak states receive within and outside communities of mutual recognition. . . .[32] What keeps the United States from conquering the Bahamas, or Nigeria from seizing Togo, or Australia from occupying Vanuatu? Clearly, power is not the issue, and in these cases even the cost of sanctions would probably be negligible. One might argue that great powers simply have no "interest" in these conquests, and this might be so, but this lack of interest can only be understood in terms of their recognition of weak states' sovereignty. I have no interest in exploiting my friends, not because of the relative costs and benefits of such action but because they are my friends. The absence of recognition, in turn, helps explain the Western states' practices of territorial conquest, enslavement, and genocide against Native American and African peoples. It is in *that* world that only power matters, not the world of today.

Finally, to the extent that their ongoing socialization teaches states that their sovereignty depends on recognition by other states, they can afford to rely more on the institutional fabric of international society and less on individual national means—especially military power—to protect their security. The intersubjective understandings embodied in the institution of sovereignty, in other words, may redefine the meaning of others' power for the security of the self. In policy terms, this means that states can be less worried about short-term survival and relative power and can thus shift their resources accordingly. Ironically, it is the great powers, the states with the greatest national means, that may have the hardest time learning this lesson; small powers do not have the luxury of relying on national means and may therefore learn faster that collective recognition is a cornerstone of security. . . .

Cooperation Among Egoists and Transformations of Identity

. . . In the traditional game-theoretic analysis of cooperation, even an iterated one, the structure of the game—of identities and interests—is exogenous to interaction and, as such, does not change. A "black box" is put around identity- and interest-formation, and analysis focuses instead on the relationship between expectations and behavior. The norms that evolve from interaction are treated as rules and behavioral regularities which are external to the actors and which resist change because of the transaction costs of creating new ones. The game-theoretic analysis of cooperation among egoists is at base behavioral.

A constructivist analysis of cooperation, in contrast, would concentrate on how the expectations produced by behavior affect identities and interests. The process of creating institutions is one of internalizing new understandings of self and other, of acquiring new role identities, not just of creating external constraints on the behavior of exogenously constituted actors. Even if not intended as such, in other words, the process by which egoists learn to cooperate is at the same time a process of reconstructing their interests in terms of shared commitments to social norms. Over time, this will tend to transform a positive interdependence of *outcomes* into a positive interdependence of *utilities* or collective interest organized around the norms in question. These norms will resist change because they are tied to actors' commitments to their identities and interests, not merely because of transaction costs. A constructivist analysis of "the cooperation problem," in other words, is at base cognitive rather than behavioral, since it treats the intersubjective knowledge that defines the structure of identities and interests, of the "game," as endogenous to and instantiated by interaction itself.

The debate over the future of collective security in Western Europe may illustrate the significance of this difference. A weak liberal or rationalist analysis would assume that the European states' "portfolio" of interests has not fundamentally changed and that the emergence of new factors, such as the collapse of the Soviet threat and the rise of Germany, would alter their cost-benefit ratios for pursuing current arrangements, thereby causing existing institutions to break down. The European states formed collaborative institutions for good, exogenously constituted egoistic reasons, and the same reasons may lead them to reject those institutions; the game of European power politics has not changed. A strong liberal or constructivist analysis of this problem would suggest that four decades of cooperation may have transformed a positive interdependence of outcomes into a collective "European identity" in terms of which states increasingly define their "self"-interests.[33] Even if egoistic reasons were its starting point, the process of cooperating tends to redefine those reasons by reconstituting identities and interests in terms of new intersubjective understandings and commitments. . . . Through participation in new forms of social knowledge, in other words, the European states of 1990 might no longer be the states of 1950.

Critical Strategic Theory and Collective Security

The transformation of identity and interest through an "evolution of cooperation" faces two important constraints. The first is that the process is incremental and slow. Actors' objectives in such a process are typically to realize joint gains within what they take to be a relatively stable context, and they are therefore unlikely to engage in substantial reflection about how to change the parameters of that context (including the structure of identities and interests) and unlikely to pursue policies specifically designed to bring about such changes. . . .

A second, more fundamental, constraint is that the evolution of cooperation story presupposes that actors do not identify negatively with one another. Actors must be concerned primarily with absolute gains; to the extent that antipathy and distrust lead them to define their security in relativistic terms, it will be hard to accept the vulnerabilities that attend cooperation. This is important because it is precisely the "central balance" in the state system that seems to be so often afflicted with such competitive thinking, and realists can therefore argue that the possibility of cooperation within one "pole" (for example, the West) is parasitic on the dominance of competition between poles (the East–West conflict). Relations between the poles may be amenable to some positive reciprocity in areas such as arms control, but the atmosphere of distrust leaves little room for such cooperation and its transformative consequences.[34] The conditions of negative identification that make an "evolution of cooperation" most needed work precisely against such a logic.

This seemingly intractable situation may nevertheless be amenable to quite a different logic of transformation, one driven more by self-conscious efforts to change structures of identity and interest than by unintended consequences. Such voluntarism may seem to contradict the spirit of constructivism, since would-be revolutionaries are presumably themselves effects of socialization to structures of identity and interest. How can they think about changing that to which they owe their identity? The possibility lies in the distinction between the social determination of the self and the personal determination of choice, between what Mead called the "me" and the "I."[35] The "me" is that part of subjectivity which is defined in terms of others; the character and behavioral expectations of a person's role identity as "professor," or of the United States as "leader of the alliance," for example, are socially constituted. Roles are not played in mechanical fashion according to precise scripts, however, but are "taken" and adapted in idiosyncratic ways by each actor. Even in the most constrained situations, role performance involves a choice by the actor. The "I" is the part of subjectivity in which this appropriation and reaction to roles and its corresponding existential freedom lie.

The fact that roles are "taken" means that, in principle, actors always have a capacity for "character planning"—for engaging in critical self-reflection and choices designed to bring about changes in their lives. But when or under what conditions can this creative capacity be exercised? Clearly, much of the time it cannot: if actors were constantly reinventing their identities, social order would be impossible, and the relative stability of identities and interests in the real world is indicative of our propensity for habitual rather than creative action. The exceptional, conscious choosing to transform or transcend roles has at least two preconditions. First, there must be a reason to think of oneself in novel terms. This would most likely stem from the presence of new social situations that cannot be managed in terms of preexisting self-conceptions. Second, the expected costs of intentional role change—the sanctions imposed by others with whom one interacted in previous roles—cannot be greater than its rewards.

When these conditions are present, actors can engage in self-reflection and practice specifically designed to transform their identities and interests and thus to "change the games" in which they are embedded. Such "critical" strategic theory and practice has not received the attention it merits from students of world politics (another legacy of exogenously given interests perhaps), particularly given that one of the most important phenomena in contemporary world politics, Mikhail Gorbachev's policy of "New Thinking," is arguably precisely that.[36] Let me therefore use this policy as an example of how states might transform a competitive security system into a cooperative one, dividing the transformative process into four stages.

The first stage in intentional transformation is the breakdown of consensus about identity commitments. In the Soviet case, identity commitments centered on the Leninist theory of imperialism, with its belief that relations between capitalist and socialist states are inherently conflictual, and on the alliance patterns that this belief engendered. In the 1980s, the consensus within the Soviet Union over the Leninist theory broke down for a variety of reasons, principal among which seem to have been the state's inability to meet the economic-technological-military challenge from the West, the government's decline of political legitimacy at home, and the reassurance from the West that it did not intend to invade the Soviet Union, a reassurance that reduced the external costs of role change. These factors paved the way for a radical leadership transition and for a subsequent "unfreezing of conflict schemas" concerning relations with the West.[37]

The breakdown of consensus makes possible a second stage of critical examination of old ideas about self and other and, by extension, of the structures of interaction by which the ideas have been sustained. In periods of relatively stable role identities, ideas and structures may become reified and thus treated as things that exist independently of social action. If so, the second stage is one of denaturalization, of identifying the practices that reproduce seemingly inevitable ideas about self and other; to that extent, it is a form of "critical" rather than "problem-solving" theory. The result of such a critique should be an identification of new "possible selves" and aspirations. New Thinking embodies such critical theorizing. . . .

Such rethinking paves the way for a third stage of new practice. In most cases, it is not enough to rethink one's own ideas about self and other, since old identities have been sustained by systems of interaction with *other* actors, the practices of which remain a social fact for the transformative agent. In order to change the self, then, it is often necessary to change the identities and interests of the others that help sustain those systems of interaction. The vehicle for inducing such change is one's own practice and, in particular, the practice of "altercasting"—a technique of interactor control in which ego uses tactics of self-presentation and stage management in an attempt to frame alter's definitions of social situations in ways that create the role which ego desires alter to play.[38] In effect, in altercasting ego tries to induce alter to take on a new identity (and thereby enlist alter in ego's effort to change itself) by treating alter *as if* it already had that identity. . . .

Yet by themselves such practices cannot transform a competitive security system, since if they are not reciprocated by alter, they will expose ego to a "sucker" payoff and quickly wither on the vine. In order for critical strategic practice to transform competitive identities, it must be "rewarded" by alter, which will encourage more such practice by ego, and so on. Over time, this will institutionalize a positive rather than a negative identification between the security of self and other and will thereby provide a firm intersubjective basis for what were initially tentative commitments to new identities and interests. . . .

NOTES

1. See Robert Keohane, "International Institutions: Two Approaches," *International Studies Quarterly* 32 (December 1988), pp. 379–96.
2. On neorealist conceptions of learning, see Philip Tetlock, "Learning in U.S. and Soviet Foreign Policy," in George Breslauer and Philip Tetlock, eds., *Learning in U.S. and Soviet Foreign Policy* (Boulder, CO: Westview Press, 1991), pp. 24–27. On the difference between behavioral and cognitive learning, see ibid., pp. 20–61; Joseph Nye, "Nuclear Learning and U.S.–Soviet Security Regimes," *International Organization* 41 (Summer 1987), pp. 371–402; and Ernst Haas, *When Knowledge Is Power* (Berkeley: University of California Press, 1990), pp. 17–49.
3. See Nye, "Nuclear Learning and U.S.–Soviet Security Regimes"; Robert Jervis, "Realism, Game Theory, and Cooperation," *World Politics* 40 (April 1988), pp. 340–44; and Robert Keohane, "International Liberalism Reconsidered," in John Dunn, ed., *The Economic Limits to Modern Politics* (Cambridge: Cambridge University Press, 1990), p. 183.
4. Friedrich Kratochwil and John Ruggie, "International Organization: A State of the Art on an Art of the State," *International Organization* 40 (Autumn 1986), pp. 753–75.

5. Keohane, "International Institutions."
6. See Nicholas Onuf, *World of Our Making* (Columbia: University of South Carolina Press, 1989).
7. On Science, see Keohane, "International Institutions"; and Robert Keohane, "International Relations Theory: Contributions of a Feminist Standpoint," *Millennium* 18 (Summer 1989), pp. 245–53. On Dissent, see R. B. J. Walker, "History and Structure in the Theory of International Relations," *Millennium* 18 (Summer 1989), pp. 163–83; and Richard Ashley and R. B. J. Walker, "Reading Dissidence/Writing the Discipline: Crisis and the Question of Sovereignty in International Studies," *International Studies Quarterly* 34 (September 1990), pp. 367–416. For an excellent critical assessment of these debates, see Yosef Lapid, "The Third Debate: On the Prospects of International Theory in a Post-Positivist Era," *International Studies Quarterly* 33 (September 1989), pp. 235–54.
8. Kenneth Waltz, *Man, the State, and War* (New York: Columbia University Press, 1959), p. 232.
9. Ibid., pp. 169–70.
10. Ibid., p. 232. This point is made by Hidemi Suganami in "Bringing Order to the Causes of War Debates," *Millennium* 19 (Spring 1990), p. 34, fn. 11.
11. Kenneth Waltz, *Theory of International Politics* (Boston: Addison-Wesley, 1979).
12. Waltz, *Theory of International Politics,* pp. 79–101.
13. For an excellent short statement of how collective meanings constitute identities, see Peter Berger, "Identity as a Problem in the Sociology of Knowledge," *European Journal of Sociology,* vol. 7, no. 1, 1966, pp. 32–40. See also David Morgan and Michael Schwalbe, "Mind and Self in Society: Linking Social Structure and Social Cognition," *Social Psychology Quarterly* 53 (June 1990), pp. 148–64. In my discussion, I draw on the following interactionist texts: George Herbert Mead, *Mind, Self, and Society* (Chicago: University of Chicago Press, 1934); Peter Berger and Thomas Luckmann, *The Social Construction of Reality* (New York: Anchor Books, 1966); Sheldon Stryker, *Symbolic Interactionism: A Social Structural Version* (Menlo Park, CA: Benjamin/Cummings, 1980); R. S. Perinbanayagam, *Signifying Acts: Structure and Meaning in Everyday Life* (Carbondale: Southern Illinois University Press, 1985); John Hewitt, *Self and Society: A Symbolic Interactionist Social Psychology* (Boston: Allyn & Bacon, 1988); and Jonathan Turner, *A Theory of Social Interaction* (Stanford, CA: Stanford University Press, 1988). Despite some differences, much the same points are made by structurationists such as Bhaskar and Giddens. See Roy Bhaskar, *The Possibility of Naturalism* (Atlantic Highlands, NJ: Humanities Press, 1979); and Anthony Giddens, *Central Problems in Social Theory* (Berkeley: University of California Press, 1979).
14. Berger, "Identity as a Problem in Sociology of Knowledge," p. 111.
15. On the "portfolio" conception of interests, see Barry Hindess, *Political Choice and Social Structure* (Aldershot, UK: Edward Elgar, 1989), pp. 2–3. The "definition of the situation" is a central concept in interactionist theory.
16. In neo-Durkheimian parlance, institutions are "social representations." See Serge Moscovici, "The Phenomenon of Social Representations," in Rob Farr and Serge Moscovici, eds., *Social Representations* (Cambridge: Cambridge University Press, 1984), pp. 3–69. See also Barnes, *The Nature of Power.* Note that this is a considerably more socialized cognitivism than that found in much of the recent scholarship on the role of "ideas" in world politics, which tends to treat ideas as commodities that are held by individuals and intervene between the distribution of power and outcomes. For a form of cognitivism closer to my own, see Emanuel Adler, "Cognitive Evolution: A Dy-

namic Approach for the Study of International Relations and Their Progress," in Emanuel Adler and Beverly Crawford, eds., *Progress in Postwar International Relations* (New York: Columbia University Press, 1991), pp. 43–88.

17. Berger and Luckmann, *The Social Construction of Reality*, p. 58.

18. See Giddens, *Central Problems in Social Theory;* and Alexander Wendt and Raymond Duvall, "Institutions and International Order," in Ernst-Otto Czempiel and James Rosenau, eds., *Global Changes and Theoretical Challenges* (Lexington, MA: Lexington Books, 1989), pp. 51–74.

19. On the role of collective identity in reducing collective action problems, see Bruce Fireman and William Gamson, "Utilitarian Logic in the Resource Mobilization Perspective," in Mayer Zald and John McCarthy, eds., *The Dynamics of Social Movements* (Cambridge, MA: Winthrop, 1979), pp. 8–44; Robyn Dawes et al., "Cooperation for the Benefit of Us—Not Me, or My Conscience," in Mansbridge, *Beyond Self-Interest*, pp. 97–110; and Craig Calhoun, "The Problem of Identity in Collective Action," in Joan Huber, ed., *Macro-Micro Linkages in Sociology* (Beverly Hills, CA: Sage, 1991), pp. 51–75.

20. See Thomas Risse-Kappen, "Are Democratic Alliances Special?" unpublished manuscript, Yale University, New Haven, CT, 1991. This line of argument could be expanded usefully in feminist terms. For a useful overview of the relational nature of feminist conceptions of self, see Paula England and Barbara Stanek Kilbourne, "Feminist Critiques of the Separative Model of Self: Implications for Rational Choice Theory," *Rationality and Society* 2 (April 1990), pp. 156–71. On feminist conceptualizations of power, see Ann Tickner, "Hans Morgenthau's Principles of Political Realism: A Feminist Reformulation," *Millennium* 17 (Winter 1988), pp. 429–40; and Thomas Wartenberg, "The Concept of Power in Feminist Theory," *Praxis International* 8 (October 1988), pp. 301–16.

21. Waltz, *Theory of International Politics*, p. 91.

22. See Waltz, *Man, the State, and War;* and Robert Jervis, "Cooperation Under the Security Dilemma," *World Politics* 30 (January 1978), pp. 167–214.

23. My argument here parallels Rousseau's critique of Hobbes. For an excellent critique of realist appropriations of Rousseau, see Michael Williams, "Rousseau, Realism, and Realpolitik," *Millennium* 18 (Summer 1989), pp. 188–204. Williams argues that far from being a fundamental starting point in the state of nature, for Rousseau the stag hunt represented a stage in man's fall. On p. 190, Williams cites Rousseau's description of man prior to leaving the state of nature: "Man only knows himself; he does not see his own well-being to be identified with or contrary to that of anyone else; he neither hates anything nor loves anything; but limited to no more than physical instinct, he is no one, he is an animal." For another critique of Hobbes on the state of nature that parallels my constructivist reading of anarchy, see Charles Landesman, "Reflections on Hobbes: Anarchy and Human Nature," in Peter Caws, ed., *The Causes of Quarrel* (Boston: Beacon, 1989), pp. 139–48.

24. See Robert Grafstein, "Rational Choice: Theory and Institutions," in Kristen Monroe, ed., *The Economic Approach to Politics* (New York: Harper Collins, 1991), pp. 263–64. A good example of the promise and limits of transaction cost approaches to institutional analysis is offered by Robert Keohane in his *After Hegemony* (Princeton, NJ: Princeton University Press, 1984).

25. Mead's analysis of gestures remains definitive. See Mead's *Mind, Self, and Society*. See also the discussion of the role of signaling in the "mechanics of interaction" in Turner's *A Theory of Social Interaction*, pp. 74–79 and 92–115.

26. . . . On attributional processes in international relations, see Shawn Rosenberg and

Gary Wolfsfeld, "International Conflict and the Problem of Attribution," *Journal of Conflict Resolution* 21 (March 1977), pp. 75–103.

27. The following articles by Noel Kaplowitz have made an important contribution to such thinking in international relations: "Psychopolitical Dimensions of International Relations: The Reciprocal Effects of Conflict Strategies," *International Studies Quarterly* 28 (December 1984), pp. 373–406; and "National Self-Images, Perception of Enemies, and Conflict Strategies: Psychopolitical Dimensions of International Relations," *Political Psychology* 11 (March 1990), pp. 39–82.

28. These arguments are common in theories of narcissism and altruism. See Heinz Kohut, *Self-Psychology and the Humanities* (New York: Norton, 1985); and Martin Hoffmann, "Empathy, Its Limitations, and Its Role in a Comprehensive Moral Theory," in William Kurtines and Jacob Gewirtz, eds., *Morality, Moral Behavior, and Moral Development* (New York: Wiley, 1984), pp. 283–302.

29. See C. Norman Alexander and Mary Glenn Wiley, "Situated Activity and Identity Formation," in Morris Rosenberg and Ralph Turner, eds., *Social Psychology: Sociological Perspectives* (New York: Basic Books, 1981), pp. 269–89.

30. See Richard Ashley, "Untying the Sovereign State: A Double Reading of the Anarchy Problematique," *Millennium* 17 (Summer 1988), pp. 227–62. . . .

31. See William Coplin, "International Law and Assumptions About the State System," *World Politics* 17 (July 1965), pp. 615–34.

32. David Strang, "Anomaly and Commonplace in European Expansion: Realist and Institutional Accounts," *International Organization* 45 (Spring 1991), pp. 143–62.

33. On "European identity," see Barry Buzan et al., eds., *The European Security Order Recast* (London: Pinter, 1990), pp. 45–63.

34. On the difficulties of creating cooperative security regimes given competitive interests, see Robert Jervis, "Security Regimes," in Stephen D. Krasner, ed., *International Regimes* (Ithaca, NY: Cornell University Press, 1983), pp. 173–94; and Charles Lipson, "International Cooperation in Economic and Security Affairs," *World Politics* 37 (October 1984), pp. 1–23.

35. See Mead, *Mind, Self, and Society.* For useful discussions of this distinction and its implications for notions of creativity in social systems, see George Cronk, *The Philosophical Anthropology of George Herbert Mead* (New York: Peter Lang, 1987), pp. 36–40; and Judith Howard, "From Changing Selves Toward Changing Society," in Judith Howard and Peter Callero, eds., *The Self-Society Dynamic* (Cambridge: Cambridge University Press, 1991).

36. For useful overviews of New Thinking, see Mikhail Gorbachev, *Perestroika: New Thinking for Our Country and the World* (New York: Harper & Row, 1987); Vendulka Kubalkova and Albert Cruickshank, *Thinking New About Soviet "New Thinking"* (Berkeley: Institute of International Studies, 1989); and Allen Lynch, *Gorbachev's International Outlook: Intellectual Origins and Political Consequences* (New York: Institute for East–West Security Studies, 1989). It is not clear to what extent New Thinking is a conscious policy as opposed to an ad hoc policy. The intense theoretical and policy debate within the Soviet Union over New Thinking and the frequently stated idea of taking away the Western "excuse" for fearing the Soviet Union both suggest the former, but I will remain agnostic here and simply assume that it can be fruitfully interpreted "as if" it had the form that I describe.

37. See Daniel Bar-Tal et al., "Conflict Termination: An Epistemological Analysis of International Cases," *Political Psychology* 10 (June 1989), pp. 233–55. For an unrelated but interesting illustration of how changing cognitions in turn make possible organizational change, see Jean Bartunek, "Changing Interpretive Schemes and Organizational Re-

structuring: The Example of a Religious Order," *Administrative Science Quarterly* 29 (September 1984), pp. 355–72.

38. See Goffman, *The Presentation of Self in Everyday Life;* Eugene Weinstein and Paul Deutschberger, "Some Dimensions of Altercasting," *Sociometry* 26 (December 1963), pp. 454–66; and Walter Earle, "International Relations and the Psychology of Control: Alternative Control Strategies and Their Consequences," *Political Psychology* 7 (June 1986), pp. 369–75.

Chapter
3

The Role of Regimes

Edward D. Mansfield

O ne of the most important developments in the study of international organization has been the proliferation of interest in international regimes. In this chapter, we analyze a variety of issues concerning the formation and effects of regimes.

Many analysts agree that norms are a central feature of international regimes. This is made explicit in what has become the most widely used definition of regimes, which is presented by Stephen Krasner in this chapter. Regimes, Krasner argues, are "sets of implicit or explicit principles, norms, rules, and decision-making procedures around which actors' expectations converge in a given area of international relations."

Regime theorists typically argue that international interactions depend on the expectations of actors, and that the norms and rules of a regime help to shape and stabilize expectations. Since regime theorists attach such importance to norms, it is useful to discuss briefly their role in international relations. Realists view norms as reflections of power, or what Hobbes referred to as the "command of the sovereign." Thus, realists often argue that norms in international relations reflect the interest of hegemonic states. In their opinion, regimes are created and maintained by hegemons because regimes yield benefits for these states. Regimes weaken when a hegemon's power declines. These explanations therefore focus on the conditions under which regimes are most likely to be *supplied*.

Many neoliberals, in contrast, focus on the conditions under which the *demand* for regimes is likely to be greatest. In their opinion, norms are not only reflections of power. Regimes are likely to be demanded regardless of whether or not a hegemon exists, because norms enable states to calculate the costs and benefits of actions more accurately than would be possible in their absence. Norms help us to interpret the behavior of states and to determine whether their behavior is in accord with agreed-upon standards. By preventing cheating and free riding, norms allow states to acquire the necessary information to enforce agreements within the context of their ongoing relationships.

Although both the realist and neoliberal views have formed the basis of much important research regarding international regimes, a variety of critiques of these views have also been advanced. First, norms may not be analogous to Hobbes's "command of the sovereign." In this sense, some scholars have argued that norms may not be outgrowths of a hegemon's interests, and that norms may be supplied in the absence of a hegemon. Second, analysts have also argued that knowledge and shared notions of legitimacy among states shape the ways in which regime issue-areas emerge. For example, Ruggie's discussion of "embedded liberalism" in Chapter 1 points out that the post–World War II compromise concerning structural adjustments in the international political economy was influenced by two factors: (1) the acceptance of full employment policies as *legitimate* state goals (instead of viewing such policies as illegitimate interferences with the market); and (2) new economic *knowledge,* based on Keynesian ideas and policies. Third, a number of analysts have argued that since the administration of regimes is seldom entrusted to a supranational bureaucracy or a hegemon, regime effectiveness is only tangentially related to the indices of power that are emphasized by realists. They maintain that regimes function not because there is a supranational or hegemonic enforcer, but because essential aspects of regimes become ingrained in the standard operating procedures of the actors' foreign policy bureaucracy. Thus, this critique suggests that both compliance with regime norms and defection from them are considerably more complicated processes than many analysts imply.

The selections of this chapter address several of these points. Stephen Krasner's article, which develops the well-known definition of regimes described above, sets the stage for our discussion of regimes. Krasner discusses a variety of leading approaches to the study of regime formation and analyzes the effects of regimes on international relations.

The other selections in this chapter stand in contrast to Krasner's argument, since they take issue both with his definition of regimes and his explanation for the emergence and stability of regimes. Oran Young analyzes the dynamics of regime creation. His model of institutional bargaining criticizes the realist approach to regime formation and expands on the neoliberal argument concerning the demand for regimes by showing the crucial role of leadership in this regard. Furthermore, he systematically examines the influence of crises, of external shocks, of salience, and of notions of equity on the formation of regimes.

Peter Haas's argument hinges on the importance of knowledge and its organization in creating and maintaining regimes. In his study of pollution abatement in the Mediterranean, Haas analyzes "epistemic communities." He argues that these scientific networks not only provided a basis of knowledge and identified the crucial causal links regarding pollution in the Mediterranean; they also made the identification of policy alternatives possible. Scientists succeeded in persuading their respective public to reformulate the interests and cooperate with other members in spite of often deep-seated political differences. In addition, by moving into positions of power, members of this epistemic community also far exceeded the usual role of advisers and became administrators of the Mediterranean Action Plan, which they designed with assistance from international organizations.

Structural Causes and Regime Consequences: Regimes as Intervening Variables

Stephen D. Krasner

DEFINING REGIMES AND REGIME CHANGE

Regimes can be defined as sets of implicit or explicit principles, norms, rules, and decision-making procedures around which actors' expectations converge in a given area of international relations. Principles are beliefs of fact, causation, and rectitude. Norms are standards of behavior defined in terms of rights and obligations. Rules are specific prescriptions or proscriptions for action. Decision-making procedures are prevailing practices for making and implementing collective choice.

This usage is consistent with other recent formulations. Keohane and Nye, for instance, define regimes as "sets of governing arrangements" that include "networks of rules, norms, and procedures that regularize behavior and control its effects."[1] Haas argues that a regime encompasses a mutually coherent set of procedures, rules, and norms.[2] Hedley Bull, using a somewhat different terminology, refers to the importance of rules and institutions in international society where rules refer to "general imperative principles which require or authorize prescribed classes of persons or groups to behave in prescribed ways."[3] Institutions for Bull help to secure adherence to rules by formulating, communicating, administering, enforcing, interpreting, legitimating, and adapting them.

Regimes must be understood as something more than temporary arrangements that change with every shift in power or interests. Keohane notes that a basic analytic distinction must be made between regimes and agreements. Agreements are *ad hoc*, often "one-shot," arrangements. The purpose of regimes is to facilitate agreements. Similarly, Jervis argues that the concept of regimes "implies not only norms and expectations that facilitate cooperation, but a form of cooperation that is more than the following of short-run self-interest."[4] For instance, he contends that the restraints that have applied in Korea and other limited wars should not be considered a regime. These rules, such as "do not bomb sanctuaries," were based purely on short-term calculations of interest. As interest and power changed, behavior changed. Waltz's conception of the balance of power, in which states are driven by systemic pressures to repetitive balancing behavior, is not a regime; Kaplan's conception, in which equilibrium requires commitment to rules that constrain immediate, short-term power maximization (especially not destroying an essential actor), is a regime.[5]

Similarly, regime-governed behavior must not be based solely on short-term calculations of interest. Since regimes encompass principles and norms, the utility function that is being maximized must embody some sense of general obligation. One such principle, reciprocity, is emphasized in Jervis's analysis of security regimes. When states accept reciprocity they will sacrifice short-term interests with the expectation that other actors will reciprocate in the future, even if they are not under a specific obligation to do so. . . . It is the infusion of behavior with principles and norms that distinguishes regime-governed activity in the international system from more conventional activity, guided exclusively by narrow calculations of interest.

A fundamental distinction must be made between principles and norms on the one hand, and rules and procedures on the other. Principles and norms provide the basic defining characteristics of a regime. There may be many rules and decision-making procedures that are consistent with the same principles and norms. *Changes in rules and decision-making procedures are changes within regimes*, provided that principles and norms are unaltered. . . .

Changes in principles and norms are changes of the regime itself. When norms and principles are abandoned, there is either a change to a new regime or a disappearance of regimes from a given issue-area. For instance, Ruggie contends that the distinction between orthodox and embedded liberalism involves differences over norms and principles. Orthodox liberalism endorses increasing the scope of the market. Embedded liberalism prescribes state action to contain domestic social and economic dislocations generated by markets. Orthodox and embedded liberalism define different regimes. The change from orthodox liberal principles and norms before World War II to embedded liberal principles and norms after World War II was, in Ruggie's terms, a "revolutionary" change.

Fundamental political arguments are more concerned with norms and principles than with rules and procedures. Changes in the latter may be interpreted in different ways. For instance, in the area of international trade, recent revisions in the Articles of Agreement of the General Agreement on Tariffs and Trade (GATT) provide for special and differential treatment for less developed countries (LDCs). All industrialized countries have instituted generalized systems of preferences for LDCs. Such rules violate one of the basic norms of the liberal postwar order, the most-favored-nation treatment of all parties. However, the industrialized nations have treated these alterations in the rules as temporary departures necessitated by the peculiar circumstances of poorer areas. At American insistence the concept of graduation was formally introduced into the GATT Articles after the Tokyo Round. Graduation holds that as countries become more developed they will accept rules consistent with liberal principles. Hence, Northern representatives have chosen to interpret special and differential treatment of developing countries as a change within the regime.

Speakers for the Third World, on the other hand, have argued that the basic norms of the international economic order should be redistribution and equity, not nondiscrimination and efficiency. They see the changes in rules as changes of the regime because they identify these changes with basic changes in principle. There is a fundamental difference between viewing changes in rules as indications of change within the regime and viewing these changes as indications of change between regimes. The difference hinges on assessments of whether principles and norms have changed as well. Such assessments are never easy because they cannot be based on objective behavioral observations. . . .

Finally, it is necessary to distinguish the weakening of a regime from changes within or between regimes. *If the principles, norms, rules, and decision-making procedures of a regime become less coherent, or if actual practice is increasingly inconsistent with principles, norms, rules, and procedures, then a regime has weakened.* Special and differential treatment for developing countries is an indication that the liberal regime has weakened, even if it has not been replaced by something else. . . .

In sum, change within a regime involves alterations of rules and decision-making procedures, but not of norms or principles; change of a regime involves alteration of norms and principles; and weakening of a regime involves incoherence among the components of the regime or inconsistency between the regime and related behavior.

DO REGIMES MATTER?

It would take some courage, perhaps more courage than this editor possesses, to answer this question in the negative. This project began with a simple causal schematic. It assumed that regimes could be conceived of as intervening variables standing between basic causal variables (most prominently, power and interests) and outcomes and behavior. The first attempt to analyze regimes thus assumed the following set of causal relationships (see Figure 1).

Regimes do not arise of their own accord. They are not regarded as ends in themselves. Once in place they do affect related behavior and outcomes. They are not merely epiphenomenal.

The independent impact of regimes is a central analytic issue. The second causal arrow implies that regimes do matter. However, there is no general agreement on this point, and three basic orientations can be distinguished. The conventional structural views the regime concept as useless, if not misleading. Modified structural suggests that regimes may matter, but only under fairly restrictive conditions. And Grotian sees regimes as much more pervasive, as inherent attributes of any complex, persistent pattern of human behavior.

. . . Susan Strange represents the first orientation. She has grave reservations about the value of the notion of regimes. Strange argues that the concept is pernicious because it obfuscates and obscures the interests and power relationships that are the proximate, not just the ultimate, cause of behavior in the international system. "All those international arrangements dignified by the label regime are only too easily upset when either the balance of bargaining power or the perception of national interest (or both together) change among those states who negotiate them."[6] Regimes, if they can be said to exist at all, have little or no impact.

Figure 1

Basic causal variables ──────→ Regimes ──────→ Related behavior
and outcomes

They are merely epiphenomenal. The underlying causal schematic is one that sees a direct connection between changes in basic causal factors (whether economic or political) and changes in behavior and outcomes. Regimes are excluded completely, or their impact on outcomes and related behavior is regarded as trivial.

Strange's position is consistent with prevailing intellectual orientations for analyzing social phenomena. These structural orientations conceptualize a world of rational self-seeking actors. The actors may be individuals, or firms, or groups, or classes, or states. They function in a system or environment that is defined by their own interests, power, and interaction. These orientations are resistant to the contention that principles, norms, rules, and decision-making procedures have a significant impact on outcomes and behavior. . . .

The second orientation to regimes, modified structural, is most clearly reflected [by] Keohane[7] and Stein.[8] Both of these authors start from a conventional structural realist perspective, a world of sovereign states seeking to maximize their interest and power. . . .

In a world of sovereign states the basic function of regimes is to coordinate state behavior to achieve desired outcomes in particular issue-areas.[9] Such coordination is attractive under several circumstances. Stein and Keohane posit that regimes can have an impact when Pareto-optimal outcomes could not be achieved through uncoordinated individual calculations of self-interest. The prisoners' dilemma is the classic game-theoretic example. Stein also argues that regimes may have an autonomous effect on outcomes when purely autonomous behavior could lead to disastrous results for both parties. The game of chicken is the game-theoretic analog. Haas and others . . . suggest that regimes may have significant impact in a highly complex world in which *ad hoc,* individualistic calculations of interest could not possibly provide the necessary level of coordination.[10] If, as many have argued, there is a general movement toward a world of complex interdependence, then the number of areas in which regimes can matter is growing.

However, regimes cannot be relevant for zero-sum situations in which states act to maximize the difference between their utilities and those of others. Jervis points to the paucity of regimes in the security area, which more closely approximates zero-sum games than do most economic issue-areas. Pure power motivations preclude regimes. Thus, the second orientation, modified structuralism, sees regimes emerging and having a significant impact, but only under restrictive conditions. It suggests that the first cut should be amended as in Figure 2. . . .

While the modified structural approach does not view the perfect market as a regime, because action there is based purely upon individual calculation without regard to the behavior of others, the third orientation does regard the market as a regime. Patterns of behavior that persist over extended periods are infused with normative significance. A market cannot be sustained by calculations of self-interest alone. It must be, in Ruggie's terms, *embedded* in a broader social environ-

Figure 2

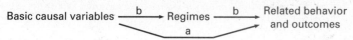

Basic causal variables —b→ Regimes —b→ Related behavior and outcomes

a

ment that nurtures and sustains the conditions necessary for its functioning. Even the balance of power, regarded by conventional structural realist analysts as a purely conflictual situation, can be treated as a regime.[11] The causal schema suggested by a Grotian orientation either closely parallels the first cut shown in Figure 1, or can be depicted as in Figure 3.

Patterned behavior reflecting calculations of interest tends to lead to the creation of regimes, and regimes reinforce patterned behavior.

The Grotian tradition . . . offers a counter to structural realism of either the conventional or the modified form. It rejects the assumption that the international system is composed of sovereign states limited only by the balance of power. . . . States are rarified abstractions. Elites have transnational as well as national ties. Sovereignty is a behavioral variable, not an analytic assumption. The ability of states to control movements across their borders and to maintain dominance over all aspects of the international system is limited. Security and state survival are not the only objectives. Force does not occupy a singularly important place in international politics. Elites act within a communications net, embodying rules, norms, and principles, which transcends national boundaries. . . .

Regimes are much more easily encompassed by a Grotian worldview. But, as the arguments made by Jervis, Keohane, Stein, Lipson, and Cohen indicate, the concept is not precluded by a realist perspective. The issue is not so much whether one accepts the possibility of principles, norms, rules, and decision-making procedures affecting outcomes and behavior, as what one's basic assumption is about the normal state of international affairs. Adherents of a Grotian perspective accept regimes as a pervasive and significant phenomenon in the international system. Adherents of a structural realist orientation see regimes as a phenomenon whose presence cannot be assumed and whose existence requires careful explanation. The two "standard cases" are fundamentally different, and it is the definition of the standard case that identifies the basic theoretical orientation. . . .

In sum, conventional structural arguments do not take regimes seriously: if basic causal variables change, regimes will also change. Regimes have no independent impact on behavior. Modified structural arguments, represented here by a number of adherents of a realist approach to international relations, see regimes as mattering only when independent decision making leads to undesired out-

Figure 3

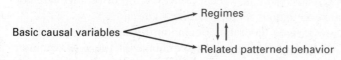

Regimes

Basic causal variables ←

Related patterned behavior

comes. Finally, Grotian perspectives accept regimes as a fundamental part of all patterned human interaction, including behavior in the international system.

EXPLANATIONS FOR REGIME DEVELOPMENT

For those authors who see regimes as something more than epiphenomena, the second major issue posed by a schematic that sees regimes as intervening variables between basic causal factors and related outcomes and behavior becomes relevant. What is the relationship between basic causal factors and regimes? What are the conditions that lead to regime creation, persistence, and dissipation? Here regimes are treated as the dependent variable.

A wide variety of basic causal variables have been offered to explain the development of regimes. The most prominent in this volume are egoistic self-interest, political power, norms and principles, habit and custom, and knowledge. The last two are seen as supplementary, augmenting more basic forces related to interest, power, and values.

1. Egoistic Self-interest

The prevailing explanation for the existence of international regimes is egoistic self-interest. By egoistic self-interest I refer to the desire to maximize one's own utility function where that function does not include the utility of another party. The egoist is concerned with the behavior of others only insofar as that behavior can affect the egoist's utility. All contractarian political theories from Hobbes to Rawls are based on egoistic self-interest. In contrast, pure power seekers are interested in maximizing the difference between their power capabilities and those of their opponent. . . .

Stein[12] elaborates two circumstances under which unconstrained individual choice provides incentives for cooperation. The first occurs when such choice leads to Pareto-suboptimal outcomes: prisoner's dilemma and the provision of collective goods are well-known examples. Stein refers to this as the dilemma of common interests. Its resolution requires "collaboration," the active construction of a regime that guides individual decision making. Unconstrained individual decision making may also be eschewed when it would lead to mutually undesired outcomes and where the choice of one actor is contingent on the choice made by the other: the game of chicken is a prominent example. Stein refers to this as the dilemma of common aversions; it can be resolved through "coordination." Coordination need not be formalized or institutionalized. So long as everyone agrees to drive on the right side of the road, little more is needed. (Stein's concept of collaboration conforms with the definition of regimes used here. It is not so clear that coordination involves regimes. Coordination may only require the construction of rules. If these rules are not informed by any proximate principles or norms, they will not conform to the definition of regimes set forth earlier.)

While Stein employs a game-theoretic orientation, Keohane utilizes insights from microeconomic theories of market failure to examine dilemmas of common interests. He is primarily concerned with the demand for regimes, the conditions under which *ad hoc* agreements fail to provide Pareto-optimal outcomes. He maintains that "Regimes can make agreement easier if they provide frameworks for establishing legal liability (even if these are not perfect); improve the quantity and quality of information available to actors; or reduce other transactions costs, such as costs of organization or of making side-payments."[13] These benefits provided by regimes are likely to outweigh the costs of regime formation and maintenance when there is asymmetric information, moral hazard, potential dishonesty, or high issue density. In addition, the costs of forming regimes will be lower when there is a high level of formal and informal communication among states, a condition more likely to be found in open political systems operating under conditions of complex interdependence.

Egoistic self-interest is also regarded as an important determinant of regimes by several other authors. Young argues that there are three paths to regime formation: spontaneous, in which regimes emerge from the converging expectations of many individual actions; negotiated, in which regimes are formed by explicit agreements; and imposed, in which regimes are initially forced upon actors by external imposition. The first two are based on egoistic calculations. . . .

2. Political Power

The second major basic causal variable used to explain regime development is political power. Two different orientations toward power can be distinguished. The first is cosmopolitan and instrumental: power is used to secure optimal outcomes for the system as a whole. In game-theoretic terms power is used to promote joint maximization. It is power in the service of the common good. The second approach is particularistic and potentially consummatory. Power is used to enhance the values of specific actors within the system. . . . In game-theoretic terms power is used to maximize individual payoffs. It is power in the service of particular interests.

a. Power in the Service of the Common Good   The first position is represented by a long tradition in classical and neoclassical economics associated with the provision of public goods. The hidden hand was Adam Smith's most compelling construct: the good of all from the selfishness of each; there could be no more powerful defense of egoism. But Smith recognized that it was necessary for the state to provide certain collective goods. These included defense, the maintenance of order, minimum levels of welfare, public works, the protection of infant industries, and standards for commodities.[14] Economists have pointed to the importance of the state for establishing property rights and enforcing contracts; that is, creating conditions that prevent predatory as opposed to market behavior. The state must create institutions that equate public and private rates of return.[15] Keynesian analysis gives the state a prominent role in managing macroeconomic variables. For all of these arguments the purpose of state action is to further general societal interests.

The contemporary economist who has become most clearly associated with arguments emphasizing the instrumental role of power for cosmopolitan interests in the international system is Charles Kindleberger. In *The World in Depression,* Kindleberger argues that the depression of the 1930s could have been prevented by effective state leadership. An effective leader would have acted as a lender of last resort and provided a market for surplus commodities. In the interwar period the United States was able but unwilling to assume these burdens, and Great Britain was willing but unable. The result was economic chaos. In a more recent statement Kindleberger has listed the following functions that states perform for the international trading system:

1. Protecting economic actors from force.
2. Cushioning the undesirable effects of an open system by, for instance, providing adjustment assistance for import-competing industries.
3. Establishing standards for products. In the absence of such standards inordinate energy may be wasted finding information about products.
4. Providing a national currency that can be used as an international reserve and transactions currency.
5. Constructing public works such as docks and domestic transportation systems.
6. Compensating for market imperfections by, for instance, becoming a lender of last resort when private financial institutions become so cautious that their conservatism could destroy global liquidity.[16]

Despite its emphasis on political action, Kindleberger's perspective is still profoundly liberal. . . . A market economy will maximize the utility of society as a whole. Political power is put at the service of the common good.

b. Power in the Service of Particular Interests   The articles in this volume are less oriented toward cosmopolitan ends; rather, they focus on power as an instrument that can be used to enhance the utility of particular actors, usually states. A game-theoretic analogy makes it easier to distinguish between two important variants of the viewpoint of power in the service of particular interests. The first assumes that pay-offs are fixed and that an actor's choice of strategy is autonomously determined solely by these pay-offs. The second assumes that power can be used to alter pay-offs and influence actor strategy.

The first approach closely follows the analysis that applies when purely cosmopolitan objectives are at stake, except that political power is used to maximize individual, not joint, pay-offs. Under certain configurations of interest, there is an incentive to create regimes and the provision of these regimes is a function of the distribution of power. . . . Hegemons provide these goods not because they are interested in the well-being of the system as a whole, but because regimes enhance their own national values.

. . . The theory of hegemonic leadership suggests that under conditions of declining hegemony there will be a weakening of regimes. Without leadership, principles, norms, rules, and decision-making procedures cannot easily be upheld. No one actor will be willing to provide the collective goods needed to make the regime work smoothly and effectively. Stein's analysis, on the other hand, suggests that as hegemony declines there will be greater incentives for collaboration because collective goods are no longer being provided by the hegemon. The international system more closely resembles an oligopoly than a perfect market. . . . For Stein, interests alone can effectively sustain order. Hegemonic decline can lead to stronger regimes.

The second line of argument associated with power in the service of specific interests investigates the possibility that powerful actors may be able to alter the pay-offs that confront other actors or influence the strategies they choose. . . .

In this context Oran Young develops the notion of imposed regimes. Dominant actors may explicitly use a combination of sanctions and incentives to compel other actors to act in conformity with a particular set of principles, norms, rules, and decision-making procedures. Alternatively, dominant actors may secure de facto compliance by manipulating opportunity sets so that weaker actors are compelled to behave in a desired way. . . .

When a hegemonic state acts to influence the strategy of other actors the regime is held hostage to the persistence of the existing distribution of power in the international system. If the hegemon's relative capabilities decline, the regime will collapse. Young argues that imposed orders are likely to disintegrate when there are major shifts in underlying power capabilities. . . .

3. Norms and Principles

To this point in the discussion, norms and principles have been treated as endogenous: they are the critical defining characteristics of any given regime. However, norms and principles that influence the regime in a particular issue-area but are not directly related to that issue-area can also be regarded as explanations for the creation, persistence, and dissipation of regimes. The most famous example of such a formulation is Max Weber's *Protestant Ethic and the Spirit of Capitalism.* Weber argues that the rise of capitalism is intimately associated with the evolution of a Calvinist religious doctrine that fosters hard work while enjoining profligacy and uses worldly success as an indication of predestined fate. . . .[17] Such values are critical constraints on self-interested calculations that would too often lead to untrustworthy and dishonest behavior.[18]

Financing by various pariah groups around the world offers a clear example of the way in which noneconomic norms have facilitated market activity. For instance, bills of exchange were devised by Jewish bankers during the late Middle Ages to avoid violence and extortion from the nobility: safer to carry a piece of paper than to carry specie. However, the piece of paper had to be honored by the recipient. This implied a high level of trust and such trust was enhanced by conventions: established practices were reinforced by the exclusionary nature of the group, which facilitated surveillance and the application of sanctions. The importance of conventions for the use of bills of exchange is reflected in the fact that they were frequently used in the Mediterranean basin in the 16th century but they were not used at the interface with the non-Mediterranean world in Syria where, according to Braudel, "two mutually suspicious worlds met face to face. . . ."

. . . John Ruggie's highly original analysis of the postwar economic regime argues that it was founded upon principles of embedded rather than orthodox liberalism. The domestic lesson of the 1930s was that societies could not tolerate the consequences of an untrammeled market. This set of diffuse values, which permeated the capitalist world, was extended from the domestic to the international sphere in the Bretton Woods agreements.

This discussion suggests that there is a hierarchy of regimes. Diffuse principles and norms, such as hard work as a service to God, condition behavior in specific issue-areas. In international relations, the most important diffuse principle is sovereignty. . . .

4. Usage and Custom

The last two sets of causal variables affecting regime development are usage and custom, and knowledge. . . . Usage and custom, and knowledge, are not treated in this volume as exogenous variables capable of generating a regime on their own. Rather, they supplement and reinforce pressures associated with egoistic self-interest, political power, and diffuse values.

Usage refers to regular patterns of behavior based on actual practice; custom, to long-standing practice. . . .[19] Patterned behavior accompanied by shared expectations is likely to become infused with normative significance: actions based purely on instrumental calculations can come to be regarded as rule-like or principled behavior. They assume legitimacy. A great deal of western commercial law, in fact, developed out of custom and usage initially generated by self-interest. Practices that began as *ad hoc* private arrangements later became the basis for official commercial law. . . .[20]

5. Knowledge

The final variable used to explain the development of regimes is knowledge. Like usage and custom, knowledge is usually treated as an intervening, not an exogenous, variable. In an earlier study Ernst Haas . . . defined knowledge as "the sum of technical information and of theories about that information which commands sufficient consensus at a given time among interested actors to serve as a guide to public policy designed to achieve some social goal. . . ."[21] Knowledge creates a basis for cooperation by illuminating complex interconnections that were not previously understood. Knowledge can not only enhance the prospects for convergent state behavior, it can also transcend "prevailing lines of ideological cleavage. . . ."[22]

For knowledge to have an independent impact in the international system, it must be widely accepted by policy makers. Stein points out that rules concerning health, such as quarantine regulations, were radically altered by new scientific knowledge such as the discovery of the microbe that causes cholera, the transmission of yellow fever by mosquitoes, and the use of preventive vaccines. Prior to developments such as these, national health regulations were primarily determined by political concerns. After these discoveries, however, national behavior was determined by an international regime, or at least a set of rules, dictated by accepted scientific knowledge. . . .[23]

New knowledge can provide the basis for . . . evolutionary change, which usually involves altering rules and procedures within the context of a given set of principles and norms. In contrast, revolutionary change, which generates new principles and norms, is associated with shifts in power. As an example of evolutionary change, . . . the fixed exchange rate system agreed to at Bretton Woods was based upon understandings derived from the interwar experience and then-current knowledge about domestic monetary institutions and structures. States were extremely sensitive to competitive devaluation and were not confident that domestic monetary policy could provide insulation from external disturbances. It was much easier to accept a floating exchange rate regime in the 1970s because the knowledge and related institutional capacity for controlling monetary aggregates had substantially increased. . . .

CONCLUSION

In approaching the two basic questions that guided this exercise—the impact of regimes on related behavior and outcomes, and the relationship between basic causal variables and regimes—the essays in this volume reflect two different orientations to international relations. The Grotian perspective, which informs the essays of Hopkins and Puchala and of Young, sees regimes as a pervasive facet of social interaction. It is catholic in its description of the underlying causes of regimes. Interests, power, diffuse norms, customs, and knowledge may all play a role in regime formation. These causal factors may be manifest through the behavior of individuals, particular bureaucracies, and international organizations, as well as states.

The structural realist orientation . . . is more circumspect. The exemplar or standard case for the realist perspective does not include international regimes. Regimes arise only under restrictive conditions characterized by the failure of individual decision making to secure desired outcomes. The basic causal variables that lead to the creation of regimes are power and interest. The basic actors are states.

. . . A more serious departure from structural reasoning occurs when regimes are seen as autonomous variables independently affecting not only related behavior and outcomes, but also the basic causal variables that led to their creation in the first place. . . .

NOTES

1. Robert O. Keohane and Joseph S. Nye, *Power and Interdependence* (Boston: Little, Brown, 1977), p. 19.
2. Ernst Haas, "Technological Self-Reliance for Latin America: the OAS Contribution," *International Organization* 34, 4 (Autumn 1980), p. 553.
3. Hedley Bull, *The Anarchical Society: A Study of Order in World Politics* (New York: Columbia University Press, 1977), p. 54.
4. Robert Jervis, "Security Regimes," in Stephen D. Krasner, ed., *International Regimes* (Ithaca, NY: Cornell University Press, 1983), p. 357.

5. Kenneth Waltz, *Theory of International Relations* (Reading, MA: Addison-Wesley, 1979); Morton Kaplan, *Systems and Process in International Politics* (New York: Wiley, 1957), p. 23; Kaplan, *Towards Professionalism in International Theory* (New York: Free Press, 1979), pp. 66–69, 73.

6. Susan Strange, "*Cave! hic dragones:* A Critique of Regime Analysis," in Stephen D. Krasner, ed., *International Regimes* (Ithaca, NY: Cornell University Press, 1983).

7. Robert O. Keohane, "The Demand for International Regimes," in Krasner, ed., *International Regimes,* op. cit.

8. Arthur A. Stein, "Coordination and Collaboration: Regimes in an Anarchic World," in Krasner, *International Regimes,* op. cit.

9. Vinod K. Aggarwal emphasizes this point. See his "Hanging by a Thread: International Regime Change in the Textile/Apparel System, 1950–1979," Ph.D. diss., Stanford University, 1981, chap. 1.

10. Ernst B. Haas, "Words Can Hurt You; or, Who Said What to Whom About Regimes," in Krasner, *International Regimes,* op. cit.

11. Bull, *The Anarchical Society,* chap. 5.

12. Stein, "Coordination and Collaboration," op. cit.

13. Keohane, "The Demand for International Regimes," op. cit., p. 338.

14. There is a lively debate over precisely how much of a role Smith accords to the state. Some (see for instance Albert Hirschman, *The Passions and the Interests* [Princeton: Princeton University Press, 1977], pp. 103–104) maintain that Smith wanted to limit the folly of government by having it do as little as possible. Others (see for instance Colin Holmes, "Laissez-faire in Theory and Practice: Britain 1800–1875," *Journal of European Economic History* 5, 3 [1976], p. 673; and Carlos Diaz-Alejandro, "Delinking North and South: Unshackled or Unhinged," in Albert Fishlow et al., *Rich and Poor Nations in the World Economy* [New York: McGraw-Hill, 1978], pp. 124–25) have taken the intermediate position endorsed here. Others see Smith trying to establish conditions for a moral society that must be based on individual choice, for which a materialistically oriented, egoistically maintained economic system is only instrumental. See, for instance, Leonard Billet, "The Just Economy: The Moral Basis of the Wealth of Nations," *Review of Social Economy* 34 (December 1974).

15. Jack Hirschleifer, "Economics from a Biological Viewpoint," *Journal of Law and Economics* 20 (April 1977); Weber, *Economy and Society,* pp. 336–37; Douglass C. North and Robert Paul Thomas, *The Rise of the Western World: A New Economic History* (Cambridge: Cambridge University Press, 1973), chap. 1.

16. Charles P. Kindleberger, "Government and International Trade," *Princeton Essays in International Finance* (International Finance Section, Princeton University, July 1978). Adam Smith was less enamoured with leadership. He felt that reasonable intercourse could only take place in the international system if there was a balance of power. Without such a balance the strong would dominate and exploit the weak. See Diaz-Alejandro, "Delinking North and South," p. 92.

17. For a recent discussion see David Laitin, "Religion, Political Culture, and the Weberian Tradition," *World Politics* 30, 4 (July 1978), especially pp. 568–69. For another discussion of noneconomic values in the rise of capitalism see Hirschman, *The Passions and the Interests.*

18. Fred Hirsch, *The Social Limits to Growth* (Cambridge: Harvard University Press, 1976), chap. 11. See also Michael Walzer, "The Future of Intellectuals and the Rise of the New Class," *New York Review of Books* 27 (20 March 1980).

19. Max Weber, *Economy and Society* (Berkeley: University of California Press, 1977), p. 29.

20. Leon E. Trakman, "The Evolution of the Law Merchant: Our Commercial Heritage," Part I, *Journal of Maritime Law and Commerce* 12, 1 (October 1980) and Part II, ibid., 12, 2 (January 1981); Harold Berman and Colin Kaufman, "The Law of International Commercial Transactions (*Lex Mercatoria*)," *Harvard International Law Journal* 19, 1 (Winter 1978).
21. Ernst Haas, "Why Collaborate? Issue-Linkage and International Regimes," *World Politics* 32, 3 (April 1980), pp. 367–68.
22. Ibid., p. 368.
23. Stein, "Coordination and Collaboration," op. cit.

The Politics of International Regime Formation: Managing Natural Resources and the Environment

Oran R. Young

Why do actors in international society succeed in forming institutional arrangements or regimes to cope with some transboundary problems but fail to do so in connection with other, seemingly similar, problems? In this article, I employ a threefold strategy to make progress toward answering this question. The first section prepares the ground by identifying and critiquing the principal models or streams of analysis embedded in the existing literature on regime formation; the second section articulates an alternative model, called institutional bargaining. The third section employs this alternative model to derive some hypotheses about the determinants of success in institutional bargaining and uses these hypotheses, in a preliminary way, to illuminate the process of regime formation in international society.

To provide a ready source of cases with which to illustrate hypotheses about regime formation as well as to lend empirical content to my argument, I draw repeatedly on evidence pertaining to institutional arrangements for natural resources and the environment. . . .[1]

EXISTING MODELS: A CRITIQUE

Two streams of analysis dominate the study of regime formation in international society. Those trained to look at the world through the prism of mainstream utilitarian models focus on the behavior of rational utility maximizers and typically assume that actors of this type will reach agreement on the content of mutually beneficial institutional arrangements, including international regimes, whenever a distinct contract zone or zone of agreement exists.[2] Working with models emanating from game theory or micro-economics, the utilitarians seek to predict (or prescribe) the locus of final settlements as well as the trajectories of sequences of offers and counteroffers leading to these settlements.[3] Because they generally regard the process of institution-building as unproductive, these analysts expect rational actors to realize feasible joint gains while simultaneously devising procedures to keep the attendant transaction costs under control.[4]

Political scientists and others trained to look to the distribution of power in society as the key to understanding collective outcomes, by contrast, regularly assume that institutional arrangements, such as international regimes, reflect the configuration of power in the relevant social system; specific arrangements come into existence when those possessing sufficient power take the necessary steps to create them.[5] These realists (or neorealists) have come to stress the role of preponderant actors or, in the current vocabulary of international relations, hegemons in the process of regime formation. Some even assert that the presence of a hegemon is a necessary condition for the emergence of institutional arrangements at the international level.[6]

Not only do these streams of analysis license disparate explanations of regime formation in international society, but advocates of each perspective also tend to treat the very factor singled out by the other as an impediment to the promotion of social welfare. . . . Whereas the realists recommend concentration of power in the hands of a preponderant actor as a recipe for success, the utilitarians prescribe the dispersal of power among a sizable number of rational utility maximizers.

How can we come to terms with these conflicting perspectives on institution-building in the interests of formulating a satisfactory account of regime formation in international society? In this section, I argue that the models of both the power theorists and the mainstream utilitarians are seriously flawed when it comes to accounting for the actual record of success and failure in efforts to form international regimes. From this, I conclude that we need to develop a more realistic model of the interactions involved in regime formation to guide our thinking in this realm.

Realist or Neorealist Models

Mesmerized by the role of Great Britain in creating regimes for international commerce and the oceans during the nineteenth century and the role of the United States in establishing monetary and trade regimes in the aftermath of World War II, many students of international relations are currently preoccupied with the place of preponderant actors or hegemons in international society. . . .[7]

Yet it is easy to demonstrate that arguments relying so heavily on the role of preponderant actors in the formation of international regimes cannot withstand the test of empirical application. Consider, in this connection, just a few significant examples. The regime for northern fur seals, established initially in 1911 and long regarded as a model for international conservation efforts, involved a mutually beneficial deal among four major powers: the United States, Japan, Russia, and Great Britain (acting on behalf of Canada).. . . [8] The more recent complex of arrangements for Antarctica and the Southern Ocean encompasses not only the two superpowers but also a number of other important powers working together as members of the Antarctic club. . . . [9] The pollution control regime for the Mediterranean Basin, by contrast, does not include either of the superpowers. It does encompass among its members, however, a number of important states that span the Arab–Israeli conflict and the Greek–Turkish conflict as well as the East–West conflict. . . . [10] What is more, in my sample of institutional arrangements, the drive to form several of the regimes was spearheaded by intergovernmental organizations or by international nongovernmental organizations, so that states did not even take the lead in the relevant processes of regime formation. There is general agreement, for example, that the International Union for the Conservation of Nature and Natural Resources (IUCN) was the motivating force in establishing the regime regulating trade in endangered species of fauna and flora spelled out in the provisions of the Convention on International Trade in Endangered Species.[11] And there is no escaping the central role that the United Nations Environment Programme (UNEP) played in the negotiating process that resulted in the 1985 convention and the 1987 protocol on ozone depletion.[12]

From the perspective of those desiring to promote international cooperation through regime formation, this is just as well, since as many observers are coming to realize, hegemony is an extreme case in international society. This is not to deny, of course, the existence of striking asymmetries among parties interested in a given issue-area both with respect to the intensity of their interest in the problem and with respect to usable bargaining strength at their disposal. Nonetheless, there are several interlocking reasons why true hegemony is the exception rather than the rule in international society.[13] There is, to begin with, the well-known fact that power in the sense of control over resources or tangible capabilities is often difficult to translate into power in the sense of the ability to determine collective outcomes. . . . [14] It will come as no surprise, therefore, that even acknowledged great powers are apt to find the opportunity costs of exercising power high in specific situations. Given the fact that great powers always strive to participate actively in a number of issue-areas or arenas simultaneously, moreover, the prospect of high opportunity costs is sufficient to induce such powers to negotiate rather than impose the terms of international regimes relating to most specific activities.[15]

What is more, contemporary international society features many situations in which a number of states possess blocking power or the capacity to veto institutional arrangements they dislike, even if they cannot impose their own preferences on others. . . . [16] In such cases, it is hard to see how any international regime could be effective if it failed to satisfy the concerns of all the . . . [important] members of international society. For all practical purposes, then, the great powers today routinely find themselves in situations in which they must negotiate the terms of international regimes covering specific issue-areas, whether they like it or not.

All of this puts a premium on a form of leadership that differs from the kind of unilateralism or imposition we ordinarily associate with the actions of a hegemon. Contrary to Charles Kindleberger's argument that "a hegemon presumably wants to do it in his own behalf" and that "a leader, one who is responsible or responds to need, who is answerable or answers to the demands of others, is forced to 'do it' by ethical training and by the circumstances of position,"[17] leadership is not simply a matter of motivation. Nor is leadership merely a form of benevolent behavior exhibited by the principal members of privileged groups who act in such a way as to supply public goods to others regardless of their unwillingness to contribute toward the supply of such goods.[18] Rather, leadership in connection with the formation of international regimes is a matter of entrepreneurship; it involves a combination of imagination in inventing institutional options and skill in brokering the interests of numerous actors to line up support for such options.[19] A leader in this context is an actor who, desiring to see a regime emerge and realizing that imposition is not feasible, undertakes to craft attractive institutional arrangements and to persuade others to come on board as supporters of such arrangements. . . .

Utilitarian Models

For their part, the mainstream utilitarians exhibit an unjustified faith in the ability of rational utility maximizers to realize feasible joint gains. As all well-trained students of international affairs now realize, even rational actors regularly experience difficulties in cooperating, with the result that suboptimal (sometimes drastically suboptimal) outcomes are a common occurrence.[20] More than anything else, this realization is what has provided the impetus for the remarkable rise of the field of public choice in recent years and made a growth industry of the analysis of institutional arrangements designed to overcome or alleviate collective-action problems.[21]

Even when there is general agreement on the existence and the dimensions of a zone of agreement, those negotiating the terms of institutional arrangements often encounter severe obstacles in their efforts to work out the details of mutually acceptable regimes: (1) Difficulties frequently ensue from widespread resort to strategic behavior or committal tactics on the part of those wanting the outcomes to favor their interests to the maximum degree possible. . . .[22] (2) Intraparty bargaining that pits powerful forces against each other within one or more of the states negotiating the provisions of an international regime can make it difficult to reach agreement at the international level. . . .[23] (3) There are commonly problems attributable to linkages among issue-areas in international society. Thus, parties are frequently loath to make concessions regarding specific issues more out of a concern for how this might affect their negotiating postures in other issue-areas than out of any commitment to the particular issue at hand. . . .[24] (4) Negotiators also regularly encounter difficulties in settling on the terms of international regimes because some of the participants do not trust others to comply with the

Figure 1 Edgeworth box diagram.

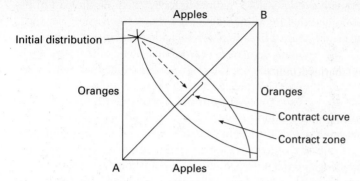

terms of the resultant arrangements rather than because they are unhappy with the substantive provisions of the arrangements themselves.[25] In some cases, this is essentially a problem of verification, as in pollution control measures relating to non-point source pollutants or in efforts to control the illegal trade in endangered species.[26] In other cases, it is more a matter of devising appropriate incentives or sanctions, as in arrangements aimed at avoiding the destruction of habitat necessary for the maintenance of biological diversity. . . .

More profoundly, mainstream utilitarian accounts of international regime foundation rest on an inappropriate, albeit well-specified and analytically appealing, model of bargaining. All this work takes as its point of departure either an Edgeworth box diagram with its depiction of a well-defined contract curve (see Figure 1) or a game-theoretic formulation with its identification of a well-defined negotiation set (see Figure 2).[27] Both of these analytic devices abstract away a great many considerations that are major preoccupations of negotiators under real-world circumstances.[28] They assume, for instance, that the identity of the participants is known at the outset and fixed during the course of negotiations, that

Figure 2 Negotiation set.

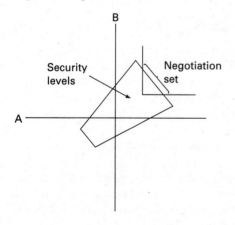

the alternatives or strategies available to the parties are fully specified, that the outcome associated with every feasible combination of choices on the part of the participants is known, and that the preference orderings of the parties over these outcomes are identifiable (at least in ordinal terms) and not subject to change. . . .

As appealing as the resultant constructs may be in analytic terms, they are of limited value in helping us comprehend the politics of international regime formation. The identity of the relevant participants in these negotiations is seldom cast in concrete. As recent experience in both the Arctic and the Antarctic suggests, the scope of the membership in international regimes can become an important focus of bargaining in its own right. It will come as no surprise, then, that efforts to spell out menus of alternatives or strategy sets in advance of these negotiations are generally doomed to failure. No doubt, there is some heuristic value in analyzing the extent to which specific collective-action problems in international society resemble prisoner's dilemma, chicken, stag hunt, or other analytic models.[29] But mapping the contours of real-world collective-action problems in terms of such analytic models is seldom a feasible proposition,[30] and our ability to foresee the consequences, unfolding over time, which result from the choice of specific options is particularly limited in connection with ongoing arrangements such as international regimes. . . .

AN ALTERNATIVE MODEL: INSTITUTIONAL BARGAINING

The principal conclusion to be drawn from the preceding discussion is that we must develop an alternative model of regime formation in order to come up with a satisfactory answer to the question posed at the beginning of this article. In my judgment, this model should retain an emphasis on negotiations among self-interested parties as a means of dealing with collective-action problems. But it should, at the same time, depart in several fundamental ways from the mainstream utilitarian accounts of the bargaining process. . . .

Multiple Actors and Unanimity Rules

While there may be disagreement (and sometimes even hard bargaining) regarding the identity of the parties that are or should be included in specific cases, efforts to devise international regimes generally involve a number of autonomous participants. This may mean a handful, such as the four states that negotiated the fur seal regime, or a modest number, such as the sixteen parties to the regime for Antarctic marine living resources or the twenty-three parties to the 1987 protocol to the ozone depletion convention. In extreme cases, it may involve over 150 states, as in the efforts to work out a deep seabed mining regime in the context of the law of the sea negotiations. And though it would certainly be helpful in analytic terms, it is seldom feasible to collapse the resultant negotiations into two-sided bargaining processes by grouping the players into two coalitions or blocs.

This means that analytic constructs closely tied to a two-party view of the world, like the Edgeworth box, cannot carry us far in coming to terms with the politics of international regime formation.[31]

Equally important, the multilateral interactions involved in regime formation do not lend themselves well to treatment in terms of the usual analytic responses to n-party situations, which center on the identification of sets of winning coalitions coupled with efforts to single out those coalitions that are most likely to form. . . .[32] [I]nstitutional bargaining in international society operates on the basis of a unanimity rule in contrast to a majority rule or some other decision rule justifying a focus on the development of winning coalitions.[33] No doubt, those negotiating the terms of international regimes may seek to exclude parties deemed likely to object to any reasonable institutional arrangements or threaten to go forward with particular arrangements regardless of the opposition of one or more parties. . . . Yet once the membership of the relevant group is set, negotiations regarding international regimes generally revolve around efforts to come up with arrangements that all participants in these negotiations can accept.

Integrative Bargaining

One thing that saves the resultant negotiations from certain failure is that regime formation in international society typically centers on integrative (or productive) bargaining in contrast to distributive (or positional) bargaining.[34] As Richard Walton and Robert McKersie observed in their early and influential discussion of integrative bargaining, the key to this distinction lies in the presence or absence of a fixed, unchanging, and generally acknowledged contract curve or negotiation set.[35] Negotiators who know the locus of a contract curve or the shape of a welfare frontier to begin with will naturally be motivated primarily by a desire to achieve an outcome on this curve or frontier that is as favorable to their own interests as possible. They will, therefore, immediately turn to calculations regarding various types of strategic behavior or committal tactics that may help them achieve their distributive goals.[36]

Negotiators who do not start with a common understanding regarding the contours of the contract curve or the locus of the negotiation set, by contrast, have compelling incentives to engage in exploratory interactions to identify opportunities for devising mutually beneficial deals. Such negotiators may never discover the actual shape of the contract curve or locus of the negotiation set, and they may consequently end up with arrangements that are Pareto-inferior in the sense that they leave feasible joint gains on the table.[37] At the same time, however, they are less likely to engage in negotiations that bog down into protracted stalemates brought about by efforts to improve the outcome for one party or another through initiatives involving strategic behavior and committal tactics.

The Veil of Uncertainty

Another factor that serves to mitigate the threat of stalemate in interactions governed by unanimity rules is what James Buchanan has described as the veil of uncertainty. It is not that those negotiating the terms of international regimes ordinarily lack information about their own roles in society, as John Rawls supposes in his concept of the veil of ignorance constraining the behavior of those negotiating social contracts under conditions approximating what he calls the original position.[38] The point is, rather, that institutional arrangements, unlike specific or self-contained choices, typically apply across a wide range of contexts and over a more or less extended period of time. . . . As Brennan and Buchanan observe, in a discussion directed toward municipal institutions, "to the extent that a person faced with constitutional choice remains uncertain as to what his position will be under separate choice options, he will tend to agree on arrangements that might be called 'fair' in the sense that patterns of outcomes generated under such arrangements will be broadly acceptable, regardless of where the participant might be located in such outcomes."[39]

Surely, this observation applies with equal force to the behavior of collective entities, such as nation-states, that dominate negotiations regarding the content of international regimes. This line of analysis undoubtedly helps to account for the fact that collections of actors have reached agreement regarding the provisions of arrangements governing whaling, the pollution of the Mediterranean Basin, and some of the problems associated with the transboundary flow of radioactive fallout. . . .

Problems and Approaches

Faced with negotiations characterized by integrative bargaining under a veil of uncertainty, the parties endeavoring to form international regimes seldom, if ever, make a sustained effort to perfect their information regarding the full range of outcomes and the dimensions of contract zones before getting down to serious bargaining. Instead, they typically zero in on a few key problems, articulate several approaches to the treatment of these problems, and seek to reconcile differences among these approaches in the course of their negotiations. In the case of deep seabed mining, for instance, the problems included matters such as the role of the Enterprise in the conduct of mining operations, production controls in the hands of the International Seabed Authority, and technology transfer. . . .[40] Similarly, the negotiations leading to the 1987 protocol on the protection of the ozone layer centered, for a time, on the relative merits of emphasizing a comprehensive ban on aerosols or of mandating an across-the-board cut in the production of chlorofluorocarbons (CFCs).[41]

There is no guarantee, of course, that the parties can reconcile divergent approaches to such problems, although it helps to be dealing with several differentiable concerns so that it becomes possible to devise trades among those who feel more or less intensely about individual problems and approaches. But when it does prove feasible to make progress in reconciling divergent approaches to relatively well-defined problems, the parties typically begin to formulate a negotiating text and to use this device to structure their ongoing efforts to develop the deals required to reach agreement on the terms of a regime.[42] Such a text can serve both to organize the negotiations involved in regime formation, as in the case of the various negotiating texts used in the law of the sea negotiations, and to provide a basis to guide the expansion or extension of a regime over time, as in the cases of the negotiation of several subsequent protocols to the 1976 convention on pollution control in the Mediterranean Basin and of the 1987 protocol to the 1985 convention on ozone depletion.[43]

Transnational Alliances

As many observers have pointed out, negotiations pertaining to the formation of international regimes commonly involve extensive intra-party bargaining, which is apt to occur simultaneously with the relevant inter-party bargaining.[44] There is nothing surprising about this when we stop to consider that states are complex collective entities encompassing numerous groups whose interests often differ widely with respect to any given issue-area. . . . Internal splits between industrialists and environmentalists are common in connection with most pollution control arrangements. And a number of members of the European Community experienced relatively sharp internal conflicts regarding the positions they took in negotiating a regime to protect stratospheric ozone.

What is interesting in connection with this discussion of institutional bargaining, however, is the potential that situations of this kind generate for the development of transnational alliances among interest groups supporting the formation of specific international regimes. An extensive network of scientific supporters located in all the Mediterranean Basin states has played an important role in bringing pressure to bear on hesitant governments to become supporters of the pollution control regime for the Mediterranean. . . .[45] In some cases, these efforts are facilitated by organizations that serve to aggregate and articulate the concerns of transnational interest groups regarding international regimes. . . . The Scientific Committee on Antarctic Research (SCAR), together with its parent organization, the International Council of Scientific Unions, has certainly been instrumental in the development of regimes relating to Antarctica.[46] And it is intriguing to consider the remarkable role of UNEP in the negotiations leading to the 1985 convention and the 1987 protocol regarding the protection of stratospheric ozone. None of this is to suggest that states no longer dominate bargaining in international society; far from it. But it would be a serious mistake to overlook the role of transnational alliances among influential interest groups in developing and maintaining regimes at the international level.[47]

Shifting Involvements

While the vision of negotiation incorporated in the mainstream utilitarian models emphasizes self-contained interactions, institutional bargaining of the type involved in the formation of international regimes almost always features a rich array of linkages to other events occurring in the socioeconomic or political environment.[48] Sometimes this poses more or less serious problems for those engaged in institutional bargaining at the international level.[49] Parties may deliberately drag their feet in hopes that their bargaining strength will increase with the passage of time. Individual participants may deliberately complicate the negotiations by linking several issues in such a way as to necessitate the development of complex bargains over an array of problems. Players may become so preoccupied with domestic matters, such as protracted election campaigns or serious civil strife, that they are not in a position to pursue institutional bargaining at the international level vigorously. Or they may simply choose to emphasize other issue-areas for the time being in recognition of their limited capacity to engage in international negotiations. . . .

In some cases, however, linkages of this type work in favor of efforts to form international regimes. Those concerned about possible erosions of bargaining strength in the future may be willing to make significant concessions to reach agreement quickly on the terms of specific regimes. Linking together disparate issues sometimes opens up possibilities for mutually acceptable arrangements by creating opportunities for the international equivalent of logrolling and the formulation of package deals.[50] Those possessing insufficient capacity to handle numerous issues simultaneously may be willing to leave much of the negotiating about the terms of certain regimes to non-governmental actors who are part of a transnational network and who have developed a considerable ability to work together in the course of prior interactions. . . . The conclusion to be drawn from this discussion, therefore, is not that these linkages necessarily make it difficult to form international regimes but, rather, that those involved in processes of regime formation must remain alert at all times to connections of this sort. That is, the natural tendency to become preoccupied with the technical aspects of the specific subject at hand can easily lead to failure in negotiating processes relating to regime formation which are highly sensitive to occurrences in the broader socioeconomic or political environment.

DETERMINANTS OF SUCCESS: HYPOTHESES ABOUT INTERNATIONAL REGIME FORMATION

The record clearly shows that institutional bargaining results in the formation of new international regimes under some conditions. Consider, just to name some recent examples, the development of institutional arrangements pertaining to transboundary radioactive fallout, stratospheric ozone, and Antarctic minerals. Yet success is far from ensured in such endeavors. Like self-interested actors in all social arenas, those attempting to work out the terms of international regimes are often stymied by bargaining impediments that prolong negotiations over institutional arrangements and can easily result in deadlocks. . . .

The next task, then, is to make use of the model of institutional bargaining to pinpoint the determinants of success and failure in efforts to form institutional arrangements in international society. . . .

1. Institutional bargaining can succeed only when the issues at stake lend themselves to contractarian interactions.

Those engaged in efforts to form international regimes experience incentives to approach this process as a problem-solving exercise aimed at reaching agreement on the terms of a social contract when the absence of a fully specified zone of agreement encourages integrative bargaining and the presence of imperfect information ensures that a veil of uncertainty prevails. . . . It is therefore critical to observe that collective-action problems in international society of the sort engendering an interest in devising arrangements to institutionalize cooperation vary in the degree to which they lend themselves to treatment in contractarian terms. And it is worth noting that those involved in efforts to form international regimes often differ markedly in terms of the skill they display in presenting problems of regime formation in contractarian terms.

To see the relevance of this factor to the success of institutional bargaining, consider, to begin with, some extreme cases. It is exceedingly difficult, for instance, to portray the problem of controlling acid precipitation in North America in contractarian terms both because the producers of the relevant emissions and the victims of acid deposition are so clearly identified at the outset and because there is not much overlap in the membership of the two groups.[51] The problem of controlling transboundary radioactive fallout resulting from nuclear accidents, by contrast, is comparatively easy to treat in contractarian terms.[52] Although a good deal is known about the dangers of radioactive fallout, individual members of international society ordinarily cannot know in advance whether they will occupy the role of site of an accident, victim state, or unharmed bystander with respect to specific accidents. This is exactly the sort of situation that gives rise to incentives to consider the common good in devising institutional arrangements.

Although they are less extreme, other cases add to our understanding of the importance of this proposition about the significance of contractarianism. There are important differences, for example, between the problems of ozone depletion and global climate change that affect the extent to which they lend themselves to formulation in contractarian terms. While the impact may vary somewhat on the basis of latitude, human populations in every part of the world will be harmed if the depletion of stratospheric ozone continues at its present rate.[53] In the case of global warming, on the other hand, there will almost certainly be winners and losers who are comparatively easy to differentiate.[54] Significant increases in sea level will cause severe damage to certain low-lying coastal areas (for example, one-half to two-thirds of Bangladesh could easily be inundated) while bestowing benefits on other regions. Global warming is expected to make some areas increasingly hospitable to large-scale agriculture even as other areas lose their current role in agricultural production. And the impact of these differences on processes of regime formation is heightened by the fact that the sources of greenhouse gas emissions are numerous and widely dispersed, whereas the producers of CFCs are few in number and located in a relatively small number of states. Under the circumstances, it is no cause for surprise that the foundations for an international regime designed to protect the ozone layer are now in place, whereas a regime to deal with global climate change is not yet in sight.

2. The availability of arrangements that all participants can accept as equitable (rather than efficient) is necessary for institutional bargaining to succeed.

Economists and others who approach the issues of regime formation as a problem in comparative statics generally place primary emphasis on the achievement of allocative efficiency in discussing the formation of new institutions as well as in evaluating the performance of existing arrangements.[55] Such analysts are apt to be highly critical of arrangements that encourage misallocations of scarce resources or that seem likely to produce outcomes lying inside the relevant welfare frontier. To be more concrete, they find much to criticize in arrangements allocating some of the choicest deep seabed mining sites to the Enterprise, imposing across-the-board percentage cuts on the production of CFCs by current producers, or reserving at least one orbital slot for each state that may become interested in satellite broadcasting.[56]

Yet those who negotiate the terms of international regimes seldom focus on these questions of allocative efficiency. In a negotiating environment featuring the rule of unanimity, they must occupy themselves, for the most part, with considerations of equity on the understanding that institutional bargaining in international society can succeed only when all of the major parties and interest groups come away with a sense that their primary concerns have been treated fairly. Allocative efficiency is an abstract concept. No one can determine whether the outcomes flowing from a given regime are in fact efficient until much later. And even then, economists often disagree vigorously in their assessments of the efficiency of observable outcomes. Equity, by contrast, is an immediate concern that evokes strong feelings on all sides. To return to the previous examples, no reasonable observer could have expected the less developed countries participating in the law of the sea negotiations to accept an arrangement that explicitly excluded the Enterprise from mining operations, thereby ensuring that a few highly industrialized states would dominate this commercial activity. There is a sense of fairness that everyone can relate to in across-the-board percentage cuts which is hard to match in more complex arrangements featuring charges or transferable production permits.[57] And it is surely easy to understand why the less developed countries regard as unjust any system that features the allocation of orbital slots on a first come, first served basis. While it is important to recognize that there are no objective standards of equity which can be applied to human affairs, it is also worth noting that identifiable community standards regarding equity do exist in specific social settings. And there is much to be said for the proposition that satisfying these standards is a necessary condition for international regime formation, whatever outside observers may think of the long-term consequences of the resultant arrangements with respect to allocative efficiency.

3. The existence of salient solutions (or focal points describable in simple terms) increases the probability of success in institutional bargaining.

Those endeavoring to craft statutes in municipal legislatures sometimes proceed, for tactical reasons, to construct formulas that are so complex or obscure that interest groups actually or potentially opposed to the relevant provisions have difficulty comprehending what is being put to a vote. No doubt, such tactics can prove useful in the efforts to form winning coalitions that dominate legislative bargaining. For the most part, by contrast, salience based on simplicity and clarity contributes to success in institutional bargaining involving numerous parties operating under unanimity rules. . . .[58] The salience of the formula of across-the-board percentage cuts in the production and consumption of CFCs certainly played a role in the successful effort to reach agreement on the 1987 protocol regarding ozone depletion. And the fact that early warning procedures are markedly simpler than provisions covering compensation for damages surely has much to do with the ease of achieving agreement on the early notification convention of 1986 as well as with the failure to incorporate compensation provisions into the two 1986 conventions relating to nuclear accidents.[59]

Conversely, it is hard to avoid the conclusion that the complexity of arrangements encompassing permits or licenses, production controls, technology transfers, the role of the Enterprise, and so forth bedeviled the effort to negotiate a regime for the deep seabed (known as the Area) in the law of the sea negotiations and played a significant role in accounting for the ambiguity of the final outcome. . . .

4. The probability of success in institutional bargaining rises when clear-cut and effective compliance mechanisms are available.

It is common knowledge among those who study collective-action problems that negotiators can fail to reach agreement on arrangements capable of yielding benefits for all parties concerned because they do not trust each other to comply with the terms of the arrangements once they are established.[60] This places a premium on the development of requirements that are easy to verify, as in the case of cuts in the production of CFCs by a small number of clearly identified producers.[61] It also accounts for the attractions of arrangements that are comparatively easy to police, such as the licensing system for deep seabed mining contemplated under the regime for the Area. . . .

At the same time, the lack of well-entrenched and properly financed supranational organizations in international society ensures that international regimes must rely heavily on the ability and willingness of individual members to elicit compliance with key provisions within their own jurisdictions.[62] A problem that has dogged the regime for endangered species, for example, is the sheer inability of many states to control the activities of poachers and others involved in the illegal trade in furs, skins, and animal parts within their jurisdictions.[63] Contrast this with the case of the fur seal regime, under which any harvest of seals was either closely regulated or actually carried out by state agencies, thereby enabling municipal governments to exercise effective control over the relevant activities whenever they chose to do so.[64] Under the circumstances, it is easy enough to understand why regime formation in international society is most apt to succeed when the participants can rely on relatively simple, nonintrusive compliance mechanisms that municipal governments can operate without undue effort or the need to expend scarce political resources. . . .

5. For the most part, exogenous shocks or crises increase the probability of success in efforts to negotiate the terms of international regimes.

Even in negotiations that allow considerable scope for integrative bargaining under a veil of uncertainty, institutional bargaining exhibits a natural tendency to bog down into a kind of sparring match in which participants jockey for positional advantages and lose track of their common interest in solving the relevant collective-action problems. All too often, the net result is a failure to reach agreement regarding feasible arrangements that would prove mutually beneficial. Given this background, it will come as no surprise that exogenous shocks or crises frequently play a significant role in breaking these logjams and propelling the parties toward agreement on the terms of institutional arrangements. . . . It is hard to overstate the shock value of the 1986 Chernobyl accident in motivating the parties to come to terms on at least some of the provisions of a regime for nuclear accidents within six months of this dramatic event.[65] And the 1985 discovery and subsequent publicization of an ozone "hole" over Antarctica emerged clearly as a driving force behind the efforts which produced the 1987 protocol on stratospheric ozone and which may well lead to additional regulatory arrangements in the near future, despite the fact that ozone depletion over Antarctica is not an immediate threat to major centers of human population.[66]

Compare these cases with the problem of global climate change. There is a good case to be made for the proposition that the disruptive impacts of nuclear accidents and ozone depletion are likely to pale by comparison with the consequences of the global warming trend over the next century.[67] To date, however, we have not experienced an exogenous shock or crisis in this realm that can compare with the Chernobyl accident or the ozone hole in capturing and galvanizing the attention of policymakers and broader publics alike. Talk of a creeping crisis with regard to global warming simply cannot produce the impact of the exogenous shocks mentioned previously as a force in breaking the logjams that commonly arise in institutional bargaining. This is no doubt frustrating to those working on a number of important collective-action problems. . . .

6. Institutional bargaining is likely to succeed when effective leadership emerges; it will fail in the absence of such leadership.

We come back, in the end, to the role of leadership in determining outcomes arising from institutional bargaining in international society. It is no exaggeration to say that efforts to negotiate the terms of international regimes are apt to succeed when one or more effective leaders emerge. In the absence of such leadership, they will fail. Those engaged in institutional bargaining must strive to invent options capable of solving major problems in a straight-forward fashion and to fashion deals that are acceptable to all. . . .

Entrepreneurial leaders in institutional bargaining are neither hegemons who can impose their will on others nor ethically motivated actors who seek to fashion workable institutional arrangements as a contribution to the common good or the supply of public goods in international society. Rather, international entrepreneurs are actors who are skilled in inventing new institutional arrangements and brokering the overlapping interests of parties concerned with a particular issue-area.[68] Such actors are surely self-interested in the sense that they seek gains for themselves either in the form of advantageous institutional arrangements if they are states or in the form of enhanced reputations or rewards if they are individuals. But this in no way detracts from the role that such entrepreneurial actors play. . . .

The preceding discussion suggests, as well, that nongovernmental organizations or even individuals can become leaders in efforts to form international regimes. The role of the Comité Spécial de l'Année Geophysique Internationale in establishing SCAR in 1958 and, through SCAR, in forming the regime for Antarctica in 1959 is comparatively well known. But the role of IUCN in promoting the regimes governing trade in endangered species and conservation of polar bears as well as the role of UNEP in creating the regime for controlling pollution in the Mediterranean Basin are also striking examples of success in international entrepreneurship. And the remarkable role of Mustafa Tolba, UNEP's executive director, in shepherding the negotiations regarding the protection of stratospheric ozone to a successful conclusion is worthy of much more systematic examination.[69] None of this means, of course, that states cannot assume leadership roles in negotiating international regimes; far from it. The activities of the United States in connection with the 1987 protocol on ozone, of France in the case of Mediterranean pollution control, and of several developing countries in the context of deep seabed mining stand out, to name just a few examples.

Neither the mainstream utilitarians nor the power theorists work with constructs capable of offering significant analytic leverage on the type of entrepreneurial leadership under consideration here. . . . It follows, therefore, that an enhanced effort to understand entrepreneurial leadership must loom large in any research program directed toward the study of institutional bargaining in international society.

CONCLUSION

The analytic perspectives currently dominating the study of regime formation in international society not only clash with one another but are also incapable of capturing some of the essential features of the processes involved in the formation of international regimes. The mainstream utilitarians fail to attach sufficient weight to an array of factors that can block the efforts of rational utility maximizers to realize feasible joint gains. Moreover, they base their accounts of regime formation on models of bargaining that are fundamentally inappropriate, even though they are well specified and appealing for their analytic tractability. For their part, the power theorists overemphasize the role of preponderant actors or hegemons in the formation of institutional arrangements at the international level. . . .

What is required to provide fully satisfactory answers to questions about regime formation is a model of institutional bargaining that takes into account the essential features of international society, including several that distinguish this social setting from the situations that prevail in domestic societies. The central section of this article, which sketches the defining characteristics of such a model of institutional bargaining, emphasizes the significance of unanimity rules, integrative bargaining, the veil of uncertainty, problem-solving activities, transnational alliances, and shifting involvements.

. . . The third section of the article initiates a process of deriving hypotheses about the determinants of success in institutional bargaining in international society. It points both to the role of structural considerations, such as the extent to which collective-action problems lend themselves to contractarian formulations, and to process considerations, such as the degree to which the parties can devise arrangements that meet the principal equity demands of all participants. Because the perspectives of the power theorists and the mainstream utilitarians have dominated prior thinking in this realm, our understanding of institutional bargaining in international society currently leaves much to be desired. . . .

NOTES

1. Regimes for natural resources and the environment presumably do not differ from other international regimes in any fundamental way, so their use as evidence entails no loss of generality in the analysis that follows.
2. For a sophisticated exposition of the concept of a contract zone or zone of agreement, see Howard Raiffa, *The Art and Science of Negotiation* (Cambridge, MA: Harvard University Press, 1982).
3. For a survey of the principal models, see Oran R. Young, ed., *Bargaining: Formal Theories of Negotiation* (Urbana: University of Illinois Press, 1975).
4. For a forceful expression of this point of view, see Gordon Tullock, *Private Wants, Public Means: An Economic Analysis of the Desirable Scope of Government* (New York: Basic Books, 1970), chap. 3.
5. See Susan Strange, "*Cave! hic dragones:* A Critique of Regime Analysis," in Stephen D. Krasner, ed., *International Regimes* (Ithaca, NY: Cornell University Press, 1983), pp. 337–54; Stephen D. Krasner, *Structural Conflict: The Third World Against Global Liberalism* (Berkeley: University of California Press, 1985); and Robert Gilpin, *The Political Economy of International Relations* (Princeton, NJ: Princeton University Press, 1987).
6. See Robert O. Keohane, "The Theory of Hegemonic Stability and Changes in International Economic Systems, 1967–1977," ACIS working paper no. 22, Center for International and Strategic Affairs, University of California, Los Angeles, 1980.
7. Although he may have come to regret it, it seems clear that Kindleberger's analysis of international economic relations in the 1930s played an important part in the development of this set of intellectual concerns. See Charles P. Kindleberger, *The World in Depression, 1929–1939* (Berkeley: University of California Press, 1973).
8. See Lyster, *International Wildlife Law,* chap. 3; and Oran R. Young, *Natural Resources and the State* (Berkeley: University of California Press, 1981), chap. 3.
9. Gillian D. Triggs, ed., *The Antarctic Treaty Regime: Law, Environment and Resources* (Cambridge: Cambridge University Press, 1987).
10. Peter M. Haas, "Do Regimes Matter? A Study of Evolving Pollution Control Policies for the Mediterranean Sea," paper presented at the annual convention of the International Studies Association, April 1987.
11. See Lyster, *International Wildlife Law,* chap. 12; and Laura H. Kosloff and Mark C. Trexler, "The Convention on International Trade in Endangered Species: No Carrot, But Where's the Stick?" *Environmental Law Report* 17 (July 1987), pp. 10222–36.
12. Philip Shabecoff, "Ozone Agreement Is Hailed as a First Step in Cooperation," *The New York Times,* 5 May 1987, pp. C1 and C7.
13. See also Duncan Snidal, "The Limits of Hegemonic Stability Theory," *International Organization* 39 (Autumn 1985), pp. 579–614.

14. Jeffrey Hart, "Three Approaches to the Measurement of Power in International Relations," *International Organization* 30 (Spring 1976), pp. 299–305.

15. The growth of international interdependencies in the modern era reinforces the argument of this paragraph, since this growth drives up the opportunity costs associated with all efforts to exercise power. See Oran R. Young, "Interdependencies in World Politics," *International Journal* 24 (Autumn 1969), pp. 726–50.

16. For an extensive analysis of blocking as well as winning coalitions, see William H. Riker, *A Theory of Political Coalitions* (New Haven, CT: Yale University Press, 1962).

17. Charles P. Kindleberger, "Hierarchy Versus Inertial Cooperation," *International Organization* 40 (Autumn 1986), pp. 845–46.

18. On privileged groups, see Mancur Olson, Jr., *The Logic of Collective Action* (Cambridge, MA: Harvard University Press, 1965), chap. 1.

19. For a discussion of political leadership as a form of entrepreneurship, see Norman Frohlich, Joe A. Oppenheimer, and Oran R. Young, *Political Leadership and Collective Goods* (Princeton, NJ: Princeton University Press, 1971).

20. See Russell Hardin, *Collective Action* (Baltimore, MD: Johns Hopkins University Press, 1982); and Kenneth A. Oye, ed., *Cooperation Under Anarchy* (Princeton, NJ: Princeton University Press, 1986).

21. For a seminal example, see James M. Buchanan and Gordon Tullock, *The Calculus of Consent* (Ann Arbor: University of Michigan Press, 1962). For a variety of perspectives on the use of public choice theory to examine institutional arrangements, see Clifford S. Russell, ed., *Collective Decision Making: Applications from Public Choice Theory* (Baltimore, MD: Johns Hopkins University Press, 1979).

22. Thomas C. Schelling, *The Strategy of Conflict* (Cambridge, MA: Harvard University Press, 1960).

23. Robert D. Putnam, "Diplomacy and Domestic Politics: The Logic of Two-Level Games," *International Organization* 42 (Summer 1988), pp. 427–60.

24. For a more general account, see James K. Sebenius, "Negotiation Arithmetic: Adding and Subtracting Issues and Parties," *International Organization* 37 (Spring 1983), pp. 281–316.

25. For an analysis of this issue, treated as the problem of cheating, see Schelling, *The Strategy of Conflict*.

26. On the illegal trade in endangered species, see Kosloff and Trexler, "The Convention on International Trade in Endangered Species."

27. See Young, *Bargaining*. Part I of this book deals with game-theoretic models of bargaining based on the concept of the negotiation set. Part II turns to economic models of bargaining stemming from the Edgeworth box construct.

28. Young, *Bargaining*, pp. 391–408.

29. See Duncan Snidal, "Coordination Versus Prisoner's Dilemma: Implications for International Cooperation and Regimes," *American Political Science Review* 79 (December 1985), pp. 923–42; and Kenneth A. Oye, "Explaining Cooperation Under Anarchy," in Oye, *Cooperation Under Anarchy*, pp. 1–24.

30. Anatol Rapoport, *Two-Person Game Theory: The Essential Ideas* (Ann Arbor: University of Michigan Press, 1966), chap. 12.

31. In principle, we can think of an Edgeworth box in n-space. But such a construct would not be analytically tractable.

32. For a classic account of the principal constructs of n-person game theory, see R. Duncan Luce and Howard Raiffa, *Games and Decisions* (New York: John Wiley, 1957).

33. Of course, this does not rule out an array of devices, threats, promises, or side pay-

ments that are aimed at inducing parties to accept particular institutional arrangements. For an account that emphasizes the attractions of the unanimity rule, see Buchanan and Tullock, *The Calculus of Consent.*

34. The term "productive bargaining" is from John G. Cross, *The Economics of Bargaining* (New York: Basic Books, 1969). The term "positional bargaining" is from Roger Fisher and William Ury, *Getting to Yes* (Harmondsworth, U.K.: Penguin, 1981).

35. Richard Walton and Robert B. McKersie, *A Behavioral Theory of Negotiations* (New York: McGraw-Hill, 1965), chaps. 2–5.

36. For a classic account of such tactics, see Schelling, *The Strategy of Conflict.*

37. The result is a kind of collective analog to Simon's notion of "satisficing" with regard to individual decision making. See James G. March and Herbert A. Simon, *Organizations* (New York: John Wiley, 1958), especially chap. 3.3.

38. John Rawls, *A Theory of Justice* (Cambridge, MA: Harvard University Press, 1971), especially pp. 136–42.

39. Geoffrey Brennan and James M. Buchanan, *The Reason of Rules: Constitutional Political Economy* (Cambridge: Cambridge University Press, 1985), p. 30.

40. For a straightforward descriptive account, see Marvin S. Soroos, *Beyond Sovereignty: The Challenge of Global Policy* (Columbia: University of South Carolina Press, 1986), chap. 8.

41. For helpful background on this case, see Allan S. Miller and Irving M. Mintzer, "The Sky Is the Limit: Strategies for Protecting the Ozone Layer," *Research Report,* no. 3 (Washington, DC: World Resources Institute, 1986).

42. For a helpful account rooted in an analysis of the law of the sea negotiations, see Robert I. Friedheim, *Negotiating the Ocean Regime,* work in progress.

43. For additional comments on the role of negotiating texts, see Raiffa, *The Art and Science of Negotiation.*

44. Putnam, "Diplomacy and Domestic Politics."

45. Haas, "Do Regimes Matter?"

46. Polar Research Board, *Antarctic Treaty System: An Assessment* (Washington, DC: National Academy Press, 1986).

47. The recent work of Peter Haas and his colleagues on the role of epistemic communities in regime formation is suggestive in this context.

48. See also Fred Charles Ikle, *How Nations Negotiate* (New York: Harper & Row, 1964).

49. For an accessible account of a number of these problems as well as techniques for coping with them, see I. William Zartman and Maureen R. Berman, *The Practical Negotiator* (New Haven, CT: Yale University Press, 1982).

50. Sebenius, "Negotiation Arithmetic."

51. The fact that some countries, such as the Federal Republic of Germany, are both major producers of acid precipitation and important victims of this form of pollution makes the problem of devising a regime to control acid precipitation more tractable in Europe than it is in North America.

52. Oran R. Young, *International Cooperation: Building Regimes for Natural Resources and the Environment* (Ithaca, NY: Cornell University Press, 1989), chap. 6.

53. See also the projections in Miller and Mintzer, "The Sky Is the Limit."

54. For some interesting projections regarding this point, see E. F. Roots, "The Cost of Inaction: An Example from Climate Change Studies," unpublished paper, 1988.

55. For a helpful introduction to the principal approaches to the concept of efficiency, see Robert Dorfman and Nancy S. Dorfman, eds., *The Economics of the Environment,* 2nd ed. (New York: Norton, 1977), pp. 1–37. For an explicit assertion regarding the appropriateness of emphasizing efficiency in this context, see Ross D. Eckert, "Exploitation

of Deep Ocean Minerals: Regulatory Mechanisms and United States Policy," *Journal of Law and Economics* 17 (April 1974), pp. 143–77.

56. See Daniel J. Dudek, "Chlorofluorocarbon Policy: Choice and Consequences," a paper distributed by the Environmental Defense Fund, April 1987; and Gregory C. Staple, "The New World Satellite Order: A Report from Geneva," *American Journal of International Law* 80 (July 1986), pp. 699–720.

57. On the distinctions among these policy instruments, see Dudek, "Chlorofluorocarbon Policy."

58. For a seminal account of the role of salience in facilitating the convergence of expectations in such settings, see Schelling, *The Strategy of Conflict.*

59. For an excellent account of the prior legal developments leading to these conventions, see Phillippe J. Sands, "The Chernobyl Accident and Public International Law," paper prepared for a conference on global disasters and international communications flows, Washington, DC, October 1986.

60. See also Schelling, *The Strategy of Conflict;* and Robert Axelrod, *The Evolution of Cooperation* (New York: Basic Books, 1984).

61. Konrad von Moltke, "Memorandum on International Chlorofluorocarbon Controls and Free Trade," a paper distributed by the Institute for European Environmental Policy, 1987.

62. For a more general discussion of compliance in decentralized social settings, see Oran R. Young, *Compliance and Public Authority, A Theory with International Applications* (Baltimore, MD: Johns Hopkins University Press, 1979).

63. Kosloff and Trexler, "The Convention on International Trade in Endangered Species."

64. Young, *Natural Resources and the State,* chap. 3.

65. Stuart Diamond, "Chernobyl Causing Big Revisions in Global Nuclear Power Policies," *The New York Times,* 27 October 1986, pp. A1 and A10.

66. Shabecoff, "Ozone Agreement Is Hailed as a First Step in Cooperation."

67. In November 1988, for example, a broad coalition of American environmental groups designated the global warming trend as the most serious environmental threat of the foreseeable future.

68. Frohlich, Oppenheimer, and Young, *Political Leadership and Collective Goods.*

69. Similar comments are probably in order regarding the role of Hans Blix, the executive director of the International Atomic Energy Agency, in promoting the 1986 conventions relating to nuclear accidents.

Do Regimes Matter? Epistemic Communities and Mediterranean Pollution Control

Peter M. Haas

Do regimes matter?[1] Much attention has been paid to regime creation and regime maintenance, but few authors have studied the substantive nature of regimes or their direct effects on national behavior. Regimes are not simply static summaries of rules and norms; they may also serve as important vehicles for international learning that produce convergent state policies. This role for regimes has been seriously underestimated in the theoretical and empirical literature, which has tended to focus on two correlates of regimes—political order and economic growth—rather than on the transformative processes that regimes may initiate or foster. The literature has also paid little attention to the fact that some regimes stem from communities of shared knowledge and not simply from domestic or transnational interest groups.

Through the examination of the Mediterranean Action Plan (Med Plan), a regime for marine pollution control in the Mediterranean Sea, I seek to demonstrate that this regime played a key role in altering the balance of power within Mediterranean governments by empowering a group of experts, who then contributed to the development of convergent state policies in compliance with the regime. In turn, countries in which these new actors acquired channels to decision making became the strongest proponents of the regime.[2]

The Med Plan is widely hailed as a success. Commentators from a variety of viewpoints cite it as the crowning achievement of the United Nations Environment Programme's (UNEP's) Regional Seas Programme and an exemplary case of interstate cooperation.[3] Its success is distinctive because of the number of compelling factors militating against it. The extensive pollution of the Mediterranean is the result of intense coastal population pressures, combined with largely unregulated industrial, municipal, and agricultural emission practices. Constructing sufficient sewage treatment facilities region-wide to handle the wastes generated by up to 200 million summertime tourists and residents would require a regional investment of $10 to $15 billion over a ten-year period. . . .

Pollution of the Mediterranean Sea was widely regarded as a collective goods problem, since one country's pollutants could wash up on its neighbor's beaches. The Riviera, for example, is polluted by discharges from Spain, France, Italy, and Monaco. If France were the only country to build sewage treatment plants and to require coastal industries to reduce their emissions, the quality of the coast would only be partially improved, and French industry would be hampered by additional production costs that would not be met by Spanish and Italian competitors. . . .

Negotiating the regime was difficult. Countries disagreed about which pollutants to control. Developed countries wanted to control all sources of pollution, whereas many of the less developed countries (LDCs) saw this as a thinly veiled attempt to control their industrialization practices and thus opted for the control of only municipal and tanker wastes. . . .

Even though the Med Plan was successfully negotiated, its maintenance poses an anomaly in terms of conventional understanding of how regimes operate. The most intriguing puzzle regarding the Med Plan's effectiveness is why states comply, given the fact that so many were initially opposed to it. . . . The highly technical dimension of the Med Plan makes it a "most expected case" for an explanation that emphasizes consensual scientific knowledge. However, the diversity of political interests in the region and the widespread political antipathy to international environmental protection initially inhibited the easy influence of scientists on their governments.

The Med Plan's successful creation was promoted by a community of ecologists and marine scientists. They served in UNEP's secretariat and were often granted formal decision-making authority in national administrations. In addition to their involvement in the policymaking process, they were given responsibility for enforcing and supervising pollution control measures. The members of this group became partisans for adopting the regime, complying with it, and strengthening it to deal with more pollutants from more sources. Following the involvement of these new actors, state interests came to increasingly reflect their environmental view, as seen in diplomats' statements and government policies, and state behavior came to reflect their interests as well, as was evident from state investment patterns and diplomatic actions. Compliance, as measured by the adoption of new policies which are consonant with the regime's norms and which ease its enforcement, has been strongest in countries in which the experts were able to consolidate their power most firmly.

As the case of the Med Plan shows, regimes may be transformative, leading to the empowerment of new groups of actors who can change state interests and practices. . . .

THE MEDITERRANEAN ACTION PLAN

. . . Within the formal framework of the 1975 Mediterranean Action Plan, the regime consists of legal, assessment, management, and administrative components. Following the adoption of the 1976 Convention for the Protection of the Mediterranean Sea Against Pollution (the "Barcelona Convention"), four protocols were negotiated to govern dumping from ships and aircraft (1976), to enhance cooperation in cases of oil spill emergencies (1976), to control pollution from land-based sources (1980), and to establish specially protected areas (1982). The Barcelona Convention and these protocols have been ratified or acceded to by all of the Mediterranean coastal states, with the exception of Albania, and are now in force. In addition, a center to develop integrated planning approaches for future coastal development was established in Sophia-Antipolis, France, and a center to coordinate seven specific projects aimed at harmonizing environmental and development objectives was established in Split, Yugoslavia. Thirteen joint research and seven monitoring projects to evaluate the quality of the Mediterranean have been carried out since 1977. Administrative arrangements include a headquarters unit in Athens, with a small professional staff and a 1987 budget of $4.1 million. . . .

. . . [The] norms [of the regime] are made abundantly clear in Paragraph 1 of Article 4 of the Barcelona Convention:

> The Contracting Parties shall individually or jointly take all appropriate measures in accordance with the provision of this Convention and those protocols in force to which they are party, to prevent, abate and combat pollution of the Mediterranean Sea Area and to protect and enhance the marine environment in that area.[4]

The rules and decision-making procedures consist of annual intergovernmental meetings at which the secretariat's administration of the joint monitoring projects is reviewed and the Contracting Parties' attempts to develop and enforce national legislation for pollution control are held up to nominal public scrutiny. A weak provision for arbitration exists but has never been invoked.

Until 1976, there was a very loose framework for evaluation. After 1976, the rules became stronger as the parties adopted protocols covering a more comprehensive range of sources and types of pollutants. The rules have grown in scope from banning marine dumping to controlling a wide variety of land-based sources of pollution, including agricultural sprays and industrial and municipal wastes. They also govern pollutants transmitted to the Mediterranean through rivers and the atmosphere. In addition to its early focus on dumping and oil spills, the Med Plan now "eliminates" the emissions of nine groups of toxic substances, "limits" the emissions of thirteen groups of less hazardous substances, and requires states to develop specific guidelines for control of these substances. The specific substances are identified in the technical annexes to the land-based sources protocol. Interim ambient quality-control standards for water in recreational areas and shellfish grounds were adopted in September 1985. An inventory of products containing the regulated substances is to be completed by the mid-1990s, along with specific ambient and emission standards. An additional annex to control pollution transmitted through the atmosphere is due to be completed in 1989. Effective control of oil pollution will require the construction of facilities to receive oily ballast material in most major Mediterranean ports, at a cost of over $150 million.

Following the evolution of a stronger regime, the quality of the Mediterranean has improved. Beaches have been protected from organic wastes, such as municipal garbage. Environmental quality data on inorganic pollutants, such as industrial wastes, remain anecdotal at best.[5] In 1976, about 33 percent of Mediterranean beaches were unsafe for swimming. Ten years later, only 20 percent were deemed unsafe by World Health Organization (WHO) and UNEP standards.[6] This improvement is largely due to the construction of sewage treatment plants inspired by the Med Plan. These plants have been built or are under construction in Tel Aviv, Aleppo, Athens, Naples, Genoa, Istanbul, Marseilles, Nice, Toulon, Alexandria, Tripoli, and Algiers.[7] In addition, ballast reception facilities are under construction or planned in ports in Greece, Yugoslavia, Egypt, Tunisia, and Turkey.[8] Between 1982 and 1984, Spain lowered the number of contaminated beaches from thirty-six to eight.[9] Between 1972 and 1982, France achieved a 93 percent reduction in chemical oxygen demand, a 90 percent reduction in suspended solids, a 95 percent reduction in hydrocarbons, a 92 percent reduction in phenols, and a 92 percent reduction in mercury emissions from some plants in the Berre Lagoon, a containment tank for wastes from the industrial zone of Fos. This was at a cost of $96 million.[10] Toxic emissions into the Rhone were reduced by 44 percent during the 1970s, and mercury emissions dropped sevenfold.[11] As the monitoring and research components of the regime collect and analyze more data and make the data available, a more sensitive evaluation of the regime's effectiveness in controlling pollution may be possible.

Although it is extremely difficult to confirm, regional scientists concur that the quality of the Mediterranean is better than it would have been without the Med Plan, and preliminary studies suggest that the pollution level has at least stabilized and is now about the same as it was in the early 1970s. In light of the rapid coastal population growth and industrialization during the past two decades,[12] maintaining the Mediterranean at a constant level of pollution is quite an accomplishment.

THE ECOLOGICAL EPISTEMIC COMMUNITY AND THE MED PLAN

The success of the Med Plan is attributable to the involvement of ecologists and marine scientists who set the international agenda and directed their own states toward support of international efforts and toward the introduction of strong pollution control measures at home.

In the Mediterranean in the early 1970s, government leaders became increasingly concerned about the extent of pollution of the Mediterranean Sea. . . . Therefore, they turned to the region's marine scientists for information and to UNEP for the development of environmental policies and the drafting of a treaty to protect the Mediterranean Sea.

UNEP officials, some secretariat members from other specialized agencies (notably WHO and the Food and Agriculture Organization [FAO]), and likeminded governmental officials in the region comprised an "epistemic community."[13] Together, they acted as an informally coordinated lobbying group. They also shared a common ecological outlook. . . . Their political values entailed a belief that all governments should actively cooperate and intervene domestically to protect the environment, including the universal adoption of more comprehensive, rational forms of economic planning to internalize environmental considerations into virtually all forms of policymaking.

UNEP officials also forged transnational alliances with regional marine scientists, who shared an interest in controlling specific pollutants but lacked the overall holistic, causal framework that ecologists accepted. Effectively acting in harmony with UNEP, these scientists had the combined impact of persuading their governments to support the UNEP measures to control as many sources and types of pollution as possible, to move for stronger measures for their control, and to comply with Med Plan policies. Later, as environmental ministries were established in the Mediterranean countries, these scientists were invited to join their staffs, as were people who were firmly in the epistemic community.

Ecological principles were embraced by members of the epistemic community as their core set of beliefs about cause-and-effect relationships. Ecology as a discipline asserts the unity of narrower scientific disciplines and conceptions of the world. . . .

Coming into popularity following World War II, ecology is fundamentally a framework in which other disciplines may be assimilated. . . . As such, it facilitated the formation of coalitions among scientists, because most contending views about what are important research questions and the appropriate levels and methods of analysis may be integrated within such a broad framework.

By promoting the adoption of a very broad definition of "pollution" which emanated from an ecological perspective, UNEP and members of the ecological epistemic community were able to encompass more parochial interests under its umbrella. The definition reads:

> "Pollution" means the introduction by man, directly or indirectly, of substances or energy into the marine environment resulting in such deleterious effects as harm to living resources, hazards to human health, hindrance to marine activities including fishing, impairment of quality for use of sea-water and reduction of amenities.[14]

Such a broad formulation of concerns blurred the distinctions between otherwise incompatible views, and this enabled UNEP and other members of its epistemic community to tie in with the broadest possible constituency by incorporating the concerns of many groups within those of UNEP. Many of the individual marine scientists and officials of specific organizations had different views about the nature of the problem of Mediterranean pollution and the appropriate remedies, reflecting their various backgrounds and expertise in disciplines such as marine biology, marine chemistry, marine geology, oceanography, microbiology, public health, and civil engineering. For instance, marine biologists and FAO officials were concerned with the positive and negative effects of organic pollutants on fishery yields. These pollutants largely come from municipal wastes. On the other hand, public health officials and WHO representatives, whose focus is on human health and communicable diseases, were concerned with the adverse effects of inorganic industrial wastes as well as the untreated municipal wastes that concerned marine biologists. These perspectives gave rise to mutually exclusive policy proposals, as FAO officials suggested that some organic wastes were useful nutrients for relatively hungry fish in the Mediterranean, whereas public health officials advocated the closure of beaches exposed to such wastes. Within UNEP's broad definition, research and policies could be developed to satisfy each group individually while avoiding a direct confrontation between them.

UNEP cemented the alliances by funding scientific research that was not supported by domestic sources, providing sophisticated monitoring equipment and training in its use, and publicizing the research findings. . . .

The external support from UNEP enhanced the scientists' domestic prestige and strengthened their domestic political base. Although their work was only loosely coordinated by UNEP, the knowledge gained through collaborative efforts established or reinforced their authority in the issue-area of marine pollution control. When consulted by their governments, the scientists provided congruent policy advice about domestic pollution control measures and encouraged them to support the norms and principles outlined in the Med Plan. . . .

Politics were also important in the negotiation of the Med Plan protocols. A number of compromises satisfied the demands of different groups. The protocols included pollutants of concern to both developed and developing countries, and the LDCs received monitoring equipment from UNEP. Arab-Israeli conflicts were downplayed as a result of the deliberately low profile stance adopted by Israeli delegates and the decision of UNEP not to invite the Palestine Liberation Organization to attend. The definition of the Mediterranean's geographic scope consciously excluded the Soviet bloc. . . .

THE EPISTEMIC COMMUNITY'S INFLUENCE ON THE MED PLAN

In 1972, there had been very few measures for pollution control in the Mediterranean states. After the regime's successful negotiation, however, member countries began to introduce measures to accomplish the Med Plan objectives. From an early antipathy to dealing with environmental problems, many LDCs became much more constructive at international meetings. . . .

The actual form of policies varies among countries. Different countries specify different emission standards, ban different substances, and point to different indicators for cleanliness. Many LDCs simply apply thresholds suggested in the WHO's *Technical Reports Series.* Yet the movement in all cases is in the same direction, in conformity with the Med Plan's enunciated norms and principles.

The countries that have been the most supportive of the Med Plan are those in which the epistemic community has been strongest. Phrased slightly differently, the variance in compliance with the Med Plan is largely explained by the amount of involvement of the epistemic community in domestic policymaking. With increasing involvement of the epistemic community, countries became more supportive of the Med Plan, became more constructive participants at international meetings, and introduced more comprehensive pollution control policies at home, often supported by increased domestic funding for pollution control. The epistemic community influenced both foreign and domestic environmental policies.

Pressures for compliance generally came from environmental ministries. . . . These ministries were either coordinative or regulatory. While coordinative ministries were merely responsible for encouraging other governmental bodies to consider environmental factors in their activities, regulatory ministries had direct responsibility for formulating and enforcing environmental policy.

In the early 1970s, most of the countries established coordinative environmental ministries, in keeping with the holistic environmental ethos galvanized by preparations for the 1972 United Nations Conference on the Human Environment. . . .

The ecological epistemic community has been able to use the administrative base provided by environmental ministries to effectively promote its own preferred vision of pollution control, which is broader in scope and more clearly delineated than the vague, formal missions assigned to the ministries in various countries. In this respect, it has been a story of putting the foxes in charge of the chicken coop. For instance, in Israel and Greece, the foreign ministries ceded responsibility for Med Plan negotiations to the Israeli environmental protection service[15] and to the Greek national council for physical planning and the environment (NCPPE), respectively, which were both staffed by members of the epistemic community. The NCPPE was instructed by its foreign affairs ministry to be "pro-environment," in essence making the Greek delegation an active environmental lobbyist and giving the scientific constituency within the government a free hand to formulate and pursue policy. With the NCPPE as a springboard, the staff introduced new domestic environmental legislation to Parliament and continually served as an "honest broker" to mediate conflicts at intergovernmental meetings.

In France, ecologists have usually been appointed as major officials of the environmental ministry, although their beliefs have not always been shared by the head of the ministry, whose appointment varies with the administration in power. In Algeria, the members of the environmental ministry and the supporting body of research marine scientists have not been members of the epistemic community, although they have shared its concerns about controlling specific pollutants.

The importance of scientific access to government decision making is underscored by the Italian experience. With a large and experienced scientific community, replete with individuals who deeply believed in UNEP's message, but without an active environmental ministry for them to channel their concerns, domestic policy did not change for several years. . . .

A more detailed analysis of the process by which Algeria and Egypt came to support the Med Plan indicates the key role played by the epistemic community. At first, both of these countries were strongly opposed to introducing measures that would inhibit industrial growth and were highly suspicious of French motivations. However, following the involvement of the epistemic community, these positions were reversed. This is particularly striking given the fact that, as small countries, both would have been able to free-ride on arrangements once they were supported by France.

Algerian leaders had always been intransigent in asserting the primacy of industrial development over environmental protection. In the early 1970s, they opposed any pollution control measures that might impede or retard economic development, and they did not send a delegation to the 1976 Barcelona Conference. Following the inclusion of marine scientists in the Algerian administration after 1975, government preferences began to change, elevating pollution control to a more equal footing with economic development. Algeria acceded to the Barcelona Convention in 1981, ratified the protocol for control of pollution from land-based sources in 1983, and also adopted national environmental legislation in 1983. . . .

The fact that the 1983 legislation includes the control of industrial wastes is an indication of the change in Algerian position from refusing to accept constraints on economic development to imposing them.

These Algerian policy changes in the early 1980s followed the entrenchment of marine scientists in the government and their provision of domestically produced analyses of marine pollution. The Algerian scientific community originally obtained access to the government through its national committee for the environment, established in 1974, and its subsequent institutionalization within the hydrologic ministry, which became the secretary of state for forests and development. In 1983, a national agency for environmental protection was formed.

Policy advice also came from scientists in the Centre de Recherches Océanographiques et des Pêches (CROP) in Algiers. CROP began monitoring pollution in 1975, in response to fears of a decrease in fishery production due to pollution. UNEP gave CROP scientists a gas chromatograph and an atomic absorption spectrophotometer to monitor industrial and agricultural wastes and also provided them with training in their use. With this new equipment, the Algerian assessment of levels of oil and other industrial wastes was consonant with that of other countries around the Mediterranean Basin. . . . The evidence of increasing marine pollution was finally accepted by the early 1980s, and policies began to change.

The Algerian position also became much more constructive at Med Plan meetings after 1979. Delegates from CROP and the hydrologic ministry began to accompany foreign ministry officials to these meetings. . . .

France provides the limiting case for the extent of an epistemic community's influence. Although the epistemic community consolidated its power in the French environmental ministry and was able to redirect domestic planning policy, it was relatively weak in influencing foreign environmental policy because the Quai d'Orsay would not cede authority to it. . . .

The environmental ministry . . . was unable to prevail with regard to French Med Plan positions. Internationally, the foreign affairs ministry had broader geopolitical ambitions in the Mediterranean to which the Med Plan was subordinated, and it therefore kept the scientists on a tight rein. The Quai d'Orsay supported overall compliance with international environmental law and was willing to defer to the environmental ministry's abiding interest in integrated environmental planning, about which it had no interest; but French delegates from the foreign affairs ministry were reluctant to accept the provisions in the protocol for control of land-based sources of pollution which covered river-borne and airborne transmission of pollutants and which banned the emission of radioactive substances, even though the environmental ministry supported them. At the Conference of Plenipotentiaries for the Land-Based Sources Protocol, scientific delegates had to telephone the Quai in Paris to authorize compromises.

Domestically, the epistemic community had a much stronger impact in France, since it was able to utilize its bureaucratic leverage. Because French scientists already had extensive domestic resources and ongoing research activities, they had much less direct interest in the Med Plan than did their colleagues from other Mediterranean countries, who could obtain needed equipment and prestige by participating. Thus, UNEP's deliberate strategy of transnational alliance building would not work well in France, and UNEP officials did not try hard to mobilize French scientists, in part because they did not want to appear to the LDCs to be closely linked to the regionally dominant French. However, although less involved than their Mediterranean colleagues in the direct policymaking associated with the Med Plan, the marine scientists in the French environmental ministry did share the beliefs of their Mediterranean colleagues about the causes of marine pollution and the need to control them, so they advocated policies similar to those advocated elsewhere by marine scientists. . . .

EPISTEMIC COMMUNITIES AND GOVERNMENTAL LEARNING

In response to new information about Mediterranean pollution, the states in which the epistemic community was most active have not only developed more sophisticated environmental policies to control more pollutants but have also sought to develop economic plans that anticipate possible environmental degradation through the preparation of environmental impact assessments. To the extent that governmental planning agencies actually follow such procedures, one may say that double-loop learning about the relative role of the environment in overall economic development occurred. In the absence of these procedures, single-loop learning is evident in efforts to incrementally manage more types and sources of pollutants.[16]

Learning occurred in two domains, through a different process in each. In the domain of foreign policy, governments committed themselves to a new environmental regime for the Mediterranean. Learning seems to have occurred by persuasion, as marine scientists and members of the ecological epistemic community informed foreign ministry officials of the need to control specific pollutants. . . .

In the domain of domestic policy, by which the states complied with the Med Plan, learning occurred through bureaucratic preemption of policy-making by the environmental ministries. The epistemic community usurped decision-making authority and promoted pollution control policies consistent with its own perspective. As observed earlier, no learning occurred in countries in which the epistemic community was unable to appropriate control.

Throughout, changes in government policy did not directly follow from objective reports of coastal pollution or from the existence of consensual knowledge. In Algeria, for instance, governmental concern about changes in environmental quality were expressed only after the domestic marine scientists were identified as authoritative experts and had become entrenched in the government. When foreign observers had reported the same phenomena in the early 1970s, the Algerian foreign ministry officials had been deaf to outside advice.[17] They had also ignored extensive domestic evidence of coastal pollution from Algerian industry.

Learning did not result solely from the persuasive force of shared understanding. Persuasion did account for a small amount of the regime's broadened scope to include more sources and forms of pollution, but national compliance came from the power acquired by a new group of actors.

CONCLUSION

The most notable aspect of the Med Plan is the domestic compliance with it. In the literature on international relations, few studies have focused on the reasons for which states actually comply with regimes. As argued above, coercion, public opinion, and anticipation of benefits do not fully explain the extent of compliance. The Med Plan's success was due to the regime's introduction of new actors who influenced national behavior and contributed to the development of coordinated and convergent policymaking in the Mediterranean states. In the face of uncertainty, a publicly recognized group with an unchallenged claim to understanding the technical nature of the regime's substantive issue-area was able to interpret for traditional decision makers facts or events in new ways and thereby lead to new forms of behavior. . . .[18]

NOTES

1. See Oran Young, "International Regimes: Toward a New Theory of Institutions," *World Politics* 39 (October 1986), pp. 115–17; Robert O. Keohane, "The Study of International Regimes and the Classical Tradition in International Relations," paper presented at the 1986 annual meeting of the American Political Science Association, p. 14; and Stephan Haggard and Beth A. Simmons, "Theories of International Regimes," *International Organization* 41 (Summer 1987), pp. 491–517.
2. For a detailed analysis of the negotiation of the Med Plan, compliance with it, and a more thorough testing of alternative theoretical explanations of its success, see Peter M. Haas, *Saving the Mediterranean: The Politics of International Environmental Cooperation* (New York: Columbia University Press, 1990). For other recent studies on environmental regimes, see Lynton Caldwell, *International Environmental Policy* (Durham, NC: Duke University Press, 1984); and Nigel Haigh, *EEC Environmental Policy and Britain* (London: Environmental Data Services, 1984). Although Haigh does not formally refer to regimes, he analyzes British compliance with the corpus of the European Economic Community (EEC) environmental directives that may reasonably be construed to constitute a regime. His conclusions about compliance, however, are equivocal.
3. See Peter Hulm, "The Regional Seas Programme: What Fate for UNEP's Crown Jewels?" *Ambio* 12 (January 1983); and George P. Smith II, "The U.N. and the Environment," in The Heritage Foundation, *A World Without a U.N.* (Washington, D.C.: The Heritage Foundation, 1984), pp. 44–45. The Med Plan serves as the model for ten other regional arrangements for controlling marine pollution.
4. UNEP, Convention for the Protection of the Mediterranean Sea Against Pollution and Its Related Protocols, 1982, p. 8.
5. The state-of-the-art estimates of levels of Mediterranean pollution are presented in UNEP's "Review of the State of the Marine Environment: Mediterranean Regional Report," GESAMP WG 26, SG 26/C/1, 19 December 1986. At present, environmental quality data are aggregated for regions of the Mediterranean Sea so as not to embarrass individual coastal states.
6. *The New York Times,* 21 October 1986, p. C3.
7. Ibid.; and Paul Evan Ress, "Mediterranean Sea Becoming Cleaner," *Environmental Conservation* 13 (Autumn 1986), pp. 267–68.

8. UNEP, *The Siren: News from UNEP's Oceans and Coastal Areas Programme*, no. 34, September 1987, p. 25.

9. See *El Pais* (Spain), 8 November 1984; and Comisión Interministerial del Medio Ambiente (CIMA), *Medio ambiente en España* (Madrid: CIMA, 1984), p. 179.

10. See Secrétariat Permanent pour les Problèmes de Pollution Industrielle de la Région de Fos-l'Etang de Berre, "Lutte contre la pollution des eaux—Etat des rejets industriels," no date; and *Presse Environment*, no. 379, 23 May 1980, p. 1.

11. *Le Monde,* 18 June 1980, p. 40.

12. Annual industrial growth from 1973 to 1984 ranged from 10.3 percent in Egypt to 1.4 percent in France, according to World Bank, *World Development Report* (New York: Oxford University Press, 1986), pp. 182–83. Tourist receipts in the Mediterranean area grew every year during this period. See International Union of Official Travel Organizations, *International Travel Statistics,* various years; and World Tourism Organization, *World Tourism Statistics,* various years.

13. The term has been used in the literature on sociology of knowledge and has been adapted for use in international relations to refer to a specific community of experts sharing a belief in a common set of cause-and-effect relationships as well as common values to which policies governing these relationships will be applied. For a good survey of the sociology of knowledge usage, see Burkart Holzner and John Marx, *Knowledge Application: The Knowledge System in Society* (Boston: Allyn & Bacon, 1979), chaps. 4 and 5, especially pp. 107–11, in which the authors present a lengthy discussion of epistemic communities, including the large community of scientists who share a faith in the scientific method. The beliefs of the ecologists which I discuss here are much more specific, since in addition to sharing a belief in the scientific method as the way to verify their understanding, they also share beliefs in specific causal models. A very similar notion is that of "thought collective," discussed by Ludwig Fleck in *Genesis and Development of a Scientific Fact* (Chicago: University of Chicago Press, 1979). See John Gerard Ruggie, "International Responses to Technology: Concepts and Trends," *International Organization* 29 (Summer 1975), pp. 569–70, in which Ruggie takes an approach similar to Foucault's use of "episteme" but associates epistemic communities with broader widespread social beliefs rather than with the more limited set of shared beliefs held by experts. See also Ernst B. Haas, "Why Collaborate? Issue Linkage and International Regimes," *World Politics* 32 (April 1980), pp. 357–405.

14. UNEP, Convention for the Protection of the Mediterranean Sea Against Pollution, Article 2, Paragraph (a). For narrower definitions of pollution which arise from other disciplinary approaches, see M. Tomczak, Jr., "Defining Marine Pollution: A Comparison of Definitions Used by International Conventions," *Marine Policy* 8 (October 1984), pp. 311–22.

15. Irving Schiffman, "The Environmental Impact Assessment Comes to Israel," *Environmental Impact Assessment Review* 5 (June 1985), p. 184.

16. For a description of single- and double-loop learning, see Chris Argyris and Donald Schon, *Organizational Learning: A Theory of Action Perspective* (Reading, MA: Addison-Wesley, 1978). Single-loop learning relates to the pursuit of new instrumental policies while the ends remain constant or unquestioned. Double-loop learning entails the recognition of new ends and the adoption of new means to accomplish them. Joseph Nye calls these "simple" and "complex" learning. See Joseph S. Nye, Jr., "Nuclear Learning," *International Organization* 41 (Summer 1987), p. 380.

17. FAO internal memo, "Report on Travel to Algeria and Tunisia to Advise Algerian Authorities on Marine Pollution Problems and to Visit the UNDP/SF Fishery Survey and Development Project TUN 33," FAO FIRM/TRAM/672, May 1972, pp. 3–4; and

FAO, "Fisheries Travel Report and Aide Memoire," no. 672, May 1972, p. 4. A UNDP consultant observed that "harbors are evil smelling places, in some places with gas and oil bubbling to the surface."

18. Note that this proposition skirts an epistemological dispute regarding the relativity and accessibility of the natural world. Does the intermediation of different cognitive frameworks and cultures preclude the possibility of achieving a single acceptable image of the natural world? Does such incommensurability imply the lack of existence of a single accessible objective reality? For a good review of the various competing philosophical perspectives on these issues, see Martin Hollis and Steven Lukes, ed., *Rationality and Relativism* (Cambridge, MA: MIT Press, 1982).

Chapter
4

Regimes and Organizations

Friedrich Kratochwil

*T*he previous chapter introduced the concept of an international regime. It examined how regimes form and some of their effects on international relations. In this chapter, we extend our discussion of regimes. More specifically, we focus on some of the organizational and institutional features of regimes.

The study of international regimes has raised a series of questions concerning the links between those institutions that consist of settled practices constituted by explicit or customary norms and formal organizations that are characterized by hierarchical bureaucratic structures. Interest in these questions was heightened by the proliferation of both formal, multipurpose organizations (such as the United Nations) and organizations that were structured along functional (issue-specific) lines, such as the International Labor Organization (ILO), or the World Health Organization (WHO). To that extent these developments seem to bear out the expectation of organization theorists such as Weber or Michels that formal organizations would displace other organizational forms because of the improved efficiency hierarchical bureaucratic structures provide for "rational" administration.

It is therefore not surprising that many scholars and decision makers expected that the establishment of hierarchical and centralized institutions in the international system would promote international cooperation and peace. These scholars viewed social order as the result of the hierarchical organization of international relations. However, as some of the selections in this chapter argue, hierarchical organizations need not be the most efficient organizational form for creating social order. For example, modern organization theory suggests that organizations which operate in rapidly changing environments are more likely to achieve their organizational goals if they are decentralized, rather than hierarchical. Thus, at first blush it seems that the extent to which hierarchical organizational arrangements foster increased efficiency crucially depends on the fit between factors which are part of the "environment" of an organization and its structure.[1] Similarly, the reliance on bureaucracies, and on a tightly organized repressive apparatus in the political sphere, might result in monumental inefficiencies—as the failures of economic planning indicate—and in social unrest or passive resistance on the part of the population.

The challenges that these scholars posed for the study of international organization have led many analysts to rely on insights provided by modern organization theory and what has been referred to as the "new institutionalism." First, as already suggested, modern organization theory was marked by a shift away from the Weberian "closed-system" approach to an "open-system" approach, that is, from the attempts of explaining outcomes in terms of the internal structure of organizations to an approach that emphasizes the interaction between organizations and their environment. Second, the new institutionalism also criticized some of the most commonly accepted justifications for governmental action, including the idea that the existence of public goods (bads) and the guarantee of property rights make governmental action necessary.[2]

This literature has raised a series of fascinating and important issues concerning what type of organizational form is best able to support a successful international regime. They lead, for example, to questions of organizational design of alternative strategies to ensure regime effectiveness. The selections in this chapter address these issues.

Beth Yarbrough and Robert Yarbrough's article provides an excellent overview of some of the central issues concerning the new institutionalism. This article reviews two books, one by Oliver Williamson, the other by Geoffrey Hodgson. Williamson's work is based more on the classical mode of economic analysis. Here the question of the "costs" of transactions provides the core concern. The efficiencies that are created by either market exchanges or by authoritative allocation through organizational hierarchies depend on the variation in "environmental" factors. Hodgson, on the other hand, is a representative of a more "sociological" (or reflexivist) mode of analysis. He suggests that the focus on "costs" might be too narrow and that a theory of institutions needs to include additional factors, such as the formation of the preferences of the actors, that are outside traditional economic analysis. This article not only provides a series of important and broad insights about the strengths and limitations of these approaches; it also suggests some of the ways in which this literature might be applied to the study of international relations.

John Conybeare is the most outspoken advocate of the "private property" school that emerged in opposition to the traditional justifications for governmental action. In applying the insights of this approach to international relations, Conybeare contrasts several decentralized solutions to problems in the international arena with what he refers to as "the international organization approach," which advocates the formation of (world) governmental or supranational bureaucracies. By focusing on the possibility of "private ordering," through the adoption of property rights and liability rules Conybeare shows that many international problems ranging from drugs to pollution and finance can be solved satisfactorily without the creation of hierarchical international organizational forms. His important article also raises some interesting issues regarding the distinction between international governance (international organization) and international *organizations* that was outlined in Chapter 1.

Edward Mansfield's contribution examines once more the context between regimes and central institutions, exemplified by the argument of hegemonic stability. According to this theory, the functioning of regimes is crucially dependent on a hegemon and its ability to provide collective goods such as enforcing the rules of a regime. To that extent the need for central institutions is again emphasized, although these structures are those of the "hegemon" rather than supranational bureaucracies or intergovernmental organizations. Mansfield shows that many of the arguments concerning the effects of the distribution of power on aspects of international trade have focused too narrowly on hegemony, while neglecting other aspects of the distribution of power. Moreover, leading theories of the international political economy generally misspecify the relationship between the distribution of power and international trade.

NOTES

1. For an important caveat concerning this environmental fit argument, see the introduction to Chapter 8.
2. Public goods (or bads, i.e., externalities such as pollution) are characterized by two features that prevent their supply (or abatement) by the market (through private transactions). One is their "joint supply," the characteristic that their consumption by one actor does not diminish the availability for others. Two, public goods are nonexclusive. National defense is a typical example of a public good. The enjoyment of security by citizen A does not diminish the supply of the good to citizens B, C, D . . . , and by defending citizen A the government also provides protection to all others. The latter problem might encourage free-rider tendencies as no individual will have incentives to contribute to the procurement of the good. Consequently, either the good will not be supplied (or only suboptimally procured), or the "government" provides the good by "taxing" the individuals, authoritatively prescribing their contribution. Similarly, in the case of a public "bad" such as pollution, no individual firm will have an incentive of installing costly pollution abatement devices in the absence of a governmental regulation.

International Institutions and the New Economics of Organization

Beth V. Yarbrough and Robert M. Yarbrough

. . . The centuries-long movement of economics away from institutional concerns has recently been interrupted. Most highly developed in its analysis of the firm, the "new economics of organization" (NEO) is notable for its range and scope, encompassing literature on the family, the state, and international relations.[1] The contributions, while diverse in perspective, share a goal of a theoretical foundation for understanding key institutions, avoiding the "black box" approach.[2] Although grounded firmly in economics, NEO is an explicitly interdisciplinary approach to social institutions and incorporates contributions from law, organization theory, and the other social sciences.

The purposes of this article are to outline the key characteristics and insights of the work of Oliver Williamson, Geoffrey Hodgson, and other NEO analysts, to bring these insights to bear on the firm and the state as central institutions of international political economy, and to assess the potential contributions of NEO to the study of international institutions. . . .[3]

NEO ORIGINS AND GOALS

The "old" institutionalism of Thorstein Veblen, John Commons, Wesley Mitchell, and Clarence Ayres had limited impact on mainstream economics.[4] Until recently, economics took a quite different path, since neither legal formalism, with its focus on state enforcement of formal rules, nor strict behavioralism, with its direct link between opportunities and behavior, left much of a role for institutions. The old institutionalist writers' limited impact is often attributed to their emphasis on methodological criticism over development of an alternative research program. . . .[5]

. . . The criticism of much of standard economic theory by NEO writers remains blunt; but the criticism is aimed less at methodology than at the focus of economics on artificial or "toy" problems existing in a social and institutional vacuum. . . .

The broad goal of NEO is to understand social institutions, which are viewed as means of facilitating cooperation in situations in which unilateral action produces inferior outcomes for the actors involved, implying the existence of potential gains from effective mutual agreements.[6] As Harvey Leibenstein notes, social organization in general faces two simultaneous problems: the "size of the pie" and the "division of the pie."[7] Actors have a common interest in expanding the size of the pie but have conflictual interests in dividing it—a problem reminiscent of prisoners' dilemma. Successful cooperation increases the size of the pie; but unilateral defection enables a party to capture a larger share of the smaller pie, and this can lead to mutual defection.

However, most NEO work does not focus on the mutual defection outcome. Instead, it focuses on the potential for a noncooperative outcome to create an incentive for actors to establish institutions to prevent that outcome. As Williamson argues,

> The benefits from cooperation notwithstanding, the achievement of cooperation is widely thought to be frustrated by the relentless logic of the prisoners' dilemma. To be sure, it has always been evident that defection can be deterred if payoffs are appropriately altered. But that strategem is held to be infeasible or is otherwise dismissed, on which account the dilemma persists or appeal is made to "exogenous norms of cooperative behavior [that are] adhered to by the actors." I submit that the feasibility of crafting superior *ex ante* incentive structures warrants more attention. A leading reason for its neglect is that the study of the institutions of contract has occupied such a low place on the research agenda. Subtle incentive features incorporated in nonstandard contracting practices have gone undetected as a consequence of this nonchalance—hence the practical significance of the prisoners' dilemma to the study of exchange has been vastly exaggerated.[8]

DISTINGUISHING CHARACTERISTICS OF NEO

In addition to its institutional focus and interdisciplinary character, two other features distinguish most NEO work from more traditional economic approaches. The first deals with the nature of the relevant environment, and the second concerns the interaction of agent and structure.

The Relevant Environment

Unlike the textbook neoclassical world of *homo oeconomicus*, the relevant world for NEO is an institutional setting in which uncertainty prevails, individuals are only "boundedly rational," legal enforcement of agreements is costly and imperfect, and opportunistic acts cannot be ruled out. In such a world, even potentially mutually beneficial relationships may require relatively complex institutional structures to support cooperation.

The NEO world is populated by individuals whom Herbert Simon would characterize as "*intendedly* rational, but only *limitedly* so."[9] Both parts of this definition of bounded rationality are taken seriously: individuals pursue goals to the best of their abilities, but those abilities are constrained by imperfect information, the complexity of the problems confronted, and limits on computational competence and foresight.[10] Bounded rationality effectively eliminates the possibility of comprehensive long-term agreements defining precisely each and every contingency, since not all contingencies can be foreseen. As a result, agreements must maintain flexibility; to use Williamson's metaphor, bridges must be crossed as they are reached rather than in advance.[11]

Individuals are also potentially opportunistic, and they can and sometimes do take advantage of others' bounded rationality, particularly in cases in which the inevitable incompleteness of agreements creates a gap between compliance in letter and compliance in spirit. As Williamson points out, opportunism can take the form of "self-interest seeking with guile" or "the incomplete or distorted disclosure of information, especially . . . calculated efforts to mislead, distort, disguise, obfuscate, or otherwise confuse."[12]

Bounded rationality and opportunism, resulting in incompletely specified and imperfectly obeyed agreements, increase the scope of uncertainty.[13] In addition to uncertainty arising from different states of the world,[14] behavioral uncertainty can arise from an actor's lack of information about other actors' preferences or actions. This makes coordination difficult, even when all parties are acting in good faith, and it therefore creates a demand for norms to enhance predictability and social institutions to support exchange and other forms of cooperation.[15] Uncertainty can also arise if actors are thought to be pursuing "strategic" behavior and deliberately concealing or disguising their preferences or actions in order to take advantage of others. This strategic behavioral uncertainty renders some institutions, norms, and actions (such as the strategy to "always cooperate" in prisoners' dilemma) infeasible.[16] The problem thus becomes one of devising institutions that will facilitate cooperation by safeguarding against opportunism, maintaining flexibility, forestalling disputes, and mediating any disputes that do arise. . . . The nature of the issues raised by the NEO environment, like those raised by international relations, focuses attention squarely on the relationship between agent and structure.

Interaction of Agent and Structure

NEO is sensitive to the problems arising in trying to define even a single observed institution. Most analysts agree, for example, that the state is an institution, but there is no consensus about its major attributes: Is it the set of individuals currently occupying government office, the constitution along with its bureaucracy and administrative apparatus, the ruling class, or the legal order emanating from recognition of sovereignty?[17] In what sense can the state act, and to what extent does the legal concept of sovereignty translate into autonomy of state action or insulation from pressures emanating from the domestic society or the international system?[18] NEO arose from analogous questions about the firm: Is it the set of individuals currently owning or employed in the firm, the legal entity created by documents of incorporation, or the management that makes operating decisions? In what sense does the firm act, and to what extent is a firm's behavior autonomous from internal and external pressures? Dealing with these questions for the case of either the state or the firm hinges on recognition of the interactive relationship between the individual and the social group. More is involved than a choice between individualism and holism; the agent-structure problem is characterized by the presence of a multilevel hierarchy in which parts are also wholes, and wholes are also parts.[19]

While the unit of analysis in textbook neoclassical economics is the autonomous individual, household, or firm, the unit of NEO analysis is the transaction, viewed as a relationship or contract. The transaction is not an instantaneous exchange in a world of perfectly specified property rights and perfectly enforced contracts; rather, it is a relationship in which performance may be nonsimultaneous and nonperformance may leave an aggrieved party with little recourse. Given these elements of anarchy, cooperation requires an institutional structure consistent with self-enforcement or self-help.

Although the emphasis of NEO analysis is on individual action, the relational focus means that careful attention is paid to the compositional principles through which individual actions produce collective action or social outcomes.[20] Individuals, rather than organizations or groups, have objectives; social wholes do not act based on aims and interests distinct from those of the constitutive individuals.[21] However, social wholes are more than the simple sum of their parts; society may affect individual objectives; and social institutions both constrain and enable individual behavior. In its endeavor to acknowledge the importance of both structure and process and of both individual and group, NEO walks the thin line between reductionism and methodological holism or reification.[22] As Hodgson argues,

> For too long economists have considered households or firms simply as unitary elements, making decisions as if they were single actors, and disregarding the real individuals involved. . . . What is left out of this approach is the continuous influence of social institutions, such as the family or the firm itself, and the social culture and roles, on the preferences and purposes of individuals involved. Whilst the aims and character of individuals help to explain the behaviour of social structures, also roles, culture and institutions have a partial effect on the goals and behaviour of individuals.[23]

Joint maximization within any group requires an institutional structure or a set of incentives and constraints (not necessarily pecuniary) that will influence individual behavior in a manner consistent with joint maximization. An example is provided by Adam Smith, who described a mechanism in which the individual is "led by an invisible hand to promote an end which is no part of his intention."[24] In Smith's view, the coincidence of individual and social interests was not automatic; it was the outcome of certain social institutions, primarily well-defined and enforced property rights and open competition, both domestically and internationally. Within that institutional context, the aggregate outcome (maximization of national wealth) mirrored the individual pursuit of self-interest (individual wealth). Smith's work was, after all, a critique of the mercantilist system, an institutional context in which, he argued, the pursuit of individual wealth reduced aggregate wealth. In today's international relations terminology, Smith's work can be considered a call for a change in regime, a redefinition of "basic property rights" and "acceptable patterns of behavior,"[25] or a change in institutions. His treatise can also be viewed as a comparative institutional exercise, since he placed individuals in two social contexts (laissez-faire and mercantilist systems) and, using theory and historical evidence, compared the aggregate outcomes that reflected the interaction of individual behavior within these contexts.

The focus of NEO on the interaction between individual preferences and behavior on the one hand and group outcomes on the other is reflected in the choice of the transaction as the basic unit of analysis. Institutionalist John Commons argued that the transaction captured the essential elements of analysis—conflict, dependence, and order[26]—by focusing on a situation in which an agreement could be mutually valuable but might be difficult to reach. . . .

The transaction represents a relationship in which the parties may find themselves in harmony, in which case unilateral action will suffice and only the simplest social institutions are required, or the parties may find themselves in actual or potential conflict, in which case different institutions will hold varying levels of promise for achieving cooperation. These institutions are viewed within NEO as various forms of contract—not an unyielding, written, and legally enforceable document but, instead, a framework of working rules. As Karl Llewellyn indicates, the contract can provide "a framework for well-nigh every type of group organization and for well-nigh every type of passing or permanent relation between individuals and groups"; this "highly adjustable" framework "almost never accurately indicates real working relations but . . . affords a rough indication around which such relations vary [and serves as] an occasional guide in cases of doubt."[27]

The law associated with contracts differs in an important respect from many other aspects of law, as Bruce Benson notes: "'Contract law' refers to the 'law' parties in exchange bring into existence by their contractual agreement rather than to the law of or about contract."[28] In other words, contract law is the law of custom and usage, the law that actors find useful in supporting their cooperation. When an unforeseen circumstance generates a dispute within a contractual relationship, the goal of the dispute-settlement process is to maintain continuity and arrive at a solution that the parties themselves might have reached if they had been able to foresee the circumstance when entering the contract.[29] This forms the basis for one of NEO's central ideas: the firm is a governance structure.[30]

NEO PERSPECTIVES ON KEY INSTITUTIONS: THE FIRM AND THE STATE

The Governing Firm

Bounded rationality and uncertainty about the future make it impossible to write long-term contracts that can govern a continuing relationship without periodic renegotiation or adjustment of terms; but opportunism makes periodic adjustment and renegotiation problematic, since parties cannot be counted on to act in "good faith." Haggling over the division of gains from any needed adjustment may result in potentially beneficial adjustments not being made. Imperfect and costly enforcement means that the legal system will, in many instances, be unable to deter or compensate for breach of contract, leaving parties vulnerable to breach and reliant on self-help or private ordering.[31]

In such an environment, transactions are differentially vulnerable to breakdown and therefore require support from institutions of varying complexity. Williamson's key dimension in explaining the assignment of certain transactions to certain types of organization is asset specificity.[32] An asset is specific if it is durable and designed for a particular use with a particular partner, thereby greatly reducing the value of the asset in another use or in use with another partner. When a relationship involves little or no investment in specific assets, the parties are safeguarded by the availability of alternative partners; if the current partner behaves opportunistically, replacement partners are available at relatively low cost. The primary task of institutions in such transactions is to support flexibility and autonomy. The "market" as an institution provides alternative partners as well as standardized norms of exchange (for example, price), and these are what is needed when continuity in any particular relationship is not highly valued.

On the other hand, when a relationship involves significant investment in specific assets, the relationship is more vulnerable. A breakdown can cause irreparable damage because the value of the specific asset (which is, by definition, useful only in the specific relationship) will be lost. All parties therefore have an incentive to maintain continuity. If conditions change, necessitating adaptation of the relationship, each party also faces an incentive to hold out for more favorable terms in an attempt to capture the full value of the relationship over the partner's best alternative.

In this type of relationship, alternative partners can no longer suffice; the anonymous trading world of neoclassical markets, in which the identity of a party is unimportant, disappears. The relationship undergoes what Williamson calls the "fundamental transformation." . . . For Williamson, the fundamental transformation works in the opposite direction, moving a relationship out of the autonomy and anonymity of the market and into a more socially embedded sphere, where the relationship is supported by relation-specific incentive structures or safeguards. Investment in such a relationship forecloses alternatives, imputing a branchlike or history-dependent structure to the choices facing the parties.[33] The primary task of institutions becomes one of supporting and signaling the parties' continuing commitment to the ongoing relationship; these institutions are by necessity unique, based in identity, loyalty, and reciprocity. . . .

The firm, from this perspective, is a mini-society with its own incentives, dispute-settlement procedures, and norms; transactions brought under control of the integrated firm are those which require a more extensive governance structure to safeguard cooperation than can be provided by the market. The firm, therefore, is an institution of governance, one in which commitment replaces (at least partially) autonomy and flexibility. The NEO governance-oriented view of the firm represents a significant departure from the textbook neoclassical view in which the firm is a technologically determined production function, a black box turning inputs into outputs, with all exchange occurring in anonymous, price-mediated markets. . . .

NEO AND INTERNATIONAL RELATIONS

Although relatively new to modern economic theory, the concept of the "governing firm" has formed the basis for a centuries-long debate concerning the interaction of firm and state. Thomas Hobbes argued that the state was potentially weakened by corporations that he likened to "many lesser common-wealths in the bowels of a greater, like worms in the entrails of a natural man."[34] Adam Smith considered the two roles of trader and sovereign as inherently incompatible:

> No two characters seem more inconsistent than those of trader and sovereign. If the trading spirit of the English East India company renders them very bad sovereigns, the spirit of sovereignty seems to have rendered them equally bad traders. While they were traders only, they managed their trade successfully. . . . Since they became sovereigns . . . they have been obliged to beg the extraordinary assistance of government in order to avoid immediate bankruptcy.[35]

More recently, Susan Strange and others have implicitly used the concept of the governing firm in developing a "web-of-contracts" model of transnational relations in which

> trade between countries in goods and services will be, and is being, sustained by a complex network or web of transnational, bilateral bargains—bargains between corporations and other corporations, between corporations and governments, and between governments. The interest of both parties to these bilateral exchanges is (and will continue to be) a far more powerful influence on the level, the direction, and the content of international trade than the puny efforts of states to interfere with market forces.[36]

Whether or not we agree with Hobbes's metaphor of firms as parasites, Smith's argument about the fundamental incompatibility of governing and trading, or Strange's characterization of the efforts of states to interfere with market forces as "puny," two points seem clear. First, international relations reflect the interaction of strategies followed not only by states but also by firms. Second, the traditional view of states as governance structures (the narrow province of political science) and of firms as traders (the narrow province of economics) provides an inadequate perspective on both institutions. As noted by the old institutionalist writers, particularly John Commons, and carried on by NEO analysts, the inextricable linkage of governing and trading is captured by a focus on the transaction, relation, or contract.

The concept of contract has a long history in political and social theory, most notably in the work of Hobbes and Locke and more recently in that of Douglass North, Margaret Levi, Geoffrey Brennan, and James Buchanan.[37] In each case, the idea of contract is a key element in explaining the state, which is viewed as trading the definition and enforcement of property rights for revenue. Thus far, however, to the extent that a contractual perspective has been used in international political economy, contracts have been notable primarily for their absence, a central element in the "anarchy" typically used to describe the international arena. According to the anarchy-based view of international relations, even mutually beneficial transactions may fail to be consummated because there is no central authority to enforce contracts and neither party can rely on the other not to behave opportunistically. The absence of the enforcement power of the state, leaving states with no recourse to higher authority in their dealings with one another, renders international relations less secure and more discordant than domestic relations.[38]

NEO, however, suggests that the dichotomous view of the domestic arena as law-ordered and the international arena as anarchic is potentially misleading. If firms are hierarchical governance structures that arise to facilitate cooperative production when law-based, anonymous, price-mediated market exchange provides inadequate safeguards to support cooperation, then the domestic and international arenas must differ in degree, not in kind, along the law-to-anarchy continuum. If so, the progress that NEO analysts have made in understanding the various institutions that individuals and firms devise to facilitate cooperation in the presence of uncertainty, bounded rationality, opportunism, and imperfect enforcement may prove helpful in analyzing international institutions as well. Williamson, whose work has thus far focused on the firm (broadly defined), is cautiously optimistic about the relevance of the approach for "noncommercial enterprise"; other writers, such as Leibenstein, explicitly claim applicability to noneconomic organizations.[39]

Despite the striking parallels between the central questions of NEO and those of international relations, the applicability of NEO to international questions is hindered by a number of difficulties. Some of these difficulties are inherent in NEO itself, at least in its current state; other difficulties relate specifically to extending the insights of NEO to international relations.

Criticisms of NEO for the Study of International Institutions

Functionalism and Efficiency   The most widely heard criticism of NEO centers on its functional approach to institutions. Mark Granovetter's statement is representative:

> The general story told by this school [NEO] is that social institutions and arrangements previously thought to be the adventitious result of legal, historical, social, or political forces are better viewed as the efficient solution to certain economic problems. The tone is similar to that of structural-functional sociology of the 1940s to the 1960s, and much of the argumentation fails the elementary tests of a sound functional explanation.[40]

This disagreement can be traced, at least in part, to a difference in usage of the word "functional." Functional explanations dominated sociology and anthropology during the mid-twentieth century, but refinement and tightening of the requirements for a valid functional theory led many social scientists to conclude that those requirements are rarely if ever satisfied in the social sciences.[41] For example, Jon Elster argues that a valid functional explanation of an institution requires both that the institution serve an unintended and unrecognized function for a group and that the function feed back to maintain or reproduce the institution.[42] The latter requirement, the survivability or natural selection element, tends to be especially weak in explanations of international institutions.[43]

A less stringent definition comes from Herbert Simon: "Institutions are functional if reasonable men might create and maintain them in order to meet social needs or achieve social goals."[44] Functional explanations under the Simon definition lose much (although not all) of their vulnerability to the teleological and compositional fallacies that plague functional explanations under the more stringent definition.[45] Under the Simon definition, a functional explanation does not require that the function served be either unintentional or unrecognized, and success in solving a problem can support survival of an institution. This looser definition of social institutions as functional corresponds closely to what institutionalists refer to as a purposive, intentional, or instrumental explanation—that is, one based in the idea of problem solving.[46]

As noted by Stephan Haggard and Beth Simmons, a key weakness of functional explanations is their failure to explain when and in what issue-areas the creation of a problem-solving institution works.[47] Some evidence suggests that human volition has an essentially episodic role in that it is important when change exceeds the capacity of current institutions to cope or when there is what Leibenstein calls "a shock to the culture."[48] This view provides one explanation for the common historical pattern of institutional change during and after wars, including the creation of the major international organizations following World War II. Varying potential for collective action provides an explanation for the varying efficacy of human volition across issue-areas,[49] but much more work is needed to understand the role of collective action (involving both state and nonstate actors) in international relations. These issues present a significant challenge to analysts working in NEO, both in its traditional areas of application and in potential new areas, and this points once again to the importance of microanalytic research that focuses on periods of institutional change and on comparisons of the efficacy of problem-solving institutions across issue-areas.

International relations theorists and NEO analysts share a tendency to regard the presence or advent of cooperation (along with any accompanying rules or norms) as desirable and the absence or breakdown of agreements as undesirable.[50] Given the functionalist, problem-solving approach to institutions offered by NEO, this conclusion is not surprising, even though it obviously hinges on adopting the perspective of a certain group. . . .[51] Consider the actions of the Organization of Petroleum Exporting Countries (OPEC) during the 1970s. What OPEC regarded as a success was hardly regarded by oil-importing economies as an example of desirable cooperation. Evaluation of the erosion or breakdown of existing systems of cooperation is similarly sensitive to the perspective or definition of the relevant group.

Once the desirability of any cooperation-supporting institution is recognized as dependent on group perspective, the NEO concept of opportunism also becomes subject to two-way interpretation. Opportunism involves failure to abide by the spirit if not the letter of an agreement, and it is, by definition, negatively evaluated by the parties to the agreement. Outsiders, on the other hand, might evaluate opportunism positively. . . . This does not, however, eliminate the usefulness of opportunism as a concept in the study of institutions. The fundamental strength of NEO is its emphasis on the role of potential *ex post* opportunism in the *ex ante* choice between alternative governance structures. It is opportunism from the viewpoint of the acting group that molds this choice and affects the outcome.[52] Evaluation of that outcome from the perspective of the larger society is a related but conceptually distinct question. The two are often obscured by the efficiency-based terminology of NEO, in which "efficiency" has meaning only in reference to a specified group, a group defined in most NEO work as those involved in the process of creating a problem-solving institution.

Private Ordering and the Law   NEO is based on empirical evidence and growing sentiment among legal scholars and practitioners that legal centralism places far too much emphasis on formal written contracts and their effective adjudication in courts of law.[53] As a result, the focus of NEO is on "private ordering" and the concept of "contract as framework."[54] Nonetheless, as Williamson points out, in the firm-centered arena with which NEO primarily deals, courts do provide "ultimate recourse" for "protection against egregious abuses of which 'might is right' is an elementary example."[55] Hodgson argues that this recourse is essential to support exchange and is given insufficient attention in Williamson's work:

> Of course, most contractual disputes are resolved without direct recourse to the courts; but this does not mean that the state has no place in the everyday process of contract. After all, the mere possibility of access to the courts is sufficient for the legal system to bear upon contractual agreements. It is not necessary that people actually appear in court for the state to have such a function. Whilst both formal and informal norms and rules play an important part in a system of exchange, in a modern society these rules are buttressed and sometimes created by law and the state.[56]

More research is needed to determine the extent to which even formal law rests necessarily on the foundation of a state, sovereign over all parties, or may evolve spontaneously based on the needs of contracting parties.[57] Although important in traditional applications of NEO, this issue obviously becomes even more troublesome in the international sphere, where the principles of *pacta sunt servanda* (treaties are binding contracts and should be observed) and *rebus sic stantibus* (substantial changes in conditions free a party from treaty obligations) are potentially incompatible. States, by nature of their sovereignty, may declare disputes "political" rather than "legal," thereby rendering them nonjusticiable and exempt from final legal settlement under international law. But such moves, especially if repeated, are unlikely to be without costs in a state system in which a relatively small number of actors engage in repeated interaction.[58] State interests are not typically served by ignoring rules and norms, a point highlighted by John Hall and G. John Ikenberry in terms of the relationship between a state and other groups within the domestic society:

> Above all it is an error to equate the strength or autonomy of the state with the ability of state elites to ignore other social actors or to impose their will in any simple manner on society. If this were the case, totalitarian states, which seek to suppress the independence of other social actors, would be most capable of realizing state goals and of promoting larger social purposes. Such a conclusion is not justified: a deeper dimen-

sion of state power has more to do with the state's ability to work through and with other centers of power. The capacity of states to act rationally is furthered and not curtailed when the state coordinates other autonomous power sources.[59]

The relative importance or efficacy of recourse to law as opposed to private ordering, both domestically and internationally, is ultimately an empirical question, one that is raised but not answered by NEO in its current state. The question goes to the heart of the nature of international law, the appropriateness of the anarchy formulation of international relations, and the nature and role of international regimes. Once again, however, it is easy to overemphasize the domestic-international dichotomy, since interpretations of the doctrines of impossibility, unconscionability, and duress which allow for "discharge" (escape from contractual obligation) rather than for charges of "breach" of a contract are central to controversies in domestic contract law.[60]

Strengths of NEO for the Study of International Institutions

Beyond Formal Legalism   Formal legalism, which assumes a central role for formal rules or laws enacted and effectively enforced by a hierarchical authority such as the state,[61] dominated both political science and economics during the late nineteenth and early twentieth centuries. In contrast, NEO recognizes the importance of informal institutions and does not posit a direct link between behavior and formalized rules.[62] Institutional approaches such as NEO suggest that formal structures represent only one part of the network or web of interactions that comprise political and economic behavior. The United Nations system, for example, is seen as a single element of the more complex state system. Similarly, the formal structure of GATT is relevant to but not determinative of behavior in the international trade policy area. From the NEO perspective, concentration on formal legal structures may prove not only incomplete but also misleading, since the effective enforcement of rules assumed by the formal approach is often missing, particularly in international relations.

This insight extends beyond the obvious point that research attention must be paid to informal institutions and norms (such as reciprocity, loyalty, identity, and ideas) as well as to more formalized and therefore more visible forms (such as treaties, legal contracts, and formal market exchange). Institutions may be so pervasive that the underlying ("institution-less") structure of a situation can be difficult or impossible to determine.[63] As noted in the earlier quote from Williamson, situations similar to prisoners' dilemma do not necessarily lead to a noncooperative outcome, since the mutually unsatisfactory nature of that outcome creates an incentive for parties to avoid it. The underlying structures of international relations in the economic, political, and security spheres have been the basis of an enduring debate.[64] While NEO, as an approach to rather than a theory of international institutions, cannot delimit the range of international relations appropriately conceptualized as having a particular structure, it can serve as a useful reminder of the web of existing institutions as a source of the ambiguity. . . .

NOTES

1. Subsets of and alternative names for the new economics of organization include the new institutional economics, transaction cost economics, and the economics of property rights. Examples of NEO treatments of various institutions include the following: Robert A. Pollak, "A Transaction Cost Approach to Families and Households," *Journal of Economic Literature* 23 (June 1985), pp. 581–608; Barry W. Poulson, "The Family and the State," in Joseph R. Peden and Fred R. Glahe, eds., *The American Family and the State* (San Francisco: Pacific Research Institute, 1986), pp. 49–80; Louis Putterman, *The Economic Nature of the Firm* (Cambridge: Cambridge University Press, 1986); Harvey Leibenstein, *Inside the Firm* (Cambridge, MA: Harvard University Press, 1987); M. Y. Yoshino and Thomas B. Lifson, *The Invisible Link* (Cambridge, MA: MIT Press, 1986); Douglass C. North, *Structure and Change in Economic History* (New York: Norton, 1981); Christopher Winship and Sherwin Rosen, eds., *Organizations and Institutions*, supplement to *American Journal of Sociology*, vol. 94, 1988; and Beth V. Yarbrough and Robert M. Yarbrough, "Free Trade, Hegemony, and the Theory of Agency," *Kyklos*, vol. 38, no. 3, 1985, pp. 348–64. A useful collection of articles can be found in four special issues of the *Journal of Institutional and Theoretical Economics* 140–43 (March 1984, March 1985, March 1986, and March 1987).

2. The "black box" terminology symbolizes (among both economists and political scientists) acknowledgement of the limitations of traditional noninstitutional approaches. See, for example, Masahiko Aoki, *The Co-Operative Game Theory of the Firm* (Oxford: Oxford University Press, 1984), pp. 4, 10, and 52; Stephan Haggard and Beth A. Simmons, "Theories of International Regimes," *International Organization* 41 (Summer 1987), pp. 497 and 513; Armen A. Alchian and Susan Woodward, "The Firm Is Dead; Long Live the Firm," *Journal of Economic Literature* 26 (March 1988), p. 65; G. John Ikenberry et al., "Introduction: Approaches to Explaining American Foreign Economic Policy," *International Organization* 42 (Winter 1988), p. 3; G. John Ikenberry, "Conclusion: An Institutional Approach to American Foreign Economic Policy," *International Organization* 42 (Winter 1988), p. 242; Richard N. Langlois, "What Was Wrong with the 'Old' Institutional Economics? (And What Is Still Wrong with the 'New'?)" Department of Economics Working Paper, University of Connecticut, 1988, p. 30; and Williamson, *Economic Institutions of Capitalism*, p. 15.

3. The "unidirectional" nature of this review article should not be construed to imply that NEO could not be strengthened by drawing on the insights of international relations theorists.

4. In "What Was Wrong?" Langlois traces the relationship between the "old" institutionalists and more modern work in NEO. A useful collection of modern papers in the institutionalist tradition can be found in two special issues of the *Journal of Economic Issues* 21 (September and December 1987). Continuing work by economists in this tradition is often referred to as "neo-institutionalism" to distinguish it from the "new institutionalism" associated with Williamson's work and other related approaches.

5. See Ronald Coase, "The New Institutional Economics," *Journal of Institutional and Theoretical Economics* 140 (March 1984), pp. 229–30. Coase's criticism is virtually identical to Keohane's admonitions to scholars of the reflective school of international relations. See Robert O. Keohane, "International Institutions: Two Approaches," *International Studies Quarterly* 32 (December 1988), pp. 379–96. On the shortcomings of the "old" institutionalism, see also Hodgson, *Economics and Institutions*, pp. 21–24.

6. As discussed in a subsequent section of this article and in note 64, NEO cannot itself delimit the range of social relations questions that fit this description.

7. Leibenstein, *Inside the Firm*, p. viii.

8. Williamson, *Economic Institutions of Capitalism*, pp. 204–5. Joanne Gowa makes a related argument about the relevance of prisoners' dilemma for international relations in "Anarchy, Egoism, and Third Images," *International Organization* 40 (Winter 1986), pp. 167–86.

9. Herbert Simon, *Administrative Behavior*, 2d ed. (New York: Macmillan, 1961), p. xxiv (1st ed. published in 1947). See also Richard N. Langlois, "Rationality, Institutions, and Explanation," in Richard N. Langlois, ed., *Economics as a Process* (Cambridge: Cambridge University Press, 1986), pp. 225–55.

10. See Williamson, *Economic Institutions of Capitalism*, pp. 30–32 and 44–47; and Hodgson, *Economics and Institutions*, chaps. 5 and 6.

11. Williamson, *Economic Institutions of Capitalism*, p. 57.

12. Ibid., p. 47; see also pp. 30–32, 47–52, and 64–67.

13. Heiner argues that uncertainty is the basic source of regularity in behavior. See Ronald A. Heiner, "Uncertainty, Signal-Detection Experiments, and Modeling Behavior," in Langlois, *Economics as a Process*, pp. 59–115.

14. In the economics literature on uncertainty, as in game theory or decision theory, a "state of the world" refers to one of many alternative situations that might arise.

15. Williamson, *Economic Institutions of Capitalism*, pp. 66–67.

16. Ibid., pp. 56–59.

17. See Roger Benjamin and Raymond Duvall, "The Capitalist State in Context," in Roger Benjamin and S. Elkin, eds., *The Democratic State* (Lawrence: University of Kansas Press, 1985), pp. 19–57; and G. John Ikenberry, "The State and Strategies of International Adjustment," *World Politics* 39 (October 1986), especially pp. 54–55. A similar question about institutions more generally is raised by Alexander J. Field in "The Problem with Neoclassical Institutional Economics," *Explorations in Economic History* 18 (April 1981), p. 183.

18. Jackson distinguishes between juridical statehood based on "negative" sovereignty, or the right of self-determination, and empirical statehood based on "positive" sovereignty, or a capacity for effective and civil government. See Robert H. Jackson, "Quasi-States, Dual Regimes, and Neoclassical Theory," *International Organization* 41 (Autumn 1987), p. 529.

19. For useful guides to these issues, see Alexander E. Wendt, "The Agent-Structure Problem in International Relations Theory," *International Organization* 41 (Summer 1987), pp. 335–70; and David Dessler, "What's at Stake in the Agent-Structure Debate?" *International Organization* 43 (Summer 1989), pp. 441–74. See also Hodgson, *Economics and Institutions*, p. 70.

20. Langlois defines a compositional principle as a proposition "about how the individual behavior links up or ties together to form the aggregate result." See "What Was Wrong?" p. 20.

21. See Langlois, "What Was Wrong?" especially pp. 25–30; and Wolfgang Seyfert, "A Weberian Analysis of Economic Progress," *Journal of Institutional and Theoretical Economics* 141 (March 1985), especially pp. 171–73.

22. Reductionism is an explanation of the whole based solely on behavior of the parts. Methodological holism claims distinct aims and interests for social wholes and suggests that they are sufficient levels of analysis. "Structure" refers to the distribution of capabilities among units, and "process" refers to the ways in which the units relate to each other; see Robert Keohane and Joseph Nye, "*Power and Interdependence* Revisited," *International Organization* 41 (August 1987), p. 745. Although neoclassical economics is strongly identified with methodological individualism, the standard economic treat-

ment of the firm as a monolithic profit-maximizing entity is vulnerable to charges of methodological holism or reification, as are many economic treatments of the household or family. For discussions of these issues and their relationship to the study of international relations, see Wendt, "The Agent-Structure Problem"; and Dessler, "What's at Stake?"

23. Hodgson, *Economics and Institutions*, p. 68.
24. Adam Smith, *An Inquiry into the Nature and Causes of the Wealth of Nations* (1776; reprint, New York: Modern Library, 1937), p. 423.
25. Stephen D. Krasner, "Structural Causes and Regime Consequences," in Stephen D. Krasner, ed., *International Regimes*, special issue of *International Organization* 36 (Spring 1982), p. 5.
26. John Commons, *Institutional Economics* (New York: Macmillan, 1934), p. 4. For a discussion of the importance of Commons' insight for the future of NEO work, see Beth V. Yarbrough and Robert M. Yarbrough, "The Transactional Structure of the Firm," *Journal of Economic Behavior and Organization* 10 (July 1988), pp. 1–28.
27. Karl N. Llewellyn, "What Price Contract?" *Yale Law Journal* 40 (May 1931), pp. 736–37. This view has obvious origins in Emile Durkheim's *The Division of Labor in Society* and in Talcott Parsons' *The Structure of Social Action*.
28. Bruce L. Benson, "The Spontaneous Evolution of Commercial Law," *Southern Economic Journal* 55 (September 1988), p. 649. This suggests parallels with international law, much of which is explicitly "created" through treaties and other forms of bargaining and agreements.
29. Williamson, *Economic Institutions of Capitalism*, pp. 68–84.
30. The nature of the firm is the question that has received the most attention from NEO analysts. The characterization of "the governing firm" in this review article draws heavily on Williamson's work, which represents the single most fully developed NEO argument. Not only has Williamson been a central contributor to NEO, but his framework is also the basis for a growing body of empirical work—a singular accomplishment. Some of that empirical work is surveyed by Paul L. Joskow in "Asset Specificity and the Structure of Vertical Relationships: Empirical Evidence," *Journal of Law, Economics, and Organization* 4 (Spring 1988), pp. 95–118.
31. Legal scholars have increasingly acknowledged the limits of legal centralism and the importance of private ordering (private negotiation and arbitration within a flexible contractual framework) as a means of dispute settlement, especially in relationships in which continuity is valued. See Llewellyn, "What Price Contract?"; Steward Macaulay, "Non-Contractual Relations in Business," *American Sociological Review* 28 (January 1963), pp. 55–70; Ian R. MacNeil, "The Many Futures of Contracts," *Southern California Law Review* 47 (May 1974), pp. 691–816; Ian R. MacNeil, "Contracts," *Northwestern University Law Review* 72 (January–February 1978), pp. 854–906; Marc Galanter, "Justice in Many Rooms," *Journal of Legal Pluralism*, vol. 19, 1981, pp. 1–47; Anthony T. Kronman, "Contract Law and the State of Nature," *Journal of Law, Economics, and Organization* 1 (Spring 1985), pp. 5–32; and Benson, "Spontaneous Evolution of Commercial Law."
32. Uncertainty and frequency of transacting are the other dimensions of transactions that play important roles.
33. For arguments along this line in international relations, see Stephen D. Krasner, "Approaches to the State," *Comparative Politics* 16 (January 1984), pp. 223–46; and Joanne Gowa, "Bipolarity, Multipolarity, and Free Trade," *American Political Science Review* 83 (December 1989), pp. 1245–56. See also R. Harrison Wagner, "Economic Interdependence, Bargaining Power, and Political Influence," *International Organiza-*

tion 42 (Summer 1988), pp. 479–80. Wagner points out "important differences . . . between negotiating a new aid or trade relationship and renegotiating an existing one," but he seemingly fails to account for the possibility of a "fundamental transformation" within a relationship. In *Economics and Institutions,* p. 301, Hodgson makes the more general point that the relative costs of various forms of organization depend in part on the status quo.

34. Thomas Hobbes, *Leviathan* (1651; reprint, New York: Macmillan, 1962), p. 245.

35. Smith, *Wealth of Nations,* p. 771.

36. Susan Strange, "Protection and World Politics," *International Organization* 39 (Spring 1985), p. 234.

37. See North, *Structure and Change in Economic History;* Margaret Levi, *Of Rule and Revenue* (Berkeley: University of California Press, 1988); and Geoffrey Brennan and James Buchanan, *The Reason of Rules* (Cambridge: Cambridge University Press, 1985).

38. Kenneth A. Oye, ed., *Cooperation Under Anarchy* (Princeton, NJ: Princeton University Press, 1986).

39. See Oliver E. Williamson, "The Economics of Organization," *American Journal of Sociology* 87 (November 1981), pp. 573–74; and Leibenstein, *Inside the Firm,* p. 1. For an evaluation of the usefulness of NEO for the study of public bureaucracy, see Terry M. Moe, "The New Economics of Organization," *American Journal of Political Science* 28 (November 1984), pp. 739–77.

40. Mark Granovetter, "Economic Action and Social Structure," *American Journal of Sociology* 91 (November 1985), p. 488.

41. The most influential functionalist works include the following: A. R. Radcliffe-Brown, "On the Concept of Function in Social Science," *American Anthropologist* 37 (Spring 1935), pp. 1–32; Bronislaw Malinowski, *A Scientific Theory of Culture and Other Essays* (Chapel Hill: University of North Carolina Press, 1944); and Walter Goldschmidt, *Comparative Functionalism* (Berkeley: University of California Press, 1966). For important criticism of functionalism in the social sciences, see Robert Merton, "Manifest and Latent Functions," in Robert Merton, ed., *Social Theory and Social Structure* (New York: Free Press, 1947), pp. 19–84; Jonathan H. Turner and A. Maryanski, *Functionalism* (Menlo Park, CA: Benjamin/Cummings, 1979); Jon Elster, *Explaining Technical Change* (Cambridge: Cambridge University Press, 1983); and Gregory K. Dow, "The Function of Authority in Transaction Cost Economics," *Journal of Economic Behavior and Organization* 8 (March 1987), pp. 13–38, especially sec. 4.

42. See Elster, *Explaining Technical Change.* See also Dessler, "What's at Stake?" for a discussion of Kenneth Waltz's narrow focus on unintended rules as opposed to intended rules.

43. Axelrod suggests that one possible "evolutionary" approach is based on the principle that "what works well for a player is more likely to be used again, while what turns out poorly is more likely to be discarded." See Robert Axelrod, "An Evolutionary Approach to Norms," *American Political Science Review* 80 (December 1986), pp. 1095–111. See also Williamson, *Economic Institutions of Capitalism.* Based on his insistence on a comparative institutional perspective, Williamson subscribes to what he calls "weak-form selection," a process whereby "fitter" institutions survive even though they may not be "the fittest" in an absolute sense (p. 23). He also notes that "'flawed' modes of economic organization for which no superior feasible mode can be described are, until something better comes along, winners nonetheless" (p. 408).

44. Herbert Simon, "Rationality as Process and as Product of Thought," *American Economic Review Papers and Proceedings* 68 (May 1978), p. 3.

45. On the teleological and compositional fallacies, see Turner and Maryanski, *Functionalism;* and Langlois, "What Was Wrong?"

46. See Walter C. Neale, "Institutions," *Journal of Economic Issues* 21 (September 1987), pp. 1177–206; Dow, "Function of Authority," especially pp. 27–28; and Andrew Schotter, "The Evolution of Rules," in Langlois, *Economics as a Process,* pp. 117–33. Among the "old" institutionalists, Commons believed that Veblen seriously underestimated the volitional or purposive component of institutions and that this led Veblen to overemphasize the extent to which institutions merely bind society to the past. See John Commons, *Institutional Economics* (New York: Macmillan, 1934); and *Legal Foundations of Capitalism* (New York: Macmillan, 1924).

47. Haggard and Simmons, "Theories of International Regimes," pp. 507–9.

48. Leibenstein, *Inside the Firm,* p. 131. See also Wendell Gordon, "Orthodox Economics and Institutionalized Behavior," in Carey C. Thompson, ed., *Institutional Adjustment* (Austin: University of Texas Press, 1967), pp. 41–67; Krasner, "Approaches to the State," especially pp. 240–43; Ikenberry, "Conclusion"; and Judith Goldstein, "The Impact of Ideas on Trade Policy," *International Organization* 43 (Winter 1989), pp. 31–72.

49. See Mancur Olson, *The Logic of Collective Action* (Cambridge, MA: Harvard University Press, 1965); Joanne Gowa, "Public Goods and Political Institutions," *International Organization* 42 (Winter 1988), pp. 15–32; Dow, "Function of Authority," pp. 32–33; and Oran R. Young, "The Politics of International Regime Formation," *International Organization* 43 (Summer 1989), pp. 349–76.

50. See Keohane, "International Institutions"; Haggard and Simmons, "Theories of International Regimes," pp. 508–9; and Gayl D. Ness and Steven R. Brechin, "Bridging the Gap: International Organizations as Organizations," *International Organization* 42 (Spring 1988), p. 248.

51. To further complicate matters, an institution may cease to serve the original beneficiary group and begin to serve another. "Capture" theories of economic regulation, for example, posit that agencies designed to regulate industries in pursuit of social goals are often captured by those very industries. See George Stigler, "The Economic Theory of Regulation," *Bell Journal of Economics and Management Science* 2 (Spring 1971), pp. 3–21. However, capture theories are largely devoid of institutional considerations, as noted by Joseph P. Kalt and Mark A. Zupan in "Capture and Ideology in the Economic Theory of Politics," *American Economic Review* 74 (June 1984), pp. 279–300.

52. Hodgson uses the possibility that the private and social valuations of "opportunism" differ to argue that the key in Williamson's work is not opportunism per se; rather, it is simply uncertainty as to whether or not a contract will be fulfilled. See *Economics and Institutions,* p. 205.

53. Note 31 provides a few examples.

54. Williamson, *Economic Institutions of Capitalism,* chaps. 7 and 8.

55. Ibid., p. 203.

56. Hodgson, *Economics and Institutions,* p. 154.

57. See Benson, "Spontaneous Evolution of Commercial Law."

58. See Robert O. Keohane, *After Hegemony* (Princeton, NJ: Princeton University Press, 1984), p. 258; and Young, "The Politics of International Regime Formation," p. 354.

59. John A. Hall and G. John Ikenberry, *The State* (Minneapolis: University of Minnesota Press, 1989), p. 95. See also Susan Strange, *States and Markets* (New York: Basil Blackwell, 1988), p. 40.

60. See Williamson, *Economic Institutions of Capitalism,* pp. 397–401. For an economics-

oriented discussion of contract enforcement and defense against breach, see Robert Cooter and Thomas Ulen, *Law and Economics* (Glenview, IL: Scott, Foresman, 1988), chaps. 6 and 7.

61. In "Spontaneous Evolution of Commercial Law," Benson uses the evolution of the medieval *lex mercatoria* as evidence to refute the argument that the state is essential even for effective formal law.
62. See Krasner, "Approaches to the State," especially pp. 229–30; and Williamson, *Economic Institutions of Capitalism,* pp. 20–21 and 164–66.
63. For example, "old" institutionalist Walton Hamilton characterized the "world of use and wont" as a "tangled and unbroken web of institutions." See Walton Hamilton, "Institutions," in Edwin R. A. Seligman and Alvin Johnson, eds., *Encyclopedia of the Social Sciences,* vol. 8 (New York: Macmillan, 1932), pp. 84–89. For several critiques of the liberal and Grotian perspective on institutions, see the following in Krasner, *International Regimes:* Stephen D. Krasner, "Structural Causes and Regime Consequences," pp. 1–21; Donald J. Puchala and Raymond F. Hopkins, "International Regimes," pp. 61–91; Oran R. Young, "Regime Dynamics," pp. 93–113; and Stephen D. Krasner, "Regimes and the Limits of Realism," pp. 355–68. See also Joseph S. Nye, Jr., "Neorealism and Neoliberalism," *World Politics* 40 (January 1988), pp. 235–51.
64. For a few of the many possible examples, see Robert Jervis, "Security Regimes," *International Organization* 36 (Spring 1982), pp. 173–94; Charles Lipson, "International Cooperation in Economic and Security Affairs," *World Politics* 37 (October 1984), pp. 1–23; Nye, "Neorealism and Neoliberalism"; Keohane, "International Institutions," p. 386; and Gowa, "Bipolarity, Multipolarity, and Free Trade."

International Organization and the Theory of Property Rights

John A. C. Conybeare

INTRODUCTION

A specter haunts the world's bureaucrats: the specter of small government. Skepticism about the expanding role of government in most industrial nations has encouraged political economists to go back to some fundamental questions about what we really need government to do for us, whether it be for reasons of efficiency or equity. The aim of this paper is to suggest that some of the theories attacking "big" government are equally applicable in the realm of international organization (IO).

. . . The traditional, and still dominant, IO view of the world is that we should aspire to create supranational, federal structures which will directly allocate the world's resources. . . .

It is the theme of this paper that such aspirations are not only impractical, but also undesirable. This paper sets out to outline the property rights theory behind the argument, suggest how these criteria for providing efficient nongovernmental solutions to problems have been incorporated into international law, and offer further IO applications in areas not traditionally considered by public choice theory. It will then deal with the international implications of the problems usually raised in discussions of property rights theory, and finally draw together the range of policy choices implied by the PR approach.

EXTERNALITIES AND PROPERTY RIGHTS

Market Failure and the Role of Government

Many political scientists tend to take for granted the efficiency, if not the legitimacy, of government intervention in market transactions. Most, therefore, simply classify policy according to the scope and aims of governments. Economists are more interested in examining the conditions under which it may be efficient for governments to directly affect the allocation of resources in society. A major focus of this interest has been on the role of governments in correcting market failures or, more particularly, externalities. . . .[1]

Externalities occur where there is a discrepancy between private and social marginal product or cost. They involve unavoidable and unintended side effects directly on the production of goods and services or the enjoyment derived from their consumption. The existence of technical or ownership externalities has provided a powerful economic rationale for the expansion of the role of government on purely efficiency grounds, even without considering equity arguments. . . .

The classic exposition of the externality correcting role of government is that of Pigou, who suggested that a major role for government should be to effect an efficient allocation of resources by inducing private actors to internalize externalities (e.g., by taxing the polluter), and in particular, by making producers of externalities liable for harmful effects. . . .[2]

The Coase Theorem

Since 1960 an area of social theory bridging the fields of law, political science and economics and known as "public choice–property rights" has evolved. . . . The PR school provides an argument that the Pigovian rationale for government directly allocating resources is unnecessary and inequitable. First, Coase shows that, in the absence of government intervention, a market system will lead to the internalization of externalities. Where transaction costs are zero, the ultimate allocation of resources will be the same regardless of which party has a property right in creating or preventing the externality. Second, he argues that to presume that the producer of an externality should automatically be liable cannot be justified on grounds of social utility and appears to him to be an arbitrarily inequitable rule. Thus, Coase attacks the two basic Pigovian arguments for government intervention—viz., that the government should automatically make producers of externalities liable for their effects, and that it should intervene to force the producer to internalize the externality. . . .

Property Rights and Liability Rules

Calabressi and Melamed have extended Coase's analysis in their typology of different methods of protecting entitlements: property rights (entitlements which must be purchased in voluntary transactions), liability rules (a party wishing to destroy an entitlement must pay an objectively determined value for it), and inalienable entitlements (rights which cannot be subject to market transactions). The importance of the article is in the attention they focus on the type of common contingencies in municipal tort and property law where the specification of property rights is insufficient to ensure socially optimal outcomes due to the objective structure of the situation or to problems of moral hazard.[3]

Liability rules may be adopted where transaction costs are high or of uncertain magnitude, where strategic behavior (e.g., extortion, non-revelation of preferences, free-riding) might constrain socially optimal outcomes, where externalities involve accidents, and to meet equity or distributional goals. Consumers are protected by product liability rules for transaction cost reasons. Pedestrians are protected from vehicle drivers by liability rules because injury to them is normally accidental (i.e., we cannot buy in advance the right to run down a specific pedestrian). . . . Liability rules in the above examples might also be justified on equity grounds. Inalienable rights serve similar purposes, though are more often used to protect equity goals involving basic norms and values (e.g., we cannot sell our children into slavery).

Liability rules involve a higher degree of state intervention than do property or inalienable rights, since the state must determine the value of an entitlement in the former. Again there are obvious parallels in the IO sphere. We need, for example, liability rules for oil tanker spills and compensation for nationalization of foreign assets. More important is that even liability rules involve less government control than is often advocated by IO scholars and practitioners. . . .

EXTERNALITIES AND THE DEVELOPMENT OF INTERNATIONAL LAW

As Coase pointed out that municipal tort law has long recognized the utility of market solutions to externalities, it may further be shown that international law has also developed in such a way as to obviate the kind of supranational powers envisaged by the IO school. This development is most salient in international environmental law where the delimitation of an externality is clearest.[4] More generally, there exist multiple legal remedies under European and North American law for the pursuit of tort actions. Many of these remedies are obtainable precisely in those areas where the IO school argues that we most need a supranational regime (e.g., uses of the sea). The development of international environmental law has shown that insofar as nations can agree upon efficient entitlement rules (liabilities or property rights) that the IO approach is unnecessary, arbitrary, and inefficient. . . .

. . . The doctrine of strict or absolute liability for externalities imposed on another state was established by a series of cases in the first half of the twentieth century. The Trail Smelter case (1935) established the liability of a Canadian iron ore smelter for damages to U.S. farmers. The Corfu Channel decision (1949) assigned liability to Albania for damage to British warships in Albanian waters. Recent development of international law has focused on criteria of equitable apportionment. The Lake Lanoux case (1960) enjoined states involved in creating externalities to "take into consideration the various interests involved, to seek to give them every satisfaction compatible with the pursuit of its own interests."[5]

The evolution of international externality law illustrates the ability of states operating in a market exchange environment to develop a system of property rights and liability rules consistent with global welfare, in the absence of any overarching supranational IO directly intervening to force states to internalize the effects of externalities. There exist today legal mechanisms for dealing with marine, freshwater, air, space, and radioactivity externalities. Hence, the development of international environmental law illustrates the point made by Coase with regard to municipal law: recognized rules regarding property rights and liability rules may not require direct governmental intervention in order to achieve an optimal allocation of resources. . . .

This brief survey of international law should serve to make it clear that, despite the difficulties in developing a workable system of market regulated entitlements in international externalities, such rules are not inherently any more unfeasible than in municipal law. . . .

APPLICATIONS OF PR THEORY BEYOND CONVENTIONAL TORT LAW

The foregoing argument may appear to be unfair to the supranationalists in the IO school, since they reserve their greatest efforts in the call for world government in areas considered to be more highly politicized (e.g., nuclear proliferation, tariff wars, drug trafficking, refugee settlement and multinational corporations). The following section will suggest that in some areas the existing situation is already globally efficient, and that in others efficient solutions could be reached by clearer delineations of property rights and liabilities. This is not to say that IOs may not play a useful role. On the contrary, there are a large number of IOs performing important information-gathering tasks. What PR theory does suggest is that their role might be limited to the providing of information and a forum for agreements on entitlements. . . .

The operative question in the PR approach is: upon whom should property rights or liability be conferred, in order to achieve socially efficient solutions. PR theory suggests that, ceteris paribus, entitlements should be vested in the party with the higher marginal transaction costs. . . . Considering some of the more contentious issues in international politics there appear to be some areas where PR criteria are already well established.

International Finance

The history of the international monetary system since 1945 has been a history of attempts to impose an IO solution on market forces. The breakdown of fixed exchange rates in 1971 has forced governments toward solutions more consistent with PR criteria. Where exchange rate movements are constrained, as in the European Monetary System (EMS), rules have been established to identify liability to intervene to keep currencies within the agreed band width. Under the old "snake" system of exchange rate management, strong currencies pulled the snake upward, forcing weak currency countries to intervene in the foreign exchange markets. Unless these small or weak currency countries had a zero marginal valuation on having to adjust macroeconomic policies or use foreign exchange reserves, the system tended to produce a suboptimal corner solution (viz., small or weak states being forced to absorb the entire adjustment cost of maintaining the snake). . . . This was perhaps due to the transaction cost to the smaller powers of bribing the large powers to accept a more interventionist role. The new EMS has attempted to distribute intervention liabilities so as to put more of the burden onto strong currency members. The liability rule approach was adopted in this case not only because of transaction costs, but also to meet demands for equity and limitations on strategic behavior, such as competitive exchange rate practices. In a wider context, the International Monetary Fund attempts to monitor rules for orderly exchange rate movements, having failed in its earlier role as a supranational IO directly controlling exchange rate changes. . . .

International Trade

The General Agreement on Tariffs and Trade (GATT) has long operated by rules consistent with PR principles. The Most Favored Nation clause is a recognition that transaction costs would be very high in the case of a large number of countries attempting to induce a country with discriminatory tariffs to reduce them. Hence, GATT confers a prohibitive liability on geographically discriminatory tariffs, though the rule breaks down in the case of customs unions or free trade areas. . . .

Anti-dumping regulations, at least in the United States, are also broadly consistent with PR principles. The U.S. Trade Act of 1974 defines liability rules for dumping: the U.S. International Trade Commission must show that increased imports have been a substantial cause of serious injury to a U.S. industry. Put in the terms of PR theory, the United States pays the transaction costs but places liability on the dumper (i.e., the dumper must "pay" in the form of tariffs or quotas). The dumper's detection costs are likely to be less (since it knows where it is dumping, the U.S. government does not), though bargaining and enforcement costs should be less for the government. Relative transaction costs do not provide a clear criterion for an efficient assignment of entitlements. The uncertainty in assessing the relative magnitude of transaction costs suggests the appropriateness of a liability rule. In this case, however, since transaction costs may be nearly equal, and since the United States automatically pays all transaction costs (i.e., its choice of an optimal supply of dumping is independent of transaction costs), the Coase theorem suggests that it does not matter who has liability. Both parties then revert to operating on their original marginal value and cost curves, not adjusted for transaction costs, and the United States treats transaction costs as an "overhead" variable cost of having an anti-dumping policy.

The application of PR theory to tariff policy needs to be treated with care, since an ordinary case of injury from import competition need not constitute justification for an anti-dumping rule based on externality criteria. The decline of an industry losing its comparative advantage to foreign competitors does not involve any dead weight loss, and hence there is no externality. It is only in the case of genuinely predatory dumping that the liability rule could be justified purely in terms of PR theory. . . .

Multinational Corporations (MNCs)

Certain effects of MNCs upon host countries may be thought of as positive (e.g., technological spinoff) or negative (e.g., political subversion, dual economy) externalities. The transaction costs, on an inter-country basis, of correcting the negative externalities are probably less for the United States (since it has administrative economies of scale in the enforcement of global behavioral criteria on its corporations) than for host countries, who would have to act in concert to limit certain forms (e.g., transfer pricing). . . .

In MNC-host bargaining, transaction costs are also likely to be less for the MNC (except those in the primary and parts of the secondary sector), which can more easily shift operations to other parts of the globe (i.e., it is hard for the host country to move away). An MNC with a low level of fixed capital investment might easily shift to another country, whereas the cost to the host of detecting, monitoring, and enforcing rules on a footloose corporation may be prohibitively high. The attempts which some nations have made to regulate foreign banks may be a case in point, since the transaction cost to the bank of moving to a more congenial domicile is minimal. Thus, it may be appropriate that MNCs should "pay" host countries to tolerate negative externalities; payment in these cases consisting of taxes, exchange controls, local equity rules, expropriation risk, and other penalties imposed by host nations. However, where the MNC's fixed investment is high (e.g., consumer goods industries), it is desirable that the host country's property right be limited in some part by rules of liability (e.g., the U.S. Hickenlooper Amendment invoking sanctions against countries which expropriate U.S. assets without due compensation). Liability rules here can also be justified by the need to deter extortion. Also, because some of the negative externalities have characteristics analogous to accidents, and because liabilities may not be fully acknowledged, the Organization for Economic Cooperation and Development (OECD) and the United Nations have put forward codes of conduct which home countries of the MNCs should impose on their corporations.

Law of the Sea

Communal ownership of the sea's resources produces numerous externalities (e.g., over-fishing, pollution). The sea is often cited as an example of the problem which Hardin has called "the tragedy of the commons," where everyone has an incentive to overuse a communal resource.[6] The typical IO solution is to call for complete governmental regulation of the uses of the sea. PR theory suggests that the establishment of property rights (e.g., expansion of territorial seas) and agreement on liability rules (e.g., for oil spills) will more efficiently lead to the internalization of these externalities. Prior to the establishment of 200 mile limits there was no incentive for countries to limit their exploitation of fishing and other resources close to other nations' shores. The only limits were loose agreements on the permissible sizes of catches in the fishing, sealing, and whaling industries. Introducing property rights internalizes externalities in a more easily enforceable manner than catch limits and forces fishing nations to pay for the externality of fishing beyond their territorial waters. . . .

Drug Traffic

Countries exporting drugs inflict an externality upon the importing nations. The externality is not the consumption of drugs, per se, since consumption is voluntary and, therefore, not a true externality, but it is rather the social costs of drug-taking (crime, health costs, lower productivity, etc.). Transaction costs are clearly lower for the intelligence networks and satellite surveillance facilities of the importing countries, since all they need do is identify the source country and monitor production. Producer countries would have the far harder task of identifying market destinations and monitoring consumption. It is entirely appropriate that the United States should pay Turkey to pass laws forcing poppy farmers to produce other crops, and to pay for Mexico's marijuana spraying operations. The same argument could be extended to cigarettes and alcohol, where the property right operates in a similar fashion: cigarette and alcohol producers have to buy the right to impose an externality, the payment being that part of indirect taxation on consumption which is paid by the producer. These taxes partly compensate the government for higher health costs, etc.

Nuclear Proliferation

The traditional IO approach of persuading countries to sign a Non-Proliferation Treaty and to be monitored by the International Atomic Energy Agency has been of questionable benefit. This may be explained in terms of the failure of the NPT to offer any side payment to the potential proliferator to induce it to give up its property right to acquire nuclear weapons. The Carter administration's policy, initially put forward early in 1977, has been to buy from countries their right to plutonium technology (viz., fuel reprocessing and fast breeder technology) by assuring them of supplies of slightly enriched uranium for peaceful uses. The problem with the Carter policy seems to have been that the payment being offered did not approximate the value which other nations place on indigenous nuclear capabilities. In any case, the transaction cost criteria suggest that this is more efficient than having a large number of countries "paying" the United States for the right to develop weapons grade technology, assuming that such a reassignment of property rights existed.

The externality in the more general case is the finite risk of war imposed on the global system as a result of any one nation acquiring nuclear weapons. . . . Should this nation pay the rest of the world for the externality it creates, or should the world pay it to remain non-nuclear? The transaction costs are likely to be prohibitively high for either party, with the exception of the previous case where the United States itself pays the transaction costs (as well as the side payment), giving the rest of the world a free good. Barring this exceptional case (and Carter's anti-proliferation policy has had little success), global liability rules (e.g., test bans) might be the only feasible policy to avoid a no-trade situation arising out of mutually high transaction costs.

International Air Traffic Authority (IATA)

This attempt to regulate externalities with a supranational IO has failed, as the major airlines resign (e.g., Pan Am) and governments negotiate air traffic routes largely on a bilateral basis. IATA had attempted to regulate the market by way of inalienable rights (the so-called "six freedoms" involving carriage rights) and price fixing. An externality was created through the need to ensure the survival of the least efficient airlines, usually the flag carriers. The externality was the welfare loss to the air traffic consumers resulting from a restricted output and higher prices. The market solution of having air travellers or nations with high efficiency airlines pay the low efficiency airline countries to close down their flag carriers never eventuated, for reasons of transaction cost and distributional equity (e.g., one may doubt the political feasibility of, say, the United States paying Australia to close down Qantas). The recent action of the United States in initiating the breakdown of IATA is resulting in a market bargaining situation, as nations pursue bilateral negotiations which should internalize the externalities resulting from the existence of low efficiency flag carriers.

There are other areas where PR principles are not explicitly recognized, but may usefully be applied. . . .

New International Economic Order (NIEO)

The range of trade and development issues on which the less developed countries (LDCs) seek redress involve, in the broadest sense, "imperialism" as an externality: the "dependencia" phenomenon, development aid, control of the world shipping market, tariffs, external debt, and commodity price fluctuations. All of the phenomena which allegedly constitute imperialism may be considered externalities insofar as they constitute unavoidable and unintended side effects imposed on the LDCs by the developed nations in the pursuit of their own national goals. As the polluter harms the pollutee, so the industrial policies of the developed country (e.g., tariff protection of a declining textile industry) may have unintended harmful side effects upon the LDC. The NIEO may be seen as an attempt by the LDCs to seek recognition of the property right and compensatory payments. Their motive is equity, but PR theory suggests that their claims could equally be made on efficiency grounds.

One reason why the LDCs have had so little success in their demands is that their policy includes seeking a supranational IO solution to the problem, via the UN Conference on Trade and Development (UNCTAD). Results of negotiations seem to be more encouraging when issues are broken down into more manageable components (e.g., EEC aid to former colonies, US tariff preferences for developing countries). In these cases, the transaction costs, as well as the marginal values of the issues, are clearer and more negotiable. On most of these individual questions, the transaction costs are less for a developed country negotiating with a group of LDCs, and payment to the latter is the frequent and appropriate result. Consolidating their interests in UNCTAD may reduce the developing countries' transaction costs, but also obscures assessment of the component issues, making negotiation and payment more difficult. In addition, UNCTAD raises the question that if transaction costs are thereby made less for LDCs, their claim to an entitlement may have a weaker justification on efficiency grounds. . . .

SOME DIFFICULTIES WITH THE PR APPROACH

Income Effects

Coase's conclusion that the allocation of resources will be invariant over differing assignments of property rights, with zero transactions costs, assumes that there are no significant income effects changing the transactors' marginal preference functions. If differing assignments of property rights affect a transactor's wealth, they will also affect the amount he is willing to pay for the internalization of the externality. Consider the case where country B causes pollution which seriously affects the wealth of country A. If a property right to pollute is assigned to B, A will be willing to pay $X for B to stop the polluting activity. However, if A has a property right in not being subjected to pollution, it might require $(X+Y) in order to tolerate pollution. This is because the property right raises A's wealth enough to make it value non-pollution more highly than it would if B had the property right (i.e., A's marginal utility for income decreases as income rises). In this case, the assignment of property rights affects the allocation of resources under zero transaction costs, and adds a further distortion where transaction costs are present. . . .

Ethics and Equity

Coase's original approach dismissed the equity problem on the grounds that there is no greater ethical imperative to give property rights to an externality receptor than to the creator. PR theorists are not generally interested in how property rights have come to be allocated, or in distributional justice, but only in whether or not the existing distribution of entitlements is efficient. . . . Equity can be taken into account in assigning property rights, and where transaction costs are zero there is no conflict between efficiency and equity. The usual method of introducing equity is by means of liability rules, already an accepted practice in international law. The statute of the International Court of Justice, for example, cites poverty of the tortfeasor as grounds for reducing damages. . . . The recent cancellation of the official external debt of some of the poorest LDCs appears to be an implicit application of this principle. In the area of international pollution control, certain LDCs (such as Brazil) have argued that they should have a greater right to pollute the globe by virtue of being less developed.[7]

Issue Linkage

. . . The effect of linkage is to reduce the marginal value of the externality to one linker (since he is getting a "free" gain on another issue) and to raise the marginal value to the other (since he must gain on this issue to compensate for taking a loss on another issue). The linkage must result in a Pareto optimal trade (i.e., one linker gains more on the current issue than he loses on the concessional issue, and vice-versa for the other). The result is to shift the outcome further toward that which would exist initially with the linker's preferred assignment of property rights.

Linkage may also be examined in terms of logrolling (or vote trading, when it occurs in real time) where there are more than two parties. The literature in this area suggests that logrolling may lead to Pareto optimal trades and improve on bilateral Coasian transactions. Problems occur with cyclical majorities and costs imposed on nondominating coalitions. However, this literature does not discuss multiparty linkage in the context of positive transaction costs and so is of limited use in considering prescriptive rules for the optimal assignment of property rights. . . .

Blackmail or Extortion

Any property right may induce the party without liability to threaten to produce an externality for the purpose of extorting gains in excess of those which would be made in the ordinary course of Coasian bargaining. France might threaten to test more nuclear weapons in the Pacific unless paid not to do so by Australia. Turkey might threaten to export more opium unless paid not to do so by the United States. How does one distinguish extortion from legitimate transactions?

Demsetz suggests that there is no useful economic distinction between the two, and that extortion is merely monopoly in reverse (viz., maximizing rent by producing too much of a good rather than too little).[8] The distinction between extortion and legitimate bargaining, he says, is a purely legalistic one. If this were the case, there would be no need to regard extortion as a problem for the Coase theorem, since the polluter and pollutee . . . are in a bilateral monopoly relationship. However, Demsetz is mistaken. . . . As Daly and Giertz note, the aggregate social utility effect of extortion is zero, when compared with the situation which would prevail under independent behavior (i.e., no extortion). All that is achieved is a redistribution of income.[9] Social utility is negative if there is a transaction cost in making, executing, or resisting the threat. This distinguishes extortion from conventional bargaining where there is an improvement in social utility.

In applying PR theory to international externalities there is some need to proscribe extortionate threats. . . .

Coercion and Enforcement

A higher propensity to deny the role of law . . . and to resort to coercion is a characteristic distinguishing international from domestic politics. Analytically, the use of force or coercion . . . poses the same problem as does extortion, since the coercing state is usually threatening to perform an act which in itself would be of no benefit. Without mechanisms to enforce property rights, states creating negative externalities will automatically retain property rights. . . . The United States refused to limit nuclear testing during the 1950s on the grounds that the costs were "reasonable," given the necessity of nuclear weapons to defend the free world. . . .[10] Powerful states may not only deny liability but reverse it. The United States for example, can force host countries to accept liability for compensating nationalized U.S. corporations, regardless of whether such an allocation of property rights is globally optimal. Similarly, Japan has been forced to accept "voluntary" quotas on some exports to the United States.

This problem may not be as serious as it appears. An emerging feature of the current "muted bipolar" system is that resort to force is an illegitimate instrument of policy. Adding to this change in global values, norms of reciprocity make resort to force more costly, particularly when force is used to violate entitlements generally regarded as inalienable (e.g., the right to political self-determination). . . .

. . . Most of the kinds of externalities considered in this paper do not involve coercion or unilateral assertion of property rights. States are more frequently waiving sovereign immunity and submitting tort actions to international tribunals. In any case, many international torts involve private parties where immunity is not at issue.

Nevertheless, the use of force or coercion is a limit to the application of PR theory. One might argue that, if a state is prepared to incur the high cost of using force, it must place such a high value on the externality that a corner solution (i.e., externality control totally in favor of the coercing state) is Pareto optimal. . . . Such an interpretation dissolves the distinction between force and legitimate bargaining. One might be tempted to conclude that the only force which would be inconsistent with PR principles would be force which did not reflect the actor's valuation of the externality. However, as Calabressi and Melamed point out in their discussion of the relationship of PR theory to criminal law, the use of force allows the unilateral conversion of all property rights into liability rules. Hence municipal law must have criminal sanctions rather than simply charging, say, a thief for the value of the article stolen.[11] Similarly, the maintenance of international property rights requires a prohibition on the use of force, regardless of whether or not the force reflected the actor's true valuation of the good.

PUBLIC GOODS: ARE THEY A SPECIAL CASE?

The Coase theorem breaks down, it has been said, where the externality has the characteristic of a public good to one of the parties.[12] A public good is one which has the property of nonappropriability (i.e., nonexcludability, because it cannot be withheld from those who do not contribute) and indivisibility (i.e., jointness of supply, since consumption by one person does not reduce the amount available to anyone else). As a result, there may be a strong rational incentive for any one actor to be a free rider, reducing his contribution to the provision of the good. The extreme case is where there is a large number of actors, each of whose benefit from the public good is infinitely small relative to the total social benefit. . . .

The next step in this line of argument is to suggest that public goods must be provided directly by governments. A major thrust of the IO approach is the argument that most international problems are of a public good nature and are therefore inherently unsolvable by market forces. IOs have an obvious bureaucratic interest in seeing public goods everywhere. IO theorists also predictably argue that international interdependence requires more supranational government to provide for an increasing number of public goods needs. . . .

The PR approach is not so easily demolished, and a number of points should be made in connection with the public goods critique:

a. The problem of providing public goods is simply a case of high transaction costs, which might be prescriptive solved simply by assigning a property right to the party with the higher transaction costs. Thus, when a large power is negotiating with a number of small powers, the issue may assume the character of a public good for the latter, raising their transaction costs to a level that would produce no trade if the large power has the property right. Some of the major international public goods problems could be dealt with in this manner (e.g., uses of the sea, nuclear proliferation, pollution). A genuine problem arises where there is no counterpart upon whom liability can be assigned (e.g., the International Year of the Child as a public good).

b. It is not necessarily true . . . that the larger a group is, the farther it will fall short of providing an optimal supply of a public good. Chamberlin shows that as group size increases, the reduction in individual contributions is at a slower rate than the increase in group size (due to income effects of the provision of the public good); hence the total amount of the public good increases with group size, up to an absolute limit. . . .[13]

Under what conditions may we expect a low level of suboptimality to obviate the need for governmental supply of the public good? The degree of suboptimality resulting . . . depends on the form of the reaction functions determining each actor's contribution. . . . The public goods literature offers several basic behavioral sources of cooperative reaction functions.

Some international public goods are supplied by virtue of "norms of reciprocity" (e.g., contributions to UN peacekeeping operations). McMillan alludes to this factor in his survey of the free rider problem. . . .[14] Experimental evidence suggests that norms of reciprocity may develop even in situations as severely non-cooperative as the Prisoner's Dilemma game, particularly when the game is played on multiple occasions, as are most public good games. . . .[15]

Many collective action problems are solved by the desire of the beneficiaries to contribute so that they will be able to influence the exact form of the public good: ". . . if they are not represented in the coalition, they may find that their cheap ride is to a destination they do not favor."[16] The point was made in connection with domestic interest groups, but is equally applicable to international public goods. A nation which free rides in a military alliance, for example, cannot expect to influence the size, structure, or deployment of military forces.

Finally, cooperation may arise from some . . . "selective incentives" in the form of side payments, persuasion, or unilateral supply by a major beneficiary. In the same vein, Coase has pointed out that public goods may often be made private to the extent necessary to ensure their supply. He cites the example of a classic "public" good, the lighthouse, showing how in seventeenth century Britain lighthouses were provided by the marketplace because port facilities could be withheld from non-contributors. . . .[17]

Despite the arguments cited above, there are undoubtedly some areas where the public good or free rider problem is severe enough to justify supranational management. However, several further caveats are in order. First, the problem may well be dealt with by means far short of the direct provision of the good by a supranational IO. Liability rules have already been suggested as a means of dealing with high transaction costs. In such cases, liability rules would be the legalistic equivalent to marginal cost sharing as a solution to the non-supply of a public good.[18]

Second, the IO solution may produce welfare losses in excess of the value of the public good. The theory of fiscal federalism suggests[19] that unless the jurisdiction which provides the public good includes the entire set of consumers, inefficiencies will result. In the case of a global IO, inefficiencies result if the entire world is not effectively a consumer of the good. . . .

Even if a global IO is the optimal size of government unit, one must also consider the costs of non-market resource allocation by bureaucratic organizations. The IO solution by itself raises transaction costs. Further costs may be introduced by what Wolf calls "non-market failure," including monopoly, inefficiency, inequity, and non-optimal supply. . . .[20]

Finally, the IO solution tends to ignore two more fundamental problems: information and ethics. The ultimate rationale for a non-market solution is the argument that governments have better information about costs and preferences than the market, presumably because their marginal cost of acquiring information is thought to be less than that of a private actor. IO solutions implicitly assume that governments have this information, a premise which is the basis for their larger assumption that governments have lower transaction costs in correcting externalities than does the market. The IO approach also incorporates an ethical perspective increasingly under question by the new philosophers of distributional justice, who argue that the cost of making actors "forced riders" is unacceptable. Hence Nozick's case that the functions of government be limited to minimal police protection.[21]

SYNTHESIS: FROM COMMUNAL OWNERSHIP TO GOVERNMENT ALLOCATION

It would be unreasonable to characterize the policy options in dealing with transnational externalities as a dichotomous choice between market regulated property rights and total allocation of resources by an IO. What is needed is a delineation of the policy continuum between the two extremes, allowing some specification of the best solution for each type of externality. The typology below offers the rudiments of such a plan:

a. Unrestrained communal ownership, where the goods involved in the externality are effectively in unlimited supply, so that no usage externalities can arise. Extraterrestrial space is a contemporary example of such a case.

b. The allocation of property rights, where there is resource scarcity and conventional externalities occur (i.e., externalities not having any of the characteristics referred to below). IOs might play a useful role as a forum for the adjudication of property rights, as do contemporary international public and private arbitral tribunals.

c. Liability rules agreed to by states and administered by an IO, where problems arise that cannot be solved by altering property right assignments (e.g., accidents, high transaction costs for all parties, strategic behavior). Some of the problems mentioned above (e.g., income and equity) may often be dealt with by property right allocations.

d. Inalienable rights, or a prohibitive liability rule for forms of behavior which would destabilize the system (e.g., the use of force or coercion), result in zero or negative utility trades (e.g., extortion), or be in some sense irreversible (e.g., a nation should not be able to sell itself into slavery).

e. The establishment of an IO to directly allocate resources where the externality involves a public good which satisfies all of the conditions below:

   i. There is no definable counterliability or property right reassignment which would result in market provision of the good.

   ii. The parties to the public good have sufficiently uncooperative reaction functions that for the relevant group size, the public good will be significantly undersupplied.

   iii. The IO solution does not itself produce welfare losses in excess of the value of the public good, as a result of higher transaction costs or further externalities introduced by government. Welfare losses may arise as a result of the non-optimal size of the IO (the fiscal federalism argument), "non-market failure," governmental knowledge inferior to that of the market, a high level of community aversion to being "forced riders" and externality control problems relating to the theory of the second best.

One might object to a PR-based taxonomy on the grounds that the assumed goal is some combination of efficiency and equity. Governments, the "realist" would argue, are concerned with neither goal but, rather, with maximizing power. The obvious, unoriginal response to such an objection is to ask "power for what?"

The most casual observation of state behavior in IOs suggests that nations use power to seek outcomes which reflect their preference for efficiency (e.g., U.S. policies toward IATA) or equity (e.g., LDC policies in UNCTAD). . . .

NOTES

1. The forms of market failure are described by F. M. Bator, "The Anatomy of Market Failure," *Quarterly Journal of Economics* 72(1978):351–79.
2. See A. C. Pigou, *The Economics of Welfare* (London: Macmillan, 1920). An up-to-date exposition of the definitional limits to the concept of externalities may be found in E. J. Mishan, *Elements of Cost-Benefit Analysis,* 2nd. ed. (London: Allen and Unwin, 1976), pp. 85–90. The theory of the second best was first stated rigorously by R. G. Lipsey and K. Lancaster, "The General Theory of the Second Best," *Review of Economic Studies* 24(1956):11–32. Pareto irrelevant externalities are described in J. M. Buchanan and W. C. Stubblebine, "Externality," *Economica* 19(1962):371–84.
3. G. Calabressi and A. D. Melamed, "Property Rules, Liability Rules, and Inalienability: One View of the Cathedral," *Harvard Law Review* 85(1972):1089–129.
4. See L. A. Teclaff and A. E. Utton, eds., *International Environmental Law* (New York: Praeger, 1974); J. Nowak, ed., *Environmental Law: International and Comparative Aspects* (Dobbs Ferry, NY: Oceana, 1976); OECD, ed., *Problems in Transfrontier Pollution* (Paris: OECD, 1974).
5. Arbitral Tribunal decision quoted in J. W. Samuels, "International Control of Weather Modification Activities: Peril or Policy," in Teclaff and Utton, p. 232.
6. G. Hardin, "The Tragedy of the Commons," *Science* 162(1968):1243–8.
7. See D. Pirages, *The New Context for International Relations: Global Ecopolitics* (North Scituate, MA: Duxbury, 1978), pp. 63–5.
8. H. Demsetz, "Wealth Distribution and the Ownership of Property Rights," *Journal of Legal Studies* 1(1972):231–2.
9. G. Daly and J. F. Giertz, "Externalities, Extortion and Efficiency," *American Economic Review* 65(1975):999–1000.
10. A. A. D'Amato, "Legal Aspects of the French Nuclear Tests," *American Journal of International Law* 61(1967):67.
11. Calabressi and Melamed, pp. 1123–27.
12. See, for example, S. Wellisz, "On External Diseconomies and the Government Assisted Invisible Hand," *Economica* 31 (1964):553–4.
13. J. Chamberlin, "Provision of Collective Goods as a Function of Group Size," *American Political Science Review* 68(1974):707–16. The limit value of expenditure on the public good is stated mathematically in M. McGuire, "Group Size, Group Homogeneity and the Aggregate Provision of a Pure Public Good under Cournot Behavior," *Public Choice* 18(1974):112.
14. J. McMillan, "The Free-Rider Problem: A Survey," *Economic Record* 55(1979):102–4.
15. A survey of the evidence is provided in C. Nemeth, "A Critical Analysis of Research Utilizing the Prisoners' Dilemma Paradigm for the Study of Bargaining," *Advances in Experimental Social Psychology,* volume 6, L. Berkowitz, ed. (New York: Academic Press, 1972), pp. 203–34.
16. G. Stigler, "Free Riders and Collective Action: An Appendix to Theories of Economic Regulation," *Bell Journal of Economics and Management Science* 5(1974):362.
17. R. H. Coase, "The Lighthouse in Economics," *Journal of Law and Economics* 17(1974):357–76.

18. M. Olson, "Increasing the Incentives for International Collaboration," *International Organization* 25(1971):871–4.
19. R. A. and P. B. Musgrave, *Public Finance in Theory and Practice* (New York: McGraw Hill, 1973), pp. 596–607.
20. C. Wolfe, "A Theory of Nonmarket Failure: Framework for Implementation Analysis," *Journal of Law and Economics* 22(1979):107–39.
21. R. Nozick, *Anarchy, State and Utopia* (New York: Basic Books, 1974).

The Concentration of Capabilities and International Trade

Edward D. Mansfield

Over the course of the previous two decades, political scientists have become increasingly interested in the relationship between international politics and global trade. Much of the literature on this topic centers on the effects of a hegemonic distribution of power on commerce. Hegemonic stability theorists argue that hegemony is a necessary condition for the existence of a liberal economic order and that in the absence of a hegemon, a liberal international economy is particularly difficult to establish and maintain. However, a growing number of theoretical and empirical critiques have been leveled against hegemonic stability theory, and the issue of whether hegemony helps shape patterns of global trade continues to be the topic of heated debate.

Despite the interest that this debate has spawned, virtually no longitudinal statistical tests of the relationship between hegemony (or, more generally, the distribution of power) and international trade have been conducted. In this article, I conduct some of the first quantitative tests of the influence that both political and economic features of the international system have on trade. The results indicate that the distribution of power strongly affects international commerce but that the nature of the relationship is much different than is commonly thought. . . .

HEGEMONY AND TRADE

Hegemonic stability theorists agree that hegemony is associated with an open trading system, while the lack of a hegemon is associated with closure. Many of them also agree that because a liberal trading system takes on features of a public good, its creation and maintenance engender collective action problems.[1] Without a state that is willing and able to act as a privileged group and unilaterally provide a liberal trading order, the establishment of a system characterized by free trade is unlikely.

Hegemonic stability theorists disagree, however, on why hegemons provide a liberal trading system. On the one hand, Charles Kindleberger suggests that hegemons provide public goods largely for altruistic reasons.[2] He maintains that the central cause of the depression during the 1930s was the absence of a benevolent "stabilizer" to coordinate the international economy;[3] Great Britain was no longer able to assume this role as it had done in the nineteenth century, and the United States was not yet willing to assume the mantle of leadership. On the other hand, Robert Gilpin, Stephen Krasner, and David Lake argue that because the hegemon derives disproportionately greater gains from such a system, it has an incentive to create and sustain a liberal international economic order.[4] They maintain that the periods of relatively free trade during the nineteenth century and after World War II can be explained best by the benefits that accrued to Great Britain and the United States from an open trading system.[5]

During the past decade, much has been written on the theoretical limitations of hegemonic stability theory. Many critics argue that systems need not be hegemonic in order to be open and, hence, no strong relationship exists between international trade on the one hand and a hegemonic or nonhegemonic system on the other. Because the theory of collective action does not preclude the provision of public goods by small (or k) groups,[6] certain nonhegemonic systems can also lead to a liberal trading order. The existence of a hegemon may ameliorate collective action problems when public goods such as a trade regime are initially supplied; but hegemony is not necessary for either their provision or their maintenance.[7] Others maintain that hegemony is unrelated to trade because hegemonic stability theory incorrectly identifies free trade as a public good. Since free trade does not meet the criterion of nonexcludability, a hegemon need not act as a privileged group to ensure its provision.[8]

Analysts have also argued that hegemony is related to trade but that the relationship is inverse rather than direct. They posit that nonhegemonic systems are likely to be relatively liberal because in the absence of a hegemon, no state possesses sufficient market power to influence world prices through the use of trade barriers. A hegemon, in contrast, has the market power necessary to improve its terms of trade by imposing an optimal tariff, and the noncooperative aspects of international commerce provide it with the incentive to take advantage of this ability.[9]

However, the extent to which the critiques described in this section undercut hegemonic stability theory remains open to question. Joanne Gowa recently argued that critics "have not deprived hegemonic stability theory of its analytic base: hegemons can reject the prescriptions of standard trade theory [to impose optimal tariffs]; . . . open international markets [often] do present public-good problems; and privileged groups enjoy a stronger advantage than small-group advocates acknowledge."[10] Moreover, not all variants of this theory ascribe equal importance to the provision of public goods in the international political economy. Those analysts who place less weight on this aspect of hegemony are less susceptible to critiques that highlight either the absence of public goods in the international system or the ability of small groups to provide these goods. This suggests that the debate over the analytic underpinnings of hegemonic stability theory remains far from resolved. Also unresolved is the issue of what, if any, empirical relationship exists between hegemony and international trade.

EMPIRICAL EVIDENCE AND ISSUES REGARDING HEGEMONIC STABILITY THEORY

In addition to the analytic critiques discussed above, hegemonic stability theory has also been challenged on empirical grounds. First, some analysts have argued that the relationship between hegemony and an open international trading system is weak. For example, John Conybeare found little cross-sectional or longitudinal evidence that hegemony is associated with national tariff levels, based on data from 1902 and 1971.[11] Similarly, Timothy McKeown concluded that no strong relationship exists between variables related to hegemony and national import levels (as a percentage of national income) of the advanced industrialized states from 1880 to 1987.[12]

Second, while others have conceded that hegemony may be associated with a relatively open trading system, they have challenged the causal linkages between hegemony and commerce. For example, Timothy McKeown, Arthur Stein, Giulio Gallarotti, and Susan Strange have maintained that a variety of international political and economic factors provide more satisfactory explanations for the existence of a liberal trading system during the nineteenth century than does British hegemony.[13] And Robert Keohane has argued that while the empirical record from 1966 to 1977 is consistent with the predictions of hegemonic stability theory, the causal relationship between American hegemony and trade in manufactured goods is weak.[14]

Third, hegemonic stability theorists have been criticized for failing to measure adequately the distribution of power. This, in the opinion of some observers, has led them to choose incorrectly the cases of hegemony that they hold up as support for the theory. For example, Bruce Russett concluded that the theory mistakenly attributes hegemonic status to Great Britain during the nineteenth century and that, contrary to the position of many critics and adherents of the theory, American control over outcomes in the international political economy has not declined since the early 1970s.[15]

Three fundamental disagreements over the definition, measurement, and operationalization of hegemony underlie much of the controversy surrounding the empirical relationship between hegemony and trade. First, there is disagreement about the scope of hegemony—that is, disagreement about the aspects of international relations over which a state must wield preponderant power in order to be considered a hegemon.[16] Some scholars argue that hegemony is characterized by a situation in which a single state dominates and orders both economic and political relations.[17] Others, however, maintain that hegemony is characterized by a situation in which a single state dominates and orders international economic relations and possesses sufficient political power to ward off military threats to the international system.[18]

Second, there is disagreement about the domain of a hegemon—that is, disagreement about the range of actors over which a state must wield preponderant power in order to be considered a hegemon.[19] Although hegemonic stability theory purports to explain *systemic* outcomes, as Stephan Haggard and Beth Simmons point out, "the relevant 'structure' is usually defined [by hegemonic stability theorists] as the distribution of power within the international capitalist system rather than within the world political system as a whole."[20]

Finally, there is no consensus regarding the inequality of power that is necessary for hegemony to obtain. While analysts agree that a hegemon is more powerful than the other actors in the system, most have been conspicuously silent on the fundamental issue of *how much more powerful* it needs to be in order to meet the requirements for hegemony.[21] A related problem is that analysts tend to treat as homogeneous all nonhegemonic distributions of power. However, the starkness of the dichotomy between hegemony and nonhegemony may mask the differential effects of various nonhegemonic distributions of power on outcomes in the international political economy.[22]

These disagreements over the definition, measurement, and operationalization of hegemony appear to influence substantially the empirical relationship between hegemony and trade. For example, Conybeare's and McKeown's statistical results indicate that hegemony is largely unrelated to trade.[23] Alternatively, my own findings suggest that hegemony is associated with the level of global commerce: the relationship is direct when Robert Gilpin's data on hegemony are used, but it is inverse when Immanuel Wallerstein's data are used.[24] Moreover, even if hegemony had an unambiguous effect on the international trading system and no disagreements existed regarding how to define, measure, and operationalize it, hegemony is only one aspect of the distribution of power. Various other features of this distribution, not only hegemony, may have effects on trade; and it would be useful to analyze the effects of hegemony in conjunction with these other features of the distribution of power before assessing the extent to which hegemony can explain outcomes in the international political economy.

THE CONCENTRATION OF CAPABILITIES

In this study, I examine how the level of global trade as a percentage of global production is affected by hegemony and by the concentration of capabilities among the major powers in the international system. Despite disagreements over how to operationalize hegemony, most analysts agree that hegemony obtains when a sufficiently "large" disparity in power exists between the *two* most powerful states in the international system (and, by extension, between the largest state and every other state in the system). But whether or not the relative power disparity between the two most powerful states has or has not reached a particular threshold provides us with no information concerning how the remaining states in the system stand in relation to one another.

On the other hand, the index of concentration (CON) used in the present study[25] is a continuous measure of the distribution of power that takes on values ranging from 0 to 1 and measures the aggregate inequality of capabilities among all of the major powers. Hence, concentration is a measure of how *all* of the major powers stand in relation to one another. The index is as follows:

$$CON_t = \sqrt{\frac{\sum_{i=1}^{N_t} (S_{it})^2 - 1/N_t}{1 - 1/N_t}} \tag{1}$$

where N_t is the number of major powers in the system in year t, and S_{it} is the proportion of the capabilities possessed by all major powers that major power i controls in year t.[26]

A recent study has shown that the level of concentration is a function of two variables: the number of major powers in the international system and the relative inequality of capabilities among the major powers.[27] In particular,

$$CON_t = \frac{V_t}{\sqrt{N_t - 1}} \tag{2}$$

where V_t is the coefficient of variation (standard deviation divided by the mean) of S_{it} in year t. When N_t, the number of major powers in the international system, is held constant, CON_t is proportional to V_t, the relative inequality of capabilities.

It is clear that concentration will increase if, holding N (and the capabilities of all but the two largest major powers) constant, the relative disparity between the two largest major powers (and, hence, V) increases. In this sense, CON is related to hegemony. But concentration will also increase if: (1) holding N constant, a "small" major power's capabilities decline relative to those of the other major powers in the system (since this will also increase V), even though no change occurs in the distribution of capabilities between the two largest states; or (2) holding V constant, the number of major powers in the system decreases.[28] Thus, the distribution of power can be influenced by a variety of factors in addition to the relative position of the largest state in the international system. For this reason, I consider separately the effects of hegemony and concentration on the level of global commerce.

In addition to the richer typology of the distribution of power that is gained by examining features of both hegemony and the concentration of capabilities, there are a variety of other reasons to analyze the relationship between CON and trade. First, CON is jointly determined by N and V; and there has been considerable interest in the effect of the interaction between these variables on outcomes in the international political economy.[29] But despite long-standing calls for empirical research on this topic,[30] few studies of this sort have been conducted. By focusing on CON, it will be possible to assess empirically the influence of some aspects of the interaction between N and V on international trade.[31]

Second, one issue that is addressed in this study is the effect of market power on commerce. As Michael Waterson points out, economists "generally agree [that any measure of market structure] should be a one-dimensional measure, incorporating the two relevant aspects of industry structure, namely firm numbers . . . and size inequalities."[32] Conybeare suggests that for the purposes of measuring a hegemon's market power, "a Herfindahl index would be the best index of hegemony, since it would discriminate between situations where a country faced a large number of small powers or a small number of medium-sized countries."[33] Indeed, this index is widely used among economists to measure industry structure and market power. CON is closely related to the Hirschman-Herfindahl index; in fact, James Lee Ray and J. David Singer have demonstrated that it "is a perfectly predictable function of [the Hirschman-Herfindahl index], as long as we know the value of N."[34] But while CON is a measure of market power, it is important to reiterate that neither it nor the Hirschman-Herfindahl index is technically a measure of hegemony, since they both measure the distribution of power among all major powers—not only the relative strength of the most powerful state. It is precisely for this reason that CON is a more comprehensive measure of aggregate market power than hegemony is and thus ought to be considered in a study of this sort. Hegemons are not uniquely able to impose optimal tariffs: large nonhegemonic states may also possess considerable market power vis-à-vis the remaining states in the system.

Third, CON possesses a number of properties that are particularly desirable for analyzing the problem at hand. For example, . . . CON is measured by using economic and military (as well as demographic) capabilities, which are the same general indices of power that hegemonic stability theorists emphasize. Analyzing the effects on trade of both hegemony and concentration thus facilitates the comparison of different features of the distribution of power, holding constant the variables used to measure power.

The use of concentration also provides insights into a number of aspects of the relationship between the distribution of power and trade that hegemony is unable to provide. For example, while hegemonic stability theory is a theory of the international political economy, it is generally used to explain international relations among only the advanced industrialized countries. In contrast, CON measures the distribution of power among all of the major powers and, as a result, is closer than hegemony to a global measure of this distribution. Moreover, because CON is a continuous measure, it allows for the examination of the effects of different nonhegemonic distributions of power on trade and mitigates the problem of how to distinguish between hegemonic and nonhegemonic distributions of power.

RELATIVE INEQUALITY AND TRADE

The preceding discussion indicates that the international distribution of power is a function of both the number of major powers and the relative inequality among them. Because of their effects via CON and for other reasons, each of these variables is likely to influence global trade when the other is held constant.

Many theories about the international political economy focus primarily on the influence of the relative inequality of power in the system and place less emphasis on the size of the group. Most prominent among these explanations is hegemonic stability theory. The theory of hegemonic stability (as well as the theory of collective action) suggests that the effect of relative inequality on trade is direct. All other things being equal, greater relative inequality enhances the prospects for collective action;[35] as V approaches its highest level, the prospects for collective action in the global trading system are greatest. Lake, for example, has found empirical support for this hypothesis. After measuring the structure of the system in terms of the relative inequality of power among a fixed group of major powers, he concluded that higher levels of inequality were associated with greater openness.[36]

Alternatively, the relationship between relative inequality and trade may be inverse. The argument that Conybeare advances rests on the premise that, all other things being equal, "the gains from . . . tariff[s] . . . are likely to be directly proportional to the countries' relative sizes."[37] When the relative inequality among the major powers is low, no major power possesses sufficient market power to influence its terms of trade. Hence, states have little economic incentive to impose tariffs or other trade barriers that would be expected to reduce global trade.[38] As relative inequality reaches higher levels, so too does the relative market power of the largest state (or states) in the system. Since this state (or group of states) has an incentive to exploit its market power by imposing an optimal tariff, relative inequality may be inversely related to the level of global trade.[39]

GROUP SIZE AND TRADE

Another set of theories about the international political economy centers largely on the impact of group size and focuses less on the relative inequality among the states that comprise the group. Proponents of small group theory, for example, maintain that, all other things being equal, smaller groups are better able than larger groups to provide collective goods in international relations.[40] Thus, N may be inversely related to international trade when V is held constant.

Other scholars, however, imply that the number of major powers is directly associated with trade. Kenneth Waltz, for example, argues that as the number of major powers decreases, each major power is likely to be larger and more economically self-sufficient.[41] Since states in an anarchic system seek to reduce their dependence on one another, trade among major powers (which comprises a large portion of global trade) may be lowest when the number of major powers is small. Under these circumstances, major powers are best able to forgo commerce with, and limit their dependence on, one another. The number of major powers may also be directly related to trade if, as the size of the major power subsystem decreases, the market power of each major power increases vis-à-vis that of the remaining states in the system. Under these conditions, fewer major powers may be associated with higher overall tariff levels and thus with lower levels of global trade.

IS THE RELATIONSHIP BETWEEN CONCENTRATION AND TRADE CURVILINEAR?

It is also likely that V and N influence trade via their effects on concentration, as well as through other channels. With regard to their influence via concentration, I posit that the relationship between CON and trade is curvilinear. Specifically, I hypothesize that when N is held constant, this relationship is quadratic.

Conybeare suggests that when market power (and, hence, concentration) rises, trade falls. For low and moderate levels of concentration, this is likely to be the case. As V increases and N decreases (and CON increases), the market power of the dominant states rises, and these states are more likely to impose an optimal tariff. All other things being equal, less international commerce is expected to be conducted under these circumstances.[42]

However, this need not imply that the relationship between concentration and trade is always inverse. Beyond some level of concentration at which trade is minimized, I hypothesize that increases in CON will tend to increase commerce. Recent work by Gowa suggests why this may be the case.[43] States with little market power have few economic incentives to impose trade barriers; and as market power increases, so too does the economic incentive to impose an optimal tariff. But when concentration is highest, a rational, nonmyopic state with substantial market power may forgo the use of such an instrument in order to maintain its monopoly power in the international economy. And, as Gowa points out, even critics of hegemonic stability theory "acknowledge that hegemons which pursue political as well as economic goals may prefer free trade for political reasons."[44] For example, a hegemon that is interested in enhancing its political power may promote free trade in an effort to foster the dependence of smaller states.[45] A hegemon may also make commercial concessions and expand its trade with certain states in order to induce political concessions from these trading partners.[46]

This suggests that there is some level of concentration at which trade is minimized; but beyond this level, powerful states may abstain from the use of trade barriers for both political and economic reasons. Indeed, the level of global protectionism may be lowest and, hence, the level of trade may be greatest both when concentration is lowest *and* when concentration is highest. And the level of international trade may be minimized when concentration lies somewhere between its highest and lowest levels.[47] Thus, I hypothesize that a U-shaped (that is, quadratic) relationship exists between concentration and trade, since this is the simplest functional form of the relationship in which both of the extreme levels of concentration are associated with the highest levels of trade. . . .

THEORETICAL IMPLICATIONS OF THE FINDINGS

The results of this study have a number of important implications for theories of the international political economy. Debates surrounding the merits of hegemonic stability theory have been at the forefront of research on the international political economy for some time. One reason why these debates remain unresolved is that scholars do not agree on how to define, measure, and operationalize hegemony and, hence, no consensus exists regarding the influence of hegemony on international relations. My findings clearly illustrate this problem. . . . They strongly suggest that until the underlying conceptual ambiguities concerning hegemony are resolved, it will be extremely difficult to assess the usefulness of hegemonic stability theory.

But regardless of whether or not the relative inequality among the two largest major powers (hegemony) is associated with trade, more attention should be devoted to the effects of features of the distribution of capabilities among all of the major powers. When the total effects of N (both via CON and via other channels) are considered, the number of major powers is directly related to . . . [the level of international trade,] . . . which is at odds with the predictions based on small group theories. It could be argued that since the number of major powers does not exceed 8 during the period covered in my study, even a large number of major powers constitutes a k-group. Under these circumstances, small groups may be able to provide an open international trading system. Even if this is the case, however, small group theory remains mute on why the value of k should be directly, rather than inversely, related to the level of trade. Indeed, one of the major shortcomings of small group theory is that it fails to specify precisely *how small* a small group is.

Another reason why the results presented here are not consistent with expectations based on small group theories may be that small group theories draw their analytic foundation from the theory of collective action, and an open trading system is not a collective good. As such, neither a small group nor high levels of inequality are required for its provision. There is considerable evidence to support the position that many of the benefits derived from an open international economic order are quite excludable. The most obvious example of this is the Soviet Union and its allies, which, as many scholars have noted, had been systematically excluded from the benefits of free trade with the advanced industrialized countries since the conclusion of World War II.

One explanation for the direct relationship between group size and trade is that as N increases, the market power of each major power declines. As a result, the ability of any major power to impose an optimal tariff may be lowest as N approaches its maximum. These results may also reflect the fact that, all other things being equal, the smaller the number of major powers, the better able each major power is to provide for its own economic needs without engaging in commerce. And since there are security externalities associated with trade,[48] states may attempt to reduce their dependence on potential adversaries once they are self-sufficient enough to do so.

A related explanation for this finding inheres in the trade-offs between relative and absolute gains among states engaged in foreign trade. Neorealists have argued that cooperation in the international political economy is inhibited by concerns over how the gains from trade will be divided, since the distribution of these gains may influence the distribution of power among the participants in commerce.[49] However, Duncan Snidal has recently suggested that, under certain circumstances, the salience of concerns over relative gains is reduced as the number of major powers in the system increases.[50] Hence, the direct relationship between N and . . . [the level of international trade] . . . may reflect the tendency for states to worry less about the security implications of commerce, and therefore to become increasingly willing to engage in foreign trade, as N increases.

In addition to the effect of the number of major powers, there is substantial evidence that the relative inequality among the major powers is also related to trade and that this relationship is U-shaped. Further, such a relationship exists between concentration and trade. To the extent that market power is a function of V, this is entirely consistent with my hypothesis. High levels of trade may obtain when the level of relative inequality (and concentration) is low because under these conditions, market power is diffused among the states in the system. As the level of relative inequality (and concentration) increases, so too does the market power of the largest states in the system. This may lead these states to impose an optimal tariff, which would be expected to decrease global trade. But when market power is highest, states may choose to forgo the use of optimal tariffs for both economic and political reasons.[51]

Since hegemonic stability theorists are concerned primarily with the influence of relative inequality (and less with group size), the fact that higher levels of relative inequality are associated with higher levels of trade is consistent with their position. However, this relationship is much richer than they hypothesize, since there is considerable variation among nonhegemonic systems in the level of trade that is conducted. Systems in which the level of relative inequality is extremely high or extremely low are characterized by high levels of trade, whereas systems in which the level of relative inequality is intermediate are characterized by lower levels of trade.

Interestingly, the existence of a U-shaped relationship between relative inequality and trade is consistent with at least one variant of hegemonic stability theory. Krasner argues that while a preponderant state will favor an open trading system because it augments this state's political power, systems comprised of many small, highly developed states may also produce an open system because the opportunity costs of closure for states in such a system are quite large.[52] He adds, however, that "a system comprised of a few very large, but unequally developed states . . . is likely to lead to a closed system" because openness would create only moderate increases in these states' income and would engender social instability and political vulnerability.[53] Thus, Krasner suggests that the system is likely to be open when relative inequality is both highest and lowest. The results of my study are in accord with his position.

These results also suggest that critics of hegemonic stability theory are correct in arguing that shifts toward a more uniform distribution of capabilities need not be associated with closure, and that the prognosis offered by those analysts who predict that the decline in American power will undermine the liberal international economic order may be overly pessimistic. If, all other things being equal, V is greater than the level that minimizes trade and is reduced, these fears may be warranted. But if, for example, Germany and Japan have already become or are becoming major powers, the combination of a decrease in relative inequality and an increase in the number of major powers may improve the prospects for freer trade. . . .

Although there is considerable evidence that features of the distribution of capabilities help shape patterns in the international political economy, different features of the distribution of capabilities are related to the level of global trade in markedly different ways. Because much of the literature on the international political economy has focused exclusively on the effects of hegemony, studies of this topic have failed to uncover much of the relationship between the distribution of power and international commerce. . . .

NOTES

1. See Mancur Olson, *The Logic of Collective Action: Public Goods and the Theory of Groups* (Cambridge, MA: Harvard University Press, 1971).
2. See the following works by Charles P. Kindleberger: *The World in Depression, 1929–1939* (Berkeley: University of California Press, 1973); and "Dominance and Leadership in the International Economy: Exploitation, Public Goods, and Free Riders," *International Studies Quarterly* 25 (June 1981), pp. 242–54.
3. In his original study on this topic, Kindleberger argued that a hegemon provides a source of countercyclical liquidity and a market for distressed goods, helps stabilize currencies, serves as a lender of last resort, and ensures an open international trading system. In a subsequent study, he indicated that hegemons also manage foreign exchange rates and coordinate domestic monetary policies. See ibid.
4. See Robert Gilpin, *U.S. Power and the Multinational Corporation: The Political Economy of Foreign Direct Investment* (New York: Basic Books, 1975); Robert Gilpin, *War and Change in World Politics* (New York: Cambridge University Press, 1981); Robert Gilpin, *The Political Economy of International Relations* (Princeton, NJ: Princeton University Press, 1987); Stephen D. Krasner, "State Power and the Structure of International Trade," *World Politics* 28 (April 1976), pp. 317–47; and David A. Lake, *Power, Protection, and Free Trade: International Sources of U.S. Commercial Strategy, 1887–1939* (Ithaca, NY: Cornell University Press, 1988).
5. Hegemonic stability theorists often posit that hegemony is a necessary, though not a sufficient, condition for the development of a liberal international economic order. For example, Gilpin argues that in addition to hegemony, a "liberal ideology [and] common interests [among the states in the system] must exist for the emergence and expansion of the liberal market system." See Gilpin, *The Political Economy of International Relations,* p. 73; and Gilpin, *War and Change in World Politics,* chap. 3.
6. See Olson, *The Logic of Collective Action.*
7. See Timothy J. McKeown, "Hegemonic Stability Theory and 19th-Century Tariff Levels in Europe," *International Organization* 37 (Winter 1983), pp. 73–91; Robert O. Keohane, *After Hegemony: Discord and Collaboration in the World Political Economy* (Princeton, NJ: Princeton University Press, 1984); and Duncan Snidal, "The Limits of Hegemonic Stability Theory," *International Organization* 39 (Autumn 1985), pp. 579–614.
8. See John A. C. Conybeare, "Public Goods, Prisoners' Dilemmas and the International Political Economy," *International Studies Quarterly* 28 (March 1984), pp. 5–22; John A. C. Conybeare, *Trade Wars: The Theory and Practice of International Commercial Rivalry* (New York: Columbia University Press, 1987); Bruce Russett, "The Mysterious Case of Vanishing Hegemony; or, Is Mark Twain Really Dead?" *International Organization* 39 (Spring 1985), pp. 205–31, and Snidal, "The Limits of Hegemonic Stability Theory."

9. See Conybeare, "Public Goods, Prisoners' Dilemmas and the International Political Economy"; and Conybeare, *Trade Wars*.

10. See Joanne Gowa, "Rational Hegemons, Excludable Goods, and Small Groups: An Epitaph for Hegemonic Stability Theory?" *World Politics* 41 (April 1989), p. 322. In addition, Spiro argues that these critiques need not undermine hegemonic stability theory, since rather than expecting a relationship between hegemony and economic outcomes, we should expect variations in the nature of power that is exercised during different phases of hegemony. See David E. Spiro, "American Foreign Policy and International Finance," in Robert Art and Seyom Brown, eds., *American Foreign Policy After the Cold War* (New York: Macmillan, forthcoming).

11. John A. C. Conybeare, "Tariff Protection in Developed and Developing Countries: A Cross-Sectional and Longitudinal Analysis," *International Organization* 37 (Summer 1983), pp. 441–67.

12. Timothy J. McKeown, "A Liberal Trade Order? The Long-Run Pattern of Imports to the Advanced Capitalist States," *International Studies Quarterly* 35 (June 1991), pp. 151–72.

13. See McKeown, "Hegemonic Stability Theory and 19th-Century Tariff Levels in Europe"; Arthur A. Stein, "The Hegemon's Dilemma: Great Britain, the United States, and the International Economic Order," *International Organization* 38 (Spring 1984), pp. 355–86; Giulio M. Gallarotti, "Toward a Business Cycle Model of Tariffs," *International Organization* 39 (Winter 1985), pp. 155–87; and Susan Strange, "The Persistent Myth of Lost Hegemony," *International Organization* 41 (Autumn 1987), pp. 551–74.

14. See Robert O. Keohane, "The Theory of Hegemonic Stability and Changes in International Economic Regimes, 1967–1977," in Ole R. Holsti, Randolph M. Siverson, and Alexander L. George, eds., *Change in the International System* (Boulder, CO: Westview Press, 1980), pp. 131–62. Gilpin also notes the inability of hegemonic stability theory "to demonstrate a close association between power and outcome." And Lake argues that because hegemonic stability theory "lacks a conception of process, or an explanation of how the constraints or interests derived from the international economic structure are transformed into decisions or political strategies within particular countries . . . the causal link between the system-level international economic structure and national-level policy is open to question." See Gilpin, *The Political Economy of International Relations*, p. 91; and David A. Lake, "International Economic Structure and American Foreign Economic Policy," *World Politics* 35 (July 1983), pp. 539–40. See also Joseph S. Nye, *Bound to Lead: The Changing Nature of American Power* (New York: Basic Books, 1990).

15. See Russett, "The Mysterious Case of Vanishing Hegemony." See also McKeown. "Hegemonic Stability Theory and 19th-Century Tariff Levels in Europe"; Keohane, *After Hegemony;* Nye, *Bound to Lead;* Strange, "The Persistent Myth of Lost Hegemony"; and Susan Strange, *States and Markets* (New York: Basil Blackwell, 1988).

16. See Russett, "The Mysterious Case of Vanishing Hegemony"; and Nye, *Bound to Lead.*

17. See, for example, Gilpin, *U.S. Power and the Multinational Corporation;* Gilpin, *War and Change in World Politics;* Gilpin, *The Political Economy of International Relations;* Russett, "The Mysterious Case of Vanishing Hegemony"; Immanuel Wallerstein, "Three Instances of Hegemony in the History of the Capitalist World-Economy," *International Journal of Comparative Sociology,* vol. 24, no. 1–2, 1983, pp. 100–108; and Paul M. Kennedy, *The Rise and Fall of the Great Powers: Economic Change and Military Conflict from 1500 to 2000* (New York: Random House, 1987).

18. See, for example, Krasner, "State Power and the Structure of International Trade"; Keohane, *After Hegemony;* and Lake, *Power, Protection, and Free Trade.* In addition, some scholars (particularly those who study war, rather than the international political

economy) place less emphasis on economic power and define hegemony as a preponderance of political-military power. See Charles F. Doran and Wes Parsons, "War and the Cycle of Relative Power," *American Political Science Review* 74 (December 1980), pp. 947–65; Jack S. Levy, "The Polarity of the System and International Stability: An Empirical Analysis," in Alan Ned Sabrosky, ed., *Polarity and War* (Boulder, CO: Westview Press, 1985), pp. 41–66; George Modelski, "The Long Cycle of Global Politics and the Nation-State," *Comparative Studies in Society and History* 20 (April 1978), pp. 214–35; George Modelski and William R. Thompson, *Sea Power in Global Politics, 1494–1983* (Seattle: University of Washington Press, 1987); A. F. K. Organski, *World Politics* (New York: Knopf, 1958); and A. F. K. Organski and Jacek Kugler, *The War Ledger* (Chicago: University of Chicago Press, 1980). Still others differentiate between economic and political-military hegemony. See, for example, Joshua S. Goldstein, *Long Cycles* (New Haven, CT: Yale University Press, 1988). Hence, the types of power that are emphasized in the definition and operationalization of hegemony appear to be determined, in large measure, by the issue-area that is being studied. Further, some scholars of the international political economy argue that dimensions of hegemony other than political and economic power must also be considered. For example, Russett and Nye highlight the importance of cultural aspects of hegemony, and Ikenberry and Kupchan argue that hegemons exercise control by socializing elites in secondary states. See Russett, "The Mysterious Case of Vanishing Hegemony"; Nye, *Bound to Lead;* and G. John Ikenberry and Charles A. Kupchan, "Socialization and Hegemonic Power," *International Organization* 44 (Summer 1990), pp. 283–316. Despite their potential importance, these dimensions of hegemony are not considered in the present analysis because of the difficulty of operationalizing and measuring them.

19. For a more complete discussion of the importance of specifying the scope and domain of power in analyses of international relations, see David A. Baldwin, "Power Analysis and World Politics: New Trends Versus Old Tendencies," *World Politics* 31 (January 1979), pp. 161–94.

20. See Stephan Haggard and Beth A. Simmons, "Theories of International Regimes," *International Organization* 41 (Summer 1987), p. 503. See also Keohane, *After Hegemony;* Stein, "The Hegemon's Dilemma"; and Nye, *Bound to Lead.*

21. See McKeown, "Hegemonic Stability Theory and 19th-Century Tariff Levels in Europe"; Russett, "The Mysterious Case of Vanishing Hegemony"; and Frederick W. Frey, "The Distribution of Power in Political Systems," paper presented at the annual meeting of the American Political Science Association, Washington, DC, 1986.

22. See Lake, *Power, Protection, and Free Trade.*

23. See Conybeare, "Tariff Protection in Developed and Developing Countries"; and McKeown, "A Liberal Trade Order?"

24. See Edward D. Mansfield, "International Trade and the Onset of War," paper presented at the annual meeting of the American Political Science Association, Atlanta, Ga., 1989. The data are found in Gilpin's *War and Change in World Politics* and *The Political Economy of International Relations* and in Wallerstein's "Three Instances of Hegemony in the History of the Capitalist World-Economy."

25. The index of concentration used in my study is based on the work of Ray and Singer. See James Lee Ray and J. David Singer, "Measuring the Concentration of Power in the International System," *Sociological Methods and Research* 1 (May 1973), pp. 403–37.

26. Hence, CON measures the "standard deviation of the percentage shares [divided by] the maximum possible standard deviation in a system of size N." See Ray and Singer, op. cit., p. 422.

27. See Edward D. Mansfield, "The Concentration of Capabilities and the Onset of War," *Journal of Conflict Resolution* 36 (March 1992), pp. 3–24.

28. Of course, this assumes that $V > 0$.
29. See Bruce M. Russett and John D. Sullivan, "Collective Goods and International Organization," *International Organization* 25 (Autumn 1971), pp. 845–65; Duncan Snidal, "Coordination Versus Prisoners' Dilemma: Implications for International Cooperation and Regimes," *American Political Science Review* 79 (December 1985), pp. 923–42; and Snidal, "The Limits of Hegemonic Stability Theory."
30. See, for example, Russett and Sullivan, "Collective Goods and International Organization."
31. One reason for examining the interactive effects of these variables via concentration (rather than via some other variable that is a function of both N and V) is that although concentration has received little attention in studies of the international political economy, many analyses of war have used concentration to measure the distribution of power. See J. David Singer, Stuart Bremer, and John Stuckey, "Capability Distribution, Uncertainty, and Major Power Wars, 1820–1965," in Bruce M. Russett, ed., *Peace, War, and Numbers* (Beverly Hills, CA: Sage, 1972), pp. 19–48; Bruce Bueno de Mesquita, "Risk, Power Distributions, and the Likelihood of War," *International Studies Quarterly* 25 (December 1981), pp. 541–68; William R. Thompson, "Cycles, Capabilities, and War: An Ecumenical View," in William R. Thompson, ed., *Contending Approaches to World System Analysis* (Beverly Hills, CA: Sage, 1983), pp. 141–63; Bruce Bueno de Mesquita and David Lalman, "Empirical Support for Systemic and Dyadic Explanations of International Conflict," *World Politics* 41 (October 1988), pp. 1–20; and Mansfield, "The Concentration of Capabilities and the Onset of War." To my knowledge, the only study that analyzes the relationship between concentration and trade was conducted by McKeown. However, his analysis differs from the present study in a number of important ways. First, McKeown uses a different set of capabilities and major powers than I do to measure concentration. Second, his model is specified differently than mine. He examines the effects of the following on the ratio of imports to gross national product for industrialized capitalist countries: (1) the concentration of capabilities; (2) the percentage of global imports that the largest importer accounts for ($TCON1$); (3) the percentage of international imports that Great Britain, the United States, France, (West) Germany, and Japan account for ($TCON5$); (4) the ratio of $TCON1$ to $TCON5$; (5) the ratios of the nominal income of Great Britain and the United States, respectively, to that of the other leading states in the system; (6) time; (7) the growth of nominal income; and (8) a lagged dependent variable. See McKeown, "A Liberal Trade Order?"
32. See Michael Waterson, *Economic Theory of the Industry* (Cambridge: Cambridge University Press, 1984), pp. 166–67. See also F. M. Scherer, *Industrial Market Structure and Economic Performance*, 2d ed. (Chicago: Rand McNally, 1979), pp. 56–59.
33. Conybeare, *Trade Wars,* p. 287, fn. 4.
34. See Ray and Singer, "Measuring the Concentration of Power in the International System," p. 430. For the original derivation of the Hirschman-Herfindahl index (HH), see Albert O. Hirschman, *National Power and the Structure of Foreign Trade* (1945; reprint, Berkeley: University of California Press, 1980), pp. xviii–xx, 87–88, and 157–62. The equation for this index is as follows:

$$HHt = \sum_{i=1}^{N_t} S_{it}^2$$

Hence,

$$CON_t = \sqrt{\frac{HH_t - 1/N_t}{1 - 1/N_t}}$$

It is clear that the primary difference between HH and CON is that the latter is somewhat less sensitive than HH to the size of N, since the lower bound of CON is 0, while the lower bound of HH is $1/N$.

35. See Olson, *The Logic of Collective Action*.

36. In particular, Lake focuses on the United States, the United Kingdom, Germany, and France. Japan is also considered, beginning in 1950. See Lake, *Power, Protection, and Free Trade*, p. 33. For a critique of hegemonic stability theory that also centers on the effects of inequality, see Russett, "The Mysterious Case of Vanishing Hegemony."

37. Conybeare, *Trade Wars*, p. 26.

38. For a fuller discussion of this issue, see ibid.; Wilfred Ethier, *Modern International Economics* (New York: Norton, 1983); and Joanne Gowa, "Bipolarity, Multipolarity, and Free Trade," *American Political Science Review* 83 (December 1989), pp. 1245–56.

39. See Conybeare, "Public Goods, Prisoners' Dilemmas and the International Political Economy"; and Conybeare, *Trade Wars*. This, of course, assumes that a state's political power is roughly proportional to its market power—that is, to its ability to influence its terms of trade. The extent to which this is the case is an empirical question beyond the scope of this article. However, it is an assumption that is made often and one that seems reasonable for the purposes of a first cut at the problem.

40. See Keohane, *After Hegemony*; Robert Axelrod and Robert O. Keohane, "Achieving Cooperation Under Anarchy: Strategies and Institutions," *World Politics* 38 (October 1985), pp. 226–54; Russell Hardin, *Collective Action* (Baltimore, MD: Johns Hopkins University Press, 1982); Charles Lipson, "International Cooperation in Economic and Security Affairs," *World Politics* 37 (October 1984), pp. 1–23; Kenneth A. Oye, "Explaining Cooperation Under Anarchy: Hypotheses and Strategies," *World Politics* 38 (October 1985), pp. 1–24; and Thomas C. Schelling, *Micromotives and Macrobehavior* (New York: Norton, 1978), pp. 211–43.

41. See the following works of Kenneth N. Waltz: "The Myth of National Interdependence," in Charles P. Kindleberger, ed., *The International Corporation* (Cambridge, MA: MIT Press, 1970), pp. 205–23; and *Theory of International Politics* (New York: Random House, 1979).

42. Of course, this assumes that larger states will not band together to deter each other from imposing optimal tariffs. Under these circumstances, the level of protectionism may remain relatively low.

43. See Gowa, "Rational Hegemons, Excludable Goods, and Small Groups"; and Gowa, "Bipolarity, Multipolarity, and Free Trade."

44. See Gowa, "Rational Hegemons, Excludable Goods, and Small Groups," p. 311, fn. 12. See also Conybeare, "Public Goods, Prisoners' Dilemmas and the International Political Economy"; and Conybeare, *Trade Wars*.

45. See Hirschman, *National Power and the Structure of Foreign Trade*.

46. See Conybeare, "Public Goods, Prisoners' Dilemmas and the International Political Economy"; and McKeown, "Hegemonic Stability Theory and 19th-Century Tariff Levels in Europe."

47. Of course, I am only considering the range of variation of concentration found in the data. For example, if the world consisted entirely of two countries, one with few inhabitants, few resources, and little capital, and the other with the remainder of the world's population, resources, and capital, one would expect practically all trade to be intranational and the level of international commerce to be relatively small, even though the level of concentration might be quite high.

48. See Gowa, "Bipolarity, Multipolarity, and Free Trade."

49. See, for example, Waltz, *Theory of International Politics;* and Gilpin, *The Political Economy of International Relations.*

50. See Duncan Snidal, "Relative Gains and the Pattern of International Cooperation," *American Political Science Review* 85 (September 1991), pp. 701–26.

51. Conybeare notes that dominant states often did not impose optimal tariffs during the nineteenth and twentieth centuries, but he argues that this era is exceptional in this regard. See Conybeare, *Trade Wars,* pp. 271–72.

52. See Krasner, "State Power and the Structure of International Trade." According to Krasner, the opportunity costs are so large because each state derives benefits from an open system and smaller powers have difficulty existing under conditions of autarky.

53. Ibid., pp. 321–22.

Chapter
5

The Functions of International Organizations

Legitimization, Norm Creation, Standard Setting

Edward D. Mansfield

*I*n Chapter 2, Robert Keohane distinguishes between reflexivist and rational choice approaches to the study of international organization. These approaches are marked by (among other things) variations concerning the role of norms in institutionalizing the behavior of states.

Rational choice approaches often view those rules and norms that define institutions and regulate international behavior as instruments for the solution of (global) problems. Reflexivists, on the other hand, argue that, in addition to these functions, rules and norms also provide "meaning" to social interaction. They maintain that this function is particularly important for the characterization and appraisal of actions. Consider, for example, the issue of how we classify a particular action that leads to the death of a person. Whether we classify this action as a murder, a manslaughter, or an accident depends not only on the observation that an individual has died because of the action of another individual, but also on factors, such as what, if any, were the motives of the perpetrator and whether or not the death was due to planned aggression or self-defense. The answers to these (and other) questions give meaning to the action that was taken and thereby shape our views concerning how the individual responsible for the death should be treated. In the absence of intersubjective understandings embodied in norms, we would have to treat all individuals that were responsible for a death (for whatever reason) in the same manner.

Reflexivists posit that these considerations are also of great importance for the purposes of understanding international relations. For example, characterizing an action on the part of a state as aggression can result in different legal and political consequences than if this action is characterized as self-defense. For this reason, and because simply observing the use of force is not sufficient to determine how an action involving the use of force should be interpreted, these characterizations are often hotly contested.

One factor that further complicates these assessments is that the norms and principles which underlie the interactions among states are "self-applied." The fact that the international system is one of self-help means not only that there is no central enforcement of rules and norms, but also that there is no authoritative means with which to determine how an action should be appraised. One party's "terrorists" are often another party's "freedom fighters." This, in turn, renders problematic the stabilization of actor expectations in the global system. Another complicating factor of this sort concerns the argument made by some reflexivists that international norms are developed through custom. Since customs often evolve quite slowly, an extended period of trial and error is generally necessary before a new norm crystallizes. Further, no effective legislative process exists in international politics in which norms can be created or adapted for the regulation of newly emerging issues.

In sum, while realists and functionalists tend to emphasize the problem-solving capacity of international organizations, reflexivists emphasize the issue of legitimacy and the "legislative" capacity of international organizations. The selections in this chapter deal with the legitimizing role that international organizations play, as well as with the ways in which the norms that underlie these organizations are developed.

Inis Claude argues that "collective legitimization" is one of the main functions of universal international organizations, particularly the United Nations. For example, Claude points out that the legitimization of policies in the absence of authoritative decisions by central institutions is fundamental to the politics of international organization. It was also central to decisions regarding how to respond to independence movements on the parts of colonies and whether and how former colonies were to be included in the United Nations after they gained independence. Because the United Nations advocated the principle of self-determination, the legitimacy of rule by colonial powers became increasingly difficult to justify. In this case, the transition from legitimization to norm creation became increasingly important.

Jack Donnelly analyzes the role of legitimacy as it pertains to human rights. The shock of genocidal policies that were implemented by Nazi Germany created a broad consensus for the Universal Declaration of Human Rights and set in motion the subsequent codification of the two covenants. While the covenants represent formal multilateral treaties, the Universal Declaration is of great interest for present purposes because it established criteria on which to judge the legitimacy of states' behavior in this issue-area. While it is clear that the United Nations possesses virtually no capabilities to enforce this Declaration, Donnelly argues that resolutions concerning human rights have influenced states' behavior by defining norms by which governments can be held accountable by their own citizens as well as by others. Thus, Donnelly maintains that the importance of the human rights regime lies less in its capacity to enforce the provisions of the treaties than in its capacity to appraise state action.

Peter Cowhey addresses the issue of technical standards and their role in the international telecommunications regime. While functionalists have argued that these areas are best administered by formal bureaucracies and technical experts, Cowhey maintains that antecedent to the interpretation of telecommunications as a technical issue was a normative political consensus buttressed by an epistemic community that believed "natural monopolies" existed in telecommunications. In particular, he argues that framing this problem as one that was technical in nature was facilitated by: (1) the political consensus to retain national monopolies; (2) the consensus that international telephone, telegram, and telex services could be used to "cross-subsidize" local services of this sort; and (3) the epistemic consensus that defined standardized access to national networks and compatibility of equipment as the "technical" issue. Cowhey suggests that changes in the interaction between the political consensus and the knowledge possessed and propagated by epistemic communities best explain the dynamics of these technical regimes and the changing tasks of international organizations.

Collective Legitimization as a Political Function of the United Nations

Inis L. Claude, Jr.

As the United Nations has developed and as its role in world affairs has been adapted to the necessities and possibilities created and the limitations established by the changing realities of international politics, collective legitimization has emerged as one of its major political functions. By this I mean to suggest that the world organization has come to be regarded, and used, as a dispenser of politically significant approval and disapproval of the claims, policies, and actions of states, including, but going far beyond, their claims to status as independent members of the international system. In this essay I shall undertake to refine and elaborate this rough definition of collective legitimization and to discuss the performance of this role by the United Nations. It is essential in the beginning, however, to provide a foundation by offering some observations about the general problem of political legitimacy.

THE PROBLEM OF POLITICAL LEGITIMACY

. . . The urge for formally declared and generally acknowledged legitimacy approaches the status of a constant feature of political life. This urge requires that power be converted into authority, competence be supported by jurisdiction, and possession be validated as ownership. Conversely, if we look at it from the viewpoint of those who attack the status quo, it demands that the *de facto* be denied or deprived of *de jure* status, that the might of their antagonists not be sanctified as right. The principle is the same whether we are dealing with those who want the *is* to be recognized as the *ought* or with those who are setting out to convert their *ought* into a newly established *is*. Politics is not merely a struggle for power but also a contest over legitimacy, a competition in which the conferment or denial, the confirmation or revocation, of legitimacy is an important stake.

. . . Political realism is always easier to entertain in the abstract than in the particular instance. The American "realist" who likes the ring of the generalization is not likely to insist that it rings true in the case of a national hero like Abraham Lincoln or of a contemporary whose human characteristics are readily visible—Dwight D. Eisenhower or Lyndon B. Johnson, for instance. When one turns from generalization about rulers to consideration of individual cases, one is struck by the observation that the urge to possess and exercise power is usually qualified by concern about the justification of such possession and exercise. . . .

In part, this reflects the fact that power holders are burdened, like other human beings, by the necessity of satisfying their own consciences. By and large, they cannot comfortably regard themselves as usurpers or tyrants but require some basis for convincing themselves of the rightness of their position.

In a larger sense, however, this argument confirms rather than denies the power-oriented character of politics. Power and legitimacy are not antithetical, but complementary. The obverse of the legitimacy of power is the power of legitimacy; rulers seek legitimization not only to satisfy their consciences but also to buttress their positions. Legitimacy, in short, not only makes most rulers more comfortable but makes all rulers more effective—more secure in the possession of power and more successful in its exercise. Considerations of political morality combine with more hardheaded power considerations to explain the persistence of concern about legitimacy in the political sphere.

Two fundamental concepts figure prominently and persistently in the history of the problem of political legitimacy: law and morality. Lawyers tend simply to translate legitimacy as *legality*, capitalizing upon the derivation and literal meaning of the word. Similarly, moralists are inclined to claim a monopoly, treating political legitimacy as a problem of moral justification. Law and morality are both well-established and important legitimizing principles, but neither singly nor in combination do they exhaust the field. Each of them requires its own legitimization; the legitimacy of the positive law, or of the prevailing moral code, is sometimes the precise issue at stake in a political controversy. Moreover, relations between law and morality are variable. They sometimes reinforce each other, as when morality enjoins obedience to law or law codifies and sanctions the demands of morality. However, they may also come into conflict, as when morality condones disobedience to an unjust law or the law commands citizens to fulfill their public duty rather than follow the dictates of their private moral convictions. In the final analysis, the problem of legitimacy has a political dimension that goes beyond its legal and moral aspects. Judges and priests and philosophers usually make themselves heard, but they do not necessarily have the last word; the process of legitimization is ultimately a political phenomenon, a crystallization of judgment that may be influenced but is unlikely to be wholly determined by legal norms and moral principles.

While different principles of legitimacy and agents of legitimization may be simultaneously operative within a given political unit and among the constituent units of the global political system, there is nevertheless a tendency for a single concept of legitimacy to become generally dominant in a particular era, to achieve widespread acceptance as the decisive standard. Indeed, the existence of such a consensus may be regarded as the essential characteristic of a cohesive and stable political system at either the national or the international level. Like most fashions, fashions in legitimization change from time to time, and the crucial periods in political history are those transitional years of conflict between old and new concepts of legitimacy, the historical interstices between the initial challenge to the established concept and the general acceptance of its replacement. Thus, the era of modern European politics was ushered in by the substitution of the Voice of the People for the Voice of God (a change thinly concealed by the myth that the Voice of the People *is* the Voice of God) as the determinant of political legitimacy. The democratic principle has achieved widespread acceptance as the criterion of legitimate government within the state, however far short of general applicability it may have fallen as an operative political principle; the democratic pretensions of undemocratic regimes do not detract from, but lend support to, the proposition that popular consent is broadly acknowledged as the legitimizing principle in contemporary political life. The modern era has also seen the establishment of national self-determination as the basis of legitimate statehood, and the global extension of the reach of this legitimizing principle has been one of the most significant developments of recent decades.

At any given time the operative significance of the dominant principle of legitimacy tends to be less than that of the agency of legitimization. This means that the crucial question is not *what* principle is acknowledged but *who* is accepted as the authoritative interpreter of the principle or, to put it in institutional terms, *how* the process of legitimization works. There is, of course, a correlation between the nature of the legitimizing principle and the identity of its applicator. For instance, the principle of divine right tends to call for an ecclesiastical spokesman, and the consent theory implies reliance upon a democratic electoral process. In the long run, perhaps, the principle may be decisive; a secular change in the ideology of legitimacy can be expected ultimately to bring about the repudiation of the old and the recognition of a new agency or process of legitimization. Thus, over time, papal decrees have lost, and plebiscite results and public opinion surveys have gained, influence in the legitimizing process. Nevertheless, in the short run, a paraphrase of the maxim that "the Constitution means what the judges say it means" can be generalized. Principles of legitimacy are necessarily rather vague and uncertain in their applicability, and the nature of the process by which their application is decided or the means by which legitimacy is dispensed can be of the greatest importance.

LEGITIMIZATION IN INTERNATIONAL RELATIONS

Against this background I should like to discuss these two propositions: (1) that the function of legitimization in the international realm has tended in recent years to be increasingly conferred upon international political institutions; and (2) that the exercise of this function is, and probably will continue to be, a highly significant part of the political role of the United Nations.

The first proposition implies that the current fashion of legitimization of the status and behavior of states in the international arena emphasizes the *collective* and the *political* aspects of the process. While statesmen have their own ways of justifying their foreign policies to themselves and their peoples, independently of external judgments, they are well aware that such unilateral determinations do not suffice. They are keenly conscious of the need for approval by as large and impressive a body of other states as may be possible, for multilateral endorsement of their positions—in short, for collective legitimization. Moreover, it is a political judgment by their fellow practitioners of international politics that they primarily seek, not a legal judgment rendered by an international judicial organ.

This is not to say that international law has no place in the contemporary procedures of legitimization. States do occasionally resort, and even more frequently propose to resort, to the International Court of Justice (ICJ) or to *ad hoc* arbitral tribunals, and still more often they invoke legal arguments in justification of their positions or denunciation of those of their opponents. One might argue that states should rely predominantly or exclusively upon judicial interpretation of international law for the handling of issues concerning legitimacy, and one might expect that in a more settled period of international relations a heavier reliance upon adjudication might develop. But my present concern is with what *is,* not with what should be or might be, and it is a fact of present-day international life that, for whatever reasons of whatever validity, statesmen exhibit a definite preference for a political rather than a legal process of legitimization.

. . . Collective legitimization has developed, for better or for worse, as essentially a political function, sought for political reasons, exercised by political organs through the operation of a political process, and productive of political results.

Even when states resort to the International Court of Justice, they often appear to seek a judicial contribution to the success of their cause in the political forum rather than to express a preference for the legal over the political process of legitimization. Thus, the request for an advisory opinion concerning certain aspects of the United Nations financial crisis, addressed to the International Court in 1961, was designed to strengthen the case for a reassertion by the General Assembly of its competence to assess Members for support of peacekeeping operations. Somewhat similarly, the South West Africa case, brought before the Court in 1960, was undoubtedly initiated by Ethiopia and Liberia with the hope of obtaining judicial support for an intensified prosecution of South Africa in the General Assembly. The use of the Court in these instances clearly reflects the intention to pursue the issue of legitimacy in the political forum, not to transfer it to the judicial forum. . . .

The function of collective legitimization is not, in principle, reserved exclusively to the United Nations. The United States has placed considerable reliance upon the Organization of American States (OAS) as an instrument for justifying its policy in various cases involving Latin American states, and the anticolonial bloc has used special conferences, beginning with the Asian-African Conference at Bandung in 1955, to proclaim the illegitimacy of continued colonial rule. However, the prominence of the United Nations in the pattern of international organization and its status as an institution approximating universality give it obvious advantages for playing the role of custodian of the seals of international approval and disapproval. While the voice of the United Nations may not be the authentic voice of mankind, it is clearly the best available facsimile thereof, and statesmen have by general consent treated the United Nations as the most impressive and authoritative instrument for the expression of a global version of the general will. The notion that the United Nations gives expression to "world public opinion" is largely a myth, propagated by the winners of diplomatic battles in the Organization in order to enhance the significance of their victories. It would be more accurate to say that the judgments of the Organization represent the preponderant opinion of the foreign offices and other participants in the management of the foreign affairs of the governments of Member States. However, the issue of what the United Nations actually represents is less important than the fact that statesmen have conferred the function of collective legitimization primarily upon that Organization.

This function has been given relatively little attention in analyses of the political role of the United Nations. Most studies have tended to focus upon the operational functions of the Organization—its programs, interventions, and peacekeeping ventures. Our action-oriented generation has concentrated on the question of what the United Nations can and cannot *do*, on the issue of its executive capacity, rather than on its verbal performance. When forced to pessimistic conclusions regarding the possibilities of United Nations action, the typical analyst or editorialist falls back upon the dismal assertion that the Organization is in danger of being reduced to a mere debating chamber, a contemptible talk-shop. Given this negative attitude toward the verbal function, it is small wonder that serious efforts to analyze its significance have been rare. . . .

Collective legitimization is an aspect of the verbal rather than the executive functioning of the United Nations, and in some sense it is a result of the Organization's incapacity for decisive intervention in and control of international relations. One might argue that the United Nations has resorted to saying "thou should" because it is in no position to say "thou shalt" and to saying "thou may" because it cannot say "thou must." It authorizes and endorses in compensation for its inability to effectuate commands, and it condemns and deplores in compensation for its inability to prohibit and prevent. However, the mood expressed in a *New York Times* editorial which, noting the danger that financial difficulties would prevent the United Nations from undertaking further peacekeeping operations, warned that "the end result would be abandonment of its Charter obligation to enforce peace and suppress aggression and a consequent slump into the status of a debating society"[1] is neither realistic nor conducive to a perceptive appraisal of the actual and potential capabilities of the Organization. It reflects an exaggerated conception of what the United Nations might have been; surely, no one who had consulted the Charter and the expectations of its framers in preference to his own hopes and ideals could ever have believed that the United Nations promised to be a dependable agency for enforcing peace and suppressing aggression in an era of great-power division. Even more, it reflects an exaggerated contempt for international debating societies and a disinclination to examine the question of what it is possible for the United Nations to do when it cannot do the impossible.

If we can learn to judge the United Nations less in terms of its failure to attain the ideals that we postulate and more in terms of its success in responding to the realities that the world presents, we shall be in a better position to analyze its development. Approaching the Organization in this spirit, we find that its debating-society aspect is not to be deplored and dismissed as evidence of a "slump" but that it deserves to be examined for evidence of the functional adaptation and innovation that it may represent. My thesis is that the function of collective legitimization is one of the most significant elements in the pattern of political activity that the United Nations has evolved in response to the set of limitations and possibilities posed by the political realities of our time.

The development of this function has not been, in any meaningful sense, *undertaken* by the United Nations, conceived as an independent institutional actor upon the global stage. Rather, it has been thrust upon the Organization by Member States. Collective legitimization is an answer not to the question of what the United Nations can *do* but to the question of how it can be *used*.

Statesmen have been more perceptive than scholars in recognizing and appreciating the significance of this potentiality for utilization of the Organization. They have persistently, and increasingly, regarded the United Nations as an agency capable of bestowing politically weighty approval and disapproval upon their projects and policies. As will be illustrated in the following section of this article, the General Assembly and, to a lesser degree, the Security Council have been used for this purpose. The debates within and negotiations around these political organs have largely concerned the adoption or rejection of resolutions designed to proclaim the legitimacy or the illegitimacy of positions or actions taken by states. Governments have exerted themselves strenuously to promote the passage of resolutions favorable to their cause and the defeat of unfavorable resolutions. In reverse, they have attempted to block resolutions giving approval and to advance those asserting disapproval of their opponents' positions.

The scale of values developed by Members of the United Nations may be represented schematically by the following device in which states A and B are assumed to be engaged in a dispute:

---

1) Approval of A's position
2) Disapproval of B's position
3) Acquiescence in A's position
4) Acquiescence in B's position
5) Disapproval of A's position
6) Approval of B's position

In this scheme A's preferences would run in descending order from the top of the list, and B's from the bottom of the list. Parliamentary battles over the endorsement, the acceptance, and the condemnation of positions taken by states are a standard feature of the proceedings of the United Nations.

One may question whether proclamations of approval or disapproval by organs of the United Nations, deficient as they typically are in both formal legal significance and effective supportive power, are really important. The answer is that statesmen, by so obviously attaching importance to them, have made them important. Artificial or not, the value of acts of legitimization by the United Nations has been established by the intense demand for them. . . .

I do not mean to suggest that states are willing to accept in principle or to follow in consistent practice the proposition that the collective judgment of the General Assembly or any other international body is decisive. While states vary in the degree to which they display respect for the function of collective legitimization, this variation appears to reflect differences in experience and expectation rather than in commitment to the principle of the validity of collective evaluation. Any state can be expected to assert the validity of acts of legitimization that support its interests and to deny that acts contrary to its interests are worthy of respect. However, the vigorous effort that states customarily make to prevent the passage of formal denunciations of their positions or policies indicates that they have respect for the significance, if not for the validity, of adverse judgments by international organs. While states may act in violation of General Assembly resolutions, they evidently prefer not to do so, or to appear not to do so, on the ground that collective approbation is an important asset and collective disapprobation a significant liability in international relations. A state may hesitate to pursue a policy that has engendered the formal disapproval of the Assembly not because it is prepared to give the will of that organ priority over its national interest but because it believes that the adverse judgment of the Assembly makes the pursuit of that policy disadvantageous to the national interest. . . .

Clearly, statesmen do not attach identical importance to all judgments of legitimacy pronounced by political organs of the United Nations but weight the significance of resolutions according to the size and composition of the majorities supporting them and the forcefulness of the language in which they are couched. This variation in the impressiveness of formal resolutions was anticipated in the Charter provisions requiring a two-thirds majority for decisions on important questions in the General Assembly (Article 18, paragraph 2), and unanimity of the permanent members of the Security Council in decisions on nonprocedural matters in that body (Article 27, paragraph 3). In practice, it is evident that a Security Council resolution supported by all the permanent members is taken more seriously than one on which three of them abstain, that the support or opposition of India is treated as more significant than that of Iceland in evaluating a resolution of the General Assembly, and that a unanimous decision of the latter body deserves and receives more attention than a narrowly passed resolution. Moreover, a clear and firm act of approval or disapproval carries more weight than a vague and ambiguous pronouncement, and a series of resolutions, pointing consistently in the same direction, is more impressive than an isolated case. While states value even narrow parliamentary victories, achieved by garnering votes wherever they may be found and diluting the language of resolutions as much as may be necessary, they obviously recognize that the most convincing legitimization is provided by the cumulative impact of repeated and unambiguous endorsements of their positions, supported by massive majorities that include the bulk of the most important and most influential states.

SOME INSTANCES OF COLLECTIVE LEGITIMIZATION

The United Nations has been heavily involved in matters relating to the question of the ratification and solidification of the status claimed, as distinguished from the policies followed, by political entities. Generally, this can be subsumed under the heading of membership business; admission to or seating in the Organization has tended to take on the political meaning, if not the legal implication, of collective recognition. New states have been inclined to regard the grant of membership as the definitive acknowledgment of their independence. . . . The prompt admission of Israel to the United Nations was clearly regarded, by both friends and foes of the new state, as a major contribution to its capacity to survive in a hostile neighborhood. The issue of conferment of status arose in a different way when Malaysia was elected to a Security Council seat by the General Assembly. Indonesia's subsequent withdrawal from the Organization, ostensibly in protest against that action, can be interpreted as a tribute to the potency of collective legitimization, for Indonesia evidently felt that the United Nations had given an intolerably valuable boost to Malaysia's international stock.

A major campaign has been waged in the United Nations to delegitimize colonialism, to invalidate the claim of colonial powers to legitimate possession of overseas territories—in short, to revoke their sovereignty over colonies. This movement culminated in the overwhelming adoption by the General Assembly of sweeping anticolonial declarations in 1960 and subsequently. The implication of this anticolonial triumph became clear in late 1961 when India was cited before the Security Council for its invasion of Goa. India's defense was, in essence, the assertion that the process of collective legitimization had operated to deprive Portugal of any claim to sovereignty over Goa and thus of any right to protest the invasion—which, by virtue of the same process, had become an act of liberation, terminating Portugal's illegal occupation of Goa.

This case illustrates the proximity of the political and the legal aspects which is frequently implicit and occasionally explicit in the operation of the process of collective legitimization. India was accused in legal terms, and it responded in similar vein. The rejoinder by and on behalf of India proclaimed, in effect, that an accumulation of multilateral denunciations of colonialism had effectively abrogated the legal right of European states to rule non-European territories; these acts had created a new law under which colonialism was invalid. Despite this exchange of legal arguments, it appears that India's real concern was not so much to clear itself legally as to vindicate itself politically. It regarded the political approval or acquiescence of the United Nations as a more important consideration than any legal judgment. In a basic sense, India won the case. Although it obtained no formal endorsement of its position, it carried through its conquest of Goa without incurring formal condemnation, and its Western critics, by declining to take the issue to the Assembly, conceded that they could not expect to win, in that organ, a political verdict unfavorable to India. . . . Thus, in one of its aspects, collective legitimacy represents a political revolt against international law.

It should be noted that ex-colonial states have not confined themselves to using the United Nations for legitimization of the campaign for definitive liquidation of the colonial system. In the economic sphere they have undertaken, in concert with other underdeveloped countries, to use the Organization to secure the establishment and general acceptance of the doctrine that they have a right to receive, and advanced states have a duty to provide, assistance in promoting economic development. Toward the same end they have invoked the support of the Organization for policies designed to free themselves from obligations and arrangements that they regard as exploitative and inimical to economic progress, including foreign ownership or control of their basic natural resources. In an era of rising economic expectations, intensive effort on the part of many new states to establish solid economic foundations for their national structures, and extreme sensitivity to vestiges of the old system of colonial domination, the legitimizing function of the United Nations has had particular significance for the realm of economic policy. . . .

The United States, like India in the Goa case, has in some instances profited from collective legitimization in its minimal form: United Nations acquiescence or avoidance of United Nations condemnation. In some of these cases the United States has pioneered in the development of the strategy of involving a regional organization in the process. When the United States became involved in the overthrow of the Guatemalan government in 1954, it vigorously asserted the claim that the United Nations should disqualify itself from considering the case in favor of the Organization of American States. This tactic, which clearly reflected American respect for the potency of United Nations disapprobation, was practically, though not technically, successful. In the Cuban crisis of late 1962 the United States altered its strategy, opting to combine the functioning of the OAS and the United Nations rather than to set them off against each other. On this occasion the American scheme, successfully executed, was to secure the legitimizing support of the regional organization and then to use this asset in the effort to obtain the approval, or avoid the disapproval, of the Security Council with respect to the measures taken against Soviet involvement in Cuba.

[Later] the United States has been conspicuously reluctant to press the

United Nations for formal consideration of the situation in South Vietnam in which American forces have become heavily engaged. This restraint has no doubt derived from lack of confidence that a United Nations organ would endorse the claim of the United States that its military commitment constitutes a legitimate counterintervention against illegitimate intrusions by Communist states. . . .

CONCLUSION

This account of selected instances in which the United Nations has been involved in the process of collective legitimization suggests that there is great variation in the effectiveness of the positions taken by the Organization. It is seldom possible to make confident estimates of the degree of influence upon state behavior exerted by United Nations resolutions, although the intensity of the concern exhibited by states about the outcome of votes in the Organization indicates that the seal of approval and the stigma of disapproval are taken seriously.

There is also room for disagreement and uncertainty concerning the merits and demerits of collective legitimization. The entrusting of this function to such an organization as the United Nations is pregnant with both valuable and dangerous possibilities, as the cases discussed may suggest. The endorsement of a United Nations organ can strengthen a good cause, but it can also give aid and comfort to a bad cause—and we can have no guarantee that international political institutions, any more than national ones, will distribute their largess of legitimacy in accordance with the dictates of justice or wisdom. Habitual utilization of the United Nations as an agency for pronouncing on the international acceptability of national policies and positions may inspire statesmen to behave with moderation and circumspection; their concern regarding the outcome of deliberations by the Organization may stimulate them to make compromises designed to improve their chances of securing collective approval or avoiding collective disapproval. On the other hand, this use of the United Nations may promote its exploitation as an arena within which propaganda victories are sought, to the detriment of its role in promoting diplomatic settlements. Collective legitimization may stimulate legal changes that will make international law more worthy of respect and more likely to be respected, but it may also encourage behavior based upon calculation of what the political situation will permit rather than consideration of what the principles of order require. In short, the exercise of the function of collective legitimization may be for better or for worse, whether evaluated in terms of its effect upon the interests of a particular state or upon the prospects for a stable and orderly world. The crucial point is that, for better or for worse, the development of the United Nations as custodian of collective legitimacy is an important political phenomenon of our time.

NOTE

1. *The New York Times,* September 16, 1963.

Human Rights and International Organizations: States, Sovereignty, and the International Community

Jack Donnelly

Human rights are traditionally understood to regulate certain relations between individuals and the states of which they are nationals. But if sovereignty means, roughly, that what a state does to its own nationals (and other resources) on its own territory is it own business, human rights practices are prima facie protected exercises of sovereign prerogative. Although this was the orthodox understanding until the end of World War II, this understanding has changed significantly over the past half century. States now operate in an environment of formal and informal legal and political constraints on their human rights practices. This essay reviews these restrictions insofar as they arise from international organizations. The question I address is the extent to which power and authority have passed from states to the international community (as represented by multilateral human rights regimes).

I make use of three ideal type models of international human rights. The traditional statist model[1] sees human rights as principally a matter of sovereign national jurisdiction. Contemporary statists certainly admit that human rights are no longer the exclusive preserve of states, and that the state is no longer (and perhaps never was) the sole significant international actor. Statists nonetheless insist that human rights remain principally a matter of sovereign national jurisdiction and a largely peripheral concern of international (inter-state) relations. International intervention on behalf of human rights is not to be expected. If it occurs, it rests on state power, not legitimate authority.

A cosmopolitan model starts with individuals, who are seen more as members of a single global political community (cosmopolis) than as citizens of states.[2] Cosmopolitans focus on the ways in which the state and its powers are challenged both from below, by individuals and nongovernmental organizations (NGOs), and from above, by the truly global community (not merely international organizations and other collective enterprises of states). Cosmopolitans often see international organizations and certain transnational NGOs as representatives of an inchoate global community of mankind. International intervention on behalf of human rights is relatively unproblematic in such a model. In fact, cosmopolitans typically reverse the burden of proof, requiring justification for *non*intervention in the face of gross violations of human rights.

The space toward the center of the continuum defined by statist and cosmopolitan models is occupied by what we can call internationalist models. Internationalists accept the centrality of states and sovereignty in international relations, but stress international social practices (such as international law and the rules and procedures of diplomacy) that regulate inter-state relations. This body of formal and informal restrictions on the original sovereignty of states creates an international social order, an anarchical society of states (Bull 1977). The international community, in an internationalist model, is essentially the society of states (supplemented by nonstate actors, to the extent that they have been formally or informally incorporated into international political processes). Intervention on behalf of human rights is permissible to the extent that it is authorized by the society of states.

Much of the rest of this essay is in effect devoted to showing that a relatively weak internationalist model, including only modest and primarily normative international societal constraints on state sovereignty, describes international human rights practices over the past half century, and is likely to continue to do so throughout the 1990s. The cosmopolitan model, to the extent that it is more than a prescription about what is desirable, is largely a prediction about the direction of change in world politics. The statist model, although accurate prior to World War II, today is at best a crude and somewhat misleading first approximation.

In developing this argument I distinguish between strong or coercive and weak or noncoercive means of intervention. All of international relations involves attempting to influence the behavior of states (as well as intergovernmental organizations and various transnational actors). This involves "interfering," in a weak sense of the term, in the domestic political processes of other states in order to alter international outcomes. Only when the interference is coercive do we have a type of international practice that can be usefully distinguished from the rest of international relations. In particular, only in this strong sense of *coercive* interference in the internal affairs of states do we have restrictions on or infringements of sovereignty.[3] I am particularly concerned with multilateral coercive interference, which does involve a significant transfer of power or political authority from states to the international community. Such interventions, however, have been virtually nonexistent in the field of human rights.

1. THE EMERGENCE OF HUMAN RIGHTS AS AN INTERNATIONAL ISSUE

Prior to World War II, human rights practices were generally considered an internationally protected exercise of the sovereign prerogatives of states. The European Great Powers and the United States did occasionally intervene in the Ottoman and Chinese Empires and in Latin America and the Caribbean to rescue nationals caught in situations of civil strife or to establish or protect special rights and privileges for Europeans and Americans. Rarely if ever, though, did they intervene to protect foreign nationals from their own government. Likewise, the "humanitarian law" of war, expressed in documents such as the 1907 Hague Conventions, limited only what a state could do to foreign nationals, not the ways a state treated its own nationals (or subject peoples over whom it exercised colonial rule).

The principal exception was slavery, which was a subject of multilateral diplomacy as early as the Congress of Vienna in 1815. In the interwar period, the International Labor Organization (ILO), created in 1919, dealt with some limited workers' rights issues and the League of Nations' Minorities System was established to protect the rights of ethnic minorities in areas where boundaries had been altered following the war. Except for these marginal exceptions,[4] prior to World War II human rights simply was not a topic of international relations. In other words, modern international relations, until relatively recently, treated international human rights in accord with a very expansive statist understanding of sovereignty.

The catalyst that made human rights an issue in world politics was the Holocaust.[5] The Nuremberg War Crimes Trials (1945–1946) introduced the novel charge of crimes against humanity. And in the United Nations, human rights became established as a standard subject of international relations.

The Covenant of the League of Nations did not even mention human rights. By contrast, the Preamble of the UN Charter includes a determination "to reaffirm faith in fundamental human rights." "Encouraging respect for human rights and for fundamental freedoms for all" is listed as one of the Organization's major purposes in Article 1. Article 55 explicitly includes human rights among the responsibilities of the Economic and Social Council (ECOSOC). Working from this mandate, the United Nations proceeded to elaborate a strong set of explicit and fairly detailed international human rights standards. In particular, the Universal Declaration of Human Rights, unanimously adopted by the UN General Assembly on December 10, 1948,[6] and the 1966 International Human Rights Covenants provide an authoritative statement of international human rights norms.

These normative successes, however, were not accompanied by comparable progress in international implementation. Although states had agreed that they ought to follow the human rights standards set out in the Universal Declaration and the Covenants, they most definitely did *not* agree to let the UN (or anyone else) enforce implementation of these norms. Norm creation was fully internationalized by the mid-1960s, but implementation of those norms remained almost entirely national.

This began to change, very slightly, in the late 1960s. In 1967 the Commission on Human Rights received authority to discuss human rights violations in particular countries, and in 1970 it was authorized to investigate complaints of human rights violations. In 1968, a Special Committee of Investigation was created to consider human rights in the territories occupied by Israel after the 1967 war. In the same year, the Security Council imposed a mandatory blockade on the white minority regime in South Rhodesia. The UN was at last beginning to move, however tentatively, from merely setting standards to examining how those standards were implemented by (at least a few) states.

Such efforts continued, and even intensified, in the 1970s. For example, the 1973 military coup in Chile led the UN to create an Ad Hoc Working Group on the Situation of Human Rights in Chile. The international campaign against apartheid in South Africa intensified. And in 1976 the International Human Rights Covenants, with their supervisory machinery (discussed below), entered into force.

The 1970s also saw human rights explicitly and systematically introduced into the bilateral foreign policies of individual countries, beginning in the United States with Congressional legislation in 1973 and 1975 that linked U.S. foreign aid to the human rights practices of recipient countries. The 1970s was also the decade in which human rights NGOs emerged as a notable international political force, as symbolized by the award of the Nobel Peace Prize to Amnesty International in 1977.

These trends toward increasing multilateral, bilateral, and nongovernmental action on behalf of human rights continued, more or less steadily, through the 1980s. New treaties on women's rights, torture, and the rights of the child were completed (in 1979, 1984, and 1989 respectively). The Human Rights Committee began to review periodic reports submitted under the International Covenant on Civil and Political Rights. The Committee on Economic, Social, and Cultural Rights was created in 1986 to improve reporting and monitoring under the International Covenant on Economic, Social, and Cultural Rights. The Commission on Human Rights not only undertook new "thematic" initiatives on disappearances, torture, and summary or arbitrary executions, but subjected a larger and more diverse group of countries to public scrutiny. And the process of incorporating human rights into bilateral foreign policy accelerated and deepened in the 1980s, even in the U.S.

At least the stronger versions of the statist model simply do not provide an accurate or illuminating picture of the place of human rights in contemporary international relations. Human rights have become a standard subject of international relations, and there are well-established international normative constraints on the human rights practices of states. The question that remains is how far these restrictions on sovereignty extend.

2. GLOBAL MULTILATERAL IMPLEMENTATION MACHINERY

Numerous multilateral human rights monitoring bodies with universal or near universal coverage have been established since the end of World War II. In this section, we look at the two most important, the United Nations Commission on Human Rights and the Human Rights Committee. In addition, we look at the work of the International Labor Organization on workers' rights, the first and most developed single-issue human rights regime, and the international campaign against apartheid, the most extensive and elaborate example of multilateral international human rights activity.

A. The United Nations Commission on Human Rights

The UN Commission on Human Rights, a permanent subsidiary body of the Economic and Social Council (ECOSOC), is the single most important international human rights body. The Universal Declaration and the Covenants, along with all the major single-issue human rights instruments, were drafted by the Commission. Its powers to supervise the implementation of these norms, however, are extremely weak.

Until 1967, the Commission was not authorized to discuss publicly human rights conditions in particular countries. And until 1970, it was not even authorized to see the details of the thousands of human rights communications received by the United Nations. ECOSOC resolution 1503, however, gave the Commission the authority to conduct confidential investigations of "communications" (complaints) that suggested "a consistent pattern of gross and reliably attested violations of human rights and fundamental freedoms."

The 1503 procedure is administratively cumbersome, involving three levels of scrutiny before a situation even reaches the full Commission. It is limited to "situations" rather than individual cases and is strictly confidential (although the Commission does release annually the names of the countries that are actively being considered). It is also very slow. Because the Sub-Commission and the Commission each meet just once a year, the procedure cannot be brought fully into play in less than two or three years after complaints are received (which may be some time after serious violations began). And the 1503 procedure is ultimately simply weak. "Enforcement," at its strongest, means making publicly available the evidence that has been acquired, along with the Commission's views on it. At most the 1503 procedure provides a certain degree of semi-independent international monitoring. This, however, is the strongest enforcement mechanism available to the Commission.

More interesting are the investigatory procedures created in the 1980s. In the late 1970s, a revitalized Western bloc, led by countries such as Canada and the Netherlands, joined by Third World states such as Senegal, began to develop a coalition pressing for a more aggressive Commission. New initiatives were undertaken on a "global" or "thematic" basis. Rather than examine the full range of abuses in individual countries, particular types of violations were addressed globally (more or less), wherever they occurred.

The decisive step was the creation in 1980 of a Working Group on Enforced or Involuntary Disappearances. In its first decade, the Working Group handled over 19,000 cases. In roughly one case in ten, government responses to Working Group inquiries have established the whereabouts or fate of the individual. Urgent action procedures, for disappearances within the past three months, have resolved about one case in five. A Special Rapporteur on summary or arbitrary executions, S. Amos Wako, was appointed in 1982. In 1985, Peter Kooijmans, the outgoing chair of the Commission, was appointed Special Rapporteur on torture. A promising Working Group on Arbitrary Detention was created in 1991. There are also Special Rapporteurs on religious intolerance (appointed in 1986) and mercenaries (appointed in 1987), but their work has been much less significant.

All of these activities reflect significant growth in the highest levels of multi-lateral human rights activities. Although most targets of these actions denounced them as unjustified intervention in their internal affairs, they have supported similar and often even stronger "interventions" against other states (especially South Africa and Israel). The activities of the Commission on Human Rights clearly reflect an internationalist, not a statist, perspective. These procedures, however, are essentially sovereignty respecting, involving only noncoercive interference. They do not represent a major transfer of power or authority from states to the international community. They reflect weak rather than strong internationalism, and the continuing (although not unchallenged) priority of sovereignty in multilateral human rights politics.

B. The Human Rights Committee and International Reporting

A number of human rights treaties have created supervisory bodies to monitor their implementation. The most important of these is the Human Rights Committee, a body of eighteen experts established to supervise the implementation of the International Covenant on Civil and Political Rights.[7]

The Committee's principal activity is to review periodic state reports on compliance. The questions posed by members of the Committee are often penetrating and critical. When the responses of state representatives are serious and thoughtful, the result can be an exchange of information and views that provides a real element of international monitoring. Cooperation by the state, however, is entirely voluntary: the representative need not answer any question, let alone provide an answer that the questioner finds satisfactory. The Committee may ask for additional information, but states actually provide only what they choose. Sometimes this is little more than extracts from laws and the constitution, or obviously evasive claims of compliance. And the Committee cannot even assure timely submission of reports. Zaire presents an extreme example: its initial report, due in 1978, was not submitted until 1987. Furthermore, the entire process applies only to the parties to the Covenant, which numbered 114 at the end of 1992.

Reporting procedures cannot force recalcitrant states to alter their practice. This does not, however, mean that they are of no value. Conscientious preparation of a report requires a national review of law and practice that can uncover areas where improvement may be needed or possible. Reporting also assures that there will be at least one international body periodically looking over the shoulders of those responsible for implementing human rights. The reports of some countries may even provide ideas or models for other countries, as may the comments of the supervisory committee.

Reporting as an implementation technique functions primarily through the good will of reporting states. As a result, supervisory bodies must walk a delicate line during their review of reports. "Weaker" and less adversarial techniques thus may actually have a greater positive effect, at least in relatively favorable circumstances. In addition, states with less bad, or even relatively good, records are particularly promising targets for international action. These states have, by their behavior, given concrete evidence of relatively good intentions and are likely to be more open to suggestions and more concerned about their international reputation.

Reporting and most other international monitoring procedures therefore are, paradoxically, likely to be most effective where they are in some sense "least needed," that is, where human rights records are relatively good (or less bad). Multilateral procedures for coercive intervention to enforce international human rights obligations simply do not exist. Recalcitrant states usually can violate human rights with impunity.[8] But even a country with a relatively good record may still violate human rights. And any victim (or potential victim) who is helped is a victory for international action, wherever that person resides.

Reporting systems fall far short of coercive intervention. They do not even involve the strongest forms of noncoercive interference. Nonetheless, in some cases at least, they can influence national human rights practices.

The Human Rights Committee may also investigate complaints from individuals in states that are parties to the Covenant's Optional Protocol. Although the 66 parties are more than half of the countries that are parties to the Covenant, this is only one-third of the countries of the world. Furthermore, democratic countries are disproportionately represented. Nonetheless, the Optional Protocol provides a strong system of monitoring. Although the list of countries on which action has been taken is hardly representative of the world's major human rights violators—Bolivia, Canada, Colombia, the Dominican Republic, Ecuador, Finland, France, Italy, Jamaica, Madagascar, Mauritius, the Netherlands, Peru, Sweden, Uruguay, and Zaire—there is some geographical diversity. Furthermore, complaints are pursued relatively aggressively, as evidenced by the Committee's innovative decision to treat a state's failure to respond as an admission of culpability.

The limitations of the Optional Protocol procedure, however, are no less noteworthy. After the Committee states its views, the process is concluded. Furthermore, most major human rights violators, not surprisingly, have elected not to be covered. This is the overriding problem of treaty-based enforcement mechanisms. Obligations apply only to parties to the treaty, and states, in the exercise of their sovereign rights, are free to choose not to accept these obligations. The stronger the monitoring and implementation procedures, the fewer the states that are willing to be covered. The Optional Protocol thus presents a striking example of the typical tradeoff between the strength of international procedures and their coverage.

C. Workers' Rights

The first international human rights regime of any sort was the workers' rights regime developed in the International Labor Organization (ILO) after World War I. Important ILO Conventions have dealt with freedom of association, the right to organize and bargain collectively, forced labor, migrant workers, and indigenous peoples, as well as a variety of technical issues of working conditions and workplace safety. And ILO monitoring procedures, which date back to 1926, have been the model for the international human rights reporting systems discussed above.

The Committee of Experts meets annually to review periodic reports submitted by states on their implementation of ratified conventions. Following this review, the Committee may issue a Direct Request, asking for additional information, or even for changes in policy. Over the last two decades, more than a thousand requests have resulted in changes in national policies. If the problem remains unresolved, the Committee may make "Observations," that is, authoritative determinations of violations of the convention. In addition, special complaint procedures exist for cases involving freedom of association or discrimination in employment.

The Conference Committee, composed of ILO delegates rather than independent experts, provides an additional level of scrutiny. Each year, it selects cases from the report of the Committee of Experts for further review. Government representatives are called upon to provide additional information and explanation.

No less important than these inquisitorial procedures is the institution of "direct contacts." Since 1969, the ILO has pursued an extensive program of consultations and advice. It is a leader in this strategy of trying to resolve problems before they become serious enough to require the attention of international monitoring bodies.

Part of the ILO's success can be attributed to its unique "tripartite" structure. Virtually all other intergovernmental organizations are made up entirely of state representatives. NGOs may participate in deliberations, but typically they have no decision-making powers. In the ILO, however, workers' and employers' representatives from each member state are voting members of the organization. It is therefore much more difficult for states to hide behind the curtain of sovereignty. The transideological appeal of workers' rights has also been important to the ILO's success.

The principal resource of the ILO, however, remains publicity, and the principal power available to its supervisory bodies is the power of persuasion. The ILO has influenced labor conditions and policies in several states over decades. Nonetheless, it lacks coercive enforcement powers.

D. Apartheid

Apartheid is the human rights issue that has received the most extensive multilateral action over the past three decades. In 1962, the General Assembly called on states to break diplomatic relations and boycott all trade with South Africa. The decisions of the General Assembly, however, are only recommendations, and until the 1980s they were largely ignored by most powerful states. The Security Council, which does have the authority to impose mandatory sanctions, established only a voluntary arms embargo in December 1963. A mandatory arms embargo had to wait until November 1977, after the Soweto riots following the death in detention of Steve Biko. Although efforts over the following decade failed to establish a more comprehensive trade embargo, several states did undertake a variety of actions to reduce or eliminate their diplomatic, cultural, and commercial relations with South Africa.

The Special Committee on Apartheid, created in 1962, has coordinated and promoted a broad international campaign against apartheid. National support committees have been formed and opinion leaders in several countries have been specially targeted. Material assistance has also been provided to victims by organizations such as the United Nations Educational and Training Program for Southern Africa, established in 1964, and the United Nations Trust Fund for South Africa, established in 1965. The 1973 International Convention on the Suppression and Punishment of the Crime of Apartheid, which came into force in 1976 and had 94 parties at the end of 1992, attempts to establish international criminal liability (although no prosecutions have occurred).

Reiteration of anti-apartheid norms, and associated condemnations of South Africa, were a regular feature in most international organizations in the 1970s and 1980s. Specialized agencies such as the ILO and the World Health Organization gave particularly close scrutiny to South African policies in their area of competence. Others adopted the alternative strategy of excluding South Africa, beginning with the International Telecommunications Union in 1965. The South African government has been prevented from taking its seat in the United Nations General Assembly since 1970. The norm of isolation was particularly effectively applied in sports, culminating in the 1985 International Convention Against Apartheid in Sports. Less systematic efforts were also made to deter, monitor, and adversely publicize concerts and other cultural contacts.

A principal influence of the apartheid regime probably has been the support, encouragement, and justification it has provided for individuals and national and international NGOs trying to alter the foreign policies of individual states. These campaigns had some success in a number of Western countries in the 1980s. The resulting initiatives, including boycotts and embargoes, crossed into the realm of coercive intervention.

All of this international activity clearly played a role in the process of reform that led to the March 1992 decision of the white electorate to abolish a race-based social and political system in South Africa. But international pressure only went as far as breaking relations, a strategy that still largely respected South African sovereignty. In particular, no Western state seriously contemplated the use of force against South Africa. Furthermore, South African governments were able to resist even these unusually strong international pressures for thirty years. And South Africa is clearly the exception, not the rule.

3. REGIONAL HUMAN RIGHTS REGIMES

So far we have looked at international procedures that in principle cover or are open to all countries. Regional human rights regimes operate among smaller, more homogeneous groups of states. Although the European regional regime provides the only case of genuine international enforcement of human rights anywhere in the world, the Inter-American regime is no stronger than the procedures we have discussed above, the African regime is weaker, and regional regimes do not exist at all in Asia and the Middle East.

A. Europe

A very strong regional human rights regime exists for the 23 (primarily Western European) members of the Council of Europe. Article 3 of the Council's Statute requires each member to "accept the principles of the rule of law and of the enjoyment by all persons within its jurisdiction of human rights and fundamental freedoms." Such provisions have been treated seriously enough to prevent Spanish and Portuguese membership until after the fall of their fascist military governments in the mid-1970s. Furthermore, Greece (in 1969) and Turkey (in 1981) have been suspended for human rights violations.

The European Commission of Human Rights receives, reviews, and evaluates "applications" (complaints) from individuals.[9] Once a case is accepted, the Commission pursues it vigorously, and a majority end with a decision against the state. Its decisions, although not technically binding, are usually accepted. Furthermore, the European Court of Human Rights has made legally binding decisions on over 150 cases dealing with a great variety of issues, including such sensitive questions as public emergencies and the treatment of prisoners in Northern Ireland.[10]

The European human rights regime has also influenced national political reforms. For example, new constitutions in Greece, Portugal, and Spain were explicitly written with the European Convention in mind. Decisions of the Commission and the Court have led to constitutional revisions in Sweden and the Netherlands. Detention practices have been altered in Belgium, Germany, Greece, and Italy. The treatment of aliens has been changed in the Netherlands and Switzerland. Britain modified its press freedom legislation. Wiretapping regulations were changed in Switzerland. Legal aid practices have been changed in Italy and Denmark. Procedures to speed trials have been implemented in Italy, the Netherlands, and Sweden. And so forth. On a day-to-day basis as well, an additional level of regional scrutiny may subtly influence national political processes.

There is also a human rights dimension to the activities of the 12-member European Community (EC), especially the European Economic Community (EEC). Economic integration in recent years has been accompanied by efforts to harmonize social policy. Because policies tend to be standardized not according to the lowest common denominator but on the basis of the better performers, this has often had a positive impact on economic and social rights. The EC has also incorporated human rights concerns into its external relations, although the means used have been relatively weak (except for the suspension of a special agreement between Greece and the EEC from 1967 until 1974, in protest against military rule).

In Western Europe, regional human rights norms are regionally enforced. But the special conditions of relatively close cultural and historical backgrounds, generally excellent human rights records, high levels of economic development, and high levels of regional and subregional cooperation on economic and other matters, suggest that the European experience is unlikely to be replicated elsewhere.

B. The Americas

As in Europe, the Inter-American human rights regime revolves around a Commission and a Court. The Inter-American Court of Human Rights, however, has decided only two contentious cases (dealing with a disappearance in Honduras and a military attack on two journalists in Peru). The real heart of the regime is the seven-member Inter-American Commission of Human Rights. Established in 1959 as a part of the Organization of American States (OAS), the authority of the Inter-American Commission does not rest on a separate human rights treaty (although there is a 1948 American Declaration of the Rights of Man, and a 1969 American Convention on Human Rights). Like the UN Commission on Human Rights, all members of the organization in principle fall under its scrutiny.

The decisions of the Inter-American Commission, however, have usually been ignored, in sharp contrast to Europe. The primary reason for this is the very different domestic human rights environment in the region.

Almost all of the countries in the European regime have excellent human rights records and a strong desire to maintain them. Communications thus typically deal with narrow or isolated violations, which are inherently unthreatening to the government. Even when there are serious systematic violations, as during the period of military rule in Greece, the government involved is seen as aberrant, and if it persists is treated as a pariah and suspended from membership in the organization.

Most countries in the Americas, by contrast, have suffered repressive military rule within the past generation. In fact, until recently, at any given time several OAS member states typically were ruled by dictatorial governments. As a result, many communications have concerned systematic human rights violations that represented an important element in the government's strategy to keep itself in power. In such circumstances, it is hardly surprising that the findings of the Commission have been ignored.

More important have been the Commission's studies and reports on human rights situations in over 20 countries. For example, the reports on Chile in the 1970s and 1980s were a significant element in the international campaign against the Pinochet government (Medina 1988: chap. 3). Although such international publicity falls far short of coercive intervention, its significance is perhaps best attested to by the diplomatic effort states exert to avoid it. For example, both Argentina and Chile devoted considerable diplomatic effort in the late 1970s and early 1980s to avoiding public criticism.[11] In addition, international publicity may aid individual victims, who are released or treated less poorly as a symbolic gesture, even if the overall situation in the country remains repressive.

In addition, we can point to one case in which the OAS did have a systematic impact on human rights. The Inter-American Commission's 1978 report on Nicaragua substantially increased the pressure on the Somoza government. And when the OAS General Assembly called on Somoza to resign in June 1979, it clearly shook his political confidence and seems to have hastened his departure (Pastor 1987: 149–151). Although not coercive intervention—the action was purely verbal and the sanction entirely normative—it is noteworthy.

In the end, though, reports and resolutions require additional action by states to have any real impact. The regional community can call on states to act in certain ways. During the Cold War era, however, except in the case of the ideologically motivated embargo on Cuba, the OAS did not intervene coercively on behalf of human rights.

C. Africa, Asia, and the Middle East

A third regional human rights regime has been established within the Organization of Africa Unity (OAU) under the 1981 African Charter on Human and Peoples' Rights. Its implementation procedures, however, are extremely weak. The eleven-member African Commission on Human and Peoples' Rights, in addition to reviewing reports, may consider communications. Only situations, however, may be discussed, not individual cases. In addition, an in-depth study of a situation requires permission from the OAU's Assembly of Heads of State and Government. This is by far the most politicized regional or international human rights complaint procedure.

The Commission has held twelve meetings through October 1992. Its initial review of state reports have not been promising, and the reports themselves have had little substance. No public action had been taken on any of the more than 100 communications that have been received. Nonetheless, the African Commission does seem to be approaching its task with seriousness, and it has not merely permitted but encouraged NGO participation.

The Permanent Arab Commission on Human Rights, established in 1968, has been notably inactive, except for occasional efforts to publicize human rights violations in Israeli-occupied territory. There are not even authoritative regional norms. Little more has been done in Asia and the Pacific. For example, the only substantial result of a 1982 UN-sponsored seminar in Colombo, Sri Lanka, seems to have been a decision to abandon a broad regional approach in favor of either the global institutions discussed above or subregional groupings. Only the Pacific Island subregion shows much promise for the development of a subregional regime.

4. HUMAN RIGHTS IN A POST–COLD WAR WORLD

The preceding sections largely chronicled the Cold War experience. The end of the Cold War and the dissolution of the former Soviet Union, along with a decade of liberalization and democratization in the Third World, have led to much talk of a new world order. I suggest, however, that whatever else it may (or may not) involve, the emerging new world order is unlikely to be characterized by a significant transfer of power or authority in the field of human rights from states to the international community. In a recent article, (Donnelly 1992) I developed such an argument in some detail. Here I briefly sketch the outlines of my position. I then consider recent activities in some of the institutions discussed above and certain recent events that might be taken as counterevidence.

At the level of the structure of the international system, the crucial change in recent years has been the end of bipolarity. In addition, the elements of power are increasingly separated, most dramatically in the military might and economic weakness of Russia and the economic prowess but military weakness of Japan and Germany. As a result, international political processes and outcomes now vary dramatically from issue to issue. Well over a decade ago, Keohane and Nye (1977) described this type of international system as one of "complex interdependence." The end of the Cold War has furthered this process.

Although the end of U.S. (and Soviet) hegemonic leadership may create new opportunities for progressive international action, complex interdependence makes it dangerous to generalize across issue areas. In particular, we must be careful not to jump from changes in international economic relations that are challenging entrenched notions of economic sovereignty to predicting comparable changes in international human rights.

For all the talk of a new world order, most states today still jealously guard their sovereign prerogatives in the field of human rights. Consider, for example, the relative weakness of the multilateral human rights procedures discussed above in contrast to, say, GATT and IMF. Even in Europe, the relatively strong regional human rights system pales in comparison to the restrictions on state sovereignty achieved through regional economic institutions. And nowhere are states advancing new proposals for major enhancements of the power of existing human rights bodies (except perhaps the CSCE) or the creation of new bodies with strong powers.

The demise of superpower ideological rivalry, the other defining feature of the Cold War order, does suggest significant human rights progress. Whatever the ultimate motivations of American (and Soviet) foreign policy, ideology played a significant part in the justification of numerous interventions that had as their consequence the systematic violation of human rights. Although U.S. intervention in the Third World certainly will continue in the post–Cold War era, without the overarching appeal to anticommunism, American administrations will find it much more difficult to muster domestic support for repressive foreign regimes. In addition, it will be easier to treat local political conflicts as local, rather than as manifestations of global ideological rivalry. These changes imply major improvements in the international human rights environment.

They do not, however, necessarily imply support for stronger international human rights procedures. There is no necessary connection between a decline in foreign policy actions that harm human rights abroad and the development of positive international human rights policies. In the United States, the Bush and Clinton administrations and the Congress have all been unwilling to expend substantial political or financial capital on behalf of international human rights. Elsewhere as well, satisfaction at recent changes has not spurred new endeavors to develop stronger international human rights procedures.

There has been modest progress at the regional level. The Council of Europe's new program of human rights assistance for the countries of Central and Eastern Europe is clear evidence of a desire to begin to prepare the former Soviet bloc states for entry into the European human rights regime. And because good human rights practices are a major condition of acceptance into "Europe," with the associated symbolic and material benefits, the efforts of the Council of Europe are likely to have a significant impact, at least in the more progressive states of Central Europe. Although this represents a geographical expansion of the coverage of the existing European human rights regime, rather than an increase in its powers, these developments are of considerable importance.

In the Americas, the overall regional environment has improved dramatically. Elected (although not necessarily democratic) governments were in office in all the mainland countries of the hemisphere throughout 1991. The OAS General Assembly, which in the early 1980s refused to even discuss the practices of gross and persistent human rights violators, has become willing to act on behalf of human rights. The embargo against Haiti, although its impact still is obscure, is a sign of relatively aggressive (although still ultimately sovereignty respecting) authorized coercive intervention. The rapid criticism of the suspension of parliamentary government in Peru is also a promising sign.

It is too early to say whether this will be a new pattern or a temporary interlude. It is unclear how the organization will respond to the imposition of military rule on the mainland; Haiti has always been something of an exception in the OAS. More seriously, there is no evidence of a new political commitment to a more aggressive pursuit of human rights violations by elected governments. The activities of the Inter-American Commission over the next few years, and in particular the responses they receive from the OAS and affected states, are likely to be an important indicator of whether the confusion of elections and human rights, so common in the U.S., is being transcended in the hemisphere. Clearly, though, the overall picture is one of modest progress, with the realistic possibility of continued incremental growth throughout the rest of the decade.

At the global level, however, not all the signs are positive. Consider, for example, the 1990 session of the Commission on Human Rights, the first in many years in which the clear majority of delegates were from countries with more or less freely elected governments. Resolutions were adopted on Cuba, El Salvador, Guatemala, Haiti, Myanmar (Burma), and the U.S. invasion of Panama. Given the state of human rights in the world at the time, the absence of resolutions on countries of the Middle East and Africa is even more striking than the Caribbean basin bias of this list. Furthermore, an almost embarrassingly mild resolution on China, which did not even explicitly condemn the Tienanmen massacres of the preceding summer, was defeated. Japan, Swaziland, and Panama were the only countries from Asia, Africa, and Latin America to vote in favor of the resolution. In addition, the Group of 77 tried (but ultimately failed) to eliminate the existing independent thematic procedures and replace them with politicized working groups of professional diplomats. And the enlargement of the Commission to 53 members will make it even more difficult for it to function as a working body, while the addition of four African, three Asian, and three Latin American and Caribbean members shifts the balance of power in a way that is likely to preclude any significant enhancement of the powers of the Commission.

The one unambiguous sign of human rights progress in the United Nations system is the observer group in El Salvador, which has unprecedented authority to engage in extensive on-site monitoring of human rights practices. This is indeed a significant transfer of authority to the international community. It is, however, an intrusion that El Salvador voluntarily accepted. There is little indication that many other states will choose to allow similar interventions. Furthermore, it is only a temporary measure, agreed to as part of a broader political settlement, intended to help smooth the transition to a new government. It should not be confused with human rights monitoring in more settled situations. The political dynamics that make a UN monitoring role acceptable, or even desirable, in such transitional situations are not likely to be replicated once a supervised election has been held.

This distinction between "normal" and transitional or other extraordinary situations raises broader questions about the international human rights significance of some other often cited examples of transfers of authority or power from states to the international community. Consider, for example, the relatively aggressive efforts to provide humanitarian assistance in Somalia, which have had at most the grudging consent of those in power. There has been a modest but very real coercive element in these UN actions. But they come in a situation in which the Somali state has effectively disintegrated. They thus represent not so much a transfer of authority as a response to a breakdown of authority. Although the resulting international action is the same—the UN now has authority in Somalia that it did not have a year ago—the political process by which this authority was obtained is unlikely to be replicated in more settled situations.

Such new activities, along with the Cambodia operation, are strikingly similar to the UN's efforts during the era of decolonization. In both cases, the UN role arose because of gaps or breakdowns in standard patterns of sovereignty. In the case of decolonization, the transition involved a fundamental formal change in legal status. (There are certainly a number of possible areas for UN or regional action of a very precisely analogous character, most notably in the former states of Yugoslavia and the Soviet Union.) In Somalia and El Salvador, civil war created a breakdown of authority. The UN has stepped into that void, providing humanitarian assistance in Somalia and transitional monitoring in El Salvador. But just as the decolonization activities of the 1960s had no direct spillover into new human rights activities of a more standard type, there is little reason to expect such a spillover today.

Where sovereignty has become problematic, as in El Salvador and Somalia, the UN may (although will not necessarily) have an opportunity to intervene coercively. We should not belittle the importance or local impact of such interventions. Nonetheless, to the extent that coercive interventions remain restricted to cases of this sort, they actually underscore the centrality of sovereignty. What has changed is not so much the balance of power between states and the international community as the opportunities for action. The end of the Cold War has made it possible for (states to allow) the UN to act in such former areas of superpower rivalry. This does indeed result in greater authority for the international community. But the transfer of authority is of a peculiarly limited sort.

Much the same is true of recent interventions in Iraq and Bosnia. In each case, the international community has treated the conflict as an inter-state conflict, despite the assertions to the contrary of Iraq and Serbia. The UN security

zone in northern Iraq is the result of a cease-fire agreement. It has the consequence of protecting the human rights of Iraqi Kurds. But it provides absolutely
no precedent for multilateral military protection of endangered minorities in
more normal circumstances. Likewise, the Bosnian intervention has been conceived of as assistance against aggression, rather than human rights intervention,
even if the result is to protect the lives of many Bosnians from a force that claims
to be their government (but whose claim is rejected by the international community).

Somalia also reminds us of the distinction between humanitarian assistance
and international human rights policies more broadly conceived. Emergency aid
to victims of natural or man-made disasters is a noble and important international
activity. The Somalia case does involve an unprecedented augmentation of the authority of the international community in the field of humanitarian assistance. But
we have no reason to expect a spillover into international human rights activities,
as they have been conventionally understood.

Even during the Cold War, massive famine usually provoked an international
response that largely transcended politics. The Reagan Administration's assistance
to Ethiopia, one of the world's most reprehensible Marxist-Leninist regimes, is
perhaps the most striking example. But there has been a huge gulf between disas-
ter relief and providing even food aid once the immediate crisis is over, let alone
international human rights intervention. We have no reason to believe that there
has been any fundamental change in perceptions or behavior in the so-called new
world order. Therefore, the value of Somalia as a precedent for human rights activity by the UN is likely to be negligible.

I do not want to belittle the importance of these interventions. Lives are being saved in ways that just a few years ago would not have seemed possible to most
observers. I do, however, want to insist that these cases have little or no implications for intervention on behalf of human rights, that is, in response to direct violations of internationally recognized human rights by recognized governments in
control of their states. We may be witnessing modest expansions of the authority
of regional communities in Europe and the Americas (but not in Africa, Asia, or
the Middle East). I see little or no evidence, however, of any transfer of power or
authority in the post–Cold War world from states to the international community.

NOTES

1. This perspective tends to be adopted by political realists. For particular human rights
   applications, see Morgenthau 1979 and Kennan 1977: 45, 214–215.
2. See Falk 1975 and Beitz 1979 (and, somewhat more broadly, Johansen 1980).
3. My own preference is to restrict the use of "intervention" to this strong sense of coercive interference. However, rather than insist on this strict usage, I will not object to
   using "intervene" to include noncoercive interference. I will, however, usually speak of
   "noncoercive interference" and "coercive intervention," to draw what I take to be an
   essential distinction.
4. The Wilsonian principle of self-determination, even had it been applied consistently in
   the Versailles settlement, was not a real exception. It applied principally to the peoples

of Europe and was never intended to apply to colonized peoples in Africa or Asia. Self-determination was seen not so much as a human right as a right of unusually "civilized" peoples.

5. J. Herman Burgers, in a privately circulated ms., has argued that efforts by H. G. Wells in the 1930s, which led to the drafting of an international declaration of human rights, helped to prepare the ground for the inclusion of human rights in the UN Charter and the early efforts of the United Nations Commission on Human Rights. He also draws attention to a 1929 declaration of the International Law Institute and a proposal in 1933 by Antoine Frangulis. These and other precursors (such as the activities of the Fédération des Droits de l'Homme in Paris in the 1920s and 1930s) should not be overlooked. Nonetheless, as Burgers readily allows, the Holocaust moved such proposals from the margins to the center of international relations.

6. Although there were no negative votes, the Soviet Union and its allies, who from the outset were unenthusiastic about the idea of an international human rights instrument, abstained on the grounds of an insufficient emphasis on economic and social rights. In addition, South Africa abstained because of the provisions on racial discrimination and Saudi Arabia abstained because of the provisions on gender equality.

7. Similar procedures exist under the 1965 International Convention on the Elimination of All Forms of Racial Discrimination, which entered into force in 1969 and had 128 parties at the end of 1990; the 1979 Convention on the Elimination of Discrimination against Women, which entered into force in 1981 and had 104 parties by the end of 1990; and the 1984 Convention against Torture and Other Cruel, Inhuman and Degrading Treatment or Punishment, which entered into force in 1987 and had 55 parties by May 1991. The Committee on Economic, Social and Cultural Rights provides a similar review of reports submitted under the International Covenant on Economic, Social and Cultural Rights, which had 97 parties at the end of 1990.

8. Even severe violators, however, may make symbolic gestures, such as the release or improvements in the treatment of political prisoners, in response to such international pressures. In addition, there may be subtle and indirect impacts on both the target state and foreign governments if the pressure persists for an extended period.

9. In recent years, the Commission has received roughly 4,000 communications a year. About four-fifths of these inquiries, though, are dropped by the individual after an initial exchange of letters, and most of the rest are clearly inadmissible. The fact that the Commission has in the end registered only about 40 new cases annually therefore is largely a testament to relatively good regional human rights records.

10. All of these procedures apply only to the civil and political rights recognized in the 1950 European Convention on Human Rights and Fundamental Freedoms and its Protocols. Economic and social rights are specified in the European Social Charter and are supervised through somewhat weaker procedures.

11. For a detailed account of Argentina's efforts in the United Nations, see Guest 1990: Part II.

BIBLIOGRAPHY

Beitz, Charles R. (1979) *Political Theory and International Relations.* Princeton: Princeton University Press.

Bull, Hedley. (1977) *The Anarchical Society.* New York: Columbia University Press.

Donnelly, Jack. (1992) "Human Rights in the New World Order." *World Policy Journal* 9 (Spring): 249–278.

Falk, Richard. (1975) *A Study of Future Worlds.* New York: Free Press.

Guest, Ian. (1990) *Behind the Disappearances: Argentina's Dirty War Against Human Rights and the United Nations.* Philadelphia: University of Pennsylvania Press.

Kennan, George F. (1977) *The Cloud of Danger: Current Realities of American Foreign Policy.* Boston: Little, Brown.

Keohane, Robert O. and Joseph S. Nye. (1977) *Power and Interdependence: World Politics in Transition.* Boston: Little, Brown.

Medina Quiroga, Cecilia. (1988) *The Battle of Human Rights: Gross, Systematic Violations and the Inter-American System.* Dordrecht: Martinus Nijhoff, 1988.

Morgenthau, Hans. (1977) *Human Rights and Foreign Policy.* New York: Council on Religion and International Affairs.

Pastor, Robert A. (1987) *Condemned to Repetition: The United States and Nicaragua.* Princeton: Princeton University Press.

The International Telecommunications Regime: The Political Roots of Regimes for High Technology

Peter F. Cowhey

AN ANALYSIS OF THE TELECOMMUNICATIONS REGIME

The telecommunications regime was largely unchallenged until the mid-1970s. How did it work? Like other service industries, telecommunications was traditionally oriented toward domestic markets, and competition in both services and equipment was limited. There were three important rationales for the system: it would increase reliability in the performance of tasks central to the public order (such as the provision of communications), would tap economies of scale or scope in the provision of services (the "network" thesis), and would advance considerations of equity expressed in the ideal of "universal service."

Most countries granted authority over communications to a single monopolist and merged their telephone company and the government ministry that regulated it. In addition, countries often mixed their postal and telephone services under one operation, which was called the postal, telephone, and telegraph authority (PTT). As a rule, telephone operations subsidized postal operations; long distance services subsidized both local telephone services and the post office; and the telephone company services subsidized the national monopolist who made the telephone equipment for them.[1] Needless to say, the system also paid high rents to organized labor.

The point-to-point nature of international telecommunications traffic (a telephone call goes, say, from New York to London) encouraged bilateral coordination among governments, particularly where there was heavy traffic flowing over cables. But unless bilateral agreements were covered under a multilateral umbrella, they could easily have contradicted each other, hampered instead of encouraged the international flow of communications, and been subject to competitive end runs.[2] Therefore, global coordination was simplified when a set of umbrella rules and standards was negotiated multilaterally.

The Regime's Institutions

The regime's most important institution [the International Telecommunications Union (ITU)] was created in 1932 by the merger of the International Telegraph Union (founded in 1865) and the signatories of the International Radio Telegraph Convention of 1906. Its three key bodies are the International Consultative Committee for Telephones and Telegraph (CCITT), the International Consultative Committee for Radio (CCIR), and the International Frequency Registration Board. These bodies are responsible for developing recommendations about telecommunications standards, developing telecommunications facilities and networks, establishing the lowest possible rates consistent with efficient service, allocating the radio frequency spectrum, registering radio frequency assignments (to avoid interference), coordinating orbital slots for communications satellites, and helping the developing countries to improve their telecommunications equipment and networks.

The ability of the ITU to carry out its responsibilities has, however, been questioned, and the ITU part of the international communications regime has traditionally been characterized as little more than a set of technical rules representing a low level of commitment by its participants.[3] Experts have mainly speculated on the adequacy of the system for allocating the radio frequency spectrum and satellite orbital slots, setting standards for new technology, and giving technical assistance to poorer nations. . . .

The most important institutional counterpart to the ITU is Intelsat, which was formed in 1964, largely as a result of U.S. efforts. Intelsat is both a communications network and a regulator. It owns and launches satellites to provide international transmission services to national telephone companies; it leases its satellite capacity for domestic communications systems; and it also is the agency that denies or approves the creation of other communications satellites that serve international markets. Scholars have considered Intelsat to be a more powerful institution than the ITU, but they have largely viewed Intelsat as the creation of an international common capability to exploit technological efficiencies while reaffirming the primacy of globalism (as opposed to regionalism) in the world economy.[4]

So far, the ITU in particular sounds like a fairly anemic, technical, and dull organization. But under its auspices, the CCITT acted as a virtual telephone cartel for the PTTs. The CCITT rules for international commerce in telecommunications services were almost absolute even though they were not binding international law. They were the anchor of a regime that facilitated bilateral monopolistic bargains, reinforced national monopolies, and limited the rights of private firms in the global market. In short, the conventional view of the telecommunications regime as primarily a technocratic exercise in technical collaboration was wrong.

The Regime's Principles and Norms

Regime theory, of course, does not rest on the analysis of specific institutions. Its starting point is the identification of regime principles. The telecommunications regime rested on the principle that monopolies of services and equipment were the most efficient and equitable way of providing public service both domestically and internationally. This principle assumed state control over international communications. The principle led to three major norms for the regime: jointly provided services, standardized networks and equipment, and organized global commons (the broadcast spectrum and satellite orbital slots).

Jointly Provided Services   This was the most important norm of the regime. Under CCITT rules, international communications by telephone, telegram, and telex (the basic services) were organized according to the norm that they were jointly provided services. This allowed the PTTs to argue that communications services did not constitute trade; rather, they were the product of a joint investment by two or more nations in a common infrastructure connecting the nations. Monopolistic communications authorities were therefore simply extending the assumed economies of scale and scope from the domestic network to the international arena through joint investment, and such economies permitted international services to cross-subsidize local services.

Each PTT struck deals with its counterparts for the exchange of international services. The receiving monopoly assumed responsibility for the message at the hypothetical midpoint between the sender and receiver; together, the PTTs assumed responsibility for investments necessary to permit the network to work (transoceanic cables, for example). Each monopoly charged its own senders, and the two monopolies settled among themselves if the traffic in both directions did not balance.

The regime rules essentially allowed each country's monopoly to charge whatever it wanted for originating an international call while paying a fixed fee to the receiving country. This made it simple to figure out revenue splits. The rules also effectively forbade all equivalents to the "group charter system" in the travel industry. Telephone companies could not route international calls through circuitous but cheaper routes, as often happens in air travel, nor could they sell services en bloc to a single purchaser at discount, who could then resell them to other parties (as in group charters on scheduled airline flights).[5] Together, these rules made international telephone service phenomenally profitable, and it allowed easy monitoring and negotiations for the cartel because all marketing deals were largely bilateral.

Satellite communications technology was the first challenge to the traditional ITU system. Satellites did not involve point-to-point systems anchored in specialized cable networks; potentially, satellites opened up point-to-multipoint communications (one sender to many destinations simultaneously and vice versa) which cut across national borders. While domestic politics led the United States to upset other countries by proposing the novel idea of Intelsat owning the service, the Americans carefully left the concept of jointly provided services unchallenged. The owners of Intelsat were national telephone monopolies, and they provided the exclusive interconnection and distribution of the satellite services. Thus, the technology was not permitted to open up competitive alternatives.

Intelsat won powerful political support by arguing that continued monopoly in communications traffic is vital for services and cross-subsidies to the Third World. It contended that competition would only skim the profitable cream from the most lucrative satellite routes while causing the performance of the system as a whole to suffer. This argument later forced advocates of competitive systems to prove that each new competitor would not harm the overall economic viability of Intelsat.

Standardized Networks and Equipment   Global universal service required standardization of the various and sometimes idiosyncratic national networks and equipment used in the telecommunications system. This norm effectively linked the provision of services to the operation of the telecommunications equipment market.

Although the CCITT assumed responsibility for the slow and careful process of developing technical standards, the recent explosion of service options made possible by digital information technologies put the standardization process under severe pressure, and many feared that incompatibilities of equipment and service designs would continue to mushroom. The ITU responded by collaborating with the International Standards Organization on the design of an integrated services digital network (ISDN) as a guide to the integration of voice, video, and data services in a comprehensive package. The process of packaging these services still allows variations in national networks but seeks a global design for the future—a much more ambitious task.[6]

Facilitating the interconnection of networks has always enjoyed strong support. What became controversial was the way in which setting standards restricted the supply of telecommunications equipment. Telephone authorities argued that the design of network equipment (central office telephone switches and communications satellites, for example) required intimate knowledge of how the network was engineered; that the transfer of knowledge between network supplier and equipment producer worked best under exclusive long-term arrangements; and that the monopolistic supply of equipment would result in maximum economies of scale and a reduction in transaction costs. The larger countries also argued that it was unacceptable for national security to rely on other countries for network equipment. These arguments led each major country to have a quasi-monopolistic national champion for equipment. A few multinational firms that were committed to extensive local production (notably ITT) became the sole source of equipment in small economies or the accepted second source in other economies.

The monopoly usually extended to customer premises equipment (CPE), which ranged from telephone handsets to office switchboards and data terminals. This supposedly ensured economies of scope, quality control, and technical inter-operability of equipment. Most telephone authorities insisted on total control over all equipment attached to the network. . . .

. . . Thus, the equipment makers were subsidized as well as shielded from competition. They were further shielded by GATT, which not only had trouble covering equipment procurement by governments and government-authorized monopolies in general but also had a specific exemption for telecommunications equipment, an exemption that persisted even after the Tokyo Round efforts to extend GATT to procurement situations. . . .

The Regime's Rules and Decision-Making Procedures

In addition to analyzing principles and norms, regime analysts examine how decisions are made, especially for the rules implementing the norms. In formal terms, the ITU and Intelsat have quite different approaches; in practice, however, both reinforce the power of the PTTs.

The ITU has a classic one-nation, one-vote system that enhances the power of developing countries. It has three sets of rules: the legally binding international law laid down in the ITU Convention, which is reviewed every five years; the regulations set forth by administrative conferences, which meet every few years; and the recommendations prepared for plenary assemblies of the CCITT and CCIR, which are not legally binding but enjoy wide acceptance. The voting power of the developing countries means that the ITU has had to satisfy their special demands without endangering the major tasks of the regime. The compromise has largely focused on two areas: frequency allocation and development assistance. The latter was not politically central to the workings of the regime.

Intelsat uses weighted voting based on a country's share of total use of the system. This gives the industrialized nations, especially the United States, a clear upper hand. For many years, the United States had more than a 50 percent share of the total votes; therefore, to prevent a unilateral U.S. decision on important questions, Intelsat was forced to require that approval or disapproval be based on more than a simple majority vote. The U.S. share has now dropped to about 23 percent of the total, but the United States remains the preeminent power in the organization.

More important than the voting rules has been the manner in which the two organizations have reinforced the power of national telephone authorities. Intelsat has always been a system owned and operated for the telephone authorities of the world. The older ITU organization created a system of international commerce among similar national bureaucratic entities, and that was half of its secret of success. It legitimated the control of the world market by specialized national bureaucracies tied to communications policy, and it delegated most of the sensitive technical and commercial work to the CCITT, which in turn delegated it to the PTTs and the recognized private operating authorities (RPOAs) such as AT&T and Western Union International.[7] Only firms licensed for entry could operate in the market, and as a practical matter these same firms dominated the working of the CCITT. In short, the regime delegated power to a particular group of specialized government bureaucracies and created a quasi-corporatist system of market entry and representation in decision making. The regime's system of norms, rules, and decision-making procedures thus increased barriers to entry to anyone who might contemplate challenging the system.

Explanations for the Origins of the Regime

Analysts of international telecommunications policy have traditionally either come from the ranks of practitioners or relied heavily on interviews with government officials involved in the regime and official documents relating to the regime. This has opened the way to a significant analytic error. While the regime literature has not delved into telecommunications extensively, it has largely pointed toward a functionalist explanation based on improving the use of technological capabilities by reducing transaction costs and creating common capabilities. The regime undoubtedly achieved this purpose, but its particular approach to technical cooperation also reinforced a monopolistic communications system. This decision was not simply a technical choice. Its explanation requires an examination of cognitive and political variables that most telecommunications analysts have slighted. . . .

Communications, it was argued, was a "natural monopoly."[8] The ideal was a single universal network, and this could not be efficiently or fairly created without having a single entity in charge of production and distribution. This was undeniably true to some degree during the early years of telephony, especially for local basic services. But it was definitely not a self-evident truth after the early years for many parts of communications, particularly the profitable long distance routes. Moreover, the stakes were sufficiently high that it is not self-evident that a virtuous policy solution (if monopoly was virtuous) should have triumphed so thoroughly when feasible technical alternatives with different payoffs existed. Indeed, one of the turning points in the regulation of communications came when economists began to grow suspicious of many of the cost claims of engineers.[9]

So powerful was the ideology of a "natural monopoly" that it even led to the creation of histories of telephone systems that are closer to myth than reality but nicely fit the political bargain underlying the regime. Governments supposedly created and expanded communications systems as an instrument of development and national security and a means to exploit technical efficiencies. But in fact governments largely nationalized private postal services for political purposes and seized telegraph services as a monopoly to consolidate the economic gains available from control of the post.[10] This suggests that a broader political explanation is needed to explain why there was no major political challenge to the prevailing cognitive framework about the telecommunications monopoly.

Politicians everywhere discovered that telephones were an attractive candidate for generating the political benefits of administering a national monopoly. In the early stages of development, technological innovation was steadily decreasing telecommunications costs, and there were some networking economies. . . . Since the most costly people to serve were in less densely populated areas and since these populations usually had disproportionate voting and political power in industrialized nations, it was attractive to politicians to build monopolistic systems that encouraged average cost pricing for a set of uniform services. . . .

Defenders of the regime also assumed that it was necessary to provide international basic services through joint investment. This was not the only or necessarily the best way to deal with the issue. Providing large initial sums (sunk investments) in a service with few alternative uses between two countries poses risks. For example, joint investment may protect the project from blackmail, but various contractual schemes could also serve this purpose. Joint investment may also be a rational way of sharing economic risks, but profits from international services were so large that a larger pool of investors than simply the PTTs probably would have been available. (Today, many U.S. telephone cables are installed and owned by companies who then sublet them to established telephone companies.) But conventional regime analysts never considered these factors, and the PTTs had no incentive to rethink conventional wisdom.

The concepts of "natural monopoly" and "the universal network" came to embody the "social fact" justifying the regime. . . . But accepting this consensus on the international telecommunications regime doomed analysts to missing its most interesting economic and political features.

Consider some of the formative episodes in the communications regime. Early in the twentieth century, the United Kingdom (the world's largest sender and receiver of messages) had become the hub of the global underseas cable system for telegraphy and the leader in the new technology of radio-telegraphy. Its Marconi Company tried to maintain a monopoly on radio-telegraphy by aggressive prosecution of patent suits and a policy of refusing to have its radio operators connect with traffic generated by other manufacturers' equipment, a policy backed by the British government.

Telecommunications analysts rightly argued that most other governments refused to accept such a market system because would-be competitors were outraged and national defense authorities disliked the Marconi monopoly. The governments therefore tried to undercut Marconi's position by instituting international rules to ensure the interconnection of radio systems, a task that became easier when several cases of maritime safety involving radio issues made global headlines.[11] Analysts ignored, however, three equally sweeping consequences of the Marconi case. First, interconnection rules for radio technology were soon used to reinforce the emerging system of government control of the electromagnetic spectrum, a system that arguably was far less efficient than an auction system would have proved to be for allocating spectrum rights. . . . Second, the attack on Marconi produced a major market bargain—an international cartel arrangement for radiotelegraphy patent rights—among the key industrialized nations. . . . Third, although radiotelegraphy had the capability of competing with transoceanic cable telegraphy by the 1920s, governments prevented this by implementing a restrictive licensing system for international carriers so as not to upset domestic systems of monopoly.[12]

The case of the international communications regime suggests that it is wise to focus attention on the dominance of domestic politics over initial regime bargains. The government officials implementing the bargain may or may not consciously articulate the political purpose of the deal, but the delegated powers of an international regime depend on it. Methodologically, making the priorities of politicians central to regime analysis suggests a different way of thinking about a regime's principles and norms. . . . Looking to the interplay of domestic politics and the international market position becomes critical for finding the conditions for nurturing the influence of epistemic communities and deducing the actual sources and boundaries of the regime's powers.

TWO PATHS TO REGIME CHANGE

No system of governance is perfect, and there has always been some quibbling about the telecommunications regime. Nevertheless, the basic bargain for monopolistic services and their technical superstructure lasted over a hundred years. Only in the 1970s did the prospect of serious change surface, and even then most analysts questioned its likelihood. . . .

Although technological innovation set the stage for policy change because it altered who could win and lose from the telecommunications systems, technology alone did not determine the type of change. This also depended on the economic and political landscape, especially the role of oligopsony in the telecommunications market.

The largest users of communications systems are relatively few in number (typically, less than 5 percent of all users constitute over half of the long distance traffic and about one-fifth of local traffic), and the cost and performance characteristics of their communications systems have become more critical to their businesses. The large users not only have the skills to abandon the public network if necessary, but they also have the motivation to influence communications regulation. When digital technology emerged, for example, it blurred the line between communications and data processing, made it possible to devise alternative flexible and inexpensive means to create and deliver many of these combined services, and gave international banks, which reckon communications and information systems to be their third highest cost of operations, the motivation to seek global reform and thereby gain an estimated savings of 30–50 percent.

Large users are also fairly easy to organize politically because of their small number. Their determined challenge to telephone monopolies led politicians to look for a compromise. One initial solution was to rewrite the regulations to allow these firms to run private internal communications networks independent of the telephone company. Typically, large firms were authorized to lease transmission capacity from the telephone company and were then provided the functions on their own. . . .

Similarly, the microchip revolution introduced many important new companies into the electronics industry, particularly in the United States and Japan. Since many of these computer companies were not traditional suppliers of the telephone company, they wanted to end the communications monopoly. . . .

Finally, many service and equipment producers concluded that the communications revolution opened up lucrative new possibilities for the production of information- and communications-based services. . . .

The Reform Coalition and the "Little Bang"

The forces for reform have emerged in most industrialized nations simply because all contain firms sharing the above interests. Because of the continental scale of its economy and its numerous multinational firms, the United States was the logical place for regulatory innovation to begin. While winning the regulatory battle at home, its firms calculated that the U.S. bargaining power made global reform feasible, and they became the most prominent exponents of regulatory reform in many countries. But in the 1980s, a transnational corporate coalition for reform emerged as firms in other countries wanted to match the terms offered to U.S. companies.

The key political reality has been that the enormous inefficiencies of traditional monopolies and the large dividends from technological innovation make it possible for new regulatory bargains to give everyone something, although not necessarily according to maximum economic efficiency or social justice. A few statistics illustrate the potential benefits of reform. Communications services and equipment are now approaching 5 percent of the gross national product (GNP) of the industrialized nations. Improving efficiency in their allocation and pricing will yield substantial social welfare returns. Since the divestiture of AT&T, the price of long distance service has declined roughly 50 percent, representing a major benefit for commercial users. Even the average local household (which was supposed to lose gradually because of curtailed subsidies) has probably had a modest decline in the overall cost of telephone services. . . .

The "little bang" approach to reform in advanced economies has five major components. The first entails the slow reduction of cross-subsidies for the average household and small businesses. Household voters and small businesses are numerous and sensitive to changing telephone prices, at least in the short run. Most governments want to avoid major new burdens on these constituents. Therefore, they retain some level of cross-subsidy, even if it is gradually reduced over time. Where and how to finance this cross-subsidy is one of the key variations in national competitive experiments.

The second component of reform is the redefinition of the role of the dominant telephone company. Countries separate postal and telephone services, thereby curtailing subsidies to the post, and then separate policymaking in the government from the actual operation of the telecommunications system. For example, France has recently created the equivalent to the Federal Communications Commission.[13] Some countries are privatizing domestic telephone services in order to increase the gulf between regulators and the national telephone company. In addition, many countries are requiring the telephone company to create separate subsidiaries for basic and enhanced communications services, with the latter ranging from computer communications services through electronic and voice mail to videoconferencing and electronic stock trading systems. The purpose is to reduce cross-subsidies from basic telephone services to the newer forms of computer and information services, thereby creating fairer and more efficient competition in enhanced services. . . .

The third component of reform focuses on the provision of CPE and enhanced services. Most countries have sharply curtailed the PTT's traditional monopoly for the sale of CPE. This has rapidly lowered prices and ended such annoyances as being forbidden to attach the optimal modem to a corporate computer network simply because it is not offered by the PTT. National authorities are also relaxing restrictions on internal corporate networks that provide for voice and enhanced services as well as restrictions on independent companies that sell some range of enhanced services (but not pure telephone services) to anyone. . . .

The fourth component of reform pertains to the provision of network equipment. The new policy nominally liberalizes procurement practices. But few countries (including the United States) will replace the majority share of a preferred local producer with whom the country has long experience, even if that producer is owned by a multinational corporation. Reform will not only open a larger minority share to new foreign suppliers on a more open competitive basis, but it will also introduce more flexible measures for certifying the technical acceptability of foreign equipment and ensuring foreign firms a right to comment on the standards.

The fifth component is that international reform mirrors domestic reform. Countries internationalize domestic change. Given the fact that less than twenty industrialized nations constitute the overwhelming share of the world telecommunications equipment and service markets, they have clearly had the market power to ensure major changes in the regime.

The "little bang" route at the international level has several features. Because it is no longer a PTT monopoly, the CPE market will now conform to traditional GATT trade rules, albeit with special measures to control nontariff barriers (such as technical standards). Network equipment will be subject to freer but not completely free trade by ending its exemption from the emerging GATT rules concerning government procurement. The European Community (EC) has introduced elaborates rules to ensure transparency and nondiscrimination in the purchase of network equipment as long as there is a minimum European content for the products. It is offering to extend these protections to other countries under a tougher GATT code or by bilateral agreements.[14]

Reformers are also tackling the global provision of services. They agree that international trade rules should cover services connecting two nations as well as services offered in any country by a foreign company, even if the service is solely provided to the local market. The rules would legitimate global private networks for multinational corporations and allow greater freedom of entry in the third party provision of enhanced services both within and between nations. However, enhanced services could still face such restrictions as ITU rules that forbid sharing the use of international circuits among several customers.

Finally, to the shock of many, even the selective competitive provision of facilities is emerging. For example, West Germany will let U.S. satellite firms compete for enhanced services with Intelsat, and many EC nations are permitting at least two competitors for the nation's cellular telephone services.

The "Big Bang"

Regulatory reformers have gone even farther in the three countries that constitute almost 60 percent of the world telecommunications market: the United States, United Kingdom, and Japan. The power of these nations to drive the world market is formidable. . . .

The only item on which the three nations do not constitute a majority of the world telecommunications market is international telephone services. But even here, the three have special advantages because they are the three most important hubs for global communications infrastructure (such as transoceanic cables) and private international corporate networks.

The United States, United Kingdom, and Japan have the principal global financial centers and are the most important originators of multinational manufacturing enterprises, which demand extraordinary advances in the use of computing and communications technologies. Thus, these countries have preferred a "big bang" in reform that introduces competition in basic telephone services and the network facilities that provide them. Political leaders in all three nations decided that market competition was the best means to allocate resources, stimulate demand for telephone services, [and] increase efficiency enough to make it possible to hold down cost increases for the average household user. . . .

Large-scale reform has not easily been accommodated by the traditional regime institutions. While proponents of each of the paths to regime change reject the status quo, they disagree on the extent of reform; therefore, some fragmentation in the formal arrangements of the international regime is predictable. This is taking two routes: a growing flexibility in the formal rules and a growing diversity of forums for discussing and handling telecommunications services.

The established international organizations have introduced more flexible rules. Intelsat streamlined its procedures for giving permission to competitive satellite systems. In return, reformers pledged to refrain from a direct attack on Intelsat's telephone services in the immediate future. The ITU had major conferences in 1988 and 1989 to rewrite its rules to address the explosion in digital technology and competition. While supporters of the status quo tried to strengthen international regulation of enhanced services and private networks to toughen the legal standing of international regulations, the United States was able to successfully champion the explicit recognition of the right of any pair of countries to introduce more competitive arrangements by mutual consent. The result was a stalemate that thwarted the goals of conservative PTTs.[15]

The growing diversity of forums has taken the form of larger numbers of bilateral trade negotiations and the introduction of a new multilateral player, GATT. With regard to bilateral trade, the United States has especially insisted on bilateral negotiations regarding communications equipment and services. . . . The U.S. Omnibus Trade Act of 1988 also singled out telecommunications for the creation of a timetable to liberalize markets in countries whose unfair trade practices were causing damage to the United States.

Similarly, the current GATT round features a major effort to bring communications and information services under its purview. The reform coalition wants GATT to extend its international review process to telecommunications services and to apply the approach used in the domestic oversight of bureaucracies. Since it is impossible to define all barriers to trade in services, they want the GATT parties to come to an agreement on markets to be liberalized and on broad principles defining fair competition. Parties would then use trade talks as a grievance procedure about any item that impinges on what the Montreal midterm review of the current GATT round defined as the principle of "market access" for services.[16]

Market access opens three items in particular for trade oversight. First, it would ensure the right of foreigners to establish business by means other than importing. The trade negotiations are creating a norm that businesses involving interactive global networks have a de facto right to local investment. The rationale is that without the right to create specialized networks, the international service network is meaningless. If IBM wants to offer its global computer network to local clients, for example, it should be able to create a local network to do so. More surprisingly, if a ticketing services firm, such as Ticketron, wants to invest in and establish a local ticketing network, it may also be protected by trade rules. Thus, GATT is creeping toward a right of foreign investment or, more precisely, controls in national restrictions on foreign investment.

Second, market access would require redefinition of national rights to create and design national networks. As noted earlier, all parties agree that there is a need for a much closer coordination of standards to ensure connectivity of networks, but they do not agree on a particular design of networks. Therefore, the reform coalition advocates that the decision-making processes for standardization as well as some of the technical dimensions of the network be subject to new forms of international oversight. It also advocates that global and national standards-setting bodies be opened to wider participation (for example, by computer firms and large users) and that a simpler and speedier process for letting foreign firms review and object to decisions on national standards be implemented.

Third, market access would require significant international oversight of national policies concerning pricing, servicing of customers, and rights of administrative appeal in the domestic market. The aim is to obtain some fairly arbitrary but easily monitored standards of conduct for domestic networks and regulations. For example, if a PTT were to deny users flat monthly rates for leasing local communications circuits, this could trigger the demand for an explanation by trade authorities. International oversight of national markets would also turn basic telephone pricing and regulation into a trade policy issue, a distinct benefit to large foreign users and suppliers of specialized services that are dependent on local telephone facilities.

The profile of the actual GATT deal will probably resemble the "little bang" with some room available for evolving to the "big bang.". . .

CONCLUSIONS

The technology of telecommunications was once conducive to a political bargain built around national telephone monopolies. The international communications regime improved the technical performance of the system while organizing an international cartel built around bilateral bargaining and guided by multilateral commercial rules. It fostered an epistemic community devoted to the idea of a "natural monopoly" for telephone services. Later, the digital technology revolution gave large users of the communications system, newer electronics companies, and would-be providers of enhanced services an incentive to challenge national regulatory systems. Once they succeeded domestically, they sought to extend the reforms to the global level. They had the market power to erode the old regime, and they turned to the organizing principle of free trade as a guide for reform. This has introduced the beginnings of an alternative epistemic community for the telecommunications regime and a new mix of institutional jurisdictions and powers to alter the old regime. More generally, it is setting a precedent for bringing most services under the umbrella of free trade rules, a significant liberalization of the world economy at a time when many fear the decline of an open economic regime.

NOTES

1. The United States was always a bit of a deviant case. While it authorized a dominant monopolistic company, it kept a separate regulatory authority, never merged postal services with telecommunications, and allowed the dominant telephone company to own its equipment supplier. These differences ultimately made reforms easier to launch in the United States.
2. The key problems in the pioneering days of international telegraphic services arose because European countries made international messages subject to inspection and tariffs at each border. This led (literally) to building telegraph stations that spanned both sides of a national boundary. The wing in Germany would receive a telegram for France, write it down, take it through customs in the middle of the building, and hand it over to the French company on the other side of the station. In response, telegraph companies lobbied for international rules that would allow the uninterrupted flow of messages across two or more nations. Hence, the forerunner of the ITU liberalized commerce in communications services. But the bargain had a second dimension. It also reinforced highly profitable national monopolies by excluding competitive entrants. See Asher H. Ende, "International Communications," *Federal Communications Bar Journal*, vol. 28, 1975, pp. 147–78.
3. See Harold K. Jacobson, "ITU: A Potpourri of Bureaucrats and Industrialists," in Robert Cox and Harold K. Jacobson, eds., *The Anatomy of Influence* (New Haven, CT: Yale University Press, 1973), pp. 59–101. Although this study did an excellent job of analyzing the processes at the ITU and noted that industrial interests were around to

lobby, it showed no systematic understanding of the political economy of the regime. For two other standard works, see David Blatherwick, *The International Politics of Telecommunications* (Berkely, CA: Institute for International Studies, 1987); and George A. Codding, Jr., and Anthony M. Rutkowski, *The International Telecommunications Union in a Changing World* (Dedham, MA: Artech House, 1982).

4. See, for example, John Gerard Ruggie, "International Responses to Technology: Concepts and Trends," *International Organization* 29 (Summer 1975), pp. 557–84.

5. The CCITT had four rules implementing the norm. First, telephone rates for international calls would be set bilaterally between the carrier of the country of origin and that of the country of ultimate destination. Carriers from the two national monopolies could establish a single "accounting rate" for calls between their countries and then split the revenues roughly "fifty-fifty" (with a fee for any third countries through which the calls passed). Second, no matter which route a call actually followed between the two countries, the accounting rate would remain the same. Thus, unlike an airline traveler, a telecommunications carrier could not take a cheap route from New York to Brussels and then take a standard short hop to Frankfurt in order to save money over the expensive direct route from New York to Frankfurt. Third, PTTs should keep prices as low as possible and should relate them to costs. Although PTTs could cross-subsidize some services for social purposes, they were obligated to avoid "harmful" competition among services. PTTs cited this latter obligation when refusing discounts for larger volume users. Fourth, there could be no "resale" of capacity. This meant that if a telephone circuit was leased to one party, that party could not resell its unused capacity to other parties. This prevented something akin to the airline charter business for telecommunications and hindered competition in enhanced services. See Jonathan D. Aronson and Peter F. Cowhey, *When Countries Talk: International Trade in Telecommunications Services* (Cambridge, MA: Ballinger, 1988).

6. It is commonplace to accept ISDN as a goal, but there are still bitter fights over what ISDN means for the design and competitiveness of telecommunications services. See William J. Drake and Lee McKnight, "Telecommunications Standards in the Global Information Economy," *Project Promothee Perspectives,* no. 5, March 1988, pp. 21–26.

7. The United States has always insisted that it could only cooperate with an organization that allowed for RPOAs in order to accommodate the fact that AT&T was a private firm and that the United States had multiple private telex and telegram carriers.

8. "Natural monopoly" as a dominant metaphor in telecommunications persisted without major controversy in a manner similar to the persistence of "naturalist realism" as a dominant motif in painting. As Bryson's brilliant analysis of "naturalist realism" notes, realism depends on the clever creation of a series of "signs" and "techniques" that are self-camouflaging so as to avoid pointing out the artificial construction of the "realist" vision. Painters have a rich agenda for paradigmatic (Bryson uses the word schematic) development of signs and techniques available to keep them and their viewers happy. But, just as vitally, successful naturalist painting depends on viewers who expect to see that type of construction of reality. In other words, "natural orders" depend on techniques that are self-effacing yet richly laden with developmental opportunities for engaged practitioners and "consumers" who have no incentive to challenge this manner of reconstructing the world. Much the same held true for the telecommunications regime. See Norman Bryson, *Vision and Painting* (New Haven, CT: Yale University Press, 1983).

9. Economists have long criticized telephone regulation as inefficient. Recent reexamination of the historical record shows that competition was possible far earlier than previously recognized. In the case of AT&T, for example, records show that the firm used

its initial control of long distance technology to stifle competition at the local level, the exact opposite of how engineers traditionally ranked the opportunities for competition. See Robert W. Garnett, *The Telephone Enterprise* (Baltimore, MD: Johns Hopkins University Press, 1985). For a compelling theory of the evolution of networks, see Eli M. Noam, "The Public Telecommunications Network: A Concept in Transition," *Journal of Communication* 37 (Winter 1987), pp. 30–48.

10. Noam, "The Public Telecommunications Network."

11. In the case of the Marconi Company, conferences in 1903 and 1906 passed ineffectual regulations to indirectly curb its monopolistic practices. After several well-publicized tragedies at sea (including the loss of the *Titanic*) were made worse by radio communications problems and after an insider stock trading scandal involving the Marconi Company and Lloyd George occurred, Britain capitulated on the interconnection issue at an international conference in 1912. See Gleason L. Archer, *History of Radio to 1926* (New York: American Historical Society, 1938).

12. Robert John Oslun, "Communications Satellite Policy: Revolutionary or Evolutionary?" Ph.D. diss., American University, Washington, DC, 1975.

13. The European Commission has also directed that this be the general rule for the EC by 1992.

14. The EC rules on local content intentionally resemble the "Buy America" policy of the United States, according to interviews with EC officials in Brussels in July 1989. The proposal indeed resembles the logic of strategic trade philosophy that Krasner has correctly endorsed for this market, although Krasner does not sufficiently note that it would also constitute a major liberalization of the market. See Stephen D. Krasner, *Asymmetries in Japanese-American Trade: The Case for Specific Reciprocity* (Berkeley, CA: Institute for International Studies, 1987).

15. Even the U.S. companies that were most critical of the outcome of the ITU World Administrative Telephone and Telegraph Conference saw no significant threat to their competitive strategies, according to interviews with officials of several data communications companies in May and June 1989.

16. For a discussion of grievance processes as a substitute for direct legislative decision, see Cowhey, "'States' and 'Politics.'" "Market access" implies that all barriers to effective global access to agreed upon service markets are subject to trade review. See Peter F. Cowhey, "Telecommunications and Foreign Economic Policy," in Paula Newburg, ed., *New Directions in Communications Policy*, vol. 2 (Durham, NC: Duke University Press, 1989).

Chapter
6

The Functions of International Organizations

Peacekeeping, Mediation, and Global Policies

Friedrich Kratochwil

*T*he purpose of this chapter is to analyze the ways in which international organizations have contributed to global security. Central to the study of international relations are analyses of the conditions under which states resort to the use of force. Advocates of world government and realists offer two of the most popular views on this topic. On the one hand, world government advocates have emphasized the importance of creating central enforcement mechanisms in the international system in order to limit the use of force. On the other hand, as was pointed out in the preface to this reader, realists emphasize the need for states to guarantee their own security in the anarchic international system. They view internal growth of capabilities and the formation of alliances as the two most viable sources of providing for states' security, and thus limiting the use of force.

The selections in this chapter offer a different perspective on this topic. They emphasize the importance of collective security arrangements and peacekeeping operations for limiting the unilateral use of force. The defining feature of a collective security system is the universal obligation of each state in the system to assist a victim in the system. The success of this type of system depends on a variety of factors. First, the maintenance of the status quo must be preferred by all relevant actors to the resort to force. Second, collective security systems are more likely to succeed when procedures exist through which a consensus can be reached regarding whether the use of force was unprovoked or an act that redressed an earlier wrong. Here the issue of legitimization, which was introduced in Chapter 5, arises again. Third, the success of these arrangements also depends on a prior agreement concerning how the burden of punishing an aggressor will be distributed among the members of a collective security system. In the absence of such agreements and their institutionalization, each state has an incentive to avoid the costly task of punishing aggressors. As a result, it is unlikely that a group of members of the collective security system will cooperate in providing this function. Since these conditions are not easily met, it is not surprising that attempts to establish collective security systems have fared poorly.

For example, a type of collective responsibility for international security was already envisaged in the Treaties of Münster and Osnabrück in 1648. But this attempt at collective security failed; and in subsequent years the growth of the law of neutrality became increasingly pervasive. Nations reserved the right to get involved in wars and enforcement actions instead of committing themselves to assisting the victims of aggression. Similarly, the Covenant of the League of Nations was also not able to solve the collective action problem in enforcement described above, since it left it up to each state to respond to aggression. The UN Charter *did* attempt to redress this problem by vesting the Security Council with the responsibility for maintaining peace and by binding UN members to adhere to its decisions. This Charter envisioned detachments of national forces, largely drawn from the "great powers," to be used for UN enforcement measures under the direct command of the UN. In this way, the Charter raised hopes that the collective security arrangement would be one "with teeth," as one of the delegates to the San Francisco Conference put it.

However, from its inception the UN faced a number of serious limitations. Primary among them were the ideological and political cleavages, particularly among the permanent members of the Security Council, that were outgrowths of divisions between the Western and the Eastern bloc. In addition, as the framers of the Charter were well aware, enforcement measures against a "great power" were likely to precipitate another world war. Peace had to rest on great-power consensus and the veto power of the five permanent members was only the outward recognition of this prudential insight. Since there rarely has been a consensus among these members concerning security-related issues, the collective security system was stillborn. Despite a variety of UN operations, none of them was taken in accordance with the provisions of Chapter VII.

But stating that the collective security system of the UN failed when assessed in terms of the aspirations of Chapter VII of the Charter is not tantamount to stating that the world organization has played an unimportant role in "peacekeeping." Substituting for the original goal of "enforcement," the notion of *peacekeeping* represented the most noticeable innovation of the UN. Peacekeeping has not only involved such traditional functions as truce supervision but also has encompassed aspects of Dag Hammarskjöld's "preventive diplomacy." The latter consisted of the interjection of troops in a crisis area with the explicit approval of the contending parties. Rather than relying on the strength of the major powers to enforce the peace, preventive diplomacy originally aimed at keeping these states out of crisis areas in order to prevent an expansion of the conflict through their intervention. Furthermore, during the last few decades, mediational activities of the Secretary-General and his representatives have also increased in frequency and salience. As the Afghan war demonstrated, "keeping" the peace increasingly involves forging consensus among the various domestic factions as well as among the outside players. But the process of forging such a consensus has to proceed even when the hostilities continue unabated. Neither classical enforcement action nor the interjection of neutral troops in order to stop the fighting is likely to be successful when neither the locals nor their outside protectors agree on an armistice on the basis of a status quo.

More recently, a new set of even more explicit *peacemaking,* rather than peacekeeping, operations has been added to the UN repertoire. These operations often involve the UN deeply in the domestic arena by charging it with the provision of some basic services and humanitarian relief for refugees or victims of ethnic violence (for example, in Somalia, Cambodia, Iraq, Bosnia) and with the monitoring of unprecedented disarmament measures (Iraq). Indeed it is the crisis of the "state" in certain areas—which is brought on by its disintegration and loss of legitimacy, rather than by classical inter-state violence—which represents, at the moment, the most pressing need. As recent events in Bosnia also demonstrate, the internal crisis not only inhibits the keeping and making of peace; it even endangers classical humanitarian relief operations. Local militia commanders hold the UN representatives hostage with their government's approval. The impotence of the organization to stop the fighting erodes the respect for UN efforts, and it endangers relief personnel and UN troops or involves them even in military engagements (Somalia).

The moderate success of the UN in the peacekeeping area seems to be paralleled by a decline in its ability to further global welfare, which represents another goal of the organization. While both bilateral and multilateral aid programs disappointed the hoped-for rapid economic growth in the Third World, during the 1970s the UN became the primary forum in which the demands for a New International Economic Order (NIEO) were voiced. The failures to institutionalize new redistributive regimes under the direct auspices of UN agencies, or as a result of ongoing global negotiations outside of the UN, have been amply documented and need not be rehearsed further. (Some of the reasons for the failure of the NIEO coalition and its inability to forge robust issue-linkages among diverse issue-areas are explored further in Ernst Haas's article in Chapter 8.)

Does this mean that "learning" has been taking place in the issue-area of peacekeeping but not in global welfare? Or are these new UN peacekeeping initiatives more the result of fortuitous circumstances than learning and organizational growth? The contribution of Ernst Haas addresses this question. He concludes that the United Nations peacekeeping activities are unlikely to provide for a new "humanitarian order" or for the permanent growth and institutionalization of a UN role precisely because the new initiatives seem more akin to adaptive responses than to genuine "learning." His careful suggestions for institutional reform provide much food for thought as they are based neither on the exaggerated hopes for a new era nor on the pessimism that nothing changes under the sun.

Given the quite limited, albeit noticeable, success in peacekeeping and the failure of global policies enhancing welfare, the pattern of UN activity shows a nearly inverse pattern to functionalist and neo-functionalist teachings. According to these theories, cooperation in low politics areas should be less problematic and more promising than in the "high politics" area of peacekeeping. But, as Ronald

Coate and Donald Puchala point out, the chances for "g
dimmed during the last decade. As opposed to the relatively
organizational routines available for peacekeeping missions,
organizational responses to poverty has proven to be conside
Other factors that account for this failure are the lack of lea
World coalition, the unpersuasiveness of some of the adv
demise of the Cold War, and the resulting loss of competition for the Third
World's allegiance.

After these critical and cautious appraisals of UN efforts in peacekeeping and
in enhancing global welfare, Donald Puchala provides a more hopeful note on UN
peacemaking. Instead of focusing on enforcement measures or normative and redistributive changes implied by global policies, Puchala's analysis centers on the
mediational role of the Secretary-General of the United Nations and his special
representatives. Puchala provides a rich account of the activities of the Secretary-
General's personal representatives and their mediational role. He argues that they
have done much to promote peace since the inception of the United Nations. But
Puchala also identifies important limitations to the further growth of these missions, ranging from overtaxing the UN staff to the inherent limitations of good offices and mediation as means of conflict resolution. He suggests, however, that the
hybrid arrangement of Article 99 of the UN Charter and Chapter VI, together
with the dispatch of special representatives, is likely to remain one of the principal
contributions to peacemaking and keeping of the peace.

Collective Conflict Management: Evidence for a New World Order?

Ernst B. Haas

TOWARD A NEW WORLD ORDER?

. . . The waning of the cold war seems to have brought with it a rebirth of the collective security practices advocated and designed in 1945 by the victors in World
War II. The fortunes of intergovernmental collective security organizations (IOs)
were at an abysmal low in 1985: referrals of new disputes were at their lowest
point since 1945; so was effectiveness at managing disputes on the agendas of IOs;
the number of unimplemented decisions was at an all-time high; on a scale of 100
(where 100 = perfect performance of all management tasks for all disputes on the
agenda) the UN stood at 10 and the major regional IOs at 15.[1]

My first task is to show statistically that these trends have indeed been mostly reversed since 1985. The remaining tasks include offering a data- and theory-based explanation of the reversal, an inquiry into the degree of permanence to be expected of these improvements, a discussion of what can be done to improve the peaceful settlement of interstate disputes and of civil wars by IOs, and a plea that the option to mount full-scale enforcement measures must be reinforced just the same.

IOs Increase Authority and Relevance

All IOs, except for the OAU, increased their effectiveness in the last five years as compared to the prior cumulative record (see Table 1), though the sharp increases on the part of the OAS and the Arab League must be discounted because so many of their cases appeared simultaneously on the UN's agenda and it was in the UN that most of the action took place.

However, UN performance during the most recent period reverses a downward slide that had gone on steadily since 1960. Ten new peacekeeping and truce observation missions, many with legally unprecedented mandates, were launched since 1988, whereas only thirteen such initiatives were mounted in the previous 43 years of the UN's life. Two election-monitoring operations were also launched. . . .

Since 1985 the number of disputes that involved fighting referred to IOs has increased sharply and the number of such disputes not so referred went down proportionately, suggesting that the legitimacy of IOs as conflict managers is improving. . . . For the first time in the history of the UN the rate of success and the rate of referral went up *together* . . . , an achievement not duplicated by the regional organizations whose aggregate effectiveness during the last five years declined, in line with an overall erratic performance. . . . The practice of unilateral intervention in civil wars on the part of the most powerful industrial states declined markedly as illustrated by events in Nicaragua, Angola, Ethiopia, Sudan,

TABLE 1   SUCCESS IN CONFLICT MANAGEMENT, 1945–1985 V. 1986–1990

	1945–1985			1986–1990		
	Total Disputes	Disputes at Once on UN and Regional Agenda	Percent Success	Total Disputes	Disputes at Once on UN and Regional Agenda	Percent Success
United Nations	148	—	23	42	—	32
Organization of American States	35	7	31	6	4	43
Arab League	27	6	20	4	2	25
Organization of African Unity	22	3	22	7	5	20

Cambodia, Afghanistan, Somalia, and Chad. The legitimacy and the authority of the UN appeared to increase spectacularly as the organization took on the mandate to monitor elections as an essential component in multilateral mediation of civil wars and in transitions to democracy, to give relief to refugees and victims of civil strife, and to take more aggressive steps than in the past with respect to the protection of human rights.[2]

Finally, there were no complaints against the Soviet Union, Britain, and France, and only one against China, in marked contrast to earlier periods in the history of the UN. Unimplemented decisions in the UN went down to 45 percent of all decisions from 54 percent for the previous forty years.

IO's Lose Authority and Relevance?

These, however, were not the only trends of interest. Disputes on the agenda of IOs were markedly less intense and dangerous than was true in previous periods, a trend even more significant when we do not include some very intense disputes carried over from previous periods but approaching solutions since 1985 (Table 2). This slight decline in relevance is also evident in the number of civil wars which were not referred to multilateral agreement since 1985 (see Table 3). . . .

During the last five years, the United States, the leader of the coalition against Iraq and the champion of a new world order, was the target of complaints no less than nine times, followed by Israel (five times) and South Africa (four times). The United States also used the veto more frequently than any other permanent member of the Security Council to ward off complaints against itself and to protect Israel.

WHY WAS THERE AN IMPROVEMENT IN PERFORMANCE? CORRELATES OF SUCCESS

Our scheme of explanation is based on a simple model. The dependent variable—success in managing conflict—is thought to be immediately explained by four "management variables": organizational decision, field operations, leadership, and

TABLE 2   INTENSITY OF OLD AND NEW DISPUTES (IN PERCENT)

	United Nations	Five Regionals
1945–1985	(N = 137)	(N = 92)
Insignificant, very low	36	59
Low, moderate	31	25
High, very high	33	16
1986–1990	(N = 32)	(N = 11)
Insignificant, very low	65	62
Low, moderate	18	23
High, very high	18	15

TABLE 3 CIVIL WARS NOT REFERRED TO MULTILATERAL ORGANIZATIONS, 1985–1990

Civil War	Outside Intervention by
Colombia	United States to government
Guatemala	
Mexico	
Peru	United States to government
Papua-New Guinea	
Philippines	United States to government
USSR (4 separate ones)	
Romania	
Tibet	
India (3 separate ones)	Pakistan to Kashmiri insurgents
Afghanistan	Pakistan/U.S./Saudi Arabia to insurgents; USSR to government
Sri Lanka	India to government; Tamil Nadu to insurgents
Maldives	India to government; Sri Lanka insurgents
Burma	
Kurdistan/Iraq	Western coalition to insurgents
Kurdistan/Turkey	
Fiji	
Mozambique	RSA to insurgents; also Malawi
South Africa	
Ethiopia	USSR to governments; Arab countries to Eritrean insurgents
Somalia	
Sudan	Ethiopia, Kenya to insurgents; Arab states to government
Rwanda	

consensus. These management variables, however, are associated with, and embedded in, six "contextual variables": degree of intensity of the dispute, seriousness of the hostilities (from simple riots to efforts to eliminate the antagonist), the extent of the geographical spread (from bilateral confrontation to global involvement), the relationship of the conflict to such global issues as the cold war and the decolonization movement, and the power dyad of the disputants (from conflict among superpowers to confrontations among the smallest states), and the alignment with power blocs of the antagonists. . . .

Contextual Variables as Correlates of Success

One plausible explanation of the rise in organizational success is the possibility that there was some systematic difference between the character of the most recent disputes . . . and the character of the disputes before 1986. In the case of the UN the difference is most striking in that successfully managed disputes were *more* threatening to world peace than earlier ones in their intensity and in the amount of heavy fighting that occurred, though not in terms of geographic spread. No systematic differences show up with respect to type of issue and alignment into blocs. As to power dyads, the most recent era differs from the earlier ones in

Third world wars.

Hurricane

Katrina

9/11

Swine flue.   FEMA

Mandatory shots.

"Shots given @ birth

natural disasters

new health plan.

rich get richer
poor get poorer.

Third world ware
call them
terrorists
to get rid
of them

Aliens: not humans.
(negative orientation
take over
earth

that the United States is more frequently cited as a threat to the peace, whereas the Soviet Union is targeted less often than before. In the regional IOs the same trends show up with respect to intensity and type of warfare, but in addition the geographic spread is widening. Members of opposing alliances and alignments challenged each other more often in recent years in regional fora. Disputes pitting a superpower (the U.S.) and such middle powers as Iran, Iraq, or Egypt against small states have sharply risen in number. In short, the salience of disputes to world and regional peace has gone up.

As salience to world peace rises, so does the success of the UN in managing disputes. Since 1986 success in management of the UN is disproportionately associated with high-intensity, violent warfare, geographic spread to the neighbors of the antagonists, with cold war issues as well as issues unrelated to any global metaissue, with parties in opposing blocs as well as among allies (whereas bloc opponents earlier usually did not resolve their disputes despite efforts at IO management), and with dyads of small-power antagonists (as opposed to larger degrees of success associated with large and middle powers earlier).

The contextual explanation that jumps to mind is that the ebbing of the cold war made it permissible for countries that had been allies but also entertained grievances against each other to take these to an international forum. Similarly, it facilitated conflict management among members of formerly opposing blocs. As the Soviet—American confrontation receded, disputes that had originally arisen, or been globalized, because of that confrontation lost their salience and thus allowed for collective management. The positive association of high-intensity, violent warfare disputes with management success is partly due to the fact that situations previously tainted by the cold war now permitted collective solutions that had not been conceivable before, as we shall see when management variables are examined. Small power dyads became more prominent than dyads including large and middle powers because of the shrinking of the decolonization issue.

The picture is quite different when we turn to regional organizations, whose overall effectiveness declined markedly during the most recent period. No significant changes in the association of the contextual variables with management success are in evidence, except when we turn to bloc alignment. Such successes as were scored were very disproportionately associated with disputes in which the antagonists were not aligned at all, whereas performance in dyads among allied disputants declined markedly. These trends are due to the numerous sharp confrontations in the OAS between the United States on the one hand and Nicaragua and Panama on the other. More basically, we suspect, the decline in organizational effectiveness is associated with a weakening of consensus in all regions, which in turn is associated with changes in bloc alignments that also reflect the waning of the cold war.

Management Variables as Correlates of Success

Improved performance by the UN was closely associated with the end of the cold war as a metaissue and with the growing irrelevance of the alignments associated with that conflict, with higher average intensity and wider spread of the disputes on the organization's agenda. These changes go along with striking changes in behavior of the member states inside the UN. The very profiles of the disputes were different. In the most recent era the organization was much more likely to launch large field operations than in the earlier periods, to make decisions that were approved by smaller majorities, and to rely much more on the leadership of the Secretary-General in shaping decisions and managing operations. Decisions to launch operations that were ultimately to prove successful, especially large operations, were far more common in recent years; no single form of leadership proved especially successful before 1986, whereas the leadership of the Secretary-General, often exercised jointly with a coalition of states including one or both superpowers, was the most prominent form of leadership associated with successful operations thereafter. In earlier eras, success demanded very wide consensus among the member states, but in the most recent period weaker forms of consensus often sufficed.

Disputes submitted to the regional organizations showed exactly the same differences in profile in the most recent era as compared to earlier cases. However, unlike the UN, the change in profile is associated with an overall *decline* in effectiveness. . . .

Improvement Analyzed in Terms of Task and Mission

Conciliation Without Large Operations   The UN's achievements in peace-keeping were not matched in efforts at mediation and conciliation that did not involve any field operations of major scope. The 22 cases of that type were distributed as shown on Table 4. Six successes in a field of 22 cases is not very impressive, though much of the failure is attributable to the fact that the United States was the victim of the complaints, or protected Israel. The actual percentage of success (16 percent) is substantially less than the average during the pre-1986 history of UN small operations, while the record for attempted conciliation with-

TABLE 4   CHARACTERISTICS OF DISPUTES CONCILIATED WITHOUT LARGE FIELD OPERATIONS, 1986–1990

	No Success	**Success**
No resolution, no operations	11 disputes; U.S., Israel, RSA sole defendants	None
Weak resolution, no operations	China human rights, Al Wazir assassination, Panama elections	Lebanese peace process, RSA death penalty
Strong resolution, small operations	Intifada, Temple Mount	Iran airliner downing, Guatemala peace process, Albanian human rights, Ending Pacific Trust

out any operations is as bad now as it was earlier. The adage that without substantial effort no impact is scored holds now as it did before, as does the finding that the membership makes little effort to mediate or conciliate in low-intensity local disputes. Conciliation efforts by the OAU to settle the Aouzou Strip and Agacher disputes came to nothing, as bilateral mediation helped ease one and an appeal to the International Court of Justice (ICJ) the other. The OAS was unable to mediate or conciliate with the help of small Secretariat missions, as it had done very often in past years, except in one trivial case. The Arab League scored only one such success since 1985, in its role in the Lebanese peace process.

Judicial Settlement and the ICJ   Like the Security Council, the ICJ came into its own after 1985 as far as the number of submissions is concerned. Before that date the Court had heard 23 cases that involved political, territorial, military, or resource issues featuring states rather than private parties; since 1985 eight new cases were referred to it. . . . Seven of the original cases were not settled for procedural reasons; in eight others one of the parties either failed to participate or declined to implement an adverse award! As if this record were not bad enough, nine advisory opinions were in effect decisions adverse to specific governments; none of the "defendants" paid any attention to the rulings! It is hardly surprising that judicial settlement of major international disputes by the world's most prominent court had a bad reputation. A number of politically very sensitive cases are now before it, the kinds of cases which, prior to the Nicaraguan complaint against the United States for supporting the Contras, the Court had rarely been called upon to hear. Mali implemented an adverse decision; Libya and Malta settled their maritime boundary dispute bilaterally, with the Court's help. One careful student of the Court's impact on the peaceful settlement of international disputes writes that "the record of international adjudication suggests that there has been a recent and significant decline in the respect nations accord the Court. . . ."[3] It is too soon to tell whether this judgment will stand.

From Peacekeeping to Peacemaking?   Pre-1986 truce observation and peacekeeping efforts resembled one another in that the mandates given by the Security Council or the General Assembly did not go beyond the ending of hostilities and the monitoring of the resulting truce, though UNIFIL when prevented from carrying out its mandate also assumed humanitarian relief duties. Typically, the mandates called for separating the belligerent forces, creating buffer zones, patrolling truce lines, reporting violations and mediating local disagreements among the parties. Things are different now. Large military and civilian forces are also given the task of disarming guerrilla groups and stopping the arms traffic (UNGOMAP, UNTAG, ONUCA, UNAVEM 2, UNIKOM, MINURSO); monitoring elections and the observance of human rights (UNGOMAP, UNTAG, ONUVEN, ONUVEH, ONUSAL, MINURSO); administering relief operations for civilians (ONUVEH, MINURSO); as well as mounting a full-scale administration of the area (UNTAG). Similar extended duties will be given to the operations planned for Cambodia. Things work out better, on the whole, if there is full agreement among all parties and organs of the UN about mandate and duration before the operations begin. There is a growing consensus that the Secretary-General alone has the power to determine the composition of the forces. While approximately 70 member states furnished personnel for these operations, a few countries stood out as consistent, continuous, and experienced participants. Many were the same as before 1986: Norway, Sweden, Denmark, Austria, Finland, Ireland, Canada; but they were joined after 1986 by Spain, Argentina, Yugoslavia, and India as core participants.

The growing autonomy of the Secretary-General is striking. Javier Pérez de Cuéllar, though lacking Dag Hammarskjöld's charismatic qualities, will be recognized as the most innovative executive head of the UN as far as conflict management is concerned. His active intervention has much to do with the increasing scope and versatility of UN peacekeeping, whether through personal intervention or by the regular use of his personal representatives. . . . The most innovative of these "coordinating" measures is his active role in negotiating a generally accepted constitutional order for countries wracked by civil war; such was his role in contributing to constitutional settlements in Namibia, El Salvador, Afghanistan, and Western Sahara. It may become a role in Guatemala, Cambodia, and Croatia.

The Secretary-General, along with others, has eloquently and repeatedly called for "peacemaking" in addition to peacekeeping. The most recent operations aim at much more than separating the warring parties because the mandates included humanitarian tasks as well as measures to aid in the introduction of democratic governance. In many of the cases the mandate called for intervention in civil wars and the introduction of democratically elected national governments to succeed the parties in conflict, a task by no means foreseen by the drafters of the UN Charter, who insisted on excluding matters "essentially within the domestic jurisdiction" of member states from the rules governing collective security and the peaceful settlement of disputes. Peacemaking came to mean, in the 1980s, that the UN has some role in mediating an end to civil strife, monitoring elections, protecting human rights in order to make a free election possible, disarming and resettling guerrillas and their families, and making sure that democratic constitutions be written and implemented. Whether the organization also has a responsibility for intervening if and when violations of such constitutions occur is still being debated. The OAS, which claims such a right, has had indifferent success in making democracy prevail.

In any event, peacemaking by UN-run democratization remains controversial. Alvaro de Soto, the UN's "man in Central America," insists that the Nicaraguan and Haitian events were not a precedent, that the UN has no regular mandate to monitor elections or assure democratization. There is a loophole, though: intervention in favor of democracy may be permissible when explicitly requested by the parties, thus waiving Article 2(7) of the Charter, when it is part of a larger peacekeeping mission and when it is approved by the Security Council or the General Assembly. Put differently, only when civil wars appear to shade into interstate conflict (as in Central America) can the mandate be expanded to include measures to implant democracy.[4]

Enforcement Measures and the Liberation of Kuwait   The UN's victorious war against Iraq and the subsequent effort to make President Saddam Hussein's government carry out the terms of Security Council Resolution 687 represent the first full-scale enforcement measures since the Korean War, and the first ever to conform to the Charter's definition of collective security. . . . What was truly innovative about the liberation of Kuwait and how likely is it that the innovations will be institutionalized?

Enforcement did not occur until gradual collective measures of warning, separate negotiations by the Soviet Union and by the Arab League, and an economic blockade (later enforced with naval forces) had proved unfruitful to bring about an Iraqi withdrawal from Kuwait. The authorization to use force was given six weeks before Operation Desert Storm began. . . . After the deadline—January 15, 1991—had passed without any move by Iraq to honor UN demands, the operation was executed exactly as threatened. Article 51 was never invoked; decisions were made unanimously by the permanent members; no UN military command was created, because the Security Council in effect delegated Operation Desert Storm to a coalition of states willing to do the fighting, just as in the case of Korea. The procedure, in short, followed the rules intended by the drafters of the Charter *and* used innovations added later under cold war conditions, but allowed under articles 48 and 106.[5] The most striking innovation, however, was Resolution 687, which orders stringent arms control and disarmament for Iraq, imposes the duty to pay reparations, and continues the trade embargo in order to compel Iraqi compliance. In addition it creates a Special Commission to supervise the disarmament of Iraq in cooperation with IAEA and WHO, gives the Secretary-General new authority to demarcate and demilitarize the Iraq-Kuwait border (the operation that became UNIKOM), repatriate refugees, and provide monitoring mechanisms for the Special Commission. . . .

The continuing difficulties experienced by the UN in getting Iraq's cooperation in implementing Resolution 687 is ample testimony to the gaps in the collective security system and the reluctance of many UN members to undertake further enforcement to compel compliance. In fact, the consensus among the governments that authorized or participated in Operation Desert Storm grew weaker as the rout of the Iraqi forces became evident. There was no consensus beyond the liberation of Kuwait. And even the official finding that aggression had been committed and had to be repelled failed to convince many people in the third world who believe that this was just another imperialistic war by the West, a position also taken by a segment of the political left in the West. The lesson is inescapable: a war, even if relabelled collective enforcement to repel aggression, is still seen as an illegitimate use of force when employed by the strong Western country against a weaker non-Western foe.

The Spotty Fortunes of Peacekeeping by Regional Organizations   The OAU was upstaged by the Economic Community of West African States (ECOWAS) in a large operation seeking to end the Liberian civil war. ECOWAS lurched from conciliation to peacekeeping to enforcement against one of the warring groups, and back to peacekeeping between the two surviving factions, in its long effort to end the turmoil. Most observers agree that ECOWAS's first foray into collective security was a great improvement over the OAU's failures in these endeavors. OAU, however, was accepted by the UN as a junior partner in monitoring the upcoming referendum in Western Sahara. The Arab League was unable to influence the course of events in the Persian Gulf, because of the deep split in its membership over whom to support. . . .

The OAS, however, enjoyed a modest revival of its waning fortunes because of its new role as election monitor. The organization was requested by some governments to monitor elections designed to choose successors for discredited authoritarian regimes, in the Dominican Republic, Guatemala, Panama, El Salvador, Paraguay, and Surinam. In addition it joined the UN in observing and certifying the election of President Jean-Bertrand Aristide in Haiti, as well as the legislature's. . . . The OAS was asked to help in the implementation of the Esquipulas agreements by disarming and resettling Contra fighters operating in Nicaragua (the bulk of the Contra forces in Honduras were disarmed by ONUCA.) But the operation was not wholly successful. OAS observers joined the UN's in ONUVEN, though coordination among the two teams was poor. On the whole, one gets the impression that OAS election monitoring has been less than energetic unless augmented by observers from other organizations.[6]

Even though sporadic efforts were made in 1987 and 1988 by members of the RIO Group of Latin American states to reform OAS collective security procedures to allow the organization a role in the Esquipulas process, nothing happened until the UN entered the area. The Central Americans had sought the support of both organizations as early as 1986 in their regional efforts at peacemaking. Mexican opposition to an OAS role foiled the intervention in Manuel Noriega's Panama urged by the United States. When the unilateral American invasion came in December of 1989, the OAS condemned it (ineffectively) by a vote of 21 to 1 with 9 abstentions. . . .

Peacemaking and Humanitarian Intervention

One consequence of the defeat of Iraq was the outbreak of a revolt in Kurdistan. The Iraqi army had no difficulty in defeating the Kurdish guerrillas, whereupon up to two million Kurds fled into the mountains where the borders of Turkey, Iran, and Iraq meet. U.S. troops then occupied northern Iraqi Kurdistan to provide food, shelter, and medical aid for the refugees and to keep the Iraqi military from advancing, all the while calling for UN humanitarian intervention to relieve the United States from acting unilaterally.

The Secretary-General was most reluctant to accept the challenge, even though some members of his staff urged him to do so in order to be able to invoke humanitarian intervention as a justification for disregarding the Charter's strictures against intervening in the domestic affairs of member states. Pérez de Cuéllar pointed to the absence of authorization by any major UN organ, denial of access by Iraq, lack of clarity about what the mandate of a UN force ought to be, the reluctance of China and the Soviet Union who wanted to create no precedent for such an excuse, and the active opposition of many third world countries.

Yet some Western European countries supported the American initiative. They went some way toward endorsing the most radical argument for disregarding national sovereignty and vesting the right of intervention in a collective effort imposed on the local government. That argument holds that there is a *right* to interfere. . . .

The UN General Assembly, always given to hyperbole, responded by announcing the creation of a "new international humanitarian order." Yet the content of that "order" remains elusive. On the one hand, the Assembly held that in the event of emergencies "the principles of humanity, neutrality, and impartiality must be given utmost consideration by all those involved in providing humanitarian assistance"; but on the other it emphasized "the sovereignty of affected States and their primary role in the initiation, organization, coordination and implementation of humanitarian assistance within their respective territories."[7] We are a long way from a consensus on the primacy of a right to intervene on behalf of refugees, starving people, or democracy.

How Solid Is the UN Consensus on Peacemaking and Enforcement?

There was some opposition from nonpermanent members of the Security Council on most of the successful peacekeeping and peacemaking operations of the last five years. In each case, however, the unanimous agreement of the permanent members, linked to considerable autonomy for the Secretary-General's mediatory activities, prevailed quite easily. In the Kuwait case, however, the dominance of resounding majorities in the Security Council (not counting the frequent opposition by Cuba and Yemen) is very deceptive. It took a long time to assemble the majority for Resolution 678 that authorized the attack, and even then China abstained. In November of 1990, Cuba, Yemen, Colombia, and Malaysia wanted to deploy UNTSO in the West Bank to protect Palestinians against the Israeli army and settlers. In December, a few days after 678 had been adopted, the same countries wanted to outflank it by deploying a peacekeeping force between Iraq and Kuwait, lift the sanctions, and withdraw all foreign forces from Saudi Arabia if only Iraq would first withdraw from Kuwait and agree to conciliation by the Secretary-General.[8] China, India, and Yemen abstained from voting on Resolution 686, which outlined the 12 principles Iraq had to accept before military operations would cease, presumably because the terms were considered too harsh and too intrusive. Ecuador and Yemen abstained from voting on Resolution 687, apparently for similar reasons. Before we can assume the permanence of a new commitment to collective security it is wise to analyze the character of the consensus on which such a commitment would have to be based.

I use the unprecedented UN administrative role in Cambodia (UNTAC) as my opening example. It is an operation in which the risk of failure is high even if we presuppose the continuity of the consensus among Indonesia, Vietnam, France, China, Russia, the United States, and Britain which has made possible the agreement in place now. UNTAC's job, in cooperation with almost all other agencies in the UN family, is to organize and conduct the election which will determine the composition of the government of a post–civil war Cambodia. The UN is also to reintroduce a normal life for Cambodians. Because of the centrality of the election as a way of permanently reconciling the four contending factions, the UN has the power to second-guess all government agencies involved, supervising the police, the courts, and ministry of the interior. Human rights monitors will play ombudsman roles. Other units will repatriate and resettle up to 400,000 civilian refugees; military units will monitor the cease-fire, disarm the guerrillas, regroup and house them, and prevent the reintroduction of imported arms.[9]

Success depends crucially on Vietnam's and on the Khmer Rouge's willingness to accept defeat. But suppose such an act of submission is delayed or opposed by either or both? Their continued cooperation depends—as before—on the positions taken by China, Russia and the United States. Will the perceptions of interest of these governments continue to converge? . . . Each might find reason to reactivate and rearm its local allies.

Other events also ought to be recalled to put the post-Kuwait euphoria into perspective. It required more than a shaky consensus among the Permanent Five to translate Resolution 598 on the Iraq–Iran war into UNIIMOG: the military defeat of Iran almost two years after the adoption of the resolution had to occur first. . . .

. . . In general, we may expect a reduction of British and French interest in third world disputes in which no immediate economic interests are at stake, and hence a growing indifference to UN interventions, which may translate into a withholding of material support.

China is an even more serious source of dissensus. Chinese arms sales violating UN policy have been routine. So have challenges to the nuclear nonproliferation regime. The Chinese have given evidence of opposing any policy or principle that might at some time be turned against them and they have been zealous in shoring up the principle of nonintervention. It is very doubtful that the United States can buy Chinese support for conflict management operations in the future in situations that Beijing sees differently than does Washington. In fact, given the irritant of differences over democracy and human rights, opposing interpretations of a given set of events is the more likely development.

Before the Soviet Union reemerged as Russia, Moscow had inundated the UN with suggestions for improving and institutionalizing peacekeeping and peacemaking. The architects of the "new thinking" in international affairs seemed to love the UN, offering a standing force of Soviet military personnel for observation, peacekeeping, and border patrol duties in troublespots. A UN naval force was proposed as well.[10] None of this proved acceptable to Washington. It is unclear whether Boris Yeltsin continues to endorse these Gorbachevian initiatives. . . .

Nor is unflinching American commitment to the multilateralism of collective security to be taken for granted. The old internationalism that identified U.S. global interests with support for international organizations and with fighting the cold war is gone. . . . The Reagan administration was ideologically opposed to multilateralism and downgraded U.S. support for the UN with a vicious vigor. . . .

The UN Is No Independent Actor Yet

Could the UN practice "coercive diplomacy," "achieve objectives in a crisis without bloodshed, avoiding the costs of war?"[11] To do so would require the carefully calculated mixture of threat and promise, and incrementally augmented deadly force, the very ladder of escalation *not* consistently climbed against Iraq. In terms of a political consensus it would require either a stable coalition of supporting states or an autonomous, strong, and respected Secretariat headed by a charismatic and brilliant Secretary-General. I have tried to show why, despite appearances, we do not now have a predictably stable coalition of core states on which institutionalized conflict management can rely. Nor is there evidence of a global public opinion that will hail UN conflict management as authoritative and legitimate irrespective of who the parties may be, no matter what the cause in question is perceived to represent.

Still, many innovations in conflict management were the result of adaptations triggered by the cold war, by the absence of a permanent consensus among the Permanent Five. The UN never functioned according to the Dumbarton Oaks blueprint and never will; the present renaissance of conflict management by no means implies the apotheosis of the founders. Past successes were achieved as a result of ad hoc and shifting coalitions producing temporary majorities. Entrepreneurial states, most often the United States, had to build these coalitions, just as the United States built the coalition that opposed Iraq. A brilliant and charismatic Secretary-General worked in close cooperation with the hegemon, never successfully in opposition to that power. That situation has not changed. A heavier agenda, the demand for new tasks and mandates, the hope for multilateral solutions do not add up to that new order everyone talks about and nobody defines.

ADAPTATION TO NEW CONDITIONS IS NOT LEARNING

The remarkable record of the UN since 1985 is a case of adapting to new challenges and opportunities *without* rethinking the basic rules of international life or considering the very foundations of international order. To adapt is to make do, to improvise, to benefit in the short run from not repeating a recently recognized error. International conflict managers have been practicing adaptation since the adoption of the "Uniting for Peace" Resolution in 1950. Conflict management has followed the organizational routine of change we label "turbulent nongrowth." The pattern is "turbulent" because new actors demand the performance of many new tasks that are not coherently linked to one another, where appropriate means for attaining constantly changing ends are not available, and where the actors are unable to rank-order their objectives consensually. "Nongrowth" prevails, not because tasks, budget, and personnel do not increase, but because they grow helter-skelter, without unifying logic or plan. In order to conclude that conflict management has evolved to something more coherent we would have to find that actors agree to reject an earlier causal scheme about war and peace as inadequate and adopt a new way of thinking about cause-effect and ends-means relationships. To learn means that such a cognitive breakthrough has taken place. Few governments think as yet in terms of a truly "new" international order.[12]

In the remaining sections of this essay I shall probe the kinds of values, and the means necessary for their attainment, that might be said to constitute a new international order. . . .

HOW TO INSTITUTIONALIZE PEACEFUL CHANGE PROCEDURES

Lessons of Peaceful Settlement Reviewed

Peacemaking has been added to peacekeeping as a multilateral response. Yet this augmentation of multilateralism is built on sand. We know that it is made possible by the revolution in the former Soviet Union, by the consequent realignment of global political forces and priorities, by the disappearance of the cold war as the metaissue. More concretely, the augmentation in multilateral authority is associated with a new consensus, with new coalitions of states backing specific operations and giving the executive head ample new space for independent initiatives in facilitating peaceful change. So far, however, the only fixed coalitional support for the mandates has been the agreement of the Permanent Five. Because this agreement cannot be considered as lasting and because Big Five hegemony is not acceptable to many other members we conclude that institutionalized support for the larger mandate is lacking. . . .

Peaceful Change: How to Improve and Not to Improve

The UN's successes (and the shortcomings of the regionals) do seem to set the scene for some true collective learning in the last decade of our millennium. States seem to be willing to aggregate issues into novel packages and to rethink older approaches to peaceful change, helped by the Secretariat and the interactions and experiences mediated through the UN. I do not think, however, that the aggregation of human rights with everything else is a safe basis for the reconceptualization of the task of peacefully changing important practices. In this section I offer my preferred version for repackaging issues and activities, aversion which minimizes the risks of the new issue package's speedy disintegration for lack of abiding consensus.

An Arms Sales Regime   Lasting democratization is heavily dependent on lasting demilitarization. Without access to modern arms most third world countries would be unable to fight wars, civil and international. Massive arms control negotiated by the NATO and ex–Warsaw Pact states makes possible a rethinking of the arms trade in general. However, it also necessitates thinking about how one may compensate third world exporters of arms for giving up on the deadly trade. Brazil, India, Argentina, Israel, Iran, and North Korea are unlikely to sacrifice the foreign exchange earnings for the love of peace alone, especially when arms sales provide a kind of substitute mission to military establishments running out of wars to fight. No regime would be acceptable unless the major merchants of death— the United States, the successor states to the USSR, France, Britain—take the initiative in getting out of the arms trade. This requires the refusal on the part of these exporting states to extend credit for arms sales. But more important, such a regime must be tied to the economic development ambitions and demands of third world countries. It must offer compensation for sales foregone in the form of some other economic benefits. . . .

Do Not Create a Metaregime for Human Rights   The cases that feature the simultaneous protection of human rights, electoral supervision, and ending civil war disruptions offer impressive but unreliable guides to the future. Idealistic endorsement of any and all human rights activities, by itself, will not usher in an interdependent community of humankind at anything but the most general level of empty rhetoric. In all likelihood there is a much better chance of advancing institutionalized respect for human rights if the advocacy and protection are embedded within the larger issue-area of peacemaking at the end of civil wars.

It would be a mistake to create an overall task area for the protection of human rights on a global scale without such an effort at nesting. Regional institutions that enjoy legitimacy and authority exist under the auspices of the Council of Europe and the OAS, while the OAU machinery has not yet displayed much life. These institutions should go their separate ways. It seems unlikely, given the lack of general consensus, that the UN's various commissions and committees will soon reach that level of attainment. In the meantime, however, harm can be done if they continue their activities under an aura of high promise and ever loftier declarations not backed by a solid consensus among the members. Neither the invention of new basic rights nor the launching of numerous new investigations is likely to be helpful unless member state performance is responsive to these impulses. To argue that every shortcoming of the state and every threat to human freedom must become subject to UN intercession is to condemn the UN to failure, not usher in a community based on recognized interdependence. . . .

Do Not Create a Metaregime for Peacekeeping and Peacemaking
Peacekeeping in the restricted sense of separating parties to an international war is a familiar and generally successful UN activity, and something regionals do not do well. Until the most recent period such peacekeeping had nothing to do with introducing and protecting democracy and human rights, though refugee relief occasionally figured in such operations. . . . Civil wars are eligible for peacekeeping only if they are part of an international conflict as well. Obviously the special mediatory role of single powerful states is compatible with this conception, such as the American role in settlements in Cyprus, Angola, Namibia, and Rhodesia. Peacekeeping in this traditional and restricted sense does not require a firm "concordat" of the Permanent Five if one or more are willing to abstain from voting on measures they do not like instead of voting negatively. However, such an agreement would certainly help to institutionalize the practice further. Nor would peacekeeping be im-

paired if suggestions for monitoring borders or troop deployment were authorized prior to the outbreak of hostilities. An early-warning system is also consistent with the further institutionalization of old-fashioned peacekeeping.

Institutionalize Peacemaking to End Civil Wars   Multi-issue peacekeeping that is designed to make the introduction of democracy possible is the most important innovation in the field of conflict management in our times. But what should the rules of engagement be in situations involving the termination of civil wars? Must all the parties agree first? Should democracy be imposed on countries lacking the institutional and human experience to make it work? Or should democratization be confined to post–civil war conditions in which all parties have opted for democracy? Should UN forces be deployed to assure national self-determination, whether democratic or otherwise? Should the creation of new nations be fostered by means of peacekeeping that integrates civilian operations, humanitarian intervention, and the protection of human rights? If the answer is "yes" to all these questions we would have to found a new organization and quintuple its budget. At the moment something like 45,000 peacekeepers are deployed even though the means for paying have not yet been devised! An overly ambitious mandate can prevent organizational learning as readily as a niggardly one. The remarks that follow are designed to advance the learning of peacemaking *while also keeping UN intervention to manageable proportions...*

Democratization should not be attempted by any international organization unless all relevant parties show commitment to freedom and pluralism, though we need hardly insist on devotion to free market principles as well even though such is American policy at the moment. All parties must request the monitoring of elections and of human rights, humanitarian intervention, and refugee relief, aid to police and the courts in order for such operations to be authorized. Hence ONUSAL and UNTAG are models of what ought to be done. MINURSO and the Cambodian relief operation are much more ambiguous; if they turn out to be offering democracy in an inhospitable setting, then both freedom and the UN become the victims of disillusionment. To encourage a permanent OAS role in intervening on behalf of democracy even though a coup against an elected government has massive support is to force democracy down the throats of unwilling consumers.

Aid to national self-determination by means of peacemaking ought not to be attempted unless a failure to act would result in genocide, as in the Kurdish case. If there is a danger of genocide or mass famine, then unilateral organizational intervention is justifiable and the organizations ought to be prepared for mounting it. Peacemaking in Yugoslavia may still turn out to have been a mistake because to determine who or what area belongs to which "nation" is often impossible. Are Croats or Serbs the more authentic nation to whom the Krajina ought to belong? How can any outsider determine this? Intervention makes sense only if the contending nations have agreed to abide by the results of a plebiscite conducted by the organization.

No intervention in any civil war ought to be attempted unless requested by all parties and/or genocide and famine are threatened in the absence of organiza-

tional intercession. It is not clear that this condition was fulfilled in the Yugoslav case. It certainly was not met in the case of the ECOWAS intervention in Liberia. This means that the organization is *not* clearly contributing to the establishment of a consensus-based government even though it may manage to separate and disarm the contending factions. The war is likely to resume as soon as the peacekeepers withdraw. Organizational intervention in civil wars makes sense only if the war is stalemated and the parties have given up hope of victory over one another. . . .

HOW TO INSTITUTIONALIZE ENFORCEMENT PROCEDURES

The reversal of the UN's fortunes have encouraged many of us to heave a sigh of relief because the realist doomsayers of a Hobbesian world seem finally to have been confounded. Contemporary idealists tend to feel that because Hobbes has finally been vanquished we should now redefine collective security as something more comprehensive and meliatory than the definition enshrined in Chapter VII of the UN Charter. Instead of merely deterring and, if necessary, reversing acts of aggression, the practice of collective security ought to be expanded to bring about peaceful change before aggression becomes a temptation for the dissatisfied.

This sense of relief should be resisted. We need not confound the Hobbesian view with recent history because its basis in theory and fact has always been weak. . . . The picture Hobbes drew and the modern realists perpetuated was always a grotesque exaggeration. States did not always posture toward one another as if they were gladiators in the arena; nor did they calculate every ounce of power in terms of relative advantage over potential antagonists. The extreme condition in international politics was mistaken for the normal one.

There surely is now more opportunity for expanding actions to bring about peaceful change, though the positive history of decolonization in the UN proves that the present is not as new as some claim. But these opportunities ought not lead us to expect the end of aggression. Even if the UN becomes a more successful agent of peaceful change, with a mandate for intervention broader than a strict interpretation of Article 2(7) allows, then we would be very foolish to expect the resultant operations to remove all temptation to belligerence. Therefore, the procedures for mounting sanctions and enforcement must not only be retained *as now defined* but also be strengthened. . . .

Reforming the Security Council

If sanctions and enforcement are to be taken as serious and permanent weapons in the arsenal of UN conflict management, procedural and substantive improvement in the machinery must be considered. More important, however, is the question of the proper composition of the Council because it will determine the coalition that will have to authorize future enforcement measures. The hegemony of the present Permanent Five will not suffice.

Some procedural changes in the Security Council's function as conflict manager would simply improve peacekeeping and pacific settlement; they do not reach the slippery slope to sanctions and enforcement. Others do pass that point. We will discuss them separately.

There is no dearth of suggestions that aim at perfecting the peaceful settlement and simple peacekeeping function. The Security Council could hold regular closed sessions at which potential future troublespots are discussed, operating on the basis of an early warning/intelligence system to be made available to the Secretary-General. Such a system might receive information from national intelligence services, do its own research, or—more ambitiously but improbably—have its own satellite surveillance capacity. What some have called a "risk reduction center" might be set up, a think tank that surveys any possible threat to security—migration, environmental, resource-related, ethnic and religious tensions, the exercise of economic intimidation—not just interstate and civil wars. (One wonders what such a center would discover that a perusal of the major newspapers does not already disclose.) Private parties ought to be used regularly as back-channel negotiators and as sources of information. Permanent observation missions might be established in special troublespots. NGO's ought to be associated with them officially. Systematic observation of developing tensions, before they reach the point of aggression or breaches of the peace or civil war, might be increased and appropriate UN machinery created therefore.[13] Mediation and conciliation become simpler when a special fact-finding mission does not have to be authorized in New York, when information flows in routinely and can be acted on without publicity.

Suggestions that have the potential for the UN's sliding into the use of force are much more controversial. Both kinds of suggestions presuppose that the abstinence rule in local conflicts and civil wars . . . be firmly accepted. UN forces could be deployed in a threatened country before the outbreak of hostilities, thus not requiring the consent of the neighboring state. The Security Council might have its own rapid deployment force in the form of standby contingents trained and equipped for the purpose; Brian Urquhart suggests reviving Article 32 of the Charter for this purpose. Permission to use offensive tactics would have to be given and the capability of Blue Helmets for offensive operations be upgraded. All of this is possible; none of it is likely unless the finances of the UN are regularized and the composition of the Security Council is changed.

There is a good deal of disagreement on how to alter the present enforcement machinery, or whether to alter it. Pérez de Cuéllar was clearly unhappy with the procedure used against Iraq. He, along with many third world governments, regretted the coalitional nature of the Desert Storm forces and the commanding role of the United States; he called for the creation of a less hegemonial mechanism and for the activation of Article 50 to assure that third countries be compensated and that force not exceed the actual need. These suggestions betoken a marked lack of enthusiasm for using Chapter VII. Those who wish to upgrade and institutionalize sanctions and enforcement advocate the creation of a multinational reserve force (identical with the rapid deployment force?) or the setting up of a permanent force under the command of the Military Staff Committee. Unless the Charter is amended this force would have to consist of personnel drawn from the armed forces of the Permanent Five.[14]

. . . In all likelihood the interest of the Permanent Five in dealing with breaches of the peace in some third world areas will decline without the cold war to stimulate concern. The threat to at least some of them must be very palpable to trigger the kind of response we saw only in Korea in 1950 and in Kuwait in 1990–1991. Small countries, especially those in the third world, have no vested concern in being ruled by the Permanent Five and harbor a good deal of resentment toward Desert Storm. Most important, however, is the envy of Germany, Japan, India, Brazil, and possibly Nigeria and Egypt. . . .

. . . I therefore propose a different formula likely to lend the legitimacy and authority to future enforcement operation which the last one lacked. *I propose that the six nations named become permanent members and that the number of nonpermanent members be raised so as to match the new number of permanent members* (probably 11). *None will have the power of veto. To pass a resolution with binding force a qualified majority in favor would have to be mobilized in each group. But the exact voting strength of the permanent members should not be equal; it should follow a weighting formula similar to that used by the IMF.*

Upgrading the Secretariat

Obviously, the autonomous power and prestige of the office of the Secretary-General must not only be safeguarded but expanded. The role played by Pérez de Cuéllar in Central America, personally and by means of his special representatives, is prototypical of what might be accomplished elsewhere. His successor, Boutros Boutros-Ghali, has already reorganized the top ranks of the Secretariat so as to adapt them to more efficient preparation for peacekeeping and peacemaking activities. . . .

U.S. Policy and the New World Order: From Hegemony to Multilateralism?

President George Bush greeted Desert Storm as the beginning of a new world order; but he also exulted on March 1, 1991, "By God, we've kicked the Vietnam syndrome once and for all." He seemed to suggest that the United States ought to lead the post-Iraq world as the new hegemon, as the only surviving superpower. . . .

. . . American leaders have three choices. They can act unilaterally by sidestepping multilateral organizations; they can anticipate or engineer a hasty consensus in such organizations and then mount the operation they prefer; or they can wait for a multilateral consensus to form on the basis of a compromise that will probably fail to meet all U.S. preferences. Internationalists of the type now in power will prefer the second alternative, hardliners the first, and accommodationists the third. I am concerned with stimulating collective learning, with helping in the development of causal conceptions that recognize complex linkages among issues. Hence I favor the third course of action for the United States. As the progression from peacekeeping to peacemaking illustrates, learning may occur when action based on initially imperfect compromise is recognized as flawed by the member states, thus triggering an improvement in mandate and mission in the next iteration.

The shrewd practice of multilateralism means that one hides one's ability to be the hegemon. Multilateralism implies quiet leadership, guidance by means of continuous consultation, and patience for producing an adequately sized coalition. It means accepting compromises that fall short of one's immediate goals. It also means not overloading international organizations with tasks that are likely to discredit them. The true mark of a multilaterally inclined superpower is its knowledge that there is no rule requiring it to lead all the time, and perhaps not even most of the time.

NOTES

1. . . . Unless otherwise noted, all statistics for the period are taken from Ernst B. Haas, *Why We Still Need the United Nations* (Berkeley: Institute of International Studies, 1986). This study was also published as "The Collective Management of International Conflict, 1945–84," in United Nations Institute for Training and Research, *The United Nations and the Maintenance of International Peace and Security* (Dordrecht: Martinus Nijhoff, 1987), pp. 3–72. Statistics referring to the period since 1984 were collected and analyzed by the author; they are reported here for the first time.

2. See Larry Minear, *Humanitarianism Under Siege* (Trenton, NJ: The Red Sea Press, 1991); Robert A. Pastor (ed.), *Democracy in the Americas* (New York: Holmes and Meier, 1989); The Council of Freely-Elected Heads of Government, *Observing Nicaragua's Elections, 1989–1990* (Atlanta: The Carter Center of Emory University, 1990); Jennifer McCoy, Larry Garber, and Robert Pastor, "Making Peace Through Mediating and Observing Elections," *Journal of Democracy* (Fall 1991).

3. Jonathan I. Charney, "Disputes Implicating the Institutional Credibility of the Court," in L. Damrosch (ed.), *The International Court of Justice at a Crossroads* (Dobbs Ferry, NY: Transnational Publishers, 1987), pp. 299–300.

4. The General Assembly approved ONUVEH over some dissent and mandated that the Secretary-General conduct complicated consultations before similar operations can be launched, perhaps in knowledge of the fact that Elliott Richardson (for the UN) and Jimmy Carter (for his Council of Freely-Elected Heads of Government) had to persuade Daniel Ortega to accept the outcome of the Nicaraguan elections monitored by the UN and the OAS. ONUSAL originated in independent requests from the Salvadoran president and the FMLN, who insisted on the UN's observing human rights violations as a confidence-building measure that had to precede the elections. Therefore the FMLN insisted that Pérez de Cuéllar give wide publicity to any violation discovered. See UN Department of Public Information and Institute of Policy Studies of Singapore, *The Singapore Symposium* (United Nations, 1991), pp. 45–49.

5. For the legal argument supporting this interpretation, see Frederick K. Lister, "Thoughts on the Use of Military Force in the Gulf Crisis," *Occasional Paper Series, No. VII* (New York: CUNY, The Ralph Bunche Institute on the United Nations, June 1991).

6. I appreciate the help given by Robert Pastor and Jennifer McCoy with respect to OAS materials.

7. A/RES/45/101, 30 January 1991 and A/RES/45/100, 29 January 1991, p. 2.

8. S/21933 and S/21986.

9. For inside information on the significant role played by the UN Secretariat in writing the Cambodia agreements on behalf of the five permanent members and the co-chairmen (France and Indonesia) of the conference of Cambodian parties, see *Singapore Symposium, op. cit.*, pp. 65–79. The Security Council late in 1991 approved the dis-

patch of the UN Advance Mission in Cambodia to prepare UNTAC operations. *UN Chronicle* (December 1991), pp. 23–27.

10. Thomas G. Weiss, ed., *The United Nations in Conflict Management* (New York: International Peace Academy, 1990), pp. 77–82 for a statement to this effect by former Soviet Deputy Foreign Minister (now UN Under-Secretary-General) Vladimir F. Petrovsky. Soviet multilateralism is interpreted as a necessary instrument of *perestroika* (and limited by its survival) by Celeste Wallender in "Soviet Policy Toward the Third World in the 1990s," Thomas G. Weiss and Meryl A. Kessler, eds., *Third World Security in the Post–Cold War Era* (Boulder, CO: Lynne Rienner, 1991), pp. 35–66.

11. The phrase is Alexander George's, as quoted in the U.S. Institute of Peace *Journal*, October 1991, p. 1. For a brilliant analysis of the limitations on the autonomy of the UN and its Secretary-General in the future see Inis L. Claude, "Reflections on the Role of the Secretary-General of the United Nations," *Occasional Paper Series, No. VIII* (New York: CUNY, The Ralph Bunche Institute on the United Nations, September 1991).

12. These concepts are discussed in detail in Ernst B. Haas, *When Knowledge Is Power* (Berkeley: University of California Press, 1990), chapters 6 and 7.

13. For these and other suggestions see Larry Minear, Thomas G. Weiss, and Kurt M. Campbell, *Humanitarianism and War, Occasional Papers, No. 8*, Thomas J. Watson Institute of International Studies (Providence, RI, 1991), and James Sutterlin's contribution to Thomas G. Weiss, ed., *Collective Security in a Changing World* (Boulder, CO: Lynne Reinner, 1992). I have also drawn gratefully on Lincoln P. Bloomfield, "International Security: The New Agenda" (Minneapolis: Hubert Humphrey Institute of Public Affairs, University of Minnesota, 1991).

14. Benjamin Rivlin, "The Rediscovery of the UN Military Staff Committee," *Occasional Papers Series, No. IV* (New York: CUNY, The Ralph Bunche Institute on the United Nations, May 1991), discusses these alternatives. So do Meryl A. Kessler and Thomas G. Weiss, in Weiss and Kessler, *op. cit.*, p. 114 ff.

Global Policies and the United Nations System: A Current Assessment

Roger A. Coate and Donald J. Puchala

1. GLOBAL POLICIES FOR BUILDING AND KEEPING PEACE

. . . The global policies of the United Nations are of two kinds. *Peacekeeping* policies prescribe courses of collective international action aimed at preventing or halting armed conflicts, while *peace-building* policies prescribe action aimed at eliminating the social and economic sources of tension that are among the causes of war. This paper examines and evaluates both varieties of global policy at the UN and in a number of the UN system's specialized agencies.

Generally speaking, recent changes in the political climate of international relations have opened new opportunities for strengthening peace by elaborating and executing peacekeeping and peace-building policies via the United Nations. The improved relations between the United States and the Soviet Union which emerged in the 1980s from the superpowers' mutual interests in nuclear arms reductions, from their reduced ideological combativeness and more particularly from Mikhail Gorbachev's 'new thinking', have contributed to a new pragmatic, problem-solving international climate. Such conditions prevailed to some extent during the US–Soviet detente of the mid-1970s, but at that time international cooperation was frustrated by implacabilities in relations between the developed and the developing countries. . . . The less ideologically charged, less combative international political climate of the late 1980s has reinvigorated the United Nations to a notable extent and permitted the organization to become more effective at peacekeeping. Yet, it does not appear that the new climate has contributed very much toward making the UN a more effective peace-building force in the world, as relatively little progress is being recorded toward alleviating human degradation via global policy and United Nations action. There are reasons for both the UN's successes and failures in the international climate of the late 1980s, and they point to a number of important lessons about the political and diplomatic requirements for improving world order.

2. UN PEACEKEEPING IN THE NEW INTERNATIONAL CLIMATE

The Charter of the United Nations established a global international organization to serve the primary purpose of promoting peaceful relations among states and peoples. Under the Charter, the UN was endowed with three principal instruments for promoting peace. It could intervene in international disputes directly and encourage pacific settlement via the Security Council (Articles 33 and 39–42); it could 'further international peace and security' by promoting 'the political, economic, social and educational advancement of the inhabitants of the trust territories' via the Trusteeship Council (Article 76); and it could work to create 'conditions of stability and well-being necessary for peaceful and friendly relations among nations', via the Economic and Social Council and the affiliated specialized agencies (Article 55). It is this third instrument of peace through enhanced human well-being that this paper mainly addresses.

In light of long-accepted Western images of the United Nations as a failed organization, it is important to point out that the trusteeship and related functionings of the UN having to do with the political independence of former colonial territories have been largely successful (Kay, 1970). 'Decolonization' became a global policy, articulated most emphatically in General Assembly Resolution 1514 (XV) in 1960, and since then more than one hundred new sovereign states have peacefully entered the international system. There were several wars for colonial independence to be sure, and indeed some particularly terrible ones as in Algeria, Indochina, and Angola. But that there were not many more is at least partly attributable to the UN's acting as an agent of peaceful transition (Kay, 1970; Claude, 1967).

It is true, for all of the reasons that the textbook writers have been keen to underline, that the United Nations has not been a very effective agent of pacific settlement in interstate conflicts or in intrastate turmoils (Claude, 1956). The Organization's record of accomplishment in the realm of peace and security (militarily construed) has been questionable. It remains so at the time of this writing; the civil war in Afghanistan rages on despite the UN-facilitated Soviet troop withdrawal; the UN-arranged Iran–Iraq armistice is presently only an armistice and not yet peace, the UNTAG arrangement in Namibia got off to a precarious start; and possible UN operations to encourage conflict resolution in Kampuchea, Western Sahara, and Central America have yet to materialize. Nevertheless, it cannot go unnoticed that the Security Council is once again operating in charter-prescribed fashion on the basis of great-power consensus, that the Secretary-General is opening more widely the doors of his 'good offices' these days, that he is getting more visitors, and that UN interventions appear to be offering face-saving ways out of increasing numbers of regional combatants.

One of the reasons that the UN has been able to rise to the peace-keeping opportunities opened by the new international climate of the 1980s is that global policies regarding the handling of international disputes which have escalated into violence have been in existence for a long time. It is rather remarkable that even after a long period during which these policies could not be pursued because of the Cold War, they still proved to be relevant and applicable in the late 1980s. As one Western European diplomat rather colorfully explained during an interview, 'the UN plumbing has been in place for many years, even though nothing was flowing through the pipes'. . . . [1]

The new effectiveness of UN peacekeeping is partly the result of Mikhail Gorbachev's 'new thinking' about the costs of his country's military occupation of Afghanistan and about the worth of the United Nations in situations where warring parties are seeking face-saving ways to extricate themselves. In the course of the negotiations over Afghanistan, receptivity in the Soviet Union to Pérez de Cuéllar's mediating efforts further elevated the already rising prestige of the Secretary-General, thus making him a more influential agent for peace (*South*, 1988). An even more fundamental element in the resuscitation of UN peacekeeping has been the newly emergent ability of the major powers, particularly the permanent members, to find consensus in the Security Council and thus to activate the global policies that prescribe the Council's mission. Five-power agreement in the Council was pivotal in the adoption of Resolution 598, which led to the Iran–Iraq armistice. Major power agreement was also important during the latter phases of negotiations that produced the plan for UN intervention in Namibia.

The cause of the new, co-operative working arrangement among the major powers are not altogether clear. One, quite obviously, is the change in Soviet officials' attitudes toward the United Nations following Gorbachev's pronouncements about the organization's importance (1987, 1988). In effect, the Soviet officials decided to be co-operative on issues of particular interest to the United

States, such as security in the Persian Gulf, and the Reagan Administration welcomed the opportunity for settling issues that Washington surely wanted settled. Beyond this, however, is the dawning recognition by policy-makers of the major powers, here including Britain and France, that over the past two decades their individual national and collective status has been slipping in our rapidly multipolarizing world.

Revitalizing the Security Council has been for these major powers both an attempt to reassert their former status and an awakening to the fact that they may have more interests in common as major powers than they might have supposed during the Cold War years. The Big Five arrangement in the Security Council anchors an advantageous status quo for the old powers that is coming under increasing challenge. Accordingly, there has also been a recent shifting of Chinese diplomacy in the direction of heightened emphasis on the PRC's status and behavior as a permanent member of the Security Council. Whereas Chinese diplomats customarily have projected the role of Third World mentor over that of major world power, this no longer appears to be the case. For the moment, at least, Peking seems to prefer to participate, and co-operate, in the processes of the Big Five focused on the settlement of regional disputes. Chinese diplomats, for example, did not join the South in criticizing the UN and the major powers for the false start in Namibia, and accommodating Chinese positions are crucial concerning possible UN peacekeeping in Kampuchea.

One further reason that the old peace-keeping 'plumbing' is working again is that with the customary Soviet and US destructiveness in the UN diminished, diplomatic opportunities have been opened to some of the middle-level powers . . . (Puchala, 1989). Diplomats from the Nordic countries, Canada, the Western European Twelve, Japan and Australia are observed these days as becoming 'more active' on peace and security questions in the UN. This increased 'activity' is an illusion inasmuch as most of these particular member governments have always been active multilaterally. But their recently increased influence in the promotion of world order is a fact. West German, Italian, and Japanese diplomatic efforts, for example, were pivotally important in the summer of 1987 when the downing of an Iranian civilian airliner by a United States naval vessel operating in the Persian Gulf nearly derailed movement toward the Iran–Iraq armistice. . . .

In sum, UN peacekeeping is working again, and global policies long on the books are being more frequently and effectively executed. It goes without saying that much of the United Nations' effectiveness in peacekeeping in the months and years ahead will depend upon the continued prevalence of superpower detente, which appears to be catalyzing the continuing ability of the Big Five to reach and sustain consensus. . . .

3. BUILDING PEACE THROUGH GLOBAL POLICY

Helping to establish social and economic conditions under which peace among peoples can flourish has been, as noted, an objective of the United Nations and its specialized agencies since their founding. After over four decades of global initiatives there is a good deal of 'plumbing' in place in the form of global policies committing the international community to work for peace through the enhancement of the well-being of mankind. This 'plumbing' includes, of course, the ECOSOC mechanism established by the United Nations Charter, and all of the elaborating resolutions adopted in the course of the North–South debates of the 1970s.[2] But there is also the foundation provided by the constitutions of the specialized agencies of the UN system, where prescriptions are made to uplift mankind in the interest of peace. The Preamble to the Constitution of the International Labor Organization, for example, affirms that 'universal and lasting peace can be established only if it is based upon social justice'. Similarly, the World Health Organization (WHO) was founded on the assumption that health is 'fundamental to the attainment of peace and security'. Even the highly technical agencies, such as the International Civil Aviation Organization (ICAO) and the International Atomic Energy Agency (IAEA), also explicitly ground and justify their work in terms of their overall contribution to building peace. The preamble to UNESCO's constitution is perhaps the most eloquent in this regard: 'Since wars begin in the minds of men, it is in the minds of men that the defences of peace must be constructed'. UNESCO's charter assignment, of course, was to enlighten men's minds.

Carrying out global policies for building peace, however, has proven to be a difficult and elusive task, even in the permissive and pragmatic international political climate of the late 1980s. The 'plumbing' may be in place, but there is still not very much flowing through the pipes. Commenting on the 43rd UN General Assembly, the *UN Observer* (1988) noted that 'the debate in the General Assembly brought out a sharp contrast between a sense of progress and achievement in the political arena and a sense of frustration and stalemate on the economic side'. It appeared as if the *peace epidemic* had no effect on the international economic environment—the bread and butter issues. Why is peace building via global policy and the implementing mechanisms of the UN so substantially more difficult than peacekeeping?

To place the situation in appropriate perspective, it should be noted that the record of the efforts and accomplishments of the specialized agencies of the United Nations system—particularly the very technical ones—in social and economic affairs is not entirely discouraging. As already alluded to, in the changed international climate of the 1980s there appears to be a new commitment among UN members to focus and act on things that are doable. The older, southern-pursued strategies of attempting to redress global structural imbalances through global negotiations between the North and South have been largely abandoned in practice, if not entirely in aspiration. Accordingly, the attention of the UN system is being increasingly directed toward treating those social and economic problems afflicting humanity which are obvious and serious and widely recognized as such.

Among the recent UN accomplishments in social and economic affairs is the initiation of the global campaign against the spread of AIDS, directed by the Global Program on AIDS (GPA) of the World Health Organization. Though there is resistance in the United Nations system to WHO's attempts to co-ordinate centrally the AIDS campaign, the program has gained the approval of a large representative number of UN members, and its urgency has loosened the tight purse strings of some large donors. Recent UN efforts to mount a global assault on trafficking in narcotics, mostly follow-ons to the global conference on narcotics held in Vienna in 1987, are also commendable. Some more technical, but nevertheless noteworthy, developments include the signing in December 1988 of the world's first treaty for integrated international telecommunications services and networks. This accomplishment of the International Telecommunications Union at its World Administrative Telegraph and Telephone Conference (WATTC-88) contributes to Third World development by lowering the costs of building modern communications infrastructures. . . .

With regard to the UN's efforts to meet basic human needs, voluntary contributions pledged to the United Nations Development Program for 1989 exceeded US$1 billion, a record (UNDP, 1989). The programs of UNICEF, particularly those concerned with primary health care, generally receive high praise from UN officials and member governments, and UNICEF, of late, has been rather generously funded by the United States, Japan, Italy, and the Soviet Union. Presently, all of the United Nations food programs, particularly the World Food Programme itself, are well thought of, with the FAO having apparently emerged from under the cloud of criticism that threatened its continued funding by the United States (Fauriol, 1984).

While a good deal of development work goes on in the United Nations system, this disparate activity seems to have done little to enhance the well-being of humankind. This is at least the prevailing perception both among those who would like the UN to become the unquestioned center of world development activities and among those who would like to see the UN get out of the aid business altogether. Much of what the UN is doing under the development rubric these days is in the form of relief measures, emergency interventions or other stopgap moves manifestly designed to stem deterioration rather than actually to promote development. While such UN undertakings are generally appreciated by their subjects, some proponents of development are faulting the UN for becoming more of an 'aid' organization and less of a 'development' one. Moreover, even for all the elaborateness of the UN's institutional mechanism for development, the amounts of resources actually allocated are modest.

Beyond its limited budgets, the most revealing indicators of the UN's current limitations in the development area are the absence of any operative global development strategy, and the organization's apparent inability to formulate one. Although a fourth United Nations 'development decade' was to be launched in 1990, the preparation of a development strategy for that decade had barely gotten underway by Spring 1989. The absence of a global development strategy, based on an agreement of the underlying causes of lagging growth and slow or sporadic modernization, and on at least a modicum of consensus about remedial policies and instruments, has produced in the UN system a prevailing 'ad hocism'. . . . Member governments are riding policy hobby horses such as 'privatization' and 'zero-growth budgets', where they seek to globalize national values regardless of whether these are actually pertinent to fostering enhanced well-being among the poor peoples of the world. Many of them are not at all pertinent for achieving this end.

4. INCENTIVES AND IMPEDIMENTS TO GLOBALISM

Why then are peacekeeping matters being handled by the United Nations reasonably well (or at least in a newly promising way), while most of the world's major social and economic issues seem not to be evoking meaningful global responses? In our estimation current differences in the performance of the United Nations in the two macro issue-areas of peacekeeping and peace building can be attributed in considerable measure to four factors: (1) the degree of consensus that can be reached in support of existing or proposed global policies, (2) the effectiveness of political leadership promoting global policies, (3) the degree of institutional co-ordination required and attainable for implementation, and (4) the complexity of both problems and policy processes.

4.1 Incentives to Effective Peacekeeping

Space limitations here will not allow detailed comparisons between peacemaking and peace-building activities in the UN, but setting some analytical benchmarks is in order. First, underlying the UN's accomplishments in peacekeeping is agreement among the five permanent members of the Security Council that United Nations' processes and instrumentalities can and should be used in efforts to halt conflicts in Third World regions. This fundamental agreement among the Big Five is also supported by the non-permanent members of the Security Council and the acquiescence of most of the rest of the UN's membership. That major-power consensus is underpinning UN peacekeeping actions is obvious. It is nonetheless crucially important.

Second, what is happening with the UN in the area of peacekeeping is happening because the major powers are actively promoting it. Leadership has been available to inject momentum, to provide diplomatic skill, and to muster clout as necessary as well as to keep the peacekeeping undertakings moving. Most of the leadership displayed has been coalitional: the most effective grouping, manifest in the Afghanistan, Iran–Iraq and Namibia cases, has been a coalition of permanent members of the Security Council and the UN Secretary-General. Intermittently operating in leadership capacities have been coalitions of non-permanent members of the Security Council, as with the Italian, West German, and Japanese teaming to keep the Iran–Iraq peace process alive in the aftermath of the *Vincennes* incident. Scandinavian, Russian, Egyptian and European Community diplomacy coalesced to set the Geneva stage for Yasir Arafat's conciliatory speech in the autumn of 1988. Apart from this, the United States government, through the efforts of Assistant Secretary of State Chester Crocker, had a great deal to do with paving the UN's way into Namibia. In addition, Mikhail Gorbachev has personally had a great deal to do with intellectually framing the context for the UN's new departures in peacekeeping and with resurrecting and rallying widespread support for the principles that legitimize the UN's peacekeeping role. Thus, to the extent that either making or enforcing global policy requires political will, there has emerged a sudden abundance of it in the UN peacekeeping realm.

Third, the UN has been able to act out its peacekeeping mandates because it has been reasonably successful at co-ordinating activities of the organs, organizations and other actors whose participation and contributions have been essential. Co-ordination has not been entirely problem free, as the initial disruption of the UNTAG operation suggested, but failures have not engendered extraordinary confusion. The UN has been fairly effective at co-ordinating the disparate elements of its peacekeeping ventures because a significant amount of organizational learning about how to co-ordinate such exercises has taken place over the years, particularly among the professional peace-keepers at what George Sherry (1986) calls 'the second UN'. United Nations co-ordination has also been reasonably effective in the peacekeeping realm because most of the co-ordination required has been of the vertical or 'chain of command' variety, which organizations like the UN can usually accomplish once they are mandated to do so. When horizontal co-ordination has been required, as in bringing national governments and non-governmental organizations usefully into the enterprises, the numbers of such formally autonomous participants have usually been small, or at least manageable. Serendipitous, but nonetheless important, is that fact that co-ordinating responsibilities in recent peacekeeping undertakings have been placed in the hands of highly able international administrators like Suddrin Aga Kahn, who is co-ordinating the international community's efforts to aid Afghanistan's reconstruction.

Fourth, without understating or belittling the significance of the UN's recent accomplishments in peacekeeping, it should be noted that in terms of global policy-making and implementation via the UN these peacekeeping issues and exercises have not been very complex. Most of the peacekeeping undertakings have, as noted, involved a relatively small number of formally autonomous or semi-autonomous participants; most of the communication and involvement has been intergovernmental; most of the required national inputs have come from single ministries, usually foreign ministries; relatively few UN organs are directly involved, and these are typically among the bureaucratically most efficient ones; all of the peacekeeping exercises extant and prospective take place in geographically delimited theaters (that is, they are not global undertakings); all of the peacekeeping exercises have readily definable, short-term goals. . . .

4.2 Impediments to UN Peace Building

Conditions within the international community and in the UN in the realm of social and economic development are almost the opposite of those now prevailing in the realm of peacekeeping. We have noted above that there is no consensus about the goals or the role of the United Nations or of many of the specialized agencies in the development realm because of differing views on the causes of underdevelopment or nondevelopment and even the very meaning of 'development'. . . .

International differences concerning the UN and social and economic development are presently compounded by disagreements about whether the UN should be primarily an *aid* institution that caters to basic human needs in critical or deteriorating situations, or a more ambitious *development* institution that acts programmatically to transform global society in accord with principles such as equality, economic justice, social and economic security, ecological equilibrium or alternatively to foster economic growth, industrialization, or technological advancement. Such issues concerning the role of international organization in dealing with the human condition have been at the heart of the controversies surrounding UNESCO, and that they cannot be resolved is hampering UNESCO's reform efforts. More broadly, these fundamental questions about the nature of development and the role of the UN makes it nearly impossible for the UN to formulate a meaningful development strategy for its Fourth Development Decade. Finally, unlike conditions surrounding the diplomacy of peacekeeping today, there is not yet a political environment within the international community conducive to building a consensus or even to engineering a convergence on the broad philosophical, substantive, and institutional issues of development. . . .

A second problem related to UN peace building is a lack of leadership. From the late 1940s to the early 1970s, US officials and diplomats exercised considerable initiative in moving the United Nations into matters of economic and social development, first with regard to war-ravaged Europe, and later with regard to the emerging South. Washington was motivated by anti-communist zeal, but even in this the prevailing logic argued that human degradation had to be alleviated before the domestic turmoil it fostered spilled outward into international warfare. US political leadership in promoting development through the United Nations continued through the 1960s, highlighted by a number of important initiatives on population, food, and health care. However, for a variety of general reasons having to do with the reduced importance of the UN as a focus of US diplomacy, a lessening of East–West competition in the South, as well as more specific reasons coming out of the North–South clashes in the UN during the 1970s, the United States' government not only abandoned its leadership in development matters, but tried, especially under the Reagan Administration, to pare back the UN's development activities (Puchala & Coate, 1988). . . .

The governments of some other industrialized countries are certainly taking the social and economic development activities of the United Nations seriously, but they are nonetheless unwilling or unable to step into the global lead. Nordic and Canadian diplomats work diligently toward making the United Nations into a more effective development organization, but they cannot rally most of their OECD partners. At the moment, moreover, Scandinavian notions of 'sustainable development', which integrate economic modernization and environmental preservation, fail to inspire many Third World governments pressed by debt and suffering from shortfalls in the wherewithal to meet basic human needs. Despite Gorbachev's professed sympathies for the plight of the South, the Soviet Union is not looked upon as a major benefactor by the South, and promoting the socialist model for economic and social development these days is not an avenue to global leadership. Chinese officials appear to be deliberately exchanging their Third World 'credentials' for superpower symbols. The Japanese government is pouring money into multilateral development agencies, but Japanese representatives insist that Tokyo is seeking neither political nor intellectual leadership in the global drive toward social and economic development. Most of the rest of the diplomatic community agrees, with some disappointment, that Japan is not aspiring to a leadership role.

The Group of 77, acting in the name of the South, emerged during the 1970s to lead politically the UN's involvement in matters of global economic and social development. Third World thinking issuing forth from the Economic Commission for Latin America, the UNCTAD, Mexican and Indian universities and elsewhere, as well as Third World political leadership on the part of Algeria, India, Mexico, Tanzania, Egypt, and other governments, fostered and promoted causes and designs for uplifting humanity via UN-sponsored economic and social development. However, by the mid-1980s the Group of 77 had faded as a consequential political force in the UN, and Third World leadership of the global drive toward development had largely disappeared. 'What we need is another Prebisch', one Third World representative said during an interview, and another noted that 'there is not at present a really charismatic Third World leader, and this makes a difference for the Group of 77'.[3] Beyond the apparent decline in the quality of political leadership in the South, there has also been a weakening of the foundations of G-77 solidarity as a result of diverging national development experiences. Moreover, after the stillbirth of the global negotiations, there has been increasing skepticism in the South both about the UN as an appropriate facilitator of development and about the very meaningfulness of global policy approaches. For political purposes in the UN there is no longer an effective Third World leadership coalition.

Some initiative in fields of social and economic development is being taken today by the executive heads and secretariats of the specialized agencies and UN departments. This is particularly the case with some of the very technical agencies such as the ITU in regard to bringing modern telecommunications to the South, and the WHO in its efforts to enhance national health care capacities. Yet there are at least two major constraints dampening executive initiatives in the UN system. First, there is a strong reluctance by most executive heads of UN agencies to usurp the prerogatives of the member states, which, for example, is keeping the UN Secretariat largely on the sidelines in the organization's struggle to produce a development plan for the Fourth Development Decade. Second, there is a prevailing anxiety about possible negative reactions from the United States. Within the agencies and the UN Secretariat, a great deal that is done now anticipates whether Washington might be offended and be prompted to reduce or terminate its financial support. Washington is not perceived to favor bold moves or new UN initiatives in the area of social and economic development. . . .

Even in issue-areas where there are global policies in place in the realm of social and economic development, implementation is often badly hampered by lack of co-ordination in the UN system. In marked contrast to the situation that prevails in the peacekeeping realm, the interagency co-operation required to execute the global social and economic policies via the UN has benefited from very little organizational learning over time, or else the lessons learned have been questionable. In addition, the required co-operation in the social and economic realm is mostly horizontal rather than vertical, and it involves many autonomous and semi-autonomous actors.

The infrastructure in the UN system for undertaking the ambitious challenge of peace building via the enhancement of human well-being is rather impressive in scale. There are sixteen formally autonomous specialized agencies, two other largely autonomous agencies—the GATT and the IAEA—hundreds of commissions, divisions, and other subsidiary bodies within the UNO itself, and thousands of regional and national representatives and field offices. . . .

The UN Charter assigns the Economic and Social Council (ECOSOC) the challenge of integrating the social and economic affairs within the UN system. Specifically, ECOSOC is to 'co-ordinate the activities of the specialized agencies through consultation with and recommendations to such agencies and through recommendations to the General Assembly and to members of the United Nations' (Article 63.2). . . .

The primary administrative mechanism for facilitating system-wide co-ordination is the Administrative Committee on Co-ordination (ACC). This body, which is comprised of the executive heads of each of the agencies and is chaired by the UN Secretary-General, is to co-ordinate the activities of the UN system regarding program and administrative matters. . . .

[Nevertheless] evaluations and expectations concerning UN system-wide co-ordination in the development field are very low. Most participants from respective secretariats and in national missions agree that there are frequent failings in attempts to promote interagency co-operation in the UN system. 'It is not that we need more co-ordinating structures', one official explained, 'we have enough of these, perhaps too many, but they don't work.'[4] Several officials reported that when interagency co-ordination works at all, it does so in the field at the country level. When co-ordination succeeds at this level it is usually because the recipient national government manages it, or it works for serendipitous reasons, such as the particular competence of the on-site UNDP representatives, or because of the compatible personalities of particular clusters of field representatives from different agencies.

Many in the UN system reason that co-ordination may not be as necessary or important in practice as it seems in theory. Redundancy in mission and organizational overlap, they say, increases the probability that tasks will be accomplished, or, it may just be that the transaction costs of trying to co-ordinate are not worth the marginal gains in efficiency that could result. . . . One UN official attempted to describe this situation in philosophical terms: 'the UN system is not a federal system; you cannot impose a centralized control structure on an inherently decentralized system.'[5] To some extent, the 'failure' of interagency co-ordination may have become a self-fulfilling prophecy: almost no one expects it to succeed; consequently it does not.

Effective system-side co-operation in the development area is also hampered by national governments. It is frequently the case that different national ministries send delegations to different UN agencies with different instructions. Or, different ministries each send differently instructed representatives to the same UN agency. Or, different national ministries foster redundancy in the UN system by asking different UN agencies to execute identical tasks. 'How can they expect us to get our act together', one official at the WHO said, 'when they can't get their own acts together at home?'[6] Presently, there is the illuminating case of UNDP, where national governments expect the UNDP to co-ordinate the UN system's development activities via control over the bulk of the system's development funds. But national governments pushing preferred projects have given a good deal more development money to other UN agencies than they have given to UNDP, thus undermining what little co-ordinating leverage UNDP might have commanded, or as one official phrased it, 'other agencies can therefore thumb their noses at UNDP and its co-ordinating efforts if they choose'.[7]

Recently the financial austerity prevailing in the UN system, plus the recent, upbeat atmosphere that is evident in Geneva, have inspired gradually changing attitudes towards co-ordination. There is both a growing appreciation of the interdependence of issues and a better understanding of the intersectoral nature of both problems and solutions. After a decade of discussions between the World Bank, the International Monetary Fund, and the ILO, to take one example, the two financial agencies have begun to take the question of the social costs of financial austerity into serious consideration in financial decision-making. . . .

5. THE LIMITS OF GLOBALISM AND INTERGOVERNMENTALISM

Three very straightforward conclusions emerge from this examination of the United Nations and global policy. The first, and perhaps least surprising, is that the United Nations can function effectively both to make or affirm and to enforce global policies when the intergovernmental political climate allows. Of course, Inis Claude said this a very long time ago concerning the UN Security Council and the organization's responsiveness on political and military issues (Claude, 1956). The requirement for consensus among governments on the transcending value and indivisibility of peace and at least a convergence among governments about the nature of threats to the peace and the appropriateness of United Nations interventions underlies the making and execution of effective global policy. This requirement has been met in the late 1980s regarding regional conflicts in the South, and the United Nations has been able to act. Historically speaking, this is rather remarkable, and must not be lost sight of. On the other hand, the requirement for political consensus has not been met in the realm of development, and the United Nations system has been hamstrung accordingly. It remains questionable whether governments will ever agree that human degradation is sufficiently threatening to peace or other transcendent values that a concerted global remedial effort is required. . . .

Second, the United Nations is capable and effective when the issues it deals with fall into the realm of traditional intergovernmental diplomacy. The UN and its agencies are, as already noted, traditional intergovernmental organizations. One of the reasons that the UN appears better able to handle peacekeeping than peace-building issues is that the former are much more amenable to intergovernmental treatment. . . . National governments are the primary targets (and beneficiaries) of peacekeeping operations. In addition, peacekeeping is facilitated by the perceived extant structure of 'power' of nations. The major powers, using the UN, initiate peacekeeping. . . .

By contrast, the UN is not very well equipped structurally or procedurally to deal with situations that are *more than traditionally intergovernmental* in their structure and dynamics, nor are the majority of the specialized agencies. Addressing most of the problems in the realm of social and economic development requires more than traditional intergovernmental institutional capabilities. Policymaking aimed at peace building in a global context is a dynamic, multifaceted, and continuous process that is by its very nature a transnational phenomenon. It is simultaneously governmental and non-governmental, centralized and inherently decentralized, co-operative and inherently conflictual. . . .

All of this may be more than a traditional intergovernmental organization can do. The technical sophistication of many development issues usually requires expertise beyond that typically possessed by diplomats, inputs beyond those which foreign ministries can provide, and calculations other than those which normally go into traditional assessments of national interest. In addition, consultative and negotiating processes concerning economic and social development frequently involve non-governmental actors and transnational actors that have no formal role in state-to-state diplomacy and no formal status in traditional intergovernmental organizations. In its development undertakings, the UN must and does deal with non-governmental actors, but it is constrained in so doing because member states resist. Most critically, because the UN is an intergovernmental organization, and because all but a very few governments today are still very provincial and narrowly self-interested in their external dealings, the UN is prevented by its members from actually addressing global problems in global terms.

It could very well be then that the fundamental reason why the UN cannot deal effectively with development issues is that its intergovernmental structure and functioning impede such effectiveness. . . . Revealingly, those among the specialized agencies that are today least intergovernmental in structure and functioning, the WHO, the ITU and the ILO for example, also tend to be among the most effective at accomplishing their missions.

Finally, just as traditional intergovernmentalism via the UN may not ultimately produce an effective response to problems of social and economic underdevelopment, neither may globalism be an ultimate formula. It is beginning to look as if global strategies, world campaigns, common approaches, and similar holistic designs may have been useful and desirable during the decades when the main objectives in global policy-making were to establish general principles for world order, to universalize standards of good citizenship in the international community and to set down rules that distinguish acceptable international behavior from barbarism. But establishing and trying to enforce guidelines for global social and economic change has false started for the increasingly obvious reason that there is too much diversity in the world to allow for concerted effective global action. . . .

NOTES

1. Personal interview, New York, 11 January 1989.
2. See, for example, UN General Assembly Resolutions: 3201 (S-VI) and 3202 (S-VI), 1 May 1974; 3281 (XXIX), 12 December 1974; and 3362 (S-VII), 16 September 1975; and

the *International Development Strategy for the Third Development Decade,* UN Document DPI/689-40460, December 1981.
3. Personal interview, New York, 19 April 1989.
4. Personal interview, New York, 19 April 1989.
5. Personal interview, New York, 20 April 1989.
6. Personal interview, Geneva, 7 March 1989.
7. Personal interview, New York, 20 April 1989.

BIBLIOGRAPHY

Claude, Inis L., 1956. *Swords into Plowshares.* New York, NY: Random House.

Claude, Inis L., 1967. *The Changing United Nations.* New York, NY: Random House.

Fauriol, Georges, 1984. *The Food and Agricultural Organization: A Flawed Strategy in the War Against Hunger.* Washington, DC: Heritage.

Gorbachev, Mikhail S., 1987. *Realities and Guarantees for a Secure World.* Moscow: Novosti Press Agency Publishing House.

Gorbachev, Mikhail S., 1988. 'The Problem of Mankind's Survival.' Speech before the United Nations General Assembly, New York, December 8.

Kay, David A., 1970. *The New Nations in the United Nations, 1960–1967.* New York, NY: Columbia University Press.

Puchala, Donald J., 1989. 'The Middle Powers, the UN and World Order in the Late 1980s.' Paper presented at the Annual Meeting of the International Studies Association, London, 28–31 March.

Puchala, Donald J. & Roger Coate, 1989. *The Challenge of Relevance: The United Nations in a Changing World Environment.* Hanover, NH: Academic Council on the United Nations System.

Sherry, George L., 1986. 'The United Nations, International Conflict, and American Security', *Political Science Quarterly,* vol. 101, no. 5, pp. 753–771.

South, 1988. 'A Model of a Mediator', no. 93, July, pp. 16–17.

United Nations, 1988. 'Political Glasnost Fails to Break Deadlock on Economic Front', *UN Observer,* vol. 10, no. 11, November, p. 2.

UNDP, 1989. 'Pledges for UNDP Reach Record High', *World Development,* vol. 2, no. 1, January, p. 29.

The Secretary-General And His Special Representatives

Donald J. Puchala

"Since my arrival in Cairo on 28th May," Count Folke Bernadotte reported to the United Nations Secretary-General in the summer of 1948, "I have striven ceaselessly to find a common basis upon which peace negotiations between the two parties might be undertaken. I have tried to bring them together in my presence or without it." He continued:

> I have studied carefully their respective positions, claims and contentions, and on the basis of such study have devised compromises which have been put to them either orally or in writing. I have employed abundantly both reason and persuasion.[1]

On his celebrated, but tragic, mission to Palestine, Count Bernadotte was a special representative of the Secretary-General of the United Nations, one of the first to function in this capacity for the new world organization. . . .

While obviously important because of its impacts on pacific settlement, the phenomenon of special representation on behalf of the Secretary-General remains an academic mystery. There is virtually no literature on the subject. The Secretary-General's special representatives as model practitioners of "quiet diplomacy" have been reluctant to reveal what they do and how they do it. . . . Therefore, even some very elementary questions remain unanswered. For example, who are the Secretary-General's special representatives? How are they selected? How are they instructed? What is their relationship to the Secretary-General, and to other UN organs? What is their relationship to parties in conflict or to other actors and theaters of activity? . . .

SELECTING SPECIAL REPRESENTATIVES

. . . In the context of commentaries on the Secretary-General's "good offices" role, special representatives are conceived as surrogates for the Secretary-General, essentially as extensions of his person who do what the Secretary-General would and could do if he were personally present. "In regard to their political and legal position," Pechota writes, "the Secretary-General's representatives enjoy the status of senior officials of the United Nations. They carry out their assignments under authority given to the Secretary-General in Article 101 of the Charter,"[2] which, quite simply, allows the Secretary-General to appoint people of his choosing. Otherwise, the special representatives find legal status in the same rather murky Charter provisions that allow the Secretary-General to open good offices, namely Article 99, which gives the Secretary-General an independent political role, and Article 33, which invites disputants to select their own conciliators.[3] Technically, there are two kinds of special representatives, those deemed "special representatives" per se, who are appointed by the Secretary-General at the behest of one of the deliberative bodies of the UN, and those called "personal representatives," who are appointed at the direct initiative of the Secretary-General. Since, in practice, there tends to be little distinction between the two kinds of representatives, the designation *special representative* refers in this paper to both. . . .

The first criterion of any special representative's eligibility is the confidence of the Secretary-General, since the appointee must be a bona fide surrogate. Consequently, Secretaries-General have tended to appoint their representatives from among personal associates or otherwise from interpersonal networks of people whose international careers have intersected. In the broadest meaning of the term, and with particular reference to Pérez de Cuéllar, the special representatives have tended to be "friends of the Secretary-General"—that is, people whom he knows personally and can count on.

Special representatives also must be acceptable to parties to the dispute into which the United Nations is intervening, and consultation with such parties always takes place before special representatives are named. It is perhaps for this reason of required acceptability that a remarkably large number of special representatives have been Swedish or Swiss nationals, and that Latin American diplomats have also been disproportionately tapped for service during Pérez de Cuéllar's incumbency. . . .

While calls for the dispatching of special representatives have most often originated in the deliberative organs of the UN, particularly in the Security Council, successive Secretaries-General have rejected interference from these bodies in actually selecting special representatives. Indeed Secretaries-General have adamantly insisted upon personally selecting the individuals who serve them. This has been partly to protect the right to appoint staff granted to the Secretary-General under Article 101 of the Charter, partly to keep special representatives as firmly and directly under the Secretary-General's control as possible, partly to buttress the credibility of special representatives in the eyes of disputing governments into whose affairs the representatives venture and partly to guard the established, but tenuous, autonomy of the Secretary-General's Office as an independent political-diplomatic organ of the United Nations.

In similar fashion, and for the same reasons, successive Secretaries-General have resisted formalizing, institutionalizing, or in any sense routinizing the appointing and dispatching of special representatives. Each mission is considered *sui generis;* each is constructed ad hoc, staffed as fully or meagerly as resources allow, and executed as ambitiously or cautiously as the Secretary-General thinks appropriate. The Secretary-General reserves the right extend or withdraw his assistance as he deems warranted by particular situations. . . .

TASKS AND FUNCTIONS OF THE SECRETARY-GENERAL'S REPRESENTATIVES

To date, the special representatives of the Secretary-General have been assigned three kinds of tasks. First, the Secretary-General is frequently asked by either the Security Council or the General Assembly to open his good offices to international disputants. Occasionally he offers his conciliation services upon his own initiative. Such attempts to move contending parties toward the pacific settlement of their disputes have invariably involved the appointing and mandating of special representatives. Second, the deliberative organs of the United Nations have frequently requested information from the Secretary-General about developments in regional theaters and other problem areas, or, more critically, the Secretary-General has sought information required to enhance his own diplomatic effectiveness. Seeking such information has also invariably involved the dispatching of special representatives. Third, as the UN has become widely and deeply involved in peacekeeping and other special operations around the world, and as the Secretary-General has been formally charged with administering such operations, it has become necessary for him to delegate executive responsibilities. His special representatives have thus become his surrogates in the field. While it is analytically useful to distinguish among the tasks of the special representatives, it should be understood that most special missions, as for example Jan Eliasson's intervention in the Iran–Iraq War and in the enforcement of the ensuing ceasefire, Marti Ahtisaari's activities in Namibia and Johannes Manz's emerging responsibilities in Western Sahara combine all three kinds of tasks.

Mediators and Conciliators

What has most frequently captured media attention—albeit in a rather minor way—have been various special representatives' performances as third-party participants in communications between international disputants. Generally speaking, one can refer to the Secretary-General's special representatives acting in such situations as "conciliators" or "mediators," and sometimes they officially are given such titles, as was Count Folke Bernadotte on his mission to Palestine. More often, however, the special representatives' third-party roles are much less formal than the technical titles denote. As a rule, these agents of the Secretary-General attempt whatever is possible to establish productive communication between disputants and remain practically indifferent to whether their efforts are called conciliation, mediation, or anything else. . . .

The Secretary-General's involvement in pacific third-party interventions via his special representatives is long, continuous, and relatively impressive. In recent experience, Diego Cordovez, the Secretary-General's special representative for Afghanistan, worked for some six years facilitating the "proximity talks" with Afghanistan and Pakistan that eventually contributed to rendering a Soviet military withdrawal from Afghanistan feasible. Before that Olof Palme, Jan Eliasson and Cordovez worked to move Iran and Iraq toward halting their decade-long border war. In similar fashion, Alvaro de Soto worked for almost two years to move the Government of El Salvador and the Farabundo Marti National Liberation Front toward an agreement concerning the international monitoring human rights in El Salvador. Earlier in the history of the United Nations, special representative Ellsworth Bunker facilitated an agreement between the Netherlands and Indonesia over the disposition of West Irian and Vittorio Winspeare Guicciardi aided in the settlement of the Anglo–Iranian dispute over Bahrain, Luis Weckmann-Munoz helped to ease border tensions between Iran and Iraq in

1974, Ambassador de Ribbing helped to settle the 1963 Anglo–Arab dispute over Oman, and Johan Beck-Friis on one occasion and Nils Gussing on another helped to defuse tensions between Thailand and Cambodia in the late 1950s. Less successfully, though no less tirelessly, a number of special representatives have been dispatched at various times to deal with the Arab–Israeli dispute, UN special representatives worked early on to promote conciliation between India and Pakistan, and a series of special representatives on Cyprus have, in the view of a recently interviewed Secretariat official, "at least kept the situation from getting worse!"[4]

The Secretary-General's special representatives can, and indeed have, brought to international disputes all of the tools, techniques, and effects customarily associated with friendly third-party interventions. As summarized by Marvin C. Ott, a third party can:

1. change for the better the behavior of the disputants just by being presented. . . .
2. facilitate communication, particularly in situations where the emotional involvement of the political leaders precludes rational face-to-face negotiation.
3. clarify the facts in a situation and thereby eliminate misunderstanding and ignorance as a source of hostility.
4. provide a break in hostilities while inquiries are made and alternatives discussed. . . .
5. suggest specific solutions, made more palatable by the presumed objectivity of their author. . . .
6. provide a partial answer to the "bargainer's dilemma," i.e., how to offer concessions while retaining the appearance of toughness . . . [and in so doing permit] the parties to save face while facilitating the necessary process of compromise.
7. . . . provide such "service activities" as supervision of a cease-fire, verification of troop withdrawals, or inspection of demilitarized zones.[5]

. . . The Secretary-General's special representatives typically make two especially important contributions to peacemaking. First, either by their mandates or through the continuity of their efforts, *they keep peace processes in motion.* Once the UN has been invited into a dispute via the proffered good offices of the Secretary-General, a peace process is set into motion, and a new dimension is thereby added to the dispute which is not under the control of the disputants. The Secretary-General by his instructions to special representatives, or as often as not the special representatives by their own inventiveness and relentlessness, can act to repeatedly remind disputants about possibilities for a negotiated peace. They may also act repeatedly to bring disputants together, to invite them to consider new or revised designs for peace, or to otherwise keep communications flowing between them. Even when settling a dispute is not the first priority of the disputants, it is the first priority of the special representative mandated to mediate, and he acts to keep the goal of peace alive. . . . Recently, at the time of the breakthroughs in the hostage situation in Lebanon in the summer of 1991, UN special representative Johnny Picco explained as being most important that "the dynamic has to be maintained at all costs."[6] He therefore specifically saw his assignment as one of keeping the process of conciliation alive. By his efforts in July and August 1991, he did this.

The crucial role of relentlessness in peacemaking was vividly underlined by special representative for Iran–Iraq Jan Eliasson. . . . When asked whether he perceived that "peace was breaking out" in the post–Cold War world, Eliasson reminded his interviewer that the several UN-brokered regional settlements emerging in 1988 were not spontaneous developments but rather the results of long-evolving, tireless efforts on the part of the Secretary-General through his special representatives. "[W]e must also remember," Ambassador Eliasson said,

> that this situation of relative success for the United Nations was preceded by a long period of hard work. Look at the discussions and talks that have taken place on Iran–Iraq. I have been involved myself since November 1980, more or less without interruption. And on Afghanistan, Mr. Cordovez's work was preceded by work by [then] Undersecretary-General Pérez de Cuéllar.
>
> On Western Sahara, we have been working for years and years. On Namibia, the resolution is unfortunately 10 years old; and on Kampuchea, we have been working for a long time. And Cyprus, also; Mr. Pérez de Cuéllar was involved in talks a number of years ago. . . .
>
> There was a sign in a Teheran hotel that Olof Palme and I saw once when we were there: "Patience is the greatest bravery." We often quoted that.[7]

A second principal contribution that the Secretary-General's special representatives typically make to peacemaking is what Secretariat officials call "conceptual." By their acquired familiarity with disputes and disputants and as a result of their credibility and impartiality, UN officials are frequently able to devise formulas for settlement that cannot emerge from the partisan thinking of the contenders. These formulas have at times become the thresholds to diplomatic movement or the actual bases for agreements, as was apparently the case with Alvaro de Soto's initiatives regarding the human rights agreement in El Salvador and Olof Palme's ideas concerning Iraqi troop withdrawals in the Iran–Iraq case. "Palme went beyond his mandate and became a mediator," a UN official explained during a recent interview. "Palme changed the whole thing in Iran–Iraq."[8] Earlier, Ellsworth Bunker's "Bunker Plan" apparently also "changed the whole thing" in the West Irian case and paved the way to settlement.[9]

Firsthand documentation showing special representatives self-consciously injecting their own ideas into attempts at pacific settlement is rare, partly because the reporting of most special representatives is contained in confidential correspondence between them and the Secretary-General. However, we do occasionally catch a glimpse of special representatives' deliberateness and inventiveness. In 1971, for example, Gunnar Jarring sent an *aide memoire* to the Arabs and Israelis, explaining that it had become appropriate for him to inject his own thinking into the negotiations. "My growing concern," Ambassador Jarring wrote,

> is that each side unyieldingly insists that the other make certain commitments before being ready to proceed to the stage of formulating the provisions to be included in a final peace agreement. . . . I therefore feel that I should at this stage make clear my views on what I believe to be the necessary steps to be taken in order to achieve a peaceful and accepted settlement in accordance with the principles of Security Council resolution 242 (1967).[10]

Even more revealing is the comprehensive report on his efforts in Palestine that Count Folke Bernadotte submitted to the Secretary-General shortly before his assassination in September 1948. "In the course of the truce negotiations," Bernadotte reported,

> the two parties had made it quite clear that they expected to receive from me, during the period of the truce, an indication of my ideas as to a possible basis of settlement. This, in their opinion, was the *raison d' être* of the truce. Notwithstanding, therefore, the complete divergence of aims and the very short time left at my disposal, I decided to submit to the two parties a set of tentative suggestions, with the primary intention to discover whether there might be found at this stage a common ground on which further discussion and mediation could proceed.
>
> On the basis of close analysis of the question and of ideas which emerged during the discussion, I presented to the parties, on 28th and 29th June respectively, under cover of my letter of 27th June . . . three brief papers, setting forth in outline my suggestions for a possible approach to the peaceful adjustment of the future situation of Palestine.[11]

Speculatively speaking, there is possibly also an important third contribution that the Secretary-General's special representatives offer to peacemaking. By their interventions as conciliators and mediators they may at times inject the interests and principles of the international community, as contained in the United Nations Charter and in UN resolutions, into the considerations of disputants and the terms of settlements. . . . There is certainly evidence that special representatives see themselves acting as agents of the international community and purveyors of United Nations norms. Ambassador Jarring in the passage quoted above, for example, perceived himself to be promoting the principles embodied in Security Council Resolution 242. Similarly, Mr. Galo Plaza, the special representative to Cyprus, articulated his philosophical position most eloquently in 1965:

> [Any settlement] must be consistent with the provisions of the United Nations Charter, of which the following in particular seems relevant: the purposes, principles and obligations relating to the maintenance of international peace and security, the peaceful settlement of disputes, respect for the principle of equal rights and self-determination of peoples, respect for human rights and fundamental freedoms, recognition of the sovereign equality of Member States, abstention from the threat or use of force against the territorial integrity or political independence of any State, and respect for treaty obligations not in conflict with those of the Member States under the Charter.[12]

Yet, while it is true that the special representatives and Secretariat officials close to the peace missions deem normative goals important, there is not very much evidence to show that disputants take "the interests of the international community" very seriously. Nor is there evidence to show that the abstract principles of the Charter have very much practical utility in peacemaking situations, particularly since disputants tend to interpret principles to their liking. Therefore, the normative influence of the Secretary-General's special representatives remains ambiguous, and the issue demands further research.

Eyes and Ears for the Secretary-General

. . . Officials close to the Secretary-General note that one of the major limitations on his ability to play a more influential political and diplomatic role, under Article 99 or otherwise, is his lack of firsthand information about conditions and developments in potential trouble spots. . . . The United Nations has no diplomatic service as such—no network of legations and consulates, no permanently stationed ambassadors with reporting obligations; no intelligence facilities of consequence. Practically speaking, the information about current affairs routinely available to the Secretary-General comes either from the governments of UN member states or from the mass media, and even under the most benign circumstances such sources are understandably biased.

Under such circumstances, the Secretary-General's special representatives function indispensably as fact-finders and monitors. Generally speaking, the first phase of every special mission is a fact-finding phase, and reporting remains centrally important throughout the undertaking. For example, at a press conference announcing his appointment as the Secretary-General's special representative for the Iran–Iraq conflict, Olof Palme explained that the major aims of the first phase of his mission were to "listen and clarify" regarding the positions of the parties and the difficult issues involved in the conflict.[13] Earlier, when Swedish Ambassador de Ribbing was dispatched to Oman in 1960 by the Secretary-General to intervene in a conflict between the United Kingdom and several Arab states, he indicated that the "primary task of the mission would be a fact-finding one. The mission would visit the area . . . and would report on such questions as the presence of foreign troops in Oman . . . [and] on the existence of any 'rebel' forces actually in control of a particular area. . . ."[14] Reporting has remained a primary responsibility of the Secretary-General's successive special representatives on Cyprus. More recently, a central purpose of Elliot Richardson's mission to Nicaragua in 1989–1990 was to monitor and report on the country's electoral campaign and national elections.[15] In the same way, Benon Vahe Sevan, the Secretary-General's current special representative in Afghanistan, is posted there in considerable measure for the purpose of providing the Secretary-General with information on current developments, as Sadruddin Aga Kahn was in Iraq to keep the Secretary-General informed about developments there. Reporting back to New York was an important part of Ahtisaari's mission in Namibia, and such reporting will be a significant aspect of Johannes Manz's mission in Western Sahara and Rafeeuddin Ahmed's mission in Cambodia.

Some have suggested that while the ad hoc information-gathering network constituted by the Secretary-General's special representatives posted to trouble spots is helpful, it hardly substitutes for a UN consular system or an official intelligence facility. A frequent complaint, voiced by special representatives themselves, is that those dispatched to crisis areas, whether insiders or outsiders, are seldom experts on the areas in question. Therefore, until they familiarize themselves with their assigned areas, their usefulness as rapporteurs is limited. In addition, the Secretary-General's special representatives, particularly the insiders who have Secretariat responsibilities as well as special missions, are actually able to spend

only a very limited part of their time in the field, which again limits their usefulness as rapporteurs. There is therefore discussion ongoing within the UN about
establishing a "foreign service" for the organization. . . . But the likelihood of a
UN "foreign service" remains low. For the foreseeable future, then, the reporting
system composed of the dispatched troubleshooters will have to suffice.

Executives in the Field

A third task of major import frequently assigned to the Secretary-General's special
representatives is the running of UN special field operations. Since the Secretary-
General cannot personally administer several operations simultaneously, and since
he certainly cannot be simultaneously physically present in different regions of the
world, the task of "field executive" has been typically delegated to a special representative. During field operations the special representative's primary assignment
is to implement the mandate handed down by the Security Council (or the General
Assembly on rare occasions). In so doing he serves as chief administrator over UN
personnel participating in the field operation, as fact-finder, monitor and rapporteur in the service of the Secretary-General, as liaison between the Secretary-General and the host government, often also as mediator among groups and factions
within the host country, sometimes as mediator between the host government and
its neighbors, as spokesman for the UN in the theater of operations and before
world media and as principal troubleshooter and crisis manager amidst the unpre-
dictabilities, complexities and confusions that UN field operations usually entail.
Marti Ahtisaari's administration of the United Nations operation in Namibia was
perhaps the epitome of special representation in a field operation. Ahtisaari operated with considerable autonomy, though the confidence and support of the Secretary-General were fully and appropriately displayed at critical times. . . .

SOME QUESTIONS OF SIGNIFICANCE

Several observations of broader import, having to do with the evolution of the
United Nations and the Office of the Secretary-General, emerge from this paper's
review of the phenomenon of special representation.

The Extended Capabilities of the Secretary-General

In the first instance, evaluating the practice and process of special representation
cannot be separated from evaluating the "good offices" function of the Secretary-
General. Appointing and dispatching special representatives is one means of providing good offices. As such, it has proven an especially powerful means because it
has notably extended the capacity of the Secretary-General to offer and implement third-party interventions, and it has thereby enhanced the authority and autonomy of the Secretary-General. Since the days of the League of Nations there
has been an evolution in the availability and efficacy of third-party mediation in
the international system. . . . Modern international organization offered "the in-

ternational community" as an eligible impartial third party, but the League of Nations was unable to produce a politically neutral entity or agency that could credibly represent "the international community." There "the Secretary-General's role was strictly limited and did not, in general, go beyond administrative and management tasks."[16] The UN Charter created a new version of the Secretary-General with autonomous political-diplomatic prerogatives, and in so doing created an international agency ideally equipped to offer impartial third-party mediation on behalf of the international community.[17] Dag Hammarskjöld recognized this and worked to establish firmly the political-diplomatic prerogatives of his office, particularly with regard to the "right to exercise good offices without a formal decision by a[nother] United Nations organ."[18] In addition, "Hammarskjöld set a pattern in using the services of his closest associates and experienced persons from outside the organization as his personal or special representatives entrusted with specific tasks in the exercise of his good offices."[19] This pattern has obviously taken hold and expanded to the extent that the Secretary-General through his surrogates is now able to conduct multiple good offices missions simultaneously, continuously, and legitimately.

> [The UN] has to a large extent simply adapted to its own requirements the techniques developed by the League. . . . It has contributed to the growing stock of pacific settlement devices the concept of the United Nations Mediator or Commissioner—the single individual of high prestige, bearing exclusively international responsibility and carrying full authority of the United Nations, who performs high-level political and administrative functions on behalf of the organization in the locality where troubled international relations exist. . . . The development of the political mechanism of pacific settlement has been a continuous process for half a century, and it may be expected to extend into the indefinite future. . . .[20]

Constraints on Third-Party Mediation

There are, however, limits on this expanded capacity. The primary physical constraints on the system of special representation have to do with staffing in New York and Geneva. Special missions are not one-man affairs: they require planning and preparation prior to field operations, complex communications during field operations and constant professional backup throughout. Each mission requires rather extensive full-time staffing, and the United Nations chronically lacks the resources to provide what is required. . . .

A further implication of the overtaxed staffing situation, as well as of the ad hoc nature of the phenomenon of special representation, is that the Secretary-General's ability to control his representatives is sometimes tenuous. As a rule, special representatives are granted considerable autonomy, partly because they have the Secretary-General's confidence and partly because time, attention and staff constraints in the Secretary-General's Office seldom permit close supervision. Even when the mandates for the special missions are composed by the Security Council, as in the case of Western Sahara, for instance, the means of implementation are largely left to the special representatives. . . .

Wide latitude granted to special representatives has reaped considerable dividends by opening avenues to creativity and inventiveness. Special representatives are surrogates for the Secretary-General, but none of them have been clones: they have brought to their missions outstanding diplomatic skills and rich, independent thinking, which have proven functional time and again. But several special representatives have also been, or aspired to be, international political actors in their own right. The permissiveness of the underdeveloped system of central control at the UN has at times tempted special representatives to ignore or go beyond their mandates or instructions, thus creating tensions in center–mission relations or otherwise raising questions about the structure of authority. "Sometimes it becomes unclear who is the tail and who is the dog." Despite the maverick behavior of some special representatives, ultimate responsibility for missions rests with the Secretary-General, who, at times, has found it necessary to defend or bear criticism for unauthorized actions taken by those in the field.[21]

A second kind of constraint on the Secretary-General's role as provider of good offices, via special representatives or otherwise, is political in two senses. First, there are instances when member states actively interfere in the Secretary-General's special missions, as, for example, when the Turkish Government disrupted UN mediation efforts on Cyprus in the mid-1970s, and more recently when the United States Government (or agencies within it) sought to discredit Alvaro de Soto's mission in El Salvador.[22]

Second, and more consequentially, there is very little evidence that third-party mediation, by the UN or any other agency, by itself ever succeeded in moving disputing parties to settle their differences. As a rule, conciliation and mediation tend to produce pacific results only after (1) disputing parties have decided to settle, as was clearly the case in Bahrain, West Irian, Oman and Afghanistan, or (2) after their major-power patrons have begun to exert irresistible pressures for settlement, as was the case in Afghanistan, Nicaragua, El Salvador, Iran–Iraq, and Namibia, or (3) after one of the disputants is satisfied with gains while the other wants no further loses, as was the case in Iran–Iraq. Even the most talented and dedicated of mediators consistently fail to resolve disputes that disputants have little interest in resolving, as was the case for a long while in the Iran–Iraq situation and has been and remains the case in Cyprus and Palestine. What this means is that third-party mediation can never be more than one element of the pacific settlement process. . . .

Institutionalized Fact-Finding

Like the proffering of good offices, the authority to engage in fact-finding is nowhere granted to the Secretary-General in the Charter. Whether or not the framers of the Charter intended the Secretary-General to conduct investigations on his own initiative remains unclear. But from the very outset during the administration of Trygve Lie the "right to take whatever steps . . . necessary to determine whether or not a matter should be brought to the attention of the Security Council has been regarded as a common-sense interpretation of Article 99."[23] This right, tested by practice and precedent, has come to include the authority to engage in "enquiry or investigation . . . to reach an objective and independent appraisal of a situation and recommend feasible ways for dealing with it."[24] Without further belaboring the constitutional history of the United Nations, the point here is that the phenomenon of special representation has greatly enhanced the fact-finding capabilities of the Office of the Secretary-General. . . . By enhancing his fact-finding capabilities, the special representation mechanism has in effect enhanced the power and autonomy of the Secretary-General vis-à-vis other UN organs and thus contributed to the evolution of the Secretary-General's Office as a political-diplomatic agency.

Another UN

It has been commonplace in the academic study of the United Nations for analysts to discover "other UNs" that have emerged serendipitously from practice and precedent while the formal UN of the Charter skidded, slipped, and stumbled through the last fifty years. Thus while it is hardly original, it is nonetheless accurate to point out that there was "another UN" functioning in the realm of pacific settlement during the long period of Cold War stalemate when the Security Council was incapacitated and during the period of North–South confrontation when the General Assembly was an inconsequential battleground. The Office of the Secretary-General was never closed. In fact, when the deliberative organs of the United Nations were most moribund, the political and diplomatic potentialities of the Secretary-General's office were most visible. It was during the Cold War and NIEO years—from the mid-1950s to the early 1980s—that the opening of good offices, the appointing and dispatching of special representatives and the conducting of third-party mediations emerged and took hold in UN practice. Consequently, there is now in existence and centered in the Office of the Secretary-General a well-developed and practiced pacific settlement mechanism the likes of which never before existed in international relations. The Secretary-General's special representatives grew in stature, credibility and accomplishment as the pacific settlement mechanism developed. They are indispensable to it, and despite the current celebration of the reactivation of Chapter VII of the Charter, the hybrid arrangement of Chapter VI plus Article 99 combined with special representation is likely to remain the UN's principal peacemaking modality.

NOTES

1. United Nations, *Progress Report of the United Nations Mediator on Palestine*, General Assembly: Third Session, Supplement No. 11 (A/648), Paris, 1948, pp. 37–38.
2. Vratislav Pechota, "The Quiet Approach: A Study of the Good Offices Exercised by the United Nations Secretary-General in the Cause of Peace," included in *Dispute Settlement Through the United Nations*, K. Venkata Raman, ed., [UNITAR] (Dobbs Ferry, NY: Oceana Publications, 1977), p. 665.
3. *Ibid.*, pp. 585–588. See also Edward Gordon, "Resolution of the Bahrain Dispute," *American Journal of International Law*, 65:3 (July 1971), p. 566.
4. Interview, United Nations, New York, July 17, 1991.

5. Marvin C. Ott, "Mediation as a Method of Conflict Resolution: Two Cases," *International Organization,* 26:3 (Summer 1972), p. 597.
6. *USA Today,* "Duo Keeps the Hostage Channels Open," August 14, 1991, p. 4A.
7. *U.N. Observer & International Report,* "UNO Talks with Jan Eliasson," 10:11 (November 1988), pp. 11–12.
8. Interview, United Nations, July 17, 1991.
9. Paul W. van der Veur, "The United Nations in West Irian: A Critique," *International Organization,* 28 (1964), pp. 54–55.
10. Raman, "The Ways of the Peacemaker," *op. cit.,* p. 466. See also "Report of the Secretary-General Under Security Council Resolution 131, 20 April 1973," S/10929 Annex II, 18 May 1973.
11. "Progress Report of the United Nations Mediator on Palestine," *op. cit.,* pp. 46–47.
12. Raman, "The Ways of the Peacemaker," *op. cit.,* p. 474.
13. *United Nations Chronicle,* "Mr. Palme Reports to Secretary-General On Results of Iran–Iraq Mission," 28:1 (January 1981), p. 9
14. Raman, "The Ways of the Peacemaker," *op. cit.,* pp. 415–416.
15. *United Nations Chronicle,* "Central America Peace Process Progresses," 27:2 (June 1990), p. 15; *The New York Times,* "Nicaragua Vote Monitors Confident," February 23, 1990, p. A3.
16. Pechota, *op. cit.,* p. 583.
17. Oran Young, *The Intermediaries: Third Parties in International Crises* (Princeton: Princeton University Press, 1967).
18. Pechota, *op. cit.,* p. 580.
19. *Ibid.,* p. 580.
20. Inis L. Claude, *Swords Into Plowshares: The Problems and Prospects of International Organization* (New York: Random House, 1956), p. 232.
21. *The New York Times,* "U.N. Under U.S. Pressure, Disavows Envoy's Statement," October 17, 1989.
22. Clifford Krauss, "U.N. Aide Assailed in Salvadoran Talks," *The New York Times,* February 1, 1991, p. A3.
23. Pechota, *op. cit.,* p. 585.
24. *Ibid.,* p. 585.

Chapter 7

The Challenges of Integration

Friedrich Kratochwil

*T*he study of integration has a long and rich tradition in the field of international relations, and it poses a variety of challenges to some theories of international politics. Central among these challenges is the primacy of the nation-state for the purpose of understanding international relations. While traditional theories of international relations emphasize the importance of sovereign nation-states, integration theorists often highlight the importance of economic, social, and other factors that join or integrate states by blurring boundaries in the stream of transactions.

Two sets of theories have been especially influential in explaining the integration process. The first is indebted to the logic of functionalism, which argues that "form follows function." In its starkest version, functionalism posits that the opportunities provided by large markets create incentives to abolish trade barriers and harmonize regulatory frameworks. Implicit in this argument is the view that economic cooperation will also foster political cooperation. Functionalists often suggest that integration is achieved "by stealth," that is, by relying on the dynamics of the integration process instead of basing it on explicit political undertakings that pose frontal challenges to sovereignty. Such a development is also, in a certain sense, inevitable, since functionalists believe that welfare considerations are increasingly important aspects of politics. Sometimes these arguments are further buttressed by the argument that scientific knowledge and the rational administration of society produce new sources of legitimization while undermining the old ones. Thus solutions to common problems arrived at by technical experts would replace the inherent arbitrariness and inefficiency of national "political" solutions.

The other approach, neo-functionalism, is less sanguine about the automaticity of the integration process and more attentive to political factors, but it still shares many important assumptions with the functional model. For neo-functionalists, solutions to global problems can rarely be arrived at with recourse only to technical rationality and expertise, since questions of competing values and trade-offs are involved in most political choices. Thus the technical experts emphasized by classical functionalism must also be adept *political leaders* in the neo-functionalist framework. Nevertheless, neo-functionalists and functionalists share an emphasis on the importance of the commitment of modern democratic governments to enhancing welfare. This commitment not only fosters expectations that welfare will increase, but it also endows technical experts, from whom decision makers are increasingly recruited, with legitimacy.

Consequently, the dynamics of integration impel leaders to change their decision-making style. Instead of relying on the lowest common denominator, or on the strategy of "splitting the difference" as is typical of bargaining, decision makers will have to seek solutions which involve "upgrading the common interest." This, in turn, will lead to an enlargement of the agenda and the involvement of more issues and participants in the integration process (meshing, or *engrenage*). As Ernst Haas argues, "We call integration the process whereby political actors in several distinct national settings are persuaded to shift their loyalties, expectations, and political activities toward a new and larger center, whose institutions possess or demand jurisdiction over the pre-existing national states."[1]

Interest in integration was heightened by the creation of supranational institutions such as the European Coal and Steel Community (ECSC), EURATOM, and in the original European Economic Community (EEC). But since economic integration was envisaged by the Treaty of Rome as a means of establishing a full-fledged "European Community," the course and pace of integration became a test case for integration theory. Although the European Community has been slowly taking shape through the creation of a unified institutional structure in which the formerly separate supranational institutions were merged, through the impetus of the Single European Act (1986), and through the accords of Maastricht (1991), the road to a "united Europe" proved more difficult and circuitous than predicted. Two issues are of particular salience in this respect. The first concerns the applicability of the lessons learned from European integration to other regions. For example, scholars became increasingly interested in whether the economic growth that had been fostered by European integration might also provide a model for economically less developed regions, such as Latin America and Africa. Given the failure of virtually all "common markets" in the developing areas it was not surprising that the European model as well as neo-classical doctrines of economic development were soon largely discarded.

The second issue concerns whether existing neo-functionalist theories provide an adequate explanation for the stop-and-go process of European integration itself. Many analysts have noted that the pace of integration slowed dramatically during the late 1960s and 1970s; and by the end of the 1970s, some scholars began to speak of "Euro-sclerosis," rather than European integration. Furthermore, the recent debates surrounding both a European Central Bank and further steps toward *political* integration suggest that, contrary to the predictions of functionalists, the nation-state is not becoming obsolete. Similarly, supranational organizations are not likely to become the nucleus of a new federal government characterized by a distinct and uniform policy process and by institutional independence from state-governments.

The example of American federalism is often the implicit template for the assessment of whether a new Europe will qualify as a "state." But such an analogy is probably misleading. Community politics and national (state) politics are *institutionally* intertwined in Europe rather than separated as in the American model. Rather than developing supranational institutions in which the institutional interest of state (national) governments are constitutionally not entrenched, the European form of governance presupposes the *representation* of state interests in community institutions and policy formulation. As Alberta Sbragia argues in this chapter, the German federal model provides a better analogy for understanding the role of the emerging structures.

The selections in this chapter address most of the issues mentioned above. Joseph Nye examines the functionalist and neo-functionalist explanations of the integration process. By basing his assessment of the integration process on a comparison of European, Latin American, and East African integration efforts, he offers a number of fundamental insights regarding integrative dynamics and its prospect for success or failure.

Christopher Brewin analyzes European integration from a legal perspective. He argues that the conventional categories of the "state" and (international) organization are not adequate for the purposes of explaining political and legal aspects of integration. The constitutional character of the Treaty of Rome, the doctrine of "direct effect" (that is, persons acquire rights directly under the treaty and not through national implementing legislation), and the doctrine of "preemption" (that is, the Community has competence within an area, thereby preempting national legislation) have created an entity which resembles a union of states in certain respects and a confederation of states in other respects.

Finally, Alberta Sbragia demonstrates that a comparative perspective on "federal" governmental arrangement is helpful in understanding the role and structure of the "central" community institutions. She challenges not only functional and neo-functional explanations but also the dichotomy between hierarchical and horizontal organization, which fails to capture some of the important aspects of the integration process.

NOTE

1. Ernst Haas, "International Integration: The European and the Universal Process," *International Organization,* vol. 15 (Fall 1961), reprinted in *International Political Communities, An Anthology* (Garden City, NY: Anchor Books, 1966), chap. 2, quote at p. 94.

Comparing Common Markets: A Revised Neo-Functionalist Model

J. S. Nye

. . . One of the pioneering political science efforts at providing a causal model of regional integration was developed under the stimulus of events in Western Europe in the late 1950's and not surprisingly it reflects these origins. . . .

In *The Uniting of Europe: Political, Social, and Economic Forces, 1950–1957* Ernst B. Haas took the partially articulated strategy of the neo-functional statesmen, related it more clearly to party and group interests, and put it in theoretical terms that have been enormously fruitful in generating further studies both in Europe and in other areas.[1] Haas, Leon Lindberg, and others have subsequently refined the original academic neo-functionalist formulations and concepts as applied to Europe; Haas and Philippe Schmitter have elaborated the approach still further in developing what is probably the most widely accepted paradigm for comparative analysis. . . .[2]

The neo-functional approach can be modified so that it is not too Europocentric to be useful as a framework for comparative analysis if the following revisions are made: (1) the dependent variable is stated less ambiguously, (2) the idea of a single path from quasi-technical tasks to political union by means of spillover is dropped and other potential process forces and paths are included; (3) more political actors are added; and (4) the list of integration conditions is reformulated in the light of comparative work that has been done on integration processes in less developed areas.

1. THE DEPENDENT VARIABLE

The ambiguities of the terms used in the study of integration are well known, and "automatic politicization," the dependent variable of the Haas-Schmitter paradigm, is no exception. . . .

Economic "liberals" restrict this operationally to what John Pinder calls "negative economic integration"[3]—the removal of discriminatory obstacles to free trade within a region. Skeptics of the liberal approach (as many economists are on the basis of the structural imperfections of markets in less developed countries) or those interested in a degree of economic interdependence which involves positive action because it costs governments some of their sovereignty or freedom of action will choose positive economic integration or economic union as the dependent variable and will measure it by the amount of shared services and degree of coordination of policies. Our choice of collective decisionmaking in the policies involved in an economic union has the virtue of closeness to the manifest motives and interests of the actors involved in integration schemes in less developed states as well as closeness to what seems to be the "neither fish nor fowl" institutional shape of the current integration process in Europe. . . .

II. ACTORS AND INTENTIONS

In the original neo-functionalist model the important actors are integrationist-technocrats and various interest groups which get governments to create a regional economic integration organization for a variety of convergent aims. Once done and depending on the degree of initial commitment this action unleashes the new forces of sector imbalance or *engrenage,* increased flows of transactions, and involvement of an increasing number of social groups which gradually focus their activities at the regional level.

These process forces or mechanisms in turn lead to two outcomes: (1) National governmental decisionmakers, under the joint pressures of the inconvenience of sector integration and of groups eager to preserve their gains from sector integration, agree to increase the initial grant of power to the regional institutions and (2) group activities and eventually mass loyalties increasingly flow to the regional center as it answers more and more of the interests previously satisfied by the national governments. The net effect is a continuous and automatic process leading to political unions if there are: (1) certain "background" conditions of symmetry between the national units, social pluralism, high transaction flows, and elite complementarity; (2) initiation conditions mentioned above; and (3) process conditions of technocratic decision-making style ("supranationality in practice"), rising transactions, and adaptability on the part of governments. . . .

The impact of Charles de Gaulle on the process of European integration led Haas to revise this theory and add another type of political actor—what he called the actor with "dramatic-political" aims.[4] Even in a setting like post-war Europe in which politics is highly bureaucratized and welfare is a predominant popular concern[5] a dramatic political leader was able to prevail over leaders with incremental economic aims and to divert the integration process from the predicted course. . . .

In the original neo-functionalist model, developed at a time when many observers were noting the bureaucratization of politics, the decline of ideology, and the growing popular concern for welfare and when foreign policies were held more closely in the vise of cold-war bipolarity, the national decisionmakers in the model were assumed to be economic incrementalists and thus be responsive to the economic logic of integration. It was thought that the technocrat-politicians could bypass the electoral or support politicians and forge links to the ever stronger regional organization until *engrenage* had proceeded so far that it was too late for anyone to change the pattern.

In this sense the neo-functionalists relied on "integration by stealth" and the positive role of popular ignorance. To a considerable extent this fit the early days of LAFTA and CACM. This picture is less accurate as a description of the *initiation* of European integration (Robert Schuman, Konrad Adenauer, and Alcide de Gaspari obviously played vital roles), but it is reasonably accurate for the workings of the ECSC. The protective cloak of noncontroversiality quickly wears out, however, as more sensitive interests are touched and as political heat generated by the integration process grows. Indeed there are some political climates in which economic issues are sufficiently highly politicized from the start that the cloak of noncontroversiality cannot be worn in the first place. Thus whatever the value of the simplified neo-functionalist model for explaining the early stages of integration in some settings, it quickly loses its explanatory value. . . .

Once we admit that (except for the early stages of integration in certain settings) important decisions affecting the integration process must be channeled through the political legitimizing leadership, we greatly enrich the model by admitting the possibility of negative as well as positive syndromes of responses resulting from the impact of the process forces upon the national decisionmakers. Actors can pull back from common tasks and institutions as well as increase their scope and authority.

There is also a third possible syndrome of responses to the impact of the process forces—the maintenance of the status quo. If the process forces are not too strong, the political leaders may prefer to tolerate the inconvenience of living with them rather than face what from their view are the political costs of negative or positive feedback. . . .

III. PROCESS MECHANISMS

A wide variety of reasons may be needed to account for the initial creation of a regional economic organization. Among the most important are the rise of a new reformist elite with incremental economic goals that is conscious of the welfare implications of existing market sizes and events in the external environment that impress upon both mass opinion and political legitimizing leaders the political cogency or usefulness of asserting their regional identity in an institutional form. . . .

As we have seen, the early neo-functionalist model gave essentially four process mechanisms that follow the creation of a common market: (1) the inherent functional linkages of tasks; (2) increasing flows or transactions; (3) deliberate linkages and coalitions; and (4) economic pressure groups, including at a later state the formation of groups at the regional level. Subsequent work by other scholars has suggested at least three other process mechanisms that may arise or be enhanced by the creation of a regional economic organization; (5) involvement of external actors; (6) regional ideology and intensification of regional identity; and (7) elite socialization.

These process mechanisms can be divided into those which follow from the liberalization or removal of state barriers to the free flow of goods and factors and those which are created by the establishment of administrative institutions. Whether political decisionmakers can ignore the pressures for decisions that the process mechanisms create or whether they will be forced into integrative or disintegrative decisions will depend upon the strength of the process mechanisms and upon conditions to be outlined below. . . .

A. Functional Linkage of Tasks

The concept of "spillover" has frequently been misapplied to cover any sign of increased cooperation, thus robbing it of its explanatory value. . . . Haas used the term to cover both perceived linkages between problems arising out of their inherent technical characteristics and linkages deliberately created or overstated by political actors (what might be called "cultivated spillover"). Despite these problems and the lesser effectiveness of the force than was originally believed to be the case, the perception that imbalances created by the functional interdependence or inherent linkages of tasks can press political actors to redefine their common tasks remains an important insight. In Walter Hallstein's words, "the material logic of the facts of integration urges us relentlessly on from one step to the next, from one field to another."[6]

For example, after tariff barriers were reduced in the European Economic Community (EEC), profit margins of firms and their competitive positions were more strongly affected by different systems of taxation, and this fact led to the adoption by the EEC countries of a common system of calculating tax on value added. When French costs began to increase relative to those of the Federal Republic of Germany (West Germany) by about 3 percent a year (i.e., inflation was higher in France than in West Germany), the initial result was the monetary crisis of November 1968 and French imposition of measures to restrain trade in order to protect its balance of payments. The longer term impact was to persuade the governments to accept a plan proposed by the Commission of the European Communities for coordination of short- and medium-term economic policies. . . .

The redefinition of tasks need not mean an upgrading of common tasks. The response can also be negative. If the conditions to be spelled out below have not resulted in a positive experience for a major coalition of actors, the inconvenience created by the imbalance may be overcome by undoing the original linkage. . . .

B. Rising Transactions

If the initiation of a regional integration scheme gives rise to an unexpected response by societal forces that result in a large rise in transactions. . . , political actors may (1) be faced with the overburdening of the institutions they have established for dealing with such transactions and with the need to curtail the transactions; (2) try to deal with them through national measures; or (3) increase the capacity of the common institutions that they have established.

. . . In other words, rising transactions need not lead to a significant widening of the scope (range of tasks) of integration but may lead rather to the intensification of central institutional capacity to handle a particular task.

Whether the feedback from rising transactions has a positive or negative effect on further progress toward economic union depends, again, on changes in the conditions below. . . .

C. Deliberate Linkages and Coalition Formation

Coalition formation tends to be based on what we called "cultivated spillover." In contrast to pure spillover in which the main force comes from a common perception of the degree to which problems are inextricably intertwined in a modern economy, problems are deliberately linked together into package deals not on the basis of technological necessity but on a basis of political and ideological projections and political possibilities. . . .

Two contrasting examples come from the EEC. A 1960 package deal hastened internal tariff cuts to satisfy those eager to advance the common market and simultaneously lowered the external tariff to satisfy those concerned about a loss of foreign trade. In contrast, in 1965 the Commission of the European Communities was unsuccessful with its proposed package deal of agricultural prices favorable to France, direct revenues for the EEC commission, and direct elections to the European Parliament.[7] The proposal touched off the 1965 EEC crisis, and there were no more successful large-scale package deals until the summit meeting at the Hague in December 1969. In other words, bureaucratic activism can also lead to bureaucratic slapdown in which packages are untied by politicians. . . .

D. Elite Socialization

The initiation of an integration scheme creates opportunities both for political decisionmakers attending meetings and bureaucrats seconded to regional institutions to develop personal ties and a possible corporate feeling. Leon Lindberg and Lawrence Scheinman have both focused attention on the increased contacts of politicians, national bureaucrats, and commission bureaucrats through the various meetings and institutions of the EEC. . . .[8]

If the conditions listed below are not favorable or change in an unfavorable direction, however, increased personal contact may enhance the potential acrimony (as it did, for example, in East Africa in 1963). Even if the contact results in socialization of political or bureaucratic decisionmakers into a system perspective, if integrative conditions become worse this may merely result in the isolation of the most prointegration actors from political effectiveness. Some accounts of bureaucrats returning from Brussels to Paris and Bonn support this view. . . .

E. Regional Group Formation

Once a regional integration scheme is established, it may serve as the stimulus for private groups to create various types of formal and informal nongovernmental regional organizations to reflect and protect their common interests at the regional level. In addition to representing a shift of political activity toward the regional level and a potential source of regional pressure on national governments these nongovernmental groupings themselves have elite socialization effects. . . .

In general, however, these regional nongovernmental organizations remain a weak force. In many cases the types of interests that are aggregated at the regional level tend to be very general, with more specific interests and structures remaining at the national level. For instance, despite the existence of regional trade union secretariats in Brussels, the idea of collective bargaining at the European level in response to the creation of a European market has not taken hold—in part because of the divisions in the labor movement but also because of the importance of national governmental power in collective bargaining. . . .

F. Ideological-Identitive Appeal

A taste shared by smaller groups to be identified as a larger group is frequently one of the factors that leads to initiation of regional integration schemes. Once established, a regional organization, by the symbol of its existence as well as by its actions (e.g., the efforts of the Hallstein commission, particularly before 1965), may heighten this sense of identitive appeal. . . .

In some cases a sense of permanence and strong identitive appeal can help groups or governments to tolerate short-term losses or sacrifices in the belief that they will be requited later. Finally, the stronger the myth of permanence, the more likely are businessmen to invest on the basis of the larger market and thus to make the myth reality in the concrete form of new industrial investments—as happened in the early days of the EEC. . . .

G. Involvement of External Actors in the Process

The original neo-functionalist formulation paid insufficient attention to the role of external factors in integration processes. . . . We are now beyond the stage of the initial criticism when we can talk of "catalysts" or "external factors" in general terms.[9] Building upon the distinction between passive and active external factors (those of a broad nature not affected by the process contrasted with those that represent deliberate action by external actors affected by the creation of a regional scheme), I include regional actor *perceptions* of the external situation as one of the integrative conditions that we will examine below and consider only *involvement* of external actors in the integration scheme as a process mechanism.

An integration process can involve various actors, including other governments, other international organizations, and nongovernmental actors such as international corporations. For example, the United States Agency for International Development and the United Nations Economic Commission for Latin America have both played important roles in the Central American Common Market. . . .

In summary, the response of political decisionmakers to the pressures generated by these process mechanisms will depend partly on the strength of the pressures—i.e., are they weak enough that the inconvenience they create is easier to tolerate than the political costs that might be incurred by a positive or negative response? . . .

IV. INTEGRATIVE POTENTIAL

The second determinant of the type of response is a set of conditions that we will refer to as the integrative potential of a region. . . . The following list of conditions that constitute the integrative potential of a region is based on the Haas and Schmitter checklist but with certain omissions, additions, and restatements. The first amendment is to drop their categorization by stages (background, initiation, process) and replace it with a distinction between structural conditions which are conceived as relatively stable variables more determined by factors other than the integration process and perceptual conditions which are quite volatile during an integration process and are determined more by the integration process itself. . . .

A. Structural Conditions

The structural conditions that affect the nature of the initial commitment and the later impact of the process forces that follow the initiation of an economic integration scheme are as follows:

I. Symmetry or Economic Equality of Units   This is restatement of Haas's and Schmitter's "size in the specific functional context of the union." At first glance it seems to contradict the proposition that "core areas" and unequal size may be helpful conditions for integration. Citing Karl Deutsch and Amitai Etzioni, Bruce Russett argues that there is no

> very convincing theory or evidence about international integration that indicates that the prospective members of a new unit should be the same size. (On the contrary, the idea of a powerful core area to provide centripetal force is rather more persuasive.)[10]

Yet others argue that economic integration cannot be successful between unequal partners. Given the tendency of industry to cluster to take advantage of the external economies available from the presence of other industries in more developed parts of a region, there is a danger that (in Gunnar Myrdal's terms) the "spread" effects of increased economic activity will be less important to the poorer areas than the "backwash" effect of the attraction of resources from the poorer to the richer areas. A case frequently cited is the deleterious effect of the unification of Italy upon southern Italy in the nineteenth century.

There are several points worth noting about this apparent theoretical dispute over the role of size in integration theory. First, it vanishes in the face of more precise formulation of what we mean by integration. What may be true of one type of integration (for example, trade) may not be of another (for example, political union). Problems of unequal size have plagued the Latin American Free Trade Association, but they did not stop the Sardinian leadership in the creation and maintenance of common institutions in Italy in the face of an elite sense of national identity and within the nineteenth century international system in which an aspect of coercion was acceptable. And it is worth remembering that Deutsch's original hypothesis about "cores" was formulated in relation to a number of historical cases of security community. . . .[11]

If inequality is interpreted not in simple terms of square miles, or even gross national product (GNP), but rather as a level of development with per capita GNP as the indicator, a simple scattergram quickly indicates a relationship between trade integration and level of development. The number of cases is few, but it seems roughly true that in nonhegemonial regional economic organizations the more equal the level of development (measured by per capita GNP), the higher the regional trade integration (intraregional exports as a percentage of total exports). . . . Moreover, no economic integration scheme (common market or free trade area) which does over 20 percent of its trade intraregionally has more than a 2:I ratio of difference in per capita incomes (Portugal, in EFTA, is the exception).

If inequality is interpreted not in terms of level of development but in terms of total size of the economy (measured in GNP), then size seems to have a very different effect in less developed than in developed areas. Relatively high degrees of trade integration have been achieved by integration schemes among developed countries in which the ratio of the largest to smallest economies (in GNP) is more than 5:I. Among less developed countries, however, the only schemes with trade integration over 20 percent have ratios of largest to smallest (in terms of GNP) of less than 2.5:I. It almost looks as if the lower the per capita income of the area, the greater the necessary homogeneity in size of economy.

While one must be cautious about using this evidence when the number of cases is so few, there are also intuitive grounds for believing that where income is lower and welfare is scarcer problems of its distribution are likely to be more strongly contested. In addition, it is more likely that backwash effects and clustering of industry to take advantage of external economies will be more politically apparent and difficult to resolve in smaller and poorer economies with fewer poles of growth. . . .

2. Elite Value Complementarity   Whether corresponding elite groups do or do not think alike makes a difference; witness the effects of the addition of a Gaullist elite to the constellation of Christian-Democratic and Socialist decision-makers in Europe in the mid-1950's. But which elites count and how much complementarity is necessary?. . .

. . . For our purpose it is the elites who control economic policy decisions that matter. These are not the same in all settings and may change over time with the politicization of a process as we shall see below. In general, the greater the complementarity of elites with effective power over economic policy as reflected in similar statements and policies toward the most salient political-economic issues in their region, the better the conditions for positive or integrative response to the pressure for decisions arising from the process mechanism.

3. Pluralism (Modern Associational Groups)   Functionally specific, universalistic, achievement-oriented groups in all member states were important components of the neo-functional path in Europe. The relative absence or weakness of such groups in many less developed countries has been shown to make integration more difficult . . . by depriving regional bureaucrats of potential allies and by depriving governments of channels of information useful in the formation of realistic economic policy.

. . . Our hypothesis is that the greater the pluralism in all member states, the better the conditions for an integrative response to the feedback from the process forces.

4. Capacity of Member States to Adapt and Respond This is a slight adaptation of the Haas-Schmitter condition to include Deutsch's concept of "internal noise" which inhibits the capacity to respond.[12] Governments in less developed countries are notoriously weak in their capacity to commit their societies. . . .

Moreover, competing demands of internal instability . . . on decisionmakers' attention may hinder the capacity of the more prosperous states to "hear" the messages from their weaker partners or to respond to them. . . .

Our hypothesis for this condition is that the greater the internal instability and other factors that diminish the capacity of the key decisionmakers in economic policy (both public and private) to adapt and respond to problems and crises, the more likely that feedback from the process mechanisms will have a negative effect. . . .

B. Perceptual Conditions

The following three perceptual conditions, on the other hand, are highly affected by the process of integration.

I. Perceived Equity of Distribution of Benefits. All students of comparative regional integration emphasize the importance of this condition. It differs from the structural condition of symmetry because it is based on perception by the actors. There is often a gap between the actual changes in economic symmetry in a region and the perception of equity among decisionmakers.

The politics of regional economic integration is not only the "politics of cooperation" but also the "politics of status" between states that have been traditional rivals. The cooperative or welfare aspect is more like a nonzero-sum game, and it is relevant . . . to use aggregate economic data to show that all states are better off or that even if a state like Honduras has not gained as much as El Salvador or Tanzania as much as Kenya, it is better off than it would have been without the common market.

The status aspect, however, is more like a zero-sum game. What matters is how decisionmakers perceive that they have gained or lost status or rank in relation to their neighbors. This is not always predictable from the hard data of economic changes. Rather it will be affected by the sensitivity of the traditional competition (such as the Franco-German rivalry) between the states and the personal predilections of particular decisionmakers. . . . The hypothesis accompanying this condition is of course that the higher the perceived equitable distribution in all countries, the better the conditions for further integration.

2. Perceptions of External Cogency.   The way that regional decisionmakers perceive the nature of their external situation and the manner in which they should respond to it is an important condition determining agreement on further integration. There are a variety of relevant perceptions such as a sense of external threat from a giant neighbor, loss of status felt by Europeans and Latin Americans as a result of bipolarity and simple demonstration effects ("everybody's doing it"). . . .

Other aspects of external dependence might be operationalized by looking at economic and military aid and perhaps also at drawings on the International Monetary Fund (IMF), at alliances, and at organizational memberships. Again, however, the important question is the existence of common perceptions of the cogency of such dependence, particularly when different dependences pull in different directions—e.g., differing French and West German perceptions of what to do about dependence on the United States and the way these differences affected their policies toward European integration. . . .[13]

3. Low (or Exportable) Visible Costs   A key tenet of neo-functional strategy is to make integration seem relatively costless by carefully choosing the initial steps. Where visible costs are low it is easier to get agreement on the first steps that will start the process of *engrenage*. Over time, of course, costs are likely to become higher and more visible. . . .

Regional integration schemes usually involve a strong protectionist element, whether it be European farmers or Central American manufacturers or nationalized industries in the LAFTA countries. Strictly speaking, this protection represents a real cost to consumers *inside* the region (compensated in the long run perhaps if there are infant industries being protected, though this is hardly the case in European coal and agriculture) as well as to foreigners in terms of their trade that is diverted (which may not be fully compensated by new trade created).[14]

Nonetheless, in accord with Harry Johnson's theory of economic nationalism the widely dispersed and less visible costs of protectionist subsidies are not as politically influential as are the concrete benefits to the specific groups being protected. Thus to the extent that it looks as though only outsiders are being hurt and the visible costs can be "exported," agreement on integration policies may be easier. . . .

V. PHASING AND CONSEQUENCES

. . . What is the likely sequence of interactions between forces, conditions, and actors over time? Do the relationships change during the course of a process? Is the process likely to be continuous, even assuming no major change in exogenous forces? Obviously, the sequences and phasing of integration process will vary with the politics of each region. Nonetheless, we can introduce some order into the study by formulating certain hypotheses about the likely shape of the integration process and try to establish the conditions under which those hypotheses are likely to be true.

We will hypothesize four conditions that are likely to characterize an integration process over time: (1) politicization; (2) redistribution; (3) reduction of alternatives; and (4) externalization. . . .

A. Politicization

If, over the course of time, positive responses to the process forces lead to higher levels of integration (stronger institutions and greater coordination of economic policy), we would expect the process to become more "political." By politics we mean the process by which conflicting visions of a common interest are agitated or settled.[15]

At the other end of the continuum of controversy are technical procedures which involve the choice of "optimal" solutions by reputed experts by apparently "rational" criteria. It is worth noting, however, that a number of subjects that are apparently technical in the sense of depending on expertise may not be amenable to purely technical procedures. For example, European cooperation in the science and technology field has been highly politicized or controversial right from the outset perhaps because of its symbolic content and the difficulties of making precise calculations of benefits in a new field.[16] Similarly, economic issues which fall closer to the technical-administrative end of the continuum of controversialism in the European context are frequently highly politicized from the outset in African settings.

We would expect politicization to increase during the course of an integration process for several reasons. More groups become involved through the effects of rising transactions, inherent linkages, or deliberate coalition formation. The larger the numbers, the more likely the possible divergent interpretations of the common interest in integration. The growth of the powers of the central institutions not only makes them more visible to mass opinion but may also stimulate action by groups opposed to integration, including national bureaucrats jealous of incursion into their powers. . . .

The greater the politicization of subjects, the less amenable they are to the quiet technocratic decisionmaking style that

> stresses the role of uninstructed experts who tend to agree among themselves with respect to the reasoning patterns and antecedent conditions relevant to a decision, *and* with respect to the outcome to be attained.[17]

This does not necessarily mean that further integration is impossible. It does mean, however, that reaching decisions may be more difficult and involve a wider range of forces. . . .

B. Redistribution

As economic integration progresses, it is likely to have an effect on the distribution of welfare, status, and power both among groups within the member states and between the member states themselves. Within states certain groups or areas are more likely than others to benefit from rising transactions, package deals and coalitions, or alliances with external actors. Certain political actors and bureaucrats will benefit more than others from their involvement in integration, particularly if public support for integration increases during the process. . . .

Redistribution is not totally bad for an integration process though it has obviously unfavorable effects in a region. . . . In Europe the prospect of redistribution is a major incentive for actors to push for further progress in integration. Roy Blough and Jack Behrman have argued that one of the causes of stagnation in LAFTA is the existence of so many guarantees against redistribution that there are few incentives for integration.[18] A certain amount of redistribution is necessary whether it be a new technocratic elite increasing its power or an area or two within a market serving as leading points of growth.

A crucial question with redistribution is the phasing of the growth of the process forces flowing from liberalization compared to those coming from the common institutions. If the role of the common institutions is increased and agreement is reached on common approaches, for example, to regional incomes policy or industrial location policy, the most severe effects of redistribution may be controlled. However, such policies involve difficult political coordination (and a more consciously perceived sacrifice of sovereign control). In the short run, governments often find it politically easier to promote integration indirectly ("negative" integration) through liberalization of their respective trade policies than to agree upon common approaches and the consequences of liberalization ("positive" integration). . . .

C. Reduction of Alternatives

An early neo-functionalist hypothesis was that integration was automatic. Once *engrenage* took place, it would become increasingly difficult and costly and thus impossible for political leaders to disentangle their nations. Although the original formulation was oversimplified and therefore misleading, the notion of automaticity was based on a useful insight. The sovereign alternatives open to political decisionmakers are reduced as an integration process goes forward.

As transactions rise and more groups (including external actors) become involved, the pressures on decisionmakers are greater. Similarly, the stronger the ideological-identitive appeal becomes. . . , the stronger the pressure on the political decisionmaker and the fewer his political alternatives. As more tasks become interrelated through inherent links or package deals the costs of disintegrative actions become greater because there is the danger of pulling the whole house of cards down.

While it would at first appear that reduced alternatives would have an unambiguously good effect over the course of the integrative process, higher costs do not necessarily determine the actions of all political decisionmakers. Having fewer alternatives is not the same as having no alternatives.

In some cases decisionmakers may not perceive or may deliberately ignore diminished alternatives and thus precipitate crises. In other cases the knowledge that other countries are equally ensnared by the diminished alternatives may be a positive incentive for the leader more willing to practice brinksmanship to provoke crises deliberately. Finally, the further integration progresses, the larger the crises are likely to become both because a greater degree of interdependence has been created and because the resistance of some political leaders may become more intense as integration approaches the security and identitive areas of greatest concern to them. . . .

D. Externalization

Schmitter has argued that whatever the original intentions, as integration proceeds member states will be increasingly forced to hammer out a collective external position vis-à-vis nonparticipant third parties because the further integration proceeds, the more third parties will react to it, either with support or hostility. . . .[19]

While a sense of external identity is important in the early stages of the process and perhaps again at higher levels of integration, it seems that too great involvement in the problems of external policies in the middle stages of integration may have a braking effect. It diverts attention, raises anticipated problems that make package deals and coalitions based on the existing structure of interests more difficult, and precipitates unnecessary crises. These in turn may stimulate opposition groups and speed up politicization through the involvement of political leaders and mass opinion in sensitive areas at too early a stage.

VI. CONCLUSIONS

What are the likely effects of the outcomes of an integration process over time? . . . First, in most settings the process of politicization means that low-cost integration and technocratic style decisionmaking procedures are unlikely to last very long and certainly not until a widespread popular support or a powerful coalition of intensely concerned interests have developed to the point at which they determine the decisions of political decisionmakers.

Second, the ability to reach difficult political agreement on "positive integration" measures to cope with the problems created by redistribution is likely to lag behind the forces created by more easily agreed upon liberalization measures. Alternatively, in settings in which market forces are weak and liberalization cannot be agreed upon it seems likely that process forces will also be weak.

Third, the sense of reduced alternatives and the precipitation of larger crises will probably fail to have an integrative effect the closer the issues come to the security and identitive areas that are of greatest concern to popular political leaders. These are also the areas in which they are least likely to have the clear overriding common interests that make crises productive rather than destructive. Finally, the pressures both inside and outside the region for a common external policy are likely to develop more rapidly than popular or group support for a high degree of integration develops in these generally more controversial fields.

In brief, unless the structure of incentives offered by the international system is seriously altered, the prospects for common markets or microregional economic organizations leading in the short run (of decades) to federation or some sort of political union capable of an independent defense and foreign policy do not seem very high. . . .

If common markets do not lead to federation, does this mean that they must slip backward or fall apart? Is there no point of equilibrium in between? The belief that common markets must go forward or fall backward is widely accepted. Indeed, it was an essential part of the neo-functional myth. . . .

While this does seem to be the case when one looks at integration from the perspective of a simple neo-functionalist model, it no longer seems necessarily to be the case according to our revised model. Indeed our basic hypothesis is that most political decisionmakers will opt for the status quo at any level as long as the process forces or popular pressures are not strong enough to make this choice unbearable for them. . . .

Moreover, as Lawrence Krause and Leon Lindberg have pointed out and the case of EFTA shows, this type of market integration need not greatly strengthen the regional institutions. In short, it seems most likely that under the current structure of international incentives dramatic-political decisionmakers will find some point of equilibrium at which they would rather tolerate the inconvenience of the existing level of process forces than incur the greater political costs of full integration or disintegration. . . .

Looked at from the perspective of our model, there are several reasons why the success of integration is limited in less developed areas. In the first place the economic structure of underdevelopment is likely to result in weaker process forces. Taking the forces resulting from liberalization—imperfect market mechanisms, lack of entrepreneurial resources, and inadequate infrastructure—all inhibit the rate at which transactions rise. Looser interdependence of economic sectors limits the pressures arising from inherent linkage of tasks. In addition, in many cases ideological biases against capitalist market mechanisms and nationalist reactions against external actors attracted by the prospects of a larger market lead to political inhibitions of the process forces resulting from liberalization.

Turning to the process forces resulting from the creation of new institutions, lack of administrative resources hampers regional bureaucracies. Premature politicization of economic issues greatly reduces the scope for bureaucratic initiative and quietly arranged package deals. . . .

This is not to say that all economic issues are emotionally laden "high politics" in less developed countries and technically soluble "low politics" in developed settings. The salience of an issue area and its susceptibility to a consensual style of decision varies with each particular political context. There is greater monetary coordination in East Africa than in Europe (where it involves questions of Franco-German balance of power).[20] Labor migration is easy for the Nordic countries but not for Central America. On the question of a common external tariff the situation is reversed. The basic point, however, is that in many less developed areas a greater number of economic issue areas tend to become highly politicized than is the case in more developed settings.

Not only is it probable that process forces will be weaker in less developed areas but the integrative potential is likely to be lower. As we saw above, the lower the income and the lower the level of industrialization, the lower the tolerance to differences in symmetry and the more sensitive the problem of equitable distribu-

tion of benefits. Not only does the problem of redistribution require more coordination of positive policy and thus involve a greater sense of loss of sovereignty, but
the resources available for compensating for redistribution are in shorter supply,
and many of the lags result from problems of human resource and infrastructure
that cannot be cured in the short run.

Low levels of modern associational pluralism restrict the role of groups in the
integration process at the same time that traditional pluralism and other problems
of internal malintegration are likely to create a setting of internal noise that re-
stricts the capacity of governments to adapt and respond. Finally, perceived external cogency is possibly higher for less developed countries because of their high
dependence on a few commodities which often have sluggish growth rates and because of their vulnerability to penetration by outside actors. But where this vulnerability differs among member states and where dependence of member states
is on different outside forces (e.g., British and French Africa and the situation in
the Caribbean),[21] external cogency may not be perceived in the same way by all
the potential partners.

NOTES

1. Ernst B. Haas, *The Uniting of Europe: Political, Social, and Economic Forces,
   1950–1957* (Standford, CA: Stanford University Press, 1958).
2. Leon N. Lindberg, *The Political Dynamics of European Economic Integration* (Stanford,
   CA: Stanford University Press, 1963); Ernst B. Haas and Philippe C. Schmitter, "Economics and Differential Patterns of Political Integration: Projections about Unity in
   Latin America," *International Organization*, Autumn 1964 (Vol. 18, No. 4), pp. 705–737.
3. John Pinder, "Problems of Economic Integration," in G. R. Denton (ed.), *Economic
   Integration in Europe* (London: Weidenfeld and Nicolson, 1969), p. 145.
4. Ernst B. Haas, "The *Uniting of Europe* and the Uniting of Latin America," *Journal of
   Common Market Studies,* June 1967 (Vol. 5, No. 4), pp. 315–343.
5. See Stephen Graubard (ed.), *A New Europe?* (Boston: Houghton Mifflin Co., 1964).
6. *European Community,* June 1967 (No. 103), p. 11.
7. See John Lambert, "The Constitutional Crisis 1965–66," *Journal of Common Market
   Studies,* May 1966 (Vol. 4, No. 3), pp. 195–228.
8. See Lawrence Scheinman, "Some Preliminary Notes on Bureaucratic Relationships in
   the European Economic Community," *International Organization*, Autumn 1966 (Vol.
   20, No. 4), pp. 750–773; and Leon Lindberg and Stuart Scheingold, *Europe's Would-
   Be Polity: Patterns of Change in the European Community* (Englewood Cliffs, NJ:
   Prentice-Hall, 1970), chapter 4.
9. J. S. Nye, "Patterns and Catalysts in Regional Integration," *International Organization,*
   Autumn 1965 (Vol. 19, No. 4), pp. 870–884.
10. Bruce M. Russett, *International Regions and the International System: A Study in Po-
    litical Ecology* (Chicago: Rand McNally & Co., 1967), p. 21.
11. Contrary to the "balance of power" theory, security-communities seem to develop
    most frequently around cores of strength. . . . Karl W. Deutsch, and others, *Political
    Community and the North Atlantic Area: International Organization in the Light of
    Historical Experience* (Princeton, NJ: Princeton University Press, 1957), p. 10.
12. See Karl Deutsch, "Communication Theory and Political Integration," in Philip Jacob
    and James Toscano (ed.), *The Integration of Political Communities* (Philadelphia: J. B.
    Lippincott Co., 1964), pp. 46–74.

13. Stanley Hoffmann, "The European Process at Atlantic Crosspurposes," *Journal of Common Market Studies,* February 1965 (Vol. 3, No. 2), pp. 85–101.

14. Harry G. Johnson, *Economic Nationalism in Old and New States* (London: George Allen and Unwin, 1968), chapter I.

15. E. C. Banfield, in *A Dictionary of the Social Sciences,* ed. by Julius Gould and William L. Kolb (Glencoe, IL: Free Press [compiled under the auspices of the United Nations Educational, Scientific and Cultural Organization], 1964).

16. See Robert L. Pfaltzgraff and James L. Deghand, "European Technological Collaboration: The Experience of the European Launcher Development Organization," *Journal of Common Market Studies,* September 1968 (Vol. 7, No. I), pp. 22–34; Also Robert Gilpin, *France in the Age of the Scientific State* (Princeton, NJ: Princeton University Press, 1968), chapter 12.

17. Haas and Schmitter, *International Organization,* Vol. 18, No. 4, p. 715.

18. Roy Blough and Jack N. Behrman, "Problems of Regional Integration in Latin America," (Committee for Economic Development, Supplementary Paper No. 22), in *Regional Integration and the Trade of Latin America* (New York: Committee for Economic Development, 1968), p. 31.

19. Philippe C. Schmitter, "Three Neo-Functionalist Hypotheses about International Integration," *International Organization,* Winter 1969 (Vol. 23, No. 1), p. 165.

20. Hans O. Schmitt, "Capital Markets and the Unification of Europe," *World Politics,* January 1968 (Vol. 20, No. 2), pp. 228–244.

21. See Aaron Segal, *The Politics of Caribbean Economic Integration* (Puerto Rico: Institute of Caribbean Studies, 1968).

The European Community: A Union of States Without Unity of Government

Christopher Brewin

The development of the European Community into the world's largest trader has forced third parties to treat it as an important actor in its own right. Yet it is plainly not a sovereign state. Therefore the Commission, the Member States and third states have all assumed that its formal status is that of an international organization. . . .

My purpose in this article is to argue that the European Community is now better conceptualized as a union of states rather than as an organization. The international law doctrine that actors are either states or organizations has become unrealistic. Not only does it cause unnecessary practical difficulties, it is conceptually misleading in implying that the Community has an inferior status as a negotiator. It may also impoverish the development of the Community unless an alternative concept is received, as can be illustrated by the history of Community law.

The development of Community law would have been crippled if the international law approach had not been defeated in the *van Gend* case of 1962. In that decision the Court of Justice established that Community law within its sphere is equal in status to national law. Further, the Court has successfully maintained that, because law should be uniform, Community law must take precedence over conflicting national law. This decision did not transform Community law into federal law because Community legislation suffers from the defect that its statutes are not legitimized by a democratic legislature. They are law in that the governments of democratic states have been authorized to make binding agreements in the Council, a procedure which accords with the union of states model discussed below. It is worth recalling that this decisive turning-point was narrowly won in 1962, and might well have been lost if the court had lacked the alternative to international law of the American constitutional law concept. . . .

In the Community's external relations there has been no such decisive turning-point. When Hallstein as President of the Commission attempted to receive ambassadors as though he were a Head of State, De Gaulle refused to countenance this claim to equal status. De Gaulle was opposed by the other five states who had already rejected the Fouchet proposals for a French-led Union as an alternative to the development of the Community. The crisis was ended through a compromise by which the credentials of heads of mission are submitted simultaneously and separately to the President of the Commission and to the President-in-Office of the Council (Groux & Manin, 1985, p. 33). This distinguishes the status of the Community from both that of international organizations and that of states. However it does not clearly answer the question whether, within its sphere, the Community is the equal of states as Community law is the equal of national law. . . .

PART ONE

International Law

I begin with international law, noting Professor Weiler's concern that stressing its foundations in international law might "carry the Community backward" (Bieber et al., 1985, p. 164, fn. 9). Since 1945, international law has fostered a conceptual simplicity and clarity which would have satisfied William of Occam. The International Court of Justice and the drafters of the Vienna Convention on the law of treaties did not have to take account of any important confederations like the Dutch states-general, the early United States of America or even the economic confederacy of the Zollverein. The simplification of state theory which accompanied the universal reception of the doctrine of state sovereignty was not held up by any consideration for the Benelux Union. It allows no half-way house between a state and an international organization. In the words of Dr Schwarze (1985),

"The legal capacity of a nation-state is original, not derived from anyone. Thus the international lawyer refers to a nation state as a 'primary legal person'. In contrast, the EEC as an international organization is not an original legal person, but was created by the Member States. Thus the legal capacity of such an international organisation 'must depend on its purposes and functions, as expressed or implied by its constituent instruments and as developed in practise', as the International Court of Justice has held.". . .

From this simple if misleading invocation of statehood, lawyers derive a basic rule about any division of powers between the organs of an international organization and their Member States. Dr Steenbergen (1985) writes, "The basic rule governing this division of powers, is that all powers which have not been conferred upon the Communities, remain with the Member-states." This relationship of creator to created normally implies a relationship of superior to inferior. Hence part of the significance of the *van Gend* case cited above is that the Court rejected this implication by its successful assertion of the applicability of Community law as national law.

A second corollary of this dichotomy between superior and inferior is that the doctrine of state succession has been developed, so far as I have discovered, only with reference to countries which have replaced former colonies (O'Connell, 1963). Lawyers have gone so far as to allow that international organizations may succeed to the powers of other international organizations. For example, by Article 7 (5) of the Parliament's draft treaty, the Union would have to respect the commitments of the European Community. However, lawyers have chosen not to consider the possibility of a non-state entity succeeding to some of the powers of states, even when those powers are identical to those previously exercised by states and which those states must now refrain from exercising. Thus in the *Spoorwegen* judgment, the Court found that "in the case of commitments arising from GATT, the Community has replaced the Member States in commitments arising from the Convention". Yet in this context replacing seems to carry the same meaning as succeeding. It cannot be that replacement refers to parts where succession implies a whole, for lawyers have no trouble in admitting that one organization can succeed to the necessarily partial powers of its precursor. . . .

A third corollary is that there is no legal doctrine of recognition for international organizations comparable to that applied to states or governments. In general terms, the point of reciprocal recognition is that the parties can no longer contest the validity of what is recognized. As an international organization the European Community has faced three sets of difficulties because of its legal status as an organization. With respect to other international organizations, notably in the UN family, there were early obstacles to accepting various aspects of Community participation, not all of which can be attributed to the political hostility of the Soviet bloc. With respect to states, when at Vienna in 1975 they legitimized their practice of asserting a right of legation to organizations of which they were not members, they did not accept that this right should be reciprocal. The third set of difficulties arises directly from the lack of a legal concept of a Union of States. In organizations whose membership is limited to states, there have been several instances in which the states members of the Community can no longer legitimately exercise their separate capacities in some areas while continuing to do so in others. The powers of the Community are identical to those previously exercised by states. Because of the Community's importance as a territorial bloc of twelve states, the organization typically needs to include it in practice if global negotiations are to succeed. If there were a legal possibility for the membership of a Union of States, with general instead of ad hoc rules on when it has one vote and when twelve, the present difficulties of Community participation, ratification and implementation set out by Groux & Manin, 1985, would be reduced.

Finally, the initial clarity of the distinction between state and organization is reduced to the extent that the concept of organization is also claimed to be flexible, with powers developed in practice with the presumed consent of the states as primary and original sources. . . .

Political Scientists

The main schools of political science have also assumed that the Community is an international organization. Functionalists and neo-functionalists do not talk of functionalist states. Gaullists insist that the nation-state is the unit of decision, capable of taxing and conscripting, while nobody would die for the European Community. Some of the best empirical studies have emphasized the different attitudes of the states, especially in the area of political co-operation (Allen & Wessels, 1982; Hill, 1983; Hill & Wallace, 1979; Hassner, 1973; . . .). These studies typically assess the usefulness to states of Community actions, or of inaction under cover of consultation. They stress the limitations consequent on the small size of the budget, the variety of national objectives, the availability of other fora, and regard for national prerogatives. Others have concentrated on the limitations inherent in the complicated central political, legal and administrative processes whereby common positions are agreed and expressed through the presidency country, or the Commission or even the Parliament (. . . Pescatore, 1979; Close, 1982; Wellenstein, 1982; . . .). These have shown that while the Commission diplomats are professionally respected, it is the states who specify the mandate and supervise every stage of the negotiations through the 'mothers-in-law' they provide. While it is true that the states have delegated exclusive competence in fisheries for example, and themselves cannot negotiate agreements on Antartica or even with Britain on the Falklands, they specify in Council the content of the common policy. Moreover any enforcement is primarily left to national warships as there are no Union warships and only thirteen Community inspectors. . . .

Economists

It is not easy to summarize the attitude of economists with respect to either the instrumental or the union thesis. In the first place they have had no difficulty in accepting the common customs tariff as a barrier around the customs union that is in all respects the equivalent of a barrier put up by a state. The difficulty is that estimates of trade creation and trade diversion rest on a model whose logic leads to the conclusion that all such barriers are not instrumental but counter-productive.

The argument for union derived from economies of scale is tempered by arguments that optimal specialization will not result. Moreover Adam Smith's recognition of patriotism as a non-economic good and his support for the Navigation acts has been considerably developed into a recognition that consideration of public policy enormously complicates the achievement of the last three stages in Balassa's typology of steps towards full integration (Pelkmans, 1980). Perhaps it would be safe to conclude that economists could accept either the union or the instrumental thesis.

The Commission

For its part, the Commission has sought international recognition as an entity in its own right, but has been quite willing to accept the status of an organization. It has generally preferred a direct reference to the European Community, as in the formula that an agreement will be open for acceptance by the European Economic Community by signature or otherwise. But where for political reasons it seemed desirable to accept a general term, it has not objected to being called an organization by a variety of names. Earlier references to 'customs and economic unions' were succeeded by variations on 'organizations for regional economic integration set up by sovereign States with powers to negotiate, conclude and apply international agreements on subjects covered by the present convention.' Recently in conventions on commodities the fashion has been to refer to 'groups of states'. A curious instance of the Commission's reluctance to make an issue of its legal status, and thereby cause friction with both Member States and third parties, arose in 1972. In its enthusiasm for European unity the People's Republic of China offered to "grant the EEC the degree of recognition it might wish to propose" (Groux & Manin, p. 21, fn.). Nothing resulted from this proposal. Similarly it might be recalled that when the Coal and Steel Community began life, the High Authority had unusual supranational powers. However it did not object when its first external mission was accredited to the British government and not to the Court of St James. When the first important agreement was signed, in 1954, the six Member States added their signatures. This certainly cast doubt on the independent external capacity of the Authority, although it is possible to argue that the new entity included its Member States as well as the Authority.

We have already discussed the compromise by which Community practice in receiving the credentials of heads of mission distinguishes Community practice from that of other organizations. However the Commission has not insisted on reciprocity with respect to its delegations in third countries. Thus, while generally its officials are accorded the same privileges as other diplomats, this can be based on a unilateral act of the host state. The more serious difficulty is that the bicephalous nature of the Community sometimes makes it unclear whether the Commission representative or the representative of the President of the Council is speaking for the Community.

With respect to organizations, the Commission's attitude to those newly established seems to differ from its attitude to those previously established. It has always responded to missives from the UN Secretary-General addressed to international organizations even though it was not granted observer status at the UN General Assembly until 1974, in a deal involving simultaneous status for the CMEA. Incrementally, it has been granted observer status at UNCTAD and UN-ESCO (1954), at ECOSOC (1967) and in the ECE (1973). It participates in the FAO global agricultural information and early-warning system, and contributes financially to the work of the ILO. Such status is clearly appropriate to that of an international organization, as is its observer status at the Council of Europe, and the OECD Council and its committees. However in new organizations it is remarkable how the Community has received full-member status; examples are the International Energy Agency, the North Atlantic Fisheries Organization (1978), and the deliberative organs set up for coffee, cocoa, tin, olive oil, rubber, etc. This does not alter the basic point that it accepts the status of an organization.

Member States

The Member States' actions have also been ambivalent. On the one hand, as of right the states have permanent high-level delegations at Brussels. These delegations work 'with and within the organisation' as specified in Article 6 of the Vienna Convention of 1975. . . . Each state is very reluctant to take another to Court, a reluctance to some extent shared by the Commission. State actions typically defend a particular state interest rather than any general interest. They fear the loss of further prerogatives, such as control over the Development Fund. A less important instance is cited by the director of the Community's legal service. He suggests that states' reluctance to agree to regulations on ships in Community ports is explained by the fear that they will be replaced by Community representatives in maritime conferences (Close, 1982). In the early stages of the Law of the Sea Conference, and in the follow-up to Helsinki, the Member States have shown a marked disinterest in the importance of Community representation.

On the other hand, and at the highest political level, there has from time to time been a willingness to promote an 'ever-closer union' of states. One can cite the initial choice of Spaak as rapporteur, the five states who supported Hallstein in 1965, the willingness to develop the permanent council known as COREPER, the Council of Heads, the Declaration of 19 June, 1983, the European Monetary System and European political co-operation. Seven states supported the proposals of the Dooge Committee.

Treaty-making Powers

The strength of the view of the Community as merely an international organization is reinforced by considering the treaty-making powers of the Communities.

Thus, in spite of the supranational powers accorded by the Treaty of Paris to the High Authority, article 6(2) states that "in its international relationships the Community shall enjoy the legal capacity to exercise its functions and to achieve its purposes". This formula is familiar to students of postwar international organizations. In the case of EURATOM it is bare title which, by Article 85, is accorded to the Community. "Special fissile materials shall be the property of the Community." Practical control however is exercised by the individual states who, by Article 87, "shall have the unlimited right of use and consumption." Article 101 of the EURATOM treaty states: "The Community may, within the limits of its competence, enter into obligations by means of the conclusion of agreements or conventions with a third country, an international organization or a national of a third country." Agreements with third countries have been made by qualified majority vote of the Council after Commission negotiations on the basis of a Council mandate. With respect to some minor agreements with international organizations, the Commission has itself concluded agreements, while keeping the Council informed. EURATOM has developed little in the way of replacing the Member States.

There is no express provision in the Treaty of Rome for the Community as such to act diplomatically at the highest level in fulfilling the responsibilities that stem from its position after enlargement as the world's largest trader. The legal personality conferred by the signatories in Article 210 is so niggardly that it is only by inference from the separate reference in the next article to municipal law that Article 210 can be understood as referring to international law. The treaty-making powers set out in the Treaty of Rome are most precise in dealing with the weaker actors in international society, potential associates, including a specific reference to unions of states (Articles 238), and international organizations, (Article 229), and specified organizations such as the Council of Europe and what was then the OEEC.

These formal powers to make treaties with third parties have not been increased by any of the treaties or executive agreements modifying the Treaty of Rome. The Single European Act, intended to "transform relations as a whole among their States into a European Union," contains no explicit reference to treaty-making powers. It remains to be seen whether putting the wide-ranging European Council and political co-operation procedures on a treaty basis will be construed as implicitly conferring such powers in securing consistency between commercial and political acts or in endeavouring to formulate a foreign policy which may include aspects of security policy.

The most important powers remain those of Articles 111 (2) and 113–114 which confer exclusive powers on the Community in succession to the Member States with respect to tariff agreements and commercial agreements. In 1984 the Council agreed to a Commercial Policy Instrument whereby a majority in the Council can impose swift retaliatory action against third parties, and by a somewhat lengthier procedure initiate diplomatic moves designed to influence the policies of third countries. The instrumental interpretation of the Community is here driven back to stressing that the procedures for using these powers, particularly under Article 228, have been modified in favour of the Member States. . . . The argument that the Community is already a Union relies instead on the fact that every Community agreement, however it is reached, further binds all the Members which their cumbersome decision-making process makes it extremely difficult for individual states to change.

The Court

The Luxembourg Court has gone a long way to making the succession doctrine a possibility by its decisions on the external implications of the adoption of common internal policies. In addition to the express competence in external affairs accorded to the Community process by the Member States in the treaties, the Court has found that there is also a competence which arises where internal rules have been adopted (ERTA competence), and further an implied competence arising even in the absence of internal rules (Opinion 1/76 competence). The key passage in the 1971 judgment on the ERTA case reads,

> "In particular, each time the Community, with a view to implementing a common policy envisaged by the Treaty, adopts provisions laying down common rules, whatever form these may take, the Member States no longer have the right, acting individually or even collectively, to undertake obligations with third countries which affect those rules.
>
> "As and when such internal rules come into being, the Community alone is in a position to assume and carry out contractual obligations towards third countries affecting the whole sphere and operation of the Community legal system."

In its Opinion 1/75 the Court rejected the doctrine of concurrent powers of Community and Member States except where a given agreement in some its parts pertained to the province of the Community while others pertained to the jurisdiction of Member States. . . . In Opinion 1/76, the Court said:

> "whenever Community law has created for the institutions of the Community power within its internal system for the purpose of attaining a specific objective, the Community has authority to enter into the international commitments necessary for the attainment of that objective even in the absence of an express provision in that connection.
>
> "This is particularly so in all cases in which internal power has already been used in order to adopt measures which come within the attainment of common policies. It is not, however, limited to that eventuality. Although the internal measures are only adopted when the international agreement is concluded and made enforceable as is envisaged in the present case by the proposal for a Regulation to be submitted to the Council by the Commission, the power to bind the Community vis-à-vis third countries nevertheless flows by implication from the provisions of the Treaty creating the internal power and in so far as the participation of the Community in the international agreement is, as here, necessary for the attainment of one of the objectives of the Community."

The doctrine of implicit powers would of course interest an American constitutional lawyer. It is restricted to the realm of necessity. . . .

For its part the Court, according to Pescatore (1979), has consistently taken the view

> "that the fulfilment of the Community's task for the furthering of the common interest cannot be jeopardised by separate actions of Member States in the international relations field. The Community must be able to show its unity not only internally; it must be enabled also to display its full negotiating power, for the common good, in its relations with third countries."

The Parliament

Although the Community thus began as an international organization, many of its protagonists intended that, internally at least, it should develop into a federal state. Disputes between its Member States and between its institutions on the nature of the Community have consequently been endemic. The 1984 draft treaty of the European Parliament, passed by 231 votes to 31 votes, is particularly interesting in that it envisages a union whose competence in external relations would, in contrast to a federal union, be limited to some but not all foreign policy areas. By article 64,

> "in its international relations, the Union shall act by common action in the fields referred to in this Treaty where it has exclusive or concurrent competence."

Article 66 goes further in that it allows for wide and successive extensions of Community competence where the states work together through one of their number as their representative:

> "The Union shall conduct its international relations by the method of co-operation where Article 64 of this Treaty is not applicable and where they involve:
> —matters directly concerning the interests of several Member States of the Union,
> —or fields in which the Member States acting individually cannot act as efficiently as the Union,
> —or fields where a policy of the Union appears necessary to supplement the foreign policies pursued on the responsibility of the Member States,
> —or matters relating to the political and economic aspects of security."

As the rapporteur for this part of the treaty, Derek Prag, has written, this attempt merely to set down the status quo in external relations was a defeat in the institutional committee inflicted by the pragmatists on the federalists (Lodge, 1986, p. 104). There is certainly no intention to establish a group of states as constituting a separate category in international law. . . . On the other hand, objectives of a treaty enable lawyers to legitimize policies as contributing to agreed ends in the sense of a framework treaty for a developing Union.

PART TWO

In his chapter on composite states, Henry Sidgwick's concern was not originality but finding criteria to distinguish confederation from a federal union on the one hand and an alliance on the other.

> "By a 'confederation', however, I shall here mean a union of states designed to be permanent; and if states unite for permanent common action in important matters, they are likely to establish a common organ having power to make decisions of importance in respect of common action."

It is interesting that Sidgwick at the end of the last century differs from earlier authors by choosing the phrase, 'important matters'. This allows for the possibility that important matters might include other matters than the obvious purpose of joint defence against a larger neighbour. He goes on to say that other common organs are likely to be created for the judicial settlement of disputes within the union, and for determining common expenses. It is the existence of a common organ which distinguishes a union from an alliance. If we consider NATO as a current example of an alliance, it has an organization but no common organ for deciding the crucial question for a military alliance of peace and war. In the event of an attack, each signatory is obliged by Article V of the North Atlantic Treaty only to take "such action as it deems necessary".

On the other hand, a union of states is distinguished from a federation by two criteria, one international and one domestic. In contrast to a federation, the states of a union retain a "substantial amount of independence in their relations with foreigners". Secondly, citizens in a union have a "habit of undivided allegiance to the government of the part-state".

The European Community seems to fit this useful, well-established if imprecise category of a composite state which is less than a federal union but more than an alliance. . . . In particular, by contracting to act as one in certain spheres, the states confer on the union an original capacity to act akin to that possessed by the sovereign state. Unlike a federal central government however, this decisive power rests not with a single government but with state representatives in the Council. In comparison with other examples of confederation, the disunity of the Community's central government is made worse in that the ministers representing the states are not permanent but change according to the subject-matter requiring joint decision. Also, their authority has been weakened by the creation of the Council of the heads of state or government, and by the variety of modes in which the Community is represented externally—by the Presidency country of the Council for the time being, by the Commission acting on a mandate from the Council, and the so-called mixed mode whereby both the Commission and the Member States separately legitimize acts to which the Community is committed. Nevertheless the "European Economic Community is an economic confederation, standing in line of descent from the economic provisions included in the Constitution of the American Union, the Zollverein established in 1834, and the Benelux Union of 1948" (p. 183). . . .

PART THREE

The normal role of a state at an international organization is either that of an observer or a participant. When third parties treat with the Community, however, their normal role is that of negotiator as though the Community were a state. Unlike their delegations to the agencies of the UN, delegations to the Community are not called observer missions by third states. On the other hand, unlike their delegations to states with a unitary government, in the case of the EC they may deal directly with the governments of Member States and seek to exploit the fragmentation of the market due to variable national aids and the like.

This would be easiest to demonstrate with respect to bilateral diplomacy especially on an ad hoc basis where the content of the negotiation was mainly a matter of exclusive competence for the Community negotiating through the Commission or where the states agreed to act collectively through the Presidency country. The pattern of high-level discussions established by the United States and Canada, in which diplomatic privileges were granted unilaterally to the Community, could be shown to have been reluctantly followed by Australia after 1976, and by Japan and Korea as protectionism on their products took on more of a Community than a national dimension. The Commercial Policy Instrument of 1984 symbolized this development. . . .

It would also be possible to argue that in multilateral agreements the convoluted attempts to involve the Community in anterooms, in appendices and declarations, in periphrases about regional economic integration organizations or groups of states, amount to a recognition that the Community has to be included as a state-like actor in its own right. I doubt if this could be demonstrated conclusively. Yet it is interesting that despite the hostility of UNCTAD and the disagreements among Member States on how to respond to UNCTAD, it is in the more recent commodity agreements that Community membership and participation as of right has been most firmly accepted.

I am not going to make such a case in detail here, but I shall concentrate instead on the argument that it is the saliency of the Community to the outside world that has made it necessary for other states to deal with it in practice as a state-like union rather than as an organization. This saliency is easy to understand in view of the size of its internal market. The Common External Tariff, the Common Commercial policy, and the Common Agricultural Policy affect the hundred-odd trading nations who are represented in Brussels.

Specifically, the enlargement of the Community to the North led to negotiations with the non-joining EFTA countries and Finland whose effect was to create an enormous and wealthy industrial free trade area. To safeguard their commercial interests, each EFTA country had to sign a treaty with the Community. In each case a bilateral committee secures conformity with Community competition policy, or rules of origin, or rules on technological co-operation, which have been determined by internal Community procedures which EFTA countries could at best only influence indirectly through a sympathetic Member State. In joining the new industrial free trade area, the ex-EFTA countries could not regard themselves as joining an international organization of which they were equal partners. They were being associated with a bloc. Secondly, enlargement extended the area of the Common Agricultural Policy, thereby increasing the asymmetrical dependence of the Community's Mediterranean neighbours on the single Community market. Since these countries could not seriously influence the development of that policy from outside, they had a strong economic incentive to negotiate accession in the case of Greece, Iberia, and Turkey, or at least to negotiate agreements which would equalize access and enable them rather than the Community to benefit from higher prices on their permitted exports. . . . The creation of a Common Fisheries Policy interested other countries, including Canada and the Soviet Union. Enlargement also increased the significance of Part Four of the Treaty of Rome for ex-colonial countries and their competitors. . . . All agricultural exporters are affected by the Community's export subsidies in third markets as well as by the detail of the Common Organization of Markets.

The protectionism of the 1970s was an important factor in the development of Community external relations. The increased importance of non-tariff barriers to trade implies that internal policies, with respect to the environment, health and other standards, are of interest to third countries. The external negotiation of agreements limiting trade in textiles, steel and chemicals, for example, became Community matters. The 1982 and 1984 negotiations on access to the United States' steel market raised the question of partial success with respect to the Treaty of Paris in practical form. This was because the Germans had both negotiated separately with the Americans and then threatened to sign a bilateral agreement. Yet they did not carry out their threat, remaining loyal to a Community agreement of December 1984 in which they were outvoted by a majority. This agreement was negotiated by two Commissioners who had unilaterally denounced the 1982 agreement (Brewin & McAllister, 1985). The development of the Community steel regime therefore might be viewed as leading to the conclusion of agreements by the Commission representing a Union, which has then allocated the Community quota among the states. This evidence is typically not conclusive, because the German threat envisaged the possibility of states negotiating unilaterally. It remains possible, therefore, to hold that the states retain sovereignty, even while transferring competence to the Community. This was the Delphic decision of the French Conseil Constitutionel of 30 December, 1976. Where the bloc character of the Community is not represented by the Commission alone, it has become represented by the sharing of powers between the states and the Commission. The GATT standards code was signed jointly by the Member States and the Community, even though there is no evidence that any third states would not recognize the Community as sufficiently representative. . . .

This is not to say that every common approach is adequate to the situation. Initially, the oil crisis exposed the inadequacy of the Community as a bloc as they were torn apart by Washington's counter-proposals to the French Energy Agency. The Community's limitations were further demonstrated by the Euro-Arab dialogue and lack of follow-up to the Venice Declaration of 1980.

But the sheer weight of the Community as a trader made it one of the Big Three in the GATT of which it was not formally a member. The significance of Community participation in GATT negotiations and committees is not so much that European protectionism was thereby less than it might have been. It is rather that by 1980 it could block the USA, transforming the GATT from an American hegemony to a balance of power situation. The USA kept the initiative as the principal locutor of both the Japanese and the Europeans, but its proposals to beef up the rules on agriculture and include services depended on the Community's acquiescence. The decision to hold ministerial talks in 1986 was made after American bilateral negotiations with the Japanese and the Community. The strength of the Community in the GATT has also been shown in the ease with which it unilaterally imposed a change in the rules over butter pricing. It undercut the price of £1200 a tonne with a matching offer of butter stored for over eighteen months at

£400 a tonne, a derogation which the GATT accepted under the guise of extending it to all exporters.

The most surprising acknowledgement of the status of the Community was the invitation to the Commission President to attend the Williamsburg economic and other subsequent summits. It is surprising in that the Community has few macro-economic powers, although within Europe its conditional lending has been substituted for that from the IMF. The invitation presumably reflected the Community's separate importance as a trading power, for the Community has not been invited to attend meetings of the financial Group of Seven, and the Commission was only an observer at the International Energy Agency.

For their part, the Member States themselves were forced to move away from the narrowly restrictive role to which they had assigned the Community at the Law of the Sea Conference, thereby raising the constitutional issue we are discussing here. As with other UN matters, the states initially took the view that they alone would take part and not the Community as such. Under Council rules, on matters of an economic nature or which are likely to affect common policies, the Member States consult among themselves and speak through the Member State holding the Presidency of the Council. The Legal Affairs Committee of the Parliament and the Commission took the view that for the Member States to act alone, whether separately or collectively, was illegal given the hybrid nature of the subject-matter under discussion (European Parliament, 1982). They were helped by two developments over the nine years of negotiations. The Community agreed the common rules of its Fisheries policy and, as the scope of the negotiations unfolded, it became clearer that the proposed Convention could affect other Community policies. It followed that the observer status accorded to the Commission was insufficient and that, at the very least, it should have been included in the delegation of the Presidency country. Third states accepted the contention that the Community status was at variance with its real powers and at the request of the EC attached Annexe 9 under which an international organization (sic) can sign and accede to the Convention provided that a majority of its Member States have done likewise. The Council in turn accepted in 1982 that the Community should sign the Final Act. In 1984 it acceded, also thereby incidentally enabling Germany as a non-signatory to continue to influence the arrangements through the Community. . . .

In terms of traditional foreign policy, the Community in the 1970s has moved a little towards the concept of confederation. . . . Enlargement to Greece and Spain has a strong political motivation. . . .

From this external perspective the Community appears as more than the sum of bargains such as are struck in the GATT, the ICAO, or in NATO. It appears to have a confederal unity in its negotiations with prospective Members, with Northern industrial countries, with Southern Mediterranean countries, with the Lomé countries and insofar as its members wish to follow a different line on the Soviet Union than that of their alliance leader. The Community has more than a distinct negotiating position on such matters as agricultural exports and food aid, fishing, chemicals, steel and textiles, in GATT rounds generally and with respect to complaints brought to the GATT or complaints about export credits in UNCTAD. The Community has replaced the Member States in that it has the leading role in these matters, whether expressed through the Commission as in the GATT, or through the Presidency country as in UNCTAD, and with respect to ASEAN, the Andean Pact or the Contadora group. On another group of issues, pollution in the North Sea and the Mediterranean (Barcelona Convention and protocols), oil storage, economic sanctions, economic summitry and bilateral informal talks with other leading traders, the Community has an important and distinct role which has not replaced that of the Member States. One might here mention a further group of economic issues where the Community has a potential external role—control of atmospheric pollution, the effective taxation of multinational corporations, and civil aviation. . . .

What all this activity does show is that the Community's importance as an actor is a consequence as much of its actions as of its legal powers. It has been the creation of a huge internal market which has made it increasingly difficult to treat the Community as an instrumental international organization. This has been the principal reason why, particularly in the decade of the 1970s, third states have negotiated directly with the Community as an autonomous actor. . . .

BIBLIOGRAPHY

Allen D. & Wessels W. eds. (1982), *European Political Co-operation* (London: Butterworth). Bieber, R. et al (1985), *An Ever-Closer Union* (Luxembourg: Office for Official Publications).

Brewin C. & McAllister R. (1985), *Annual review of the Activities of the European Communities, 1984* (London: UACES).

Close G. (1982), 'Self-restraint by the EEC in the exercise of its external powers' in *Yearbook of European Law*, 1982, p. 60.

European Parliament (1982), Doc 1—793/82.

Forsyth M. (1981), *Unions of States* (Leicester: Leicester University Press).

Groux J. & Manin P. (1985), *The European Communities in the International Order* (Luxembourg: Office for Official Publications).

Hassner P. (1973), *Europe in the Age of Negotiation* (London: Sage).

Hill C. (ed.) (1983), *National Foreign Policies and European Political Cooperation* (London: Allen & Unwin).

Hill C. & Wallace W. (1979), 'Diplomatic trends in the European Community' *International Affairs*, Vol. 55 No. 1, January 1979.

Lodge J. (ed.) (1986), *European Union* (London: Macmillan).

O'Connell D. (1963), 'State succession and the effect upon treaties of entry' in *British Yearbook of International Law*, 1963, pp. 54–132.

Pelkmans J. (1980), 'Economic theories of integration revisited' in *Journal of Common Market Studies*, Vol. XVIII, No. 4, June 1980.

Pescatore P. (1979), 'External relations in the case-law of the Court of Justice of the European Communities' in *Common Market Law Review*, November, 1979, pp. 615–647.

Schwarze J. (1985), 'Towards a European foreign policy—legal aspects' given at the Europa Instituut, Amsterdam, 12 December, 1985, p. 3.

Shlaim A. & Yannopoulos G. (eds.) (1986), *The EEC and the Mediterranean Countries* (Cambridge: Cambridge University Press).

Steenbergen J. (1985), 'Legal instruments and external industries of the E.C.' given at the Europa Instituut, Amsterdam, 12 December, 1985.

Weiler J. (1982), 'Community, member-states and European integration: is the law relevant?' in *Journal of Common Market Studies,* special edition, 1982.

Wellenstein E. (1979), *25 Years of European External Relations* (Luxembourg: Office for Official Publications).

Thinking About the European Future: The Uses of Comparison

Alberta M. Sbragia

... The European Community is not a political entity that is easily understood. Unique in its institutional structure, it is neither a state nor an international organization. The lack of the normal political lubricants, such as transnational political parties, renders the Community, to use Helen Wallace's words, "a part-formed political system.". . . [1]

Given the current institutional structure, the issue of how much national governments should shape Community policymaking rests at the heart of debates about the long-term future of the Community. As the Community institutions (propelled by the decisions taken at Maastricht in December 1991) take on responsibility for an increasing number of policy competences, as the European Parliament presses for an ever-stronger role in the structure of governance, as the European Court of Justice continues to exercise judicial review, and as the institutional challenges posed by future enlargement become clearer, so the role of national governments in Community decisionmaking will be constantly debated. As the "nation-state" truly becomes the "member state" in the post-Maastricht Community, it is the fate of national governments that will shape the Community's political future.

Is it possible to "federalize" the Community significantly while retaining a key policymaking role for national governments? This chapter considers some relevant ideas about comparative federalism, which may help in thinking about some of the critical issues in future institution building. Since territory is central to federal arrangements, the chapter focuses on the implications for Community governance of the Community's strong territorial dimension. In particular, it outlines the conflict between the representation of territory and the representation of voters as a crucial element in the debate over the appropriate decisionmaking role of national governments.

FEDERALISM IN COMPARATIVE CONTEXT

. . . The debate over an appropriate role for national governments in decisionmaking is linked to the issue of making the Community somehow accountable to the electorate so that it is rendered more democratic. A federal structure, based on a "citizens' Europe," stands as the alternative to a Europe of nation-states. The question of how to balance the weight of the national governments and that of the "European electorate" is central to the debate about institutional power. In addressing this balance, the future institutional architecture of the Community will be making a statement about how democracy is defined within the Community.

The striking feature of the debate about the future institutional shape of the Community is the way in which the participants use the terms "federalism" or "federal.". . .

Although the academic literature on the subject often argues that federalism as such has common constitutional characteristics, actual federations vary significantly in how they organize the power of constituent units within the overall framework of power in the system.[2] Further, the widespread federalization of once unitary systems introduces still more variation in any possible definition of federalism. Using the United States as the referent for debates about federalism, therefore, obscures the dynamism, the complexities, and the strikingly wide range of potentially federalist institutional arrangements. . . .

Missing from the current political and scholarly debate is an appreciation of the various institutional arrangements possible under federalism. Further, there is a lack of acknowledgment of the "silent dialogue" that has gone on among the founders of federations and that accounts for the uniqueness of each system in the way it deals with the claims of territory. That self-consciousness about designing institutions in response to the problem of territory makes the study of federations useful in thinking about the Community's future.

For example, the American, Canadian, and Australian founders of their respective federations deliberately designed institutions in reaction to models of which they disapproved. Negative models (often imperfectly understood) were important in these attempts at institutional design. J. W. Schulte Nordholt concludes that, in the American case, "the Founding Fathers, especially James Madison, studied the Dutch past and used it, or better, rejected it, for their own purposes.". . . [3]

The Canadian Fathers of Confederation, for their part, rejected what they understood as the American model of federalism. The Australians in turn rejected Canada's model.[4] In Canada and Australia, however, the wishes of the founders were contradicted by the evolution of the respective systems. Canada, designed to have a strong national government, is now "one of the most decentralized operative federations in the world," while Australia, which "knowingly emphasized states rights," is now comparatively centralized.[5] Self-consciousness about designing institutions does not ensure they will evolve as planned. . . .

THE PROBLEM OF NATIONAL GOVERNMENTS

The dichotomy pervading much European debate on the future of the Community is evident in Christopher Tugendhat's discussion of the tensions within the Community: "Federalism and intergovernmentalism, supranationalism and cooperation between different nationalities: two different concepts of Europe . . . have been vying with each other since the earliest days of the Community."[6] Typically, federal arrangements have been viewed as being in opposition to "intergovernmentalism"—the two are seen as mutually exclusive. In that vein, integration within the Community is assumed to be correlated with the weakening of the role of national governments.

In both neofunctionalist and federalist analysis, a strengthening of a center or of the general power has become linked to the subordination, the weakening, of the current member states' powers, a ceding of sovereignty by the states. In both models, the Community's institutions would be strong to the extent they were insulated from the reach of national governments. Neofunctionalist theory, for example, gradually came to be understood as positing that a supranational government would gradually take over many of the powers of the national government. In federal models, a center, acting independently of its constituent units, takes over certain functions even if those units retain significant powers. The federal government is sovereign in its domain as specified by a constitution establishing the federation.

Under both models, sovereign institutions in the new entity will be sovereign precisely because they are independent of the control of the constituent units' governments. They are responsible to voters rather than to governments. An entity in which sovereign "general" institutions do not exist is assumed to be simply a confederal body.

The building of European institutions, therefore, has been conceptualized as an enterprise in which national governments had to be circumvented, weakened, or otherwise displaced from their preeminent place. Both pro- and anti-integrationists have identified the representation of the Community interest with the Commission and, more recently, with the European Parliament, not with those institutions representing national interests such as the Council of Ministers and the European Council. The Community is thought to be strong to the extent that its policies transcend the collectivity of national interests, and the strength of the Commission has been seen as a rough approximation of the likelihood of such transcendence occurring.

A strong Community has not been envisaged as involving the assertive representation of the institutional self-interests of each member government. Similarly, a situation like the present one in which each national government shares power *with other national governments* rather than have power exercised over them by a political center does not constitute integration as originally imagined. Founders of the Community such as Jean Monnet wanted far more than the "joint exercise of pooled sovereignty."

. . . The Commission does have some powers normally attributed to a center. Yet the national governments have, through the use of qualified majority voting, accepted the sharing of power with one another rather than with the Commission. Integration has thus proceeded through the willingness of national governments to submit to one another—not to the Commission. The supposed motor of European integration has not been allowed to displace national prerogatives.

The successful protection by national governments of their collective role has led those committed to further integration to regard national governments as necessarily part of the problem and not part of the solution. Governments are especially problematic because the electorate is conspicuous by its absence. The European Parliament is the ultimate check on executive power only insofar as that power is manifested in the Commission. The member states, acting in the Council of Ministers, are consequently the ultimate decisionmakers. Introducing qualified majority voting under the Single European Act has not changed, constitutionally, the *collective* weight of the nation-state.[7] Even after Maastricht the Parliament will depend on the Commission and the Council of Ministers for much of its policy impact.

Why did many scholars interested in the phenomenon of integration misjudge the power of national governments? I would argue that they underestimated the importance of both the fact that the Community was a creature of a treaty rather than a constitution and the strength of the territorial dimension within the Community. The latter was exceptionally strong on its own as well as being mobilized and represented by national governments. . . .

The Territorial Dimension

The national governments that sign treaties are governments of a specific territorial unit. Governments, institutionally, represent the territorial cleavages in the Community that have received international recognition. Yet even if national governments as such did not exercise institutionalized strength in the Community, politics would still have a powerful territorial dimension. The legacy of the European sovereign state is that national boundaries are extraordinarily important shapers of most aspects of life. The territorial claims that national governments represent, therefore, are exceedingly strong.

It is nearly impossible to overestimate the importance of national boundaries as key organizers of political power and economic wealth within the Community.

National identity, political party organizations, party systems, partisan identity, interest groups, taxing and spending arrangements, educational systems, electoral constituencies, the internal organization of the state, executive-legislative relations, the appointment of commissioners and European Court justices, the role of the judiciary, legal systems, and administrative apparatuses are all defined by national territory.

The ties across territory are relatively weak in critical areas. Most individuals in the Community, for example, speak only their national language and thus cannot communicate across territory. Feelings of social solidarity are also constrained by national boundaries in the central area of taxation. . . .

The territorial dimension is so strong, therefore, that based on the experience of other federal systems characterized by territorial diversity, it would be felt even if sovereign Community institutions were agreed to. That is, even if national governments as such did not participate in the Community's policymaking process, Community politics would certainly be shaped, and probably dominated, by territorial considerations.[8] National boundaries would continue to matter enormously if a federal Europe were constructed.

The Impact of Treaty and Territory on Institutions

The evolution of institutions in the Community illustrates the impact of treaties and national governments. . . .

It is useful here simply to point out that the intersection between the use of treaty negotiations and the role of national governments is nowhere more present than in the agreements made at Maastricht about the EuroFed. . . . The proposed central bank is far more federal than the Federal Reserve System in the United States. Whereas national central banks will be represented in the EuroFed's governing structure, neither American governors, state banking commissioners, nor state legislatures are represented on the governing councils of the Federal Reserve. The proposed bank resembles the constitution of the Bundesbank, which is governed in such a way that all the territorial units of the German federation are formally represented. . . . The central bank agreed to at Maastricht thus will not be a sovereign institution (that is, insulated from its constituent units) in the way the American Federal Reserve is. Rather, the member governments' central banks will pool sovereignty—they will all participate in its governance. They will not cede sovereignty to a European institution that excludes their direct participation.

The effect of the territorial dimension on the European Court of Justice, the most sovereign of the Community's policymaking institutions, perhaps best illustrates the power of territorial claims even when not mobilized by national governments. . . . The Court was created by the Treaty of Rome and has come to exercise significant powers of judicial review over the laws of the member states. Yet the Court has done so by using the highest (as well as lower) national courts as its partners.

Through a procedure in which the national courts ask the European Court of Justice for preliminary references and preliminary rulings, which they then render as their own verdict, the Court has been able to impose the supremacy of Community law. Such a procedure, however, distinguishes the Court from, for example, the Supreme Court in the United States. In the Community's legal system, national judiciaries play a pivotal role in contrast to, for example, the subordinate role played by American state judiciaries.

In the United States, the Supreme Court delivers its own verdict, which is then binding on both federal and state courts. In the Community, the European Court uses the national judiciary to render its verdicts, thus harnessing the national judicial and legal order to the Court's interpretation of whether national and Community law are compatible. . . .

The Court, then, incorporates territorially based judicial systems into its decisionmaking structure in a way alien to, for example, the American system of judicial review. The Community's legal order has been constructed with the active cooperation and partnership of the national courts as opposed to their subordination.

TERRITORY VERSUS ELECTORATE

. . . The "democratic deficit" [of European institutions] is causing widespread concern among scholars and policymakers. The deficit, in the eyes of many, is due to the lack of power exercised by the European Parliament. In this view, the institution representing the individual citizens of the member-state countries does not have enough of a say in the workings of the Community. The weaknesses of the European Parliament are somewhat less than they were before the Single European Act and the decisions taken at Maastricht, but nonetheless the Parliament is too weak to provide the kind of democratic accountability conventionally implied by the term *democracy*. Further, the creation of a EuroFed . . . will make such a deficit even more striking. . . .

Analysts who give overriding importance to the representation of individuals regard the representation of the "institutional self-interests of governments"[9] as belonging to a confederation rather than to a federation. In a federal system, according to this view, a sovereign Community must by definition represent individual voters as opposed to the governments of member states. In brief, national governments are associated with confederation, while electoral representation is linked to the development of Community institutions independent of national governments. . . .

The focus on electoral representation as the pivot around which the hoped-for federal constitutional order would revolve has its roots in the desire for a political center that would anchor the corporate development of the Community. That center is not rooted in territorial cleavage and the representation of that cleavage but, in this view, is meant to transcend such divisions, to represent the European interest. . . .

From a comparative point of view, such an analysis is problematic. Territorial politics is so important in politics characterized by territorial cleavages that the representation of territorial claims is bound to be a likely feature of politics in similar contexts. Because of the role of territorial boundaries as the central organizing units of Community political and economic life, it is extremely difficult to imagine a federated Community represented. Nor is the representation that does exist in the Senate disproportionate to population. Finally, for many reasons, Canadian members of Parliament exhibit high degrees of party discipline (higher than British members of Parliament). Such party cohesion minimizes the representation of constituencies territorially defined or of the interests of provincial governments as such.

Nonetheless, finding a constitutional ally in the (British) Judicial Committee of the Privy Council during the nineteenth century, the provinces have been able to increase their powers in the Canadian system. The requirement that provincial governments must unanimously approve amendments to the Constitution (contrasted with the three-fourths majority required in the United States) has given the provinces a strong position in the federal system.

Still a different model of federalism is presented by Germany's federal system. In fact, German federalism illustrates the elasticity of federal arrangements in two important ways. First, it shows how unique institutions can be created at the national level. . . .

Second, the German federation differs from other federal systems in how power is divided among governments. . . . In the policymaking process, the federal government legislates, and the state governments implement policy. The federal level does not administer its own policies, for administration falls under the states' jurisdiction.

The power of the states in the system comes from their near monopoly in administration and, more interestingly for current purposes, from their direct participation in the decisionmaking process at the federal level. Such participation is linked to the unique system of representation that underlies the German federation. The German federal system recognizes the representation of two distinct entities—voters and governments. Voters are represented in the Bundestag, to which the executive is accountable. The state governments themselves are represented in the Bundesrat, the second chamber, which exercises an absolute veto over legislation affecting the Länder. . . .

The system of representation within the German system, therefore, differs significantly from that found in other federal systems. The German second chamber represents what Fritz Scharpf terms the "institutional self-interests"[10] of the executive branch of the Länder governments, the Länder's dominant political authority. Rather than having the members of the upper house selected either by the state legislature or by voters, the German system puts the selection process in the hands of the German states' executive. The Länder cabinets select and instruct the members of the Bundesrat.

By contrast, even when nineteenth-century American senators were chosen by state government, they were chosen by the state legislature and not by the governor. Further, the degree of instruction received from the legislature was neither high nor well enforced. Gunter Kisker concludes that "the Bundesrat speaks for the 'States as States' even more than the U.S. Senate did before 1913, when its members were elected by the state legislatures."[11]

The German model, therefore, represents an important institutional innovation in federalism and helps us to grasp how the constituent units of a system may, as institutions, participate in central decisionmaking. . . .

The German model of federalism raises an alternative to the way representation and territory are traditionally linked. Rather than considering territory as a "package" in which individual voters exercise their choice in choosing the members of sovereign institutions, the Bundesrat offers an example of an institution wielding general power in which the interests of territorial governments (defined as executives rather than legislatures) are protected by those very governments. The "general" power does not need to be thought of as separate from the power of the constituent units—the latter is integral to the construction of the former.

The representation of governments rather than individuals is so unusual that it does not fit conventional notions of democracy. Even though those governments are responsible to directly elected legislatures, indirect representation is viewed with deep suspicion by current theorists of democracy. In a similar vein, the participation of constituent units in the exercise of the general or federal power is so atypical that scholars of federalism have felt impelled to categorize it as a deviation from normal federalism.

Yet the representation of territorially based governments does provide a method of facilitating integration, of achieving federalism, without submerging the interests of the constituent units. It does offer the possibility of federalization through indirect rather than direct representation—or of combining direct and indirect representation in a way that gives the collectivity of national governments (but not individual governments) the right of absolute veto. It thus presents an alternative to models that assume that federalization must necessarily be characterized by either a supranational executive or by parliamentary sovereignty. It essentially allows one to think about the exercise of public authority without imposing a center-periphery model on such an exercise.

Although the Bundesrat is universally referred to as unique, its significance for possibilities in designing federal institutional structures has probably been underestimated. The German system offers an alternative way of conceptualizing federalism, for the Bundesrat offers an alternative way of thinking about how constituent units of a federation can participate in the work of the "center." The German system raises the possibility that, at the Community-level, a federal-type organization could operate without a center as traditionally conceptualized, so long as the national governments are willing to abide by qualified majority voting, abide by judicial review in case of disputes, allow the Commission to exercise policy leadership, and permit the Parliament to exercise some (even coequal) power. In that sense, a center could conceivably be constructed by member governments without its being detached from the collectivity of constituent units, in this case national governments. . . .

NOTES

1. Helen Wallace, "The Best Is the Enemy of the 'Could': Bargaining in the European Community," in Secondo Tarditi and others, eds., *Agricultural Trade Liberalization and the European Community* (Oxford: Clarendon Press, 1989), p. 205.
2. Arend Lijphart argues that at least a rough consensus exists in the literature on the

constitutional characteristics of federalism. The primary characteristic is "a guaranteed division of power between central and regional governments." He goes on to conclude that "five secondary characteristics of federalism can be identified: a written constitution, bicameralism, equal or disproportionately strong representation of the smaller component units in the federal chamber, decentralized government, and the right of the component units to be involved in the process of amending the federal constitution but to change their own constitutions unilaterally." Arend Lijphart, "Consociation and Federation: Conceptual and Empirical Links," *Canadian Journal of Political Science*, vol. 12 (September 1979), p. 502. Murray Forsyth, however, indicates how difficult it is to cleanly distinguish between a so-called confederation or federal union, on the one hand, and a federal state on the other. Forsyth distinguishes between a political union having a federal government and a "federal state." For example, Forsyth argues that the United States from 1789 until the Civil War was not unequivocally a federal state. Murray Forsyth, *Unions of States: The Theory and Practice of Confederation* (Leicester University Press, 1981), p. 4. . . .

3. J. W. Schulte Nordholt, "The Example of the Dutch Republic for American Federalism," in J. C. Boogman and G. N. Van der Plaat, eds., *Federalism: History and Current Significance of a Form of Government* (The Hague: Martinus Nijhoff, 1980), p. 67. . . .

4. Bruce W. Hodgins, "The Plans of Mice and Men," in Bruce W. Hodgins, Don Wright, and W. H. Heick, eds., *Federalism in Canada and Australia: The Early Years* (Waterloo, Ontario: Wilfrid Laurier University Press, 1978), p. 14.

5. Hodgins, "Plans of Mice and Men," p. 4.

6. Christopher Tugendhat, *Making Sense of Europe* (Viking, 1986), p. 71.

7. In brief, the votes of each member country are not equal—it is not a system of "one country, one vote." France, Germany, the United Kingdom, and Italy each have ten votes; the other member countries each have fewer, with Luxembourg having only two votes. For a proposal to be approved under the rules of qualified majority voting, fifty-four (out of a total of seventy-six) votes need to be cast in favor. Twenty-three negative votes are sufficient to kill the proposal. The introduction of qualified majority voting does not alter the constitutional position of the Commission in comparison with the Council of Ministers. However, it does increase the Commission's tactical position compared with the Council's because the Commission has a wider range of negotiating tactics it can use to advance its positions. It can threaten to discount the votes of a particularly obstructionist member government and can anticipate coalition behavior in its formulation of proposals presented to the Council.

8. Although it is important to remember that in the United Kingdom the centralized unitary state has indeed been able to minimize the political role of strong territorial differences, it is unlikely that the Community could develop that degree of "central" authority. For a seminal history of the territorial dimension in the United Kingdom, see Hugh F. Kearney, *The British Isles: A History of Four Nations* (Cambridge: Cambridge University Press, 1989). See also Richard Rose, *The Territorial Dimension in Government: Understanding the United Kingdom* (Chatham, NJ: Chatham House, 1982).

9. The term is used by Fritz W. Scharpf in a seminal article on the Community, one from which I have drawn liberally. Fritz W. Scharpf, "The Joint-Decision Trap: Lessons from German Federalism and European Integration," *Public Administration*, vol. 66 (Autumn 1988), p. 254.

10. Scharpf, "Joint-Decision Trap," p. 254.

11. Gunter Kisker, "The West German Federal Constitutional Court as Guardian of the Federal System," *Publius*, vol. 19 (Fall 1989), p. 37. In a similar vein, Hans-Georg Wehling states, "One could speak of the *Bundesrat* as an assembly of *Land* ambas-

sadors, but the *Land* governments cannot entrust just anyone with this task: the members of the *Bundesrat* as well as their representatives have to be members of their *Land* cabinet. . . . Because the members are subject to instructions by their *Land* government, the votes of one *Land* can only be cast as a bloc. . . . The right to vote, then, is not given to the individual members of the *Bundesrat* but to the *Länder* represented by the *Land* governments." Hans-Georg Wehling, "The Bundesrat," *Publius,* vol. 19 (Fall 1989), p. 54.

Chapter
8

Structures and Transformations

Friedrich Kratochwil

*I*n a way our discussion has come full circle. This reader began with an inquiry into the way in which international politics is organized. By focusing on the issue of international governance rather than on the activities of various international organizations, the scope of our inquiry was broadened to include regimes as well as formal institutions. To that extent, it was argued that international organization is not simply a subfield of international politics but rather a distinctive mode of inquiry. Since this orientation does not take for granted those assumptions that underlie both realism and world government approaches,[1] the concern with international governance necessarily becomes part of "critical theory" in the sense that Robert Cox refers to in his article in this chapter.

A whole host of important questions arises when order is no longer identified with the existence of hierarchy or when the organization of force is no longer the predominant explanatory factor in a theory of international politics. Beginning with such an alternative pre-theoretical understanding of politics and order has important implications for the task of building better theories. By displacing power—conceived of in terms of capabilities—from its central place in a theory of international politics, subsequent theorizing could become less parsimonious and elegant. But many of the arguments advanced by authors in earlier chapters and in the selections below suggest that the ideal of parsimony in theory building can prove doubly debilitating if not pursued with extreme caution. For example, the parsimony of structuralism eliminates the interaction between agents and structure from the set of puzzles that a theory of international relations should explain, and accords primacy to the international system. Furthermore, since structuralists usually are not concerned with the realism of their basic assumptions, but make prediction and explanation the central goals of their theories, this approach inhibits empirical analysis. After all, good predictions can often be derived from false theories. For getting a person to the moon, for predicting the positions of stars, and for determining one's position on the high seas, a "false" Newtonian or Ptolemeic theory will often suffice; but this does not demonstrate that the theory in question is correct.

Much of this reader is concerned with illuminating the complexities of the organization of international life. Instead of assuming that there is one best way of organizing (as, e.g., functionalism does), many of the organizational approaches described in this reader help the analyst to inquire into the (dis)advantages of different organizational designs for the implementation and effectiveness of regimes. In addition, by placing the question of regime effectiveness in the broader frame of both the notions of legitimacy and of epistemic agreement, the usefulness of apolitical "technical" cooperation as the paradigm for cooperation in general can be criticized and the reasons for the breakdown of technical regimes can be pinpointed. Peter Cowhey's contribution above made this point eloquently. While a regime might come under pressure when any one of these factors (technology, consensual knowledge, legitimacy) experiences change, the cumulative effects of both shifts in the patterns of consensus concerning state/market relations *and* of technologies transforms the placid environment of functional agencies into turbulent fields. Protracted negotiations are then necessary to forge a new consensus.

The approach of many papers in this reader also raises questions as to the "evolutionary" paths organizations allegedly follow in their growth/adaptation and as to the determination of the reasons for their failure and decay. Precisely because efficiencies from hierarchically structured decision making in formal organization occurs only under the conditions of highly stable environmental conditions, the efficiency and effectiveness of hierarchical organizations are more complicated than adaptation and cannot be answered by recourse to evolutionary arguments. In a rapidly changing environment, it is not the "fit" between organization and environment, but rather the spreading of risk—and that means often inefficient redundancy—that might be more advantageous. In other words, whether institutions are successful and survive does not depend on a simple fit or adjustment to a preexisting niche but rather on the (in)ability of these institutions to control or transform their environment. In any case learning and leadership are crucial elements in organizational survival. Both of these crucial problems are neglected when we view organizational activity merely as an adaptive response.

All of these arguments, in a way, reinforce the argument made by Wendt, and by Kratochwil and Ruggie in Chapter 1, that ultimately the fruitfulness of a research program depends not so much on method as on the realism[2] and richness of its "ontology." The final selections below take up many of these themes as they relate to building better theories of international politics.

David Dessler's article is perhaps the most explicit about the need for an enriched, rather than parsimonious, ontology in building theories of the international system and of the patterns of international politics. Arguing that the classical neorealist model of the international system represents a truncated understanding of structures, Dessler shows that only special cases of systemic change can be investigated by its "positional model." Furthermore, he argues that these explanations can easily be subsumed under a more general model which accounts for the co-constitution of both agents and structures and their persistence or (radical) modification.

Robert Cox's contribution begins with a Marxist materialist perspective. For Cox, what is being "organized" is not political life, national or international, not even their conjunction. For him, all organizational activity is basic to the problem of *production*. Only against this background can the distinctions of what is political and what is economic, what is in the domain of the state or of society be understood. Since the understandings and categories we use in our analyses are not neutral and immutable but constituted by this productive process, they have to be problematized in our theoretical reflections.

But different from classical Marxism (particularly Engel's version), Cox's analysis pays special attention to the power of ideas as well as their constitution of and interaction with practices. Here Gramsci's conception of "hegemony" is helpful, although it sometimes comes close to "idealism." Cox's research program begins with the social forces engendered by the production process, then examines the social formations (state-society complex), and finally investigates "world orders" (defining the problematic of war and peace for the ensemble of states). It is historically rich and analytically suggestive, linking individuals and groups with domestic structures, which, in turn, condition the system of states.

Ernst Haas takes up the question of practice from a different perspective. His concern is not the productive process but rather the decision making of actors who face the choice of (non)cooperation. This vantage point makes the framing of issues into issue-areas and the effects of interdependence upon decision makers the crucial variables. An investigation into the impact of interdependencies and of efforts linking different issues into one new "whole" (issue area) represents the main contribution of this article. Haas not only distinguishes between different styles of decision making depending on the issue-linkage; he also is able to generate challenging hypotheses about the strength of regimes and their capacity to adapt. In addition, he examines the interaction between regimes and organizations and develops a typology of organizational forms.

NOTES

1. It is an often overlooked fact that world government approaches and realism both share most of the Hobbesian premises concerning social order. They differ only in their assessment of whether or not it is "realistic" to expect the establishment of viable supranational institutions, or whether one has to be content with traditional instruments of statecraft (alliances, balancing, negative and positive sanctions) for creating order in international politics.
2. It should be clear that I use the term "realism" here in an epistemological sense and not as a descriptive label for the tenets of a particular approach to international politics.

What's at Stake in the Agent-Structure Debate?

David Dessler

. . . In this article, I seek to determine how philosophical insight might yield an empirical payoff and, specifically, to show how the metaphysical victories claimed by scientific realism over its philosophical rivals might be exploited to generate a progressive research program in the structural analysis of international politics. I take as a baseline for this analysis what in current parlance is known as the "agent-structure problem" in social theory. This problem is, strictly speaking, a philosophical one. It emerges from two uncontentious truths about social life: first, that human agency is the only moving force behind the actions, events, and outcomes of the social world; and second, that human agency can be realized only in concrete historical circumstances that condition the possibilities for action and influence its course. . . .

The remainder of this article is divided into five sections. The first section argues that a theory's *ontology* (the substantive entities and configurations the theory postulates) is both the basis of its explanatory power and the ultimate grounding of claims it may have to superiority over rival theories. Imre Lakatos's methodology of theory-choice is consistent with this conception of the link between ontology and theory. The second section assesses Waltz's approach to structural theory, termed here the *positional model.* Unlike other critiques of Waltz, the one developed here firmly differentiates between the ontology of Waltz's structural approach and the theory based on it. The positional ontology is shown to recognize only the unintended features of systemic organization. The third section of the article outlines an alternative ontology of international structure, called the *transformational model,* premised on the philosophy of scientific realism. The transformational model views structure as a means to action rather than as an environment in which action takes place. It gives central ontological position to social rules, both constitutive and regulative, intended and unintended. The fourth section offers a direct comparison of the positional and transformational models and discusses the empirical promise of a transformational research program. It also demonstrates that the positional model recognizes the structural status of unintended rules only, suppressing or ignoring the role of intended rules, and hence is incapable of generating full structural explanations of state action. Here the main thesis of the article is fully articulated: *Because the transformational model of structure provides a more comprehensive ontology than the positional model and is capable of grounding discussion of a wider range of phenomena than any positional theory, it provides a more promising basis for progressive theoretical research.* The fifth section of the article concludes that the stakes in the agent-structure debate are indeed high and that they deserve the attention of all those interested in developing explanatory theories of international politics and, in particular, theories of peaceful change.

THE RELATION BETWEEN THEORY, ONTOLOGY, AND EXPLANATORY POWER

In this section, I consider the distinction between theory and ontology and advance the scientific realist contention that ontology is the basis of a theory's explanatory power. I take "theory" to refer generally to testable explanations of observed behavior. Theory does not merely locate or describe associations between observable phenomena; it explains them. What is tested in testing a theory is not an association but the explanation of it. . . .

"Ontology" refers to the concrete referents of an explanatory discourse.[1] A theory's ontology consists of the real-world structures (things, entities) and processes posited by the theory and invoked in the theory's explanations. The ontology of a discourse constrains but does not determine correct explanations in that discourse.[2] In classical physics, the ontology consists of space, time, and matter, meaning that all the entities or processes to which a classical explanation refers are embodiments of or relations between space, time, and matter. Newton's laws, for example, refer to mass, force, and acceleration. It should be stressed that an ontology is a *structured* set of entities; it consists not only of certain designated kinds of things but also of connections or relations between them. . . . In international relations theory, the statement "A system consists of a structure and interacting units" represents an ontological claim.

According to scientific realism, theories explain by showing how phenomena are products or aspects of an underlying ontology.[3] For example, a fever is explained as a by-product of the biochemical processes induced by a virus in the body. . . . A theory's explanatory power comes from its ability to *reduce* independent phenomena—that is, to show how apparently unconnected phenomena are actually products of a common ontology.[4] Biochemical explanations of disease are powerful because they show how apparently independent symptoms and signs are co-products of a single underlying process. For example, a cough and fever (among other clinical signs) are shown to be common aspects of, say, influenza. In this case, reduction is achieved by showing how independent phenomena—symptoms and signs that could and do appear independently in other circumstances, such as cough, fever, muscular aches, and so on—are features of a given ontological process (the workings of a virus). . . .

In general, the greater the number of independent phenomena a theory reduces, the better that theory is. That is, the richer and more comprehensive the underlying ontology, the better the theory. Newton's physics showed there was a connection between the variables in the law of free fall and Kepler's laws, thus reducing (ontologically uniting) terrestrial and planetary phenomena. The fall of an apple and the orbit of the moon, previously considered entirely unrelated phenomena, became just two examples of how collections of atoms behave when subject to gravity.[5] Einstein's general theory of relativity unified temporal, spatial, gravitational, and dynamical phenomena within a single ontological framework.[6] Indeed, one reason relativity theory earned widespread acceptance even before much experimental support had been collected was its ability to reduce many more independent phenomena than classical mechanics could. This feature of relativity theory was not one simply of correspondence with the facts; what made the theory convincing was not only that it explained well but also that it explained so many different phenomena within one ontological framework. The lesson is that theories which reduce more independent phenomena are, *ceteris paribus,* preferable to those which reduce fewer.[7]

This conclusion converges with important arguments advanced by Lakatos in his studies of the methodology of theory-choice in science. Lakatos is critical of the methodology of "naive falsificationism," which involves simple tests of a given theory against the empirical record at a given point in time. Lakatos argues, first, that a theory is not to be evaluated alone against the evidence, holding it up against arbitrary standards of parsimony, elegance, power, and so on. Instead, it is properly evaluated only in comparison to other theories, in terms of standards not exogenously imposed but generated through the process of comparison itself.[8] Second, Lakatos argues that theories should be assessed not at a single point in time but in dynamic profile as part of an ongoing research program. Research programs are to be evaluated in terms of their ability to generate, in ongoing studies, increasingly powerful explanations from a stable core of standards and assumptions. In sum, according to Lakatos, theory-choice is both *comparative* and *dynamic.* . . .

THE POSITIONAL MODEL OF INTERNATIONAL STRUCTURE

Waltz's ontological model of the international system is based on an explicit analogy with economics. . . . "International-political systems, like economic markets, are individualist in origin, spontaneously generated, and unintended."[9] This statement suggests a fundamental ontological distinction between structure at one level of the international system and interacting units at another.[10] Waltz develops a number of terms to describe these levels and their differences. Structure refers to the "arrangement," "positioning," "organization," or "situation" of the units in the system. The units, which can be characterized and differentiated by their "attributes" or "properties," exhibit "interactions," "interconnections," and "relations" in their actions or behavior. Corresponding to the ontological distinction between the arrangement of units and their interaction is an epistemological distinction between systemic and reductionist theories.[11] A systems-level theory shows how "the organization of units affects their behavior and their interactions," while reductionist theories "explain international outcomes through elements and combinations of elements located at the national or subnational level." . . . [12]

Ontologically, then, structure is viewed as the unintended positioning, standing, or organization of units that emerges spontaneously from their interaction. To describe and understand structure—the initial step in constructing a theory of international politics—we must be careful to distinguish it, Waltz insists, from the underlying behavior of the units. We must separate the *interaction* of units from their *arrangement*. Both features, Waltz notes, might be described by the term "relation," but only the latter is permitted in a definition of structure: ". . . To define a structure requires ignoring how units relate with one another (how they interact) and concentrating on how they stand in relation to one another (how they are arranged or positioned)."[13] The arrangement of units, unlike their attributes and interaction, "is a property of the system," not of the units.[14] Therefore, while the attributes and interactions of states must be confined to the unit-level, Waltz argues, the arrangement of those states is properly considered a systemic feature.

It is important to stress that according to this ontology, structure refers only to the spontaneously formed, unintended conditions of action generated by the coactivity of separable units. Structure is, so to speak, a by-product rather than a product of interaction. Not only is it unintended, but it is essentially impervious to attempts to modify it or control its effects. . . . In sum, the positional model views structure as those conditions of action that are (1) spontaneous and unintended in origin, (2) irreducible to the attributes or actions of individual units, and (3) impervious to attempts to change them or escape their effects.

Having outlined the ontology of his approach, Waltz begins the move from model to theory, from a description of the ontology of structure to a theoretical definition of it. We know what structure *is*—the unintended arrangement, organization, or positioning of units in a system—but we have not yet determined how best to describe it and deploy it in causal explanation. . . .

Waltz directs us to three questions about the configuration of units in the system, the answers to which he offers as a tripartite theoretical definition of structure.[15] (1) What is the principle by which the parts of a system are arranged? In the international system, it is anarchy. (2) What functions are specified for the units? The functions of states are not formally differentiated. (3) What is the distribution of capabilities across the units of the system? In the international system, bipolar and multipolar distributions exhaust recent historical experience. Waltz then argues that because states are functionally similar, "the second part of the definition drops out" in characterizing systems change[16]; hence, international structures are to be defined and compared according to two basic dimensions of state placement: anarchy and the distribution of power.

Waltz's structural theory is meant to explain recurring patterns of actions and outcomes in the interstate system.[17] The persistence of interstate war is attributed to anarchy, and the enduring stability of the postwar international order is attributed to the bipolar distribution of power.[18] Waltz also links structure to specific actions and outcomes. For example, the American–Soviet arms race after World War II, peace within postwar Europe, China's intervention in the Korean War, and Soviet negotiations with Germany in the 1920s and 1930s are all claimed by Waltz to be specific consequences of the workings of structure in international politics.[19] How are we to assess these claims? . . . Lakatos insists that these questions must be answered not through simple appeal to the evidence but, rather, in terms of comparisons with a rival approach. This rival approach, rooted in scientific realism, must first be explicated.

THE TRANSFORMATIONAL MODEL OF INTERNATIONAL STRUCTURE

The Ontology of Society According to Scientific Realism

The scientific realists' agent-structure solution, as described by Roy Bhaskar, starts from a simple premise—namely, that "all [social] activity presupposes the prior existence of social forms."

> Thus consider *saying, making,* and *doing* as characteristic modalities of human agency. People cannot communicate except by utilizing existing media, produce except by applying themselves to materials which are already formed, or act save in some or other context. Speech requires language; making materials; actions conditions; agency resources; activity rules. . . . [S]ociety is a necessary condition for any intentional human act at all.[20]

"Structure" refers, in this ontology, to the social forms that preexist action, these forms being conceived as analogous to language. Social structure stands in relation to social action as language stands in relation to discourse (speech and writing). . . .

According to [this] transformational model, action is to be viewed by the social scientist as speech is viewed by the linguist: as the skilled accomplishment of actors utilizing the available media through which action becomes possible. The primitive entities comprising this ontology are actors, actions, and the materials for action (in contrast to the positional ontology, which consists of actors, actions, and the arrangement of actors). The transformational model suggests two important connections between action and the materials (structure) presumed by it. First, structure both enables action and constrains its possibilities. Second, structure is the outcome as well as the medium of action. Consider the language model. As a set of semantic and syntactic rules, language is the medium making communication possible; at the same time, it constrains the ways in which that communication can be effected. The rules of language make it possible to speak sensibly, and they put limits on what counts as sensible speech. Furthermore, language is not only the medium of discourse—being drawn upon and instantiated in speaking and writing—but it is also the outcome of that discourse, being "carried" through space and time by its usages. Thus, all social action presupposes social structure, and vice versa. An actor can act socially only because there exists a social structure to draw on, and it is only through the actions of agents that structure is reproduced (and, potentially, transformed). . . .

The structural relation between part and whole, which in the positional model reflects the distinction between units and their arrangement, becomes in the transformational view akin to the relation between message and code or between speech and language. Note the particular conception of structural causality the latter approach implies. Again, the language analogy is useful. The English language does not cause or bring about discourse in the way that a spark, stimulus, or vector force causes resultant behavior. Rather, it affects action by enabling certain possibilities of discourse and disabling or excluding others. In Aristotelian terms, structure is a *material cause* rather than an *efficient cause* of behavior.

Structure alone explains only the possibilities (and impossibilities) of action.[21] As with the positional approach or any other structural model, a transformational explanation cannot alone explain outcomes. Structure cannot provide a complete explanation of action any more than the English language completely explains a given use of it or any more than the material from which a statue is crafted completely explains the statue itself. A complete explanation must appeal not only to the material but also the efficient causes of action, which can be located only within a theory of the agents.

The starting point of the scientific realist approach to international structural theory is therefore the recognition that state action is possible and conceivable only if there exist the instruments through which that action can in fact be carried out. Two sorts of instruments or media of action are necessary.[22] First, nations must have *resources*, the physical attributes that comprise "capability." A military strategy requires military forces; monetary policy, financial instruments; trade policy, the goods and physical infrastructure of trade; and so on. Second, nations must have available *rules*, the media through which they communicate with one another and coordinate their actions. For policy not only relies upon physical capability, but it also requires a framework of meaning through which use of that capability becomes recognizable as policy (as intended, meaningful behavior) and through which these intended meanings can form the basis for patterned state interaction. The importance of resources is acknowledged in the positional model, which defines "arrangement" in terms of the distribution of capability. But the role of rules in state action remains untheorized in that approach, and therefore some initial remarks toward a theory of rules would be appropriate at this point.

Constitutive and Regulative Rules

The notion of "rule" occupies a central spot in the ontology of the transformational model. . . .

A rule is, in its most basic sense, an understanding about how to proceed or "go on" in given social circumstances. . . . [Rules] are "procedures of actions, aspects of praxis" that "appl[y] over a range of contexts and occasions" and "allow for the methodical continuation of an established sequence."[23] Now this is necessarily a broad definition, not least because it must encompass at least two types of rules, constitutive and regulative.[24] *Regulative rules* prescribe and proscribe behavior in defined circumstances. As John Searle notes, they "regulate antecedently or independently existing forms of behavior; for example, many rules of etiquette regulate interpersonal relationships which exist independently of the rules."[25] Traffic laws, building fire codes, and the requirements set down in an arms control treaty all exemplify the regulative dimension of rules. The penalty for not following such rules typically involves some sort of sanctioning behavior on the part of another. *Constitutive rules*, on the other hand, "create or define new forms of behavior."[26] The rules of chess, for example, define an activity by setting down explanations of what counts as a move of the knight, what constitutes a checkmate, and so on. Not to follow constitutive rules is to make oneself misunderstood or incomprehensible—to perform a social action incorrectly or to fall outside the boundaries of a meaningful "form of life."[27] Constitutive rules take the form, "X counts as Y in context C," while regulative rules fit the form, "Do X in context C."

Although I will continue here with the well-established practice of considering constitution and regulation as products of two different types of rule, it is worth noting that constitutive rules have regulative implications, and vice versa. . . .[28] To be following constitutive rules is to participate in a form of life, to make oneself understood according to the structure of meanings that defines action in that realm. . . .

The constitutive/regulative typology can be applied usefully in the analysis of international structure. Constitutive rules, which I will also term here "conventions," are standardized, relatively unchanging practices that constitute a "vocabulary" (a stock of meaningful actions, or signs) for international communication. Conventions enable signals of support, opposition, hostility, friendship, condemnation, indifference, commitment, resignation, and so on.[29] For example, military exercises can be timed and located either to signal a nation's commitment to supporting a specific policy or outcome or to signal its hostility or opposition to the policies of another nation.[30] Conventions include verbal as well as "physical" practices. . . .

Regulative rules are defined here as public claims, backed by sanctions, that prescribe, proscribe, or permit specified behavior for designated actors in defined circumstances. Such rules take the form, "Actor A should do X in context C." They are backed by sanctions and thus are to be distinguished from mere regularities or routines. The internality of sanctions to rules implies a division between followers (or violators) and enforcers of rules—the "targets" and "sources" of sanctioning behavior. The dynamics of rule-making bind followers and enforcers together in a relationship which, though usually asymmetrical, constrains in both directions.

Rules need not be stated explicitly. Cohen introduces an important distinction between *tacit* and *formal* regulative rules, which he conceives on a continuum: "At one end of the spectrum are found rules arrived at by tacit agreement and which are not directly negotiated either in writing or by word of mouth. At the other end of the spectrum are rules deriving from formal negotiations and expressed in formal, binding agreement. In between are rules of the game contained in the 'spirit' of formal agreements, verbal 'gentlemen's' agreements, and 'nonbinding,' though written, understandings.". . . [31]

COMPARING THE POSITIONAL AND TRANSFORMATIONAL MODELS

The Positional Model's Implicit Reliance on Social Rules

The transformational model's focus on rules may suggest that it is best suited to the study of a certain type of conduct—namely, institutional conduct—while the positional model is more appropriate for the study of interaction within anarchy. For is the interstate system not uniquely the political realm in which rules have little, if any, role to play in determining behavior? . . . However, to the scientific realist, this conclusion is misplaced. Scientific realism insists that *all* social action depends on the preexistence of rules, implying that even under anarchy, rules are an essential prerequisite for action.[32] It asserts the impossibility and inconceivability of social behavior without rules; the issue of whether a centralizing authority exists or not is beside the point. Rules are, in the transformational model, both logically and praxiologically necessary for social action. . . . The positional theory is a case in point. Structure is defined there only as anarchy and a distribution of power. But, clearly, anarchy and power distribution cannot alone and in themselves lead to any behavior. Some link between this environment and the realm of action is needed. Here the concept of rationality is introduced. As Keohane points out, "The link between system structure and actor behavior is forged by the rationality assumption, which enables the theorist to predict that leaders will respond to the incentives and constraints imposed by their environments.". . . [33]

The scientific realist would stress that the rationality assumption brings rules into the explanatory framework without acknowledging them as such. According to the transformational model, if it is true that the international imperative is survival, it is also true that knowing how to survive means knowing the rules of the game. For example, a nation in a position of declining power may act rationally by allying itself with other powers. This rational action presumes the existence of the rules of interstate communication and coordination utilized in any treaty-making process. Rationality is thus not merely an assumption about the *manner* in which nations calculate and act; it is also an assumption about the *means* through which those actions are carried out. The rationality assumption in the positional model thus presupposes the existence of rules in international relations. Structure must consist of something more than anarchy and the distribution of power. It must also encompass the media through which rational action is effected.

A brief example from Waltz's work illustrates this important point. Waltz puts great emphasis on the notions of competition and socialization, two "pervasive processes" that "encourage similarities of attributes and of behavior."[34] To show how structure molds behavior through socialization, Waltz gives the example of Soviet behavior just after the Russian Revolution. . . .

. . . [But] what are the units socialized *to,* if not (at a minimum) understandings of conventions? If Waltz's theory did not presume the existence of a set of rules constitutive of "the system" to which nations are socialized, it could not explain how state behavior is constrained by structure. What compelled the Soviets to take action so similar to that of other states, even though it was at odds with their own ideology, was, in Waltz's terms, the rationally directed motive to survive in an anarchic realm. But this is just a shorthand for saying that the Soviets, having recognized the precariousness of their security position, resorted to use of the existing system of conventions through which great powers communicate and negotiate with one another, and they were thus able to bolster their security position by making deals with foreign powers. Waltz sees as evidence of the Soviets' socialization the deals undertaken with "that other pariah power and ideological enemy, Germany."[35] The scientific realist would stress that such deals can be made only between nations who can communicate, who draw on a shared set of constitutive rules with which alliances can be forged and through which they gain meaning. Without at least an implicit presumption of such rules, no sense can be made of rationality in international relations, and no bridge can be forged theoretically between positional structure and action.

Thus, the difference between the transformational and positional ontologies is not that one recognizes the existence of rules and the other does not. Both models recognize the efficacy of rules in international politics, and theories based on either model must appeal to the existence of rules, even if only implicitly. The difference between these ontologies lies in their conception of the *relation* between rules and action. In the positional ontology, rules (conventions and norms) are fixed parameters of action, unintentionally reproduced, which constrain and dispose behavior so as to preserve the rule structure. In the transformational ontology, they are the material conditions of action which agents appropriate and through action reproduce or transform, possibly intentionally. It is worth exploring this difference in some detail.

Recall that in the positional ontology, structure is an unintended by-product of rational, self-interested efforts to survive. Rules, which give shape and meaning to rationality and thereby make survival possible, are a necessary (if theoretically suppressed) component of structure. . . .

In the transformational view, by contrast, structure is a medium of activity that in principle can be altered through that activity. Any given action will reproduce or transform some part of the social structure; the structural product itself may be intended or unintended. In general, social action is both a product (an intended action) and a by-product (the reproduction of rules and resources implicated in the intended action). The linguistic analogy is again useful. When people speak a language, they are typically carrying out an intentional action (such as ordering a meal or supporting a philosophical argument) and at the same time are unintentionally reproducing the conditions which make that intentional action possible (reproducing language itself). . . .

The possibility that rules may become the objects of intentional action and that they may be transformed through action returns us to the issue of how such real-world entities as alliances, trade pacts, and arms control agreements are to be treated by structural theory. The positional ontology limits structure to what is both irreducible to action and unintentional in origin. Thus, entities that are intentionally produced, such as alliances, cannot be part of structure. Waltz is explicit on this point. Alliances are a feature not of the organization of systems, he argues, but of "the accommodations and conflicts that may occur within them or the groupings that may now and then form.". . . [36] This theoretical conclusion is entirely consistent with the underlying positional ontology. Intentional action and the products of intentional action, such as alliances and treaties, must be relegated to the unit-level in this ontology.

However, according to scientific realism, this conclusion is mistaken. While it is true that such things as alliances emerge from state interaction, they are not simply *aspects* of that interaction; they are *products* of it. . . . The rules that make up an alliance or trade agreement may be reproduced or transformed by subsequent activity, but they cannot be reduced to it. NATO, for example, rather than being just an aspect of the (unit-level) interaction among a select number of states is a real (system-level) structure of rules that regulates and gives meaning to a wide range of current and contemplated behavior by those states. NATO cannot be reduced to the activities carried out in its name, such as military exercises and meetings of foreign ministers. It consists also of relatively enduring rules and norms that these actions draw upon, reproduce, and transform. These rules, inscribed in a written treaty that exists independently of the activities it enables and regulates, are a legitimate component of structure, deserving to be treated as such by structural theory.

According to scientific realism, then, the positional model offers a *truncated* ontology of structure. . . . By conflating the unintended with the irreducible, the positional model is incapable of recognizing those features of the system's organization that are both irreducible to interaction and intentially produced (intended products). It thus bars from structural theory an entire class of structural elements in international politics. . . . The transformational ontology, by contrast, shows why all rules deserve structural status and provides a basis for integrating them in structural explanation. Because the ontology it postulates is richer and more comprehensive than its positional rival, the transformational model promises theory that is more powerful than its positional counterpart.

The Empirical Promise of a Transformational Research Program

The problem with Waltz's theory is not the explanatory schema it sets forth but the ontology on which it is based. . . .

Waltz is reluctant to concede that other structural theories, even those based on a positional ontology, might be advisable. . . .

. . . [He] fears that broadening the definition of structure to include other systemic features will introduce a "reasoning [that] makes the criteria of inclusion infinitely expansible," rendering structural theory a mishmash of causal considerations best treated separately. . . .[37]

Waltz is correct to stress the importance of parsimony. The more efficient the means to given explanatory ends, the better the explanation, other things being equal. But Waltz mistakenly defines parsimony only in terms of the number of independent variables in a theory, ignoring the ontology from which those variables are drawn. The number of independent variables one wishes to include in an explanation is generally a matter of subjective choice, dictated by what sort of explanation one wishes and how accurate it must be. To explain the path of a falling object, we may need only the law of gravitation if our requirements are not too severe. But if we wish to know the path of the object's fall in great detail, we will need to include consideration of the wind, rain, air resistance, Coriolis force, and the like. The choice between a single-variable theory that explains a little and a multivariable theory that explains a lot will generally be determined by the requirements of engineering rather than by the standards of science. . . .

Parsimony, in any case, is not gauged simply by the number of variables in a theory. Ontology too can prove more or less efficient in grounding explanatory efforts. After all, if parsimony were simply a matter of minimizing the number of variables in an explanation, Newton's explanation of the planets' orbital paths would be better than Einstein's. The Newtonian calculations require only the universal law of gravitation, and they leave only a small portion of the orbits unexplained. Einstein's calculations introduce complex relativistic corrections to the Newtonian laws, and in so doing explain only slightly more than those laws. If we need to know only the rough paths of the planets, say for purposes of telescopic tracking, the simpler Newtonian theory may be preferable on practical grounds. But Einstein's remains a better theory, and not only because it explains some planetary motion that Newton's cannot. Einstein's theory is better because it is more parsimonious in a basic ontological sense: it grounds explanations not only of planetary orbits but also of a number of unrelated and otherwise unexplainable phenomena. . . .

But why is a transformational model needed to examine the nature of rules and rule-following behavior in the interstate system? Why can we not simply take Waltz's theory as a starting point and then bring rules into the analysis when and where they are warranted? The basic problem was explained earlier in this section: the ontology underlying Waltz's theory makes no room for intentional rules as structural features of the system. If we start with Waltz's theory, we have no way of grounding a consideration of such rules without appealing to an outside ontology and thereby losing the parsimony of that theory. The transformational ontology grounds consideration of intentional rules not only by making their existence explicit but also by providing a useful model of how they exist in relation to action. . . . To appreciate the power of the transformational model, it is worth examining the differences in these configurations more closely.

In the positional model, structure is an *environment* in which action takes place. Structure means the "setting" or "context" in which action unfolds. In a positional approach, international structure stands in relation to state action much as an office building stands in relation to the workday activities that take place within its walls: it is a fixed, enduring set of conditions that constrains and disposes, shapes and shoves behavior. . . .

In the transformational approach, by contrast, structure consists of *materials for action*. Rather than being an environment or "container" in which behavior takes place, it is a medium, a means to social action. An office building, in this view, is not so much a setting for the activities of workers as it is an enabling structure that workers make use of to get their jobs done.[86] Certainly, structure is a constraint on action; the insights of the positional model are not sacrificed in the scientific realist approach. Travel through air-conditioning ducts and out of upper-story windows will be sanctioned, either by the rules of the workplace or by the law of gravitation. But by configuring structure as a means to action, rather than as an environment in which action takes place, a more powerful and comprehensive treatment of the conditions of action becomes possible. Rules are not concrete girders constraining action but, instead, are media through which action becomes possible and which action itself reproduces and transforms.

Action is constrained and enabled by rules; the rules are the outcome as well as the medium of that action. . . .

What might be the shape of a research program predicated on the ontology of scientific realism? One established research area in which the advantages of the transformational model can be immediately exploited is that dealing with the creation and maintenance of international institutions. The ontology of the transformational model provides the conceptual tools to describe and explain institutions and to investigate their enabling and constraining qualities. . . . In transformational terms, institutions consist of *formal, regulative* rules. In contrast to the positional approach, the transformational model supplies an ontology that not only is suitable for the study of such rules but also is capable of showing the continuities (as well as the discontinuities) between institutionalized and noninstitutionalized behavior.

Keohane notes that institutions are embedded in enduring "practices" of international politics, the most important of which is sovereignty.[38] The idea of embeddedness suggests a *stratification* of the international rule structure, which can be understood as a hierarchical dependence of both constitutive and regulative rules in which higher-order rules presume the existence of more sedimented (lower-order) ones. That is, some rules underpin not only action but also other rules or rule-structures. For example, when two nations sign an arms control treaty, they not only adopt a set of operative arms control regulations, but they also reproduce the rules associated with the underlying practice of sovereignty (rules that give the nations the very identity required to make treaties possible). Thus, the rules associated with the practice of sovereignty, which regulate a good number of "surface" activities (for example, the activities of diplomatic personnel around the world), also underpin and support a great number of other regulative rules in international politics. This suggests why the violation of any of the deeply sedimented rules that define sovereignty, such as in the seizing of hostages at the American Embassy in Teheran in 1979, will be met with profound resistance within the system. . . .

The immediate challenge to the transformational research program is to provide an initial framework for identifying and classifying rules of various sorts. The integrative power of a transformational program will depend on developing an encompassing schema showing relations and connections between various types of rules. Such a framework cannot be constructed through a priori analysis nor through a purely inductive strategy. Instead, initial ideas must be ventured and then applied in research, and the results used to modify and extend the initial concepts. As this classificatory framework is developed, several empirical questions need to be addressed. How are rules recognized by actors? How are they made, reproduced, and transformed? Why do states sometimes adhere to rules and at other times break or ignore them? Why do states sometimes enforce rules by sanctioning violators and at other times ignore the rule-breaking of others? These basic questions, as well as others, are aimed not at generating a static list of rules associated with behavior in various circumstances but at bringing to light *how* it is that rules, which are both the medium and the outcome of action, affect action the way they do. . . .

CONCLUSION: STAKES IN THE AGENT-STRUCTURE DEBATE

The history of science shows that when a new theory confronts well-established scientific thought, it typically faces two difficulties. First, the scientific community's familiarity with established theory works to obscure the new theory's powers and possibilities.[39] Second, the new theory's initial state of underdevelopment leaves it vulnerable to skeptical attacks from those who correctly perceive the theory's ambiguities and uncertainties. But, as the corpus of Lakatos's work demonstrates, any attempt at single-point "naive falsificationism" would be a mistake. . . .

. . . The transformational model merits our confidence because it is derived from the basic principles of scientific realism. It will take time to develop the model and amass the empirical results necessary to judge its usefulness. In the meantime, we can look forward to at least three advantages of adopting the transformational approach.

First, because many of the research questions entailed by a transformational model can be answered only by looking at the policymaking processes within states, a transformational approach can draw explicit links between structural and unit-level theories. The elaboration and testing of some of the structural theory must take place at the level of foreign policy decision making. Recall that no structural theory can alone predict state behavior, and therefore no such theory can be tested by referring to the outcomes of state action alone. However, a transformational structural theory claims to explain the forces within the decision- and policy-making processes that generate state behavior, and thus the theory can be tested against the record of these processes. . . .

Second, in addition to the "vertical" linkages between unit- and system-level theory, the transformational approach grounds the development of "horizontal" linkages between issue-areas in international politics. The concern for reputation, for example, cuts across processes of both conflict and cooperation. The importance of reputation to the "high" politics of national security is well appreciated. For example, when discord arises, a reputation for being "tough"—for showing a willingness to bear costs in pursuit of goals—may help secure the cooperation or acquiescence of others. But reputation is important in the "low" politics of trade and finance as well. . . . Insofar as reputation derives from rule-enforcing and rule-following reliability, it requires structural exposition and analysis. The transformational model provides a comprehensive ontology for such analysis. While the positional ontology favors the study of "high" over "low" politics, the transformational model integrates the two realms. . . .

Third, and perhaps most significant, the transformational approach to structural theory provides a promising basis for constructing explanations of peaceful change, a task that has been identified as the most pressing contemporary challenge to theorists of international relations. . . .[40] Waltz sees the efforts of theorists concerned with understanding the possibilities for change in the state system ("critical theory") as different in kind from his attempts to explain recurring patterns of action ("problem-solving theory").[41] Critical theorists, he maintains, "would transcend the world as it is; meanwhile we have to live in it."[42] But must our efforts to explain the world as it is condemn us to giving up hope of changing it? Scientific realism insists not. . . . Therein lies perhaps the most crucial stake in the agent-structure debate.

NOTES

1. See Stephen Gaukroger, *Explanatory Structures: Concepts of Explanation in Early Physics and Philosophy* (Atlantic Highlands, NJ: Humanities Press, 1978), p. 39; and Roy Bhaskar, *Scientific Realism and Human Emancipation* (London: Verso, 1986), p. 36. In this article, I use "model" interchangeably with "ontology."

2. Gaukroger, *Explanatory Structures*, p. 64.

3. See Jerrold Aronson, *A Realist Philosophy of Science* (New York: St. Martin's Press, 1984); Rom Harre, *The Principles of Scientific Thinking* (Chicago: University of Chicago Press, 1970); Rom Harre, *Varieties of Realism*, part 4 (Oxford: Blackwell, 1986); and S. Korner, *Categorical Frameworks* (Oxford: Blackwell, 1974). The terminology of "common ontology" is Aronson's. Harre speaks of "source analogues," Korner of "common categorical frameworks."

4. In *A Realist Philosophy of Science*, p. 174, Aronson states that "two phenomena are independent in that it is (physically) possible for one to occur without the other and vice versa."

5. Ibid., p. 271.

6. Ibid., pp. 182–83.

7. Einstein used this lesson to protect one of his theoretical predictions from countervailing empirical evidence. In late 1905, the experimental physicist Walter Kaufmann reported measurements of the mass of the electron at variance with claims Einstein had set forth in earlier research. Einstein rejected Kaufmann's measurements, claiming that the "systematic deviation" reported between those measurements and Einstein's predictions likely indicated an "unnoticed source of error" in Kaufmann's work. Kaufmann's data were to be dismissed because, in Einstein's professed "opinion," they supported theories that were not convincing alternatives to Einstein's own. And what made Einstein's theory more convincing was its ontological breadth. Einstein thus cited, as an independent criterion of theory-choice, the ontological power of his theory, in order to reject as implausible the data that contradicted his theory. Significantly, Einstein proved to be correct (though this was not shown for three decades). See the account in Arthur I. Miller, *Imagery in Scientific Thought* (Cambridge, MA: MIT Press, 1986), chap. 3; quotes are from pp. 118–19.

8. According to Lakatos, "There is no falsification before the emergence of a better theory." See Imre Lakatos, *The Methodology of Scientific Research Programmes: Philosophical Papers*, vol. 1 (Cambridge: Cambridge University Press, 1978), p. 35.

9. Kenneth Waltz, *Theory of International Politics* (Reading, MA: Addison-Wesley, 1979), p. 91.

10. Ibid., p. 40.

11. Ibid., p. 18.

12. Ibid., pp. 39 and 60.

13. Ibid., p. 80.

14. Ibid.

15. Ibid., pp. 81–99.

16. Ibid., p. 101.

17. Ibid., p. 69.

18. See the following works of Waltz: *Theory,* p. 66; "The Stability of a Bipolar World," *Daedalus* 93 (Summer 1964), pp. 882–87; and *Man, the State and War* (New York: Columbia University Press, 1959).

19. Waltz, *Theory,* pp. 125 and 127–28; and Waltz, "Reflections on *Theory of International Politics:* A Response to My Critics," in Robert Keohane, ed., *Neorealism and Its Critics* (New York: Columbia University Press, 1986), p. 332.

20. Roy Bhaskar, *The Possibility of Naturalism* (Atlantic Highlands, NJ: Humanities Press, 1979), p. 43.

21. Alexander Wendt, "The Agent-Structure Problem in International Relations Theory," *International Organization* 41 (Summer 1987), p. 362.

22. Anthony Giddens, *Profiles and Critiques in Social Theory* (Berkeley: University of California Press, 1983), chap. 3.

23. Anthony Giddens, *The Constitution of Society* (Berkeley: University of California Press, 1984), pp. 20–21.

24. The seminal article on this subject is that of John Rawls, "Two Concepts of Rules," *Philosophical Review* 64 (January 1955), pp. 3–32. See also W. V. O. Quine, "Methodological Reflections on Current Linguistic Theory," in Donald Davidson and Gilbert Harmon, eds., *Semantics of Natural Language* (Boston: Riedel, 1972), pp. 442–54; and the broader discussion in Friedrich Kratochwil and John Gerard Ruggie, "International Organization: A State of the Art on an Art of the State," *International Organization* 40 (Autumn 1986), pp. 753–75. The present essay draws primarily on the influential work by John R. Searle, *Speech Acts: An Essay in the Philosophy of Language* (Cambridge: Cambridge University Press, 1969).

25. Searle, *Speech Acts,* p. 33.

26. Ibid.

27. Peter Winch, *The Idea of Social Science and Its Relation to Philosophy* (London: Routledge & Kegan Paul, 1958).

28. Anthony Giddens, *Central Problems in Social Theory* (London: Macmillan, 1979), p. 66.

29. ... See ... David S. Clarke, Jr., *Principles of Semiotic* (London: Routledge & Kegan Paul, 1987), especially chap. 4, "Communication," pp. 73–103.

30. See Barry M. Blechman and Stephen S. Kaplan, *Force Without War: U.S. Armed Forces as a Political Instrument* (Washington, DC: Brookings Institution, 1973); and Stephen S. Kaplan, *Diplomacy of Power: Soviet Armed Forces as a Political Instrument* (Washington, DC: Brookings Institution, 1981).

31. Raymond Cohen, *International Politics: The Rules of the Game* (London: Longman, 1981), p. 50. See also Paul Keal, *Unspoken Rules and Superpower Dominance* (New York: St. Martin's Press, 1983), chap. 3.

32. The claim that "system" presupposes "rules" is distinct from the argument that the international political system represents a "society" reflecting shared norms. In Bull's version of this latter argument, an international society "exists when a group of states, conscious of certain common interests and common values, form a society in the sense that they conceive themselves to be bound by a common set of rules in their relations with one another, and share in the workings of common institutions." Bull conceptualizes "rules" in the regulative sense only—"general imperative principles which require or authorize prescribed classes of persons or groups to behave in prescribed ways"—and links rules to the achievement and maintenance of "order," implying "a pattern of activity that sustains the elementary or primary goals of ... international society."

Thus, when Bull declares the existence of "a common set of rules" in international politics, he means a common dedication to the achievement of shared values, interests, or norms. By contrast, when the scientific realist speaks of a common set of rules, all that is necessarily implied is the shared conventions of meaning that the very idea of social action in international relations presupposes. Above quotes are from Hedley Bull, *The Anarchical Society* (New York: Columbia University Press, 1977), pp. 13, 54, and 8. . . .

33. Robert Keohane, "Theory of World Politics: Structural Realism and Beyond," in Keohane, *Neorealism and Its Critics*, p. 167.
34. Waltz, *Theory*, pp. 74 and 76.
35. Ibid., p. 128.
36. Ibid., p. 98.
37. Waltz, "Reflections on *Theory*," p. 329.
38. Robert Keohane, "International Institutions: Two Approaches," *International Studies Quarterly* 32 (December 1988), p. 384.
39. See Norwood Russell Hanson, *Patterns of Discovery: An Inquiry into the Conceptual Foundations of Science* (Cambridge: Cambridge University Press, 1958), chaps. 1, 2, and 4.
40. See Robert Gilpin, *War and Change in World Politics* (New York: Cambridge University Press, 1981); and Robert Keohane, "Theory of World Politics." For an important theoretical and historical analysis of the determinants of peaceful systemic change, see Charles F. Doran, *The Politics of Assimilation: Hegemony and Its Aftermath* (Baltimore, MD: Johns Hopkins University Press, 1971).
41. Waltz, "Reflections on *Theory*," p. 338. The distinction is Robert Cox's, presented in "Social Forces, States, and World Orders: Beyond International Relations Theory," in Keohane, *Neorealism and Its Critics*, pp. 204–54.
42. Waltz, "Reflections on *Theory*," p. 338.

Social Forces, States and World Orders: Beyond International Relations Theory

Robert W. Cox

Academic conventions divide up the seamless web of the real social world into separate spheres, each with its own theorising; this is a necessary and practical way of gaining understanding. . . .

. . . The segments which result, however, derive indirectly from reality insofar as they are the result of practices, that is to say, the responses of consciousness to the pressures of reality. Subdivisions of social knowledge thus may roughly correspond to the ways in which human affairs are organised in particular times and places. They may, accordingly, appear to be increasingly arbitrary when practices change.

International relations is a case in point. It is an area of study concerned with the interrelationships among states in an epoch in which states, and most commonly nation-states, are the principal aggregations of political power. It is concerned with the outcomes of war and peace and thus has obvious practical importance. Changing practice has, however, generated confusion as to the nature of the actors involved (different kinds of state, and non-state entities), extended the range of stakes (low as well as high politics), introduced a greater diversity of goals pursued, and produced a greater complexity in the modes of interaction and the institutions within which action takes place.

One old intellectual convention which contributed to the definition of international relations is the distinction between state and civil society. This distinction made practical sense in the Eighteenth and early Nineteenth centuries when it corresponded to two more or less distinct spheres of human activity or practice: to an emergent society of individuals based on contract and market relations which replaced a status-based society, on the one hand, and a state with functions limited to maintaining internal peace, external defence and the requisite conditions for markets, on the other. Traditional international relations theory maintains the distinctness of the two spheres, with foreign policy appearing as the pure expression of state interests. Today, however, state and civil society are so interpenetrated that the concepts have become almost purely analytical . . . and are only very vaguely and imprecisely indicative of distinct spheres of activity.

. . . There has been little attempt within the bounds of international relations theory to consider the state/society complex as the basic entity of international relations. As a consequence, the prospect that there exist a plurality of forms of state, expressing different configurations of state/society complexes, remains very largely unexplored, at least in connection with the study of international relations. . . .

Some historians, both Marxist and non-Marxist, quite independently of theorising about either international relations or the state, have contributed in a practical way towards filling the gap. . . . In France, Fernand Braudel has portrayed these interrelationships in the Sixteenth and Seventeenth centuries on a vast canvas of the whole world.[1] Inspired by Braudel's work a group led by Immanuel Wallerstein has proposed a theory of world systems defined essentially in terms of social relations. The exploitative exchange relations between a developed core and an underdeveloped periphery, to which correspond different forms of labour control (e.g. free labour in the core areas, coerced labour in the peripheries, with intermediate forms in what are called semi-peripheries).[2] Though it offers the most radical alternative to conventional international relations theory, the world systems approach has been criticised on two main grounds: first, for its tendency to undervalue the state by considering the state as merely derivative from its position in the world system (strong states in the core, weak states in the periphery); second, for its alleged, though unintended, system-maintenance bias. . . .

The above comments are . . . warnings prior to the following attempt to sketch a method for understanding global power relations: look at the problem of world order in the whole, but beware of reifying a world system.[3] Beware of underrating state power, but in addition give proper attention to social forces and processes and see how they relate to the development of states and world orders. Above all, do not base theory on theory but rather on changing practice and empirical-historical study, which are a proving ground for concepts and hypotheses.

ON PERSPECTIVES AND PURPOSES

Theory is always *for* someone and *for* some purpose. All theories have a perspective. Perspectives derive from a position in time and space, specifically social and political time and space. . . . Of course, sophisticated theory is never just the expression of a perspective. The more sophisticated a theory is, the more it reflects upon and transcends its own perspective; but the initial perspective is always contained within a theory and is relevant to its explication. There is, accordingly, no such thing as theory in itself, divorced from a standpoint in time and space. . . .

To each such perspective the enveloping world raises a number of issues; the pressures of social reality present themselves to consciousness as problems. A primary task of theory is to become clearly aware of these problems, to enable the mind to come to grips with the reality it confronts. Thus, as reality changes, old concepts have to be adjusted or rejected and new concepts forged in an initial dialogue between the theorist and the particular world he tries to comprehend. This initial dialogue concerns the *problematic* proper with a particular perspective. . . .

Beginning with its problematic, theory can serve two distinct purposes. One is a simple, direct response: to be a guide to help solve the problems posed within the terms of the particular perspective which was the point of departure. The other is more reflective upon the process of theorising itself: to become clearly aware of the perspective which gives rise to theorising, and its relation to other perspectives (to achieve a perspective on perspectives); and to open up the possibility of choosing a different valid perspective from which the problematic becomes one of creating an alternative world. Each of these purposes gives rise to a different kind of theory.

The first purpose gives rise to *problem-solving theory*. It takes the world as it finds it, with the prevailing social and power relationships and the institutions into which they are organised, as the given framework for action. The general aim of problem-solving is to make these relationships and institutions work. . . . Since the general pattern of institutions and relationships is not called into question, particular problems can be considered in relation to the specialised areas of activity in which they arise. . . . The strength of the problem-solving approach lies in its ability to fix limits or parameters to a problem area and to reduce the statement of a particular problem to a limited number of variables which are amenable to relatively close and precise examination. The *ceteris paribus* assumption, upon which such theorising is based, makes it possible to arrive at statements of laws or regularities which appear to have general validity but which imply, of course, the institutional and relational parameters assumed in the problem-solving approach.

The second purpose leads to *critical theory*. It is critical in the sense that it stands apart from the prevailing order of the world and asks how that order came about. Critical theory, unlike problem-solving theory, does not take institutions and social and power relations for granted but calls them into question by concerning itself with their origins and how and whether they might be in the process of changing. It is directed towards an appraisal of the very framework for action, or problematic, which problem-solving theory accepts as its parameters. Critical theory is directed to the social and political complex as a whole rather than to the separate parts. As a matter of practice, critical theory, like problem-solving theory, takes as its starting point some aspect or particular sphere of human activity. But whereas the problem-solving approach leads to further analytical sub-division and limitation of the issue to be dealt with, the critical approach leads towards the construction of a larger picture of the whole of which the initially contemplated part is just one component, and seeks to understand the processes of change in which both parts and whole are involved.

Critical theory is theory of history in the sense of being concerned not just with the past but with a continuing process of historical change. Problem-solving theory is non-historical or ahistorical, since it, in effect, posits a continuing present (the permanence of the institutions and power relations which constitute its parameters). The strength of the one is the weakness of the other. Because it deals with a changing reality, critical theory must continually adjust its concepts to the changing object it seeks to understand and explain.[4] These concepts and the accompanying methods of enquiry seem to lack the precision that can be achieved by problem-solving theory, which posits a fixed order as its point of reference. This relative strength of problem-solving theory, however, rests upon a false premise, since the social and political order is not fixed but (at least in a long-range perspective) is changing. Moreover, the assumption of fixity is not merely a convenience of method, but also an ideological bias. Problem-solving theories can be represented, in the broader perspective of critical theory, as serving particular national, sectional, or class interests, which are comfortable within the given order. . . .

The perspectives of different historical periods favour one or the other kind of theory. Periods of apparent stability or fixity in power relations favour the problem-solving approach. The Cold War was one such period. In international relations, it fostered a concentration upon the problems of how to manage an apparently enduring relationship between two superpowers. However, a condition of uncertainty in power relations beckons to critical theory as people seek to understand the opportunities and risks of change. . . . To reason about possible future world orders now, however, requires a broadening of our enquiry beyond conventional international relations, so as to encompass basic processes at work in the development of social forces and forms of state, and in the structure of global political economy. Such, at least, is the central argument of this essay.

REALISM, MARXISM AND AN APPROACH TO A CRITICAL THEORY OF WORLD ORDER

Currents of theory which include works of sophistication usually share some of the features of both problem-solving and critical theory but tend to emphasise one approach over the other. Two currents which have had something important to say about inter-state relations and world orders—realism and Marxism—are considered here as a preliminary to an attempted development of the critical approach.

The realist theory of international relations had its origin in an historical mode of thought. Friedrich Meinecke, in his study on *raison d'état,* traced it to the political theory of Machiavelli and the diplomacy of Renaissance Italian city-states. . . . Meinecke's interpretation of *raison d'état* is a contribution to critical theory. . . .

Since the Second World War, some American scholars, notably Hans Morgenthau and Kenneth Waltz, have transformed realism into a form of problem-solving theory. Though individuals of considerable historical learning, they have tended to adopt the fixed ahistorical view of the framework for action characteristic of problem-solving theory. . . .[5]

The generalised form of the framework for action postulated by this new American realism (which we shall henceforth call neo-realism, which is the ideological form abstracted from the real historical framework imposed by the Cold War) is characterised by three levels, each of which can be understood in terms of what classical philosophers would call substances or essences, *i.e.* fundamental and unchanging substrata of changing and accidental manifestations or phenomena. These basic realities were conceived as: (1) the nature of man, understood in terms of Augustinian original sin or the Hobbesian "perpetual and restless desire for power after power that ceaseth only in death"[6]; (2) the nature of states, which differ in their domestic constitutions and in their capabilities for mobilising strength, but are similar in their fixation with a particular concept of national interest (a Leibnizian *monad*) as a guide to their actions; and (3) the nature of the state system, which places rational constraints upon the unbridled pursuit of rival national interests through the mechanism of the balance of power.

Having arrived at this view of underlying substances, history becomes for neo-realists a quarry providing materials with which to illustrate variations on always recurrent themes. The mode of thought ceases to be historical even though the materials used are derived from history. Moreover, this mode of reasoning dictates that, with respect to essentials, the future will always be like the past.[7]

In addition, this core of neo-realist theory has extended itself into such areas as game theory, in which the notion of substance at the level of human nature is presented as a rationality assumed to be common to the competing actors who appraise the stakes at issue, the alternative strategies, and the respective payoffs in a similar manner. This idea of a common rationality reinforces the non-historical mode of thinking. Other modes of thought are to be castigated as inapt, and incomprehensible in their own terms (which makes it difficult to account for the irruption into international affairs of a phenomenon like Islamic integralism, for instance).

The "common rationality" of neo-realism arises from its polemic with liberal internationalism. For neo-realism, this rationality is the one appropriate response to a postulated anarchic state system. Morality is effective only to the extent that it is enforced by physical power. This has given neo-realism the appearance of being a non-normative theory. It is 'value-free' in its exclusion of moral goals (wherein it sees the weakness of liberal internationalism) and in its reduction of problems to their physical power relations. This non-normative quality is, however, only superficial. There is a latent normative element which derives from the assumptions of neo-realist theory: security within the postulated inter-state system depends upon each of the major actors understanding this system in the same way, that is to say, upon each of them adopting neo-realist rationality as a guide to action. Neo-realist theory derives from its foundations the prediction that the actors, from their experiences within the system, will tend to think in this way; but the theory also performs a proselytising function as the advocate of this form of rationality. . . .

The debate between neo-realists and liberal internationalists reproduces, with up-to-date materials, the Seventeenth century challenge presented by the civil philosophy of Hobbes to the natural law theory of Grotius. Each of the arguments is grounded in different views of the essences of man, the state and the inter-state system. An alternative which offered the possibility of getting beyond this opposition of mutually exclusive concepts was pointed out by the Eighteenth century Neapolitan Giambattista Vico, for whom the nature of man and of human institutions (amongst which must be included the state and the inter-state system) should not be thought of in terms of unchanging substances but rather as a continuing creation of new forms. . . .

This should not be taken as a statement of radical idealism (*i.e.* that the world is a creation of mind). For Vico, ever-changing forms of mind were shaped by the complex of social relations in the genesis of which class struggle played the principal rôle, as it later did for Marx. Mind is, however, the thread connecting the present with the past, a means of access to a knowledge of these changing modes of social reality. Human nature (the modifications of mind) and human institutions are identical with human history; they are to be understood in genetic and not in essentialist terms (as in neo-realism) or in teleological terms (as in functionalism). One cannot, in this Vichian perspective, properly abstract man and the state from history so as to define their substances or essences as *prior to* history, history being but the record of interactions of manifestations of these substances. A proper study of human affairs should be able to reveal both the coherence of minds and institutions characteristic of different ages, and the process whereby one such coherent pattern—which we can call an historical structure—succeeds another. . . . The error which Vico criticised as the "conceit of scholars", who will have it that "what they know is as old as the world", consists in taking a form of thought derived from a particular phase of history (and thus from a particular structure of social relations) and assuming it to be universally valid.[8] This is an error of neo-realism and more generally, the flawed foundation of all problem-solving theory. . . .

How does Marxism relate to this method or approach to a theory of world order? . . . For our purposes, it is necessary to distinguish two divergent Marxist currents, analogous to the bifurcation between the old realism and the new. There is a Marxism which reasons historically and seeks to explain, as well as to promote, changes in social relations; there is also a Marxism, designed as a framework for the analysis of the capitalist state and society, which turns its back on historical knowledge in favour of a more static and abstract conceptualisation of the mode of production. The first we may call by the name under which it recognises itself: historical materialism. It is evident in the historical works of Marx, in those of present-day Marxist historians such as Eric Hobsbawm, and in the thought of Gramsci. . . . The second is represented by the so-called structural Marxism of Althusser and Poulantzas ("so-called" in order to distinguish their use of "structure" from the concept of historical structure in this essay) and most commonly takes the form of an exegesis of *Capital* and other sacred texts. Structural Marxism shares some of the features of the neo-realist problem-solving approach. . . . Historical materialism is, however, a foremost source of critical theory and it corrects neo-realism in four important respects.

The first concerns dialectic, a term which, like Marxism, has been appropriated to express a variety of not always compatible meanings. . . .

Both realism and historical materialism direct attention to conflict. Neo-realism sees conflict as inherent in the human condition, a constant factor flowing directly from the power-seeking essence of human nature and taking the political form of a continual reshuffling of power among the players in a zero-sum game, which is always played according to its own innate rules. Historical materialism sees in conflict the process of a continual remaking of human nature and the creation of new patterns of social relations which change the rules of the game and out of which—if historical materialism remains true to its own logic and method—new forms of conflict may be expected ultimately to arise . . . .

Second, by its focus on imperialism, historical materialism adds a vertical dimension of power to the horizontal dimension of rivalry among the most powerful states, which draws the almost exclusive attention of neo-realism. This dimension is the dominance and subordination of metropole over hinterland, centre over periphery, in a world political economy.

Third, historical materialism enlarges the realist perspective through its concern with the relationship between the state and civil society. Marxists, like non-Marxists, are divided between those who see the state as the mere expression of the particular interests in civil society and those who see the state as an autonomous force expressing some kind of general interest. This, for Marxists, would be the general interest of capitalism as distinct from the particular interests of capitalists. Gramsci contrasted historical materialism, which recognises the efficacy of ethical and cultural sources of political action (though always relating them with the economic sphere), with what he called historical economism or the reduction of everything to technological and material interests.[9] Neo-realist theory in the United States has returned to the state/civil society relationship, though it has treated civil society as a constraint upon the state and a limitation imposed by particular interests upon *raison d'état*, which is conceived of, and defined as, independent of civil society.[10] The sense of a reciprocal relationship between structure (economic relations) and superstructure (the ethico-political sphere) in Gramsci's thinking contains the potential for considering state/society complexes as the constituent entities of a world order and for exploring the particular historical forms taken by these complexes.

Fourth, historical materialism focuses upon the production process as a critical element in the explanation of the particular historical form taken by a state/society complex. . . . Historical materialism examines the connections between power in production, power in the state, and power in international relations. . . . [It] is sensitive to the dialectical possibilities of change in the sphere of production which could affect the other spheres, such as those of the state and world order. . . .

FRAMEWORKS FOR ACTION: HISTORICAL STRUCTURES

At its most abstract, the notion of a framework for action or historical structure is a picture of a particular configuration of forces. This configuration does not determine actions in any direct, mechanical way but imposes pressures and constraints. . . .

Three categories of forces (expressed as potentials) interact in a structure: material capabilities, ideas and institutions. No one-way determinism need be assumed among these three; the relationships can be assumed to be reciprocal. The question of which way the lines of force run is always an historical question to be answered by a study of the particular case [see Figure 1].

Material capabilities are productive and destructive potentials. In their dynamic form these exist as technological and organisational capabilities, and in their accumulated forms as natural resources which technology can transform, stocks of equipment (*e.g.* industries and armaments), and the wealth which can command these.

Ideas are broadly of two kinds. One kind consists of intersubjective meanings, or those shared notions of the nature of social relations which tend to perpetuate habits and expectations of behaviour.[11] Examples of intersubjective meanings in contemporary world politics are the notions that people are organised and commanded by states which have authority over defined territories. . . .

The other kind of ideas relevant to an historical structure are collective images of social order held by different groups of people. These are differing views as to both the nature and the legitimacy of prevailing power relations, the meanings of justice and public good, and so forth. Whereas intersubjective meanings

Figure 1

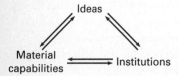

are broadly common throughout a particular historical structure and constitute the common ground of social discourse (including conflict), collective images may be several and opposed.[12] The clash of rival collective images provides evidence of the potential for alternative paths of development and raises questions as to the possible material and institutional basis for the emergence of an alternative structure.

Institutionalisation is a means of stabilising and perpetuating a particular order. Institutions reflect the power relations prevailing at their point of origin and tend, at least initially, to encourage collective images consistent with these power relations. Eventually, institutions take on their own life; they can become either a battleground of opposing tendencies, or stimulate the creation of rival institutions reflecting different tendencies. . . .

There is a close connection between institutionalisation and what Gramsci called hegemony. Institutions provide ways of dealing with internal conflicts so as to minimise the use of force. . . . There is an enforcement potential in the material power relations underlying any structure, in that the strong can clobber the weak if they think it necessary. But force will not have to be used in order to ensure the dominance of the strong to the extent that the weak accept the prevailing power relations as legitimate. This the weak may do if the strong see their mission as hegemonic and not merely dominant or dictatorial, that is, if they are willing to make concessions that will secure the weak's acquiescence in their leadership and if they can express this leadership in terms of universal or general interests, rather than just as serving their own particular interests.[13] Institutions may become the anchor for such a hegemonic strategy since they lend themselves both to the representations of diverse interests and to the universalisation of policy. . . .

The method of historical structures is one of representing what can be called limited totalities. The historical structure does not represent the whole world but rather a particular sphere of human activity in its historically located totality. The *ceteris paribus* problem, which falsifies problem-solving theory by leading to an assumption of total stasis, is avoided by juxtaposing and connecting historical structures in related spheres of action. Dialectic is introduced, firstly, by deriving the definition of a particular structure, not from some abstract model of a social system or mode of production, but from a study of the historical situation to which it relates, and secondly, by looking for the emergence of rival structures expressing alternative possibilities of development. . . . Historical structures are contrast models: like ideal types they provide, in a logically coherent form, a simplified representation of a complex reality and an expression of tendencies, limited in their applicability to time and space, rather than fully realised developments.

For the purpose of the present discussion, the method of historical structures is applied to the three levels, or spheres of activity: (1) the organisation of production, more particularly with regard to the *social forces* engendered by the production process; (2) *forms of state* as derived from a study of state/society complexes; and (3) *world orders, i.e.* the particular configurations of forces which successively define the problematic of war or peace for the ensemble of states. Each of these levels can be studied as a succession of dominant and emergent rival structures.

The three levels are interrelated. Changes in the organisation of production generate new social forces which, in turn, bring about changes in the structure of states; and the generalisation of changes in the structure of states alters the problematic of world order. . . .

The relationship among the three levels is not, however, simply unilinear. Transnational social forces have influenced states through the world structure, as evidenced by the effect of expansive Nineteenth century capitalism, *(les bourgeois conquérants)* upon the development of state structures in both core and periphery. Particular structures of world order exert influence over the forms which states take. . . . Forms of state also affect the development of social forces through the kinds of domination they exert, for example, by advancing one class interest and thwarting others. . . .[14]

HEGEMONY AND WORLD ORDERS

How are these reciprocal relationships to be read in the present historical conjuncture? Which of the several relationships will tell us the most? A sense of the historicity of concepts suggests that the critical relationships may not be the same in successive historical periods, even within the post-Westphalian era for which the term "state system" has particular meaning. The approach to a critical theory of world order, adumbrated here, takes the form of an interconnected series of historical hypotheses.

Neo-realism puts the accent on states reduced to their dimension of material force and similarly reduces the structure of world order to the balance of power as a configuration of material forces. Neo-realism, which generally dismisses social forces as irrelevant, is not much concerned with differentiating forms of state. . . , and tends to place a low value on the normative and institutional aspects of world order. . . .

An alternative approach might start by redefining what it is that is to be explained, namely, the relative stability of successive world orders. This can be done by equating stability with a concept of hegemony that is based on a coherent conjunction or fit between a configuration of material power, the prevalent collective image of world order (including certain norms) and a set of institutions which administer the order with a certain semblance of universality (*i.e.* not just as the overt instruments of a particular state's dominance). In this formulation, state power ceases to be the sole explanatory factor and becomes part of what is to be explained. . . .

The two periods of the *pax britannica* and the *pax americana* . . . satisfy the reformulated definition of hegemony. In the mid-Nineteenth century, Britain's world supremacy was founded on its sea power, which remained free from challenge by a continental state as a result of Britain's ability to play the rôle of balancer in a relatively fluid balance of power in Europe. The norms of liberal economics (free trade, the gold standard, free movement of capital and persons) gained widespread acceptance with the spread of British prestige, providing a universalistic ideology which represented these norms as the basis of a harmony of interests. While there were no formal international institutions, the ideological separation of economics from politics meant that the City could appear as administrator and regulator according to these universal rules, with British sea power remaining in the background as potential enforcer.

This historical structure was transformed in its three dimensions during the period running from the last quarter of the Nineteenth century through the Second World War. During this period British power declined relatively, losing its undisputed supremacy at sea, first with the German challenge and then with the rise of US power; economic liberalism foundered with the rise of protectionism, the new imperialisms and ultimately the end of the gold standard; and the belated and abortive attempt at international institutionalisation through the League of Nations, unsustained either by a dominant power or a widely-accepted ideology, collapsed in a world increasingly organised into rival power blocs.

The power configuration of the *pax americana* was more rigid than that of the earlier hegemony, taking the form of alliances (all hinging on US power) created in order to contain the Soviet Union. The stabilisation of this power configuration created the conditions for the unfolding of a global economy in which the United States played a rôle similar to that of Britain in mid-Nineteenth century. The United States rarely needed to intervene directly in support of specific national economic interests; by maintaining the rules of an international economic order according to the revised liberalism of Bretton Woods, the strength of US corporations engaged in the pursuit of profits was sufficient to ensure continuing national power. The *pax americana* produced a greater number of formal international institutions than the earlier hegemony. The Nineteenth century separation of politics and economics had been blurred by the experience of the Great Depression and the rise of Keynesian doctrines. Since states now had a legitimate and necessary overt rôle in national economic management, it became necessary both to multilateralise the administrative management of the international economy and to give it an intergovernmental quality.

The notion of hegemony as a fit between power, ideas and institutions makes it possible to deal with some of the problems in the theory of state dominance as the necessary condition for a stable international order; it allows for lags and leads in hegemony. For example, so appealing was the nostalgia for the Nineteenth century hegemony that the ideological dimension of the *pax brittanica* flourished long after the power configuration that supported it had vanished. Sustained, and ultimately futile, efforts were made to revive a liberal world economy along with the gold standard in the inter-war period. . . .

SOCIAL FORCES, HEGEMONY AND IMPERIALISM

Represented as a fit between material power, ideology and institutions, hegemony may seem to lend itself to a cyclical theory of history; the three dimensions fitting together in certain times and places and coming apart in others. . . . [However], what is missing is some theory as to how and why the fit comes about and comes apart. It is my contention that the explanation may be sought in the realm of social forces shaped by production relations.

Social forces are not to be thought of as existing exclusively within states. Particular social forces may overflow state boundaries, and world structures can be described in terms of social forces just as they can be described as configurations of state power. The world can be represented as a pattern of interacting social forces in which states play an intermediate though autonomous rôle between the global structure of social forces and local configurations of social forces within particular countries. This may be called a political economy perspective of the world: power is seen as *emerging* from social processes rather than taken as given in the form of accumulated material capabilities, that is as the result of these processes. . . .

It is, of course, no great discovery to find that, viewed in the political economy perspective, the *pax britannica* was based both on the ascendancy of manufacturing capitalism in the international exchange economy, of which Britain was the centre, and on the social and ideological power, in Britain and other parts of northwest Europe, of the class which drew its wealth from manufacturing. The new bourgeoisie did not need to directly control states; its social power became the premiss of state politics.[15]

The demise of this hegemonic order can also be explained by the development of social forces. Capitalism mobilised an industrial labour force in the most advanced countries, and from the last quarter of the Nineteenth century industrial workers had an impact on the structure of the state in these countries. The incorporation of the industrial workers, the new social force called into existence by manufacturing capitalism, into the nation involved an extension in the range of state action in the form of economic intervention and social policy. This in turn brought the factor of domestic welfare (*i.e.* the social minimum required to maintain the allegiance of the workers) into the realm of foreign policy. The claims of welfare competed with the exigencies of liberal internationalism within the management of states; whilst the former gained ground as protectionism, the new imperialism and ultimately the end of the gold standard marked the long decline of liberal internationalism.[16] The liberal form of state was slowly replaced by the welfare nationalist form of state.

The spread of industrialisation, and the mobilisation of social classes it brought about, not only changed the nature of states but also altered the international configuration of state power as new rivals overtook Britain's lead. Protectionism, as the means of building economic power comparable to Britain's, was for these new industrial countries more convincing than the liberal theory of comparative advantage. The new imperialisms of the major industrial powers were a projection abroad of the welfare nationalist consensus among social forces sought or achieved within the nations. As both the material predominance of the British economy and the appeal of the hegemonic ideology weakened, the hegemonic world order of the mid-Nineteenth century gave place to a non-hegemonic configuration of rival power blocs. . . .

James Petras, in his use of the concept of an imperial state system, has posed a number of questions concerning the structural characteristics of states in the present world order. The dominant imperial state and subordinate collaborator states differ in structure and have complementary functions in the imperial system; they are not just more and less powerful units of the same kind, as might be represented in a simple neo-realist model. A striking feature in his framework is that the imperial state he analyses is not the whole US government; it is "those executive bodies within the 'government' which are charged with promoting and protecting the expansion of capital across state boundaries."[17] The imperial system is at once more than and less than the state. It is more than the state in that it is a transnational structure with a dominant core and dependent periphery. This part of the US government is at the system's core, together (and here we may presume to enlarge upon Petras' indications) with inter-state institutions such as the IMF and the World Bank, symbiotically related to expansive capital, and with collaborator governments (or at any rate parts of them linked to the system) in the system's periphery. It is less than the state in the sense that non-imperial, or even anti-imperial, forces may be present in other parts of both core and periphery states. The unity of the state, posited by neo-realism, is fragmented in this image, and the struggle for and against the imperial system may go on within the state structures at both core and periphery as well as among social forces ranged in support and opposition to the system. The state is thus a necessary but insufficient category to account for the imperial system. The imperial system itself becomes the starting point of enquiry.

The imperial system is a world order structure drawing support from a particular configuration of social forces, national and transnational, and of core and periphery states. One must beware of slipping into the language of reification when speaking of structures; they are constraints on action, not actors. . . .

At this point, it is preferable to revert to the earlier terminology which referred to hegemonic and non-hegemonic world order structures. To introduce the term "imperial" with reference to the *pax americana* risks both obscuring the important difference between hegemonic and non-hegemonic world orders and confusing structurally different kinds of imperialism (*e.g.* liberal imperialism, the new or colonial imperialism, and the imperial system just outlined). The contention here is that the *pax americana* was hegemonic: it commanded a wide measure of consent among states outside the Soviet sphere and was able to provide sufficient benefits to the associated and subordinate elements in order to maintain their acquiescence. Of course, consent wore thin as one approached the periphery where the element of force was always apparent, and it was in the periphery that the challenge to the imperial system first became manifest.

It was suggested above how the particular fit between power, ideology and institutions constituting the *pax americana* came into being. Since the practical issue at the present is whether or not the *pax americana* has irretrievably come apart and if so what may replace it, two specific questions deserving attention are: (1) what are the mechanisms for maintaining hegemony in this particular historical structure? and (2) what social forces and/or forms of state have been generated within it which could oppose and ultimately bring about a transformation of the structure?

THE INTERNATIONALISATION OF THE STATE

A partial answer to the first question concerns the internationalisation of the state. The basic principles of the *pax americana* were similar to those of the *pax britannica*—relatively free movement of goods, capital and technology and a reasonable degree of predictability in exchange rates. . . . The post-war hegemony was, however, more fully institutionalised than the *pax britannica* and the main function of its institutions was to reconcile domestic social pressures with the requirements of a world economy. The International Monetary Fund was set up to provide loans to countries with balance of payments deficits in order to provide time in which they could make adjustments, and to avoid the sharp deflationary consequences of an automatic gold standard. The World Bank was to be a vehicle for longer term financial assistance. Economically weak countries were to be given assistance by the system itself, either directly through the system's institutions or by other states nominally certified by the system's institutions. These institutions incorporated mechanisms to supervise the application of the system's norms and to make financial assistance effectively conditional upon reasonable evidence of intent to live up to the norms.

This machinery of surveillance was, in the case of the western allies and subsequently of all industrialised capitalist countries, supplemented by elaborate machinery for the harmonisation of national policies. Such procedures began with the mutual criticism of reconstruction plans in western European countries (the US condition for Marshall aid funds), continued with the development of annual review procedures in NATO (which dealt with defence and defence support programmes), and became an acquired habit of mutual consultation and mutual review of national policies (through the OECD and other agencies).

The notion of international obligation moved beyond a few basic commitments, such as observance of the most favored nation principle or maintenance of an agreed exchange rate, to a general recognition that measures of national economic policy affect other countries and that such consequences should be taken into account before national policies are adopted. Conversely, other countries should be sufficiently understanding of one country's difficulties to acquiesce in short-term exceptions. Adjustments are thus perceived as responding to the needs of the system as a whole and not to the will of dominant countries. External pressures upon national policies were accordingly internationalised. . . .

The practice of policy harmonisation became such a powerful habit that when the basic norms of international economic behaviour no longer seemed valid, as became the case during the 1970s, procedures for mutual adjustment of national economic policies were, if anything, reinforced. In the absence of clear norms, the need for mutual adjustment appeared the greater.[18]

State structures appropriate to this process of policy harmonisation can be contrasted with those of the welfare nationalist state of the preceding period. Welfare nationalism took the form of economic planning at the national level and the attempt to control external economic impacts upon the national economy. To make national planning effective, corporative structures grew up in most industrially advanced countries for the purpose of bringing industry, and also organised labour, into consultation with the government in the formulation and implementation of policy. . . .

The internationalisation of the state gives precedence to certain state agencies—notably ministries of finance and prime ministers' offices—which are key points in the adjustment of domestic to international economic policy. Ministries of industries, labour ministries, planning offices, which had been built up in the context of national corporatism, tended to be subordinated to the central organs of internationalised public policy. As national economies became more integrated in the world economy, it was the larger and more technologically advanced enterprises that adapted best to the new opportunities. A new axis of influence linked international policy networks with the key central agencies of government and with big business. This new informal corporative structure overshadowed the older more formalised national corporatism and reflected the dominance of the sector oriented to the world economy over the more nationally-oriented sector of a country's economy. . . .[19]

THE INTERNATIONALISATION OF PRODUCTION

The internationalisation of the state is associated with the expansion of international production. This signifies the integration of production processes on a transnational scale, with different phases of a single process being carried out in different countries. International production currently plays the formative rôle in relation to the structure of states and world order that national manufacturing and commercial capital played in the mid-Nineteenth century.

International production expands through direct investment, whereas the rentier imperialism, of which Hobson and Lenin wrote, primarily took the form of portfolio investment. . . . The essential feature of direct investment is possession, not of money, but of knowledge—in the form of technology and especially in the capacity to continue to develop new technology. The financial arrangements for direct investment may vary greatly, but all are subordinated to this crucial factor of technical control. . . . These enterprises become suppliers of elements to a globally organised production process planned and controlled by the source of the technology. Formal ownership is less important than the manner in which various elements are integrated into the production system. . . .

INTERNATIONAL PRODUCTION AND CLASS STRUCTURE

International production is mobilising social forces, and it is through these forces that its major political consequences *vis-à-vis* the nature of states and future world orders may be anticipated. Hitherto, social classes have been found to exist within nationally-defined social formations, despite rhetorical appeals to the international solidarity of workers. Now, as a consequence of international production, it becomes increasingly pertinent to think in terms of a global class structure alongside or superimposed upon national class structures.

At the apex of an emerging global class structure is the transnational managerial class. Having its own ideology, strategy and institutions of collective action, it is both a class in itself and for itself. Its focal points of organisation, the Trilateral Commission, World Bank, IMF and OECD, develop both a framework of thought and guidelines for policies. From these points, class action penetrates countries through the process of internationalisation of the state. The members of this transnational class are not limited to those who carry out functions at the global level, such as executives of multinational corporations or as senior officials of international agencies, but includes those who manage the internationally-oriented sectors within countries, the finance ministry officials, local managers of enterprises linked into international production systems, and so on.[20]

National capitalists are to be distinguished from the transnational class. The natural reflex of national capital faced with the challenge of international production is protectionism. It is torn between the desire to use the state as a bulwark of an independent national economy and the opportunity of filling niches left by international production in a subordinate symbiotic relationship with the latter.

Industrial workers have been doubly fragmented. One line of cleavage is between established and non-established labour. Established workers are those who have attained a status of relative security and stability in their jobs and have some prospects of career advancement. Generally they are relatively skilled, work for larger enterprises, and have effective trade unions. Non-established workers, by contrast, have insecure employment, have no prospect of career advancement, are relatively less skilled, and confront great obstacles in developing effective trade unions. Frequently, the non-established are disproportionately drawn from lower-status ethnic minorities, immigrants and women. The institutions of working class action have privileged established workers. . . .

The second line of cleavage among industrial workers is brought about by the division between national and international capital (*i.e.* that engaged in international production). The established workers in the sector of international production are potential allies of international capital. . . .

Established workers in the sector of national capital are more susceptible to the appeal of protectionism and national (rather than enterprise) corporatism in which the defence of national capital, of jobs and of the workers' acquired status in industrial relations institutions, are perceived to be interconnected.[21]

Non-established labour has become of particular importance in the expansion of international production. Production systems are being designed so as to make use of an increasing proportion of semi-skilled (and therefore frequently non-established) in relation to skilled (and established) labour.[22] This tendency in production organisation makes it possible for the centre to decentralise the actual physical production of goods to peripheral locations in which an abundant supply of relatively cheap non-established labour is to be found, and to retain control of the process and of the research and development upon which its future depends.

As a non-established workforce is mobilised in Third World countries by international production, governments in these countries have very frequently sought to pre-empt the possibility of this new social force developing its own class-conscious organisations by imposing upon it structures of state corporatism in the form of unions set-up and controlled by the government or the dominant political party. . . .

SOCIAL FORCES, STATE STRUCTURES, AND FUTURE WORLD ORDER PROSPECTS

. . . The social forces generated by changing production processes are the starting point for thinking about possible futures. These forces may combine in different configurations, and as an exercise one could consider the hypothetical configurations most likely to lead to three different outcomes as to the future of the state system. The focus on these three outcomes is not, of course, to imply that no other outcomes or configurations of social forces are possible.

First, is the prospect for a new hegemony being based upon the global structure of social power generated by the internationalising of production. This would require a consolidation of two presently powerful and related tendencies: the continuing dominance of international over national capital within the major countries, and the continuing internationalisation of the state. Implicit in such an outcome is a continuance of monetarism as the orthodoxy of economic policy, emphasising the stabilisation of the world economy (anti-inflationary policies and stable exchange rates) over the fulfilment of domestic socio-political demands (the reduction of unemployment and the maintenance of real wages levels).

The inter-state power configuration which could maintain such a world order, provided its member states conformed to this model, is a coalition centering upon the United States, the Federal Republic of Germany, and Japan, with the support of other OECD states, the co-optation of a few of the more industrialised Third World countries, such as Brazil, and of leading conservative OPEC countries, and the possibility of revived détente allowing for a greater linkage of the Soviet sphere into the world economy of international production. The new international division of labour, brought about through the progressive decentralisation of manufacturing into the Third World by international capital, would satisfy demands for industrialisation from those countries. Social conflict in the core countries would be combatted through enterprise corporatism, though many would be left unprotected by this method, particularly the non-established workers. In the peripheral countries, social conflict would be contained through a combination of state corporatism and repression.

The social forces opposed to this configuration have been noted above. National capital, those sections of established labour linked to national capital, newly mobilised non-established workers in the Third World, and socially marginal in the poor countries are all in some way or another potentially opposed to international capital, and to the state and world order structures most congenial to international capital. These forces do not, however, have any natural cohesion, and might be dealt with separately, or neutralised, by an effective hegemony. . . .

A second possible outcome is a non-hegemonic world structure of conflicting power centres. Perhaps the most likely way for this to evolve would be through the ascendancy in several core countries of neo-mercantilist coalitions which linked national capital and established labour, and were determined to opt out of arrangements designed to promote international capital and to organise their own power and welfare on a national or sphere of influence basis. The continuing pursuit of monetarist policies may be the single most likely cause of neo-mercantilist reaction. Legitimated as anti-inflationary, monetarist policies have been perceived as hindering national capital (because of high interest rates), generating unemployment (through planned recession), and adversely affecting relatively deprived social groups and regions dependent upon government services and transfer payments (because of budget-balancing cuts in state expenditures). An opposing coalition would attack monetarism for subordinating national welfare to external forces, and for showing an illusory faith in the markets (which are perceived to be manipulated by corporate-administered pricing). . . .

A third and more remotely possible outcome would be the development of a counter-hegemony based on a Third World coalition against core country dominance and aiming towards the autonomous development of peripheral countries and the termination of the core-peripheral relationship. A counter-hegemony would consist of a coherent view of an alternative world order, backed by a concentration of power sufficient to maintain a challenge to core countries. While this outcome is foreshadowed by the demand for a New International Economic Order, the prevailing consensus behind this demand lacks a sufficiently clear view of an alternative world political economy to constitute counter-hegemony. The prospects of counter-hegemony lie very largely in the future development of state structures in the Third World. . . .

NOTES

1. Fernand Braudel, *Civilisation matérielle, Economie et Capitalisme, XVe–XVIIIe Siècle*, 3 vols. (Paris: Armand Colin, 1979). Braudel's theory and method are outlined in his essay first published in 1958 in *Annales E.S.C.* "Histoire et sciences sociales. La longue durée" (republished in Braudel, *Ecrits sur l'histoire*, Paris: Flammarion, 1969).
2. There is now quite a large literature produced by this school. The basic work is I. Wallerstein, *The Modern World-System: Capitalist Agriculture and the Origins of the European World-Economy in the Sixteenth Century* (New York: Academic Press, 1974). A brief summary of the world systems theory is in Wallerstein, "The rise and future demise of the world capitalist system: Concepts for comparative analysis", *Comparative Studies in Society and History* (vol. 16, no. 4, Sept. 1974), pp. 387–415.
3. I use the term "world order" in preference to "inter-state system" as it is relevant to all historical periods (and not only those in which states have been the component entities) and in preference to "world system" as it is more indicative of a structure having only a certain duration in time and avoiding the equilibrium connotations of "system". "World" designates the relevant totality, geographically limited by the range of probable interactions (some past "worlds" being limited to the Mediterranean, to Europe, to China, etc.). "Order" is used in the sense of the way things usually happen (*not* the ab-

sence of turbulence); thus disorder is included in the concept of order. An inter-state system is one historical form of world order. The term is used in the plural to indicate that particular patterns of power relationships which have endured in time can be contrasted in terms of their principal characteristics as distinctive world orders.

4. E.P. Thompson argues that historical concepts must often "display extreme elasticity and allow for great irregularity". His treatment of historical logic develops this point in his essay "The Poverty of Theory" in *The Poverty of Theory and Other Essays* (London: Merlin Press, 1978), esp. pp. 231–242.

5. This is most clearly expressed in K. Waltz, *Man, the State and War* (New York: Columbia University Press, 1954).

6. *Leviathan,* Part I, chap.xi

7. Kenneth Waltz, in a paper presented to a panel discussion at the American Political Science Association in August 1980 for which a first version of the present essay was written, asked the question "Will the future be like the past?", which he answered affirmatively—not only was the same pattern of relationships likely to prevail but it would be for the good of all that this should be so. It should be noted that the future contemplated by Waltz was the next decade or so.

8. *The New Science of Giambattista Vico* trans. from the third edition by Thomas Goddard Bergin and Max Harold Fisch (Ithaca and London: Cornell University Press, 1970), p. 19, para. 127.

9. Antonio Gramsci, *Selections from the Prison Notebooks* edited and trans. by Quintin Hoare and Geoffrey Nowell Smith (New York: International Publishers, 1971), esp. pp. 158–168. The full critical Italian edition *Quaderni del carcere* (Torino: Einaudi editore, 1975) contains additional passages on this point, *e.g.* pp. 471, 1321, 1492. Gramsci saw ideas, politics and economics as reciprocally related, convertible into each other and bound together in a *blocco storico* [historic bloc]. "Historical materialism", he wrote, "is in a certain sense a reform and development of Hegelianism. It is philosophy freed from unilateral ideological elements, the full consciousness of the contradictions of philosophy." (Einaudi edition, p. 471, my rough translation).

10. As in Stephen Krasner, *Defending the National Interest: Raw Materials Investments and U.S. Foreign Policy* (Princeton: Princeton University Press, 1978) and Peter Katzenstein, ed., *Beyond Power and Plenty. Foreign Economic Policies of Advanced Industrial States* (Madison: University of Wisconsin Press, 1978). The United States is represented by these authors as a state which is weak in relation to the strength of civil society (or more particularly of interests in civil society), whereas other states, *e.g.* Japan or France, are stronger in relation to their societies. Civil society is thus seen in the US case as limiting the effectiveness of the state.

11. On intersubjective meanings, see Charles Taylor, "Hermeneutics and Politics", in Paul Connerton, ed., *Critical Sociology* (Harmondsworth, Middlesex: Penguin Books, 1965), chap. VI. Also relevant is Peter L. Berger and Thomas Luckman, *The Social Construction of Reality* (Harmondsworth, Middlesex: Penguin, 1971).

12. Collective images are not aggregations of fragmented opinions of individuals such as are compiled through surveys; they are coherent mental types expressive of the world views of specific groups such as may be reconstructed through the work of historians and sociologists, *e.g.* Max Weber's reconstructions of forms of religious consciousness.

13. Gramsci's principal application of the concept of hegemony was to the relations among social classes, *e.g.* in explaining the inability of the Italian industrial bourgeoisie to establish its hegemony after the unification of Italy and in examining the prospects of the Italian industrial workers establishing their class hegemony over peasantry and petty bourgeoisie so as to create a new *blocco storico* (historic bloc)—a term which in Gram-

sci's work corresponds roughly to the notion of historic structure in this essay. The term "hegemony" in Gramsci's work is linked to debates in the international Communist movement concerning revolutionary strategy and in this connection its application is specifically to classes. The form of the concept, however, draws upon his reading of Machiavelli and is not restricted to class relations but has a broader potential applicability. Gramsci's adjustment of Machiavellian ideas to the realities of the world he knew was an exercise in dialectic in the sense defined above. It is an appropriate continuation of his method to perceive the applicability of the concept to world order structures as suggested here. For Gramsci, as for Machiavelli, the general question involved in hegemony is the nature of power, and power is a centaur, part man, part beast, a combination of force and consent. See Machiavelli, *The Prince*, Norton Critical Edition, Robert M. Adams, ed. (New York: W.W. Norton, 1977), pp. 49–50; Gramsci, *Selections op. cit.*, pp. 169–170.

14. A recent discussion of the reciprocal character of these relations is in Peter A. Gourevitch, "The Second Image Reversed", *International Organization* (Vol. 32, No.4, Autumn 1978), pp. 881–911.

15. E. J. Hobsbawm writes: "The men who officially presided over the affairs of the victorious bourgeois order in its moment of triumph were a deeply reactionary country nobleman from Prussia, an imitation emperor in France and a succession of aristocratic landowners in Britain." *The Age of Capital, 1843–1875* (London: Sphere Book, 1977), p. 15.

16. Among analysts who concur in this are Karl Polanyi, *The Great Transformation* (Boston, MA: Little, Brown, 1957); Gunnar Myrdal, *Beyond the Welfare State* (New Haven: Yale University Press, 1960); E. H. Carr, *Nationalism and After* (London: Macmillan, 1945); and Geoffrey Barraclough, *Introduction to Contemporary History* (London: Penguin, 1968).

17. "The Imperial State System" paper presented to the American Political Science Association, Washington, D.C., August 1980.

18. Max Beloff was perhaps the first to point to the mechanisms whereby participation in international organisations altered the internal policy-making practices of states in his *New Dimensions in Foreign Policy* (London: Allen and Unwin, 1961). R. W. Cox and H. K. Jacobson, et al., *The Anatomy of Influence: Decision-making in International Organisation* (New Haven: Yale University Press, 1972) represented the political systems of international organisations as including segments of states. R. O. Keohane and J. S. Nye, "Transgovernmental Relations and International Organizations", *World Politics* (Vol. 27, October 1974) pointed to the processes whereby coalitions are formed among segments of the apparatuses of different states and the ways in which international institutions facilitate such coalitions. These various works, while they point to the existence of mechanisms for policy co-ordination among states and for penetration of external influences within states, do not discuss the implications of these mechanisms for the structure of power within states. It is this structural aspect I wish to designate by the term "internationalisation of the state". Christian Palloix refers to "L'internationalisation de l'appareil de l'Etat national, de certains lieux de cet appareil d'Etat. . . ." (*L'internationalisation du capital*, Paris, Maspero, 1975, p. 82) by which he designates those segments of national states which serve as policy supports for the internationalisation of production. He thus raises the question of structural changes in the state, though he does not enlarge upon the point. Keohane and Nye, subsequent to the work mentioned above, linked the transgovernmental mechanism to the concept of "interdependence", *Power and Interdependence*, (Boston: Little, Brown, 1977). I find this concept tends to obscure the power relationships involved in structural changes in

both state and world order and prefer not to use it for that reason. Peter Gourevitch, *op. cit.*, does retain the concept interdependence while insisting that it be linked with power struggles among social forces within states.

19. There is, of course, a whole literature implicit in the argument of this paragraph. Some sketchy references may be useful. Andrew Shonfield, *Modern Capitalism* (London: Oxford University Press, 1965) illustrated the development of corporative-type structures of the kind I associate with the welfare-nationalist state. The shift from industry-level corporatism to an enterprise-based corporatism led by the big public and private corporations has been noted in some industrial relations works, particularly those concerned with the emergence of a 'new working class', *e.g.* Serge Mallet, *La nouvelle classe ouvrière* (Paris: Scuil, 1963), but the industrial relations literature has generally not linked what I have elsewhere called enterprise corporatism to the broader framework suggested here (*cf.* R. W. Cox, "Pour une étude prospective des relations de production", *Sociologie du Travail*, 2, 1977). Erhand Friedberg, "L'internationalisation de l'économie et modalités d'intervention de l'état: la 'politique industrielle' ", in *Planification et Société* (Grenoble: Presses universitaires de Grenoble, 1974), pp. 94–108, discusses the subordination of the old corporatism to the new. The shift in terminology from planning to industrial policy is related to the internationalising of state and economy. Industrial policy has become a matter of interest to global economic policy makers, *cf* William Diebold, Jr., *Industrial Policy as an International Issue* (New York: McGraw-Hill for the Council on Foreign Relations, 1980) and John Pinder, Takashi Hosomi and William Diebold, *Industrial Policy and the International Economy* (Trilateral Commission, 1979). If planning evokes the spectre of economic nationalism, industrial policy, as the Trilateral Commission study points out, can be looked upon with favour from a world economy perspective as a necessary aspect of policy harmonisation: "We have argued that industrial policies are needed to deal with structural problems in the modern economies. Thus, international action should not aim to dismantle these policies. The pressure should, rather, be towards positive and adaptive industrial policies, whether on the part of single countries or groups of countries combined. Far from being protectionist, industrial policy can help them to remove a cause of protectionism, by making the process of adjustment less painful." (p. 50). It may be objected that the argument and references presented here are more valid for Europe than for the United States, and that, indeed, the very concept of corporatism is alien to US ideology. To this it can be replied that since the principal levers of the world economy are in the United States, the US economy adjusts less than those of European countries and peripheral countries, and the institutionalisation of adjustment mechanisms is accordingly less developed. Structural analyses of the US economy have, however, pointed to a distinction between a corporate international-oriented sector and a medium and small business nationally-oriented sector, and to the different segments of the state and different policy orientations associated with each. *Cf* John Kenneth Galbraith, *Economics and the Public Purpose* (London: Andre Deutsch, 1974) and James O'Connor, *The Fiscal Crisis of the State* (New York: St. Martin's Press, 1973). Historians point to the elements of corporatism in the New Deal, *e.g.* Arthur M. Schlesinger, Jr., *The Age of Roosevelt* (London: Heinemann, 1960).

20. The evidence for the existence of a transnational managerial class lies in actual forms of organisation, the elaboration of ideology, financial supports, and the behavior of individuals. Other structures stand as rival tendencies, *e.g.* national capital and its interests sustained by a whole other structure of loyalties, agencies, etc. Individuals or firms and state agencies may in some phases of their activity be caught up now in one, now in another tendency. Thus the membership of the class may be continually shifting though

the structure remains. It is sometimes argued that this is merely a case of US capitalists giving themselves a hegemonic aura, an argument that by implication makes of imperialism a purely national phenomenon. There is no doubting the US origin of the values carried and propagated by this class, but neither is there any doubt that many non-US citizens and agencies also participate in it nor that its world view is global and distinguishable from the purely national capitalisms which exist alongside it. Through the transnational managerial class American culture, or a certain American business culture, has become globally hegemonic. Of course, should neo-mercantilist tendencies come to prevail in international economic relations, this transnational class structure would wither.

21. Some industries appear as ambiguously astride the two tendencies, *e.g.* the automobile industry. During a period of economic expansion, the international aspect of this industry dominated in the United States, and the United Auto Workers union took the lead in creating world councils for the major international auto firms with a view to inaugurating multinational bargaining. As the industry was hit by recession, protectionism came to the fore.

22. R.W. Cox, "Labour and Employment in the Late Twentieth Century", in R. St. J. Macdonald, et al., eds., *The International Law and Policy of Human Welfare* (Sijthoff and Noordhoff, 1978). This tendency can be seen as the continuation of a long-term direction of production organisation of which Taylorism was an early stage, in which control over the work process is progressively wrested from workers and separated out from the actual performance of tasks so as to be concentrated with management. See Harry Braverman, *Labor and Monopoly Capital* (New York: Monthly Review, 1974).

Why Collaborate?
Issue-Linkage and
International Regimes

Ernst B. Haas

I. WHY STUDY REGIMES?

THIS essay is yet another attempt to specify the particular mode of international collaboration we call a "regime."...

...Under what conditions do convergences of interest arise that call for the creation of regimes? How can there be international collaboration despite the persistence of conflict and of differentials in the power of actors?

Institutionalized collaboration can be explored in terms of the interaction between changing knowledge and changing social goals. It seems axiomatic that parties in conflict will, under conditions of changing understanding of their desires and of the constraints under which they must act, seek to define an area of joint gains. The definition of joint gains must be based on the goals of the actors *and* on the calculations ("knowledge") that influence the choice of goals. What, then, about the social power of certain groups and the hegemonic position of strong states in world politics?

If it were possible to predict the outcome of international negotiations by projecting the power of the parties, our question would be answered. If social classes and governments never changed their minds about individual and joint gains, there would be no question. But under conditions of complex interdependence, no such projection is possible. The existence of an unstable hierarchy of issues on the international agenda means that minds are being changed all the time. Hence we focus on changing knowledge and changing goals. . . .

We will begin by exploring relationships between types of interdependence, issues, and the need for collaboration. Next, we will inquire how issues become "linked" into packages called "issue areas." By examining the role of changing knowledge and social goals in defining the content of such packages, four patterns of cognition for choosing regimes are developed. Finally, we will look into the type of organizational arrangements that correspond to various types of regimes. . . .

II. INTERDEPENDENCE, ISSUES, ISSUE-AREAS

Negotiations may be controversial or smooth, laden with conflict or free of it. As long as the parties agree on the benefits to be derived from collaboration, conflict does not arise. During the 19th century, for instance, it was taken for granted by all concerned that British investment in Argentine beef production and electric utilities was beneficial for both Britain and Argentina. Negotiating the capital and technology transfers considered appropriate then did not pose a problem. No *issue*, no controversy arose until Britain sought to intervene, diplomatically or militarily, to protect the British investment against Argentine efforts to change the understanding under which it had been introduced earlier. Collaboration becomes conflictual only when the parties begin to disagree on the distribution of benefits to be derived. . . .

Interdependence

. . . If Britain considers herself relatively insensitive to a change, we say that Argentina is *more vulnerable* than Britain. Sensitivity is measured by the perceived effects of interrupting a pattern of interdependence. Vulnerability is measured by the opportunity costs incurred by making alternative arrangements for collaboration when the initial arrangement breaks down. Unequal sensitivity and vulnerability amount to *asymmetrical interdependence:* Britain is less dependent on Argentina than Argentina is on Britain. . . . The construction of international arrangements regulating interdependence—which we call regimes—under conditions of complex interdependence depends on how the asymmetries are perceived by the participants. Their definition of the issues requiring regulation is a function of the perceived costs of asymmetrical interdependence. Calculations of sensitivity and vulnerability therefore inform the discussion of remedial measures.

Any two countries may collaborate on a number of topics at the same time. There is not necessarily a connection between these topics in the minds of the actors. Some may become controversial issues while others remain free of conflict. . . .

Our first step must be to clarify what is meant by "issue" and by "linking issues." The discussion of linkages will enable us to specify what we mean by "issue-area." We will then be able to discuss how knowledge may or may not be used in the establishment of linkages, and how issue-areas differ from each other.

Issues and Issue-Areas

Issues are separate items that appear on the agenda of negotiators. In the [Law of the Sea] (LOS) negotiations, some of the issues are concerned with the width of the territorial sea and the national economic zone, who can mine the deep sea for manganese nodules and under what conditions, who can draw up rules for fisheries conservation, and whether marine pollution should be controlled by national or multilateral means. The issues in international monetary collaboration include the size and type of reserve assets held by the International Monetary Fund, the conditions under which members can draw on them, and the proportion to be used for maintaining international liquidity, protecting the balance-of-payments positions of certain members, and compensating other members for losses incurred because of foreign trade vicissitudes. The agenda also includes, of course, the question of whether there should be fixed, flexible, or floating exchange rates. In what sense are these issues connected with each other?

It is possible to think of monetary management as being made up of separate issues. Central banks will negotiate to increase liquidity, shore up each other's currencies, and fix the rate of exchange between currencies either by manipulating the currency market or through administrative regulation. In negotiating a conflict, each issue can be handled separately. Monetary management was largely handled this way prior to the Bretton Woods Agreement. Efforts were made to deal with monetary issues as packages only when it was generally recognized that the resolution of *each* of these issues had an effect on the overall economic health of the participants. Degrees of currency fluctuation were no longer considered in terms of the short-term balance of payments alone but also in conjunction with overall rates of growth, inflation, and deflation. Previously separate monetary issues had been converted by the actors themselves into an *issue-area*, a recognized cluster of concerns involving interdependence not only among the parties but among the issues themselves. . . . We can speak, since 1944, of the existence of an internationally recognized monetary issue-area. . . .

Things are more complicated in ocean management because no consensus on knowledge has emerged to give coherence to the consensus on goals. The ocean matters to governments because their citizens use it to fish, sail ships, extract oil, fight wars, and conduct research; they also now recognize that the oceans help determine the weather and that it may not be a good idea to use them as the world's garbage dump. Each of these activities has given rise to conflicts among countries. Governments have sought to resolve them by means of bilateral treaties and multilateral conventions establishing basic ground rules for behavior. But until very recently, each issue was approached separately. . . .

In 1967 a new doctrine was announced: the oceans were to be considered "the common heritage of mankind," and the totality of their resources a means for redistributing income and welfare among all countries. To achieve this, it was no longer possible to consider issues separately since each issue was thought to contribute to increased equality among states. More importantly, effects of interdependence *among* issues were now recognized: changing marine technology could result in over-fishing, unacceptable pollution, greater ship disasters; and the mining of deep-sea minerals could depress the price of the same minerals mined on land. As a result, the Law of the Sea Conference was convened by the United Nations to resolve the cluster of issues by means of a single treaty. Ocean matters became, for the first time, a tentatively recognized issue-area. But, as we shall see, there is a considerable distance between the cognitive event of issue-area recognition and the institutional event of regime construction: the inter-issue Law of the Sea negotiations . . . dragged on for a decade.

There are important differences between the construction of regimes for money and for the oceans. Knowledge relevant to ocean management is far less consensual than the macroeconomic professional consensus that existed between 1950 and 1970. Although oceanographers, fisheries specialists, and mining engineers accumulated a great deal of technical information during these decades, neither they nor government officials have succeeded in *integrating* this information into a strategy for realizing the common heritage of mankind. Global welfare is indeed recognized as an overriding social goal; but there is no consensus on *how* the management of specific resources can be aggregated into attaining it in the form of joint gains. . . .

State power is a vital mediating agent in the absence of consensual knowledge. Those who claim the knowledge and the ability to act can negotiate for private goods they are able to control. When they want others to be barred from the benefits of fisheries conservation and prevented from polluting the shoreline, they create exclusive national zones; when they want to exploit a high-sea resource, they invoke the principle of open access. Nobody has the power to impose a global regime, but many have the power to impose private spheres; and a few have the capability to monopolize deep-ocean mining.

The LOS negotiations (like the parallel effort to construct the NIEO) constituted a case of "premature" issue-packaging. The package was the result of a negotiating strategy adopted by the weak—first in UNCTAD and later in all international economic forums. In addition, the character of the resources to be subjected to a regime may explain the difference in outcomes. Ocean-related resources constitute a very heterogeneous group of concerns, united only by the fact that they are situated on or under the water. Money, on the other hand, is a universal medium on which all economic activity depends; for better or for worse, the management of money responds to some widely accepted theories. The management of ocean resources does not. . . .

Knowledge

Knowledge has emerged in our argument as a basic ingredient for exploring the development of issue-areas. A further explication of this notion is essential if I am to avoid being labelled a technocratic determinist. I do *not* mean that knowledge is a synonym for the discoveries of natural science, the opposite of ideology, the sole basis for establishing objective truth, superior to politics, or a substance that makes experts wise and politicians clowns.

Knowledge is the sum of technical information and of theories about that information which commands sufficient consensus at a given time among interested actors to serve as a guide to public policy designed to achieve some social goal. Knowledge incorporates scientific notions relating to the social goal. Such notions are rarely free from ideological elements. Nor are they necessarily free from the self-interest of their proponents. . . . None of this matters for our purposes. As long as these activities are accepted as a basis for public policy by groups and individuals professing varying political ideologies, we consider such notions as consensual. Knowledge is the professionally mediated body of theory and information that transcends prevailing lines of ideological cleavage.

Internationally, then, the sharing of a fund of knowledge among governments otherwise in opposition to each other is a form of cognitive convergence. When Soviet and American engineers agree on the properties of strategic weapons, and economists on the determinants of the business cycle and how to model it (and there is evidence that such agreement has occurred), certain ideological differences are being bridged by converging modes of thought. The same happens when pollutants are identified, measured, and related to the quality of life, or when the trade-offs among various sources of energy are assessed. . . .

But *who* is knowledgeable—the technical expert, the businessman, the politician, the peasant? Another way to put this question is to ask at what point knowledge is consensual. The monetary theory underlying the Bretton Woods regime existed in the professional literature before 1945; an effort to put it to work internationally was made in 1933. The management doctrine underlying the LOS negotiations had been developed by Arvid Pardo before 1967. Neoclassical economic development doctrine was challenged before 1974. What matters is not when a given view was first developed, but when it attains general acceptance as a guide to public policy. It is normal that technical specialists originate a particular body of knowledge and claim relevance for it. Knowledge becomes salient to regime construction only after it has seeped into the consciousness of policy makers and other influential groups and individuals.[1] In 1945, Keynesian economics was widely accepted by economists and labor leaders, had made important inroads into the U.S. bureaucracy, but was still being resisted by the business community; a few years later, some key business groups made their peace with it. Pardo's approach to ocean management has not been accepted by specialists or governments. The "basic human needs" doctrine has officially taken the place of older development views without completely pre-empting them; it is not yet consensual, but it has its adherents. A claim to knowledge becomes consensual whenever it succeeds in dominating the policy-making process—and that implies acceptance by all major actors involved in that process. In the NIEO negotiations, no such consensus exists. The *dependencia* doctrine is the property of the poor; it is *their* way of organizing the appropriate knowledge, but not the lore on which the rich rely. It is therefore not knowledge in the sense in which the term is used here.

Knowledge constitutes only one dimension of our exploration into issue-areas and issue-linkages. Regimes are constructed by states through the medium of multilateral negotiation. The linking of issues that remained separate in earlier periods can be interpreted as a kind of learning. But learning is but another word for reinterpreting one's interests. Interests may—but need not—change with more consensual knowledge. We now inquire into negotiations and learning as an aspect of issue-linkage that takes into account the varying interests and goals of the parties.

Knowledge, Linkages and Issue-Areas

Issue-specific negotiations usually deal with topics on which there is an accepted body of knowledge. Economists in general agree on the effects that exchange rate systems have on the benefits derived from trade; fisheries specialists subscribe to the principle of the "maximum sustainable yield.". . . This means that in issue-specific negotiations on these topics there is a high degree of certainty about the efficacy of the *immediate* solution; benefits can be calculated fairly reliably as long as the existing base of knowledge remains unchanged. All other things being equal, the narrower the scope of issues to be negotiated, the higher the degree of certainty about efficient solutions. However, when we assume a dynamic situation of rapidly changing knowledge, the pattern is reversed. Experts can no longer be sure that accepted solutions will bring certain benefits. They will be tempted to expand the scope of topics as they suspect that knowledge in cognate fields has something to tell them about the efficacy of broader types of solutions. For instance, fisheries specialists concerned only with optimal harvesting of a fixed stock may begin to think about artificially manipulating the size of the stock when (1) the means for doing this become known, and (2) fish stocks are considered as a constituent of overall dietary calculations. Under such conditions, inter-issue negotiations offer a greater hope of efficient solutions even though the knowledge base is itself changing and far from conclusive. Greater certainty is a hope, not a scientific given.

Why link issues? Since changes in knowledge and social goals do not necessarily go together we have no warrant for arguing that all economic regimes relying on scientific and technological information *must* owe their origin to this confluence. Nor are we entitled to argue that issues *will* be linked simply because we live under conditions of complex interdependence. Successful negotiations for institutionalizing international collaboration depend on the congruence of interests as much as on changes in consensual knowledge. It follows that issue-linkage will not succeed if the states with a strong stake in the existing distribution of benefits, and the capability to control it, prefer to keep things as they are. The United States and the Soviet Union, for example, saw no reason to link the issues of peaceful nuclear energy and the proliferation of nuclear weapons as long as each was able to control the process of technological diffusion. The desire to construct the non-proliferation regime arose only when the process seemed to pass out of their control. Issue-specific negotiations tend to favor the coalition of states who have long had an interest in the issue and who dominate the resource. Issue-linkage, on the other hand, is favored by those who want "in": a regime that links issues will come into existence only if the "outs" somehow manage to persuade the "ins."

There are three ways of persuasion. (1) One can link issues by introducing into the agenda of multilateral negotiations items that are not connected by any intellectual coherence at all; we call this "tactical linkage." The objective is simply to obtain additional bargaining leverage, to extract a *quid pro quo* not obtainable if the discussion remains confined to a single issue. (2) Issue-linkage may also be attempted, however, to maintain the cohesion of one's coalition. The coalition is held together by a commitment to some overriding social goal, even though the partners disagree with respect to the knowledge necessary to attain it. . . . We call this behavior pattern "fragmented linkage." (3) Issue-linkage may also proceed on the basis of cognitive developments based on consensual knowledge linked to an agreed social goal. This is the pattern of greatest interest to the construction of regimes; we call it "substantive linkage."

Power is present as a mediating agent in all three modes. The credibility of a tactical linkage depends on the "linkee's" perception of the linker's ability and willingness to withhold collaboration if the linkage is refused. In fragmented linkage situations, the potential defectors from the coalition must be held in line by means of side-payments or promises, and the opposing coalition must be effectively threatened. Even in situations of substantive linkage, knowledge is rarely so consensual as to eliminate the role of threat and reward as a way of persuading the weaker negotiating partners. But the use of power is always limited by the perception of complex interdependence that motivates the parties to negotiate in the first place.

Tactical issue-linkage is a negotiating ploy that eschews reliance on intellectual coherence among the issues linked. . . . Deep-sea nodule mining can be regulated without also worrying about the right of passage through straits. Yet these issues were in fact linked because the victims of asymmetrical interdependence wished to link them and had enough leverage to succeed. Tactical linkage is a cheap way to increase pay-offs because it expands the agenda of possible benefits to be derived. . . . What is called "package dealing" and "linkage politics" in journalistic accounts of foreign policy conforms to this pattern; so does the legislative practice of log-rolling. Tactical issue-linkage, then, is simply a way of maximizing the separate gains of the parties, even though the outcome of the negotiations may be an agreement that establishes a new regime.

Fragmented linkages are best illustrated by the NIEO negotiations, which constitute an attempt to realize some joint gains, even though it is far from clear how the gains will be distributed.[2] Uncertainty over distribution *is* a reason for issue-linkage. If the linkers are uncertain about the interdependence effects of the issues, it is safer to link, in the interest of gaining maximum concessions and holding their coalition together—even in disregard of knowledge that may suggest that linking is unwise substantively and unacceptable to the opposition politically. Thus we find in the NIEO that every outstanding economic grievance of the South is linked to an overarching argument for global redistribution of resources, ranging from such immediate matters as aid and debt relief to the long-range considerations of technology transfer, commodity price stability, and nonreciprocal tariff treatment. The intellectual justification for the package was worked out by the UNCTAD economists in a series of studies that were widely challenged by economists in the developed countries. Professional knowledge is far from consensual. . . . In general, the entire package *is* related to the global redistribution of resources. There is some coherence from the point of view of the coalition attempting the linkage; but if there is none for the opposing party, we still lack a base of consensual knowledge.

Hence it is the principle of substantive linkage that is of greatest interest to us. We are concerned with explaining how negotiators link issues into packages in deference to some intellectual strategy or evolving awareness of causal understanding. . . .

This proposition must not be overstated: substantive knowledge *alone* cannot legitimate a holistic package of issues. The legitimation depends on the acceptance of a new understanding on the part of key political actors. Governments—even when exposed to novel insights about energy, growth, pollution, or food—cannot be expected to stop considering their policies within the perspective of what passes for the national interest. Substantive issue-linkage depends on learning that the national interest can be redefined or broadened, and that international collaboration is *required* for the realization of national goals. *Knowledge can legitimate collaborative behavior only when the possibility of joint gains from the collaboration exists and is recognized.*

All modes are "rational" in the sense that the actors show concern over cause and effect, and the relationship between ends and means, in seeking to attain a specific goal. But the types of rationality differ. . . .

Substantive issue-linkages lend themselves to holistic prescriptions of salvation. Many holists consider them to be the most conscious of complex systems of cause and effect, most sensitive to many ends and purposes, and most attuned to scan the full range of the means available for solving "the problem." Hence, they consider only this mode "rational" in the common use of the term, and issue-packages agreed upon by any process less rational as just another case of sub-optimizing. This view is not helpful if we wish to understand how regimes come into being; substantive issue-linkage can be effected by cognitive means short of the holistic extreme.

We now apply these propositions about issue-areas and issue-linkage to the way actors order their goals and apply knowledge in the construction of regimes. Issue-linkage refers to negotiating behavior. Our next concern is with the negotiators' structure of perceptions.

III. KNOWLEDGE AND GOALS: HOW TO ORDER THEM TO CHOOSE REGIMES

Knowledge and Goals in Overcoming Dependency

The actors whose cognition is of interest are thinking beings: they do not normally act randomly. . . . Actors can be expected to utilize whatever knowledge is available to help them in the calculation of advantage, whether they do so efficiently or not.

The regimes of concern here all have to do with wealth, welfare, and economic equality among nations. All the goals that matter to the actors are articulated in the global debate about the New International Order. That debate encompasses the conflict over goals associated with an open international economy and the Bretton Woods regime on the one hand, and the revolt of the Third World against that regime on the other. It pits the "liberal" ideology of the wealthy North against the antidependency ideology of the South. Asymmetrical, complex interdependence, as perceived by the underdeveloped countries, provides the basis for the confrontation; the shared goal of the South is to overcome dependency. That goal contains several different development strategies which provide the occasion for the introduction of knowledge.

Import-substituting industrialization is one of the strategies. Its proponents are concerned with raising aggregate national income; they expect the benefits accruing to a few successful enterprises to trickle down into the rest of the society eventually. . . .

Others propose the strategy of economic and technological self-determination. They associate dependency with the structure of capitalism and its global division of labor. The factors causing dependency are thought to include education, the media, the habits of the "center" classes in the "periphery" and their unholy alliances with the elites of the North, as well as the behavior of foreign investors. . . . No single goal can be attained without paying attention to a wide variety of economic, scientific, and social policies now considered relevant. Hence, goals "expand" and "become interconnected."

Redefining Goals

Changes in goals and in knowledge are crucial to our argument. But in the real world neither one changes all the time. We summarize the two processes under discussion without assuming covariation. The goals of governments, in modern times, change because new groups, parties, opinions, and demands enter the national political arena rapidly and in large numbers, reflecting the process of accelerating social mobilization. . . . But this expansion of goals may occur *without* a coherent intellectual understanding of causes and effects, and *without* a complete mastery of the means considered necessary and sufficient to attain the ends. . . .

Similarly, knowledge about causes and effects, means and ends, may expand rapidly and command an increasing consensus among the experts who generate it. Consensual knowledge may or may not infect the politicians. . . .

The hallmark of complex interdependence is uncertainty: there are too many goals, all competing for attention; there is no agreement on the best means for attaining them; the understanding of causes is subject to ideological disputation, not consensus; what is a cause to one actor is an effect to another. In short, *goals cannot be ordered into a hierarchy of importance or salience equally acceptable to all.* International collaboration, the effort to regulate asymmetrical interdependence, is an attempt to reduce uncertainty when a multiplicity of values are at stake and the simplest strategy for reducing uncertainty—autarky—is not practicable. Linking issues is fallible man's way of marshaling what knowledge he has in order to attain his goals. Constructing issue-areas by way of substantive linkages implies some ordering. . . .

We can now come back to our discussion of how linkages among issues are negotiated. Issue-specific negotiations do not involve these kinds of uncertainties and coping mechanisms because I do not associate them with complex interdependence. They do not refer to situations in which the need for a new regime is felt, though they are commonly used for adapting and maintaining existing institutional arrangements. We may therefore disregard issue-specific negotiations. In tactical linkage negotiations, knowledge is either not consensual or irrelevant; therefore it cannot inform the negotiations in a systematic fashion. . . .

Linking issues on the basis of fragmented or complete substantive awareness of applicable knowledge is our real concern: actors espousing an "expanding" set of goals seem doomed to relying on what is known or knowable about the physical and social world. . . . They therefore share a commitment to consensual knowledge, whether on a partial or a more complete basis. . . .

Four Cognitive Styles

Goals and knowledge may be combined. Figure 1 suggests schematically how issue-areas develop from separate issues. Each cell captures a particular cognitive style, a particular convergence of ways of thinking about knowledge and action. One may think of the units in the cells as individuals or decision-making teams such as delegations to conferences. . . .

The distinction between static-specific and interconnected-expanding goals has been explained. A clarification about "consensual" knowledge is now needed.

Figure 1

| | | Goals considered by politicians are: | |
		Specific, static	Interconnected, expanding
Beliefs of experts about knowledge become:	More consensual	Pragmatic	Rational
	Not more consensual	Eclectic	Skeptic

What matters is not that substantive knowledge about soil chemistry, ocean currents, or the biology of fish stocks is changing, but that there be a constant and active evolution of ideas about how scientific knowledge can and should be related to politics and policy making. Not merely information, but the management of *knowledge for action* is the vital consideration for the growth of issue-areas. . . . "More consensual" knowledge includes efforts to pick and choose, from among scientific disciplines and endeavors, those items that can be combined in a comprehensive effort to achieve the social or political goals of concern to us. The two modes opt for different principles of organization. They also use different ideologies to justify one procedure or the other.

The Rational Mode   In the rational mode, there is covariation between changes in knowledge and changes in goals. Experts increasingly agree on the management of knowledge for action; politicians accept their consensus as they make it part of their striving to attain more ambitious goals. The combination implies an acceptance of synoptic planning as the appropriate administrative technique. . . . The rational mode presupposes inspiration by a comprehensive doctrine which is the source of the planners' optimism. . . . Rationalists consider themselves masters of technique and substance, means and ends, causes and effects.

Of course, an ordering of goals is achieved by such means—however temporarily. *This ordering depends on the acceptance of the goals and the knowledge by all important actors,* or the exclusion from decision making of any actors who do not share the faith. Has such a situation ever existed in the history of international collaboration? One can think of experts who advocated doctrines of this kind and failed to convince all of the key actors of their vision: such was Arvid Pardo's fate in the Law of the Sea negotiations, Robert Triffin's in the reform of the international monetary system, and Lord Orr's in the field of food.

In the heyday of the Northern economic boom after World War II, Keynesian macroeconomics came close to providing such a consensus. . . .

We now know that the consensus was temporary. The goals of many of the actors changed; the NIEO reflects the change. Consensual economics disintegrated into "left" and "right" Keynesianism, neoconservativism and neo-Marxism. Each school has its own way of linking issues, or of not linking them. The rational mode has not demonstrated its staying power—whether the knowledge comes from economics, oceanography, or nuclear engineering.

The Eclectic Mode   Eclecticism is the logical obverse of rationalism. Knowledge is not used in decision making so as to arrive at a more integrated understanding among sectors and disciplines. Fisheries experts, geophysicists, petroleum engineers, and naval architects go their separate professional ways; they make little effort to reinterpret their specialized knowledge under the conceptual roof of "managing the common heritage of mankind." Politicians and administrators also make no concerted effort to change the social objectives to which they are committed. They continue to conserve fish stocks instead of planning to meet nutritional needs; they encourage the construction of supertankers, issue leases for ocean mining, exclude foreign polluters from straits and harbors—all without integrating these objectives into an ordered set of priorities for the oceans.

"Eclectics" comprise the large number of actors who are content to continue doing what they have always done. They believe neither in salvation by way of more consensual knowledge about techniques nor in the possibility of fashioning more integrated and ambitious goals. . . . Such actors may engage in package-dealing when they encounter one another in international negotiations; but the deals feature the *tactical* linking of issues.

Whether or not conceptual integration takes place is a matter judged by the outside observer on his own terms. The participants, unmindful of the distinctions made by us, may well consider their activities as constructing issue-areas in line with the best scientific knowledge available to them. The key is the mode of decision making they adopt; eclecticism prevails if no attempt is made to transcend disjointed incrementalism. The participants do not use methods of synoptic assessment; they do not construct formal models of the oceans including *all* activities of concern; they do not attempt to make a joint simulation of cost-benefit alternatives covering fishing, mining, shipping, and pollution control (and hence, there is no real appreciation of trade-offs). Politicians package issues in line with coalitional and bargaining dynamics, rather than in terms of agreement on integrated objectives to be attained. . . .

The Skeptic Mode   What if goals entertained by politicians do become broader, more interconnected, and more consensual, but the accompanying knowledge remains or becomes fragmented? The effort to order issues along a hierarchy of priorities is made, but there is no adequate, accepted body of knowledge informing the order. The ordering is merely rhetorical: one set of negotiators is committed to one line of analysis with its source of certainty while another set professes quite a different approach. Agreement among actors on the hierarchy is not likely to be long-lived. . . .

"Skeptics," therefore, are either impatient or unconcerned with knowledge. They do not believe in, or are unwilling to wait for, the arrival of consensus among the experts. . . . Synoptic planning and analytic techniques coexist with disjointed incrementalism in making decisions. . . . The larger goals are approached through hit-or-miss programs and single-shot solutions that are not consistently justified in terms of some overarching logic or method.

The Pragmatic Mode   But what if there is an increasing body of consensual knowledge among experts, which is not fully matched among politicians with an expanding set of social goals recognizing intellectual interconnections? The situation prevails when publics and policy makers become aware of unwanted and unanticipated consequences of industrialism while also wanting its benefits. Goals do change in recognition of more consensual knowledge, but not all actors agree on how the goals ought to be ordered. Pragmatists attempt to use the analytical techniques associated with what Lindblom calls "strategic planning." They do seek to contrive substantive linkages on the basis of such efforts at integrating knowledge. But pragmatic experts can never be sure to find an understanding and sympathetic audience among all of their political masters.

While rationalists strive for the aggregating of goals into issue-areas, pragmatists tend to experiment with combining two or three issues; they may consent to decompose them into separate issues once they are convinced that the aggregation is conceptually faulty or politically ineffective. Pragmatists would prefer to link issues substantively at all times, but will settle for partial substantive linkage when they must. . . . As single goals change and coalitions among actors shift, so does the order of priorities among goals. Improved knowledge may help in the ordering; but knowledge, too, is rarely final and uncontested. Pragmatists must work on the border of relative and temporary certainty and of occasionally ordered social goals. Hence, they must settle for stop-and-go tactics—attempts at grasping larger wholes, followed by periods of retrenchment. . . .

IV. COGNITIVE PROCESSES, CHANGE, AND REGIMES

My purpose is to suggest an ideal-typical definition of regimes, to inquire how, in our era, international collaboration can flourish in a setting of conflict, how islands of order can form in an ocean of disorder. Different modes of cognition can suggest how men redefine their interests to attempt the realization of joint gains in some fields while continuing to play the zero-sum game in others. Negotiation on the basis of substantive linkages does not guarantee successful regimes. Cooperation on an informal basis can certainly take place in the absence of full-fledged regimes. . . .

Hypotheses of Change

. . . The four hypotheses that follow make claims about cognitive styles, issue-linkage, the prominence of state power in the linkage, and the capacity of any resulting regime to survive. We assume that the cognitive style informing the negotiations characterizes all the important parties: all are rationalists, skeptics, eclectics, or pragmatists. The more complex situation of mixtures of prevalent styles will be taken up when we discuss "learning through negotiation."

1. If the negotiating conference is characterized by *eclecticism,* issues will be linked exclusively in a tactical manner. The credibility of the linkage is largely a function of the will and the ability of key parties to impose it, including the manipulation of technical information. It is unlikely that a regime will emerge; if it does, it will not outlive the first important technological innovation.

2. If the negotiating conference is dominated by the *rational mode,* substantive issue-linkage on the basis of agreed doctrines will prevail. Power differentials among states are not important as mediating instruments. The

resulting regime will be as stable as the doctrinal consensus on which it rests.

3. If the negotiators are *skeptics,* fragmented issue-linkage will prevail, and the will and capability of powerful states can be expected to remain important as instrumentalities for rewarding coalition partners and paying off opponents. The resulting regime will be weak and unstable.

4. If the negotiators are *pragmatists,* they will first attempt substantive issue-linkage and withdraw to fragmented linkage when this becomes politic. State power is a factor in reaching an agreement, but not an essential one. The resulting regime, though including fewer issues than had been hoped, will nevertheless be fairly stable. It will also be capable of being adapted and adjusted so as to include additional issues later.

Regime stability implies several things. The norms, rules, and procedures that make up the regime will not be challenged by the members so as to throw the existence of the arrangement into doubt. The rights of the parties will be generally respected and obligations will be carried out. Challenges will take the form of conduct specified by the regime's procedures. . . .

Structural Explanation of Change

Students of international regimes are in disagreement as to whether changes in the rules of collaborative games among nations are best explained in "structural" or in "cognitive" terms. While my explanation is cognitive, the burden of this section is to suggest that the differences can be reconciled with the help of the notion of the "national interest," albeit not a platonic ideal interest, but interest perceived by actors and identified by analysts.

In the structural explanation, we seek to identify deep-seated patterns or conditions in the international system and to ask whether these have or have not changed. We can then explain new institutional patterns in terms of such changes. The differential in power, influence, and stratification among states is the condition of greatest interest to the structuralist. He sees the world in terms of changing balances between "weak" (or new, or underdeveloped) states and "hegemonic" (or strong, industrialized, and—potentially or actually—militarily dominant) states. International regimes flourish when hegemonic states define them, operate them, and pay for them; they decline when hegemons change their minds. Naturally, the rules of a regime are tailored to the national interests of the hegemons. The law of the sea was dictated by those who owned big navies, merchant marines, and fishing fleets before 1967; monetary order was maintained by the economically most powerful: Britain before 1914, the United States between 1945 and 1971. When the relative power position of the hegemon eroded—for whatever reasons—the regime had to change. Structuralists do not worry about differences in *how* the national interest may be understood by various groups, bureaucracies, and individuals within a state. The strength of the state is taken as the key ingredient of the explanation, and the balance of power among states as the predictor of specific regimes.

This approach can be applied to our way of explaining regime construction. It explains fully the situation in which no new consensual knowledge enters the negotiating process. Interests are considered fixed. When a given state lacks the capability to make its interests prevail and new actors challenge its former primacy, the game changes. One may then say that international collaborative arrangements that reflect *static* knowledge of cause-and-effect patterns and *settled* views about the relationship of means to ends *are* a reflection of established stratification patterns. Since there are no influential ideas challenging the prevailing technical wisdom of how to manage money or fish stocks, choice is effectively constrained by prevalent schedules of opportunity costs. When the distribution of power and influence among states changes—as it surely has since 1960—national interests that had previously lacked the opportunity to be heard, now become very audible indeed. But since these "weak" states lack the ability to challenge the prevailing technical knowledge they must seek a better deal on the basis of the negotiating processes we have identified with tactical and fragmented linkages. The weak must rely on their numerical strength and their ability to forge coalitions by granting or withholding benefits desired by the "strong." More voices mean more interests, more demands, and more complex negotiations; they are made more complicated still if, at the same time, changes within the hegemonic states undermine their ability to take a clear position. Expressed in terms of the cognitive modes presented above, the structural explanation of change is consistent with the skeptical and the eclectic types of process. The absence of new knowledge in the model forces reliance on less-than-substantive ways of linking issues. . . .

Cognitive Explanation of Change

In the pragmatic and rational modes of negotiating, emphasis is put on the use of increasingly consensual new knowledge in making more ambitious policies. An explicit additional variable is introduced to explain change—a variable that accentuates new ways in which actors think. Since actors can be expected to make use of whatever help they can get in reducing their uncertainty about how to attain their increasingly complex and ambitious objectives, this knowledge will be put to use through cognitive means. . . . The addition of new knowledge is . . . associated with new communications channels, think tanks, international research institutes, and efforts to model "world systems" at national and international, public and private institutions. Substantive issue-linkage then prevails, though it may be mixed with fragmented linkage. State power remains in the picture to the extent that the pure rationalist style does not prevail.

Learning Through Negotiation

To students of international organizations condemned to follow the debates of United Nations bodies, it may seem odd to associate these discussions with the idea of learning. In fact, the iteration of familiar patterns of behavior suggests the analogy of the anthill rather than that of the academy. . . . [But] insects cannot transcend stereotyped behavior without genetic change, [yet] people can by drawing on experience. One kind of experience consists of making use of information that becomes available. Another kind integrates various bodies of information to construct theories and other intellectual aids. Such processes can be experienced by individuals, groups, organizations, and even states. . . . Learning, in the context of regime construction, is the cumulative recognition of knowledge necessary for realizing joint gains; learning must be Pareto-optimal. We know that learning has taken place when the actors adopt new rules of behavior that make use of new information and knowledge, or adopt ways for the search for such knowledge. . . .

Actors who seek to use new knowledge to link issues substantively cannot be said to act contrary to their national interests. There is no need to assume the sudden victory of dispassionate wisdom over selfish interest. But why assume the contrary—that actors will continue to cut off their noses to spite their faces when it is within their power to enjoy both wisdom and self-interest? New knowledge, then, is used to redefine the content of the national interest. Awareness of newly understood causes of unwanted effects usually results in the adoption of different, and more effective, means to attain one's ends. . . . If we adopt this perceptual notion of the national interest, we must discard the idea of "structurally necessary" regimes; nothing is *absolutely* necessary. Necessity is a function of perception, of knowledge; it is time-bound. . . .

How can we conceptualize the process of learning to use new knowledge in the redefinition of national interests? Obviously, the impulse may come from many sources in domestic political systems and may be diffused through many international agencies, public and private. The knowledge, however, does not become politically relevant until it shows up as an ingredient in the formulation of national demands for altering the existing pattern of interdependence. The empirical locus for the next encounter is the process of negotiating new regimes.

Hence, learning is a form of persuasion, and persuasion implies an initial disagreement among the parties, which is gradually resolved or settled by compromise. Learning through negotiation is more likely to take place in a setting in which *no single* cognitive style characterizes the negotiators, but where pragmatists encounter skeptics or eclectics. Learning is associated with mixed cognitive settings rather than with the pure types hypothesized above. The knowledge is unevenly diffused and not completely consensual; there is conflict over goals; power is perceived to be asymmetrically distributed, though not concentrated in one country for purposes of all issues and sectors of concern. In the negotiations that ensue for resolving conflicts over clashing national interests so as to find a zone of joint gains, learning takes place if and when the bargaining positions of the parties begin to *converge* on the basis of consensual knowledge tied to consensual goals (or interests), and when the *concessions* that are exchanged by the parties are perceived as instrumental toward the realization of the joint gains.

. . . *Learning as conceptualized above occurs only when pragmatists and rationalists have the edge over their eclectic and skeptic colleagues. . . .*

But what if the pragmatists and rationalists are not successful? If no convergence occurs on any dimension, there will be no regime. The LOS is again our example, and it demonstrates the prevalence of a process that is just as much part of the creation and diffusion of new knowledge as the forging of substantive issue-linkages. New information may actually sensitize negotiators to possible future gains that are best realized without a regime. New knowledge on fisheries conservation, pollution control, and off-shore mining had the effect of making several Third-World governments determined to reap these advantages for themselves alone, to the exclusion of others. Their example was soon followed by all countries that espoused the formula of a 200-mile economic zone. . . .

The mixture of cognitive styles leads us to a second set of hypotheses about regime construction.

1. If the negotiations are dominated by a conflict between rationalists and pragmatists, the solution will still feature the use of substantive issue-linkage dominated by consensual knowledge. There is no clear case that illustrates this pattern, though approximations to it are found in the U.N. Environmental Program. A relatively stable regime will result.

2. If the negotiations are dominated by a conflict between eclectics and pragmatists and the new information is unpersuasive with respect to joint gains, any issue-linkage will be purely tactical. That case is illustrated by the LOS negotiations. If there is a regime, it will be unstable.

3. If the negotiations are dominated by conflict between skeptics and eclectics, fragmented issue-linkage will dominate, and various partial regimes will be built. None will be stable because the controversy over goals to be achieved continues even if knowledge does not become more consensual. The NIEO is in this situation now.

4. If the negotiations are dominated by conflict between skeptics and pragmatists, the possibility exists that fragmented issue-linkage will yield to substantive linkages, though these may well be temporary and dependent on the next turn of the screw of knowledge. Regimes will be more stable than in case 3 and less stable than in case I because this hypothesis incorporates the notion of learning-by-negotiation; skeptics respect new knowledge though they do not wish to wait for it. The food regime comes close to presenting a current example.

V. REGIMES AND ORGANIZATIONS

. . . Historically, regimes have been created for regulating single issues rather than issue-areas. Hence, lawyers speak of regimes for fishing, allocation of radio frequencies, pure food and drugs, money, or foreign investment. Norms, rules, and procedures—centralized in international organizations or left to the decentralized network of national officials—have existed for many years. Such arrangements are not of interest here. The term "regime" as used here is reserved to the situation in which rapid changes in scientific knowledge and political expectations combine to produce the types of visions represented in the contemporary debate about the global economic order.

Regimes are norms, procedures, and rules agreed to in order to regulate an issue-area. Norms tell us *why* states collaborate; rules tell us *what,* substantively speaking, the collaboration is about; procedures answer the question of *how* the collaboration is to be carried out. Procedures, therefore, involve the choice of whether specific administrative arrangements should be set up to regulate the issue-area. Administration involves organization. . . .

Norms

Why would states wish to collaborate with respect to managing and regulating the process of improving their technological positions? The purposes of those who demand a regime—and hence the norms underlying collective action—can be summarized as the *acquisition of a capability* to act in a specific domain, either nationally or collectively. This includes creating the ability to make decisions, to analyze a situation, to set up new relationships, as well as to fashion physical goods, and perfect, adjust, or change decision making norms or manufacturing facilities or habits of action so as to better exploit something already in place.

Procedures

Whatever the strength of the norm, the next question must be: *How* shall the norm be implemented? I distinguish between four procedural modes. (I) A *common framework* seeks to affect national behavior through exchanges of information and common rules of reporting and record-keeping. In the language of organization theory, the division of labor sought here is confined to "pooling" separate capabilities without re-arranging them in the search for a common product. (2) A *joint facility* is a more ambitious and demanding way of pooling capabilities by seeking to harmonize and standardize the behavior of the participants through the imposition of common routines. The actors agree to a loose division of labor, not merely by keeping each other informed but by changing routinized ways of doing things so as to meet an agreed standard. (3) A *common policy* is more demanding still. It calls for the ordering and scheduling of national behavior in such a way that the participants agree to adjust their action to the planned needs of the collectivity by re-arranging prior patterns—a type of division of labor called "sequencing" in organization theory. (4) A *single policy* substitutes a centralized set of plans and objectives for the national ones. Since in doing so it absorbs the pre-existing commitments of the national actors, the resulting pattern of interaction (and the division of labor among the parts) is far more complex than in the other instrumentalities: the interaction is "reciprocal."

The pooling of instrumentalities of action through a common framework calls for very simple coordinating bodies. Interbureaucratic committees of high civil servants suffice. When a joint facility is to be operated, however, a research staff may be necessary to devise the appropriate standards and norms; the staff need be no more than a working party of independent experts, convened when necessary. But it often develops into an international secretariat, which then comes to service the interbureaucratic committee. These institutions are sufficient for setting out common ground rules for national action. Sequencing is more ambitious, since priorities for action must be established. Some parts of the whole must act before others; some kinds of previously legitimate action will become illicit. Creation of a common policy thus demands a capacity to make joint commitments; that is the task of councils of ministers and summit conferences, aided by lower-level committees of national civil servants and rudimentary international staffs. It must be understood, however, that these lower-level bodies are incapable of making commitments without the agreement of their superiors. A single policy, and the relationships of reciprocity it implies, calls for a full-fledged "government," whether in the federal tradition or in some other approximation. In short, there is no need for a formal organization if the actors opt merely for a common framework; but there is need for a very elaborate organization if a single policy is deemed necessary.[3]

Types of Regimes

When the norm is accepted with roughly equal fervor among all participants in a regime, the varieties of rules and procedures give us the types presented in Figure 2.

The five possible regimes are labelled in conformity with what organization theory has to say about the character of the activities: pooling/aiding, standardizing/scheduling, forecasting, targeting, and planning. (1) Actors proceeding within a common framework engage essentially in collecting and exchanging information. Their pooling of information is supplemented with technical assistance from the better- to the poorer-endowed countries when existing capabilities are unevenly distributed among the members. (2) If they wish to do more than share information, they must choose a joint facility. If they so choose, information is not only pooled, but new information requested and the substantive area of concern is subjected to standardized monitoring procedures. The standardization of information processing amounts to "shaping" the information into accepted bodies of knowledge used in making policies. If capabilities are unevenly distributed, the richer are expected to aid the poorer by allocating a disproportionate share of common resources to them. Allocation implies that joint action is "scheduled"; there has to be some understanding on who is to give whom how much before the activity can be carried out effectively.

A common policy also requires the sharing of information and the increasing of knowledge. In addition, it carries with it understandings that each actor will seek to attain a desirable outcome by a certain time. The outcome is decided collectively, but each participant remains in charge of implementing the decision.

Figure 2 Types of regimes

Procedures	Rules		
	Share information	Increase knowledge	Channel/foreclose action
Common framework	Yes (1)	No	No
Joint facility	Yes	Yes (2)	No
Common policy	Yes	Yes (3)	Yes (4)
Single policy	Yes	Yes	Yes (5)

(3) One way of accomplishing this involves forecasting without setting targets for achievement. The collective forecasting of the future is an exercise in increasing knowledge, but the forecasts need not call for action. (4) If action is desired, the results of the forecasts are translated into targets for each of the participants. Targeting without forecasting and the sharing of information is not conceivable. (5) Finally, a single policy for a set of states presupposes all of the above, plus commitment to a firm plan of action which is implemented by the central organization. . . .

How to Choose Regimes

In choosing among the possibilities, a decision maker must weigh a number of factors. What is his cognitive stance? What is the stance of the opposing coalition? How should evolving knowledge be incorporated into his political strategy or ideology? What is the norm?. . .

These questions can be combined in one overarching concern: what is the appropriate membership for a regime? The choice is between centralization and decentralization. One can think in terms of a uniform and global regime, with procedures placed under the guardianship of a single organization, as opposed to the coexistence of several regionally diverse regimes, with a diffuse set of rules binding different types of states to different obligations, and a congeries of overlapping organizations. Moreover, diverse regional regimes can also coexist within global arrangements. Everything still depends on the norm selected and the cognitive stance associated with it.

The committed rationalist must opt for a planning regime: he depends on increasingly consensual knowledge—obtained by way of pooling, standardizing, and allocating informational resources—to attain his social and economic goals. Targeting, forecasting, and planning presuppose the success of increasing and managing knowledge. The skeptic, though depending on whatever knowledge is currently at hand, wants to attain his complexly linked social goals without waiting for an increased consensus on knowledge. His choice would then be a standardizing-scheduling regime. The pragmatist will swing back and forth between the forecasting and targeting regimes, attempting at first to choose as the rationalist would, but compelled to fall back on the less powerful regimes if he is unable to arrive at a satisfactory method of connecting the issues calling for collaboration. For the eclectic, only a pooling-aiding regime is appropriate.

In terms of the more familiar organizational dynamics, we must conclude that the rationalist will seek institutional solutions that are centralized in a single organization integrating all activities thought germane to the issue-area. His desire for institutional coherence suggests no other solution. Skeptics and pragmatists, however, are compelled to sacrifice institutional coherence to less precise arrangements. Skeptics may well prefer to forgo the creation of formal organizations altogether, as may eclectics. When confronted with the possibility that a no-organization regime will fail to attain the objectives suggested by its norm, the skeptic and the pragmatist will agree to hit-or-miss institutional tinkering that may take a multi-organizational and multi-level format. They therefore face the practical problem of how to achieve coherence among the programs and norms of the multiple organizations that they will spawn.

Even if all our hypotheses were shown to be correct, and if all the typologies found universal acceptance, we would not be able to predict which regime would be chosen. But we *are* able to advise the policy maker which regime he ought *not* to select, by excluding possibilities and limiting choice. . . .

The best service to be expected from an ideal-typical discussion of regimes is to make people pause and think.

NOTES

1. But, it is said, experts always disagree with each other; how can we speak of a consensus? In the early stages of any shift in paradigm, they certainly do disagree, and there is no consensus. Even later, experts will continue to disagree on certain aspects of their field, but not on all. In the early stages of discussion regarding the creation of regimes, the use of knowledge will be no more consensual than is the current U.S. debate among the experts on the future of nuclear energy. Experts disagree with each other on the facts *and* on the social goals to be realized. Moreover, they do tailor the factual discussion to whatever goal they espouse. But that is not the case during the entire lifecycle of a technology or a theory. At times there is consensus (as there was with respect to nuclear energy in the 1950s and 1960s because the dissidents were few in number and outside the policy-making process); it is permanent consensus that is inconsistent with the process of scientific investigation itself. See Howard Margolis, *Technical Advice on Policy Issues,* Sage Professional Paper No. 03-009 (Beverly Hills, CA.: Sage, 1973).
2. I rely greatly on Robert L. Rothstein *Global Bargaining* (Princeton: Princeton University Press, 1979), in this section, even though he considers the inter-issue linkage in the Integrated Commodity Program to be essentially tactical, used solely to hold the heterogeneous Group of 77 together. Rothstein also shows that, while the parties agreed on many specific economic arguments and demonstrations, they continued to disagree on whether to act in accordance with them in the creation of the UNCTAD-designed Common Fund. What mattered was whether they thought in terms of "best-case" or "worst-case" scenarios. The issue that divided them was whether, in the process of commodity price stabilization, equity (the goal of the G-77) or efficiency (the goal of Group B) should be maximized. The Common Fund that they eventually agreed to differs from the proposal UNCTAD had used to link the issues.
3. The typology and the rationale on which it is based are adapted from John Gerard Ruggie, "International Responses to Technology: Concepts and Trends," *International Organization,* xxix (Summer 1975), 570–74. For various ways of matching the typology with cognitive modes in explaining institutional variation, see Ernest B. Haas, Mary Pat Williams, and Don Babai, *Scientists and World Order* (Berkeley: University of California Press, 1977), chap. 6.

Credits

4 Friedrich Kratochwil and John Gerard Ruggie, "International Organization: A State of the Art on an Art of the State," *International Organization*, 40 (1986): 753–775. Reprinted by permission of The MIT Press, Cambridge, Mass. Copyright © 1986 by the World Peace Foundation and the Massachusetts Institute of Technology.

32 John Gerard Ruggie, "Multilateralism: The Anatomy of an Institution," *International Organization*, 46 (1992): 561–598. Reprinted by permission of The MIT Press, Cambridge, Mass. Copyright © 1992 by the World Peace Foundation and the Massachusetts Institute of Technology.

44 Robert O. Keohane, "International Institutions: Two Approaches," *International Studies Quarterly*, 32 (1988): 379–396.

61 Duncan Snidal, "Coordination Versus Prisoners' Dilemma: Implications for International Cooperation and Regimes," *American Political Science Review*, 79 (1985): 923–942.

77 Alexander Wendt, "Anarchy Is What States Make of It: The Social Construction of Power Politics," *International Organization*, 46(1992): 391–425. Reprinted by permission of The MIT Press, Cambridge, Mass. Copyright © 1992 by the World Peace Foundation and the Massachusetts Institute of Technology.

97 Stephen D. Krasner, "Structural Causes and Regime Consequences: Regimes as Intervening Variables," *International Organization*, 36 (1982): 1–21. Reprinted by permission of The MIT Press, Cambridge, Mass. Copyright © 1982 by the Massachusetts Institute of Technology.

109 Oran R. Young, "The Politics of International Regime Formation," *International Organization*, 43(1989): 349–376. Reprinted by permission of The MIT Press, Cambridge, Mass. Copyright © 1989 by the World Peace Foundation and the Massachusetts Institute of Technology.

128 Peter M. Haas, "Do Regimes Matter? Epistemic Communication and Mediterranean Pollution Control," *International Organization*, 43 (1989): 377–404. Reprinted by permission of The MIT Press, Cambridge, Mass. Copyright © 1989 by the World Peace Foundation and the Massachusetts Institute of Technology.

143 Beth V. Yarbrough and Robert M. Yarbrough, "International Institutions and the New Economics of Organization," *International Organization*, 44 (1990): 235–259. Reprinted by permission of The MIT Press, Cambridge, Mass. Copyright © 1990 by the World Peace Foundation and the Massachusetts Institute of Technology.

159 John A. C. Conybeare, "International Organization and the Theory of Property Rights," *International Organization*, 34 (1980): 307–334. Reprinted by permission of The MIT Press, Cambridge, Mass. Copyright © 1980 by the Board of Regents of the University of Wisconsin System.

174 Edward D. Mansfield, "The Concentration of Capabilities and International Trade," *International Organization*, 46 (1992): 731–764. Reprinted by permission of The MIT Press, Cambridge, Mass. Copyright © 1992 by the World Peace Foundation and the Massachusetts Institute of Technology.